Constitution, Public Finance, and Transition

Finanzsoziologie

Herausgegeben von Jürgen G. Backhaus

Band 4

PETER LANG
Frankfurt am Main · Berlin · Bern · Bruxelles · New York · Oxford · Wien

Ringa Raudla

Constitution, Public Finance, and Transition

Theoretical Developments in Constitutional Public Finance and the Case of Estonia

PETER LANG
Internationaler Verlag der Wissenschaften

Bibliographic Information published by the Deutsche Nationalbibliothek
The Deutsche Nationalbibliothek lists this publication in the Deutsche Nationalbibliografie; detailed bibliographic data is available in the internet at http://dnb.d-nb.de.

Zugl.: Erfurt, Univ., Diss., 2009

This book is a doctoral dissertation
that has been defended at the University of Erfurt.

547
ISSN 1610-059X
ISBN 978-3-631-59945-7

www.peterlang.de

Table of Contents

PART II: Constitutions as *Explanantia* in Public Finance

List of Tables

List of Figures

List of abbreviations

CA	Constitutional Assembly
CAB	Cyclically Adjusted Balance
CBS	Close to Balance or in Surplus
CEE	Central and Eastern Europe
CIT	Corporate Income Tax
CPR	Common-Pool Resource
CRC	Constitutional Review Chamber
EDP	Excessive Deficit Procedure
EMU	European Monetary Union
EU	European Union
EC	European Communities
FSU	Former Soviet Union
GDP	Gross Domestic Product
IFI	International Financial Institution
IMF	International Monetary Fund
LR	Largest Remainder
MOF	Ministry of Finance
MP	Member of Parliament
NMS	New Member States
OECD	Organisation for Economic Cooperation and Development
PD	Prisoner's Dilemma
PIT	Personal Income Tax
SAO	State Audit Office
SGP	Stability and Growth Pact
TEL	Tax and Expenditure Limit
USSR	Union of Soviet Socialist Republics

Abstract

This dissertation explores the role of constitutions in public finance, with a special focus on transitional context in Central and Eastern Europe. The two general questions addressed by this study are: How do formal constitutional provisions that matter for public finance come about? How do constitutions shape policy choices in public finance? By drawing on existing literature in positive constitutional political economy, part I of this book puts forth an analytical framework for analysing how fiscal constitutional provisions come about and tests the conjectures with the case of constitution-making in Estonia in 1991–1992. The Estonian case study demonstrates that alongside institutional self-interests of the framers, the constitutional choices were strongly influenced by the inter-war constitutions of Estonia and symbolic considerations. Part II summarises, synthesises and criticises the emerging orthodoxy in positive constitutional public finance and examines whether it can explain the commitment to fiscal discipline in Estonia between 1992 and 2007. The main shortcomings of the emerging orthodoxy are the failure to account for configurational effects of constitutional elements and the tendency to resort to over-simplified metaphors without exploring closer the problem structures in political reality. Part III puts forth an analytical framework for exploring how constitutions shape the main laws governing the policy arena of public finance through constitutional review, autolimitation and constitutional deliberations. The case study of Estonia demonstrates that the constitution can indeed play a significant role in influencing the development of the organic budget law and tax laws.

Keywords: constitutional public finance, constitutional political economy, constitutional economics, institutional economics, budgetary institutions, fiscal rules, Central and Eastern Europe, transition economies, Estonia, constitution-making, constitutional review, constitutional deliberation, budgetary policy, tax policy, veto players, common-pool resources.

Acknowledgements

In writing my Ph.D. dissertation, I have benefited from the help of a number of people. In particular, I would like to thank my supervisor Prof. Jürgen Backhaus for his valuable time, expertise and helpful criticism on this manuscript. The discussions with him added significantly to my understanding of the topic and the issues involved. Writing this dissertation at the University of Erfurt would have been impossible without the grant of the Estonian Ministry of Education for doctoral studies abroad.

I am also grateful to Prof. Wolfgang Drechsler and Prof. Tiina Randma-Liiv for encouraging and inspiring me to pursue the doctoral studies. I would also like to express my gratitude to the Institute of Public Administration at Tallinn University of Technology and especially to Prof. Rainer Kattel, who has allowed me to take advantage of extremely flexible work schedule. This dissertation has benefited from the valuable comments and helpful criticisms of the participants of the doctoral colloquia at the Chair of Public Finance and Fiscal Sociology and at the Chair of Institutional Economics and Economic Policy, in particular from Prof. Helge Peukert, Prof. Gerhard Wegner, Dr. Enrico Schöbel and Arne Wei_.

Various chapters of this dissertation have received valuable input from the participants of various conferences and workshops, including the 6th Erfurt Conference on Fiscal Sociology (Rudolstadt, 13 October 2006), the 20th Consecutive Workshop in Law and Economics (Erfurt, April 4–5, 2007), the Annual Conference of Association of Budgeting and Financial Management (Washington, DC., 25–27 October 2007), the 7th Erfurt Conference on Fiscal Sociology (Rudolstadt, 19 October 2007) and the 21st Consecutive Workshop in Law and Economics (Erfurt, 19–20 March 2008). Special thanks in this regard are to Prof. Richard Wagner, Prof. Francesco Forte, Prof. Kenneth Kriz and Prof. Daniel Williams.

I am also really grateful to Jens Claussen, who was always willing to listen when I wanted to discuss some issues related to the dissertation, who drew me back to reality when I had receded too far from it and who provided me with immense emotional support throughout the journey of writing this manuscript. I am thankful to my father Heiki Raudla, who was always happy to explain me the enigmas of Estonian politics and enlighten me about what was going on behind the curtains of the Estonian political scene. The remaining mistakes are, of course, entirely my own responsibility.

Ringa Raudla

Introduction

In the recent decades, the constitution has been "brought back in" to public finance (to allude to an expression that has become almost a cliché in some circles of political inquiry). This is mirrored by an increasing number of publications that pursue the "constitutional" (or Wicksellian) approach to public finance, which competes with the more conventional welfare economic (or Edgeworthian) approach.[1] Alongside normatively oriented constitutional studies of public finance, there has been a notable surge in positively oriented inquiries, inspired by the conviction that in order to explain why the public finances of a polity look like they do, one needs to explore the institutional (including constitutional) setting that characterises the policy-making arena of public finance. Thus, this book does not need to start with a long justification why one should *at all* consider the role that constitutions play in public finance and why it would be insufficient to remain in the cosy confines of the orthodox welfare economic understanding of what public finance is about. The questions are rather: How far has the recent positively oriented literature of constitutional public finance come? What are the potential obstacles? Which questions have been neglected? Where can one look for potentially fruitful avenues of research?

Most broadly put, this book is concerned with the role of constitutions in public finance, with the term "constitution" referring to the most literal (and also every-day) understanding of the word. In particular, the general research questions that the current study aims to address are the following: First, how do formal constitutional provisions that matter for public finance come about? Second, how do constitutions shape policy choices in public finance? This two-fold division draws on the logic of the research programme of positive constitutional political economy, which, following Buchanan (see, for example, 1987, 1990), focuses on two main questions: how are constitutional rules chosen (constitution as *explanandum*)[2] and how do they influence policy choices and outcomes (constitution as *explanans*)? (Voigt 1997; Voigt and Wagener 2000)[3]

Since a substantial part of studies in positive constitutional political economy – especially in the *explanans* stream – deal with issues of public finance

1 The distinction between the Wicksellian tradition and Edgeworthian tradition, or the "old" and "new" public finance, has been explained by Backhaus and Wagner (2004, 2005), Brennan and Eusepi (2004) and Backhaus (2002a).

2 According to Voigt (1999, p. 2), the *explananda* stream of positive constitutional political economy is primarily concerned with developing hypotheses about how different factors in constitution-making influence the resulting content of the constitution and analysing how polities factually choose their constitutional rules.

3 Though in its early phases of development, constitutional political economy was primarily "a normative endeavour interested in legitimising the state and its actions in terms of fairness, justice, or efficiency", in which the constitution was viewed as a social contract, then by now the research programme has clearly expanded and includes an increasing number of works of positive analysis (Voigt and Wagener 2002, p. xv).

(which should not be surprising, given that the pioneers of constitutional political economy came from the field of public finance),[4] it would make sense to talk about "positive constitutional public finance" as a sub-field of positive constitutional political economy.[5] A look around in the existing literature shows that the *explanans* stream of constitutional public finance has been taken up by an entire "industry" of researchers and one can even speak of "an emerging orthodoxy", while the *explanandum* stream is still in an embryonic phase of development. When navigating in the *explanans* stream, one is likely to be dizzied by the volume of studies and can hence "afford" to take stock of the existing research, criticise it and put forth alternative approaches. In the *explanandum* stream, however, one is a rather lonely sailor and is faced with a task to breathe life into the quest.

Hence, the different parts of the book deal with literatures that are at very different stages of development. Part I draws on the general literature of positive constitutional political economy in order to come up with an analytical framework for exploring how constitutional provisions that pertain to public finance come about; part II summarises, synthesises and criticises the emerging orthodoxy in positive constitutional public finance; part III puts forth an alternative way of analysing how constitutions influence public finance.

Although the two questions – how do constitutions come about and what is their impact – are analytically distinct and could, in principle, be examined separately, a number of advantages arise from combining them in a single inquiry. The knowledge of how particular rules have come about can contribute to deeper understanding of their impacts. Indeed, the motivations that drive the constitutional phase can be carried over to the post-constitutional phase, and the constitutional theories employed in the making of the constitution can influence the interpretation of the constitutional rules later on.

To emphasise once more, in this book, the term "constitution" refers *primarily* to the formal written constitution, but, when considered analytically useful, also to the "extended constitution", which encompasses the formal rules of the game (like budgetary institutions) established on a statutory level. Thus, though some strands of constitutional political economy employ the term "constitution" in a very broad sense, using it to refer to any institutions, rules or norms (see Voigt 1999 for an overview), then, in this inquiry, the term constitution is regarded more "literally", especially in parts I and III of the book.[6] Though part II treats the term "constitution" in a somewhat more relaxed way and considers governing arrangements that emerge from constitutional rules as

4 See, for example, Brennan and Eusepi (2004) for that argument.

5 The term "constitutional public finance" has been employed by Backhaus (1996, 2002b, 2004), and Backhaus and Krabbe (1991).

6 Thus, conceptually, the understanding of constitutional political economy in this book has the closest affinity to that of constitutional law and economics, which also regards the "constitution" as the legal document (Backhaus 1998, p. 83).

falling under *constitutional* public finance, part III emphasises the need to distinguish between the core constitution and the extended constitution in order to explore their interactions.

Alongside the terms "constitution" and "public finance", there is a third element in the title of this book – "transition". Although, indeed, an important goal of this book is to contribute to the development of "general" constitutional public finance, the primary focus of the empirical (but also theoretical) analysis in this book is on the transition in Central and Eastern European countries in general and on one country – Estonia – in particular. The focus on inter-relations between constitutions and public finance in *transitional* context has been inspired by a number of factors. First, by the belief that in order to be meaningful, social inquiry should be situated in time and space and strive towards more elaborate middle-range theories rather than towards nomothetic laws. Second, given their potentially important roles as focal points, constitutions in transition countries can provide a useful testing ground for finding out whether the ambitious role that constitutional political economy attributes to constitutions actually holds. Third, an inquiry of the challenging task to "rebuild a boat on the open sea", as Elster (1993) has aptly characterised the making of the constitutions in the CEE region at the outset of transition, would be useful for exploring what aspects of public finance constitutional framers pay attention to, when everything is in flux and a large number of options are open.

Throughout the chapters, a connecting thread is the question – to what extent can the behaviour and decisions of the political actors, either in the design of constitutional institutions or in the post-constitutional phase, be explained by strategic calculations and to what extent by symbolic motivations? As discussed in greater detail in chapter 4, the distinction between the "calculus" and the "cultural" perspective is an important dividing line between the different institutionalist approaches in social sciences (Hall and Taylor 1996), and, inevitably, this question is carried over to constitutional analysis as well.

Outline of the Book

Part I of this book (chapters 1–3) focuses on constitutions as *explananda*: it explores how constitutional provisions that matter for public finance come about. Since the strand of positive constitutional public finance that is concerned with constitutions as *explananda* is still in a very early phase of development, part I of this book draws extensively on the existing literature in positive constitutional political economy, in the hope that it can provide a useful starting point for constitutional public finance as well.

Chapter 1 gives an overview of the testable hypotheses pertaining to constitution-making, brought up in the recent literature, with a special focus on conjectures concerning the impacts of different kinds of framers, their motivations and the constraints they face on the resulting constitution (especially on the general features of *political institutions* that are considered relevant for public finance). Chapter 2 gives an overview of the constitution-making in Estonia in 1991–1992 and tests the hypotheses with this case. Chapters 1 and 2 have in fact two different goals. First, they contribute to positive constitutional political economy by testing the existing theoretical propositions and bringing to the fore the shortcomings of the hypotheses (and the needs for refinements).[7] Second, more importantly for this book as a whole, the hypotheses outlined in chapter 1 form a basis for deriving a list of conjectures in chapter 3, which is concerned with the making of *fiscal constitutional* provisions; chapter 2 also serves an important role for understanding both the making of the fiscal constitutional provisions analysed in chapter 3 and for having background knowledge of the general constitutional framework in Estonia (and how it came about), necessary for comprehending the other case studies undertaken in parts II and III of the book.

Chapter 3 explores the formal fiscal constitution as *explanandum*; in other words, it examines how constitutional provisions pertaining to public finance come about. Although fiscal aspects of constitutions (especially substantive fiscal rules establishing debt and deficit ceilings) have received extensive (and increasing) attention in the recent literature, the analyses have hitherto focused primarily on the *impacts* of these provisions rather than on how these rules have emerged. The few studies that have viewed fiscal constitutional provisions as *explananda* are, for most part, concerned with provisions that have been added to *existing* constitutions rather than analysing how constitutional provisions pertaining to budgeting and taxation come about when an *entire constitution* is written afresh (for example, after a regime change).[8] Therefore, chapter 3 focuses on how formal fiscal constitutional provisions come about in the context where a whole new constitution is designed. In the existing literature, no comprehensive analytical framework has been put forth for examining fiscal constitutional provisions as *explananda*; thus, the first goal of chapter 3 is to propose an approach for examining how constitutional provisions that pertain to budgeting and taxation come about. By drawing on the hypotheses that concern constitution-making in general, a list of conjectures is put forth. The second goal is to test these conjectures with the case study of Estonia and to analyse whether the existing approaches in positive constitutional political economy can shed light on fiscal constitutional choices made by framers in a transitional context.

---

7 Although some of the hypotheses outlined chapter 1 have already been tested with the cases of almost all Central and Eastern European (CEE) countries (see Adamovich 2004; Elster 1996a, 1997a,b), the constitution-making in Estonia and in the other two Baltic countries has not been analysed in the light of these hypotheses.

8 The studies that have analysed the making of fiscal constitutional provisions in the context of drafting an entirely new constitution include Tang (1991) for the Hong Kong Constitution, and Brennan and Pardo (1991) for the Spanish Constitution. These studies, however, have primarily a normative orientation and do not seek to test any specific hypotheses.

Part II (chapters 4–7) and part III (chapters 8–10) focus on the role of constitutions as *explanantia* in public finance; that is, on the question of how constitutions shape policy choices in public finance. While part II focuses on the emerging orthodoxy in constitutional public finance (and its shortcomings), part III proposes an alternative venue for approaching the role of constitutions in public finance.

Part II of this book has three main goals. First, it gives an overview of how existing studies that can be categorised as falling under positive constitutional public finance answer the question, "How does a constitution influence budget discipline, expenditure levels, spending mix, tax revenues, features of tax systems and fiscal adjustments?" Second, it examines whether the core theoretical propositions of the emerging orthodoxy in constitutional public finance can provide insights for understanding a particular case: the commitment to fiscal discipline in Estonia between 1992 and 2007. Third, it criticises the emerging orthodoxy, points out the main shortcomings of the existing studies and puts forth alternative venues of research for positive constitutional public finance.

The term "constitution" in part II encompasses three different kinds of "constitutional institutions": first, the formal constitution itself (in particular, the political institutions, budget procedures and fiscal rules entailed in it); second, the "extended" constitution, which is, in its functions, very similar to the formal constitution and encompasses budgetary institutions (usually outlined in organic budget laws) and statutory fiscal rules; third, the governing arrangements that emerge from the political institutions (especially electoral rules), reflected in the number of parties on the political arena and the government type.

Chapter 4 provides the groundwork for chapters 5–7. First, it outlines the assumptions that underlie positive analysis in constitutional public finance. Since most of the studies have hitherto paid rather limited attention to the *mechanisms* linking constitutional provisions and policy outcomes, chapter 4 elaborates on the links between constitutional rules and substantive choices in public finance with the help of insights from different institutionalist approaches. Drawing on Hall and Taylor (1996), the discussion points to two main approaches (to explaining the role of institutions in shaping the behaviour of political actors) that different streams of institutionalism subscribe to: the "calculus" approach and the "cultural" approach. Second, chapter 4 puts forth a concise analytical framework that can be used for summarising, synthesising and criticising the theoretical propositions and empirical findings of the emerging orthodoxy in positive constitutional public finance.

The framework outlined in chapter 4 is employed for structuring the discussions in chapters 5 and 6. Chapter 5 looks at the effects of political institutions: that is, at the impacts of the main features of the "machinery of government", as defined directly or shaped indirectly by the constitution, on public finances. It considers the effects of presidentialism versus parliamentarism, electoral rules and governing arrangements (the size of the legislature and cabinet, the number of parties in the legislature and the cabinet, unicameral versus bicameral legislatures), direct democracy mechanisms and judicial institutions. Chapter 6 focuses on the effects of extended fiscal constitutions: the impacts of fiscal rules (e.g., balanced budget requirements and deficit limits) and budgetary institutions (rules of procedure governing the preparation, adoption and implementation of the budget) on public finances. Both chapters take stock of the existing studies, offer a synthesis of the prevalent models and propositions in existing theoretical literature, summarise the results of the empirical studies conducted so far and criticise the existing literature.

Whereas discussions in chapters 5 and 6 assume that institutions *matter* in explaining budgeting and taxation and the question is rather, *which* institutions matter and *how* they matter,[9] chapter 7 starts with the question "To what extent can the political institutions and the extended fiscal constitution explain a particular case, namely, adherence to fiscal discipline in Estonia from 1992 to 2007?" Among the transition countries, Estonia has hitherto stood out as an exemplary case of fiscal discipline, with the lowest level of government debt and the best indicators for budget balances. Chapter 7 thus explores to what extent the commitment to budgetary discipline has been driven by constitutional factors, like particular features of political institutions, fiscal rules and budgetary institutions, and what other factors have been relevant.

While part II of this book is concerned with the "emerging orthodoxy" of constitutional public finance and its shortcomings (as exemplified, *inter alia*, by the Estonian case study in chapter 7), part III of this book (chapters 8–10) offers an alternative way of approaching the question "How do constitutions influence public finance?" The recent literature of constitutional public finance is primarily concerned with exploring the associations between particular constitutional features and aggregate fiscal indicators. Confining inquiry to such an exercise, however, would present only a very limited picture of the role of constitutions in the policy arena of public finance and neglect other forms of influence that the constitution can have. In order to gain a more complete overview of the effects of a constitution on a polity's public finance, one should also consider how the constitution can shape the main laws of public finance – especially the organic budget law, other framework laws governing the budget procedures, framework laws for taxation and tax acts themselves. Further, the studies in the emerging orthodoxy usually confine themselves to the "calculus approach" in explaining how a constitution (as a particular type of institution) shapes the behaviour of political actors, while neglecting the insights from the "cultural approach". Given that both the cultural approach and calculus approach help to explain im-

9 Therefore, the discussion in these chapters does not start with specific budgetary outcomes, followed by attempts to list all possible factors explaining these outcomes. Rather, the discussion takes up different kinds of constitutional institutions and discusses how each of these institutions would influence policy choices and outcomes in public finance.

portant parts of reality, constitutional public finance would benefit from both of them. The goal of chapter 8 is therefore to offer an analytical framework that integrates both the calculus approach and cultural approach in exploring the role of constitutions in public finance. The analytical framework outlined in chapter 8 is then used in chapters 9 and 10 for examining how constitutional review, auto-limitation and constitutional deliberations have shaped the main public finance laws in Estonia between 1992 and 2007.

Methodological Remarks

In contrast to the prevailing predilection for large-n studies and regression analyses in the emerging orthodoxy of positive constitutional public finance, this book employs case study approach as an empirical research strategy. While methodological preferences are obviously influenced by the ontological and epistemological standpoints of the author, opting for case study approach in this book has also been motivated by dissatisfaction with the current state of research in constitutional public finance. In particular, it is acknowledged that the case study method offers a number of advantages by allowing the researcher to "retain the holistic and meaningful characteristics of real-life events" (Yin 2003, p. 1) and by providing more ample opportunities for tracing causal mechanisms and interaction effects of various factors (Gerring 2007; Ragin 2000, 2008; George and Bennett 2005).

The conception and design of the case studies in this book has drawn extensively on what Blatter and Blume (2008, p. 316) call "an unprecedented reflection on case study research", mirrored in recent works discussing the characteristics, advantages, sub-types and design issues of case study approach as a research strategy (see Gerring 2004, 2007; George and Bennett 2005; Bennett and Elman 2006; Yin 2003; Gomm, Hammersley and Foster (eds.) 2000; Brady and Collier (eds.) 2004). The case studies in this book thus consciously combine elements from "causal process-tracing" approach and "congruence analysis". While congruence analysis is theory-centred and seeks to make use of a case study to address a "*broader* theoretical discourse",[10] process-tracing approach is more case-centred and strives to attain "*deeper* and *denser* insights" by focusing on "the temporal unfolding and dense interactions of causal factors in specific

10 Congruence analysis "focuses on drawing inferences from the (non-)congruence of concrete observations with specified predictions from abstract theories to the relevance or relative strength of these theories for explaining/understanding the case(s) under study" (Blatter and Blume 2008, p. 325). In congruence analysis, the case studies are used to "indicate the relevance of a specific theoretical framework or to modify a theoretical framework" (p. 343).

cases" (Blatter and Blume 2008, pp. 316–317, emphases in original).[11] In particular, the case studies in this book proceed from an assumption that an in-depth analysis characteristic to process-tracing is useful and often even necessary for illuminating the causal mechanisms that the theoretical propositions are concerned with. In deciding over how detailed the case study should be, the level of existing theoretical discourse has been taken as a guiding point: if there already is a sufficient theoretical framework and theoretical propositions that can be tested (like in chapters 2 and 7), the congruence approach takes a lead; if, however, one has only a set of conjectures (as in chapters 3, 9 and 10), rather than a full-fledged theories, the process-tracing elements dominate.

Thus, for the purposes of chapter 2, the Estonian case of constitution-making can be regarded as a "crucial" case (Eckstein 1975) for testing the prevalence of institutional self-interest in the constitutional design of Central and Eastern European (CEE) countries. Since the 1992 Constitution was prepared by a separate assembly, convened for the specific purpose of drafting the constitution, and which worked in the knowledge that the resulting document would be ratified by referendum, the Estonian case can be regarded as the "least likely" case for the dominance of institutional self-interest among framers. Thus, if institutional self-interests were found to play a significant role in the constitution-making of the Estonian case, such interests can be expected to have been even more prevalent in the constitutional design of the other countries in the region.

In chapter 7, the Estonian case can be categorised in a number of ways. First, for *political institutionalists* in constitutional public finance, it would represent a "deviant" case: according to the general predictions of this stream of inquiry, Estonia should have problems with commitment to fiscal discipline, but it does not. Second, for *budgetary institutionalists*, Estonia would represent a "typical" case (in the sense that in large-n studies it would lie on the regression line) or a crucial case (a "most likely" case, in the sense that if the centralised budgetary institutions do not lead to budget discipline in Estonia, which has the most centralised budgetary institutions in CEE, they would be even less likely to secure budget discipline in other countries in the region). As it turns out, however, the case study in chapter 7 has primarily a *revelatory* nature: it shows how both political and budgetary institutionalists miss out an important part of the explanation.

The case studies in chapters 3, 9 and 10 have a more exploratory nature, in the sense that they probe the plausibility of the conjectures that this book itself puts forth; they also indicate the relevance of further theoretical (and empirical) studies on the issues concerned.

---

11 Causal process-tracing attempts to "identify traces for every step between the cause and the outcome" in order to gain a better understanding of causal mechanisms, complicated interactions of causal factors and causal pathways (Blatter and Blume 2008, p. 320).

With regard to general disciplinary orientation, this book proceeds from a set of questions that are considered to be important and looks for answers across disciplinary boundaries, rather than letting oneself to be restricted by canons of a single discipline. Indeed, the inquiry attempts to employ a "complex-free" approach to the questions posed and turns to a broad range of studies that have dealt with these questions, irrespective of whether they can be categorised as belonging to the realm of economics, political science, sociology, law or public administration. Indeed, the topic at hand – the role of constitutions in public finance – by its very nature, calls for *staatswissenschaftliche* approach (an approach of the sciences of the state) to inquiry, and, in that way, going back to the roots of public finance.[12]

12 This understanding has been inspired by Drechsler (2001), and Backhaus and Wagner (2004, 2005).

PART I: Constitutions as *Explananda*

Chapter 1: Constitutions as *Explananda*: Hypotheses from the Existing Literature

1.1. Introduction

The first part of the book (chapters 1–3) is concerned with the stream of constitutional political economy that analyses constitutions as *explananda*. This strand of analysis is primarily concerned with developing hypotheses about how different factors in constitution-making influence the resulting content of the constitution and analysing how polities factually choose their constitutional rules (Voigt 1999, p. 2).[13] Although the "*explananda* stream" of positive constitutional political economy is still in its early stages of development, it has received increasing attention (owing to constitution-making in the European Union, among other factors) in recent years.[14] Of particular interest have been the following questions: How do the process of constitution-making, the constellation of actors involved, their preferences and bargaining power, time limits and historical constraints (like previous constitutions or political experiences) influence the resulting *content* of the constitution? Another, also important, stream of positive analysis focuses on the effects of different factors on the *quality* of constitutional debates and the implications of the nature of the debate on the resulting document.[15] It is concerned with questions like: What factors are conducive to deliberative constitution-making?[16] What aspects facilitate the achievement of consensus in constitutional debates? Does the quality of constitutional debates influence the resulting constitution?[17] Although driven by important normative

---

13 For a more detailed overview of the research agenda for positive constitutional political economy, its precursors and related disciplines, see Voigt (1997).

14 For discussions on constitution-making in the European Union, see Magnette and Nicolaidis (2004), Crum (2004) and Bohman (2004), among others.

15 The main starting point for analyses of the quality of constitutional debates is the distinction between arguing and bargaining. *Arguing* (or *deliberation*) entails engaging in communication for the purpose of persuading opponents: making them change their beliefs about factual or normative matters by offering impartial arguments that seek to further common interest, public good, individual rights and democratic values. *Bargaining* entails communication for the purpose of forcing or inducing the opponent to accept one's claim by relying on threats and promises. (Elster 1991, 1993, 1995a) For a critique of this dichotomy, see Holzinger (2004).

16 Elster (1998a) suggests that the main variables that play a role in influencing whether constitution-making is characterised by arguing or bargaining are the following: the size of the body, publicity, the presence or absence of force and the importance of interest as the motivation of the framers.

17 Elster (1998a, p. 104) argues that "A deliberative setting can shape outcomes *independently* of the motives of the participants." (emphasis in original) Voigt (2004, p. 211) notes that Elster's distinction between arguing and bargaining suggests a question: "Are there any systematic consequences concerning the content of the constitutional document

standpoints (desirability of consensus and deliberation rather than bargaining), these are also important *positive* questions, but will not be the focus in this study.

This chapter is primarily concerned with the effects of the *kinds* of participants involved in constitution-making process and the *constraints* they face on the content of the provisions proposed and included in the resulting constitution. Analysing these aspects of constitution-making in real-life context can facilitate the achievement of a more holistic understanding of constitution-making as a phenomenon. In addition, such positive analysis can contribute to normative discussions about how constitution-making should look like by exploring the validity of underlying causal assumptions of the normative propositions.

The goal of this and the subsequent chapter is to contribute to the literature in positive constitutional political economy by bringing together the hypotheses on constitution-making, suggested in the existing literature, and testing them with a specific case: constitution-making in Estonia in 1991–1992. While most of the hypotheses outlined below are not tied to a concrete historical context, some would be formulated with a specific reference to constitution-making in Central and Eastern European (CEE) countries at the outset of transition. The present chapter gives an overview of the testable hypotheses pertaining to constitution-making, brought up in the literature, with a special focus on the conjectures concerning the impacts of different kinds of framers, their motivations and the constraints they face on the resulting constitution. The hypotheses outlined here will also serve as a basis for deriving a list of conjectures in chapter 3, concerned with the making of fiscal constitutional provisions.

1.2. Hypotheses on Constitution-Making

The existing theoretical and empirical works in positive constitutional political economy have offered a number of hypotheses about the effects of the constellation of actors involved, their motives and the constraints they face on the resulting provisions in the constitution.

1.2.1. Modes of Constitution-Making

In his discussion on different modes of constitution-making, Elster (1997a) distinguishes between eight types: constitutions can be internally or externally imposed, come in the form of a contract, be made under imposed constraints, by a minority, by elite accommodation, by indirectly or directly elected assemblies. With regard to the last form, the constituent body can be called into being only

that can be explained with the differential use of arguing and bargaining?" These questions are closely related to the general discussion on whether the quality of deliberation exerts influence on substantive outcomes. For a concise overview of existing theoretical and empirical literature on that question, see Steiner *et al.* (2004).

for the purpose of preparing the constitution or it can simultaneously serve as an ordinary legislature. Normative discussions on constitution-making have emphasised the advantages of having a separate constitutional assembly rather than using the existing legislature (Elster 1997a, 1998a; Ackerman 1992; Salzberger and Voigt 2002; Mueller 1996).[18]

An important question, therefore, before analysing the specific procedures of constitution-making is: When is it likely that a separate constitutional assembly is convened for drafting the constitution (rather than using an existing legislature or giving a newly elected assembly the double task of drawing up a constitution and adopting ordinary legislation)? What are the factors that are conducive to that? Elster (1998a, p. 117) considers it "highly unrealistic" that a country can afford to have two sets of elites, one for writing the constitution and another for governing the country. Drawing on Ackerman (1984, 1991), Voigt (2004, p. 223; 1997, p. 26) suggests a hypothesis that a decision to convene a constitutional assembly would take place during "constitutional moments", in which a group does not make decisions according to the standard self-interest rationale but proceeds from special considerations that are only valid in that very moment. Buchanan has also used the term "constitutional moments", which are identified "by their singularity, by their extraordinary presence, by their intrusion of sorts into the ongoing compromises of conflicting interests that describe and define ordinary political experience" (Buchanan 1997a, p. 186).

1.2.2. The Actors Involved in Constitution-Making

Moving on to the composition of the constitution-making body, the kinds of actors involved and their motives are considered to be important for the resulting constitution. In their analysis of constitutional preferences, Vanberg and Buchanan (1989) distinguish between "constitutional interests" and "constitutional theories". A person's constitutional theories are his or her predictions about the

---

18 There seems to be a general agreement that having a separate constituent assembly is more conducive to deliberation than using existing structures. Elster (1993, p. 182; 2000, p. 140) argues that since "a main task of a constituent assembly is to strike the proper balance between the legislative and executive branches of power", assigning that mission "to an assembly that also serves as an ordinary legislative body would be to ask it to act as judge in its own cause". In other words, "To reduce the scope for institutional interest, constitutions ought to be written by specially convened assemblies and not by bodies that also serve as ordinary legislatures." (Elster 1998a, p. 117) Ackerman (1992) emphasises that having a separate assembly would prevent the mixing of constitutional law with ordinary legislation, which is likely to happen when parliament draws up the constitution. He also argues that such a form of constitution-making would lead to a constitution that enjoys high legitimacy. Mueller (1996, pp. 316–317) adds that when legislators draft a constitution, they may allocate a disproportionately high percentage of time to deciding short-term issues, especially when the country faces a crisis, and neglect constitutional issues that are more relevant in the long run.

prospective outcomes of alternative rules; constitutional interests are person's subjective evaluations of the expected outcomes of the rules. Constitutional interests, in turn, can be carried by different kinds of motivations. Elster (1993, 1995b, 1996b, 1997a) distinguishes between personal, institutional and partisan interests in constitution-making. The extent to which these interests come to the fore in constitution-making, would depend on the nature and set-up of the constitution-making body.[19]

1.2.2.1. Members of the Constituent Body

Elster (1993, 1995b, 1996b, 1997a) argues that when the constitution-making body coincides with the existing legislature (or is a sub-committee thereof) and/or other branches of government are involved, institutional self-interest would play an important role in constitution-making: the framers would be inclined to enhance their own position in the constitutional framework, at the expense of the other organs of state. As Elster (1996a) explains, the institutional interests can reflect different kinds of considerations, like the intention to stay in political life beyond the constituent parliament or identification with the institution that the actors belong to (e.g., because of the need for cognitive consonance).[20]

Proceeding from the assumption of institutional self-interest, Elster (1996a) puts forth a number of hypotheses that can be tested with empirical cases. The first hypothesis is that constituent assemblies that simultaneously serve as ordinary legislatures will assign more extensive constitutional powers to the legislative branch than to the executive and the judiciary. The second hypothesis posits that constituent parliaments will assign a central role to the legislature in the amendment process of the constitution, at the expense of referenda or other forms of extra-parliamentary ratification. The third hypothesis is that unicameral and bicameral constituent assemblies will create, respectively, unicameral and bicameral legislatures. The fourth hypothesis is that if the president is involved in the constitution-making process, he will promote strong presidency.

To the extent that the constituent body is made up of groupings clearly identified with particular parties, partisan interests are likely to play a role in constitution-making, alongside with institutional interests. Voigt (2004), Mueller (1996, ch. 21) and Elster (1993) conjecture that the involved political parties will try to influence the constitution (in particular the electoral rules) in a way that enhances their chances of being (re-)elected. Thus, small parties will favour proportional representation with a low threshold, while large parties will endorse

19 Elster (1995b, p. 377) notes that, usually, the personal interest of the framers in specific constitutional provisions is relatively marginal, although it may play a role in some cases.

20 In the normative discussion, Elster (1998a) emphasises that actors or institutions whose behaviour is to be regulated by the constitution – such as the executive, the judiciary and the military – should not be part of the constitution-making process.

a plurality (or majoritarian) system. Politicians who are already well-known and popular will endeavour to establish rules that allow voters to cast a ballot for specific individuals, while disliked leaders of the main parties will advocate party-list procedures. Elster (1993, p. 182) also suggests that a party that has a strong presidential candidate will argue for a strong presidency, whereas other parties will seek to limit the constitutional powers of the president.

Similar hypotheses, reflecting the assumptions of institutional and partisan interests, as put forth by Elster, Voigt and Mueller, have been suggested by Geddes (1996), Lijphart (1992), Ordeshook (1990), Rakove (1997) and Schnellenbach (2004) for constitutional choices in general; Magalhaes (1999), Smithey and Ishiyama (2000), Ginsburg (2002) and Romeu (2006) for constitutional provisions pertaining to judiciary; and Frye (1997) with regard to the design of the executive branch. A common proposition in these studies is that actors involved in constitution-making attempt to design such political institutions that would enable them to exercise the power to the greatest possible extent in the post-constitutional phase. Smithey and Ishiyama (2000, p. 171) conjecture, for example, that because of institutional self-interest, framers would be "predisposed against limiting themselves, particularly in the form of oversight by other actors" and predict that factors that give rise to stronger powers of legislature and executive in the constitution would lead to constrained powers of judiciary.

Further, a common assumption in the studies of Magalhaes (1999), Smithey and Ishiyama (2000), Ginsburg (2002), Romeu (2006) and Frye (1997) is that institutional choices result from the interaction between institutional self-interests of the framers, their bargaining position in the constituent assembly and uncertainty with regard to the post-constitutional composition of different institutions.[21] Frye (1997) notes that when faced with *certain* post-constitutional electoral outcomes, actors with a strong position in constitutional negotiations can translate their bargaining power into a set of political institutions more easily; in the face of uncertainty, however, this task becomes more complicated. He argues that "High uncertainty encourages expectant winners and losers to hedge their bets more than they would under low uncertainty." (p. 531) Frye conjectures that constitution-making is likely to result in a strong executive, if the electoral favourite for the executive position has strong bargaining powers in the constituent assembly and the electoral outcome is fairly certain. Conversely, if the electoral favourite has weak bargaining powers and/or the electoral outcome is highly uncertain, the framers will design an executive office with few specific powers and tightly constrained residual powers.[22]

21 Although uncertainty can be viewed as a constraint that the actors face, then because of the close interaction between constitutional interests and uncertainty, this factor will be discussed under the "actors" section than under the "constraints" section.

22 Frye (1997) finds empirical support for these conjectures in his comparative study of four post-communist countries.

Drawing on Frye (1997), Smithey and Ishiyama (2000) argue that if the prospective "electoral favourite" for the executive office has a strong position in constitutional negotiations and is certain of the electoral outcome, the prospective executive will not be motivated to establish a strong judiciary, which may limit his or her freedom of action. Conversely, if the degree of competition between prospective candidates for the office is high and the electoral outcome is uncertain, the framers would endeavour to create a strong judicial branch, which would serve as a strong arbitrator of political conflicts.[23] In a similar vein, Ginsburg (2002) hypothesises that framers would only be motivated to grant the judiciary strong powers of constitutional review if they are uncertain of their post-constitutional power positions.[24] Romeu (2006) conjectures that constitutional designers would opt for a separate constitutional court (rather than choosing institutional arrangements according to which constitutional review is integrated with the rest of the judiciary), if the future composition of the legislature and the executive is uncertain.

1.2.2.2. Constitutional Experts

Alongside representatives from existing governing institutions, external constitutional experts can be involved in drafting the constitution.[25] The analytical value of looking at the role played by constitutional experts has been emphasised by Elgie and Zielonka (2001, p. 39), among others. Voigt (2004, pp. 23–24) conjectures that constitutional experts who are involved in constitution-making will not attribute a dominant role to the legislature *vis-à-vis* the other two branches. In addition, he suggests that if the experts involved are constitutional lawyers, they will advocate extensive guarantees of independence for the

23 In addition to this inter-institutional factor, Smithey and Ishiyama (2000) outline a number of other potential factors that can, in principle, shape the institutional choices pertaining to the strength of the judiciary. They hypothesise that the emergence of powerful judiciary is less likely, the more statist the political culture, the deeper the economic recession at the time of drafting the constitution, the weaker the judiciary at the pre-transition period, the smaller the degree of competition and the smaller the number of actors involved in the initial constitutional negotiations. Their empirical study of 20 post-communist countries indicates that of the factors considered, only the number of parties involved in constitutional negotiations played a significant role in influencing the degree of judicial independence, although it had an opposite effect compared to the hypothesised one: the larger the number of actors involved, the less independent the resulting constitutional court.

24 Ginsburg's (2000) study of 18 post-communist countries confirms this prediction.

25 In normative discussion, Elster (1995b, pp. 395–396) suggests that the role of experts should be kept to a minimum because solutions tend to be more stable if dictated by political rather than technical considerations. As Elster puts it, "Lawyers tend to resist the technically flawed and deliberately ambiguous formulations that may be necessary to achieve consensus." (p. 395)

judiciary; and if the experts' role in constitution-making is dominant, the constitution will entail strong guarantees of judicial independence.

1.2.2.3. The General Public

Both normative and positive literatures in constitutional political economy have discussed the role of general public in constitution-making. The main questions here are: How does public involvement and publicity of constitution-making impact on the quality of constitutional debates?[26] How does public involvement in constitution-making influence the content of the resulting constitution? The current study is primarily concerned with the latter question. Voigt (2004) propounds that if a referendum is necessary to ratify the constitution, the possibility of popular referenda for issues other than constitutional ones will be included in the constitution. In addition, he argues that the use of referendum for ratifying the constitution will lead to a document that takes the preferences of citizens at large explicitly into account.[27] Elster (1995b, p. 374) has also emphasised the

---

26 With regard to the question of whether open or closed discussions on the constitution enhance deliberation (rather than bargaining), Elster (1998a) points to diverging propositions. On the one hand, the presence of the public makes it hard to appear motivated merely by self-interest. Thus, when the process is under strong scrutiny from the public, the members would be likely to replace the language of interest by the language of reason and present their argument in terms of common good or the public interest. On the other hand, Elster argues, publicity can have undesirable effects: framers may find it more difficult to back down from a position already stated and are, therefore, less likely to change their mind as a result of reasoned objections (p. 109). Therefore, Elster proposes that the constitution-making process ought to contain elements of both secrecy (e.g., in the form of committee discussions) and openness (in the form of plenary assembly discussions) (p. 117). Ordeshook (2002, p. 183) commends that the preparation of the constitution should occur outside of public view, but its subsequent ratification should involve as broad a segment of society as possible. Mueller (1996, p. 326) suggests that the openness of the proceedings should depend on how the members of the constitutional convention were selected. He recommends openness in the case of a specially elected or randomly chosen convention and using secrecy when the members come from the existing parliament. For a general discussion of whether publicity is conducive to deliberation, see Chambers (2005).

27 Normative literature has also discussed the question of whether the constitution should be ratified by referendum or not. Elster (1998a) argues that the constitution ought to be subject to popular ratification by referendum. The same viewpoint is endorsed by Ordeshook (2002, p. 183). Mueller (1996, pp. 320–322), however, suggests that the form of ratification should depend on how the members of the constitutional assembly were selected. He argues that when the members have been elected to the constitutional assembly or chosen randomly, the agreement of the convention on the constitution would be sufficient. In the case, however, where the members of the convention come from the existing parliament, the resulting draft constitution should be put on referendum. For an overview of the discussions of whether ratification by referenda would have been desirable in the context of CEE countries, see Elgie and Zielonka (2001, pp. 40–42).

importance of "downstream constraints", arising from the process of ratification: "If the framers know that the document they produce will have to be ratified by another body, knowledge of the preferences of that body will act as a constraint on what they can propose."

Besides the role as the body of *ratification*, the public can be involved in *preparing* the draft constitutions. Voigt (2004) discusses the effects of inclusive participation in the constitution-making on the resulting provisions. Inclusive participation involves elements like giving different groups or individuals the right to make proposals concerning the constitution, informing the public regularly on the progress of the proceedings of the assembly and having broad media coverage on the activities of the assembly (p. 214). Voigt hypothesises, first, that inclusive participation in constitution-making will lead to high levels of power delegation in the constitution. Second, Voigt suggests that if the public at large can participate in the drafting of the constitution by submitting proposals, the resulting constitution will be less coherent compared to the one that is negotiated behind closed doors, where conflicting interests can be resolved by compromises involving package deals (p. 219). He conjectures that single-issue participation will lead to a constitution that contains contradictory provisions. Schauer (1998a, pp. 5–6) has also put forward some hypotheses concerning how publicity and public involvement may impact on the resulting constitution. He suggests that publicity makes it harder to make tough choices and more difficult to eliminate (or to decide not to include) provisions; hence, the resulting constitution will contain more provisions. Schauer argues that publicity may make vagueness more difficult, because the perpetual "what if?" forces may produce increased pressure towards specificity.

1.2.3. Constraints and Models

Besides the *actors* involved in constitution-making, the *constraints* they face and the *models* they can draw on are considered to be important factors that influence the content of the constitution.[28] In the context of regime transitions in general and in Central and Eastern Europe in particular, the two main (and interrelated) constraints that have been discussed in the literature are first, the time constraint, and second, the previous constitutions and historical experiences of the country. Besides being viewed as constraints, the previous constitutions can be perceived as models, sources of inspiration and points of reference for constitutional theories. Similar role can be exercised by constitutions of other countries. The desire to belong to a particular cultural, political or economic sphere

28 The line between the *actors* involved in constitution-making and the *constraints* they face cannot, of course, always be clearly drawn. The need to have the constitution ratified by the public could, on the one hand, be considered as a *constraint* on the framers. To the extent that the general public can also be involved in constitution-making, however, would justify counting it as an *actor* in the constitution-making process.

may bring along pressures to include specific institutional choices, characteristic to this sphere, in the constitution as well. Hence, framers in CEE countries can be expected to have felt pressures to draw extensively on the "example constitutions" of other (Western) European countries.

McFaul (1999, pp. 30–31) suggests that the scarcity of time and the need to decide simultaneously on many issues of constitutional design compel actors to prioritise.[29] However, when focusing on one set of questions of institutional design, the framers may discard other issues, with unintended consequences for the future. Further, McFaul argues that when time is scarce, there would be little space for constitutional innovation, since the designers of institutions do not have "the temporal luxury of searching for ideal solutions" (p. 31). Thus, they are likely to draw upon the examples that they are already familiar with – past institutional arrangements.

Salzberger and Voigt (2002, p. 26) argue that, in the context of constitution-making in Central and Eastern Europe, the historical constitutions of these countries, which are often symbols of national pride or unity, can be expected to have amounted to an essential constraining force. Salzberger and Voigt also claim that the preceding communist constitutions would be another constraint, despite the fact that they were often not taken very seriously under communism. They suggest that the communist constitutions may acquire certain relevance, since the constitutional conventions have to start their deliberations on the basis of *some* set of rules and, in this regard, the communist constitutions have the advantage of being the status quo (p. 30). McFaul (1999, p. 31) also conjectures that "The most recent preceding institutional order will have the greatest effect on new institutional design." Drawing on Riker (1996, p. 123), he argues that "the more remote an institution, temporally or spatially", the less likely it is that the framers would choose it (p. 31). According to Riker (1996, p. 123), a temporally remote institution can become significant for current institutional choices, if "the great bulk of the participating framers comprehend its relevance" and the institution is mutually well-understood (cited in McFaul 1999, p. 31).

Elster, Offe and Preuss (1998, p. 35) argue that the post-communist societies have three different pasts exercising causal influence on institutional choices: in addition to the communist period and the more remote pre-communist period, there is the "very immediate period of extrication from the communist regimes"

29 The time constraint for the constitution-making body has played an important role in discussions that are primarily normatively oriented. Voigt (2004, p. 214) suggests that the more generous the time limit given to a constitutional assembly, the more weight would be given to deliberation. Similar argument, although for legislative settings in general, has been made by Lascher (1996, p. 513). On the other hand, Elster recommends that the assembly should work with a time limit, so that no group can use delaying tactics to get its way. Drawing on McWhinney (1981), Elgie and Zielonka (2001) suggest that constitutional settlements tend to be quick, when either exhilarating or traumatic political events bring about constitutional consensus.

(p. 35). Elster, Offe and Preuss (1998, p. 60) emphasise, in particular, the significance of the experiences from the inter-war period for constitutional design choices made in CEE. They suggest that past regimes may serve as models and cognitive points of reference in framers' search for new political institutions.[30] Elster (1992) conjectures, drawing on the work of Schelling (1960), that these historical constitutional precedents serve as "focal points", especially with regard to the establishment of the "machinery of government": the relations between president, government, parliament and courts. Alongside the previous constitutions themselves, the historical experiences with these constitutions and the kinds of political systems that they gave rise to (and evaluations thereof) can be expected to have played an important role, both as constraints and positive models.

Returning to the distinction between constitutional theories and constitutional interests, put forth by Vanberg and Buchanan (1989), past experiences are likely to be sources for constitutional theories. Offe (1997, p. 212) has emphasised that framers "will typically seek inspiration and legitimacy in a construed model of the past of their own society". He adds that the past is often divided into "a rejected, though immediate 'dark' past and a more distant but celebrated 'golden' past" (p. 212). Further, Offe (1997, p. 213) argues that "borrowing" across space or time is facilitated by the desire of the framers to "shy away from accepting responsibility for what they are really doing"; therefore, the framers would be tempted to hide "behind the often fictive notion of imitation or transplantation". In contrast, Schauer (2005) has argued that framers would be reluctant to engage in spatial transplantation: besides anticipated "transplant effects", whereby borrowed constitutional concepts lead to problematic mismatches when applied in indigenous context, spatial borrowing in constitution-making is likely to be complicated by the symbolic value of constitution-making. As Schauer puts it, "To make a constitution is to declare independence in the strongest sense of that term, and a nation that is not perceived – by itself and others – as having made its own constitution is likely to be perceived as being for that reason just so much a less independent and less mature country." (p. 912) Therefore, he conjectures that although framers in newly independent and transforming nations draw on the constitutional models and designs of other countries, then given the symbolic connotations of constitution-making, the drafting of a new constitution is likely to be an internally driven and indigenous process. When the framers are faced with contradictory pressures – the need to cover up institutional engineering and the desire to remain indigenous – borrowing from previous constitutions can be expected to be especially likely, given that this enables the framers to accommodate both of these pressures.

30 "In a situation where options are numerous and everything must be accomplished at once, the return to the 'golden' pre-communist past can serve as a clue to come to an agreement." (Elster, Offe and Preuss 1998, p. 62)

1.3. Summary

Taken together, the list of hypotheses of constitution-making that will be tested in the next chapter is the following:

H_1: A decision to convene a constitutional assembly presupposes a "constitutional moment".
H_{2a}: Constituent assemblies that simultaneously serve as ordinary legislatures will assign more extensive constitutional powers to the legislative branch, at the expense of the executive and the judiciary branches.
H_{2b}: Constituent assemblies that simultaneously serve as ordinary legislatures will assign a central role to the legislature in the amendment process of the constitution, at the expense of referenda or other forms of extra-parliamentary ratification
H_{2c}: Unicameral and bicameral constituent assemblies will create, respectively, unicameral and bicameral legislatures.
H_{2d}: If the president is involved in the constitution-making process, he will promote a strong presidency.
H_{3a}: Members of the constituent assembly who expect to hold a political office in the post-constitutional phase opt for constitutional rules that foster their chances for re-election.
H_{3b}: Constitution-making will result in a strong executive if the electoral favourite for the executive position has strong bargaining powers in the constituent assembly and the electoral outcome is fairly certain. Conversely, if the electoral favourite has weak bargaining powers and/or the electoral outcome is highly uncertain, the framers will design an executive office with few specific powers and tightly constrained residual powers.
H_{3c}: Framers will design a strong and independent judiciary if the future composition of the legislature and the executive is uncertain.
H_{3d}: Framers will grant the judiciary strong powers of constitutional review only if the future composition of the legislature and the executive are uncertain. Conversely, if the post-constitutional electoral outcomes are certain, framers will not grant the judiciary strong powers of constitutional review.
H_{4a}: Constitutional experts who are involved in constitution-making will not attribute a dominant role to the legislature *vis-à-vis* the other two branches.
H_{4b}: If the experts involved are constitutional lawyers, they will argue for extensive judicial independence.
H_{5a}: If popular referendum is necessary to ratify the constitution, the possibility of popular referenda for issues other than constitutional ones will be included in the constitution.
H_{5b}: The use of referenda in order to ratify the draft constitution will lead to a document that takes the preferences of the citizens at large explicitly into account.

H_{5c}: Inclusive participation in constitution-making will lead to high levels of power delegation.
H_{5d}: Single-issue participation will lead to a constitution that contains contradictory provisions.
H_{5e}: Public involvement in constitution-making will result in a longer constitution and more specific provisions.
H_{6a}: If the time limit given for constitution-making is short, only a small number of areas will receive extensive attention.
H_{6b}: If the time limit given for constitution-making is short, the resulting constitution will draw extensively on previous constitutions.
H_{6c}: The framers will draw on institutional models that are the closest in terms of space or time. The more distant an institutional model, temporally or spatially, the less likely that the framers will include it in the constitution.
H_{6d}: The experiences with previous constitutions of the country will be the prevailing source of constitutional theories for participants in constitution-making.
H_{6e}: In the context of constitution-making in CEE, the constitutions of the pre-communist period were the main models the framers draw upon, given their symbolic importance.

With regard to the communist constitutions existing in CEE at the time of constitution-making, the prediction could go both ways. On the one hand, the communist constitutions can be expected to play a prevalent role as a constraint or model, given their advantageous position as status quo. On the other hand, the communist constitutions had been stigmatised, which can be expected to have made the framers reluctant to draw on these constitutions.

H_{6f}: In CEE countries, the framers drew extensively on the existing constitution.
H_{6g}: In CEE countries, the framers avoided using the existing constitution as a model.

With regard to constitutional transplants, the prediction for constitution-making in CEE could also go both ways. On the one hand, the framers can be expected to have drawn extensively on the examples of Western European constitutions, given their desire to demonstrate the affinity to European cultural and political sphere. On the other hand, the framers can be expected to have been reluctant to transplant provisions from Western European constitutions, given the desire to prove the ability to design indigenous constitutions.

H_{6h}: In CEE countries, framers avoided legal transplants in constitution-making.
H_{6i}: In CEE countries, framers used legal transplants extensively.

More broadly put, one can also raise the question of whether the institutional choices in constitution-making are driven more by strategic calculations or by symbolic meanings attached to particular institutional features. While most of the hypotheses outlined above proceed from the assumption that decisions of the framers are primarily motivated by strategic calculations, hypotheses H_{6d}, H_{6e}, H_{6f}, H_{6g}, H_{6h} and H_{6i} also take into account the symbolic meanings that different constitutional choices may convey. Therefore, when exploring constitutional choices framers make, one should also look for trade-offs that have been made between strategic calculations and symbolic choices and whether the framers have had to sacrifice pursuits of institutional self-interest if symbol-driven discourses require that.

Chapter 2: Testing Hypotheses on Constitution-Making: The Case of Estonia

This chapter seeks to test the positive hypotheses put forth in chapter 1 with a specific case: constitution-making in Estonia in 1991–1992. Some of the hypotheses outlined in chapter 1 have already been tested with the cases of almost all CEE countries (see Adamovich 2004), but constitution-making in Estonia (and the other Baltic countries) has not been analysed in the light of these hypotheses so far. What makes the Estonian case special compared to other instances of constitution-making in Central and Eastern Europe is that the 1992 Constitution of Estonia was prepared by a separate constitutional assembly (rather than by an existing legislature)[31] *and* the resulting constitution was approved by means of a referendum,[32] implying that it could be viewed almost as an "ideal" case from a normative point of view. Therefore, the Estonian constitution-making can be considered to be a particularly interesting case for constitutional political economy. It can be regarded as "a crucial case" (in the sense conceived by Eckstein 1975) for testing the impacts of partisan and institutional self-interest: if these interests play a role in such a setting, they are likely to play even greater role in other settings that are characterised by the existing legislature acting as the constituent body and/or where the constitution is not subject to ratification by referendum.

Doing an in-depth case study of constitution-making (in the light of theoretical propositions) complements the existing large-n studies (Smithey and Ishiyama 2000; Ginsburg 2002; Romeu 2006) and comparative studies (Elster 1993, 1995b, 1996a; Frye 1997). An in-depth case study offers a more holistic perspective, allows the consideration of interaction effects of the various independent variables considered and provides a more thorough basis for elaborating

---

31 Although in Romania and Bulgaria, new bodies – with a purpose to draft the constitution – was elected, these bodies were also entrusted with the task of passing ordinary legislation and acting as interim parliaments in parallel to preparing the constitution. Although the Estonian Constitutional Assembly also included members from the existing legislature (the Supreme Council), it was a separate body and was explicitly given the task of drafting the constitution.

32 Constitutions were ratified by a referendum also in Romania, Lithuania and Poland. What sets the Estonian case apart from these three cases is that unlike in Lithuania, where the public had only twelve days to consider the Constitution, in Estonia, the public had almost two months; unlike in Poland, where only 43 percent of eligible voters participated and of whom only 53 percent voted in favour, in Estonia 67 percent of the electorate participated, of whom 91 percent supported the Constitution. While in the Estonian case it was clear for the Constitutional Assembly that the draft Constitution would need to be ratified by plebiscite, in Romania, the decision to put the draft Constitution on referendum was adopted only shortly before the referendum (see Adamovich 2004, p. 213).

upon the causal mechanisms in play.[33] Elster (1993, p. 194) has even argued that we would never be able to come up with "a law-like theory of constitution-making"; rather, the elements considered to be important in influencing constitution-making should be used as "raw material for the specification of *mechanisms* – frequently occurring patterns of causal interaction" (emphasis in original). In his discussion on the tools of constitutional political economy, Voigt (1996, 1997, 1999) notes that historical analysis is especially apt for analysing constitutional change and for providing empirical tests of the theories developed. He emphasises that analysing in detail the singular events would refrain the analysis from ignoring too many relevant details and of generalising too broadly (1999, p. 54).

Further, the empirical aspects brought up in this case study can be used as an input for a further in-depth comparative study of constitution-making involving a larger number of countries. A more comprehensive comparative study of constitution-making in CEE countries – for example, in the form of "structured, focused comparison" (George and Bennett 2005, ch. 3) – would be particularly promising, since, as Elster has noted, "the many simultaneous transitions in Eastern Europe offer a gigantic natural experiment" (1993, p. 170).

The main sources of information for the case study in this chapter were the verbatim reports of the plenary sessions of the Constitutional Assembly, the memoirs of the members of the Assembly, archival materials and secondary materials describing and discussing the constitution-making in Estonia.

For the context of this book as a whole, the overview of the constitution-making and the resulting constitution in Estonia serves as a useful background for understanding further case studies on Estonia undertaken in chapters 3, 7, 9 and 10 of this book.

2.1. Constitution-Making in Estonia in 1991–1992

During the coup in Moscow on 20 August 1991, the Supreme Council of Estonia declared the independence of Estonia and decided to convene the Constitutional Assembly (CA), which would include members from the two competing parliamentary bodies in Estonia at the time: the Supreme Council and the Estonian Congress. The Supreme Council (105 members) had been elected in the first multiparty parliamentary elections in 1990 by the electorate that consisted of all inhabitants registered in Estonia. The Estonian Congress (499 members) had been elected in February 1990 by all who had been citizens of Estonia prior to Soviet occupation (and their descendants). The elections to the two bodies reflected the rivalry between two different pro-independence groups that had been competing against each other since 1989 (Raitviir 1996, p. 353). On the one

33 Yin (2003, p. 1) has underlined, "The case study method allows investigators to retain the holistic and meaningful characteristics of real-life events."

hand, the Estonian Popular Front favoured a more flexible approach to independence, making use of the existing institutions by gradually taking over and restructuring the existing organs of state power, seceding from the Soviet Union and proclaiming a new Estonian Republic. On the other hand, the movement called the Citizens' Committees (promoted by the Estonian Heritage Society, the Estonian National Independence Party and the Christian Union) opposed such a conciliatory strategy and working within the "illegitimate" institutions; they demanded establishing new institutions, called for the registering of the citizens who would elect the Estonian Congress, and advocated the *restitution* of the pre-war Estonian Republic.[34] The Popular Front participated in the competitive elections for the Supreme Council in 1990, won a plurality of seats and became a ruling force in the Council.[35] The National Independence Party, together with the Estonian Heritage Society, became a dominant force in the Estonian Congress.[36] Although the Estonian Congress remained a kind of "a shadow parliament" to the Supreme Council, it had an important moral weight and could not be defied by the Council.[37] (Pettai 2001, pp. 112–114; Taagepera 1993, ch. 7, 1994, pp. 213–214; Raitviir 1996, p. 353; Lauristin and Vihalemm 1997, p. 90)

The decision of the Supreme Council to convene the Constitutional Assembly has been termed as a "miracle compromise" (Pettai 2001, p. 111), given that it managed to strike a balance between the diverging plans of the Supreme Council and the Estonian Congress with regard to how to proceed with constitution-making. Some members of the Supreme Council called for declaring the Supreme Council a constitution-making body, while the leaders of the Estonian Congress insisted on new elections for a constitution-making body (Pettai 2001, p. 114).[38] With the resolution of the Supreme Council on the election of the

34 As a result of the initiative of the Citizens Committees, 845 000 citizens were registered (Taagepera 1993, p. 174).

35 The Estonian National Independence Party and some of its allies refrained from participating in the elections for the Supreme Council since they perceived it as an "illegitimate" institution (Taagepera 1993, p. 174).

36 Among the registered citizens, the turnout at the elections of the Estonian Congress was 98 percent of the adults who had registered (Taagepera 1993, p. 174).

37 Although most Estonians supported cooperation between the two bodies, little of it materialised (Taagepera 1993, pp. 176–177). Throughout 1990–1991, there was "never-ending jousting" between the Congress and the Council (p. 185). Lauristin and Vihalemm (1997, p. 93) note that although such a split could have had disastrous consequences for Estonian independence, fortunately, considerations of common interest prevailed, and the conflict between the two bodies remained rather low profile. Vahtre (1996, p. 79) explains that the role of the Congress was "deterrant" in the sense that any "Soviet-minded" decision by the Supreme Council would have increased the popularity of the Congress.

38 The decision of the Supreme Council did not go uncontested, however. A group of members of the Supreme Council submitted an alternative proposal to the Supreme Council, according to which the Constitution would be drafted by a group of 20–30 legal experts, together with foreign experts. The proposal suggested that after the preliminary version

Constitutional Assembly (3 September 1991) it was decided that the Constitutional Assembly should have 60 members (30 from the Estonian Congress and 30 from the Supreme Council).[39] Those 43 candidates who were members of both the Supreme Council and the Estonian Congress had to decide in which body they would stand as candidates. The resolution required that the election of the members to the CA would follow the principle of proportionality, but the exact procedure was to be determined by the bodies themselves. The Assembly was given the right to contract experts and scientists for advice. The draft Constitution was to be submitted to the Supreme Council (by 15 November 1991), which was to decide on putting the draft on referendum. As Taagepera (1994, p. 218) points out, an important feature in the Council's resolution was the stipulation that the decisions in the Constitutional Assembly were to be reached by simple majority voting (rather than by absolute majority).[40] The final draft Constitution, however, had to receive the support of the majority of all members of the Constitutional Assembly. On 7 September 1991, the Supreme Council and the Estonian Congress elected their representatives to the Constitutional Assembly. Taagepera (1994, p. 217) notes that the election outcomes in both bodies were fairly proportional to the strength of the various groupings in the respective bodies. Among the total of 60 CA members, about 20 were connected to the Popular Front, another 20 could be counted as national radicals, 13 were various Estonian moderates and reform Communists, and 7 were representatives of the Russians. Among the 30 representatives elected from Supreme Council, 15 were also members of the Estonian Congress, among the 30 representatives elected from the Estonian Congress, 3 were also members of the Supreme Council (Aaskivi and Pärnaste 2002, p. 49).

As Taagepera (1994, p. 218) explains, based on his own experience as a member of the CA, the tactics of those CA members interested in a constructive outcome (including members both from the Supreme Council and the Congress) were to settle on procedural issues before the CA convened, with a view to the very tight deadline (only two months, which was very short time, given that the Assembly could only meet on Fridays and Saturdays). The rules of procedure were to ensure that the CA would be able to concentrate on preparing the text of

---

of the Constitution has been drafted, it would be submitted for public discussion that would involve the Estonian Congress, the representatives of local governments, county governments and associations. This proposal was, however, rejected by the Supreme Council.

39 The number of members in the Constitutional Assembly was also a compromise. The Estonian Congress favoured a larger assembly of 80 representatives, while the Supreme Council supported a smaller one of 40 members. Some members of the Supreme Council demanded a higher representation for the Supreme Council as the "senior partner" (Taagepera 1994, pp. 216–217).

40 Taagepera (1994, p. 218) points out that the Supreme Council itself had often been bogged down by the requirement of absolute majority for making decisions.

the Constitution and not get bogged down by current political disputes (Aaskivi 2002, p. 123). For that purpose, a small group met informally and, at the opening session of the CA, presented a set of procedural rules (Taagepera 1994, p. 218). For most part, the rules of procedure reflected an existing legislative approach to passing a law, including the submission of draft(s), three readings where amendment proposals were voted on and committee work. An important decision with respect to the rules of procedure was the decision not to establish a quorum requirement. Thus, the Constitutional Assembly could begin its sessions irrespective of how many members were present.[41] According to the rules of procedure, the chairman of the Assembly had the right to discontinue all speeches that did not regard the Constitution. The rules of procedure stated that draft constitutions were to be submitted to the Assembly by the beginning of October 1991, and, from the submitted proposals, the Assembly would choose one as the basis for further deliberation.[42]

The rules of procedure foresaw the creation of committees, in order to facilitate a more detailed discussion on the different chapters of the Constitution.[43] At the first meeting of the Constitutional Assembly, on 13 September 1991, seven committees were formed. The first committee was responsible for the preamble, general provisions and people; the second committee for fundamental rights, freedoms and duties; the third committee for the *Riigikogu* (the parliament), the Government, the state budget, legislation and amending the Constitution; the fourth committee for the head of the state and international treaties; the fifth committee for defence; the sixth committee for the courts, the State Audit Office and the legal chancellor; the seventh committee for local governments. The committees were formed on a voluntary basis: the members could sign up for the committee that interested them most. In November 1991, an eighth committee – a redaction committee – was elected, with the task to edit and coordinate the various chapters in order to ensure consistency and coherence of the draft.

41 Taagepera (1994, p. 222) emphasises that the lack of quorum requirement was essential for the successful functioning of the CA, since it avoided giving power to the absentees.

42 The idea of including specific deadlines was suggested by Peet Kask (a member of the Supreme Council), who recalled how the Supreme Council had wandered aimlessly during its first months in 1990 (Taagepera 1994, p. 219). To several members, the requirement to submit draft constitutions came as a surprise: they expected that the Assembly would proceed like the Constitutional Convention of the United States, where first the general principles had been agreed upon and then specific provisions drafted (Adams 2002; Pärnaste 2002).

43 The rules of procedure gave the committees a very important role. It was stipulated that the amendment proposals to the draft Constitution would be submitted to the committee dealing with the particular topic, the committee would then discuss the proposal, pass a decision and present the decision to the general assembly. Members of the Assembly not satisfied with the decision of the committee could request a vote on the decision at the plenary session.

At the second session of the CA, two draft constitutions were submitted. The first one had been drafted by a working group of legal experts led by the Minister of Justice Jüri Raidla. The second draft was the 1938 Constitution of Estonia. By the end of September, three further draft proposals were submitted.[44] The Constitutional Assembly voted on 11 October 1991, which of the drafts would be taken as the basis for continued work. The main competing drafts were the draft of Raidla and his team (putting forth a more presidential system)[45] and the draft of Jüri Adams (putting forth a more parliamentary system by mending the 1920 Constitution of Estonia with some more balanced provisions and incorporating some provisions from the 1938 Constitution).[46] The Constitutional Assembly chose the draft of Adams (a member of the Estonian Congress and the chairman of the Estonian National Independence Party) as the basis for further deliberations (with 29 versus 22 votes). Although the draft of Adams was taken as the basis, during the course of the Assembly's work, the draft was extensively revised and many articles and wordings were taken over from Raidla's draft.[47]

At the end of October 1991, a delegation of foreign experts visited the Assembly and commented on the draft.[48] The Constitutional Assembly did not

44 For an overview of the different drafts and the differences between them, see Taagepera (1994) and Pettai (2001).

45 The group of 12 leading legal experts had been working on the draft Constitution (or a "temporary" Constitution) for several months. Raidla, when presenting the draft Constitution to the Constitutional Assembly, emphasised the thorough preparation and broad base of ideas that had been used for putting together the draft, including the Estonian Constitutions of 1920 and 1938, constitutions of other (as he emphasised "cultural") states, the theoretical works and media publications of several legal scholars and practitioners from Estonia, the draft constitutions proposed by the leading legal scholars in Estonia in 1990 and early 1991, the pre-constitutional acts of the Supreme Council pertaining to public law and the constitutional positions of the Estonian Congress (*Põhiseadus ja Põhiseaduse Assamblee* 1997, pp. 56–57).

46 As Adams (2002) admits in his memoirs, he wrote this draft essentially in one week. Still, he had been interested in constitutional issues for a longer time and had written several memoranda concerning constitutional issues to the Estonian Congress during 1990–1991. As pointed out by Pettai (2001) and Taagepera (1994), Adams had no formal training in law, but a degree in forestry. Because of his dissident background, he had been working as a boiler-man.

47 Ruutsoo (2002a, p. 201) even argues that the adopted Constitution was more similar to the draft of Raidla than to the draft of Adams.

48 The delegation of foreign experts (under the auspices of the Council of Europe) included: E. Harremoes (Denmark), the director of legal affairs at the Council of Europe; R. Herzog (Germany), the President of the Constitutional Court of Germany; K. Berchtold (Austria), expert in the Council of Europe; P. Germer (Denmark), professor of constitutional law at Aarhus University; I. MacPherson (Canada), the dean of the legal faculty of Toronto University; M. Russell (Ireland), expert in the Council of Europe; G. Carcassonne (France), a member of the Constitutional Council of France; H. Ragnemalm (Sweden), a member of the Venice Commission for Democracy through Law, a member of the

manage to meet the initial deadline (set for 15 November) and asked for extending the deadline for submitting the final draft. The Supreme Council took notice of that information and decided that the CA must present the draft Constitution by 20 January 1992. The first draft of the Constitution was released to the public on 21 December 1991. During the first three months of the Assembly's work, relatively little had been reported on its deliberations to the public.[49] The redaction committee was given the task to sort through the proposals submitted by the public. Some 500 persons, groups and organisations sent their recommendations. In January 1992, the Supreme Council decided that the Constitutional Assembly should continue its work but cooperate more closely with the "expert group" led by Raidla (Aaskivi and Pärnaste 2002, p. 60). The expert group consisted of seven members: all of them had been the members of the team that had formulated the draft of Raidla. As a result of the cooperation, several additions were made to the draft, in particular to the chapter on the fundamental rights and duties (Hänni 2002a, p. 164).

The final version of the draft Constitution was approved by the Constitutional Assembly on 14 February 1992 (by a margin of 32 to 3 votes, with 6 abstentions) and was submitted to the Supreme Council for consideration. In March the Supreme Council decided that it would not start changing the draft Constitution but returned it to the Assembly, claiming that it lacked consensus among the Estonian people and had no backing of the majority of the Assembly. The CA was again asked to "coordinate" its draft with the "expert group" of the Supreme Council lawyers, take into account the proposals of the Supreme Council and submit a new draft by mid-April. (Taagepera 1994, pp. 226–227; Aaskivi and Pärnaste 2002; p. 68; Adams 2002, p. 151; Hänni 2002a, p. 166) During the following month, a host of minor wording changes were made to the Assembly's draft, but, in terms of content, not much was changed. A more substantive change was the right given to the president to appeal to the Supreme Court after his veto is overridden by the parliament. The Assembly reaffirmed its support for the document at the 30th session (on 10 April 1992), and the Supreme Council decided to put the Constitution on referendum. On 28 June 1992, the Constitution was approved in a referendum where only Estonian citizens could vote. The list of citizens included 669 080 persons; 446 708 took part in the referendum, of whom 91 percent voted in favour of the Constitution.

Swedish parliament; A. Suviranta (Finland), the president of the Administrative Court of Finland. In addition, a number of foreign experts were asked to submit their written opinions on the draft Constitutions, including H. Schwartz, from American University, Washington.

49 The only exceptions were some articles published in the newspapers by the members of the Assembly (for an overview, see Jarne 2002).

2.2. Testing the Hypotheses

The goal of this section is to test the hypotheses outlined in chapter 1 with the case of constitution-making in Estonia. The hypotheses that are confirmed would have a strengthened position in the theoretical framework on constitution-making.[50] Further, this section seeks to elaborate on the underlying causal mechanisms and indicate possible directions for the refinement of the hypotheses.

2.2.1. Mode of Constitution-Making

As mentioned above, what makes the Estonian case of constitution-making special in the context of Central and Eastern Europe, is that the Constitution was prepared by a constituent body that was formally separate from the existing legislature (although including representatives from there). In other CEE countries, the constitution-making bodies were at the same time also functioning as ordinary legislatures or were sub-committees thereof. The Estonian Constitutional Assembly (1991–1992) comes closer to the ideal proposed by normative discussions than any of the other constituent bodies in CEE and should therefore be of special theoretical interest for constitutional political economy.

The Estonian case provides corroboration for the hypothesis H_1, stating that the decision to convene a constitutional assembly presupposes a "constitutional

50 Some of the hypotheses outlined in chapter 1 have already been tested. Based on 13 country reports from CEE and FSU, Elgie and Zielonka (2001, p. 39) claim that the cases provide "sufficient evidence to claim that framers tend to adopt constitutional solutions to their own institutional interests". Elster (1993, 1996a, 1997b) has tested the hypotheses proceeding from institutional self-interest with the cases of constitution-making in Poland, Hungary, the Czech Republic, Slovakia, Bulgaria and Romania. He finds that, for most part, the hypotheses termed H_{2a}-H_{2d} in section 1.3. are corroborated. There are only few notable exceptions: the legislative constituent assembly in Hungary created a very strong constitutional court and adopted constructive vote of confidence (that strengthens the power of the government *vis-à-vis* the legislature) and in Romania constitutional amendments are subject to mandatory referendum. Elster (1993, pp. 193–194) also finds support for H_{6a} and H_{6b}: the pre-communist constitutions of these countries played an important role as positive or negative models in the design of the constitutions. In his study of ten CEE countries (Albania, Bulgaria, Poland, Romania, Hungary, Slovakia, the Czech Republic, Croatia, Macedonia and Slovenia) Adamovich (2004, ch. 5) confirms H_{2a}-H_{2d} and H_{3a}. In addition, based on the country reports in Zielonka (ed.) (2001), some of the other hypotheses outlined in chapter 1 can also be tested. The making of the Polish 1997 Constitution provides evidence for H_{5d} (see Wyrzykowski 2001). As for H_{3a}, several cases from CEE show that the framers may choose not to fix the electoral system in the constitution (e.g., Hungary) or provide only very general outlines (e.g., Poland and Czech Republic) (Elgie and Zielonka 2001, p. 44; Elster 1997a, p. 125). The Lithuanian case clearly confirms H_{4b}, H_{6b} and H6d (see Gelazis 2001). The case of Ukraine confirms H_{4a} (see Wolczuk 2001, p. 253).

moment". The moment at which the Supreme Council of Estonia decided to convene the Constitutional Assembly can certainly be characterised as a "constitutional moment": it took place during the coup in Moscow and the decision was adopted together with the declaration of independence. The main objective of the declaration was to draw a legal demarcation line between Estonia and the Soviet Union, in case the coup succeeded (Taagepera 1994, p. 215). The demonstration of unity between the Supreme Council and the Estonian Congress was needed to secure both domestic and international credibility of the declaration of independence. In order to reach the compromise, both sides were willing to make concessions that would have been difficult (or even impossible) during the times of "normality", which is why it has been termed a "miracle compromise" (Pettai 2001, p. 115).[51] By agreeing to share the constitution-making with the Congress, the Supreme Council ceded a significant amount of its formal power and gave up the proposal to declare the Council as a constitution-making body. In return for being included in the making of the new Constitution, the representatives of the Congress gave up their ideas of re-enacting the 1938 Constitution or calling for general elections of a new constitution-making body (to be elected by citizens of Estonia). Taagepera (1994, p. 216) remarks that after the threat of the coup passed, some representatives on both sides began to feel they had conceded too much, but the agreement had already been signed. Given that the resolution to convene the Assembly was in the same decision with the declaration of independence, contesting one would have jeopardised the other. In addition to the "constitutional moment", historical experiences can be argued to have played a role in the choice of the constitution-making body. Marju Lauristin, one of the authors of the compromise, noted in her speech in the Supreme Council that the idea of Constitutional Assembly had been inspired by the National Assembly that had drafted the 1938 Constitution in Estonia (Verbatim Record of the Supreme Council, 3–5 September 1991, p. 91). Although Elster (1998a, p. 117) argues that it is highly unlikely that a country can afford to have two sets of elites – one for writing the constitution and another for governing the country – especially in the context of transition, the Estonian case shows that even in a situation of urgency, a country may be able to afford "two elites". This, however, was made possible by a idiosyncratic situation in Estonia where there were two representative assemblies: the Supreme Council (the formal legislative body) and the Estonian Congress that was more like a body for deliberation on constitutional issues. As Taagepera (1993, p. 174) notes, "Among the many odd happenings in Eastern Europe around 1990, the elections of the Esto-

51 As Marju Lauristin, one of the authors of the compromise, noted later in a speech in the Supreme Council (as a response to objections regarding the creation of the Constitutional Assembly), "In moments of crisis, apparently, not only persons but also assemblies of persons are ethically and politically more mature and enlightened." (Verbatim Record of the Supreme Council, 3–5 September 1991, p. 90)

nian Congress … ranked among the strangest."[52] Therefore, one should not be too hasty in drawing a lesson for future cases.

2.2.2. Actors Involved in Constitution-Making

2.2.2.1. Members of Constituent Body

The Estonian case of constitution-making confirms hypothesis H_{2a} for most part. More than half of the framers came from an existing legislature (the Supreme Council)[53] and the resulting Constitution is parliamentarian (with the president as a symbolic head of the state with limited executive powers). The Constitution gives the residual powers to the legislature, and, as Frye (1997) notes, the presidency in Estonia is among the weakest in the region. Schneider (1999, p. 419) even argues that the Constitution gives the *Riigikogu* (the Estonian legislature) several tasks that are untypical functions for a parliament and belong usually to the realm of the executive.

The underlying mechanisms behind this institutional choice, however, need further investigation. Of special theoretical interest is the question of whether the representatives from the Estonian Congress (which did not pass laws but acted as a deliberative body for outlining the contours of constitutional laws) also preferred a strong parliament to a strong president and why. In terms of proportions, more representatives from the Estonian Congress than from the Council preferred a strong parliament and a weak president. On the one hand, it should be noted that already the first party programme of the Estonian National Independence Party (from year 1988) had indicated a preference for a strong parliament (Niitsoo 2002, p. 91). Hence, the preference for a strong legislature could be seen as having been driven by principled commitment to parliamentarism. On the other hand, the CA delegates from the Estonian Congress were prominent figures in the Estonian political scene (including former dissidents, independence activists, writers and academics) and could be considered as very likely candidates for the next parliamentary elections. Thus, the hypothesis linking the membership in an existing legislature to a constitutional preference for a strong parliament should be complemented with a hypothesis linking the *expected* membership (even without the existing membership) in the future parliament to the respective constitutional preference.

52 "Here was a country the Kremlin still considered as part of the USSR, yet its brash citizens committees carried out full-fledged elections that bypassed the entire Soviet administrative structure. … The approach was amazingly successful in that genuine countrywide elections materialized – perhaps the only privately organized general elections in world history." (Taagepera 1993, p. 174)

53 Although both the Supreme Council and the Estonian Congress could send 30 representatives to the CA, several representatives sent to the CA by the Estonian Congress were also members of the Supreme Council.

In addition to the pursuits of institutional self-interest, other explanatory factors for the design choices should be considered and their importance assessed. Malova and Haughton (2002, p. 103) point out that "the European inheritance of parliamentarism" played an important role in the constitution-making of the CEE countries, tilting the preferences towards parliamentarism. In Estonia's case as well, the will to "return to Europe" appears to have played a role in institutional choices. Most framers assumed from start that a choice would be made among hybrid systems rather than between a pure presidential and a pure parliamentary regime. There were, however, some framers who argued for a presidential regime: the adherents of the 1938 Constitution. Malova and Haughton suggest that more elevated status of parliaments in CEE countries is, in part, a product of the legacy of communist rule, under which, theoretically at least, the constitutions invested all power in parliament (p. 109). At the same time, however, one needs to keep in mind that the parliamentary bodies during the Soviet regime were only a political façade. In the Estonian case, it was only the Supreme Council elected in the democratic elections in 1990 that became a "real parliament", vested with actual decision-making powers. During the debates of the CA, the existing (Soviet) constitution was viewed negatively as giving excessive de facto powers to the executive; its supposed "exemplary parliamentarism" was not mentioned at all.

In explaining the choices of the Constitutional Assembly in Estonia, Schneider (1999) suggests that the "excessive burdening" of the parliament reflected the historical experience: on the one hand, there was the fear of the authoritarianism of the "silent epoch" of the 1930s, on the other hand, there was the memory of the super-democratic 1920 Constitution, which had acquired the nature of a revered "myth" and gave rise to the attitude among a number of the members of the Constitutional Assembly that the more tasks the parliament has, the more parliamentarian the state is. When looking at the debates in the Constitutional Assembly, the main argument of the proponents of parliamentarism in the CA was that parliamentarism is more conducive to the survival of a young democracy; references were often made to the studies by Matthew Shugart and his colleagues. It was feared that strong presidentialism would give rise to conflicts between the president and the parliament, leading to instability. Based on the verbatim records of the debates in Assembly alone, one could conclude that the empirically proven constitutional theories and the desired goal of a stable democracy played a major role in the constitutional design in Estonia. The memoirs of the members of the Constitutional Assembly, however, point to a different conclusion. As a prominent member of the Constitutional Assembly Peet Kask (2002, p. 180) admits in his recollections of the work of the Assembly, the constitutional preference of the majority of the Assembly for a strong parliamentary system was driven by the current interests of the members rather than by the weight of the arguments. Rein Lang (2002, p. 219), who was an expert to the Assembly, states that in preparing the Constitution, there was a competition between the different forces who wanted to secure their power for the future: "Therefore, every legal construction that concerned the mechanisms of power were viewed through a political prism." Liia Hänni (2002a, p. 164), another prominent member of the Assembly, notes that although the members of the Assembly had given an oath not to consider the issues of current politics, these considerations rose high in discussions over the institution of president.

As mentioned in section 2.1., the parliamentarian draft of Adams won only by a margin of seven votes against the more presidential draft of Raidla. Those members of the Congress who were in favour of strict legal continuity of the inter-war republic wanted to adopt the 1938 Constitution, according to which the president had very strong powers. Further, there were several members from the Supreme Council who supported a strong president on the grounds that this would enhance their chances to remain in power (since they were affiliated with the most likely candidate for that position, Arnold Rüütel). Thus, the hypothesis that framers who are members of an existing legislature will always prefer strong constitutional powers of the future legislature does not necessarily hold. As the Estonian case shows, for some framers, trade-offs may have to be made between institutional self-interest and adhering to historical tradition; for others, future positions in other branches may appear more likely.

Still, increasing the powers of the president and the cabinet (*vis-à-vis* the initial draft of Adams) came about primarily as a result of the pressure from the presidium of the Supreme Council (with the chairman of it, Arnold Rüütel, hoping to become the next president) and the local constitutional experts (some of whom were members of Government at the time). As pointed out in section 2.1., the Supreme Council sent the draft Constitution back to the Assembly on 19 March 1992 and ordered it to coordinate the draft with the expert group of the Supreme Council. Had it only been up to the decision of the Assembly itself, the resulting Constitution would have been even more parliamentarian.

Altogether, the Estonian case confirms the hypothesis H_{2a} to a large extent. More refined versions of the hypothesis should, however, emphasise the different motives of the members of the constituent body: those who are members of an existing legislature, but view their position in the executive branch more likely, will have constitutional preferences for a strong executive; those who are not members of the existing legislature, but expect to be elected to the future legislature, will prefer a strong legislature. Further hypotheses should point to interplays between historical experiences (including commitment to previous constitutions) and institutional self-interest. In addition, interactions between the constituent body and other existing governmental institutions would warrant closer inspection. The interaction between the different bodies would depend on the nature of the "upstream constraints" (Elster 1996b) imposed on the constitution-making body (like the Supreme Council in the Estonian case), which may constrain the expressions of institutional self-interest of a particular branch in constitution-making. On the other hand, the actors or agencies imposing the upstream constraints may have their own institutional interests that they pursue in constitution-making. Elster (1996b, p. 96) has conjectured that "The creators will try to exercise an influence over their creature, by imposing constraints on the constitutional document or by reserving a right of veto." To what extent the "creator agency" can be successful in pushing through its own interests depends, *inter alia*, on the veto power it has, its perceived legitimacy by the public and the extent to which its members are represented in the constitution-making body.

The Estonian case confirms partially the hypothesis H_{2b}. The Estonian Constitution provides for referendum as one possible mechanism for amending the Constitution. There are, however, two other possibilities that emphasise the role of the legislature in amending the Constitution, which are certainly easier than the use of referenda. A more refined version of the hypothesis should outline that even if a referendum is foreseen as an option for amending the Constitution, the options given to the legislature are likely to be easier.

The hypothesis H_{2c} is confirmed by the Estonian case: the unicameral Assembly opted for a unicameral legislature. Interestingly, however, at the beginning of the discussions of the Assembly, several members of the first committee (five out of seven) supported a bicameral legislature, like it had been foreseen by the 1938 Constitution. The chairman of the first committee Vello Salum (from the Estonian Congress) argued that the parliament should be bicameral, since most of the parliaments in the world are bicameral. He referred to the second chamber of the 1938 Constitution, which had included older experienced people and improved the quality of legislation. (*Põhiseadus ja Põhiseaduse Assamblee* 1997, p. 145) The third and fourth committee, however, supported a unicameral parliament. Unicameralism versus bicameralism was one of the issues that was touched upon by several foreign experts as well. They were all very critical of bicameralism and advised against it (*Põhiseadus ja Põhiseaduse Assamblee* 1997, speeches by Russell, pp. 327–328, Berchtold, p. 328–329, Suviranta, p. 330, MacPherson, p. 335). The arguments of the foreign experts against bicameralism were often referred to during subsequent debates.

The hypothesis H_{2d} is supported by the Estonian case. Although Estonia did not have an institution of president during the time of the constitution-making, there was a position – the Chairman of the Presidium of the Supreme Council – that was in many ways perceived as an equivalent to that of a president or a head of the state. Arnold Rüütel, who held this position at the time, was also a member of the Constitutional Assembly but could not participate in its work very actively, given his numerous obligations elsewhere. Several groupings in the Supreme Council, however, were interested in guaranteeing that Rüütel would become president after the Constitution is passed (Laar 2002; Ruutsoo 2002a,b). The representatives from these groupings (together with the local expert group) clearly promoted a stronger president and direct elections of the president.

The Estonian case provides confirmation for the hypothesis H_{3a}. Those who wanted to see Rüütel as the president, advocated direct popular elections of the president (given the popularity of Rüütel among the people), while his opponents argued for electing the president in the parliament (which implied at least some possibility of Rüütel not becoming a president).[54] None of the parties participating in the Constitutional Assembly had an overwhelming majority and there were no proposals to introduce a majoritarian system for parliamentary elections.[55] It was in the interest of all parties to have a proportional electoral system, which was also included in the Constitution.[56]

The Estonian case corroborates hypothesis H_{3b}, suggesting that if the electoral favourite for the executive position has weak bargaining powers and/or the electoral outcome is highly uncertain, the framers will design an executive office with few specific powers and tightly constrained residual powers. Frye (1997) also argues that in Estonia the president was attributed so limited powers as a result of the combination of electoral uncertainty and the bargaining position of those supporting a strong president.[57] Indeed, those supporting Rüütel had a lower bargaining power in the Constitutional Assembly than his opponents and although Rüütel was the electoral favourite according to opinion polls, the electoral outcome was not certain. Still, the causal mechanisms at play behind the institutional choices made by the Assembly with regard to the power and election mode of the president were more complicated than suggested by Frye. First, institutional self-interest of the framers (discussed above) and historical experiences played a role in opting for a strong parliament (and by implication, for a weaker president). Second, assessing the electoral chances of Rüütel – and hence designing the powers of the president – was complicated by the fact that the very *mode* of electing the president was under continuous discussion and was not established until the very end of the CA's work. The opponents of Rüütel feared that direct presidential elections would allow him to become the president, while elections in the legislature would lessen his chances. Hence, it could be argued that it was the uncertainty with regard to the *electoral rule* for electing the president that made the framers more cautious in attributing specific and residual powers to the institution of president. Strategic calculations were further complicated by the fact – as decided in March 1992 – that the first presidential elections were to take place in a different way than the mode entailed in

54 "I remember a debate with an important member of the Estonian Congress who declared that the Constitution has to make sure that Arnold Rüütel will not become a president" (Lang 2002, p. 219).

55 While the draft of Raidla left the characteristics of the electoral system to be determined by statutes, the draft of Adams already provided for proportional electoral system.

56 It is interesting to note here that 24 out of the 60 members of the CA became members of the first *Riigikogu* elected in 1992.

57 Frye (1997) remarks that according to prevalent theories of institutional choice – emphasising that the framers would prefer a strong executive when the polity faces an economic downturn (Przeworski 1991), has a parliament dominated by weak parties (Shugart 1993) or is characterised by ethnic fragmentation (Horowitz 1985) – Estonia should have a strong president, but it does not.

the Constitution: in order to appease the public, the Implementation Act of the Constitution foresaw that the first presidential elections would be direct in the first round and only if no candidate received more the 50 percent of the votes, the parliament would elect the president.[58]

The Estonian case provides evidence for hypotheses H_{3c} and H_{3d}. The framers were faced with electoral uncertainties concerning the first elections pursuant to the new constitution and the Estonian 1992 Constitution provides for a strong and independent judiciary and extensive constitutional review. At the same time, however, the causal mechanisms in play appear to have been different than conjectured by Ginsburg (2002), Smithey and Ishiyama (2000) and Romeu (2006), who focused on framers' strategic calculations. In the Estonian case, most of the provisions pertaining to the independence and powers of the judiciary were already included in the first drafts submitted to the assembly and the provisions in these drafts had been mostly taken over from the inter-war constitutions. Also, as will be discussed in section 2.2.2.2., the proposals to further increase the powers of the judiciary, compared with the initial drafts, came primarily from constitutional experts (both foreign and local), while the Constitutional Assembly played a rather passive role in drafting the provisions pertaining to judiciary. Only on very few occasions were objections voiced by the members of the CA to these suggestions.

For example, the provision "Judges shall be appointed for life" (Article 147 Section 1) was included already in the drafts of Raidla and Adams. This provision was accepted by members of the CA; only once was a concern expressed with regard to the applicability of this provision in the immediate post-constitutional phase because of the lack of well-qualified and professional judges (*Põhiseadus ja Põhiseaduse Assamblee* 1997, pp. 207–208).[59] The general attitude among framers was that guaranteeing the independence and autonomy of judiciary was extremely important for establishing a genuinely democratic order and avoiding the politicisation of courts, which had characterised the Soviet period. Most of the members concurred with the chairman of the sixth committee (in charge of the chapter on courts) Jüri Rätsep in that the politicisation of the courts had been responsible for many tragic experiences of the Soviet period (*Põhiseadus ja Põhiseaduse Assamblee* 1997, p. 445).

On the whole, the debates on the court system were relatively brief; most of the discussions focused on minor issues (like how much longer than the established retirement age would the judges be allowed to remain in office). The issue

58 As Ruutsoo (2002a, p. 204) points out, this provision was "engineered" by the representatives of the Congress to guarantee that Rüütel would not become president. The supporters of Rüütel, however, still expected him to become president, even with a system like that.

59 Ants Erm (from the Estonian Congress) suggested foreseeing a transitional phase during which judges would be appointed for seven years (*Põhiseadus ja Põhiseaduse Assamblee* 1997, pp. 207–208).

that appeared to receive most extensive attention and emotional feedback was the question of whether lay members of the courts would be foreseen or allowed by the Constitution. The vice chairman of the sixth committee Ülo Seppa persistently brought up the need to preclude the use of lay members in court proceedings by a constitutional provision establishing that judges have to be professional. Rätsep, however, favoured the continuation of using lay persons in court proceedings and argued that the foreign experts had also regarded such a system positively. In the final version of the Constitution, the issue of lay persons is not dealt with: this was left for lower level acts to regulate.[60]

With regard to constitutional review, Pettai (2005b, p. 93) notes that during the discussions of the CA "the need for some kind of constitutional review was never disputed", and the debates were confined to the specific "mechanics" of how the procedures and institutions would look like. The only provision that was contested with regard to constitutional review concerned the right of the president to turn to the Supreme Court – after the law the president has returned to the *Riigikogu* (on the grounds of unconstitutionality) is passed unamended – and ask the Court to declare the law unconstitutional. Such a right of the president was recommended by expert Matthew Russell, who drew on Irish experience with such a mechanism of constitutional review (*Põhiseadus ja Põhiseaduse Assamblee* 1997, p. 325). Although the draft of Adams had included the right of the president to exercise a veto on the grounds of unconstitutionality, it stipulated that when the *Riigikogu* passes the law unamended, the president *has to* proclaim it. The fourth committee proposed to add the right of the president to turn to the Supreme Court, but the CA decided not to include this provision in the draft Constitution in November 1991 (*Põhiseadus ja Põhiseaduse Assamblee* 1997, pp. 382–383).[61] However, this provision was proposed by the redaction committee in April 1992 (at the thirtieth session of the CA) and was included in the Constitution.[62]

The discussions on constitutional review in the CA appear to corroborate the arguments by Shapiro (1999, p. 218), who has noted that constitutional review has been adopted by framers in many countries partly because constitutional review has become an obligatory component of currently prevailing conception of constitutionalism. Like in the other CEE countries, the successful experience of Western European countries with constitutional review played a role in the institutional choices of Estonian framers (see Elgie and Zielonka 2001, p. 30).

60 This solution was also recommended, for example, by expert Suviranta, from Finland (*Põhiseadus ja Põhiseaduse Assamblee* 1997, pp. 329–330).

61 Instead of discussing the president's right to turn to the Supreme Court, the CA focused on the issue of what the required majority should be for the *Riigikogu* to override the president's veto. (*Põhiseadus ja Põhiseaduse Assamblee* 1997, pp. 382–386)

62 Hänni justified this provision by stating that it would be unfair if the president were forced to proclaim a law that he considers unconstitutional (*Põhiseadus ja Põhiseaduse Assamblee* 1997, p. 1005).

Altogether, strategic considerations with regard to the judiciary appeared to play a lesser role compared to the "constitutional theories" pointing to the need to break with the Soviet heritage and to establish a European-type judicial system.

The Estonian case also contradicts the pattern found by Smithey and Ishiyama (2000), according to which the larger the number of parties involved in the constitutional negotiations, the less independent the resulting constitutional court would be. Despite the fact that almost all existing parties were represented at the constituent assembly, the Estonian 1992 Constitution provides for a strong and independent judiciary and extensive constitutional review.[63] Also, one should note that although Ginsburg's theoretical model would predict the adoption of centralised constitutional review with a separate constitutional court in Estonia's case, the framers in fact opted for a decentralised approach, with the constitutional review chamber being an integral part of the judiciary.[64]

2.2.2.2. Constitutional Experts

With regard to the hypotheses H_{4a} and H_{4b}, the Estonian case provides more evidence in favour than against. The case study indicates, however, that one should distinguish between different ways constitutional experts can be involved in constitution-making. The experts can be elected as members of the assembly, submit draft constitutions, be contracted as advisors to the assembly (e.g., to the committees of the assembly or to the assembly as a whole), be involved through special sessions where experts present their opinions, and the constituent body can even be compelled – by upstream constraints – to work with a task-force of experts. When analysing the role of experts in constitution-making in Estonia, a distinction should be made between foreign and local experts. Among local experts, one should differentiate between those who were contracted by the Assembly itself (to aid the work of the committees) and those with whom the Assembly was, in later phases of its work, "compelled" to cooperate by the Supreme Council.[65] Therefore, the overview below looks at the different kinds of experts in discussing the role they played in the constitutional discussions and the advice they gave.

---

63 A more detailed overview of the Estonian constitutional review is given in chapter 9.

64 Although on the proposal of the redaction committee, the CA left out the provision according to which "in a court proceeding, the court shall not apply any law that is in conflict with the Constitution", this provision was included in the Constitution again in March 1992. With regard to the idea of having a separate constitutional court, although this was suggested by some foreign experts, this was admitted as a possibility only once at the debates of the CA (see the speech by Peet Kask, *Põhiseadus ja Põhiseaduse Assamblee* 1997, p. 385). For most part, the CA proceeded from the provision in the draft of Adams, according to which the Supreme Court is also the court of constitutional review.

65 These experts were, for most part, the same who had submitted one of the draft constitutions – the so-called Raidla's draft – to the CA in September 1991.

Concerning the role of the local experts in *preparing* the draft Constitution, Ruutsoo (2002a, p. 202), a member of the CA, has argued that one of the reasons why the Assembly rejected the draft of the legal experts (Raidla's draft) was "the distanced confidence" of the team. When the draft was presented, an impression was given that changing the draft too much would be problematic. Raidla's team served the concept of a strong president as the only possible one and threatened to withdraw the draft when this was changed (Kask 2002, p. 179). Also, as Ruutsoo (2002b, p. 160) argues, several members of the Assembly resented the fact that Raidla was the Minister of Justice in the Government of Edgar Savisaar, who was very unpopular among several delegates from the Estonian Congress.

The visit of the delegation of foreign experts was viewed very positively by the Assembly members (Adams 2002). Some considered it even as a highlight of the work of the Assembly (Kask 2002, p. 179) and their opinions were often referred to in subsequent discussions of the Assembly. The foreign experts, who were for most part constitutional lawyers, advocated a parliamentary system and warned against too strong a president. Further, some foreign experts emphasised the need to strengthen the powers of the parliament *vis-à-vis* the cabinet. Russell (from Ireland), for example, pointed out that the parliament should have a stronger position *vis-à-vis* the government in asking questions and information.[66] He suggested that any individual member of the parliament should have the right to ask questions from the government. (*Põhiseadus ja Põhiseaduse Assamblee* 1997, p. 325) Several foreign experts also criticised the high majority requirements for the parliament (e.g., the two-thirds majority required for electing the president). Only Carcassone, an expert from France, was concerned with the weakness of the executive *vis-à-vis* the legislature (p. 324).

All the foreign experts favoured strong and independent courts with extensive powers of constitutional review. Expert Russell, drawing on Irish experience, suggested strengthening the role of the constitutional court by giving the president the right to refer a law to the court, if the parliament passes it unamended after the president has sent it back to the parliament (*Põhiseadus ja Põhiseaduse Assamblee* 1997, p. 325).[67] Expert Berchtold recommended having a separate constitutional court, like it is in Austria (p. 328). Expert Schwartz emphasised the importance of specifying in the Constitution how constitutional issues can get to the Supreme Court (Archival document no. RA-23-24-1-5, pp. 21, 23). Russell also emphasised the importance of having an independent and respected system of courts and judges. Interestingly, some foreign experts even considered the Estonian Constitution to give too strong guarantees to the judiciary. Schwartz, for example, pointed out that life tenure for judges is too long

66 In the draft of Adams it was stipulated that only if one-fifth of the parliament presents an inquiry, the Government must answer.

67 The same suggestion was put forth by Schwartz (Archival document no. RA-23-24-1-5, p. 22).

(Archival document no. RA-23-24-1-5, pp. 6d, 23).[68] Also, some experts, including Ragnemalm and Berchtold, expressed a concern that the institution of legal chancellor – one of the institutions involved in constitutional review – appeared to have unusually extensive powers (*Põhiseadus ja Põhiseaduse Assamblee* 1997, pp. 322, 328). All in all, however, the foreign experts advocated establishing a strong parliament and an independent judiciary with extensive powers of constitutional review; hence, the Estonian case provides support for the hypothesis H_{4b} but contradicts the hypothesis H_{4a}.

Among the experts who were *contracted* by the committees of the Assembly, legal specialists dominated. There were very few political scientists; Matthew Shugart, who advised the committee working on the chapter on the president, was a clear exception. Rein Taagepera, another prominent political scientist, was himself a member of the Constitutional Assembly. Both Taagepera and Shugart clearly favoured a more parliamentarian system and warned against too strong powers of president, whereas the legal specialists contracted by the committees had diverging views on the powers of the different branches.

The local constitutional experts who had written one of the draft constitutions (the so-called Raidla's draft) and who were "compelled" to work with the Assembly in later phases sought to attribute less power to the legislature *vis-à-vis* the other branches and endeavoured to increase the power of the president and the judiciary. While foreign experts had advised to lower the majority needed for electing the president by the parliament, the local experts argued (successfully) for increasing it to two-thirds again. Experts Rebane and Kiris (who were not members of the expert team but who were asked to submit written opinions on the different drafts of the Constitution) both suggested in their opinions to give the president the right to initiate legislation (Archival document no. RA-23-24-1-5, p. 44, 53, 84). In addition, Kiris recommended giving the president the authority to appoint the legal chancellor, the auditor general and the chief justice of the Supreme Court, like it had been in the 1938 Constitution (p. 50). On the whole, the constitutional experts of Estonia were very fond of the 1938 Constitution and the way it divided the power between the parliament, the government and the president; in particular, they saw the president as having an important "balancing role".

As a result of the input of the experts to drafting the Constitution, the judiciary was given extensive powers and strong guarantees of independence.[69] Estonia is the only country in CEE where judges are guaranteed life tenure by the constitution. The Estonian system of constitutional review, for example, gives

68 Schwartz noted, "I continue to have doubts about appointing all judges for life, particularly in early stages when you may still have judges whom you don't fully trust for either their competence or independence." (Archival document no. RA-23-24-1-5, p. 23)

69 It is worth noting here that many of the local constitutional experts involved in the constitutional discussions became members of the Supreme Court (or affiliated with it) in the post-constitutional phase.

the Supreme Court the right to exercise not only *ex post* and concrete control, but also *ex ante* and abstract control (through the mediation of the president or the legal chancellor). The local constitutional experts sought and succeeded to give the president the right to turn to the Supreme Court when his suspensive veto is overridden by the parliament, which can be seen as increasing both the power of the president and the Supreme Court. Salzberger and Voigt (2002, p. 41) also note that among the eight CEE countries they studied, the Estonian constitutional court has the highest *de jure* independence.

With respect to the provisions on judiciary in the Constitution, it is worth noting that the preparation of the acts regulating the courts and the status of judges had started already before the Declaration of Independence and they were passed by the Supreme Council on 23 October 1991, shortly after the Constitutional Assembly had convened. As Schneider (1999, p. 414) points out, the Constitution adopted the main principles reflected in these acts. There was, however, some confusion over how extensive the regulation of the courts in the Constitution should be, given that the main act regulating the judiciary already existed. The members of the Assembly sought to avoid contradicting the provisions in the existing acts but were, at the same time, hesitant to take over specific provisions from these acts (Schneider 2002).

Summing up, the local experts, who were constitutional lawyers, were suspicious of giving too many powers to the parliament and suggested increasing the powers of the president.[70] The foreign experts, in contrast, supported a strong parliament and warned against a strong president. Both local and foreign experts emphasised the importance of strong and independent judiciary. Refined hypotheses would distinguish between foreign and local experts, and emphasise the importance of the countries the experts come from (and their experiences with the constitutional arrangements in their respective countries). In addition, the hypotheses should distinguish between "contracted" (or invited) and "imposed" advice, which is likely to have different effects on discussions and resulting decisions.

---

70 With respect to the role of the local experts in constitutional discussions, a member of the Assembly Kaido Kama (2002, p. 177) puts it like following, "The best results were achieved when the opinions of the legal experts and politicians were balanced." On the other hand, Sibul (2002, p. 226) points out that the experts and the members of the CA never really came to trust each other. He suggests that one of the reasons was that the legal experts regarded the constitution more as a legal text than societal agreement. Hallaste (1996, p. 441) suggests that although the local experts usually "dressed" their arguments in the form of juridical expert opinion, their were often motivated by political considerations.

2.2.2.3. The General Public

The hypothesis H_{5a} was confirmed by the Estonian case – at least formally. In reality, however, it is difficult to bring about referenda. Only the parliament has the right to submit a bill to a referendum. Furthermore, if a bill that is submitted to a referendum does not receive a majority of votes in favour, the president shall declare extraordinary elections to the parliament. There are a number of reasons why the Constitutional Assembly decided to constrain the use of referenda. In part, it was motivated by distrust towards the public; in part, by the experiences with the ultra-democratic Constitution of 1920 (Maruste and Schneider 1996, p. 85; Arjakas 2002, p. 34). Another hypothesis in a similar line of discussion should look at whether the constitution provides for popular initiative. Based on the analogy with referenda, one can conjecture that if the constitution has to be ratified by the people, it will provide for popular initiative. The Estonian case, however, would not confirm this hypothesis. Adams explained leaving out popular initiative by pointing out that the Constitution gives the right to initiate laws to every member of the *Riigikogu* (*Põhiseadus ja Põhiseaduse Assamblee* 1997, p. 137). Thus, he could not conceive of a situation where there would be an important problem in the society and no member of the parliament to bring up the issue. In addition, Ernits (1999, p. 473) points out that the Assembly drew a lesson from the year 1933: the constitutional amendments that had led to authoritarian regime had been adopted as a result of a popular initiative. Again, the experiences of the inter-war period appear to have played a special role in shaping the constitutional choices in Estonia.

With regard to the hypothesis H_{5b}, the Estonian case points to ambiguous evidence. On the one hand, several members of the Assembly emphasised the importance of taking into account the public opinion, given that the Constitution would be put on referendum. Ülo Uluots (*Põhiseadus ja Põhiseaduse Assamblee* 1997, p. 336), for example, remarked, “We are facing an important filter – the referendum – so we should not ignore the proposals that have come from outside the assembly.” Lauri Vahtre (p. 612) also argued that the public opinion should be listened to, because people themselves think that they know what they want, and if the Assembly did not follow the public opinion, the people would consider the Assembly to be ignorant and would not approve of the Constitution. Andres Tarand (p. 708) also emphasised that the Assembly should be very careful with the paragraphs that go against the public opinion. He argued that people should have the right to determine what kind of political system they want to live in, and even if they make wrong decisions, they can only realise it through experience. At the same time, several members of the Assembly were apprehensive of public discussions on the draft Constitution. Ivar Raig (p. 543), for example, emphasised that it was important to prevent the public discussion from turning into fights on current political issues. Viktor Korrovits (p. 545) reminded the Assembly of the negative experiences the public had had with public discussions on the Soviet Constitution or party programmes, where the opinions of the public had actually not been taken into account. He argued that although this case would be different, there would still be some dangers with the public discussion since it may bring up the issues of current politics. In particular, he pointed out that public discussion would enable the forces in the Supreme Council and its presidium to launch propaganda for increasing the president's power. Hando Runnel (p. 547) even argued that in his opinion the whole idea of public discussion was so reminiscent of the Soviet times that it would be better to forgo it. Further, he stated that having public discussion would be uneconomical and it would extend the period of constitutional vacuum. He suggested that it would be better to give the people the right to decide between different formulations of certain chapters or provisions.

As pointed out in section 2.1., about 500 persons, groups and organisations sent their recommendations to the Assembly. Hänni pointed out, when summarising the letters and proposals sent by the public, that many of the letters were very emotional and touched upon issues of current politics (*Põhiseadus ja Põhiseaduse Assamblee* 1997, p. 694). The two main demands that dominated in the letters were to call the head of the state "president" rather than "*riigivanem*" ("the state elder", the term for the head of the state in the 1920 Constitution) and to have direct popular elections of the president instead of electing the president by parliament (Taagepera 1994, p. 225). Hänni (*Põhiseadus ja Põhiseaduse Assamblee* 1997, pp. 694–695) noted that, on the whole, the public seemed to be very trusting of the institution of the president and very sceptical of the parliament (the *Riigikogu*). Many letters expressed the fear that the draft Constitution was super-parliamentary and would give rise to factionalisation and conflicts between parties, which, in turn, would lead to the kind of political trafficking that had dominated the Estonian politics in the 1920s. The Assembly followed the opinion of the public and changed the term "*riigivanem*" to "president". With regard to the method of electing the president, the Assembly decided to go *against* the prevailing popular opinion, which supported direct elections of the president (in addition to the letters sent to the Assembly, the public opinion polls indicated that more the 70 percent of the public supported direct elections of the president) and opted for indirect elections of the president (by the parliament or by an electoral college comprising of the members of the parliament and representatives of local government councils, summoned when the parliament does not manage to elect the president). Peet Kask (the head of the fourth committee) argued that the question of whether the president should be elected by the people was not a question that should be asked from the people: "It is obvious that people want to elect the president themselves. But if we ask from people whether they want to pay income tax, they would say that they don't want to. ... The same logic applies to the question of how the president should be elected." (*Põhiseadus ja Põhiseaduse Assamblee* 1997, p. 610)

However, in order to appease the public, the Implementation Act of the Constitution foresaw that the very first elections of the president in 1992 would be direct in the first round; the legislature were to come into play only if none of the candidates received more than 50 percent of the votes in the first round.[71] Some of the powers of the president that were not included in the first draft were added after the public discussion, including the right of the president to initiate the amendment procedure of the Constitution and to appoint judges. Giving the president the right to initiate ordinary legislation, as suggested by many letters, was not included, however. Several letters by the public pointed out that the units of local government should be stipulated in the Constitution. In the final draft of the Constitution this was done: it was stated that local governments are cities and rural municipalities. A number of letters also suggested including the possibility of popular initiative in the Constitution, but that was not taken into account by the Assembly. The Assembly did not include a proposal made in a number of letters to increase the quorum requirement for the parliament (set at one-fourth in the draft) but left the quorum requirement out altogether; instead, it outlined a list of important acts that need a qualified majority to be passed. Another step taken to appease the public was a provision (in the implementation chapter) according to which, for three years following the ratification of the Constitution, constitutional amendments could be made with relaxed majorities in the *Riigikogu* or initiated by popular initiative (requiring 10 000 signatures).[72] Altogether, though there were some serious discussions in the Assembly expressing fears that the public may reject the Constitution, one can conjecture that the expected likelihood of rejection was rather low, given the problems that would have been created by constitutional vacuum and the symbolic importance that the Constitution had in affirming the independence of Estonia and breaking with the communist legacy.

The hypothesis H_{5c} appears to be corroborated by the Estonian case, but the underlying mechanisms are different from the hypothesised ones. The Estonian constitution-making process, for most part, satisfies the conditions of inclusive participation and openness as outlined by Voigt (2004, p. 214), in terms of allowing for public discussion, ratification by referendum and broad media cover-

---

71 The "official" explanation for this option was that since the party system in Estonia was still in the process of being formed, it would have been unrealistic to expect the political groupings to agree immediately on a common president. Given that the Constitution requires two-thirds majority in the parliament for electing the president, it was suggested that the political system was too young to achieve such compromises only after the very first elections. (see explanations by the chairman of the Constitutional Assembly Tõnu Anton, Verbatim Record of the Supreme Council, 16–19 March 1992, pp. 42–43).

72 In 1994, as a result of the popular initiative, two constitutional amendment proposals were submitted to the *Riigikogu*: the first suggested introducing direct elections of the president and second proposed stipulating the right to receive old-age pension according to the work contribution of the person. In the parliament, however, these initiatives did not find support.

age. The Estonian Constitution has been evaluated as having one of the most extensive delegations of power among the CEE constitutions (Salzberger and Voigt 2002, p. 35). The constitutional provisions pertaining to the delegation of power to the Supreme Court, the Legal Chancellor, the State Audit Office and the Bank of Estonia, however, did not result from inputs from the general public. Salzberger and Voigt (2002, p. 35) conjecture that the extensive constitutional delegation of powers in Estonia can be attributed to having a constituent assembly, the composition of which did not reflect actual powers but was an "artificial" equal division of seats. One could argue, however, that the Assembly *did* in fact reflect the actual distribution of powers and the reasons behind extensive constitutional delegation of power lie elsewhere. As discussed above, the experts (both foreign and local) had certainly a role in influencing the powers of the president and the judiciary. In particular, the foreign experts emphasised the importance of independent judiciary and a strong constitutional court. The provisions on the Bank of Estonia in the Constitution are in fact very brief and the provisions guaranteeing its autonomy are stipulated in statutes. The idea of the institution of legal chancellor was taken (although in a rather modified form) from the 1938 Constitution. The institution of the State Audit Office had already been established in 1990, before the drafting of the Constitution. Thus, the extensive delegation of powers came about as a result of a mixture of factors: drawing on historical experiences and previous constitutions, the advice of constitutional experts, and the desire to reverse the heritage of the Soviet times (where the power had been in the hands of only one institution).

The hypothesis H_{5d} appears to be too crude in the light of the Estonian case, since single-issue participation does not necessarily translate into incorporating the suggested provisions in the constitution. However, had the proposals by the public pertaining to the mode of electing the president been taken into account by the framers, the constitution would have embodied inconsistencies between the formal powers of the president and the way he is elected. The public demanded direct elections of the president, despite the relatively limited authority the president was assigned in the draft Constitution. Conversely, had all the proposals by the public to increase the powers of the president been taken into account, this would have created inconsistencies with the indirect mode of elections (which implies lower de facto powers).

The hypothesis H_{5e} is for most part not confirmed by the Estonian case. The draft submitted to public discussion included 153 articles; the final draft adopted by the Assembly and submitted to referendum comprised 168 articles. Most of the articles that were added to the initial draft, however, came about as a result of the cooperation with the expert group on chapter 2 of the Constitution (fundamental rights, freedoms and duties). The proposals by the public did not concern so much the broad wording of the provisions but touched upon more basic choices pertaining to the machinery of government. Different forms of public discussion are likely to have very different impacts. Had the public been indeed physically present on the balconies of the Assembly, a pressure towards including more and more specific provisions would have been more likely. Given that the participation was in the form of letters, whereby a special committee read through the letters and selected the prevailing suggestions for further discussion, a host of proposals suggested by different groups and individuals did not come up for consideration.

2.2.3. Constraints

The hypothesis H_{6a} is partially confirmed by the Estonian case. One should, however, distinguish between the time constraint for the submission of draft constitutions, the initially envisaged deadline for the adoption of the Constitution and the actual time constraint. In the Estonian case, the deadline for the submission of drafts was very short (only some weeks) and, as shown above, the drafts submitted drew extensively on the inter-war constitutions. The initially foreseen deadline for the Assembly was also very short: only two months. During the first two months, when the Assembly felt a big time pressure, the Assembly clearly sought to look for focal points.[73] This was reflected in the willingness to settle on the procedural aspects of the Assembly's work as fast as possible in order to proceed with substantive discussions. The decision to adopt one particular draft as a basis of the work made looking for focal points easier, despite the fact that many members of the Assembly would have preferred the competing draft. The Assembly was compelled to prioritise among the issues – and most of the sessions were dominated by discussions on issues that were seen as the most controversial ones, especially the powers and the election mode of the president. Among 30 topics that were discussed at least in 10 meetings, the tasks of the president were discussed at 22 meetings (Pärnaste 2002, pp. 275–277), about a quarter of the time of the Assembly was spent on discussions over whether the president should be elected directly by the people or by the parliament (Hänni 2002a, p. 163), and the question of how the president should be called ("president" or "*riigivanem*") was discussed at 10 meetings (Pärnaste 2002, pp. 275–277).

73 Comparatively speaking, the time pressure to adopt a constitution was clearly more present in the newly independent CEE countries (e.g., Estonia, Latvia, Lithuania, Slovenia and Slovakia) than in other CEE countries that were independent states already before the start of transition. For a newly independent country, having a new constitution was strongly related to indicating a clear break from the federal unions they belonged to. In the Lithuanian case, for example, although most of the participants involved in drafting the constitution were unhappy with the document, it was simply passed because of the sense of urgency (Gelazis 2001).

The hypotheses H_{6b}, H_{6d} and H_{6e} are confirmed by the Estonian case, while the hypothesis H_{6c} is refuted.[74] Although the 1992 Constitution is a new document rather than a copy of any of the previous constitutions, several ideas were taken over from the constitutions of the inter-war period. As noted above, the 1938 Constitution was submitted as one of the drafts to the Assembly, primarily in order to reinforce the principle of legal continuity and emphasise the point that the Estonian Republic was *restored* rather than newly established.[75] On the whole, the debates in the Assembly were clearly influenced by the country's constitutional history of the inter-war period (Taagepera 1994, p. 211). The authors of the main competing drafts in the CA also emphasised the need to draw on historical constitutional traditions. Raidla, when presenting his draft Constitution to the Assembly, emphasised that "the source of the Constitution should be the traditions and ways of being of the people, but not the constructions of politicians or legal scholars" (*Põhiseadus ja Põhiseaduse Assamblee* 1997, p. 52).[76] Adams suggested, "Constitutions cannot be made according to theories. Good constitutions can only be done in the way a tailor makes a suit: it has to match the request of the client, but at the same time the measurements of the client. We have to proceed from existing texts, previous experiences, national customs, existing conditions and future endeavours." (Adams 2002, p. 137) During the debates of the Constitutional Assembly, the experiences with the inter-war constitutions were constantly referred to and lessons drawn: the ultra-democratic 1920 Constitution was seen as leading to excessive fractionalisation and instability of governments;[77] the 1933 amendments, creating a post of a strong president, were seen as facilitating the emergence of an authoritarian regime; the 1938 Constitution (drafted by a constitutional assembly largely fol-

74 For comparison, these hypotheses are clearly confirmed in the case of the other Baltic states as well. Latvia re-adopted the 1922 Constitution instead of drafting a new one (Sprudzs 2001) and the Lithuanian framers sought to produce a draft document from the three constitutions adopted during the inter-war period (Gelazis 2001, p. 166).

75 The re-enactment of 1938 Constitution was supported, paradoxically, by the extreme nationalists and by the ex-communist faction, although for different reasons. The nationalists followed the principle of juridical continuity, while the ex-communists hoped, with the help of the 1938 Constitution, to secure the presidency for Rüütel (Lauristin and Vihalemm 1997, pp. 100–101).

76 In presenting the draft Constitution to the Supreme Council in March 1992, Raidla also emphasised that the more the new Constitution carries in it the legal-political culture of the inter-war period, the stronger and more reliable it is (Verbatim Record of the Supreme Council, 16–19 March 1992, p. 55).

77 According to the 1920 Constitution, the prime minister served as head of state. A third of the parliament could request a two-month delay in promulgating any law adopted by majority vote, in order to give time to organise a request for a popular referendum. Such a referendum could be initiated by 25 000 citizens and if it went against the parliament, new parliamentary elections were mandatory. Extremely proportional representation contributed to fractionalisation; the average cabinet duration was eight months. (Taagepera 1994, p. 212)

lowing the guidelines set by President Konstantin Päts) also indicated some dangers of having too strong a president. With respect to the division of powers, the 1992 Constitution is closest to the suggested constitutional amendments of 1932, which were rejected by referendum.[78]

The Estonian case corroborates the hypothesis H_{6g}, while confuting hypothesis H_{6f}. The Constitution that had been in force during the communist regime was regarded only as a negative example during the debates of the Constitutional Assembly, indicating a desire to have a clear break with this past. With regard to hypotheses concerning legal transplants from the constitutions of other countries, the Estonian case provides more evidence for H_{6h} than for H_{6i}. While the constitutions of West European countries were occasionally taken as points of reference and examples for assessing possible impacts,[79] the inter-war constitutions of Estonia appeared to play a more explicit role in the design of the 1992 Constitution than the constitutions of other countries.

2.3. Conclusions

Altogether, the Estonian case does indeed provide evidence for the hypotheses proceeding from institutional self-interest of framers. Thus, although the Constitutional Assembly was called into being for the specific purpose of drafting the constitution, this did *not* prevent the members from pursuing institutional self-interest. The majority of the members of the Assembly came from a legislative body and, as hypothesised, the parliament was given an overriding importance in the Constitution, including an important role in amending the Constitution. There were, however, members of the Assembly who supported a stronger president: some were motivated by partisan interests, some by historical considerations. The head of the state at the time of the constitution-making (and the most likely candidate to become the new president) supported a stronger president. More refined versions of the hypotheses pertaining to institutional self-interest would have to emphasise the different motives of the members of the constituent body (e.g., depending on in which branch they see their political future), the role of historical experiences in weighing the arguments and the interaction

78 Given that the constitutional amendments passed in 1933 were so extensive, these amendments have often been considered as the "second constitution" (and thus, the 1938 Constitution as the "third"). As Arjakas (2002, p. 35) explains, while historians tend to view the 1933 amendments as amounting to a new constitution, some legal scholars tend to view them as amendments rather than a new constitution (since about one-third of the 1920 Constitution was changed, while the rest remained in place).

79 With regard to constitutional lesson-drawing, the right of the president to turn to the Supreme Court when he considers a law passed by the *Riigikogu* unconstitutional, appeared to be inspired, at least partly, by the Irish system (and the recommendations of expert Russell from Ireland).

between the constituent body and other branches of government (including upstream constraints).

It was hypothesised that the constitution is designed so that it would enhance the electoral chances of framers who hope to hold a political office. The party-system in Estonia at the time of constitution-making was at an early stage of development, characterised by a large number of parties and party-like organisations. In such a situation, it was clearly the interest of all parties involved to adopt a proportional rather than plurality (or majoritarian) electoral system in the Constitution. With regard to the rules of electing the president, the framers tended to support the rules that would give (or respectively not give) the post to a preferred (or not preferred) candidate.

The Estonian case corroborates the hypothesis suggesting that when the electoral favourite has weak bargaining powers and/or the electoral outcome is highly uncertain, the framers will design an executive office with few specific powers and tightly constrained residual powers. At the same time, the causal mechanisms were somewhat different from those suggested by Frye (1997). It was uncertainty with regard to the *electoral rule* for electing the president made the framers more cautious in attributing specific and residual powers to the institution of president.

The Estonian case provides evidence for the hypotheses suggesting that framers will design a strong and independent judiciary (and grant the judiciary strong powers of constitutional review) if the future composition of the legislature and the executive are uncertain. The members of the Constitutional Assembly were faced with electoral uncertainties and the Estonian 1992 Constitution provides for a strong and independent judiciary and extensive constitutional review. At the same time, the causal mechanisms appear to be different than conjectured by Ginsburg (2002), Smithey and Ishiyama (2000) and Romeu (2006), who focused on the strategic calculations of the members of the constituent body. The proposals to increase the powers of the judiciary came primarily from constitutional experts (both foreign and local) and the Constitutional Assembly played a rather passive role in drafting the provisions pertaining to judiciary. Strategic considerations with regard to the judiciary hence appeared to play a lesser role compared to the "constitutional theories" pointing to the need to break with the Soviet heritage and to establish a European-type judicial system.

It was hypothesised that experts in constitutional issues would not attribute a dominant role to the legislature *vis-à-vis* the other two branches. Further, it was conjectured that if the experts involved are constitutional lawyers, the constitution would provide for more extensive judicial independence. The Estonian case provides more evidence in favour than against these hypotheses, but in order to make the analysis of the role of experts more precise, the theoretical framework should distinguish between different *kinds* of experts (local and foreign) and different *ways* they can be involved in constitution-making (as members of the assembly, contracted advisors to help the committees, international advisors or "obligatory" advisors). As the Estonian case shows, interaction between the members of the constituent assembly and the experts (and the perceived legitimacy and objectivity of the advice of the experts) can play an important role with regard to how and to what extent the experts' advice is taken into account. The Estonian case demonstrates that those experts who were closely involved with the executive branch and with whom the Assembly was "ordered" to work together were viewed with suspicion, while foreign experts and local experts who were *invited* to give their opinion were viewed more positively. Further, the Estonian case indicates that the opinions of different kinds of experts with regard to the relative powers of the parliament and the executive can diverge. While most of the local experts were against giving too large powers to the parliament and supported a stronger president, the foreign experts emphasised the merits of parliamentarism and warned against too strong president. The local experts were partly motivated by their political preferences but also by the historical traditions and their fondness of the 1938 Constitution of Estonia, with which they were all very familiar with (and which had been the dominant line of constitutional thinking in the "Schneider school of constitutional law" to which most of the local experts belonged to). The constitutional experts (both foreign and local) were in favour a strong and independent judiciary and advocated the attribution of extensive powers of constitutional review to the courts.

With regard to the role of the general public in constitution-making, it was hypothesised that the use of referendum to ratify a draft constitution will lead to a document that takes the preferences of citizens at large explicitly into account. The Estonian case offers only partial evidence for this hypothesis. While some of the suggestions of the public were taken into account in putting together the final draft of the Constitution, some of the most loudly voiced ones were not included in the Constitution. Most importantly, despite a large number of letters (and opinion polls) that indicated the wish to have *direct* popular elections of the president, the final draft of the Constitution still stipulated *indirect* elections by the parliament. To appease the public, however, the very first presidential elections were foreseen to be direct (at least in the first round). More refined hypothesis here would have to look at the chances that the public would indeed reject the constitution, were the public preferences not taken into account. If the new constitution is an important symbol for affirming independence and the constitutional vacuum is perceived to be damaging, the rejection of it by popular referendum would be less likely, which, in turn, should make the framers more immune to the pressures of public opinion.

It was hypothesised that inclusive participation in constitution-making will lead to high levels of power delegation. With some reservations, the Estonian constitution-making can be termed as inclusive and the Estonian 1992 Constitution has been evaluated as entailing most extensive delegation of powers among the CEE constitutions (Salzberger and Voigt 2002, p. 35). The reasons behind it, however, appear to be different from those suggested by Salzberger and Voigt.

Extensive delegation of powers in the Estonian constitution came about as a result of the input from the experts (both local and foreign) and the inter-war constitutions, on which the framers drew extensively. As the Estonian case shows, the hypothesis that single-issue participation leads to contradictory constitutional provisions does not necessarily hold, since the suggested provisions would not be automatically included in the constitution. Also, public participation did not result in a significantly longer constitutional document. Rather, the Constitution was made longer and the provisions more specific as a result of the proposals of the constitutional experts.

The hypotheseses concerning the effect of a short time limit on constitution-making was mostly confirmed by the Estonian case. The time pressure was immense at the beginning of the work of the Assembly, forcing the members to look for focal points. The Assembly was compelled to prioritise among the issues: most of the sessions were dominated by discussions on issues that were seen as the most controversial ones, especially the powers and the election mode of the president. In later phases of the work, when the time pressure was somewhat eased, the Assembly did look at areas that were considered to be of lesser importance, but the discussions were still dominated by the few areas of debate (e.g. the method for electing the president) that had been the focal points at the beginning of the Assembly's work.

The Estonian case clearly confirmed the importance of previous constitutions in constitution-making, especially in the face of time constraints. Many provisions in the 1992 Constitution were taken over from 1920 and 1938 Constitutions (and proposed changes to the 1920 Constitution in the inter-war period). During the debates of the Constitutional Assembly, the experiences with these constitutions were constantly referred to and lessons drawn. It should be noted, however, that in Estonia's case (like in the cases of Lithuania and Latvia), drawing on inter-war constitutions also served the purpose of emphasising the legal continuity of the republic and underlining the legitimacy of the claims of independence.

Altogether, the Estonian case corroborates most of the hypotheses proceeding from the assumption of institutional self-interest, the role of the experts in constitution-making and the importance of historical experiences. The case provides contradictory evidence to the hypotheses concerned with public participation in constitution-making.

More broadly put, the Estonian case provides evidence for the *interaction* between strategic calculations and symbolic meanings that the actors attach to particular choices in the making of the constitution. Although the framers were often driven by institutional self-interest in their choices of constitutional provisions (in particular with regard to provisions pertaining to the powers and election mode of the president), strategic calculations do tell only *part* of the story. Indeed, already in trying to explain the decision to convene the Constitutional Assembly, the "calculus" approach would run into difficulties. This "miracle compromise" was facilitated by the "constitutionality" of the moment (Ackerman 1984, 1991; Voigt 2004, p. 223; 1997, p. 26; Buchanan 1997a), which suppressed the self-interest rationale of the political actors and brought to the fore loftier considerations.

Further, explicating the debates and decisions of the Constitutional Assembly calls for going beyond the strategic calculations of the framers. As the discussions in the Constitutional Assembly indicate, the symbolic meanings attached to the historical constitutions of the inter-war period played an important role in the institutional choices. The framers' conception of the Constitution as a quintessentially symbolic document was also mirrored by lengthy discussions on the preamble. While Offe (1997, p. 213) suggested that the "borrowing" across time is would be motivated by the desire of the framers to "shy away from accepting responsibility for what they are really doing", the framers in Estonia admitted their role as "designers" of the new constitution. Rather, the extensive borrowing from the inter-war constitutions was driven by time constraints and the symbolic connotations that the historical constitutions had for asserting the continuity of the Estonian statehood. The desire to represent a clear break with the communist past – carried by strong symbolic motivations – also shaped the institutional choices (like strong guarantees of independence for the judiciary).

Understanding the role of experts in Estonian constitution-making also calls for looking beyond the strategic calculations of the framers. The proposals put forth by local constitutional experts were often viewed by many framers with a priori scepticism, as if the affiliation with the existing government had "tainted" the proposal, irrespective of its specific content. Also, the scepticism with regard to the role of public discussion in constitution-making had a lot to do with the connotation that the public discussion had had during the Soviet times. The decision of the Constitutional Assembly to go against the prevailing public opinion with regard to the mode of electing the president appears counterintuitive at first sight, but is understandable, when one takes into account that given the symbolic importance of the constitution in affirming independence, the likelihood that the public would have actually rejected the constitution was rather low.

A more complete theoretical conception of constitution-making should hence also account for the symbolic meanings that the framers (and the public) attach to particular choices and analyse how the symbolic meanings are able to shape the strategic calculations of the participants involved.

Chapter 3: Fiscal Aspects of Constitutions as *Explananda*: Theoretical Propositions and the Estonian Case

Fiscal aspects of constitutions have received extensive attention in constitutional political economy; in particular, the analyses have focused on constitutional provisions concerning balanced budget requirements, tax and expenditure limitations, borrowing restrictions and debt ceilings. Hitherto, however, the main focus of research has been on the *impacts* of these provisions: these constitutional provisions have been treated as *explanantia*. The studies that have regarded fiscal constitutional provisions as *explananda* have been, for most part, concerned with provisions that have been added to *existing* constitutions rather than analysing how constitutional provisions pertaining to budgeting and taxation come about when an *entire* constitution is written afresh (for example, after a regime change).[80] The two studies that have analysed the making of fiscal constitutional provisions in the context of drafting an entirely new constitution are Tang (1991) for the Hong Kong Constitution, and Brennan and Pardo (1991) for the Spanish Constitution. These studies, however, have primarily a normative orientation and do not seek to test any specific hypotheses.

In this chapter, the focus is on how formal fiscal constitutional provisions come about in the context where *a whole new* constitution is designed. In the existing literature, no comprehensive analytical framework has been put forth for examining fiscal constitutional provisions as *explananda*. Therefore, the first goal of this chapter is to propose one possible approach for examining how fiscal constitutional provisions come about. By drawing on the hypotheses concerning constitution-making in general, outlined in chapter 1 of this book, a list of conjectures about how constitutional provisions pertaining to budgeting and taxation come about is put forth. Subsequently, these conjectures are tested with the case study of Estonia. Given the exploratory nature of this chapter, the list of conjectures put forth is not claimed to be definitive and exhaustive. Rather, the goal is to inquire, to what extent the existing approaches in positive constitutional political economy can shed light on the fiscal constitutional choices made by framers in a transitional context.

80 In particular, the factors behind the decisions to add fiscal constitutional provisions to an existing constitution have been considered. Of special interest have been the provisions pertaining to balanced budget requirements, debt limits, borrowing restrictions and tax limitations. Most of the studies exploring this issue have focused on the U.S. states and, among the factors behind fiscal constitutional choices, the following ones have received particular attention: the antecedent fiscal balances, tax burden, debt level, fiscal preferences of the electorate and the existence of direct democracy mechanisms (see, *inter alia*, Helland 2000; Gordon 2008; Kousser, McCubbins and Rozga 2008; Debrun and Kumar 2007; Poterba 1996; Inman 1996).

3.1. Theoretical Propositions

Drawing on the review of theoretical propositions and hypotheses given in chapter 1 of these book, this section seeks to derive specific conjectures about how the actors involved in constitution-making, their preferences and the constraints they face influence the resulting constitutional provisions on budgeting and taxation.

3.1.1. Actors Involved in Constitution-Making

Analogously to other constitutional provisions (discussed in section 1.1.2.), constitutional preferences of the framers can be expected to play a major role in the resulting constitutional provisions pertaining to budgeting and taxation. Constitutional preferences concerning budgeting and taxation would be shaped by both constitutional theories and constitutional interests (Vanberg and Buchanan 1989). Constitutional interests, in turn, can be carried by personal, institutional and partisan interests (Elster 1993, 1995b, 1996b, 1997a), the prevalence of which would be influenced by the make-up of the constituent body. Elster argues that institutional self-interest would dominate, if the framers come from existing governing institutions. Assuming institutional self-interest of the members of the constituent body, as discussed in section 1.1.2.1., one can conjecture that if the framers are also members of the existing legislature, the parliament will be attributed a more important role in the budget procedure *vis-à-vis* the government and the president or other state institutions. Conversely, if the president, the government or other institutions are involved in the constitution-making process, they will seek to promote a greater role of their respective institutions in budget process.

Analogously to constitutional review, framers can be conjectured to be "predisposed against limiting themselves, particularly in the form of oversight by other actors" (Smithey and Ishiyama 2000, p. 171) in the area of budgeting and taxation. Hence, when framers come from existing governing institutions or hope to be elected to the legislature or government in the post-constitutional phase, they can be expected to be reluctant to impose *substantive* constitutional limitations (in the form of balanced budget requirements, for example) or strong *procedural* limitations (like supermajorities) on decisions concerning public finance. At the same time, however, given the need to convey a sense of objectivity and orientation to the general public good, the framers are likely to present the arguments for their positions in the form of constitutional theories rather than constitutional interests (Elster 1997a, p. 133). Therefore, appealing to constitutional theories can be expected to dominate over arguments appealing to constitutional interests in constitutional discussions on budgeting and taxation.

To the extent that the framers have already been involved in legislative and governmental budgeting and tax policy, as members of the respective institutions, one can predict that constitutional theories concerning budgeting and taxation put forth during discussions in the constitutional assembly will draw on preceding experiences, and solutions offered will be oriented to existing problems. McFaul (1999, p. 31) reminds us that "reaction to an immediate political circumstance is usually the impetus for new institutional designs". In a similar vein, Holmes and Lucky (1994, pp. 121–122) argue that constitutions tend to be retrospective documents rather than prospective ones, "designed to solve the most pressing problems of the past, not the future".

With regard to the role of partisan interests in the design of constitutional provisions concerning budgeting and taxation, a number of tentative conjectures can be put forth. Representatives of small parties are likely to argue for an active role of the legislature in budgeting, since that would preserve the possibility for parties outside the governing majority to provide input for the state budget during legislative proceedings. Members of large parties, conversely, may favour budgetary procedures that give the executive extensive powers and constrain the amendment rights of the legislature, given that this would give the government in office more leeway and discretion to pursue its budgetary policies. At the same time, of course, even members of larger parties, expecting to be in opposition at least part of the time in the future, may want to preserve the rights of opposition parties to participate actively in shaping the state budget. Ideological motivations of partisan actors may also shape constitutional provisions on budgeting and taxation. Parties on the economic right may advocate constitutional articles entailing balanced budget requirements or constraints on borrowing, while left-oriented parties are likely to oppose such limitations.

As discussed in subsection 1.1.2.2., alongside with representatives from existing legislative and executive institutions, constitutional experts can be involved in designing the constitution. Voigt (2004, pp. 23–24) conjectures that constitutional experts who are involved in constitution-making will not attribute a dominant role to the legislature *vis-à-vis* the other two branches. Hence, one would expect experts to argue for balanced powers (between the executive and legislature) in budgeting and taxation as well.

Drawing on the general conjectures put forth in subsection 1.1.2.3., concerning the role of the general public in constitution-making, one can conjecture that if the constitution is subject to ratification by referendum, the framers will be motivated to take the constitutional preferences of the public with regard to budgeting and taxation explicitly into account in drafting fiscal constitutional provisions. Further, if the general public is actively involved in preparation of the draft constitution, more extensive delegation of power in public finance can be expected as well, alongside with other forms of power delegation (see Voigt 2004). Hence, inclusive participation by the public in constitution-making can be predicted to lead to more extensive limitations of the central government power in public finance (e.g., guarantees of financial autonomy for local governments and larger majorities prescribed for public finance decisions). Further, inclusive participation can be predicted to give rise to provisions that foresee an extensive role of the public with regard to taxation and budgeting (e.g., allowing referenda, popular initiatives or extensive public consultations on these issues). Analogously to the effects of inclusive participation on the coherence of the resulting constitution (Voigt 2004, p. 219), one can presume inclusive participation to induce less coherent (and potentially contradictory) constitutional provisions on budgeting and taxation. Reflecting the general propositions by Schauer (1998, pp. 5–6), inclusive participation by the public is likely to result in more specific provisions on taxation and budgeting in the constitution.

3.1.2. Constraints and Models

As discussed in section 1.2., alongside with the kinds of actors involved in constitution-making, the constraints they face and the models they can (or are expected to) draw upon can be assumed to play a role in influencing the content of the constitution. Analogously to other provisions in the constitution, it can be conjectured that if the time-limit for designing the constitution is tight, there would be little space for constitutional innovation concerning provisions on budgeting and taxation and the framers would be inclined to draw extensively upon the past institutional arrangements and provisions in the previous constitutions of the country (McFaul 1999, pp. 30–31). In addition, since framers have motives to cover up "institutional engineering", pointing to provisions in previous constitutions enables them to employ more "objective" justifications for institutional solutions proposed (Offe 1997).

As mentioned in section 1.2., drawing on historical constitutions would be especially plausible in CEE countries because of the additional sense of legitimacy that the inter-war constitutions convey (Salzberger and Voigt 2002, p. 26). Thus, as was conjectured about other provisions in CEE constitutions, provisions on taxation and budgeting are likely to be taken over from the constitutions that were in force in the pre-communist period. Also, whether viewed positively or not, the existing institutional arrangements for budgeting and taxation can be presumed to be important points of reference for devising new constitutional provisions (McFaul 1999, p. 32; Salzberger and Voigt 2002, p. 30). Further, in discussions over constitutional provisions on budgeting and taxation, both the immediate institutions and the historical experiences with previous constitutions can be conjectured to be important sources of constitutional theories employed by the framers. With regard to constitutional lesson-drawing across space, although framers may face pressures to draw on the "positive examples" of other countries, the desire to have "one's own" constitution (Schauer 2005) may render constitutional transplantation difficult also in the area of public finance.

When the time-constraint is strong, the need to prioritise may imply that provisions on budgeting and taxation will receive only limited attention in constitutional discussions. Hence, one can conjecture that if the time-limit for drafting the constitution is tight, the resulting constitution will include numerous and detailed provisions on budgeting and taxation *only* if fiscal issues are high on the political agenda. If not, provisions on taxation and budgeting will be fewer and vague.

3.1.3. Fiscal Provisions in Constitutions as *Explananda*: A List of Conjectures

Since the propositions presented below are still rather tentative and exploratory, they are called "conjectures" rather than "hypotheses".

Conjecture 1: The members of the constituent body who are also members of the existing legislature, they will seek to grant the parliament a more important role in budget procedure compared with the roles of the government and the president or other state institutions. If the president or the government or other institutions are involved in constitution-making process, they will seek to promote a greater role of their respective institutions in budget procedure.
Conjecture 2: To the extent that the framers come from existing governing institutions or expect to be elected to the legislature or government in the post-constitutional phase, they will be reluctant to adopt substantive constitutional limitations or strong procedural limitations for decisions concerning public finance.
Conjecture 3: Appealing to constitutional theories will dominate over arguments appealing to constitutional interests in constitutional discussions on budgeting and taxation.
Conjecture 4: To the extent that framers have already been involved in legislative and governmental budgeting and tax policy (as members of the respective institutions), constitutional theories concerning budgeting and taxation put forth during the discussions of the constituent body will draw on the preceding experiences, and the solutions offered will be oriented to existing problems.
Conjecture 5: Representatives of small parties will argue for an active role of the legislature in budgeting. Members of large parties will favour budgetary procedures that give the executive extensive powers and constrain the amendment rights of the legislature.
Conjecture 6: Constitutional experts will argue for balanced powers between the executive and legislature in budgeting and taxation.
Conjecture 7: If the constitution is subject to ratification by referendum, framers will take the constitutional preferences of the public into account in drafting constitutional provisions pertaining to public finance.
Conjecture 8: Inclusive participation by the public in constitution-making will lead to more extensive limitations of the central government power in taxation

and to provisions that foresee an extensive role of the public in taxation and budgeting.

Conjecture 9: Inclusive participation will lead to less coherent constitutional provisions on budgeting and taxation.

Conjecture 10: Inclusive participation will lead to detailed constitutional provisions on budgeting and taxation.

Conjecture 11: The provisions on taxation and budgeting will be taken over from the previous constitutions.

Conjecture 12: Existing institutional arrangements for budgeting and taxation will be the main points of reference for devising new constitutional provisions.

Conjecture 13: Constitutional transplantation of provisions concerning public finance will be avoided.

Conjecture 14: When the time-limit for drafting the constitution is tight, the constitution will include numerous and detailed provisions on budgeting and taxation only if fiscal issues are high on the political agenda. If not, provisions on taxation and budgeting will be few and vague.

These conjectures are tested with the case of constitution-making in Estonia in 1991–1992. In order to provide a basis for testing these conjectures, section 3.2. gives an overview of the constitutional provisions concerning budgeting and taxation in the Estonian Constitution of 1992 and how these provisions came about during the work of the Constitutional Assembly. Section 3.3. evaluates the conjectures with the help of the case study on Estonia and section 3.4. discusses the main findings in the light of societal conditions prevailing at the time of constitution-making in Estonia.

3.2. Making of Constitutional Provisions Pertaining to Budgeting and Taxation in Estonia

The questions that will be analysed in this section are the following: What kind of provisions pertaining to budgeting and taxation are stipulated in the Constitution of Estonia? How did they come about? What were the underlying constitutional preferences behind the provisions that remained in the final version of the Constitution and behind those that were voted out? The main sources of information for analysing the emergence of different provisions pertaining to budgeting and taxation are different draft constitutions submitted to the Assembly, the previous Constitutions of Estonia and verbatim records of the plenary sessions of the Constitutional Assembly. As pointed out by Adams (2002, p. 146), since most of the Assembly members focussed their attention to the work of the committee they belonged to or even on some sub-topic in it, the speeches held at the general assembly played an important role: their function was to convince the members of the Assembly who were not dealing with a particular topic to vote for or against the controversial provisions.[81] In addition, the published memoirs of the participants in the Constitutional Assembly and archival materials on the work of the Constitutional Assembly (including proposals and suggestions sent to the Assembly by the public and written opinions of the experts) have been used for compiling the case study. Section 3.2.1. gives an overview of the constitutional provisions on the state budget and section 3.2.2. focuses on the constitutional provisions on taxation.[82]

3.2.1. Making of Provisions Pertaining to Budgeting

Three of the draft Constitutions submitted to the Constitutional Assembly by 1 October 1991 included a separate chapter called "Finance and the State Budget" and, on the whole, dedicating a separate chapter to the issues of public finance was seen as reasonable.[83] In the Constitution adopted in 1992, there are altogether 12 articles pertaining to the state budget. Five of them are brought out in the chapters on the *Riigikogu* (ch. 4), the Government (ch. 6), Legislation (ch. 7), and the rest in chapter 8, called "Finance and State Budget".

Article 65 sub-point 6 stipulates that the *Riigikogu* shall pass the state budget and approve the report on its implementation, sub-point 10 states that on the proposal of the Government the *Riigikogu* will decide on borrowing by the state and on the assumption of other proprietary obligations by the state. Article 87 states that the Government shall prepare the draft of the state budget and submit it to the *Riigikogu*, administer the implementation of the state budget and present a report on the implementation of the state budget to the *Riigikogu*. Article 104 stipulates that the State Budget Act and Acts pertaining to foreign and domestic borrowing and to proprietary obligations of the state can only be passed and amended by a majority of the membership of the *Riigikogu*. Article 106 establishes that, *inter alia*, issues regarding the budget, taxation and financial obligations of the state shall not be submitted to a referendum. Article 110

---

81 Of course, the protocols of committee meetings (especially those of the third committee, which dealt with the issues of public finance) would have been a useful source of information, but most of the work of the committees was not recorded. The few records of the work of the third committee that were produced (according to the list of archival materials), have, unfortunately, disappeared from the Estonian State Archive. As Kask (2002, p. 178) explains, however, the committees did not take final decisions but prepared the discussions for the Assembly, and the chairmen of the committees reported regularly on what had been going on in the committee. Hence, indirectly, the work of the committees has been recorded in the general Assembly discussions.

82 For a general overview of constitution-making in Estonia, see chapter 2.

83 In presenting his draft Constitution, Ando Leps pointed out that although Raidla's draft had a separate chapter on the state budget, then, in his opinion, the "whole budget buffoonery" would require a separate act and should not be outlined in the Constitution (*Põhiseadus ja Põhiseaduse Assamblee* 1997, p. 113). That, however, was not a prevailing position among the delegates.

states that laws that establish state taxes and the state budget shall not be enacted, amended or repealed by a decree of the president.

In a separate chapter called "Finance and the State Budget" (ch. 8), budget procedure is outlined in more detail. Article 115 states that the *Riigikogu* shall pass as a law the budget of all state revenue and expenditure for each year (section 1); the Government of the Republic shall submit a draft state budget to the *Riigikogu* not later than three months before the beginning of the budgetary year (section 2); and, on the proposal of the Government, the *Riigikogu* may pass a supplementary budget during the budgetary year (section 3). Article 116 requires that if a proposed amendment to the state budget or to its draft has the effect of decreasing estimated revenue or increasing expenditure or reallocating expenditure, the proponent of the amendment has to append financial calculations to the proposed amendment that demonstrate the sources of revenue necessary to cover the expenditure (section 1).[84] Section 2 requires that the *Riigikogu* shall not eliminate or reduce expenditures in the state budget or in its draft that are prescribed by other laws.[85] Article 117 states that the procedures for the drafting and passage of the state budget shall be provided by law. Article 118 stipulates that the state budget passed by the *Riigikogu* shall enter into force at the beginning of the budgetary year and if the *Riigikogu* does not pass the state budget by the beginning of the budgetary year, expenditure of up to one-twelfth of the expenditure of the preceding budgetary year may be made each month. Article 119 establishes that if the *Riigikogu* has not passed the state budget within two months after the beginning of the budgetary year, the president shall declare extraordinary elections to the *Riigikogu*.

In addition, in the chapter on the Auditor General, Article 135 provides that the Auditor General shall present to the *Riigikogu* an overview on the use and preservation of state assets during the preceding budgetary year at the same time as the report on the implementation of the state budget is debated in the *Riigikogu*. In the chapter on local government, Article 154 states that expenditure related to duties of the state imposed by law on a local government shall be funded from the state budget. Table 3.1. provides an overview of the sources of the dif-

84 Given that only the Government has the right to submit the draft budget, this provision implies that the level of expenditures, given expected revenues, is determined by the Government. Increasing expenditures from this "baseline" level requires that the members of the *Riigikogu* who make such proposals have to indicate where the increases of revenue would come from.

85 As Lehis (2002, p. 518) points out, this provision assumes that the draft budget submitted by the Government includes all expenditures prescribed by laws. If the draft budget by the Government implies changes to other acts (e.g., tax laws), the Government has to submit the draft acts of all these changes together with the draft budget and the *Riigikogu* should pass all these acts before passing the state budget. Lehis adds that contradiction between the state budget and an act could come about as a result of changes made to an act, but the Constitution does not regulate such a situation (p. 519).

ferent articles pertaining to budgeting and taxation in the 1992 Constitution of Estonia.

Table 3.1.: Sources of fiscal constitutional provisions in the 1992 Constitution of Estonia

Provision	Source
Article 65 sub-point 6	1920 Constitution, 1938 Constitution, complemented by Raidla's draft
Article 65 sub-point 10	1920 Constitution, 1938 Constitution
Article 87	1920 Constitution, complemented by Raidla's draft
Article 104	1920 Constitution, complemented by Raidla's draft
Article 106	1920 Constitution, 1938 Constitution
Article 110	1938 Constitution
Article 113	1920 Constitution, complemented by Raidla's draft
Article 115 Section 1	1920 Constitution, 1938 Constitution
Article 115 Section 2	1938 Constitution
Article 115 Section 3	Raidla's draft
Article 116 Section 1	1938 Constitution, Adams' draft, modified by the Assembly
Article 116 Section 2	1938 Constitution
Article 117	Raidla's draft
Article 118	1938 Constitution
Article 119	Adams' draft, Raidla's draft
Article 135	1938 Constitution
Article 154	Raidla's draft
Article 157 Section 2	Adams' draft

When comparing the final version of the Constitution with the drafts submitted to the Assembly, it is clear that most of the provisions pertaining to budgeting came from the draft submitted by Raidla's team (despite the fact that the draft of Adams was taken as the basis for the work of the Assembly). The only provisions that were in a similar form in the draft of Adams were Article 115 section 2, Article 116 section 1 and Article 119. When presenting his draft to the Assembly, Adams admitted that he was not a specialist in economics and that he had used Raidla's draft for coming up with the deadlines for the budget procedure.[86] Aaskivi (2002, p. 125) points out that when the third committee was working, it always had both drafts together on the table; on many occasions, the solutions and the wordings were compared and the best one used.

The articles in Raidla's draft, in turn, came for most part from the previous constitutions of Estonia. Article 65 sub-point 6 existed in a similar form in the 1920 Constitution and in the 1938 Constitution, only "approving the report on the implementation of the state budget" was added by Raidla's team. Also, the

86 Also, given that Adams had a very short time to prepare the draft and that his focus in drafting the proposal was on giving larger powers to the parliament (in comparison with the Raidla draft), it is understandable that he could not focus on the aspects of public finance in greater detail.

1920 Constitution said that the *Riigikogu* would approve the making of loans and the 1938 Constitution added that the Government would make a proposal for it. The addition "other proprietary obligations by the state" was proposed by Raidla's team. The provision that the Government would submit the draft state budget was taken from the 1920 Constitution and Raidla's team added that the Government would also "administer the implementation of the state budget and present a report on the implementation of the state budget to the *Riigikogu*".[87] Article 106 was taken from the 1920 Constitution; it was also in the 1938 Constitution. Article 110 was taken from the 1938 Constitution. The provisions pertaining to the budget procedure in chapter 8 of the Constitution have for most part been taken over from the 1938 Constitution. Article 115 section 1 was taken from the 1938 Constitution (a similar provision existed also in the 1920 Constitution); the word "all" was added by Raidla's team. Section 2 of Article 115 was similar in the 1938 Constitution: it was stated that the Government has to submit the draft state budget 70 days before the beginning of the next budgetary year. Section 3 was added by Raidla's team. Article 116 section 1 is discussed at length below. Section 2 was taken from the 1938 Constitution. Article 117 was added by the team. Article 118 and 135 were taken from the 1938 Constitution. Articles 119 and 154 were added by Raidla's team.

For most part, the discussions on provisions concerning budgeting were confined to what was brought up in Raidla's draft. Thus, the initial drafts set the frame for discussions and the Assembly did not add very much with regard to issues pertaining to the state budget. The only article that was "new", in the sense that it was added to the Constitution during the debates of the Constitutional Assembly, was Article 104. This article was not included in the draft Constitution that was adopted in December 1991 but was included as a result of the public discussion. Many protest letters were concerned with the low quorum requirement for the *Riigikogu* (set at one-fourth in the draft of December 1991) and suggested higher quorum requirements, varying from one-third to nine-tenths. (*Põhiseadus ja Põhiseaduse Assamblee* 1997, p. 722) Also, several letters were concerned with the fact that only a simple majority was required for passing legislation and the requirement of absolute majority was suggested. Given that the Assembly was reluctant to introduce a higher quorum requirement (in the final version of the Constitution, Article 70 stipulates that the quorum for the *Riigikogu* shall be provided by the *Riigikogu* Procedure Act), a "compensation" for that was offered: an absolute majority requirement was set for a list of important acts, including the State Budget Act (the organic budget law) and acts pertaining to foreign and domestic borrowing and to proprietary obligations of the state.

---

87 A similar provision existed already in the organic budget law adopted in 1989, but here the responsibility for putting together the report on the implementation of the budget was given to the Minister of Finance, who was to submit the report to the Council of Ministers, which would, in turn, submit it to the Supreme Council.

Most of the articles pertaining to the state budget that are included in the final version of the Constitution did not give rise to debates in the Constitutional Assembly. In fact, most of the debates regarding the state budget concerned articles that were included in the initial drafts but were eventually left out of the Constitution. The issue giving rise to most controversies in the Assembly was whether and how relations between the state budget and the legislation should be provided for in the Constitution, and, in particular, whether those introducing new legislation should bring out the implications it would have on the budget.

The 1938 Constitution, which was also submitted as one of the drafts for initial discussion, included an article stipulating that the draft acts of legislation (initiated by members of parliament) that bring about additional expenditures in the budget or reduce or abolish state revenues have to be accompanied with financial calculations, showing what the source of revenue for covering the costs would be. In addition, those drafts could only come to debate in the parliament after receiving consent from the Government.[88] With regard to the state budget procedure itself, it was stipulated that the parliament could increase expenditures and introduce new revenues to the state budget only after receiving consent from the Government. The same provisions (together with the stipulation that calculations need to be appended if the act brings about *reallocation* of expenditure) were included in the draft Constitution submitted by the working group of Raidla. A similar provision (but without the requirement to receive the consent from the Government) was also included in the draft Constitution submitted by Adams and it was worded as following: "For all draft acts and amendments to the budget that increase the expenditures or decrease the revenues the initiators have to append financial calculations to the proposed amendment, which demonstrate the sources of revenue necessary to cover the expenditure."[89] The draft of Adams, however, did *not* require receiving prior consent from the Government when parliament wanted to increase expenditures or reduce revenues during the readings of the state budget in parliament. While the 1938 Constitution and Raidla's draft required that only those draft acts that are initiated by mem-

88 Interestingly, this is similar to Article 113 Section 1 in the German Constitution, which states, "Laws that increase the budget expenditures proposed by the Federal Government, or entail or will bring about new expenditures, shall require the consent of the Federal Government. This requirement shall also apply to laws that entail or will bring about decreases in revenue. The Federal Government may demand that the *Bundestag* postpone its vote on bills to this effect. In this event the Federal Government shall submit its comments to the *Bundestag* within six weeks."

89 It is worth noting that a similar provision was included in the Latvian 1922 Constitution (re-enacted in 1991); Article 66 Section 2 states that "If the Parliament makes a decision that involves expenditures not included in the Budget, then this decision must also allocate funds to cover such expenditures." The 1992 Constitution of Lithuania also has an offsetting provision; Article 131 Section 2 states that "Upon considering the draft Budget, the Parliament may only increase expenditures upon specifying financial sources for said expenditures."

bers or committees of parliament have to indicate the sources of finance, the draft of Adams required such calculations to be appended for *all* draft acts, regardless of whether they originate from parliament or cabinet.

Since it was the draft of Adams that was taken as the basis of further work of the Constitutional Assembly, the main focus was on the requirement to append financial calculations for *all initiated acts* (and not only those initiated by the parliament) and not on whether the consent of the Government needed to be secured before acts with budgetary implications could be brought up in parliament. Although the provision stating that all changes to the draft state budget that increase expenditures or reduce revenues need the consent of the Government was brought up as a possible alternative during the sixth session, it did not gain sufficient support and was not debated upon in further sessions. Also, the question of whether such calculations should be appended when changes are made to the *draft budget* during the readings of the budget in parliament did not give rise to disagreements. Thus, the main provision that was debated upon during subsequent sessions was whether initiators of draft legislation have to append the financial calculations when the act would have implications for the budget. This issue was discussed altogether at five different sessions of the Constitutional Assembly. The main proponent of this provision was the vice chairman of the third committee of the CA Kalju Koha (also the head of the Economic Affairs and Budget Committee of the Supreme Council) and the main opponent of it was the chairman of the third committee Illar Hallaste (from the Estonian Congress, but also a member of the Supreme Council). The suggestions made to the Assembly by the third committee reflected the internal developments in the committee: the recommendations varied depending on who had been present at the meetings of the committee and who had been chairing the meeting. For most part, although the chairman was against this provision, the committee as a whole supported the requirement. The arguments on that provision reflected the conception the different sides had of relations between government and parliament.

The relation between legislation and state budget came up for the first time at the third session of the Assembly (on 27 September 1991), when the draft of Raidla's working group was discussed. Hallaste pointed out that the provision according to which all draft acts that have budgetary implications should be accompanied with cost calculations (and indications of which revenues would be used to cover these costs) and all such drafts would need to secure the consent of the Government, would reduce the role of the parliament in legislation to zero and turn the *Riigikogu* into a puppet parliament, since all drafts would increase or redistribute costs. Raidla answered that such a requirement is necessary, because the Government has a more comprehensive overview and more information of the factual situation of the budget than the parliament. Therefore, he emphasised, the draft acts that have budgetary implications should be under Government's control, so that only such decisions would be adopted that can be feasibly implemented. *(Põhiseadus ja Põhiseaduse Assamblee* 1997, p. 80)

These arguments reflect both theories and interests of the participants. The "theory" underlying the provision requiring the Government's consent in Raidla's draft was that the Government is better informed about the implications of the different acts for the budget and the Government's consent would secure the feasibility of the proposals. Given that Raidla was himself a member of the cabinet, it is perhaps not surprising that in his draft the Government was given a much stronger role in the legislative process. The need to secure Government's consent would have significantly increased the power of the Government at the expense of the *Riigikogu*. In addition, Raidla was able to draw on the 1938 Constitution, which, despite its authoritarian nature, was still popular among many of the Assembly members. Hallaste, who was himself a member of both the Supreme Council and the Congress, clearly represented the interest of the legislature in securing its power *vis-à-vis* the Government.

As mentioned above, since Raidla's draft was not taken as the main basis of the Assembly's discussions, the subsequent discussions did not focus on Government's consent but on the need to append financial calculations to *all* legislative drafts. At the sixth session of the CA, Hallaste pointed out that it would be better to abolish this requirement and suggested that the financial calculations should be done instead by the Government, when putting together the following year's budget. At the same session, Koha explained why the requirement of appending financial calculations should still cover *both* the amendments to the state budget and draft acts. He pointed out that during the preparation of the state budget, the spenders have to present their cost estimates and there is a discussion over how much money they receive. He argued that the same logic should apply to all acts that bring about costs: before the parliament passes an act, it should know how large the costs brought about by this act are. (*Põhiseadus ja Põhiseaduse Assamblee* 1997, pp. 186, 190)

The lengthiest discussion on that issue was held during the 20th session. First, Hänni pointed out that the redaction committee doubted the practicality of this requirement, since at the beginning of the legislative process, it may be difficult to evaluate what the budgetary implications of the act are. She stated that such a restriction would amount to an unnecessary filter in the legislative process and make the legislative process too cumbersome, by bringing about lengthy discussions on whether the prognoses about the costs are correct. In his answer, Koha emphasised that the budget is the second most important document in the life of the state (after the Constitution), because it would concern all inhabitants of Estonia and form the basis for implementing domestic and foreign policies. He argued that the budget is a very precise document: it is submitted by the Government, behind whom there is a huge apparatus that makes the calculations of expenditures and revenues. He stated that the constraining condition is necessary in order to prevent populism in the passage of laws:

When we change a tax law, some expenditure would remain outstanding. This cannot be done in a populist way and therefore it is necessary that those who initiate an act prove that the act does not change the structure of the expenditures and, if it does, where funds would be taken to cover the expenditures. (*Põhiseadus ja Põhiseaduse Assamblee* 1997, pp. 667–668)

After Koha's speech, Tiit Käbin (a member of the third committee) pointed out that although the principle of such a requirement is correct, it should not be stipulated in such an absolute way in the Constitution. He brought an example of declaring an emergency situation and how it would be absurd, if the resolution were to be accompanied with exact calculations. To that Koha answered, "Even when an emergency situation is declared, we still have to take a decision on which expenditures have to be curtailed. … We cannot make a decision that we have an emergency situation and simply spend." (*Põhiseadus ja Põhiseaduse Assamblee* 1997, pp. 668–669)

Peet Kask (chairman of the fourth committee, delegate from the Supreme Council) pointed out in his subsequent speech that, in reality, it would be difficult to verify whether the calculations satisfy the conditions set out in such constitutional provision. As he put it, "Formally, these calculations can be required, and a piece of paper, on which a number is written, is a calculation." He argued that if a certain legislative draft entailed a danger of hurting the state purse, the Government or a respective minister would bring up this issue anyway. In his opinion, it should be the task of the minister to demonstrate that the draft act hurts the budget and to provide the appropriate calculations, instead of making the one initiating the act responsible for providing the calculations. He admitted that while the principle in itself is acceptable, it requires more detailed specification in further acts and it should not be such a categorical requirement for all initiators of draft acts. (*Põhiseadus ja Põhiseaduse Assamblee* 1997, p. 669)

In the following speech, Ülo Uluots (a member of the fourth committee, delegate from the Supreme Council) brought an example of discussions on supplementary budget in the Supreme Council:

A rather innocent-looking proposal came from the assembly room, but, at a closer inspection, it turned out that this would instantly imbalance the budget. … But because our reglement, which is for us a like a constitution, allowed it, the Supreme Council had to work for two additional days in order to balance the budget again.

He claimed that the requirement to append financial calculations is necessary for preventing such populist proposals. He suggested that perhaps after three or four years such an article could be abolished (after the organic budget law has been passed), but until then it should be provided for by the Constitution. (*Põhiseadus ja Põhiseaduse Assamblee* 1997, pp. 669–670)

The chairman of the seventh committee Kalle Jürgenson (delegate from the Estonian Congress) argued against this provision by pointing out that a draft act goes through several readings, during which the experts have time to review it and find out whether the act fits in the framework of the existing budget or not; if it does not, this question would be taken up by the budget committee. He added, "I do not think that a legislator should be required to do calculations regarding fields that may be rather alien for him." Valeri Kois (member of the Economic Affairs and Budget Committee of the Supreme Council, member of the fourth committee of the CA) also argued against this provision,

> We often have situations in the Economic Affairs Committee in which the Committee wants to make changes to a Government project. Then the representatives of the Government start contravening and ask questions about money: where to take the money from and where to put it. Since the Government already has the whole information, they have a very strong weapon. If we put this provision into the Constitution, we cannot do anything with them. *(Põhiseadus ja Põhiseaduse Assamblee* 1997, p. 670)

Following this discussion at the 20th session, the Assembly voted against this provision (it received 21 votes against and 6 votes in favour) and it was left out of the Constitution. What remained was the requirement that if a proposed amendment to the *state budget* or to its *draft* has the effect of decreasing estimated revenue or increasing expenditure or reallocating expenditure, the proponent of the amendment has to append financial calculations to the proposed amendment, which demonstrate the sources of revenue necessary to cover the expenditure. For the rest of the legislation, this requirement did not apply anymore.

In sum, the constitutional "theories" underlying the position that supported requiring financial calculations for all draft acts were the following:

- The same logic that applies to the budget should apply to the proceeding of all draft acts that bring about costs.
- Members of parliament should know how large the costs of legislative acts are.
- Such a requirement would prevent the passing of populist proposals that unbalance the budget or the passing of acts that cannot be implemented because of lacking sources of funding.

The "theories" against this provision were:

- Such a requirement would make legislative process too cumbersome.
- Members of parliament may not be able to make such calculations.
- Such a requirement would unduly increase the power of government at the expense of parliament.

- The parliament (e.g., the budget committee) would discuss the costs associated with a draft act anyway; therefore, no such requirement is necessary in the Constitution. Even if the parliament did not discuss it, the concerned ministers would bring up the cost implications.
- Since it would be difficult to specify the quality of such calculations in the Constitution, such a requirement may become a formality that cannot be enforced.

Most of the delegates who were involved in the discussions over this requirement were members of the Supreme Council[90] and, as could be seen, the arguments of the different delegates clearly reflected their own experiences with legislation and state budget in the Supreme Council and their conceptions of the balance of powers between parliament and cabinet in legislative activities.[91] The remarks made by Kois, for example, mirror very clearly the power fights going on between the Economic Affairs and Budget Committee of the Supreme Council and the Government, which contributed to his reluctance to give the Government an additional tool for exerting its power.[92] The speech by Uluots, on the other hand, mirrored the frustration with the messy proceedings of the state budget in the Supreme Council. Still, the arguments presented by Koha (who was the chairman of the Economic Affairs and Budget Committee of the Supreme Council) were more strongly driven by constitutional theories about how relations between the state budget and legislative activities should look like.

Since many delegates of the CA had a legislative background or could see themselves as future members of the parliament, they were reluctant to endorse a requirement that would have clearly constrained the initiation of draft acts by members of the parliament. Interestingly though, this provision was voted out of the draft Constitution only at the 20th session – until then it had remained there (and had the support of the third committee, apart from its chairman).

As for the opinions of foreign experts, this provision was touched upon only by two persons. On the one hand, Ragnemalm (from Sweden) noted in his written opinion on the draft constitution that the requirement to append financial

90 Also, in the third committee that discussed the topic of finance and budget, six members out of seven were members of the Supreme Council (although some of them had been elected by the Estonian Congress).

91 On the whole, as can be seen from the verbatim records of the sessions of the Supreme Council, the members were becoming increasingly dissatisfied with the situation that the Council itself lacked capacity to draft laws and had to rely primarily on legislative drafts coming from the Government.

92 The Economic Affairs and Budget Committee was the committee in the Supreme Council that, *inter alia*, dealt with issues pertaining to budgeting and taxation. The Rules of Procedure of the Supreme Council required that all legislative proposals that have implications for the budget have to be commented upon by the Budget and Economic Committee. This committee was also responsible for looking through and coordinating the amendments to the draft budget in the legislative budget procedure.

calculations to all draft acts is unrealistic (Archival document no. RA-23-24-1-5, p. 123). On the other hand, Carcassonne (from France) remarked that the provisions in the draft constitution would not protect public finances sufficiently. He argued that such calculations (as required by the provision) are usually unimpressive and the indications of the sources of finance may turn out to be economically absurd. He suggested that in order to avoid demagogy in difficult situations, it would be better to leave only the Government the right to increase expenditures or even to decrease expenditures, like it is stipulated in the constitutions of France and Germany. (Archival document no. RA-23-24-1-5, p. 150)

As mentioned above, other articles pertaining to the budget received only rather limited attention from the Constitutional Assembly. The provision stating that "the *Riigikogu* shall not eliminate or reduce expenditure in the state budget or in its draft which is prescribed by other laws" was not included in the draft of Adams but was taken over from Raidla's draft. Interestingly, this provision was criticised by some foreign experts, since it could be interpreted in several ways; consequently, it was voted out of the draft Constitution. At the 18th session it was, however, re-introduced, as a result of the recommendations from the local expert team. As Hänni explained, this provision means that *Riigikogu* has to include the expenditures that are foreseen by a pension law, for example, very accurately in the budget. She noted, "If, on the whole, there is a principle that a later norm replaces an earlier norm, then adding this provision means that in the case of the state budget this principle does not apply." Hänni added that the necessity to include such a provision had been emphasised by local expert Heinrich Schneider. (*Põhiseadus ja Põhiseaduse Assamblee* 1997, p. 554)

What was also taken over from Raidla's draft was the word "all" in Article 115, resulting in the wording "The *Riigikogu* shall pass as a law the budget of *all* state revenue and expenditure for each year." At the 18th session, Hänni explained that the word "all" was considered to be necessary, because the state should not have extra-budgetary revenues or expenditures. (*Põhiseadus ja Põhiseaduse Assamblee* 1997, p. 554)

With regard to Article 119 (stating that if the *Riigikogu* fails to pass the state budget within two months after the beginning of the budgetary year, the president shall declare extraordinary elections to the *Riigikogu*), Adams, when introducing his draft, admitted that this was inspired by recent experiences in the Supreme Council. He noted that although most of the constitutions in Europe appear to assume that the legislature would not run into trouble with adopting the budget in due time, the Estonian practice had shown otherwise. (*Põhiseadus ja Põhiseaduse Assamblee* 1997, p. 142) The redaction committee proposed at the 16th session (on 22 November 1991) to soften this provision and to leave it up to the president to decide whether extraordinary elections would be declared or not, instead of foreseeing it as a compulsory move. Although such a "softer" provision was included in the draft Constitution at first, it was again changed back to the original formulation in February 1992 (as a result of the recommendations of the local expert team). The final version states that the "president declares" – rather than "may declare" – extraordinary elections, if the *Riigikogu* has not passed the state budget within two months after the beginning of the budgetary year.

Another debate that touched upon the state budget concerned the issue of whether the establishment of certain parliamentary committees should be fixed by the Constitution. At the seventh session, Uluots pointed out that two committees should be brought out by the Constitution: the budget committee and the legal committee. He feared that, otherwise, political games may end in a situation where there is no budget committee or legal committee.[93] Ülle Aaskivi (a member of the third committee) stated that the third committee had discussed this issue and although the idea seemed attractive at first, then, as a result of further deliberations, the committee had voted against that provision. She added, however, that this issue should be discussed further, since it would be necessary for the electorate and candidates to know what kind of work the members of the *Riigikogu* have to do. Juhan-Kristjan Talve stated that since the competences of the budget committee would not be specified in the Constitution, just mentioning the committee would remain rather abstract and hence unnecessary. Vello Saatpalu argued that the future parliament would be clever enough to establish such committees on its own initiative. Andres Tarand argued that it is difficult to foresee what kind of committees would be needed in 25 years, for example, and it should be the task of the *Riigikogu* to organise its work in a way it considers appropriate. Hando Runnel, however, emphasised, "Some statesmen have said that the right of budget is the main right of the representative body." He pointed to two tendencies that might threaten this right: "one tendency that says that the budget should be put together by the government and another that says that parliament is useless in that process". Therefore, in his view, fixing the budget committee in the Constitution was practical and not redundant. (*Põhiseadus ja Põhiseaduse Assamblee* 1997, pp. 266–267) The issue was voted upon and received 8 votes for and 25 against and was hence left out of the Constitution.

3.2.2. Making of Provisions Pertaining to Taxation

In the 1992 Constitution of Estonia, there are four articles that concern taxation. Article 106 establishes that issues regarding the state budget, taxation and financial obligations of the state shall not be submitted to a referendum. Article 110 stipulates that laws that establish state taxes and the state budget can not be enacted, amended or repealed by a decree of the president. Article 113 stipulates that state taxes, duties, fees, fines and compulsory insurance payments shall be

93 This proposal might have been inspired by the fact that in the Supreme Council there was no separate committee on budgeting or taxation. The Economic Affairs and Budget Committee dealt, in addition to other issues of economic policy, with budgeting and taxation.

provided by law. Article 157 Section 2 establishes that a local government has the right, on the basis of law, to levy and collect taxes, and to impose duties. While Article 104 requires that the State Budget Act and Acts pertaining to foreign and domestic borrowing and to proprietary obligations of the state can only be passed and amended by a majority of the membership of the *Riigikogu*, this requirement does not apply to tax laws.

Where did these provisions come from? In the draft submitted by Adams, there were no equivalents of Articles 106, 110 and 113. These articles were taken over from Raidla's draft or were suggested in the course of the debates. Articles 106 and 113 were taken from Raidla's draft. In the draft of Raidla, the equivalent of Article 110 in the current Constitution (regarding the decrees of the president) did not include tax laws; that was added during the course of the debates. The provisions in Raidla's draft were for most part taken from the previous constitutions of Estonia. As mentioned above, Article 106 was taken from the 1920 Constitution, Article 110 from the 1938 Constitution. Article 113 existed in a similar form in the 1920 Constitution.[94] Raidla's team added to that "fees, fines and compulsory insurance payments".

Altogether, there were very few discussions on the topic of taxation in the Assembly. When discussing the provisions on referenda, Kask mentioned that no country has referenda on issues of taxation (*Põhiseadus ja Põhiseaduse Assamblee* 1997, p. 232). There was also a short discussion on whether the duty to pay taxes should be stipulated in the Constitution. The obligation to pay taxes ("Everybody has the duty to participate in covering the governing costs of the state and the local governments by paying taxes and duties that have been stated by the law") was included in one of the early drafts but was voted out by the CA. During the 14th session, Sergei Sovetnikov proposed to include it again. The chairman of the second committee Vardo Rumessen stated that the committee had discussed this provision but voted against it because such obligation is self-evident. As he put it, "We should not stipulate all the obligations separately, like brushing one's teeth in the morning." (*Põhiseadus ja Põhiseaduse Assamblee* 1997, p. 480). Sovetnikov, however, argued that he had looked at the constitutions of Latvia and Russia and they had such a provision. He claimed, "In our Constitution there are too many rights and too few obligations." Lauri Vahtre pointed out that the word "everybody" in this provision was very disturbing, since in other countries, a tourist is not obliged to pay taxes but can buy from a tax-free shop. Adams pointed out that the wording "covering the governing costs" was not appropriate, since the budget would not only include governing

---

94 In the 1938 Constitution, however, there was no such requirement, implying that tax acts could be established by presidential decrees as well (Lehis 2002, p. 501). Also, before the coming into force of the 1992 Constitution, establishing taxes by governmental decrees was common: this was allowed by the Taxation Act that was in force between 1990 and 1993 (p. 508).

costs. He emphasised that such a duty is anyway covered by the duty to obey the law. (*Põhiseadus ja Põhiseaduse Assamblee* 1997, pp. 481–482)

The interest of the general public in constitutional issues of public finance was very limited. From all the letters and opinions sent by the public to the Constitutional Assembly, only three touched upon the chapter on Finance and the State Budget: one pointed out that the word "emission" sounds too foreign, the second suggested that the use of state property should be regulated by the Government, and the third proposed that the State Audit Office and the Bank should submit their reports to the Government. In addition, there was a suggestion put forth by 23 workers of a factory, according to which citizens of other countries who live in Estonia should pay a tax for the purposes of defence and government, amounting to 10 percent of the person's income. With regard to the chapter on the State Audit Office, the Conservative party suggested that the Office should also monitor the implementation of the state budget. (Archival document no. R-23-24-1-6, pp. 294–295).

3.3. Testing the Conjectures

In this section, the conjectures outlined in 3.1.3. are evaluated in the light of the Estonian case study.

The Estonian case for most part corroborates Conjecture 1 stating that if the members of the assembly are members of an existing legislature, they will seek to grant the parliament a more important role in the budget process compared to the executive branch. The 1992 Constitution of Estonia does indeed attribute an important role to the legislature in the budgetary process. Although the Government submits the draft budget, the *Riigikogu* has the right to change it before it approves it. Further, the role of the president regarding the budget is explicitly limited: the Constitution stipulates that presidential decrees cannot concern the issues of the state budget or the State Budget Act. An important provision concerning the budgetary powers of the *Riigikogu vis-à-vis* the Government is Article 65 sub-point 10, stating that on the proposal of the Government, the *Riigikogu* will decide on borrowing by the state and on the assumption of other proprietary obligations by the state. This provision entails clear constraints on "independent" borrowing by the executive and requires all loans to be approved by the legislature. As could be seen from the overview in section 3.2.1., most of the members of the Assembly were reluctant to constrain the *Riigikogu*'s role in making the budget and rejected the provision allowing Government's veto on amendments to the budget and on draft acts that have implications for the budget. Also, many members of the Assembly – apart from some notable exceptions – considered it problematic to restrict the legislators by requiring them to show budgetary implications and sources of financing for the draft acts that they initiate. As could be seen from the discussions of the Constitutional Assembly reviewed in section 3.2.1., the members of the Assembly were afraid that this requirement would constrain legislative freedom and give the Government an informational advantage in discussing draft acts.

At the same time, however, the Constitution imposes some clear constraints on the legislature in the budget process. In particular, Article 116, requiring the amendments to the draft budget to be offsetting, and Article 119, implying high costs of failing to pass the budget for the legislature (extraordinary elections), can be considered to constrain the powers of the *Riigikogu vis-à-vis* the Government. As the discussion above shows, this puzzle can at least partly be explained by the heritage of the 1938 Constitution: it was an important source of inspiration for public finance provisions in Raidla's draft, which played a major role in shaping the public finance provisions in the final version of the Constitution. Since the 1938 Constitution gave very strong powers to the executive, the "borrowed" provisions pertaining to budgeting carried some of the legislative constraints also over to the 1992 Constitution. Still, despite the historical example in the 1938 Constitution, the Government's veto on budgetary amendments did not find its way to the 1992 Constitution, indicating trade-offs that the framers had to make between institutional self-interests and historical models.

As discussed in section 3.2.1., the representative of the executive, Minister of Justice Jüri Raidla sought to attribute stronger budgetary powers (including veto power on legislative amendments to the budget and on draft acts with budgetary implications) to the Government in his draft. To what extent this preference was inspired by his team's fondness of the 1938 Constitution, to what extent by institutional self-interest, is difficult to ascertain, but the provisions in Raidla's draft were *perceived* to represent the institutional self-interests of the executive by the members of the Assembly (see also section 2.2.) and were rejected as such. At the same time, the draft constitution proposed by Raidla entailed clear limitations of the executive power *vis-à-vis* the legislature: Article 65 sub-point 10 prevents the Government from taking independent decisions on state loans; this can be regarded as evidence against Conjecture 1.

The Estonian case also offers evidence for Conjecture 2: the majority of the framers came from existing governing institutions or expected to be elected to the legislature or government in the post-constitutional phase and the resulting constitution does not entail substantive constitutional limitations (e.g., in the form of balanced budget requirements) or strong procedural limitations (like supermajorities for acts concerning public finance). As section 3.2. indicates, the constraints embodied in provisions on public finance in the 1992 Constitution of Estonia are only procedural (rather than substantive) and, as such, relatively moderate: an absolute majority is required for the organic budget law and framework laws pertaining to borrowing, but not for the organic tax law or specific tax laws. Provisions concerning substantive constraints were not proposed by any member of the Assembly.

Conjecture 3 finds partial confirmation in the Estonian case. Although the discussions on issues of public finance were relatively brief, some tendencies can be brought out. Appealing to constitutional theories for most part dominated over arguments appealing to constitutional interests in the constitutional discussions on budgeting and taxation, although there were also notable exceptions (see remarks by Uluots and Kois, brought out in section 3.2.1.). Conjecture 4 is confirmed by the Estonian case: all the participants in the discussions over budgeting were members of the existing legislature (the Supreme Council) and their arguments, presenting either "theories" or "interests", reflected prior experiences and offered solutions to existing problems. The word "all" added to Article 115 mirrored framers' dissatisfaction with the opacity of existing state budgets. For instance, the expenditure side of the 1990 state budget included only 14 items; 37 percent of the expenditures were planned for "financing the national economy" without further details. Further, the transparency of the budget was reduced by complicated interrelations between the budget of Estonia and the budget of the Soviet Union.[95] As Tang and Nilgo (1995, p. 92) point out, because of the interrelations with the Soviet budget, it was almost impossible to know the total expenditures or revenues in any given year. The arguments in favour of requiring the initiators of draft acts to append budgetary calculations (indicating the sources for financing the act), repeatedly brought up by Koha, reflected his dissatisfaction, as a head of the Economic Affairs and Budget Committee of the Supreme Council (responsible for evaluating the budgetary implications of the proposed draft acts), with the proceedings of draft acts in the Supreme Council at the time.

The testing of Conjecture 5 is somewhat complicated in the Estonian case, given that the party system was still in an embryonic phase of development. Since there was a large number of parties and party-like organisations, it would have been the interest of the representatives of all these parties to argue for a stronger role of the legislature in budgeting. There were, however, also framers who supported more stringent constraints on legislature in issues concerning public finance. Although, in principle, one could have expected the representatives of different parties to include their ideological preferences concerning budgeting and taxation in the constitution, no explicitly ideological proposals were made during constitutional discussions.

Although the foreign experts paid very little attention to issues of public finance, the few remarks that were made indicated their preference to grant stronger budgetary powers to the executive *vis-à-vis* the legislature, providing evidence for Conjecture 6. The preferences of the local constitutional experts, expressed most clearly in Raidla's draft, also indicated the wish to constrain the

95 For example, payments from the profit of all-Union enterprises located in Estonia, as well as part of the turnover tax, personal income tax and social security contributions were transferred as revenues to the Soviet Union's budget. There were also direct contacts between the budgets of all-Union enterprises and all-Union ministries: many enterprises were closely tied to their ministries in Moscow and received their financial resources from there. (Tang and Nilgo 1995, p. 93; Taaler 1995, pp. 112–113)

budgetary freedom of the legislature by foreseeing Government's veto on legislative amendments to the draft budget, which also corroborates Conjecture 6.

Conjecture 7 predicted that when the constitution is subject to ratification by referendum, framers would take the constitutional preferences of the public into account in drafting constitutional provisions pertaining to public finance. Testing this conjecture is complicated in the Estonian case, since the public paid very little attention to constitutional provisions on budgeting and taxation. The few proposals made in the letters sent to the Assembly were not included in the Constitution. The main impact of the general public on the resulting provisions concerned the requirement of absolute majority for a list of important acts, including the organic budget law and acts on state borrowing. The list of acts for which absolute majority is required was introduced after the public discussion – as a "compromise" for not stipulating a more stringent quorum requirement for the parliament.

Conjecture 8 stated that inclusive participation in constitution-making would lead to constitutional provisions that foresee a decentralised budget process and an extensive role of the public in taxation and budgeting. The Estonian constitution-making does not provide evidence for this conjecture. In the Estonian case, although one can consider the constitution-making – especially in its later phases – as inclusive, that played no important role with regard to the provisions on the state budget: no proposals of more extensive decentralisation or limitations of the central government power in the budget process or taxation were put forth by the public. With regard to the local governments, the Constitution stipulates that they have independent budgets. This provision, however, was already included in the draft Constitution that was submitted to public discussion. Further, despite inclusive participation in the constitution-making, the Constitution does not impose any limitations on the state with regard to taxation, apart from the requirement to establish taxes by law. Indeed, for passing or amending tax laws, not even an absolute majority of the membership of the *Riigikogu* is required – tax laws can be changed with a simple majority. Although the list of acts for which qualified majority is required includes the State Budget Act and acts pertaining to foreign and domestic borrowing and to proprietary obligations of the state, the discussion in the media after the "official" public discussion did not bring up the issue of including tax laws in that list. Further, in Estonia's case, inclusive participation did not lead to provisions that give a greater role to the general public with regard to taxation and the budget (e.g., allowing popular initiatives or referenda on issues concerning budgeting or taxation). In fact, the public discussion did not protest at all against the provision that forbids submitting issues pertaining to taxation and the state budget to a referendum.

Conjectures 9 and 10 proposed that more extensive public involvement in constitution-making would lead to more specific (and potentially contradictory) provisions pertaining to taxation and budget-making in the constitution. These propositions were not confirmed by the Estonian case. The main provision of the

Constitution pertaining to taxation – Article 113, which states that state taxes, duties, fees, fines and compulsory insurance payments shall be provided by law – is rather vague and essentially only bans establishing taxes with Government regulations and other lower level acts.

Conjecture 11, suggesting that the provisions on taxation and budgeting are likely to be taken over from the constitutions that were in force in the pre-communist period was clearly confirmed in the Estonian case. Two-thirds of the provisions pertaining to taxation and budget in the 1992 Constitution were taken from the 1920 and 1938 Constitutions. Some of the added provisions were similar to those included in the organic budget law passed in 1989 (although this was not mentioned by the participants), providing some evidence for Conjecture 12.

Conjecture 13, suggesting that constitutional transplants from the constitutions of other countries are unlikely, was also confirmed in the Estonian case. Although the German Basic Law was often cited as one of the main examples for the Estonian Constitution, very little from it was taken over with regard to taxation and budgeting. For example, establishing the "golden rule" in borrowing never came up in the discussions.[96] A possible explanation for this omission is that the concept of balanced budget prevailing at the time was a merely a "formal" notion. The State Budget Act (passed in 1989) required the Government to submit a balanced budget to the parliament, but the list of budget revenues also included loans, which meant that the budget would always be "balanced". Another possible explanation is that since the constitution-making took place amidst economic crisis, introducing a balanced budget requirement (in its real sense), a golden rule or a debt limit would have been perceived as unwanted constraints in a tight fiscal situation. On the other hand, the budgets in 1990–1991 had been in surplus (Shen 1994, p. 119),[97] which implies that the issue of budget deficits was not a very burning issue at the time. In August 1991, a month before the Constitutional Assembly was convened, a supplementary budget was passed, since tax revenues had significantly exceeded the forecasted expenditures. At the end of 1991 and beginning of 1992, however, the Government and the Supreme Council had to resort to repetitive budgeting because of the hyperinflationary conditions. That meant that the budget could only be

---

96 As mentioned above, the German Basic Law requires prior consent of the Government for passing laws that increase expenditures or decrease revenues, which is similar to a provision that was put forth in Raidla's draft. Still, an analogous provision was already in the 1938 Constitution of Estonia, which was a more likely source of "inspiration" for that provision in Raidla's draft.

97 Estonia's state budget was independent from that of Moscow since early 1990. The independence implied that net revenue transfers to the central budget of the USSR were ended and were used for the domestic budget. In 1990, the surplus-to-revenue ratio was 9.4 percent (which was the highest in the Baltic states for that year). The positive ratio was 9.5 percent in 1991 and 1.07 percent in 1992. (Shen 1994, pp. 124–125)

adopted for one month or few months at a time. The Ministry of Finance at that time sought to keep a conservative fiscal stance and budget deficit only became an apparent "threat" in spring 1992, but the Government immediately took action and restored budget balance by summer. By that time, however, substantive debates on the Constitution were already over. On the whole, balanced budget became an overriding principle in the Estonian economic policy only after the currency reform and introduction of the currency board system in June 1992.

Conjecture 14, emphasising the importance of the time constraint in constitution-making, was confirmed in the Estonian case. The very short deadline set by the Supreme Council meant that draft constitutions had to be submitted very fast and the Assembly had to work very swiftly. Given the time pressure, the structure presented in the winning draft Constitution changed very little and the additions that were made came chiefly from the main competing draft. Both of the draft constitutions that influenced the final outcome had a separate chapter on finance and the state budget. In both drafts, the provisions in this chapter were rather brief and concerned mainly the budget procedure, while having only one article on taxation. Bringing up new articles for that chapter would have been the task of the third committee. Given that besides the chapter on finance and the state budget, the third committee had to deal with very important chapters concerning the parliament, government and legislation, it had to prioritise. Naturally, the issues regarding the parliament and government received much more attention. Since the draft of Adams was very vague on the exact duties and powers of the legislature, government and the president (Pettai 2001, p. 122), it was seen as needing extensive revision, which in turn left less time for discussing the chapter on finance and the state budget. Thus, a further conjecture for the theoretical framework could be: if there is a specific committee in the constitutional assembly, focusing on the issues of public finance, there would be a larger number of more specific provisions pertaining to budgeting and taxation.

3.4. Discussion

Altogether, the discussions of the Estonian Constitutional Assembly indicate that the issues of budgeting and taxation received relatively little attention. The issues of public finance were discussed at ten sessions of the assembly, warranting about the same (or even less) amount of attention as the question of whether the institution of the president should be called "president" or "*riigivanem*" (state elder).

A possible explanation for the lack of interest with regard to taxation in the Assembly could be that there already was the 1990 Taxation Act: a framework law that created the new system of taxes.[98] Since this Act was the basis for

98 The 1990 Taxation Act established the list of taxes, gave the state the right and duty to collect them, established the right of the state to control the funds collected and made tax

Western type tax system that came into force in January 1991, including further provisions on taxation in the Constitution was not perceived as urgent. It is also conceivable that taxation was seen as an area where, given quickly changing circumstances, flexibility and ability to react fast were seen as desirable and, thus, any limitations would have been unwanted.[99] The experience with changing the tax laws in 1991–1992 showed that, for most part, the Government wanted to introduce changes very swiftly, but the readings in the Supreme Council took very long time.[100] On the whole, it seems that the framers viewed the Constitution rather as a purely political document, separated from what were seen as more "technical" economic policies or overly "ideological" tax policies.[101] In 1991–1992, extensive economic reforms were undertaken and the work in the Assembly and in the committees preparing and implementing the economic reform (liberalisation, privatisation and currency reform) took place in parallel rather than interactively.

In trying to explain why there were no appeals from the public suggesting provisions of taxation, a number of possible explanations can be offered. When the constitution-making started, Estonia had just moved from a Soviet-type tax system to a modern Western-style tax system. Thus, both the longer-term experiences with the Soviet tax system and the very recent experiences with the newly introduced taxes played a role in how the population perceived the issues of taxation. One of the main characteristics of the Soviet tax system was the invisibility of taxes. As Rose (1992, p. 22) explains it, centrally planned economies did not need to "worry" about taxation, because "the state took its cut of the funds before they ever reached the hands of individuals". Kopits (1993, pp. 232–233) also reminds us that in the planned economy, financial policies did not have a distinct function: they were entirely subservient to the annual economic plan. Most tax revenues came from profit, turnover and payroll taxes levied on state-owned enterprises. Turnover taxes captured the difference between administratively set prices, and profit taxes took the (remaining) surplus generated by socialised enterprises. Wage and payroll taxes were withheld at the enterprise

evasion a violation of the law (Tang and Nilgo 1995, p. 94). The list of taxes included personal income tax, corporate income tax, VAT, activity license tax, land tax, excise tax, natural resources tax, pollution tax and local taxes.

99 For example, the Personal Income Tax Act was changed several times during 1991–1992, given the need to adjust the tax brackets to high inflation.

100 On one occasion, the Government was so frustrated with the slowness of the proceedings that it took the initiated draft act back and passed the changes with governmental decrees (which was possible, according to the existing Taxation Act).

101 Despite the apparent lack of interest in issues related to taxation in the Constitutional Assembly, debates on tax laws in the Supreme Council – taking place at the same time – were very intensive. For example, in October–November 1991, which was the most intensive working period of the Constitutional Assembly, the reform of personal income tax was discussed in the Supreme Council. One of the main issues discussed already then was whether the tax system should be proportional or progressive.

level and individual income taxation was relatively unimportant. (Martinez-Vazquez and McNab 1997; Schaffer and Turley 2002; Tanzi and Tsibouris 2000) Several authors have noted that since the state did not rely on personal income tax for the bulk of its revenue and people had no active experience in directly paying taxes (e.g., submitting tax declarations or paying taxes during transactions), there was a lack of tax consciousness among ordinary people and little awareness of the actual tax burdens (see Kodrzycki 1993; McKinnon 1993; Martinez-Vazquez and McNab 1997, 2000; Tanzi and Tsibouris 2000).

Based on the experiences with the Soviet tax system, one could expect that individuals would be relatively uninterested in the issue of taxation, while the enterprises would be more concerned. Given the arbitrariness of taxation at the level of enterprise, one could have expected the enterprises to speak up more loudly about possible constitutional provisions on taxation. It has to be kept in mind, however, that by 1991–1992, only small businesses had been privatised, while large firms were still state-owned. Until then, there had been little opposition to otherwise controversial tax measures, because the state served a dual role as the owner of enterprises and as the tax collector (Martinez-Vazquez and McNab 2000, pp. 274–275). Thus, they did not yet have direct interests in including any clear limitations on taxation in the Constitution.

The new tax system that came into force in January 1991 constituted an important change for individual taxpayers: in addition to paying personal income tax on the income from their main job, they also had to start paying income tax on earnings from contractual jobs, grants, receipts from entrepreneurship and property income. Compared with the previous levels, the tax rates were higher (16, 24 and 33 percent for the different brackets). Thus, one could have expected that the very "fresh" experiences would make the issues of taxation rather prominent in the mind of the population and encourage the public to submit proposals on constitutional provisions on taxation. When the Deputy Finance Minister Enn Roose was presenting the draft Personal Income Tax Act in the Supreme Council in August 1990, he noted that the draft act had received rather contradictory opinions in the public discussion. "Some thought that the personal income tax, the principles of the tax and the tax rates are completely normal, some thought that the personal income tax should not be included in the tax system at all. We have also read purely emotional opinions according to which this draft act robs the nation, undermines private initiative and is against agricultural production." In addition, he noted that the main protests had come from those for whom the marginal tax rates increase or who have to start paying it for the first time (including individual enterpreneurs, cooperatives, farmers, veterans). (Verbatim Record of the Supreme Council, 22 August 1990, pp. 87–89) When discussing the changes to the Taxation Act in February 1991, Roose noted,

> Hopefully in the future we will have a special working group, formed by the Supreme Council and the Government, which would work out and explain to people the nature of our tax system. So far it has not been done. People have to know why one or another tax is as high as it is or why the proportions between different taxes are how they are. At the moment we do not have propaganda regarding the tax laws. (Verbatim Record of the Supreme Council 18–21 February 1991, p. 139)

None of these considerations were reflected in the work of the Constitutional Assembly or the proposals sent to the CA by the public, however. At the same time, one needs to keep in mind that the introduction of the whole new tax system had also a symbolic connotation for the inhabitants of Estonia: the economic independence from the Soviet economy. As Tang and Nilgo (1995, p. 95) put it, designing a new tax system "was aimed at creating a civilised tax system independent of the Soviet Union". Thus, Estonia's "own taxes" were seen as being better than having to paying taxes to the Soviet budget. For the firms, tax rates were kept low at the beginning to encourage the former all-union firms to pay their taxes into the Estonian budget and not into the Soviet Union budget (Tang and Nilgo 1995, p. 95). After a while, however, such a "patriotic" view of taxes gave a way to seeing even "own" taxes as a burden. Tax arrears and tax evasion became more widespread after the currency reform in June 1992, which raised the tax rates considerably. By that time, however, the Constitution had already been passed. Hence, it can be conjectured that if the drafting of the constitution had taken place later, it would have been likely to include more fiscal provisions.

When putting the case of Estonia into comparative perspective, it should be noted that the constitutions of the other CEE countries adopted at the beginning of transition also include very few provisions concerning budgeting and taxation. The only CEE country whose constitution entails detailed provisions on budgeting (including fiscal rules) is Poland[102] – but these provisions were only included in the "big Constitution" that was adopted in 1997 and not in the interim (also called "little") Constitution that was passed 1993.[103] Bruszt (2002, p.

102 Just for comparison, the chapter of the 1997 Polish Constitution that deals with public finances has about 1200 words, while the corresponding chapter has about 300 words in Estonia, 400 words in the Lithuania, 300 words in Slovenia, 150 words in the Slovak Republic and 570 words in Romania. The constitutions of Latvia, the Czech Republic, Hungary and Bulgaria do not even have a separate chapter on public finance.

103 For example, Article 216 Section 5 of the 1997 Constitution of Poland establishes that "It shall be neither permissible to contract loans nor provide guarantees and financial sureties which would engender a national public debt exceeding three-fifths of the value of the annual gross domestic product." Article 220 Section 1 states that "The increase in spending or the reduction in revenues from those planned by the Council of Ministers may not lead to the adoption by the House of Representatives (*Sejm*) of a budget deficit exceeding the level provided in the draft Budget." Article 220 Section 2 stipulates that "The Budget shall not provide for covering a budget deficit by way of contracting credit

56) reckons that in the Central and Eastern European countries, fears and hopes related to the remaking of the *political field* dominated in the constitutional debates, and the agenda of constitutional change was structured by questions related to political legitimacy. Given the invisibility of taxes during the Soviet times, the issues of taxation were not seen as something that should be regulated by the Constitution. For framers, the question of "citizens" was much more important than the question of "taxpayers".

For developing a better understanding of constitutions as *explananda* in public finance, further in-depth studies of constitution-making in different countries are needed. The list of conjectures put forth in this chapter can certainly provide a starting point for examining the other CEE countries.

---

obligations to the State's central bank." Article 221 establishes that "The right to introduce legislation concerning a Budget, an interim budget, amendments to the Budget, a statute on the contracting of public debt, as well as a statute granting financial guarantees by the State, shall belong exclusively to the Council of Ministers.

Part II: Constitutions as *Explanantia* in Public Finance

Chapter 4: Why and How Do Constitutions Matter in Public Finance?

While part I of this book was concerned with constitutions as *explananda*, parts II and III focus on the role of constitutions as *explanantia* in public finance. Analysing effects of alternative constitutions has long been an important research topic in political science, as exemplified by contributions of Sartori (1994), Powell (1982) and Lijphart (1994), among many others. However, as Persson and Tabellini (2003) point out, the research of comparative politics has primarily focused on *political* consequences and less on *economic* effects of constitutions. Studies in constitutional political economy and constitutional economics seek to fill this gap by exploring the effects of constitutions on economic indicators.[104]

In his outline of the research agenda of positive constitutional economics, Voigt (1997) lists the following "economic effects" as foci of analysis: transaction costs, interdependence and external costs (see Buchanan and Tullock 1962, ch. 16), economic output, economic growth, tax rates, public expenditure and taxpayer honesty. As can be seen from this list, alongside the most general economic indicators (like economic output and economic growth), the effects pertaining to public finance are considered to belong to the "core research agenda" of positive constitutional political economy. This should not be surprising, since many pioneers of constitutional political economy (for example, Wicksell, Buchanan, Tullock, Olson) were, first and foremost, specialists in public finance.[105] Besides the public finance indicators pointed out by Voigt, the streams of positive constitutional political economy that are concerned with public finance – shortly put, "constitutional public finance" – have focused on indicators of budget discipline (deficits, surpluses, debt levels), spending mix, tax mix, fiscal adjustments, pro- or counter-cyclicality of fiscal policies. Going beyond specific aggregate indicators, studies in constitutional public finance should also analyse the impacts of constitution on inclusiveness (the range of interests encompassed), stability and social optimality of policies in public finance (see Scharpf 1989).

With regard to the specific constitutional features that are considered as *explanantia*, Voigt (1997), in his outline of the research agenda for positive constitutional political economy, enumerates the following aspects: the separation of powers (unicameralism versus bicameralism, executive veto, federalism), direct versus representative democracy and individual rights. Besides these insti-

104 For a discussion on the differences between the "political economics" camp and "public choice" camp in constitutional political economy, see Blankart and Koester (2006, 2007).

105 However, as Blankart and Koester (2006, 2007) have noted, the more recent pursuits of positive constitutional political economy – political economics, represented most prominently by Persson and Tabellini – tend to dismiss the intellectual ancestors of the kind of research they are doing.

tutional elements, studies in constitutional public finance have considered the effects of different electoral institutions (and governing arrangements arising thereof), characteristics of judiciary (including constitutional review), budgetary procedures and fiscal rules.

Part II of this book focuses on the effects of constitutions on budget discipline, expenditure levels, spending mix, tax revenues, features of tax systems and fiscal adjustments. However, before looking at the effects of constitutions on these particular aspects of public finance (which is done in chapters 5 and 6), it is essential to outline more general arguments about *why* and *how* constitutions affect public policies in general and policy choices and outcomes in public finance in particular. Since studies of constitutional public finance have hitherto paid rather limited attention to the *mechanisms* linking constitutional provisions and policy outcomes, insights from different institutionalist approaches are used for elaborating the links between constitutional rules and substantive choices in public finance. Hence, sections 4.1. and 4.2. serve the role of eliciting the presumptions regarding the causal mechanisms that underlie the discussions in chapters 5 and 6. Section 4.3. addresses the basic question of constitutional public finance: Do constitutions really matter for outcomes in budgeting and taxation? The short answer is: they do. Given the large amount of studies on constitutional public finance undertaken in recent years, a unified framework for a structured overview of the existing propositions and empirical findings is called for. Therefore, in section 4.4., an analytical framework for summarising, synthesising and criticising existing studies in constitutional public finance is outlined. This framework constitutes the "analytical skeleton" for chapters 5 and 6.

4.1. Mechanisms of Influence: Insights from Institutionalist Approaches

On the whole, the underlying *mechanisms* of how constitutional rules shape resulting decisions (and policy outcomes) have received less attention in the current literature of positive constitutional public finance than the assumed *associations* between constitutional rules and policy effects themselves. Voigt (1997, p. 19) reminds us, however, that the correlations one may be able to detect between certain institutional arrangements and particular policy patterns are alone not sufficient for drawing causal inferences. What makes ascertaining the causal impacts of a constitution particularly difficult is that, ideally, one would have to show that *without* the existing constitution, the resulting outcomes would have been different (Voigt 2004). Despite these difficulties, or perhaps exactly *because of* such challenges in ascertaining causal relationships between constitutions and public policy, one should inquire into the mechanisms that link constitutional rules and policy choices.[106] Elster's (1999b) argument that social sci-

106 See Scharpf (1989) for the general argument on the necessity to specify the causal linkages between political institutions and policy choices.

entific analysis should be focused on specifying the "mechanisms" that produce certain outcomes ought to be of particular concern for constitutional public finance as well.

Given that constitutional political economy (including constitutional public finance) can be seen as a part of the broader spectrum of approaches called institutional economics, the answers provided by different institutional approaches about how institutions influence the behaviour of political actors can certainly inform the analysis.[107] In studies of constitutional public finance, certain "modes" of influence are often simply assumed, taken as given, depending on the stream of institutionalism the authors are aligned with. Keeping in mind *different* kinds of explanations for the effects of institutions, however, would be useful for evaluating theoretical models developed and empirical results obtained in constitutional public finance. In addition to institutional approaches in economics, constitutional public finance – in its pursuits to explain how constitutions affect policy decisions – can draw on institutional approaches in political science.[108]

The explanations of how constitutional rules influence policy can focus on different elements in the chain depicted in Figure 4.1.

Figure 4.1.: Links between constitutional rules and policy outcomes

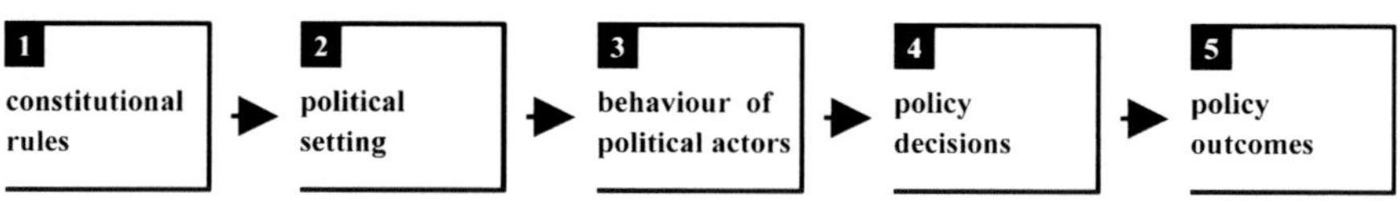

The links "constitutional rules – political setting" and "political setting – behaviour of the political actors – policy decisions" are explored closer in the following subsections. The strength of causal influence between the different elements in this chain becomes weaker as one moves down the chain, since more and more factors come into play. Therefore, when drawing a connection between constitutional rules and policy decisions (and outcomes), one should keep in mind that the causal relations between the sub-chains can be complex, subtle, indirect and contingent (March and Olsen 2005; Weaver and Rockman 1993; Scharpf 1989, p. 149). The same constitutional rule can have different impacts when combined with different rules under different conditions. Therefore, constitutional rules can only be presumed to "constrain and enable outcomes without being the immediate and direct cause of public policy" (March and Olsen

107 For overviews of institutionalisms in political science and sociology, see Koelble (1995).

108 Hall and Taylor (1996) distinguish between three strands of institutionalism in political science: historical institutionalism, rational choice institutionalism and sociological institutionalism. They note that rational choice institutionalism in political science overlaps heavily with new institutionalism in economics.

2005, p. 9). Pursuits to disentangle institutional effects become increasingly difficult, the larger the number of levels and centres in institutional settings is and the more these settings are characterised by interactions among multitudinous autonomous processes (Orren and Skowronek 2004; March and Olsen 2006). Further, in exploring the links between the elements in the chain, one cannot remain oblivious to contextual factors, including, *inter alia*, normative and cognitive orientations of the political actors (e.g., belief systems of the political actors with regard to means-ends and causes-effects relationships in policy problems), situational factors and the very nature of the specific policy problem (Scharpf 1989, p. 150; 2000, p. 767).

4.1.1. Constitutional Rules and Political Setting

As indicated in Figure 4.1., constitutional rules can be considered to be important in shaping the *political setting* in which political actors interact. The link between constitutional rules and political setting is often neglected in the existing literature of constitutional public finance, which tends to consider immediately the link between constitutional rules and actors' behaviour. Although in some cases, indeed, constitutional rules can impose direct constraints "on the repertoire of permissible policy choices" (Scharpf 2000, p. 774), then, for most part, the effects of the constitution on policy choices are mediated through the political *setting* that is structured by constitutional rules. Ostrom (1986, p. 7) emphasises that "Viewing rules as directly affecting the structure of a situation, rather than as directly producing behavior, is a subtle but extremely important distinction." Drawing on Diermeier and Krehbiel (2003, p. 126), one can view constitutions as establishing "contextual features of a collective choice setting that defines constraints on, and opportunities for, individual behaviour in the *setting*" (emphasis added).

Ostrom (1986, p. 19) distinguishes between seven different types of rules that operate *configurationally* to affect the structure of an action situation: position rules, boundary rules, scope rules, authority rules, aggregation rules, information rules and payoff rules. Although Ostrom does not speak specifically of constitutional rules, the spectrum of different kinds of rules she elaborates on also covers the kinds of rules constitutions usually entail. Thus, constitutional rules shape political action situations by defining the following aspects of a political setting: the kinds of positions, the number of persons that can hold a particular position, how participants are chosen to hold the positions and how they have to leave, the set of actions assigned to different positions, decision functions to be used at particular nodes, the channels of communication between participants in positions, the costs or external inducements associated with sets of outcomes, and how benefits and costs have to be distributed to those holding the positions (p. 19). Shortly put, constitutional rules can influence resulting policy choices by determining the actor constellations involved in decision-making and the modes (or "baseline conditions") for their interaction (Scharpf 2000, pp. 775–776; Nelson and Sampat 2001, p. 33). For example, constitutional rules can impact on political decision-making by influencing the time-frames for taking decisions and giving guidance for gathering facts and information (Berggren and Karlson 2003, p. 115).

Further, by defining power relations between the positions (and thus between actors filling these positions), constitutional rules influence whose preferences are likely to prevail. According to Dahl (1956, p. 135), the primary role that constitutions play in shaping the political setting is by establishing the methods of control for political actors. By distributing "control rights" among actors, constitutional rules can exercise a significant role by determining "what particular groups are to be given advantages or handicaps in the political struggle" (Dahl 1956, p. 137). In sum, constitutional rules can be viewed as having "an ordering effect on how authority and power is constituted, exercised, legitimated, controlled and redistributed" (March and Olsen 2005, p. 9).

Scharpf (1989) points out that, among the rules outlined by Ostrom (1986), boundary rules and aggregation rules (termed "decision rules" by Scharpf) are particularly relevant for predicting policy choices. According to Scharpf (pp. 152–153), boundary rules (defining the units of collective action) are important, since they define units within which "contracting" is replaced by "governance" as a procedure for transforming preferences into decisions; decision rules, in turn, are essential since they specify the processes of "governance" in terms of "who is entitled to participate in which decisions, and how collective choices are to be reached in the face of disagreement among legitimate participants".

In his 1989 article, Scharpf distinguished between three main decision mechanisms: hierarchy, majority and unanimity.[109] Drawing on Tsebelis (1995a), Scharpf (2000, pp. 775–776) underlines that boundary rules and decision rules "determine the most basic and policy-relevant characteristic of the institutional setting, namely, the number of formal veto positions".[110] Thus, according to Scharpf (2000, p. 776), at one extreme end of the continuum is a single actor (or a "unified action centre"), whose preferences and perceptions determine policy choices. At the other end of the continuum are multiple-actor constellations, in which policy decisions are influenced by choices and negotiations of several independent actors.

These main features of the institutional setting, in turn, influence the inclusiveness, inter-temporal stability and allocative efficiency of policy choices (Scharpf 1989, p. 157). For example, hierarchical decision systems are more likely to consider both long-term and short-term concerns and majoritarian systems tend to focus on short-term benefits, while implications of unanimity are

---

109 In a later book, Scharpf (1997) suggested using a broader notion of "modes of interaction" and classified the various modes of interactions as following: mutual adjustment, negotiated agreement, voting and hierarchical direction (see also Scharpf 2000).

110 See also Tsebelis (1995b, 1999, 2002).

ambiguous. In a similar vein (although using somewhat different terminology), Cox and McCubbins (2001) argue that the "effective number of vetoes"[111] in a polity greatly influences the two key trade-offs inherent in policy-making and policy outcomes: first, the trade-off between a political system's *decisiveness* (its ability to make policy decisions) and its *resoluteness* (its ability to commit to established policy decisions); and second, the trade-off between the *public*- and *private*-regardedness of the policies produced. In a polity where the effective number of vetoes is large, changing a policy will be difficult (because the transaction costs that must be overcome are larger),[112] but committing to a policy (i.e., being more resolute) will be relatively easier. Conversely, a polity with a smaller effective number of veto players is more able to make or implement policy changes, but it is less resolute (and thus less likely to be able to maintain the new status quo). With respect to public- and private-regardedness of the policy produced, Cox and McCubbins (2001) argue that the greater the number of effective vetoes, the more private-regarding will be the policies enacted: this outcome is a consequence of bargaining among veto players, if each veto player is in a position to demand and receive side-payments (in the form of narrowly targeted policies).

Adding the link "constitutional rules – political setting" to an analysis of impacts of constitutions helps to structure the analysis and to distinguish the features that characterise a particular *setting* from the *behaviour* of political actors in that setting. Such a distinction can be particularly useful in comparative institutional and constitutional analyses seeking to disentangle the *structures* created by rules from the participants' *reactions* to these structures. At the same time, one should not dismiss the link between the political setting and policy outcomes: How exactly do the elements of institutional setting and the structure of the situation influence the behaviour of political actors? From the accounts of Cox and McCubbins (2001), among others, one may get the impression that the characteristics of the political setting almost automatically translate into particular tendencies in policy choices. A closer look at individual-level behaviour in an institutional setting, however, would substantially complement the inquiry into causal mechanisms between the links in the chain connecting the constitution to policy choices in public finance.

4.1.2. Decisions and Actions of Actors in Political Setting

Moving on to the next element in the chain: How does the political setting, the structure of the situation created by constitutional rules, influence the decisions and actions of political actors? Most simply put, by defining the setting where

111 The "effective number of vetoes" refers to two salient aspects of the political process: the number of political actors that possess a veto over policy change and the extent to which there is conflict of interest between these actors (Cox and McCubbins 2001).

112 On that point, see also Posner (1987) and Berggren and Karlson (2003).

political actors interact, constitutional rules can influence the behaviour of political actors in the following ways: they can constrain, enable, simplify and guide. As Diermeier and Krehbiel (2003, p. 127) put it, institutions can provide incentives for and impose constraints on certain types of behaviour. Alongside the usually assumed constraining and encouraging functions, constitutions can be expected to "simplify political life by ensuring that some things are taken as given" (March and Olsen 2005, p. 9), "reduce the range of potential behaviour" (Ostrom, Gardner and Walker 1994, p. 38) by defining "a set of allowable actions" (Ostrom 1986, p. 6). As Immergut (1998, p. 13) puts it, political institutions (outlined in constitutions) "allow political choices to be made because they do not allow every conceivable political choice to be considered".

In order to provide a more fine-grained answer to the question of how the political setting, defined by constitutional rules, shapes the behaviour of political actors, a distinction put forth by Hall and Taylor (1996) is employed. In their discussion on different strands of institutionalism, Hall and Taylor (1996) divide the different responses to this question into two broad categories: the "calculus approach" and the "cultural approach".[113]

4.1.2.1. The Calculus Approach

As Hall and Taylor (1996) explain, the "calculus approach" focuses on strategic interaction and those aspects of behaviour that are instrumental and grounded in strategic calculation to achieve a set of goals (presumed to be exogenous).

At the most basic level, constitutional rules can be viewed as affecting the costs and benefits associated with undertaking certain actions and hence making particular actions more or less likely. Ostrom, Gardner and Walker (1994, p. 38) state that rules "change the costs and benefits that an actor can expect when following a certain course of action". As Buchanan (2002, p. 14) puts it, "Constitutional rules have the effect of increasing the costs of taking certain actions. It is more costly to take action in violation of a rule than it is to take the same action in the absence of the rule. ... An increase in the cost of any choice alternative will reduce the resort to that alternative."

Going beyond decisions where the actor's payoff depends only on his or her independent decision, the calculus approach points to a substantial role that institutions play in shaping the *strategic interactions* of interdependent actors. According to the calculus approach, constitutions affect behaviour "by providing actors with greater or lesser degrees of certainty about the present and future behavior of other actors" (Hall and Taylor 1996, p. 939). By supplying relevant information about the behaviour of others, enforcement mechanisms for agree-

113 Hall and Taylor (1996) note that rational choice institutionalism tends to subscribe to the calculus approach, sociological institutionalism to the cultural approach, while historical institutionalism is eclectic and uses both of these approaches to explain the relationships between institutions and actions.

ments and penalties for defection, constitutional rules can influence *actions* and *responses* of an individual in the political arena. As pointed out in section 4.1.1., constitutional rules establish the *modes of interaction* between political actors; thus, by affecting the range and sequence of alternatives on the choice-agenda, for example, the rules can shape the resulting decisions and actions (Hall and Taylor 1996, p. 945). In the words of Shepsle (1989, p. 135), constitutional rules can be seen as providing "the strategic context in which optimizing behaviour takes place". Drawing on Eggertsson's (1997, p. 1192) account of rational choice institutionalism, constitutions can affect transaction costs, the information available to actors and their incentives, which, in turn, affect behaviour and outcomes. In sum, according to the calculus approach, constitutional rules can play an important role by shaping the *incentive structure* of political actors.

Scharpf (2000, p. 777) takes the analysis a step further and explores closer the links between particular kinds of political *settings* and the *incentive mechanisms* the settings give rise to. He explains that in issue areas dominated by a single actor, "the incentives that have the most direct effect on policy choices are constituted by the mechanisms of political accountability", whereas in issue areas with multiple actors (i.e., with several effective veto points), accountability is weakened and policy choices are more likely to be influenced by "incentives favoring cooperation or conflict between the veto actors". A similar starting point has been adopted by Spiller and Tommasi (2003) and Spiller, Stein and Tommasi (2003) in their "policy-making capabilities" (or "state capabilities") approach, employed for mapping the effects of political institutions into properties of public policies (e.g., whether the policies are stable and predictable, can adjust to volatile conditions and lead to broad or concentrated benefits). They argue that the incentives and constraints on political actors, established by constitutional rules, play an important role in shaping the political process, which, in turn, influences the policy-making processes and capabilities. Proceeding from the "calculus approach", they argue that several relevant characteristics of public policies depend essentially on whether political actors are able to achieve cooperative outcomes or not. In settings where concluding inter-temporal political agreements is possible, public policies are likely to be more effective, sustainable and more flexible in responding to changing circumstances in the economy. Summing up the same idea, Weaver and Rockman (1993, p. 9) state that constitutional rules "encourage or discourage certain attributes of decision-making process that enable or deter the emergence of policymaking capabilities that influence government's ability to make strategic policy choices".

4.1.2.2. The Cultural Approach

Alongside the calculus approach, constitutional public finance should also acknowledge the insights from the "cultural approach", when explaining the role that constitutions play in shaping the behaviour of political actors. The "cultural approach", according to Hall and Taylor (1996, p. 939), emphasises that, besides purely instrumental "calculations" and strategic considerations, the chosen courses of action can be strongly influenced by the interpretation of the situation. The cultural approach underlines that institutions play a role by offering moral and cognitive templates (e.g., in the form of cognitive scripts, models and routines), filters for interpretation, frames of meaning and guides for action. Besides providing strategically useful information, institutions can influence "the identities, self-images and the very goals of the actors". (Hall and Taylor 1996, p. 939) While the calculus approach assumes that the preferences of the individuals, acting within the constraints institutions impose on them, are *exogenous* to the institutions, the cultural approach points to the essential function institutions serve in *shaping* the individual preferences. In particular, institutions can play an important role in constituting and forming the individual preferences with regard to feasible options, by defining how the outcomes will be evaluated by the actors involved (Scharpf 1997, p. 39; Schmid 2004, p. 1). According to Steinmo (1993), institutions offer a context that enables individuals to interpret their self-interest and their policy preferences arising thereof. In a similar vein, Hodgson (2006, p. 7) notes, "By structuring, constraining, and enabling individual behaviors, institutions have the power to mold the capacities and behavior of agents in fundamental ways: they have a capacity to change aspirations instead of merely enabling or constraining them." Drawing on March and Olsen (2005, pp. 5, 10), one can view constitutions as "carriers of identities and roles" and "markers of a polity's character, history and visions", which offer interpretive frames for political actors. Since "politics is a place for discovering, elaborating, and expressing meanings" constitutional law can serve as an essential "instrument of interpretive order" (Burgess 1993, p. 447). Constitutional rhetoric and constitutional discourse can entail "transformative power" (Burgess 1993, p. 450) in shaping the orientations of political actors.

At the same time, the cultural approach reminds us that openness in interpretation implies that though constitutions structure the political setting and create certain "biases" (Schattschneider 1960) or tendencies, constitutional rules cannot determine policy choices or outcomes in detail. Political actors may not always be sure of what exactly constitutional rules prescribe in specific situations, as "there may be competing rules and competing interpretations of rules and situations" (March and Olsen 2005, p. 10). When faced with the same sets of hurdles posed by constitutional rules, "self-reflective actors can make creative decisions about how to proceed" (Immergut 1998, p. 26).

Further, proceeding from cultural approach, one has to keep in mind that the relationship between constitutions and individual action is "highly interactive and mutually constitutive": when conforming with a particular constitutional norm or interpretation thereof, the political actors reinforce the very norm by attesting the social meaning it has (Hall and Taylor 1996, p. 948).

Given that both the cultural approach and calculus approach help to explain important parts of reality, constitutional public finance would benefit from both of them. For most part, however, recent studies in constitutional public finance have been confined to the calculus approach and rational choice institutionalism, which, as will be seen in chapters 5–7, is able to bring out some patterns, but leaves a lot unexplained. Therefore, there is a strong need for complementary studies that also encompass the notions of the cultural approach in explaining the links between constitutional rules and choices of political actors. One way of integrating the cultural approach more extensively into analytical pursuits of constitutional public finance – via the means of encompassing the role played by constitutional deliberations and constitutional constructions in policy-making – is presented in part III of this book.

4.2. Why Are Constitutional Rules Followed?

Section 4.1. was primarily concerned with the question: How do constitutional rules, either directly or by shaping the political setting, influence the behaviour of political actors and the policies they choose? A related but still a separate question is: *Why* would constitutional rules be followed by political actors? Often, in studies looking at the effects of constitutions on resulting decisions and policies, compliance with constitutions is simply *assumed*: it is presupposed that political actors follow the constitutional rules, without bringing up the question why they would do that. Brennan and Buchanan (1980, pp. 9–10), for example, state that, for the purposes of their analysis, compliance with constitutional rules is simply assumed, because historical experiences demonstrate that governments have complied with constitutional rules and their actions have been constrained by constitutions. Curiously, although they are not concerned with the reasons why this has been so, their "whole construction is based on the belief, or faith, that constitutions can work, and that tax rules imposed within a constitution will prevail" (p. 10). Ostrom (1986, p. 6) also remarks that most formal models in institutional inquiries entail a tacit assumption that individuals are, for most part, rule-followers. Such *deus ex machina* assumptions are puzzling, since the question "Why do political actors follow constitutional rules?" touches upon a core issue in an analysis of constitutional institutions and their effects. Ordeshook (1992, p. 138) has even remarked that the question of how constitutional rules are maintained and enforced constitutes "[a] central mystery of democratic theory". Thus, constitutional public finance should also be concerned with constitutional compliance and inquire into the mechanisms that help to explain compliance or defection.

Once more, the distinction used by Hall and Taylor (1996) in characterising different institutionalist approaches – the "calculus approach" and the "cultural approach" – can be employed for explaining why constitutional rules are followed by political actors.[114]

The *calculus* approach would suggest that an actor complies with a constitutional rule, because deviation would make him or her worse off than adherence. In other words, compliance or non-compliance would be subject to a similar "calculation" as making choices *within* institutional constraints. Davidson (1984), for example, conjectures that politicians are most likely to break those constitutional rules in the case of which non-compliance will only imply a small reduction in their future legitimacy. The calculus logic is also inherent in game-theoretic approaches of constitutional analysis, according to which political actors are expected to adhere to constitutional rules, if compliance strategies constitute a Nash equilibrium (i.e., if deviation from constitutional rules would make individual actors worse off than adherence). Drawing on Hall and Taylor (1996, p. 940), one can argue that the more a constitutional rule contributes to resolving collective action dilemmas, the more likely is adherence and the less likely deviations from it.

One factor that can influence the "payoff" from deviating from a constitutional rule is whether and how constitutional rules are enforced by third parties. Although conceptualising the judicial review as a mechanism of guaranteeing compliance begs the question of how the rules that define the jurisdiction of the court are enforced in turn (Ordeshook 1992, p. 138), constitutional review can be expected to play an important role in guaranteeing compliance with the constitution. Sutter (1997, p. 147), for example, notes that "Judicial review is a relatively efficient means of enforcing a constitution." He argues that the court reports can provide substantial alleviation for collective action and coordination problems, by providing a focal point for ascertaining constitutional violation. In addition to constitutional courts, constitutional review can be exercised by other institutions in the political system: the president, ombudsmen, the legal chancellor and other institutions with the authority to review legislative acts and to call attention to possible violations of the constitution.[115]

Alongside the enforcement of rules by a third party, constitutional rules can be maintained if they are "self-enforcing". The importance of self-enforcement of constitutional rules has been emphasised by Ordeshook (1992), Hardin (1989) and other authors who view constitutions as coordination devices rather than contracts. Coordination rules usually provide incentives for all actors in the game to conform to the convention (Hodgson 2006, p. 14). A coordination equilibrium is likely to be self-policing because participants in the political game lack incentives to change strategy (to violate the constitutional rule) and, at the same time, each actor wishes that other players keep to their strategy as well

114 In a similar vein, March and Olsen (2005) distinguish between "the logic of appropriateness" and "the logic of consequences" in explaining compliance.

115 The role that constitutional courts and other institutions of constitutional review play in shaping legislative choices in public finance is elaborated in chapter 8.

(Schotter 1981, pp. 22–23). Hardin (1989, p. 119) argues that "Establishing a constitution is a massive act of coordination that creates a convention that depends for its maintenance on its self-generating incentives and expectations." Proceeding from the conception of constitutions as coordination devices, Lehne (2004) provides an extensive game-theoretic analysis of why constitutional rules would be complied with. He suggests that although game-theoretic analysis predicts that it is highly improbable that *every* provision of a constitution would be complied with on its own, *across-the-board* constitutional compliance is nevertheless possible, since what happens in one game has repercussions in other games within the overall constitutional game. The complexity of the overall constitutional game "facilitates the stabilization of any existing ordered constitutional system as an actual equilibrium" (p. 237). Lehne also emphasises that "in a complex setting like the overall constitutional game, a written constitution has particular advantages, which help it to gain and maintain focal point power as coordination device, e.g. its 'writtenness' and its comprehensiveness" (p. 237).

According to Hall and Taylor (1996, p. 940), the *cultural approach* suggests that rules would be followed because they may be so "conventional" or "taken-for-granted" that the question of whether to follow or not to follow the rule is not even raised (see also Berger and Luckman 1967). As Hodgson (2006, p. 15) emphasises, though, one should distinguish between rule-following out of convenience and rule-following ensuing from a normative belief in the rightfulness and legitimacy of the rule (see also Vanberg 1994; March and Olsen 1989, 2006). According to March and Olsen (2005, p. 8), the adherence to rules can be induced by ethos, by "a sense of rights and obligations derived from an identity and membership in a political community". When constitutional rules are capable of influencing the aspirations of political actors, the rules would be reinforced and perpetuated because these very rules have played a role in moulding the endeavours of those actors (Hodgson 2006, p. 7). As Smith (1988, pp. 89, 95) puts it, constitutional rules can "influence the self-conception of those who occupy roles defined by them"; through influencing the "senses of purpose and principle" political actors adhere to, constitutional rules can convey a sense of duty and identify "inherently meaningful actions".

4.3. Do Constitutions Matter for Budgeting and Taxation?

Constitutional institutions have received increasing attention as an important factor in explaining policy decisions in budgeting and taxation.[116] An emerging

116 Other theoretical models for explaining budgetary outcomes include the following: tax-smoothing models, business-cycle models, partisan-cycle models, electoral-cycle models, models of strategic use of debt. The tax-smoothing model (see Barro 1979; Lucas and Stokey 1983) predicts that budget deficits follow economic cycles: the budget balance is used as a buffer to allow tax rates to be approximately constant at the level that keeps the

consensus is that economic, demographic and ideological factors do play some role in influencing budgetary choices but cannot tell the entire story: a significant proportion of the variation is left unexplained.[117] Another emerging consensus points to the role of institutional variables in explaining both the fiscal scale (levels of expenditure and revenues) and fiscal balance (deficits and debts). Imbeau and Chenard (2002, p. 17) conclude, after reviewing 39 empirical studies (until 2001), that "Budgetary performances are affected by electoral cycles and by institutional arrangements."[118] Thus, in order to explain budgetary outcomes, looking at the constitutional arrangements that define the political and fiscal institutions is warranted. The same standpoint has been endorsed by Bails and Tieslau (2000), Poterba (1996), Alesina and Perotti (1995), Eslava (2006), Freitag and Sciarini (2001), Franzese (2002b), de Wolff (1998), Pinho (2004), Woo (2003), Persson and Tabellini (2003, 2004a,b) and many others. Gersl (2007, p. 67) even goes as far as to say that "The only appropriate way of how to treat the issue of public deficit and its reduction or elimination must inevitably include a deep analysis of the political process and especially the fiscal constitution, i.e.

---

budget in inter-temporal balance. These predictions are similar to Keynesian models of deficit determination, according to which fiscal tools are used to stabilise cyclical fluctuations and to boost the economic activity during recession. Partisan-cycle models assume that politicians are primarily motivated by ideology and predict that there is a systematic relationship between the partisan composition of governments and budgetary outcomes (see Hibbs 1977; Schmidt 1996; Wagschal 1998). Models of strategic use of debt assume that debt levels are used for influencing the policy choices of subsequent governments (Alesina and Tabellini 1990; Persson and Svensson 1989; Aghion and Bolton 1990; Milesi-Ferretti and Spolaore 1994; Milesi-Ferretti 1995). The core idea of these models is that when an incumbent government is anticipating electoral defeat and does not like the policies potentially adopted by the successor government, it may opt for accumulating debt and, by doing that, is able to force the successor government to spend resources on debt service instead of on policies motivated by ideological goals.

117 For findings showing that partisanship matters under various other conditions, see Cameron (1985), Carlsen (1997), Cusack (1997, 1999), Garrett and Lange (1991), Garrett (1997), Hibbs (1977) and Bräuninger (2005), van Dalen and Swank (1996) among others. For findings suggesting that it does not, see Alesina and Roubini (1997, ch. 7), Cowart (1978), Hahm, Kamlet and Mowery (1996), Robertson (1982), Haan and Sturm (1994), and Leachman *et al.* (2007), among others. For empirical studies confirming the strategic use of debt model, see Pettersson-Lidbom (2001). Several studies, however, have not found support of this hypothesis; see, for example, Franzese (2000), Andrikopoulos, Loizides and Prodromidis (2004) and Helland (2000).

118 For early discussions on the impacts of electoral cycles, see Nordhaus (1975), Frey and Lau (1968), Kramer (1971), Goodhart and Bhansali (1970), Frey and Schneider (1978a,b), Tufte (1978), Cukierman and Meltzer (1986), Rogoff (1990), Rogoff and Sibert (1988), MacRae (1977). For reviews of literature on electoral cycles, see Paldam (1997), Gärtner (2000), Mueller (2003), Wagner (2001), Franzese (2002c) and Drazen (2000). The role of electoral cycles has also been confirmed by the following recent studies: Amorim Neto and Borsani (2004), Shi and Svensson (2006), and Brender and Drazen (2005).

the rules that set incentives for political representatives in the realm of fiscal policy."

With regard to taxation, Steinmo and Tolbert (1998, pp. 166–168) note that, surprisingly, macroeconomic explanations – population of a country, imports-exports as a percentage of GDP, wealth measured by per capita GDP, growth measured by change in GDP – provide little or weak explanations for variation in tax burdens. Further, differences in public opinion towards taxation also yield insufficient explanatory power. Steinmo and Tolbert emphasise, therefore, that possible explanations should be looked for in the differences of political institutions. The same standpoint is endorsed by Merrifield (1991) and Gould and Baker (2002).[119]

In analysing the effects of constitutions on public finance, chapters 5 and 6 assume that institutions *matter* in explaining budgeting and taxation; the question is rather, *which* institutions matter and *how* they matter. In other words, the discussion in the following chapters does not start with specific budgetary outcomes and attempt to list all possible factors explaining these outcomes. Rather, the review takes up different kinds of constitutional institutions and explores how each of these institutions influences policy choices and outcomes in public finance. In chapter 7, in turn, a more "idiographic" approach (see Brower, Abolafia and Carr 2000) is taken and the question is: To what extent can the political institutions and the extended fiscal constitution explain a particular case, namely, the commitment to fiscal discipline in Estonia from 1992 to 2007?

One can distinguish between three streams of literature in positive constitutional public finance, each looking at different kinds of "constitutional institutions". One stream of literature looks at the effects of various political institutions: parliamentarism versus presidentialism, proportional electoral system versus plurality (or majoritarian) system, bicameralism versus unicameralism, and so forth. The second stream looks at "fiscal rules", including balanced budget requirements, debt ceilings, tax and expenditure limits. The third strand, starting with Weingast, Shepsle and Johnsen (1982) and von Hagen (1992), looks at how decision-making procedures regarding budgeting and taxation affect policy choices. The procedural rules pertaining to budgeting and taxation can be stipulated either in the constitution or in laws that are usually considered "constitutional laws" (e.g., the organic budget law and the rules of procedure for the parliament). Constitutional laws can be viewed as part of the "extended constitution" (see Berggren and Kurrild-Klitgaard 2002) and different provisions entailed in these laws regarding budgeting and taxation can be viewed as the "extended fiscal constitution", complementing the "fiscal constitution" in a narrow sense (entailing only the fiscal provisions in the constitution).[120] Chapters 5 and

119 For reviews of different models explaining how political variables affect tax policies, see Gould and Baker (2002). For a review of political economy of taxation, see Swank and Steinmo (2002).

120 A systematic depiction of these different terms is presented in section 6.1.

6 take up these different streams in turn. Given the vast amount of literature that has emerged on the impacts of constitutions on public finance in recent years, a system for categorising the propositions they entail is called for. The next section outlines an analytical framework that is taken as a basis for examining the effects of different kinds of constitutional institutions on public finance in chapters 5 and 6.

4.4. Analytical Framework for Constitutional Public Finance

This section outlines a concise analytical framework that can be used for summarising, synthesising and criticising existing studies in constitutional public finance and for providing directions for future research. This framework should be helpful for categorising and comparing the existing (and also future) studies on the effects of constitutions on public finance and for linking the different models and theoretical perspectives they entail. Figure 4.2. summarises the analytical framework and the main predictions made with regard to how constitutional rules that make up the political setting shape the policy choices in public finance. The figure indicates the links that the prevalent models in constitutional public finance (principal-agent models, common-pool models and veto players models) make between the main mechanisms in the action arena of public finance (as shaped by the political setting) and the effects on policy choices in public finance, contingent on the particular features of the institutional settings (strong versus weak accountability, many versus few participants on the policy arena).

The existing literature exploring the effects of different constitutional institutions on budgeting and taxation can be viewed as focusing on two mechanisms that arise from the political setting and shape interactions between political actors: accountability mechanisms and coordination mechanisms.
Accountability mechanisms concern vertical relations between voters and their elected representatives, and the approaches used here often draw on principal-agent models. Although this distinction is often neglected in the existing literature, one should discern between different levels of accountability here. The locus of accountability can be on individual level (e.g., an individual legislator or a member of cabinet), party level or institutional level (referring to the accountability of the executive as a whole, for example).

Figure 4.2.: Analytical framework for constitutional public finance

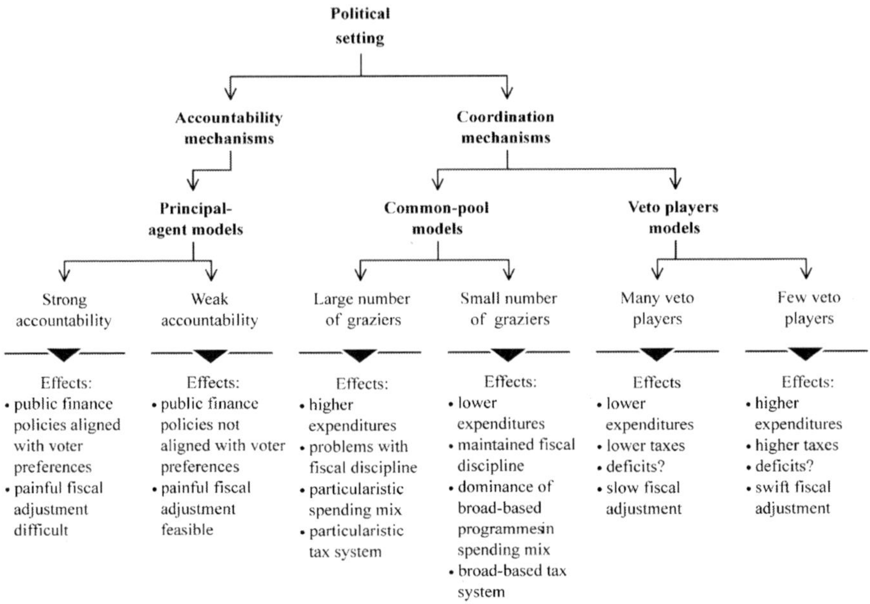

One particular constitutional arrangement can influence the accountability mechanisms on these different levels in complementary but also in discrepant ways. For example, a proportional electoral system may enhance the accountability of *parties* to the electorate but at the same time weaken the accountability of *individual* legislators and the *executive* as a whole to the electorate. In addition to vertical accountability mechanisms between *elected officials* and *voters*, it is analytically necessary to consider the effects different constitutional arrangements have on the accountability of an *individual legislator* to the *party*: that is, to what extent parties command control over their individual members.

What implications would stronger or weaker accountability of policy-making entities to the electorate have for policy choices in public finance? Most generally put, when the accountability mechanisms between policy-makers and the electorate are strong, one can expect the policy choices in public finance to be more in line with the preferences of the electorate (or the majority thereof). What exactly that would mean for the levels of expenditure, revenues, spending mix and the features of the tax system, would depend on the fiscal preferences of the voters. If voters are assumed to be fiscal conservatives (Peltzman 1992; Moak 1982; Alesina, Perotti and Tavares 1998; Skilling and Zeckhauser 2002), stronger accountability should lead policy-makers to opt for more constrained expenditure levels, lower taxes and lower budget deficits. When voters value fiscal prudence, stronger accountability should give rise to more prudent choices in public finances. If one follows Buchanan's (1957, 1987) assumption that voters favour expansion of current expenditures – but without corresponding increase in taxes – one would expect higher expenditures, lower tax revenues and higher deficits in polities with stronger accountability mechanisms. When accountability mechanisms, as established by constitutional arrangements, are weak, one can expect the policy choices to be poorly aligned with the preferences of the voters. While stronger accountability has usually positive connotations, one should keep in mind that blurred accountability can sometimes be conducive to the taking of distressing measures; hence, stronger accountability may make the decision-makers more unwilling to undertake necessary but unpopular reforms, like the adoption of painful fiscal adjustments.[121]

The *coordination* mechanisms pertain to horizontal relations and transactions between different government branches, partisan actors or elected representatives: for example, between the legislature and the executive, between the different chambers of the legislature, between the parties in the government or the legislature, or between the elected representatives in the legislature. The main models used for conceptualising horizontal relations and the ensuing coordination problems between institutional, partisan or individual political actors are *budgetary commons* (or common-pool) models and *veto players* models.

Budgetary commons models emphasise the role of political fragmentation (also called size fragmentation) in shaping fiscal outcomes and predict that the larger the number of participants in budgetary decision-making process, the higher will be resulting expenditures, tax expenditures and budget deficits and the more particularistic will be the spending mix and the tax system.

Although most of the authors cite Hardin's (1968) "tragedy of the commons" as their inspiration for conceptualising the general tax fund as "budgetary commons", subject to the same problems as other common-pool resources, the idea that fiscal policy is faced with common-pool resource problems goes back to Tullock (1959). According to Tullock (1959, p. 577), the logic of common-pool resource problem would be applicable to "any governmental activity which benefits a given individual or group of voters and which is paid for by general taxation". The common-pool resource metaphor can hence be expected to be "insightful" whenever one deals with "distributive" or "divisible" policies, where benefits are targeted and costs are diffused among the general population (see, among others, Ferejohn 1974; Collie 1988; Brubaker 1997; Wagner 2002; Buchanan and Yoon 2001, 2002).

The gist of budgetary commons models is that the participants involved in budgeting internalise full benefits of a spending proposal but bear only a fraction of the cost, since it is financed from the common tax fund. The divergence be-

121 At the same time, of course, one should keep in mind that in polities where inability to achieve fiscal consolidation is punished by voters (and the policy actors anticipate that correctly), stronger accountability would also lead to prompter fiscal consolidation.

tween *perceived* and *actual* costs of programmes, in turn, would lead the graziers on the commons to demand higher levels of particularistic expenditures than would be efficient, leading to increasing expenditures, and, in a dynamic context, to higher deficits (see Velasco 1999, 2000). Weingast, Shepsle and Johnsen (1981), who put forth the first formal model of decision-making on budgetary commons, pointed to the "law of $1/n$", which predicts that the larger the number of graziers (the n) on the budgetary commons, the smaller is the fraction of costs that each grazier internalises. The smaller the fraction that each grazier has to bear, the smaller become the perceived costs compared with the actual costs and the more severe the common-pool problems involved in budgeting are likely to be. Overgrazing the commons can also take the form of tax expenditures (reflected, *inter alia*, in the special provisions, exemptions and loopholes in the tax laws). In the case of tax expenditures, too, one can expect a divergence in the perceived benefit arising from the exemption that the target-constituency receives and the costs it imposes.

Who exactly the graziers on the commons are, can be conceptualised in different ways. Some models focus on *individual* graziers (legislators in the legislature or members of cabinet), some on *partisan* graziers (parties in the legislature or in the government) and some on *institutional* graziers (e.g., the two chambers in a bicameral legislature). The seminal formal model of the tragedy of budgetary commons, put forth by Weingast, Shepsle and Johnsen (1981), demonstrated how common-pool problems of budgeting arise in a legislative setting where each legislator represents the interests of his or her home-district. Inspired by this basic model that is applicable to a U.S. type presidential form of government with a majoritarian electoral system, a number of modified versions of budgetary commons models have been proposed in order to conceptualise the common-pool problems also in parliamentary settings and proportional electoral systems. Thus, while the article by Weingast, Shepsle and Johnson (1981) focused on individual legislators and geographically concentrated interests, further models have extended the notion of "graziers" to partisan actors and socially concentrated interests they represent (including socio-economic, demographic or sectoral interests). Analogously to the geographic representation of interests, the underlying idea is that while many public programmes or services can be targeted to particular constituencies or groups of voters, taxes are spread across the entire electorate. In the case of such targeted programmes, those who benefit from particular programmes (be it a social group or a particular sector), bear only a fraction of the costs needed to finance these programmes and have, therefore, incentives to demand increasing levels of such expenditures. The political parties that represent the socially concentrated interests, in turn, have incentives to seek increased expenditures on programmes benefiting their respective constituencies but without having to take into account the full cost of increases in spending. Therefore, for example, coalition governments with parties representing different socio-economic interests are conjectured to face common-pool problems of budgeting more often than single-party governments. Common-pool models focusing on individual ministers in the cabinet, in turn, predict that the larger the number of spending ministers, the larger the common-pool problems are likely to be.

The gist of *veto players* models (see Tsebelis 1995a,b) is that the more there are veto players (or veto actors)[122] that can block a policy choice, the more difficult it is to reach a common agreement for adopting policy changes and the more biased policies are towards status quo.[123] Like there can be various types of graziers on budgetary commons, there can be different kinds of veto players in budgetary decision-making: institutional, partisan and individual actors. As mentioned in section 4.1.1., the larger the number of veto points in the polity, the lower is its capability to be decisive, in terms of adopting policy decisions that depart from status quo, but the higher is its resoluteness in committing to adopted policy decisions (Cox and McCubbins 2001). For public finance, this would mean that systems with *fewer* veto points are able to adopt *more* expenditure programmes and increase taxes more easily than polities with many veto points. At the same time, systems with few veto points would be able to reverse the adopted programmes more easily, while polities with a higher number of veto points would be more likely to sustain the expenditure programmes or tax systems already enacted. When faced with a need to undertake fiscal adjustment, systems with more veto points would have difficulties in acting decisively; however, once the corrective fiscal measures have been adopted, such polities would be more likely to stick to them, while systems with few veto points would have problems with credible commitment. In addition, Cox and McCubbins (2001) argue that the larger the number of effective veto points in the political system, the more private-regarding will be the enacted policies, implying more particularistic spending and lower expenditures for public goods and broad-based programmes.

Both *accountability* and *coordination* mechanisms entailed in different constitutional institutions can be examined with regard to how they structure the incentives of political actors and whether these incentives are conducive to cooperation or competition between the actors. The incentive structure and the competitive or cooperative orientations arising thereof are likely to influence *governing capabilities* that foster prudent policy choices in public finance. Schick (1993), drawing on Weaver and Rockman (1993), suggests that maintaining fiscal discipline and curbing budget deficits requires two governmental capabilities: setting and maintaining priorities when policy objectives are in conflict and resources are limited, and imposing costs on concentrated interests. He underlines that these capabilities are likely to have special relevance in economically

122 According to Tsebelis (1999, p. 593) "a veto player is an individual or collective actor whose agreement is necessary for a change of the status quo".

123 For a critical review of the existing theoretical and empirical studies employing the veto players approach, see Ganghof (2002).

difficult times: when the governments have to opt for larger deficits or higher taxes, and curtail expenditures or increase taxes (p. 189). Different constitutional institutions influence these particular capabilities in different ways. How exactly, is explored in chapters 5 and 6.

The three-fold division of the streams of literature in constitutional public finance – concentrating, respectively, on political institutions, fiscal rules and budgetary institutions (outlined in section 4.3.) – is the basis for structuring the following two chapters. Chapter 5 looks at the effects of political institutions (i.e., the main features of the "machinery of government" as defined directly and shaped indirectly by the constitution). Chapter 6 focuses on the effects of fiscal constitutions: the impacts of fiscal rules (e.g., balanced budget requirements) and budgetary institutions (rules of procedure governing the preparation, adoption and implementation of the budget) on public finances. The chapters consider theoretical propositions about effects of different constitutional arrangements on accountability and coordination mechanisms in a polity and what implications they would have for public finances. Also, overviews are given of the existing empirical studies that have looked into the effects of the different constitutional rules on fiscal indicators. Finally, a critique of the "emerging orthodoxy" of constitutional public finance is put forth.

The critique is presented at two different levels. First, a number of shortcomings, gaps and inconsistencies can be found *within* the dominant discourse; if one subscribes to the prevailing discourse of the emerging orthodoxy in constitutional public finance, there are a number of theoretical and empirical problems that need to be addressed. At the second level, the critique is taken one step further and is addressed *at* the dominant discourse: the hidden normative assumptions that underpin the theoretical propositions, models and metaphors employed (especially the "tragedy of budgetary commons" metaphor) are brought out and their problematic implications for inquiry discussed. The idea of the review of literature in chapters 5 and 6 is to let the discourse of the emerging orthodoxy to "come through" to the reader in the way it is presented in the existing literature – that is, to pass on the impression one gets from the literature, without commenting extensively on the problematic premises, hidden normative assumptions and ideological orientation of the existing studies *in the course* of giving the overview. The critique of the discourse is left for the concluding sections in chapter 6.

Chapter 5: Political Institutions as *Explanantia* in Public Finance

There is an increasing volume of literature analysing the effects of political institutions (entailed in constitutions) on budgeting and taxation. These studies pose questions like the following: Does it matter for public finance whether the form of government is presidential or parliamentary? Would fiscal outcomes be systematically different under proportional as opposed to majoritarian (or plurality) electoral systems? Does the size of the legislature matter for budget size and composition? Can one expect bicameral legislatures to adopt different budgets than unicameral legislatures?

Drawing on the analytical framework that focuses on the accountability and coordination mechanisms that shape policy-making in public finance (outlined in section 4.4.), this chapter takes stock of the existing literature on the effects of political institutions on budgeting and taxation. The overview offers a synthesis of the existing models and propositions in existing theoretical literature, and outlines and summarises the results of the empirical studies conducted so far. First, the effects of presidentialism versus parliamentarism are considered, followed by the effects of electoral rules and governing arrangements (the size of the legislature and cabinet, the number of parties in the legislature and the cabinet, unicameral versus bicameral legislatures). Finally, the effects of direct democracy mechanisms and judicial institutions are discussed.[124] Often, the studies in constitutional public finance consider the effects of constitutional rules on expenditures and taxation separately, focusing *either* on budgetary outcomes like expenditure levels and budget deficits *or* on taxation (tax burden, tax structures). If taxes are viewed together with the budget outcomes, then the studies confine themselves to the level of tax revenue rather than other aspects of the tax system. The overview given in this chapter serves to bring the disparate strands of literature together and to present a more complete picture of the effects of political institutions on public finances. While for most part, sections 5.1.–5.6. let the existing literature "speak its own message", then the discussion in section 5.7. criticises the existing studies and puts forth alternative venues of research that future studies examining the role of political institutions in public finance could consider. While the critique in section 5.7. remains for most part a "within-discourse" criticism, the "above-discourse" critique is presented together with the appraisal of fiscal constitutionalist literature in section 6.5.2.

---

124 Though, in principle, a study exploring the effects of political institutions on public finance should also consider the effects of unitary versus federalist arrangements, this constitutes already a large and separate topic in public finance and is closely intertwined with issues like fiscal federalism. Because a large body of literature discussing and synthesising this topic already exists, this issue will be left out of the discussion here.

5.1. Presidentialism versus Parliamentarism

5.1.1. Theoretical Propositions

Approaches exploring the effects of presidential and parliamentary regimes on budgeting and taxation focus on how these different institutional arrangements influence the accountability of elected officials to the electorate and to what extent coordination problems can emerge between executive and legislative branches.

With regard to the question of whether accountability mechanisms are stronger in a presidential system or in a parliamentary system, one can distinguish between two opposite positions: the "presidentialist" position and the "parliamentarist" position (Schick 1993; Weaver and Rockman 1993).[125] The presidentialist position, advocated, among others, by Persson, Roland and Tabellini (1997) and Persson and Tabellini (2000, 2003), assumes that since the executive and the legislature are elected separately in a presidential system, the accountability mechanisms of the executive are stronger in a presidential system than in a parliamentary system with fused executive and legislature. In a presidential system, the chain of delegation is shorter, since the executive is directly answerable to voters, which should mitigate principal-agent problems between the electorate and the executive. As Padovano, Sgarra and Fiorino (2003, p. 52) put it, a parliamentary system, where the executive is only indirectly accountable to the voters, leads to more "slack" in the principal-agent relationship between voters and policy-making entities, for any given amount of information that voters can gather. When the competencies and responsibilities of separate branches are clearly defined, voters are able to identify more easily the institutional actor responsible for particular policy choices and "exercise the electoral control with lower information costs for any given slack in their principal agent relationship with the policy making bodies" (Padovano, Sgarra and Fiorino 2003, p. 52). The parliamentarist position – in contrast – argues that owing to the fusion of legislature and executive in a parliamentary system, the accountability mechanisms are centralised and, therefore, stronger than in a presidential system, where accountability is decentralised between the two institutions (Weaver and Rockman 1993, pp. 11–12).

Depending on whether one subscribes to the presidentialist or the parliamentarist position about the accountability mechanisms, one would make opposite predictions about public finance choices under different forms of government. On the one hand, proceeding from the presidentialist position, the fusion of the executive and the legislature in a parliamentary regime (which weakens the accountability of both branches to voters) can be expected to lead to higher

125 As Weaver and Rockman (1993, pp. 16–17) explain, these are "ideal type positions that are intended to highlight the issues in dispute".

rents, reflected in higher levels of budgetary expenditures. At the same time, blurred accountability in a parliamentary system may help to diffuse the blame for cutting expenditures or increasing taxes when fiscal consolidation is needed. Proceeding from the parliamentarist position, one would expect that more centralised accountability in a parliamentary system would be conducive to adopting policies that are responsive to the preferences of the electorate. At the same time, concentrated accountability would make the government more reluctant to impose losses, since voters can clearly blame the governing party or parties for their losses. (Weaver and Rockman 1993, p. 17)

With regard to the question of whether *coordination* problems of budgetary decision-making are more prevalent in parliamentary or presidential regimes, again, the presidentialist and parliamentarist positions point to diverging propositions (Schick 1993, pp. 187–190). The parliamentarist position reckons that coordination of policy-making is easier in parliamentary systems: the cabinet offers a centralised forum where policy alternatives can be directly compared, disputes over priorities resolved, conflicting standpoints coordinated and resource constraints imposed. The presidential systems, in contrast, are characterised by decentralisation and the absence of definitive mechanisms for resolving conflicts between executive and legislative priorities, which can undermine fiscal discipline.

The presidentialist position, however, contends that the institutional advantages of a parliamentary system, in the form of offering a centralised forum for priority setting, are likely to be illusory rather than having real effects. The proponents of the presidentialist position claim that, despite the centralised forum of a cabinet, the government will be unable to easily reorient priorities and impose costs on constituent groups, because of pressures from programme beneficiaries and norms of reciprocity, expressed in the reluctance of spending ministers to cut the expenditures of other ministries. It is also pointed out that cabinets in parliamentary systems have immense workloads, which means that the taking of substantive decisions is still left to individual departments and the alleged benefits of coordination within the cabinet may not materialise. The presidentialist position underlines that setting priorities and imposing costs is especially difficult when cabinets are multiparty coalitions or when cabinet ministers are closely identified with specific interests or regions. (Schick 1993, pp. 187–190)

In addition, the presidentialist position emphasises that common-pool problems of budgeting would be smaller in presidential systems, since the president has a nation-wide constituency, which gives him incentives to consider a larger portion of the total tax burden accompanying expenditures than is considered by individual actors in parliamentary systems (Hallerberg and Marier 2004, p. 575; Shugart and Haggard 2001). Hence, the president can be expected to act as a countervailing force to particularistic biases of legislative politics; for example, he can pick apart inefficient legislative logrolls by exercising line-item veto (Carter and Schap 1987; Dearden and Husted 1990; Fitts and Inman 1992). On the other hand, McCarty (2000, p. 118) points to reasons why the assumption of "presidential universalism" might be suspect. Driven by electoral motives, the president may have incentives to engage in targeted spending: to channel resources to strategic "swing" regions or to direct distributive benefits to certain legislators in order to further his legislative agenda. As Cox and McCubbins (2001, p. 30) put it, if both the executive and legislative branch prefer to engage in logrolling in order to get the spending *it* wants rather than act as a blocker for spending the other branch wants, the result could be increasing expenditures and deficits. To what extent presidential incentives to favour particularistic spending can be translated into actual budgetary choices, depends, *inter alia*, on the specific role attributed to the president in the budget process.[126]

Veto players models (see Haggard, Kaufman and Shugart 2001; Schick 1993) conceive of presidential systems as having more institutional veto players than parliamentary systems, where the executive and legislature are fused. Having an additional veto player implies that the adoption of further expenditure programmes and increasing taxes would be more difficult in presidential systems, leading to lower levels of spending and taxation. Persson, Roland and Tabellini (1997) emphasise that the separation of powers, with "checks and balances" between the executive and the legislature, is likely to impose more discipline on budgetary process, because the two power-centres monitor each other and prevent the abuse of power. They also argue that in a parliamentary regime, it is easier for politicians to collude with each other, which can lead to higher rents than in a presidential regime. With regard to the emergence of deficits, making predictions becomes more difficult: lower expenditures would imply lower likelihood of deficits, but reduced willingness to increase taxes could also necessitate deficit financing.

When deficits have already emerged or when fiscal consolidation is needed because of external shocks, veto players models would predict that presidential regimes have more difficulties in undertaking fiscal adjustments, because corrective measures can be blocked either by the president or the legislature (see, for example, Persson and Tabellini 2003, p. 28). As Haggard, Kaufman and Shugart (2001, p. 77) underline, because of the additional veto gate the institution of the president amounts to, coherent fiscal policy is less likely, since such a system would be less able to act in a decisive manner in the face of crises and is more likely to delay the adjustment. Especially in situations with divided government, mutual vetoes can lead to a stalemate, exacerbating difficulties in priority-setting, which are inherent in the separation of powers, and thus impair the capacity of the government to deal with budget deficits (Schick 1993, pp. 190–191).

126 McCarty (2000) argues that if presidential budgetary powers are confined to veto powers, the president would act as a break on government spending, regardless of whether he has particularistic or universalistic preferences.

With regard to tax policies, the veto players approach would predict more stable and less innovative tax policies in presidential regimes than in parliamentary regimes, *ceteris paribus* (Weaver and Rockman 1993, p. 17).[127] Hallerberg and Basinger (1998, 1999) conjecture that presidential systems (with divided governments) are less likely to lower top marginal tax rates for personal and corporate income taxes. Hettich and Winer (1999, ch. 11) hypothesise that since the existence of checks and balances in presidential systems increases the costs of reaching and enforcing agreements, political actors would be motivated to remove particularly contentious issues from the regular decision-making process. This, in turn, would imply that presidential systems will make more extensive use of earmarking and trust funds in designing the tax system than parliamentary regimes.[128] Further, they argue that because of a lengthier process of proposing and adopting tax policies, presidential regimes would make less extensive use of discretionary tax policy (e.g., for stabilisation) than parliamentary regimes. This means that presidential regimes would respond slower to exogenous economic shocks by restructuring taxation than parliamentary regimes. Third, Hettich and Winer hypothesise that because of the separation of powers in a presidential regime, it would be more difficult for the legislature to control the administration of tax laws; therefore, legislatures in presidential regimes (compared with legislatures in parliamentary regimes) would be impelled to write tax laws that are more complex and comprise more special provisions.

Confining the analysis of mechanisms of accountability and coordination only to *institutional* level, however, would present an oversimplified view of the incentive structures that characterise political settings in presidential as opposed to parliamentary systems. An analysis of accountability mechanisms, in particular, should not be restricted to the chain of accountability between the *institutions* and the *electorate*; one should also consider the impacts on the accountability of an *individual* legislator to the *party*. The confidence requirement characteristic to parliamentary regimes (meaning that the cabinet needs to have the confidence of a majority in the legislature) creates strong incentives to maintain party discipline: the parties supporting the executive possess treasured proposal powers (owing to the linkage to ministerial portfolios and connection to the cabinet as a whole), which give them advantages *vis-à-vis* the parties in the opposition (see Shugart and Carey 1992; Huber 1996; Diermeier and Feddersen 1998; Baldini 2000; Persson and Tabellini 2003). Therefore, parties usually command significantly stronger control over their members in parliamentary regimes than in presidential regimes. That, in turn, should make the coordination

127 Here, again, the presidentialist position would argue that owing to multiple sources of policy proposals, the presidential system would augment the capacity to innovate in tax policy (Weaver and Rockman 1993, p. 17).

128 Although they word the hypotheses as pertaining to predicted tax policy choices in the United States and Canada, one can extend these hypotheses to apply to presidential versus parliamentary systems in general.

of fiscal policy choices *within* the legislature significantly easier and faster in parliamentary systems than in presidential regimes, where individual legislators are subject to weaker party discipline. While in a parliamentary system, the number of participants who have to coordinate their budgetary decisions is equal to the number of parties represented in the legislature or the government, then in a presidential system, the number of participants can equal to the total number of legislators. Hence, assuming the validity of the "law of 1/*n*", common-pool problems of budgeting are likely to be more severe in legislatures of presidential systems compared with parliamentary systems. Also, the imposition of difficult measures is likely to be more difficult when party discipline is weaker, which would make fiscal adjustment slower.[129]

Proponents of the presidentialist position, however, view the common-pool problems of budgeting in the legislature to be more severe in parliamentary systems, exactly *because* of party discipline, which makes it easier for organised interest groups to put forth proposals for grazing the budgetary commons. Mueller (2002), for example, argues that in a presidential system, where the elected representatives are less dependent on their parties and the connection to the executive is weaker, redistribution activities are politically costlier than in a parliamentary system; therefore, government expenditures are higher in parliamentary systems. He claims that in a presidential system, it is more difficult to create a majority supporting transfers to interest groups, whereas in a parliamentary system, where the adherence of the legislators to the party line is usually strong, it is sufficient for the representatives of interest groups just to establish a point of contact with the party rather than having to persuade a larger number of individual legislators. As Mueller argues, the relationships between interest groups and parties in parliamentary regimes are not only "cheaper" to establish, they are also more durable: even if there is a turnover in the individual membership represented in the legislature, the parties represented often remain the same.

Alongside the indicators of fiscal scale and fiscal balance, the effects of confidence requirement (in a parliamentary regime) and the separation of powers (in a presidential regime) on spending mix and budget composition is explored as well. Huber, Ragin and Stephens (1993) conjecture that the dispersion of power in presidential regimes would act as an obstacle to the expansion of the welfare state. Shugart and Haggard (2001, p. 66) point to the countervailing incentives of the executive and legislators in presidential regimes: the president in a presidential system should, because of his nation-wide constituency, be concerned with providing *public* goods rather than particularistic programmes, but the separation of legislators from the executive renders the representatives less mo-

129 Further, as Weaver and Rockman (1993, p. 17) argue, the independence and decentralisation of legislative power in a presidential system can make the individual legislators highly susceptible to outside pressures, making coordination and priority setting even more difficult.

tivated to focus on genuinely *public* programmes. Because the legislature and the executive are elected separately and are not mutually dependent on each other for survival, legislators do not need to demonstrate their "loyalty to a party label" and legislators "can represent narrow interests without sacrificing the connection between voters and the executive" (p. 68). Persson, Roland and Tabellini (2000) conjecture that in parliamentary regimes, spending is likely to be directed toward broad programmes (e.g., social transfer programmes and public goods), while in presidentialist regimes, where legislative majorities tend to be less stable and re-form according to the issues discussed, spending is likely to be allocated to particularistic projects rather than to broad spending programmes. To what extent the incentives provided by separation of powers translate into the domination of private-regarding programmes in the budget depends, *inter alia*, on the specific features of the electoral system, which are discussed in section 5.3. Candidate-centred electoral formulas are likely to aggravate the parochial bias of budgets in presidential systems, while party-centred systems can be expected to mitigate it.

5.1.2. Empirical Evidence

There are a number of empirical studies exploring the effects of parliamentarism versus presidentialism on expenditures, revenues, deficits, spending mix and features of tax systems. The review below considers first the results of large-n studies, followed by small-n comparative studies and case studies. The most extensive empirical study looking at the effects of the form of government on budgetary outcomes has been the one conducted by Persson and Tabellini (2003).[130] Persson and Tabellini (2003) test the hypotheses about the effects of presidentialism versus parliamentarism on fiscal policy with the help of two data sets: a pure cross section, with average observations for 85 democracies over the 1990s, and a panel with annual observations for 60 democracies going back to 1960. They find that presidential systems have lower levels of spending than parliamentary systems. They also suggest that presidential democracies have lower deficits, but here the estimated constitutional effects are less robust: it is difficult to identify the constitutional effect separately from other policy determinants (p. 274). Persson and Tabellini (2003) also find that in presidential democracies, spending and deficits are pro-cyclical rather than counter-cyclical. Altogether, they conclude that presidential regimes are associated with smaller government, lower taxation, less redistribution and inefficiently low spending on public goods.

There has been only one study that has found different effects from those referred to by Persson and Tabellini. Voigt, Müller and Blume (2007), in their study of 30 countries, find that presidential systems have higher total govern-

130 For a detailed review and critique of the book, see Acemoglu (2005).

ment expenditures (as a percentage of GDP) than parliamentary systems.[131] Other empirical studies have endorsed the findings by Persson and Tabellini. Crepaz (1998) shows, in a study of 18 industrialised countries from 1965 to 1986, that parliamentary systems have higher welfare expenditures as a proportion of GDP than presidential systems. Scartascini and Crain (2002) find, in a world sample of countries over the period 1980–1996, that presidential systems have negative effects on the level of government spending. Boix (2001) concludes, in a study of 65 countries from 1965 to 1990, that presidentialism had a strongly negative direct effect on government revenues through a status quo bias in an otherwise upward-trending series; in other words, parliamentary systems were able to raise more tax revenues than presidential systems. Woo (2003) examines the effects of presidentialism and parliamentarism on budget deficits in a study of 57 developed and developing countries from 1970 to 1990, and concludes that the effect is insignificant.[132] Gerring, Thacker and Moreno (2005) also find that countries with "centripetal" constitutions (characteristic to parliamentary systems), entailing incentives for "voice" rather than "veto", could collect higher levels of taxes than countries with "centrifugal constitutions" (characteristic to presidential regimes). Hallerberg and Basinger (1998, 1999) observe that systems with more veto players (including presidential systems) lowered the top marginal income tax rates less than countries with fewer veto players. Fredriksson and Millimet (2004) examine the effects of presidentialism and parliamentarism on environmental taxation in 80 democracies and show that presidential systems tend to have lower gasoline and diesel taxes than parliamentary systems.

In evaluating the results of these cross-country studies, it has to be kept in mind, of course, that the dichotomous classification of political systems into parliamentary and presidential ones is a gross simplification. Besides the fact that this classification does not capture the hybrid systems, there are also clear differences within the pure types. Shugart and Carey (1992), among others, have shown that the specific powers of the president (e.g., executive control, legislative veto powers and constitutional powers to call new elections) can be very different in different presidential democracies. Also, parliamentary systems differ with regard to legislative procedures and rules for forming and dissolving governments (see Laver and Shepsle 1996). As Myerson (2000) emphasises, these differences may be associated with systematically different patterns of political behaviour and resulting policy choices.

In addition to the large-n studies undertaken more recently, a number of case studies and small-n comparative studies have explored the effects of presiden-

131 At the same time, however, Voigt, Müller and Blume (2007) find that the effects of presidentialism versus parliamentarism lose their significance if the degree of direct democracy characterising the polity is estimated simultaneously.

132 Woo (2003) finds, however, that public deficits are lower in presidential systems than in parliamentary systems, once electoral law and other variables are controlled for.

tialism and parliamentarism on budgeting and taxation. McCubbins (1991a,b), Cox and McCubbins (1991), Fiorina (1992) and Kiewiet and McCubbins (1991) discuss the effects of divided government in the United States and show that this has led to significant increases in spending and to excessive deficits. Drawing on the case studies of the United States, Sweden and the Netherlands, Schick (1993, pp. 224–232) concludes that the separation of powers (especially when combined with divided government) undermines the capability to set clear priorities among economic objectives, which is critical for achieving deficit reduction. Specifically, he argues that the divided government in the United States impaired the capacity of the government to resolve the problem of budget deficits in the 1980s: the persistent stalemate inhibited effective setting of priorities (pp. 190–191, 227). A number of case studies exploring the effects of different kinds of presidential regimes are presented in Haggard and McCubbins (2001). The overall conclusion of the case studies (on Chile, Argentina and Taiwan) is that the specific characteristics of the presidential systems play an important role in budgetary decision-making.

A number of case studies and comparative studies have explored the effects of the form of government on characteristics of the tax system. Steinmo (1993) argues that the division of powers between legislative and executive branches in the United States helps to explain the highly particularistic, relatively progressive and low revenue-yielding tax system: such a setting leads political actors to strive for policies that serve their short-term interests, reflected in exemptions and loopholes in tax codes and in resistance to tax increases.[133] Ganghof (2007) shows that the centripetal political institutions (including parliamentarism) in Denmark help to explain the maintenance (and even increase) of aggregate income tax levels. Hettich and Winer (1999, ch. 11) test the hypotheses pertaining to tax policies in presidential versus parliamentary systems, outlined in section 5.2.1., by comparing Canada and the United States. They show that the United States does indeed use earmarking and trust funds more extensively than Canada. They also find that between 1970 and 1980, Canada undertook twice as many extensive discretionary tax changes than the United States and tax policy lags were longer in the United States. Finally, Hettich and Winer compare the tax forms and tax legislation in the two systems and, in line with the predictions, find that the tax system in the United States is more complex than that of Canada.

133 As Steinmo (1993, p. 137) puts it, the political stalemate between the legislature and the executive has rendered the politics of taxation to "the micro politics of special interest wrangling".

Table 5.1.: Effects of presidentialism on public finances (compared with parliamentarism)

	Higher	Lower	No effect
Level of expenditure	Voigt, Müller and Blume (2007)	Persson and Tabellini (2003) Persson, Roland and Tabellini (2000) Scartascini and Crain (2002)	
Level of public goods		Persson and Tabellini (2003)	
Level of tax revenues		Persson, Roland and Tabellini (2000) Steinmo (1993) Boix (2001) Gerring, Thacker and Moreno (2005)	
Particularism and complexity of the tax system	Hettich and Winer (1999) Steinmo (1993)		
Deficit	Schick (1993) McCubbins (1991a, 1991b) Cox and McCubbins (1991) Fiorina (1992)		Persson and Tabellini (2003) Woo (2003)

Table 5.1. summarises the results of the empirical studies considering the effects of presidentialism versus parliamentarism on public finance. Altogether, the existing cross-sectional and case studies indicate that presidential systems tend to be associated with lower levels of expenditure and lower levels of taxation than parliamentary systems. This can be interpreted either as evidence for stronger institutional *accountability* in a presidential system (if one assumes preference for lower taxes by voters) or as a result of more *veto players* in the budgetary process or a combination of both. The legislative *common-pool problems* arising from lower party discipline in a presidential system are reflected in a spending mix that is biased towards parochial goods, at the expense of public goods. At the same time, the mechanisms of stronger executive accountability, diverging policy preferences between veto actors and higher transaction costs of policy-making appear to prevent the translation of legislative common-pool problems into higher expenditures. Although the case studies

demonstrate that presidential systems have disadvantages in achieving and maintaining fiscal discipline, the large-n cross-country studies indicate that presidentialism has no significant effect on budget deficits.

The main caveat of the cross-sectional studies conducted so far is that they do not distinguish between different kinds of parliamentarism and presidentialism and hybrid forms thereof; the dichotomous division of political systems may well conceal more than it reveals. Though the case studies and small-n comparative studies face problems of over-determination, they can certainly do a better job in "process-tracing" (see Bennett and Elman 2006; George and Bennett 2005; George and McKeown 1985; McKeown 2004) and elaborating on the underlying causal mechanisms that play a role in translating the characteristics of a presidential or parliamentary system into specific features of political setting, which in turn influence interactions between political actors and the outcomes of their interactions. Further studies should also investigate differences in the capabilities of the different regimes to put forth (and adopt) innovative tax policies and adapt existing tax systems to exogenous shocks.

Another caveat of cross-sectional empirical studies following the research programme by Persson and Tabellini is that the effects of various features of political institutions are likely to be configurational rather than additive (Scharpf 1997), which can make the isolation of the effects of a single variable – like presidentialism – methodologically very challenging. In particular, the interactions between the general form of government and the specific features of the electoral system are likely to play a significant role in influencing the capacity of a presidential or a parliamentary system to solve problems in public finance.

5.2. Proportional versus Majoritarian Electoral Systems

Electoral rules and the kind of governing arrangements in governments and legislatures they give rise to have received more extensive attention than other political institutions in institutional, constitutional and political economy approaches to public finance. Since electoral rules usually shape the governing arrangements and not vice versa, electoral rules as "more constitutional" are taken up first and the effects of the governing arrangements they give rise to are examined in section 5.3.

Electoral systems differ with regard to three main elements: district size, electoral formula and ballot structure. *District size* (also called district magnitude) refers to how many legislators acquire a seat in a voting district. At one extreme, each district can have only one representative. At another extreme, the entire country can be a single district with all representatives elected in this country-wide district. *Electoral formulas* determine how votes are translated into seats: under plurality (also called first-past-the-post) rule, the winner of the highest vote share gets a seat in a given district; under majority rule, the candidate needs a majority of the votes in the district in order to get elected; under proportional rule, seats would be awarded in proportion to votes gained in each district. *Ballot structures* indicate how citizens can cast their ballot: for individual candidates, for party lists or a combination of the two. (Lijphart 1994; Farrell 2001; Mueller 1997)

As Persson and Tabellini (2004a, p. 79) put it, although these three aspects are theoretically distinct, they are correlated: plurality rule often goes together with voting for individual candidates in single-member districts and proportional representation is often implemented through a system of party lists in large districts. Given the clustering of the features, electoral systems tend to be divided simply into proportional and plurality (or majoritarian) systems.[134] But, as Persson and Tabellini rightly point out, these features are not always correlated and one can find different mixes of them.[135]

5.2.1. Theoretical Propositions

The overview of theoretical propositions looks first at the effects of *accountability* and *coordination* mechanisms characteristic to different types of electoral systems on fiscal scale and fiscal balance, followed by impacts on spending mix and features of tax systems.

In studies investigating the effects of electoral institutions on the *accountability* of elected representatives in their budgetary decisions, principal-agent models are often taken as the starting point. In a democratic setting, elections constitute the most important mechanism for the voters as principals to make their agents answerable for choices that have been made on their behalf. As von Hagen (2003) underlines, two elements of electoral institutions warrant closer examination in that respect: First, to what extent are policy makers made personally accountable to voters for their past policy choices? Second, to what extent do the electoral rules encourage competition among politicians?

Most studies claim that majoritarian systems are more conducive to *individual* (or personal) accountability of elected representatives (see Myerson 1993; von Hagen 2002; Persson 2002; Persson, Roland and Tabellini 1997; Persson and Tabellini 2000, 2002, 2003, 2004b; Bawn and Rosenbluth 2006). Plurality (or majoritarian) electoral rules (especially the combination of small district magnitude, plurality rule and votes cast for individual candidates) are considered to bring to the fore the personal performance of individual candidates and hence maximise personal accountability. Proportional electoral systems (especially when combining large district magnitude, proportional representation and votes

134 Although plurality and majoritarian systems differ with regard to the share of district votes that the candidate needs to gather to get elected, these systems are often considered to be equivalent in the ideal-typical division of electoral systems into plurality and proportional types.

135 For overviews on different electoral systems in the world, see Blais and Massicotte (1996) and Cox (1997), among others.

cast for party lists), in contrast, are considered to weaken personal accountability of the candidates, since voters can only assess the average performance of all candidates elected from the party list. Scartascini and Crain (2002) underline that as the district size increases, the anonymity of the individual legislator increases, implying decreased costs of not serving the interests of the specific geographic area the district covers. Diluted individual accountability may imply that incentives to provide an efficient level of spending, adhere to fiscal discipline and react adequately to a worsening fiscal situation are weakened among individual legislators. Further, Helland (2000, p. 131) argues that proportional electoral rules (with list votes, large district magnitude, distribution of votes in upper tiers) are more complicated and therefore make it challenging for voters to achieve effective coordination and to act in a concerted way to penalise governments for engaging in costly deficit financing.

Given the incentives for stronger individual accountability in majoritarian systems, approaches focusing on accountability mechanisms entailed in different electoral systems usually predict that majoritarian systems would foster more prudent fiscal policies than proportional systems. At the same time, von Hagen (2003) argues that individual accountability problems in proportional systems are, at least in part, alleviated by a higher level of political competition between parties in such systems (owing to lower entrance barriers for new parties). He suggests that increased competition encourages identification of waste (and rent extraction) by other parties in the electoral competition process, which should exercise countervailing effects to diluted individual responsibility of the legislators.

Besides *personal accountability* of the individual representative to voters, one should also consider how the electoral system influences the principal-agent relations between the *voters* as principals and *parties* as agents with respect to actual policy choices. Here, predictions point to diverging directions. On the one hand, one could expect stronger accountability of parties in majoritarian electoral systems. As Mueller (1996, p. 128) argues, in a majoritarian system, which usually leads to a single party holding the majority of seats in the legislature, voters can expect the winning party to be able to implement the policy platform presented in the campaign (especially in parliamentary systems). In a proportional system, which often leads to multiparty legislatures with no dominant majority, in contrast, voters have difficulties in making predictions about how their choice in the ballot would influence the *actual* policy choices that the legislature will be able to make, since the policy choices would depend on the relatives strengths of the parties that gain representation in the legislature. Hence, drawing on Mueller, because of their ability to implement the policy programme as promised, one would expect stronger accountability of the parties to their electorate in majoritarian systems, leading to public finance policies that correspond to the preferences of the majority of the electorate. On the other hand, since majoritarian systems give parties incentives to focus spending on marginal districts rather than on all districts, the parties may have weaker motivations to address the "safe" districts in their spending decisions, which would lead to lower overall level of spending but may move the total spending level away from the preferences of the majority of the electorate.[136]

Although majoritarian systems may facilitate stronger individual *accountability* of elected officials to their voters, the incentives provided by a majoritarian system may make the *coordination* of budgetary decision-making *within* the legislature more complicated. In other words, there may be a trade-off between stronger accountability on a vertical level and better coordination capabilities on a horizontal level: stronger individual accountability does not necessarily translate into better coordination in budgetary decision-making. This trade-off emerges from a weaker accountability of an *individual* legislator to the *party* it belongs to. In a majoritarian system, individual representatives have incentives to cultivate a personal vote; therefore, they have stronger motives to serve the interests of their specific constituency than to foster the reputation of the party they belong to (Fenno 1978; Cox and Rosenbluth 1993; Carey and Shugart 1995). For representatives of single-member districts, re-election can be best secured by explicitly serving the home-district and advancing its specific interests when putting forth spending proposals. In proportional electoral systems with party lists, where the political fates of individual candidates depend on the decisions of the party (e.g., with regard to how high up on the party list they would be placed), the costs of not serving the party are higher for an individual legislator, which enhances the accountability of individual legislators to the party they belong to.

Because of weaker party discipline in legislative votes in majoritarian systems (see Rose 1983; Cain, Ferejohn and Fiorina 1987), one would expect *common-pool problems* of budgeting to be more severe in legislatures in majoritarian systems than in proportional systems. While in legislatures elected according to a proportional system with party lists, the number of graziers on the legislative budgetary commons can be considered to be equal to the number of parties in the legislature, then in legislatures where officials have been elected on majoritarian (or first-past-the-post) basis, the number of graziers can amount to the number of legislators. Von Hagen (2003) has taken the analysis one step further and argues that *extremely proportional* electoral systems, which lead to a large number of parties (each standing for a specific social group or sector) being represented in the legislature, may become subject to common-pool problems similar to legislatures in majoritarian systems. As he explains, since representatives from different districts or of different social groups are likely to engage in logrolling and games of reciprocity to find majorities for policies fa-

136 For the evidence of the tendency of governments in majoritarian systems to target marginal districts in order to enhance their chances of re-election, see Denemark (2003) and John and Ward (2002).

vouring their constituencies, both plurality rule and proportional representation with many small parties aggravate common-pool problems in budgeting by giving incentives to graze (and potentially overgraze) the fiscal commons for the benefit of specific geographical or social groups. Therefore, higher levels of spending and larger deficits can be expected in countries with plurality rule or proportional representation with many small parties than in countries with proportional representation and few broad-based parties.

Although most of the literature exploring the role of electoral institutions in public finance assumes that majoritarian systems encourage personal vote more than proportional systems, Hallerberg and Marier (2004) argue that proportional electoral systems with *open lists* (i.e., where voters can determine the order of the party's candidates on the list) are more conducive to personal vote than majoritarian systems. They argue that since the open-list system shifts the electoral focus from parties to individual representatives, the candidates have to appeal to voters in their home-district in order to get elected and re-elected (see also Grofman and Reynolds 2001).[137] When open lists are combined with a large district magnitude, intra-party competition for votes in a specific district increases and the incentives to cultivate a party reputation (and campaign for broad national public policy issues) are weakened, since the candidates have to appeal to some other basis than the party label in order to attract votes at the expense of other candidates from the same party (Carey and Shugart 1995; Shugart and Haggard 2001, p. 87; Cox and McCubbins 2001, p. 43). Therefore, in systems with candidate-centred electoral formulas, which cultivate personal vote (and undermine party discipline), the candidates would have incentives to focus on particularistic promises made to (sub)groups of voters in the district and act as individual graziers on fiscal commons. Hence, Hallerberg and Marier (2004) argue that common-pool problems of budgeting, in terms of higher deficits, would be most severe in proportional electoral systems with open lists and large district magnitude, followed by majoritarian systems, and least severe in proportional systems with closed lists and large district magnitudes.

Both the mechanisms of *accountability* and *coordination* entailed by different electoral systems are likely to have significant impacts on the *spending mix*, on the kinds of programmes and expenditures included in the budget. Elected officials in majoritarian systems, who view their primary responsibility to lie within their home-district, have fewer incentives to support expenditures on public goods and broad-based programmes than elected officials in proportional systems. While individual legislators in majoritarian systems would not be able

137 Grofman and Reynolds (2001), drawing on Carey and Shugart (1995), challenge the classification of electoral systems according to the degree of proportionality in transferring the votes to seats and call for alternative classification of the systems according to the degree to which they foster candidate-centred focus rather than party focus (including intra-party competition) in electoral competition and party discipline in the ensuing policy-making.

to claim significant credit for changes in nation-wide policies, they can credibly claim credit for particularistic spending projects targeted to their home-district (Cox and McCubbins 2001, p. 38; see also Fiorina and Noll 1979; Arnold 1990; Fenno 1978; Ferejohn 1974). As Mueller (1996, pp. 13, 140) underlines, geographic representation makes the following of the "parochial imperative" an attractive strategy for representatives: voters in the district may have diverging positions on national issues, but most of them are likely to favour an increase in the portion of national spending targeted to their district. The coordination problems that such electoral incentives give rise to would aggravate the reaching of agreements on provision of public goods. Furthermore, in majoritarian systems, the competition between parties focuses on marginal districts, which makes it politically more profitable to focus on particularistic spending targeted to these districts than on provision of nation-wide public goods (Persson and Tabellini 1999). Hence, one would expect a higher proportion of spending on parochial goods, particularistic projects and pork, and lower level of spending on public goods in majoritarian systems (Cox and McCubbins 2001; Reed 1994; Lizzeri and Persico 2001; Milesi-Feretti, Perotti and Rostagno 2002; Persson and Tabellini 1999a,b, 2003, 2004a,b; von Hagen 2002).

In contrast, in proportional systems (especially with closed list systems), the primary "units" of budgetary decision making are parties, which generally have incentives to gain support from broad coalitions of interests in the population. Such incentives, in turn, would encourage the provision of broad, non-targeted public programmes (e.g., universalistic redistributive programmes like public pensions or other welfare state programmes) and public goods (Persson and Tabellini 1999; Milesi-Ferretti, Perotti and Rostagno 2000; Lizzeri and Persico 2001). As Crepaz (1998, p. 68) puts it, parliamentary polities with proportional electoral rules "have a higher capacity to respond to diffuse issues such as health care, unemployment insurance, and social assistance".

Von Hagen (2003) adds that the degree of proportionality of the electoral rules should also be considered: extremely proportional systems and majoritarian systems may have similar effects on the general nature of expenditure programmes. As he argues, if a proportional system is combined with many small parties, the resulting policy choices are likely to be targeted to specific electoral groups (e.g., professional groups, particular business sectors and minorities).[138] Conversely, von Hagen expects more public goods and non-targeted public programmes in proportional systems that are dominated by a small number of broad-based parties. In a similar vein, Scartascini and Crain (2002) predict that with increasing proportionality of the electoral system, the share of subsidies and transfers (directed to demographic or socio-economic groups) in public expenditures increases.

138 For a formal model of this argument, see Lizzeri and Persico (2005).

In addition to the degree of proportionality reflected in the district magnitude, the extent to which the electoral system encourages the cultivation of personal vote is likely to play an important role in the spending mix of the budget. Shugart and Haggard (2001, p. 88) underline that party-centred electoral rules (with closed lists) would make the legislators more sympathetic to the provision of public goods and broad-based programmes, but candidate-centred electoral rules (i.e., majoritarian systems and proportional systems with open lists) would motivate the legislators to cater to the local or sectoral interests, even if that would amount to "cheating" on the party label.

While the effects of electoral rules on fiscal discipline and types of public programmes have received extensive attention in the literature, studies that consider the effects of an electoral system on specific features of *tax systems* are still very few. Hettich and Winer (1999) argue that majoritarian voting systems lead to less taxation (and less income taxation in particular). Austen-Smith (2000) predicts that proportional systems would lead to higher and more redistributive taxation. McKenzie (2001), in his political economic model that explicitly incorporates the incentive effects of electoral rules for the tax system, suggests that the electoral process can affect the resulting tax mix by influencing the political weight that parties attribute to different groups of taxpayers. In particular, he argues, since the political calculus gives a larger weight to groups of swing voters in a majoritarian system, then, analogously to spending mix, majoritarian electoral rules are likely to lead to a tax mix that targets swing voters more extensively compared with proportional systems. Since targeting swing groups is likely to go hand in hand with increasing complexity of the tax system, polities with majoritarian rules can be expected to have more complex tax systems than polities with proportional electoral rules. Further, McKenzie conjectures that since tailoring tax laws to specific group attributes is easier in the case of direct taxes than indirect taxes, majoritarian systems are likely to have tax mixes where direct taxes are prevalent. In addition to the focus on marginal districts in majoritarian systems, the complexity of the tax system and the level of exemptions and exceptions in tax laws are likely to be influenced by the extent to which individual legislators have incentives to cultivate personal vote. If representatives have incentives to follow the parochial imperative, they would be more likely to provide their constituencies with tax expenditures (targeted either sectorally or geographically) reflected in tax exemptions and higher degree of complexity in tax laws.

5.2.2. Empirical Evidence

The review of empirical evidence considers first the results of cross-national studies in which electoral systems are divided dichotomously to proportional and majoritarian systems. Next, the effects of specific elements of proportional systems and the degree of proportionality are considered, followed by the level of personal vote encouraged by an electoral system. After an overview of the large-n studies, the results of case studies and small-n studies are presented.

A common finding of the large-n studies that divide electoral rules dichotomously to majoritarian and proportional electoral systems is that majoritarian systems are associated with lower taxes, expenditures and deficits and higher levels of particularistic spending. Powell (1982) shows that majoritarian electoral systems are associated with lower levels of and smaller increases in income taxes than systems with proportional electoral rules. Grilli, Masciandro and Tabellini (1991) analyse the net debt among OECD countries in 1989 and primary deficits from 1950 to 1989 and find that in almost all instances, the countries that had high debt and deficit levels also had highly proportional electoral systems. Persson and Tabellini (2000) and Milesi-Ferretti, Perotti and Rostagno (2002) ascertain that proportional systems spend relatively more on broader, socially based transfers, while majoritarian systems spend relatively more on the purchase of goods and services that can be regionally targeted. Persson and Tabellini (2003) explore the effects of electoral systems on a range of fiscal outcomes: overall size of government, budget deficits, broad versus narrow programmes and adjustment to shocks. Their central finding is that electoral rules have a strong effect on fiscal policy outcomes: welfare states, overall government spending and budget deficits are larger in countries with proportional electoral rules than in those with majoritarian systems. They even go as far as to say that "The electoral rule emerges from this research as one of the primary determinants of fiscal policy in modern democracies." (p. 270)[139]

Several other studies have come to the same conclusions as Persson and Tabellini (2003). Scartascini and Crain (2002) show, with a large sample of world countries, that countries with plurality electoral systems have lower public expenditures than those with proportional systems. Boix (2001) also finds that systems with proportional representation have bigger governments. Woo (2003) ascertains that deficits and gross debts were higher in countries with proportional electoral institutions than in countries with plurality rules.[140] Lagona and Padovano (2007) indicate, in their study of 12 EU countries from 1980 to 2003, that plurality systems are associated with lower expenditures and lower deficits. Gould (2001) observes that majoritarian democracies collect lower tax revenues than proportional democracies.[141] Gerring, Thacker and Moreno (2005) demonstrate that countries with "centripetal" constitutions (including proportional electoral rules) could collect higher levels of taxes than "centrifugal" polities

139 These results have been further discussed in Persson and Tabellini (2004a,b).

140 Interestingly, Woo (2003, p. 401) finds that a presidential regime is associated with larger surpluses under a proportional electoral system than under a majoritarian one.

141 As Gould and Baker (2002, p. 105) explain it, "Constituents of majoritarian parties that expect to govern alone may support beggar-thy-neighbour competitive taxation that in the long run produces lower revenue, whereas constituents of parties that expect to govern in coalition favor broader revenue bases."

(with majoritarian rules). Lavigne (2006) finds that, among developing countries, countries that have not been able to undertake a needed fiscal effort tend to have proportional electoral systems; among developed countries, countries that pursue fiscally responsible policies tend to have first-past-the-post electoral systems and countries that fail to undertake fiscal adjustments in the face of a fiscal crisis tend not have proportional electoral systems. There has been one study, though, that has found clearly different results than the pre-mentioned studies. Sakamoto (2001), in his study of 18 OECD countries from 1960 to 1994, shows that the average deficit among countries with proportional electoral rules was *lower* than in majoritarian countries.

Some authors have also considered the effects of different kinds of proportional electoral systems and the *degree* of proportionality of the electoral systems on fiscal outcomes. Stein, Talvi and Grisanti (1999) find, in their cross-section study of 26 Latin American countries, that higher district magnitude is associated with higher budget deficits. Gould (2001) observes a difference in revenue levels across OECD democracies that use proportional representation: proportional countries with at least one large party collected more tax revenues than did proportional countries with only small parties. Scartascini and Crain (2002) show that the electoral system influences the composition of government expenditures: the share of subsidies and transfers in the overall government expenditure increases as the system becomes more proportional. Milesi-Ferretti, Perotti and Rostagno (2002), in their study of 20 OECD and 20 Latin American countries, also obtain the result that larger districts are associated with higher overall spending. Persson and Tabellini (2000) and Milesi-Ferretti, Perotti and Rostagno (2002) find that more proportional systems spend relatively more on broader, socially based transfers, while more majoritarian systems spend relatively more on the purchase of goods and services that can be regionally targeted. Ricciuti (2004a) analyses 19 OECD countries from 1975 to 1995 and ascertains that an increasing number of representatives per district harms fiscal balances, while closed lists and thresholds counteract this tendency. Crepaz and Moser (2004), studying 15 OECD countries from 1960 to 1996, find that a higher degree of proportionality of the electoral system is associated with larger expansion of public expenditures: the higher the degree of proportionality of the electoral system, the higher the level of current disbursements (as a percentage of GDP). Fabrizio and Mody (2006) show, in their study of ten new member states of the EU (between 1997 and 2003), that district magnitude has significant effects on budget surplus: the larger the magnitude, the smaller the long term surplus. They also find that more proportional systems have higher levels of social transfer payments.

Hallerberg and Marier (2004) explore the effects of the extent to which the electoral system encourages personal vote on budget deficits. Drawing on the index created by Carey and Shugart (1995) for measuring the level of personal vote,[142] they examine the effects of electoral systems on budgetary outcomes in 20 Latin American and Caribbean countries between 1988 and 1997. They conclude that increases in the level of personal vote encouraged by the electoral system have negative effects on budget balances. Edwards and Thames (2007), in their study of 77 democracies between 1970 and 2000, observe that the level of personal vote has positive effects on government expenditures. Scartascini and Crain (2002) find, on the other hand, for a sample of OECD countries (1971–1996) and for a sample of world countries (1980–1996), that proportional electoral systems with closed lists had higher government expenditures than those with open lists.

There have also been a number of country-studies analysing the effects of electoral institutions on budgetary outcomes. Italy, in particular, has received attention in association with the electoral reform from proportional to plurality system. Hallerberg (2000a), for example, discusses the effects of the Italian electoral reform on the budget and shows that the change in the electoral system *itself* did not immediately lead to reduction in deficits: fiscal adjustment only came about after the reform of budgetary institutions (especially the centralisation of budgetary decision-making in the Treasury). The question of whether majoritarian systems give incentives for more pork-barrel spending than proportional systems has been explored in a case study of Germany by Stratman and Baur (2002). They argue that exploring the incentives provided by electoral rules in a cross-country context is complicated by unobserved differences between countries, which cannot be easily encompassed by various model specifications; hence, it is difficult to disentangle effects of electoral institutions from country effects. Therefore, the German case – where legislators are elected with two different ballots, a list ballot and a district ballot – can be viewed as especially appropriate for exploring the effects of different electoral rules, since other contextual factors influencing the incentives can be kept constant. Stratman and Baur (2002) find that the mechanism under which a legislator has been elected does indeed influence his or her choices. Those representatives who have been elected under first-past-the-post mechanism usually choose to be members of such committees that allow them to service their geographically based constituency by influencing the allocation of benefits (e.g., committees for construction, traffic, agriculture), while those legislators who have been elected under proportional rule are members of committees that can service constituencies of the party (defined according to social or demographic characteristics) rather than geographically based constituencies.[143]

142 In constructing the personal vote index, Carey and Shugart (1995) take into account the amount of power party leaders have in determining who appears on the ballot, how votes are pooled (across the party, at sub-party level or no pooling) and the number of votes that voters can cast.

143 The study by Stratman and Baur (2002) confirms the findings of Lancaster and Baur (1990), who find, based on a survey data, that legislators who have been elected under

In his small-n comparative study, Steinmo (1993) shows how cross-national variation in tax policy can be explained by differences in political institutions. He argues that Swedish authorities have been able to develop a stable, relatively regressive and high revenue yielding tax system (that imposes a high tax burden on the average citizen but not on corporate enterprises) owing to the stable and non-majoritarian political institutions (reflected in a proportional electoral system with D'Hondt formula) and compromise-seeking minority cabinets. In the case of the United Kingdom, the centralised single-member, first-past-the-post electoral system resulting in powerful majoritarian governments with few incentives for compromises and cooperation, has led to a highly unstable tax structure, subject to frequent reforms and so-called "yo-yo" effects. In the United States, Steinmo argues, the electoral incentives, combined with the decentralised structure of the legislature (where legislative committees have great autonomy and decision-making power) have played a significant role in the emergence highly complex tax system (characterised by a large number of exemptions and loopholes). As Steinmo (1993, p. 139) notes, the members of the Congress, driven by electoral motives, have viewed tax exemptions as "political plums", rather than considering them as incentives for investment and tools of economic management.

As can be seen from Table 5.2., the studies exploring the effects of the electoral system on spending, revenues and deficits, on the whole, point to converging results: proportional electoral systems are associated with higher expenditures, higher taxes and higher deficits. Most of these empirical studies point to evidence that the more proportional the system is, the higher are expenditures and deficits. In addition, proportional electoral systems are associated with higher proportions of public goods and broad-based transfers in the budget than majoritarian systems, where parochial and geographically targeted expenditures dominate. Although the existing studies have not explored it explicitly, one can conjecture that higher deficits in proportional systems can be at least partly fostered by the kind of expenditures that such systems are conducive to. Proportional systems tend to give rise to higher levels of social transfers, which often acquire the status of legal entitlements and may be more difficult to cut in the face of fiscal difficulties. Further studies should explore this link more thoroughly.

---

plurality rule view it more important to provide geographically focused projects in order to become re-elected than legislators elected under proportional rule.

Table 5.2.: Effects of electoral systems on public finances

	Spending	Revenues	Deficit
Proportional system (vs majoritarian)	Higher spending: Persson and Tabellini (2003) Lagona and Padovano (2007) Scartascini and Crain (2002) Boix (2001) Higher spending on public goods, broad programmes, social transfers: Persson and Tabellini (2000, 2003) Milesi-Ferretti, Perotti and Rostangno (2002)	Higher revenues: Powell (1982) Gould (2001) Steinmo (1993) Gerring, Thacker and Moreno (2005)	Higher deficit: Persson and Tabellini (2003) Grilli, Masciandro and Tabellini (1991) Woo (2003) Lagona and Padovano (2007) No effect: Lavigne (2006) Lower deficit: Sakamoto (2001)
Larger degree of proportionality	Higher spending: Milesi-Ferretti, Perotti and Rostagno (2002) Scartascini and Crain (2002) Crepaz and Moser (2004) Higher proportion of subsidies and transfers: Scartascini and Crain (2002)	Lower revenues: Gould (2001)	Higher deficit: Stein, Talvi and Grisanti (1999) Ricciuti (2004a) Fabrizio and Mody (2006)
Higher level of personal vote	Higher spending: Edwards and Thames (2007) Lower spending: Scartascini and Crain (2002)		Higher deficit: Hallerberg and Marier (2004)

Altogether, there seems to be more empirical evidence for theoretical propositions concerning stronger accountability mechanisms than for those predicting common-pool problems in majoritarian systems – at least when looking at the indicators of fiscal scale and fiscal balance. At the same time, common-pool problems expressed in excessive *parochial* spending (at the expense of public goods) appear to find manifestation in majoritarian systems. Further studies should compare the strength of these mechanisms under different regimes: common-pool problems associated with majoritarian systems are likely to be stronger in presidential systems than in parliamentary systems, where party discipline over individual members is stronger. The study of Woo (2003) is certainly indicative in that respect, providing evidence that under presidential regimes, majoritarian systems have lower surpluses than proportional systems.

The main shortcoming of the studies that have just compared the effects of majoritarian and proportional rules is that such a dichotomy is a gross oversimplification: there are many forms of both proportional and majoritarian rules (see, for example, Cox 1997; Taagepera and Shugart 1989). Therefore, the studies exploring the effects of specific elements of electoral systems (e.g., open lists versus closed lists, district magnitude, different electoral formulas) can be viewed as steps in analytically fruitful direction. Given the configurational effects of the different elements, however, exploring the effects of these elements in a partial approach may be misleading, which is why closer attention should be paid to interaction effects. Also, collapsing the different elements of an electoral rule into an index of proportionality faces the problem that district magnitude, for example, may have very different effects on the incentives of individual candidates, depending on whether open or closed lists are employed.

Future studies should take a closer look at the links between the degree of proportionality of the electoral system and features of the tax system. The tendency indicated by the study of Gould (2001), for example, warrants further exploration: Why would a more fractionalised party system (associated with more proportional electoral systems) collect lower tax revenues than a proportional system with a dominating party? Also, an in-depth exploration of the effects of the level of personal vote on public finance decisions would be a fruitful avenue of research. While some studies have already examined the effects of the level of personal vote on aggregate fiscal indicators, further studies should examine closer the impacts on spending mix and tax expenditures.

In addition to the direct effects that electoral systems have on the incentives of elected officials, electoral rules play an important role in shaping the party system and the type of governments elections usually result in. There is an extensive literature linking the party system and the governmental structure to the electoral system. The Duverger's Law (based on the ideas presented in Duverger 1954) predicts that plurality-based elections in single-member districts will give rise to a political system with two main parties. Duverger's Hypothesis predicts that proportional electoral systems lead to multiparty politics.[144] Duverger's (1954) ideas have been empirically endorsed and further elaborated by Sartori (1968), Rae (1967), Taagepera and Shugart (1989, 1993) and Lijphart (1990,

144 The distinction between Duverger's "Law" and "Hypothesis" was made by Riker (1982).

1994), among others.[145] An important elaboration of Duverger's Hypothesis is the prediction that the larger the district magnitude, the larger will be the number of political parties (Sartori 1968). The number of parties that gain representation in the legislature, in turn, influences the number of parties that make up the government. Hence, coalition governments are more likely under proportional representation than under first-past-the-post (or majoritarian) systems.[146] Besides being more likely to produce coalition governments, minority governments are also seen as more likely under proportional electoral system (Strom 1990). Further, the particular formulas used for translating the votes into seats can play a role in influencing the power constellations and fractionalisation of parties in legislature and government. The employment of less proportional formulas, like the D'Hondt method, which treats the dominant parties more favourably, is likely to lead to lower party fragmentation of legislatures and governments than some other "more proportional" formulas, like the LR-Hare method (see e.g., Gallagher 1991; Taagepera and Laakso 1980; Lijphart 1994; Schuster *et al.* 2003). Comprehensive constitutional political economy models of the effects of electoral systems on budgeting and taxation should therefore address both the *direct* and *indirect* effects of electoral institutions. The impacts of different governing arrangements (that different electoral systems give rise to) on policy choices in public finance is the topic of the next section.

5.3. Governing Arrangements: Number of Individual and Partisan Decision-Makers in Legislature and Executive

5.3.1. Theoretical Propositions

In Ostrom's (1986) terminology, electoral institutions play an important role in constituting the position and boundary rules of a political setting. As emphasised in section 4.4., the number of participants involved in taking decisions on budgeting and taxation is likely to have important bearings on policy choices in public finance. In part, the number of participants can be determined already in the constitution, for example, with regard to how large the legislature is. In part, the number of participants is influenced by electoral rules. The number of partisan decision-makers in the *executive* is likely to be larger in polities with proportional electoral rules (which usually give rise to multiparty coalition govern-

145 A number of criticisms of Duverger's Law and Hypothesis have also been put forth. For example, Taagepera and Grofman (1985) claim that in a mature democracy, it is the number of issue divisions in the society that does a better job of predicting the number of political parties rather than the electoral laws. For an overview of critical evaluations, see Grofman and Reynolds (2001).

146 For empirical studies confirming it, see, among others, Ordeshook and Shvetsova (1984), Cox (1997) and Amorin Neto and Cox (1997). For a thorough review on the determinants of the number of parties, see Lijphart (1999).

ments) than in majoritarian systems. On the other hand, as mentioned in section 5.2.1., majoritarian electoral rules (especially when combined with a presidential system) can lead to a larger number of participants in *legislative* budgetary process than proportional rules, by enabling individual legislators, rather than parties represented in the legislature, to be the primary decision-making units on budgetary commons. In other words, electoral institutions influence both the *kind* of participants that would be the primary decision-makers on a legislative level (individual legislators or parties) and the *number* of partisan participants in both legislature and executive.

There is a large (and increasing) body of literature discussing the effects of the number and kinds of participants in the budgetary process on choices and outcomes in public finance. The main models used for explaining the effects of the number and kinds of participants on budgetary outcomes are *budgetary commons* models and *veto players* models. Subsection 5.3.1.1. gives an overview of the theoretical positions of *budgetary commons* models that have sought to explain budgetary outcomes by looking at the size of the legislature, the number of legislators in the governing majority, the number of parties and committees in the legislature, the number of parties in the governing coalition and the number of spending ministers in the cabinet. Section 5.3.1.2., in turn, surveys the theoretical propositions of *veto player* models of budgeting and juxtaposes the predictions of these models with the predictions of budgetary commons models. Section 5.3.1.3. discusses the effects of *accountability* mechanisms entailed in different governing arrangements on policy choices of public finance.

5.3.1.1. Budgetary Commons Models

Budgetary commons models emphasise the role of size fragmentation in determining fiscal outcomes and predict that the larger the number of participants in budgetary decision-making process, the higher will be resulting expenditures and budget deficits and the higher the proportion of particularistic spending in the budget. Budgetary commons models have explored the effects of the number of decision-makers both in legislature and executive. Some models concentrate on the individual level (individual legislators and ministers in the cabinet), while others have taken parties (in the legislature or in the cabinet) as the focus of analysis. The overview below considers first the legislative level and then the executive level of budgetary decision-making; within each level, the effects of the number of different kinds of participants (individual and partisan) on policy choices and outcomes in public finance are considered.

5.3.1.1.1. Size of Legislature

The size of legislature, as an element of constitutional setting, was the main focus in the seminal studies exploring the common-pool problems of budgeting.

The *tragedy of budgetary commons* was first formally modelled by Weingast, Shepsle and Johnsen (1981), who demonstrated the possible effects of geographical concentration of interests in a legislative setting where legislators have been elected in single member districts and, in order to ensure re-election, have motives to provide targeted spending to their home-district. Since the publicly funded goods provided to each district are financed from a common tax base, those who benefit from a particular project bear only a fraction of the costs needed to finance this project. Therefore, legislators have incentives to seek increased expenditures on projects benefiting their respective districts – without having to take into account the full costs of increases in spending. The divergence in the perceived and actual costs is likely to lead to an inefficient level of spending: the districts receive parochial goods at a higher cost than the value attached to these goods. As Weingast, Shepsle and Johnsen (1981) show, the larger the number of districts (and hence legislators), the larger will be the discrepancy between perceived costs and benefits. The larger the number of districts, the smaller is the district-specific cost burden of any publicly funded project and the larger the demand for district-specific expenditure. Weingast, Shepsle and Johnsen (1981, p. 654) have termed this insight the "law of $1/n$". When there are n districts and tax burden is dispersed uniformly among the districts, the cost each district has to bear for the parochial good is a fraction of $1/n$ of the actual cost of the good. The larger the n (i.e., the larger the number of representatives in the legislature), the smaller is the marginal cost incurred to each legislator (or to his district) from increased expenditure. Faced with falling marginal costs of expenditure, each individual legislator internalises a smaller portion of the increased expenditure and would have incentives to demand more expenditure on pork; altogether, this may lead to the adoption of projects for which the marginal costs are higher than marginal benefits.

Weingast, Shepsle and Johnsen (1981) demonstrate how the "law of $1/n$" holds in a decentralised setting. However, in order to get the particularistic spending (targeted to one's home-district) adopted by the legislature, an elected official needs to procure support from other legislators, often in the form of promising support for parochial projects benefiting the districts of the other legislators. Hence, the costs that the individual legislator (and the district) incurs when securing a targeted project for his own district may also have to include tax costs of financing the projects of other districts included in the legislative deal. For an individual legislator, the costs of engaging in a legislative deal in order to procure support for his own district's project would depend on two (inter-related) factors. First, the costs would depend on the number of participants in the legislative coalition involved in the package deal. Second, the costs would be conditioned by the possibility to externalise tax costs of the deal to legislators outside the legislative coalition. The larger the coalition needed for adopting the package of projects, the larger the total tax costs that each district has to bear, *ceteris paribus*. If all the members of the legislature are involved in the coalition (i.e., the package is adopted by a universalistic coalition) and tax costs are distributed uniformly between the districts, each district would bear the cost *C/n* associated with each project and the cost C for all *n* projects (assuming that each district will get a project with the cost C). If the decision on the package of particularistic projects would be adopted by a majority coalition and the tax burden is distributed uniformly, the winning majority can externalise at least part of the tax costs to districts outside the coalition. If tax costs can be distributed unevenly – by shifting the tax costs of the package to non-coalition districts – the members of the legislative coalition may be able to escape the tax costs of the projects adopted.

Hence, in analysing the distributive politics on budgetary commons, an important question is: Would distributive politics be characterised by minimum-winning coalitions or universalistic coalitions? Although according to Riker (1962), one would expect vote-trading coalitions to be minimum-winning coalitions, since every "unnecessary" member included in the deal would reduce the payoff for the members in the coalition, these predictions have not found consistent confirmation in actual distributive policy-making (e.g., Fiorina 1981). In pursuit of approximating the legislative realities and formal modelling, Weingast (1979) argues that the norm of universalism[147] is driven by inherent instability of minimum-winning coalitions, arising from the absence of legally binding agreements between legislators. According to Weingast, because each legislator is faced with uncertainty over being included in the minimum-winning coalition, legislators would favour the universalistic coalition: they would rationally prefer a *certain* (although smaller) net benefit obtained from universalistic decision-making over the possibly larger but *uncertain* net benefit accruing from a minimum-winning coalition.

Proceeding from the assumption that distributive politics is subject to the norm of universalism, a further puzzle arises: Why would the "law of 1/*n*" still hold in such a context? In other words, why would legislators (and their home-districts), anticipating the universalistic coalition, still use the 1/*n* of the cost of their district-specific project rather than the total C as the basis for demanding district-specific spending? Why would a universalistic coalition adopt packages of projects that are inefficient (with marginal costs exceeding marginal benefits)?

As Collie (1988, p. 433) rightly points out, the main problem with the model put forth by Weingast (1979) was that it failed to address the rational-choice prediction that the passage of inefficient particularistic expenditures (where the marginal costs of the project exceeded its marginal benefits) is individually rational only when legislators can form a minimum-winning coalition and exter-

147 Weingast (1979, p. 24) has defined universalism as "the tendency to seek unanimous passage of distributive programs through inclusion of a project for all legislators who want one".

nalise at least part of the project costs to the excluded constituencies by making use of the general tax fund. Shepsle and Weingast (1981) sought to address this puzzle by reinterpreting the "costs" and "benefits" associated with a given project for a specific district. They argued that the funds allocated from the general budget for a district-specific project would be presented by the legislators as "benefits" to the constituencies in the district rather than "costs". Further, they showed that owing to the transformation of "economic" costs into "political" benefits, universalism in the legislature was compatible with economically inefficient legislation.[148] Hence, they argue that although the need to accommodate the project costs of other partners in the universalistic coalition (or any coalition, for that matter) should reduce the "illusion of $1/n$", the divergence in the political and economic conceptions of project costs would help to maintain this "illusion".

Buchanan and Yoon (2002) put forth an alternative model that attempts to reconcile rational choice, universalism and inefficient distributive policies. While the model proposed by Weingast, Shepsle and Johnsen (1981) assumes that the norm of universalism gives rise to a single stable coalition, including most of the legislators, which acts as a monolithic collective decision-authority (by implicitly adopting quasi-unanimity rules) in a single fiscal period, Buchanan and Yoon (2002) consider the possibility of multiple majorities that can take fiscal action independently in the same fiscal period. They show that in constitutional settings that allow the authorisation of collective action upon the formation of *any* majority, the fiscal capacity of the polity becomes a commons for which different coalitions have open access to and can graze the general tax fund for providing particular benefit programmes or transfers. Buchanan and Yoon argue that, because of the common access and majority voting rule in every emerging coalition, fiscal commons will become subject to the same problems of externalities as is the case with common-pool natural resources. They predict that fiscal decision-making by multiple majority coalitions would lead to larger budgets and higher tax rates than a single majority acting as a "fiscal monopoly" (p. 513). Further, since larger legislatures permit the formation of a larger number of possible majorities, the aggregate tax rate (and associated excess burden) can be expected to increase with the size of the legislature. Thus, in Buchanan and Yoon's (2002) model, the number of graziers is captured by the number of possible majority coalitions that can be formed: the larger the size of the legislature, the larger is the number of coalitions grazing the commons. Since each minimum-winning coalition would internalise less of the project costs than a universalistic coalition, the divergence in the perceived costs and benefits of particular projects is likely to be larger in such a setting rather than in

148 For an alternative formal explanation of the emergence of universalism in a legislative setting, see Niou and Ordeshook (1984). For a discussion and critique of the different models, see Collie (1988).

a setting with a monolithic universalistic coalition in charge for the entire fiscal period. Combined with the translation of economic costs into political benefits (as proposed by Shepsle and Weingast 1981), the "illusion of 1/*n*" is even more pronounced in such a setting than in a universalistic setting.

Primo and Snyder (2008) reconsider the robustness of "the law of 1/*n*" and explore its validity under different conditions. They demonstrate formally that the link between the size of the legislature and the level of spending depends on a number of factors, including the types of goods that are being distributed and the dead-weight costs of taxation. Specifically, their analysis indicates that under some conditions, a "reverse law of 1/*n*" can prevail: the larger the number of districts, the smaller becomes the total spending size. They bring an example of different spending proposals for public transportation under varying district sizes. When districts are large, a representative for a specific district would prefer to propose an expensive area-wide rail system. When districts are small, however, the representatives of these districts would prefer to propose subsidy programmes for bus services in their corresponding districts. Since the costs of the rail system are likely to be higher than the subsidy programme for bus services, a smaller number of districts would translate into lower level of spending on public transport. Based on their formal analysis, Primo and Snyder (2008) argue that while the "law of 1/*n*" would be valid in smaller legislatures (i.e., adding an additional legislator to a small legislature would bring about an increase in expenditures), its effects on the margin may be the opposite in very large legislatures.[149]

In addition to the nature of goods provided and the degree of distortions brought about by taxation, the validity of the "law of 1/*n*" in a particular setting can be influenced by further factors pointed out by interest group theories of government, represented, for example, by Stigler (1976), Crain (1979), McCormick and Tollison (1981) and Shugart and Tollison (1986). Fiorino and Ricciuti (2007, pp. 118–119) have summarised the predictions of this line of research with regard to the effects of legislature size on spending as following. On the one hand, the larger the size of the legislature, the lower are the costs of lobbying for interest groups because of higher competition between vote suppliers (the legislators), which, in turn, would encourage more interest groups to seek transfers from legislative activities. Further, the larger the number of members in the legislature, the more each can specialise on law-production in a specific area, which should lead to more legislative output (including more expenditure programmes). On the other hand, the size of the legislature can have constraining effects on spending: as the number of decision-makers increases, the higher

149 Primo and Snyder (2008) also argue that the "law of 1/*n*" applies to the project sizes only when there is at least some degree of congestion in the goods being provided and the dead-weight costs of taxation are sufficiently low.

become the transaction costs for finding a viable majority of votes for each proposed programme. Thus, as Fiorino and Ricciuti (2007, p. 118) underline,

> A larger legislature could be associated either with higher production costs required for assembling legislative majorities or, alternatively, with lower decision making costs if the returns from increased labor specialization in the committee apparatus dominate the effect of larger sized groups on decision making costs.

This makes a priori predictions of the effects of the size of legislature on spending ambiguous. In a similar vein, Thornton and Ulrich (1999, p. 592) argue that from transaction costs perspective, one would expect a larger legislature to increase the costs of producing legislation; since in "collusive" activities, smaller numbers are preferred, a larger legislature would reduce legislative production and government spending. Although Weingast, Shepsle and Johnsen (1981) argued that the norm of universalism plays an important role in achieving the passage of expenditure bills, they did not sufficiently address the question of higher transaction costs that may be associated with legislative bargaining when the number of actors increases.

Since the model proposed by Weingast, Shepsle and Johnsen (1981) proceeds from assumptions characterising a legislative setting in a U.S. type presidential regime, it is not applicable in a parliamentary setting where party discipline is more pronounced. The logical extensions of the model have sought to adjust it, to take into account the particularities of different kind of polities and legislative settings. The conception of n in the "law of $1/n$" has hence been modified to encompass the number of legislators in the majority, the number of parties in the legislature and the number of parties in the governing coalition.

5.3.1.1.2. Size of Governing Majority

The size of the governing majority can be gauged in different ways. First, the absolute number of legislators in the governing majority can be counted. Second, the relative size of the majority – the proportion of the legislative seats belonging to the governing majority – can be employed. A third approach would combine both aspects and measure the excess number of seats that the governing majority has. The employment of the absolute size, in particular, is haunted by a number of problems. Counting the absolute number of seats that the government has in the legislature as a measure of the number of graziers in the commons is especially problematic in the case of minority governments: given the reduced bargaining power of the government, members of the opposition parties have to be included in policy-making. Also, the absolute number does not reflect accurately the decision-making dynamics in the legislature. Therefore, for most part, the relative or combined measures have been preferred in empirical studies.

Though the basic intuition of the budgetary commons models is that the larger the number of participants in the budgetary process, the higher the expenditures, the existing theoretical inquiries have pointed to more complicated (and even reverse) relationships.

Inman and Fitts (1990) modified the model developed by Weingast, Shepsle and Johnsen (1981) and argued that, given the disciplining effects of parties, the prevailing norm in legislative bargains is "constrained universalism", implying that the common-pool resource problem depends on the number of legislators in the *governing majority* rather than on the *total* number of members in the legislature. They argue, however, that the effect of the size of the majority party on expenditure levels is curvilinear. They predict that when the number of legislators in the majority party rises to a particular threshold level, government expenditure increases correspondingly, because of incentive mechanisms provided by the "law of 1/*n*". Above that threshold level, however, the tax costs that the members of the majority party have to incur start rising, since less of the tax costs can be shifted to the supporter groups of legislators outside the governing majority. In other words, up to a certain level, the costs of increased expenditures can be externalised to a legislative minority, but as the minority gets smaller and smaller, the members of governing majority have to internalise the tax costs themselves and have therefore reduced incentives to demand higher expenditures.

Mukherjee (2003) conjectures that the size of the governing majority and the level of expenditures have a "cube relationship". He predicts that government expenditure first decreases when the majority party's size grows above 50 percent, then increases when its size is between 56 and 68 percent, and decreases again when its size is greater than or equal to 68 percent. As Mukherjee argues, when the margin of majority grows from a bare 50 percent majority to 56 percent, the hedge against potential defections increases and the need to include other parties in the winning coalition is reduced, which, in turn, implies that the need to incorporate additional pork-barrel expenditures to gain the support of other minority parties declines. The reason why expenditures start growing again (beyond a threshold of 56 percent) is that the marginal costs incurred by *each* majority party member from higher expenditure become lower (the 1/*n* effect) and the tax costs of expenditures can be externalised to legislators belonging to opposition parties. When the margin of majority reaches about 68 percent, however, the possibilities to externalise tax costs to opposition members start declining and the governing majority has to internalise most of the costs implied by increased expenditures, which, in turn, would lead them to prefer lower levels of expenditures.

Volkerink and de Haan (2001) argue that the larger the excess number of seats the government has in the parliament, the smaller the common-pool problems of budgeting: the stronger the position of government *vis-à-vis* the legislature, the less likely the government is to comply with expenditure demands from the legislature.

5.3.1.1.3. Number of Parties in Legislature

The next step – in line with the legislative realities in parliamentary settings with proportional representation – was to focus on common-pool resource problems that arise when *parties* (rather than individual *legislators*) are viewed as the primary decision-making units in budgeting. Combining the notions of socially concentrated interests and parties as decision-making units, it is argued that the more parties there are "grazing" the budgetary commons (i.e., the more parties there are in the legislature) and the more each is focused on increasing the spending items that favour the group(s) of voters supporting it, the more likely it is that common-pool resource problems emerge. An important aspect that has to be taken into account when counting the parties in the legislature as graziers on budgetary commons is that the *absolute* number may not reflect the actual dynamics of legislative decision-making.[150] Most political science literature, therefore, advocates a counting measure of parties represented in the parliament that takes into account their relative shares of seats, called the "effective number of parties" (proposed by Laakso and Taagepera 1979; for a discussion see also Taagepera and Shugart 1989, pp. 78–81; Lijphart 1994, pp. 67–70).[151]

Scartascini and Crain (2002) and Mukherjee (2003) consider multiparty legislatures without a majority party and argue that such a legislative setting is characterised by the norm of universalism between parties because of inherent instability of coalitions. Therefore, party leaders would attempt to achieve unanimous ratification of expenditure programmes by accommodating the budget proposals of all parties in the parliament, including opposition parties. Mukherjee (2003) posits, drawing on the "law of $1/n$", that the larger the effective number of parties in the legislature (the larger the n), the higher is central government expenditure, because the total number of projects that have to be incorporated in the budget is larger. Similar predictions are obtained by Scartascini and Crain (2002). Mukherjee (2003) also argues that in a multiparty legislature with no majority party, parties would be motivated to propose spending programmes that are targeted to their specific supporter groups (demographic, socio-economic or sectoral) and would have few incentives to propose spending

---

150 As Mueller (2003, pp. 272–273) elucidates, in a legislature with five parties, each holding 20 percent of the seats, it would be sound to speak of a five-party legislature. If these five parties, however, hold respectively 70, 30, 7, 2 and 1 percent of seats, it would be more difficult to call this a five-party legislature.

151 As Eklit and Robert (1996, p. 225) put it, "The effective number of parties can best be understood as the *hypothetical* number of parties of equal size which would have resulted in the same level of fractionalization as have the *actual* number of parties of varying sizes." (emphases in original)

on public goods from which all constituencies can benefit. Hence, he hypothesises that an increase in the effective number of political parties represented in the parliament will lead to a decrease in the level of expenditures allocated for public goods and to an increase in the level of subsidies and transfers that can be targeted to specific constituencies. Similar arguments are presented by von Hagen (2003), who conjectures that legislatures entailing a large number parties can become subject to common-pool problems of budgeting.

Crepaz and Moser (2004, p. 271) also argue for using the effective number of parties in the *parliament* rather than the number of parties in the *governing coalition* when exploring the effects of the number of participants in the budgetary game on levels of expenditure, because this captures better the compromises and logrolls that take place between governing and opposition parties. In particular, they posit that conceptualising the number of parties in the legislature as the *n* is especially relevant in the context of minority governments, which are subject to continuous pressures to solicit support from non-government parties by making "side-payments" in order to get the budget passed (see Blais, Blake and Dion 1993). Further, as Crepaz and Moser (2004, p. 271) emphasise, the number of parties in the legislature reflects the fragility of the governing coalition. When the total number of alternative coalition partners – were the existing coalition to break down – is low, the coalition can be expected to be more stable. Conversely, when the number of alternative partners with whom it is possible to form a new coalition is large, it is easier for a partner to quit the existing coalition and build a new one. The very fragility of the coalition, in turn, increases pressures to submit to intra-coalition bargains, side-payments and logrolls put forth by coalition partners.

5.3.1.1.4. Number of Committees in Legislature

Weingast and Marshall (1988) argue that in legislative settings where parties command only limited control over their members, legislative committees can assume the role of primary decision-making units. They note that committees serve an important function in enforcing legislative trades: by mitigating problems of *ex post* enforceability of legislative bargains that would otherwise plague vote-trading. Weingast and Marshall (1988, p. 160) add that committees would be composed of "high demanders" in particular policy jurisdictions, since legislators would have incentives to become members of a committee in which they have a highest stake (reflecting the concerns of their geographic or sectoral constituency). When the appropriations authority is decentralised, the committees would view tax revenues as a common resource, leading to common-pool problems in budgeting (Dharmapala 2003, p. 350). When committees can act as graziers on budgetary commons, the "law of $1/n$" would predict that common-pool problems would increase when the number of committees increases (see Fiorina 1981).

5.3.1.1.5. Number of Parties in Governing Coalition

Most of the studies exploring the problems of budgetary commons have focused on the number of parties in the *government* rather than in the *legislature*. Coalition governments, with parties representing different socio-economic interests, are hypothesised to face larger common-pool problems of budgeting than single-party governments. The larger the number of parties in the coalition, the more severe the common-pool problems in budgeting are conjectured to be. (von Hagen and Harden 1995; Kontopoulos and Perotti 1999; Stein, Talvi and Grisanti 1999; Perotti and Kontopoulos 2002) There are two analytically distinct elements that contribute to the emergence of common-pool problems in budgetary decision-making by coalition governments. First, in order to hold the coalition together, there are pressures to cater to the budgetary needs of all coalition parties. The larger the number of parties in the coalition, the more difficult it becomes to maintain fiscal restraint. Second, as the number of parties in the government grows, the marginal cost of a particular expenditure item for a party (and its supporters) that proposes this item falls, leading to higher levels of expenditures demanded. While large parties, striving for support from a broader electorate, have incentives to internalise the tax costs of increasing expenditures on public programmes, smaller parties that serve particular electoral groups have weaker incentives to do so, and they tend to externalise the costs of the expenditure programmes they propose (Inman 1988; Inman and Fitts 1990; Borge and Rattso 2002).

Bawn and Rosenbluth (2006) emphasise that "a coalition of parties" acts differently from "a coalition party", because of electoral accountability mechanisms. They argue that while a single party in government is electorally accountable for all policy decisions it makes, parties that participate in coalition governments are held responsible for a subset of policy decisions: for the policy areas in which they have the biggest stake and the strongest influence. Thus, although one would, in principle, expect a coalition of parties, each of which represents a single interest, to make similar decisions to a single party that represents a coalition of interests, when the interests they represent are identical, the separate electoral accountability of each party in a coalition government would lead it to make different policy decisions than a single-party majority government. Further, Bawn and Rosenbluth claim that decisions of coalition governments are likely to reflect the policy preferences of the coalition partner that places the highest priority on a policy issue, because voters would attribute this coalition party the main responsibility for the issue. That, in turn, implies that in each policy decision, the external costs would be internalised to a lesser extent than in a single-party government. The smaller the support base of each party in the coalition, the larger is the fraction of costs that would be externalised in each policy decision subject to the control of a particular member of the coalition. Though increasing the number of parties in the coalition does not necessarily translate into an increase in the number of interest groups that are represented altogether, it does influence the degree to which policy choices weigh diffuse costs against targeted benefits. As a result of a more extensive divergence in the perceived costs and benefits of spending programmes, coalition governments are more likely to become subject to common-pool problems of budgeting than single-party governments.

Tornell and Lane (1999) and Lane (2003) argue that because of a voracity effect, pressures for increased spending resulting from the common-pool problem may become stronger when the economy is doing well and budgetary resources are in abundance. As Lane (2003) explains, when faced with surpluses, the incentive for individual parties in the coalition to act prudently is low: each party knows that if it refrained from increasing its demand for part of the surplus (in order to implement a desired policy or provide targeted spending for its supporter groups), the result would not be larger surplus, since other parties would increase their appropriation rate by even greater amount. Hence, Lane predicts that coalition governments would be more likely to run pro-cyclical fiscal policies during good times than single-party governments.

Owing to a larger number of players, coalition governments are considered to be less durable than single-party governments and therefore more likely to both think and act in their short-term self-interest, whereas effective budgeting requires long-range planning and implementation (Freitag and Sciarini 2001). De Haan and Sturm (1994), for example, argue that short-lived governments are more prone to budget deficits, since they try to stabilise the political system and their position by increasing transfer payments. Harrinvirta and Mattila (2001) hypothesise that because of the tendencies to increase spending without matching revenue increases, government instability is likely to lead to higher deficits. Debrun and Kumar (2007) argue that a deficit bias in fiscal policy is likely to be stronger when partisan policy-makers are uncertain about their re-election chances (which in turn increases their discount rate); therefore, they predict that higher political instability should lead to higher deficits.

5.3.1.1.6. Number of Spending Ministers in Cabinet

Taking the analysis of budgetary decision-making in the cabinet one step further, a set of approaches (especially prevalent in the literature on budgetary institutions and procedures, discussed in detail in chapter 6) views the number of individual *ministers* rather than the number of *parties* represented in the cabinet as the primary decision-making units. Hallerberg (2000b), among others, has argued for counting the number of ministers in the cabinet rather than just the parties, given that ministers from the same party can have diverging views on spending items. Further, he suggests that ministers would usually be evaluated according to how well they manage to safeguard the interests of the constituents of the ministry. Proceeding from the "law of $1/n$", it is argued that the larger the number of spending ministers in the cabinet, the more severe common-pool problems in budgeting would be. These approaches assume that ministers have incentives to seek increased expenditures on programmes benefiting their respective ministries, since they do not have to take into account the full cost of the increases in revenues. (Kontopoulos and Perotti 1999; Schaltegger and Feld 2008)

As Schaltegger and Feld (2008) point out, the ministerial demands for increasing portions of the state budget may originate from different sources. Like individual legislators, individual ministers are motivated to serve their own constituencies. Further, in making proposals for budget appropriations, ministers may represent the demands of specific interest groups with which the ministry has close links. Finally, the requests for larger budgets may arise from the ministerial bureaucracy. As Schaltegger and Feld (2008) underline, the norms of reciprocity (implying that ministers are motivated to support each other's budget proposals) might even be stronger between individual *ministers* than between individual *legislators* because of the smaller circle of participants involved in the cabinet.

Proceeding from the assumption of voracity effect, Lane (2003) predicts that governments with a larger number of spending ministers would be more likely to run pro-cyclical fiscal policies during good times. In a similar vein, Brosens and Wierts (2007) argue that, because of voracity effect, surpluses would be associated with fewer spending ministers. To what extent the *potential* common-pool problems entailed in governmental budgeting are *actually* translated into overgrazing the budgetary commons depends on the budgetary institutions and the existence (or non-existence) of coordination mechanisms that facilitate the internalisation of costs associated with expenditures (either in a form of a strong minister of finance or binding fiscal contracts), which are discussed in chapter 6.

5.3.1.2. Veto Players Models

While the budgetary commons models described in section 5.3.1.1. posit that the larger the number of participants in budgetary decision-making, the larger the resulting expenditures (and, in a dynamic perspective, the larger the budget deficits), veto players (or veto actors or veto points) models argue that the *larger* the number of participants with a veto power, the more likely is policy gridlock and the more biased the resulting policy choices would be towards status quo (see Tsebelis 1995a,b, 1999, 2002; Immergut 1992; Cox and McCubbins 2001). Although, in principle, the larger the number of individual legislators in the legislature, the higher the transaction costs of reaching an agreement, individual legislators (either in the legislature as a whole or in the legislative majority) are usually not conceived as veto players. Most of the veto players approaches analysing the number and kinds of participants in budgetary decision-making process focus on parties in coalition governments. Some veto players approaches also take into consideration the number of opposition parties in the legislature and how fractionalised the partisan veto players are. Further, in considering the role of veto players in budgetary process, one needs to keep in mind that the impact of veto players is likely to vary with a specific fiscal situation that the government is faced with.

In the review below, section 5.3.1.2.1. discusses the role of coalition partners as veto players and juxtaposes the contradictory predictions that budgetary commons models and veto players models make about coalition governments with regard to expenditures, taxation and deficits in fiscally "good times". Section 5.3.1.2.2. discusses the obstacles coalition governments face in dealing with fiscal crises and undertaking fiscal consolidation in "difficult times". While sections 5.3.1.2.1. and 5.3.1.2.2. consider the effects of partisan veto actors by simply "counting" the absolute number of parties that make up the coalition government, section 5.3.1.2.3. takes a step further and considers the effects of the fractionalisation of partisan veto players (both in the government and in the parliament) on public finances. Section 5.3.1.2.4. discusses the impacts of minority governments and contrasts the predictions that the budgetary commons models and veto players models make in this regard.

5.3.1.2.1. Coalition Parties as Veto Players in "Good Times"

Proceeding from the basic assumptions of veto players models, one would predict that the larger the number of coalition partners (and the more diverging their preferences), the more difficult it would be to change the status quo and introduce new expenditure programmes. Therefore, one would expect *lower* expenditures in polities where coalition governments dominate than in systems with single-party majority governments; this is a *contrary* prediction to what common-pool models make about coalition governments (see section 5.3.1.1.5.). Thus, one puzzle that the veto players approach to budgeting and taxation has to address is the question of how budget increases can come about in a setting with many veto players in the government, which, in principle, should lead to status quo bias in existing expenditures.

Crepaz (1998) and Crepaz and Moser (2004) have sought to address this puzzle by distinguishing between *collective* veto points (e.g., parties in the governing coalition) and *competitive* veto points (e.g., chambers in a bicameral system);[152] they predict that competitive veto points are likely to constrain "budgetary expansion", while collective veto points are likely to promote it. The core of their argument is that in the case of competitive veto points, the blame for decisions is not "personalised", as in the case of parties, but "institutionalised". As Crepaz and Moser (p. 266) put it, in competitive veto points, political actors can

152 Tsebelis (1995) distinguishes between partisan veto points (such as the number of parties) and institutional veto points (such as federalism and bicameralism).

shift the responsibility for the veto to the "faceless" institution: it is these institutions that are blamed rather than the parties or party leaders. Owing to the possibility to shift the blame, such "institutionalised" vetoes are less costly; thus, they are likely to be used more often, making it more difficult to change the status quo. Collective veto points, in contrast, are more "personalised" (linked to specific party leaders, for example), which makes the use of vetoes costlier. As Crepaz and Moser (2004) argue, each coalition partner seeks to ensure that one's own party is not blamed for the fall of a government. Therefore, collective vetoes are likely to be used less frequently, which lessens the status quo bias and helps to explain why the existence of several veto players in the government does not necessarily lead to constrained expenditures. Crepaz and Moser also underline the role of collective responsibility (whereby all coalition parties would be held accountable for the successes and failures of the government) and the importance of coalition agreements in discouraging the members of coalition to exercise a veto after the coalition has been formed. The willingness of the parties in the coalition to employ their veto power *after* the coalition has been formed and coalition agreement reached depends on the norms of political culture with regard to how negatively a violation of coalition agreement is perceived.

Alongside the line of reasoning pertaining to political or electoral costliness (in terms of negative public backlash) of using the veto power that a veto player is endowed with, one should consider other motivations of intra-coalition veto players to exercise (or refrain from exercising) their veto in any given budgetary decision. A coalition party is likely to be motivated to use its veto power in budgetary expansion, if a particular decision implied costs (in terms of additional tax burdens) for its supporter groups. If, however, there are possibilities to externalise the immediate tax costs of a spending programme to supporters of parties outside the coalition, the incentives to impose a veto on a spending proposal are weakened. Further, opportunities for deficit financing imply that the costs can be either postponed or blurred, which can further curtail the motives to exercise a veto. Also, the role of veto players in influencing budgetary outcomes depends on whether they can engage in bargaining with other veto players and demand side-payments in return for their consent. If veto players can threaten the decision-making with gridlock and demand side-payments (e.g., in the form of increased expenditures directed to their specific constituencies) for granting their consent, the number of side-payments demanded would increase with the number of participants, resulting in higher levels of expenditures (and higher deficits). If budget constraints are soft, a coalition partner would generally prefer to *get* the spending it prefers rather than to *deny* the spending that other parties prefer (Cox and McCubbins 2001, p. 30). As Cox and McCubbins explain it, vetoing another party's spending would usually confer a diffuse benefit on all taxpayers, whereas spending can be targeted to one's own constituency groups;

hence, the use of the vetoes in budgetary decision-making may be regarded as an unattractive electoral strategy.

Although, at first sight, the *budgetary commons* and the *veto players* models give rise to diverging predictions with regard to the level of expenditures in coalition governments, a more elaborate model would regard these theoretical perspectives as complementary. The more the veto players have incentives and possibilities to demand side-payments and the more they have opportunities to externalise the costs of increased expenditures to constituencies of other players, the more similar would be the effect of the number of veto players to the effect of *n* graziers on budgetary commons. The smaller the parties are and the narrower their support base, the more likely they are to behave as graziers.

With regard to the emergence of deficits, simple veto-players models would have difficulties in making a priori predictions. Since a larger number of veto actors is likely to constrain both spending and revenues, the effects on deficits may be ambiguous, unless the nature of the veto players is specified. Peters (1991, pp. 10, 113–114) regards coalition partners as graziers in spending and veto players in taxation. He argues that since coalition governments are induced to spend more (due to the side-payments needed for keeping the coalition together), and, at the same time, reaching an agreement on raising taxes for budgetary expansion is difficult (since coalitions seek to minimise the tax burden that falls on their constituent groups), coalition governments tend to run larger deficits than single-party governments. Harrinvirta and Mattila (2001) also conjecture that the larger the number of parties in the coalition, the more difficult are spending cuts and tax increases, because each party seeks to shield its supporters from lower benefits and increased tax obligations; these two tendencies make coalition governments more prone to deficits. According to Sakamoto (2001, p. 533), on the other hand, coalition parties act as graziers in taxation; referring to Steinmo and Tolbert (1998), he argues that since coalition governments (especially with dominant coalition polities) tend to tax more, their inclination towards higher expenditures would not necessarily translate into higher deficits.

5.3.1.2.2. Coalition Parties as Veto Players in "Difficult Times"

In analysing the role of coalition parties as veto players in public finance, one needs to keep in mind that the dynamics leading to increases in expenditures and the *emergence* of public deficits is different from the dynamics leading to the inability to *curb* budget deficits. When the government faces a fiscally difficult situation, the general prediction of veto players models would be: the larger the number of participants, the more difficult it is for the government to curb the deficit. As Tsebelis (1995a,b, 1999, 2002) contends, a larger number of veto players tends to "lock in" economic policy and reduce its ability to respond to outside shocks. Hence, one can expect coalition governments to have more difficulties, compared with single-party governments, in *curbing* the deficit in a situation when the government faces a permanent shock (leading to persistence of budget deficits and debt accumulation). The same viewpoint is endorsed by Hallerberg and Basinger (1998) and Bawn (1999), among others. As mentioned in section 4.4., according to Schick (1993, pp. 187–188), curbing budget deficits usually requires two governmental capabilities: setting and maintaining priorities when policy objectives are in conflict and resources are limited, and imposing costs on concentrated interests. He hypothesises that single-party majority governments are likely to have advantage over coalition and minority governments in setting and maintaining priorities (p. 190). In a similar vein, Haggard, Kaufman and Shugart (2001, p. 88) argue that when governing coalition is fragmented, it is likely to be more difficult take decisive action and adopt coherent policies. Reflecting these general considerations, a number of formal models has been put forth to describe the structure of incentives and interaction between parties in the governing coalition faced with a need to reduce budget deficit.

The *prisoner's dilemma model* of budgeting (see Roubini and Sachs 1989a,b; Alesina and Perotti 1995) considers the coalition partners as having different interests and constituencies. By analogy with the standard version of the model, even though all parties in the coalition favour reduction of the deficit, each coalition partner may have incentives to protect the programmes that benefit its constituency against austerity measures. In other words, curbing the budget deficit can be viewed as a "public good": every party would like to enjoy the public good (deficit reduction), but without having to pay for it (by cutting expenditures favouring its supporters). The more parties there are in the coalition, the more difficult the attainment of collectively efficient fiscal policies is likely to be. In the absence of strong coordination mechanisms, the non-cooperative solution is likely to prevail; the resulting equilibrium is that no budget cuts would be made and deficits persist. Roubini and Sachs (1989a) add that the rapid turnover of multiparty governments reduces the incentives for participating parties to cooperate among themselves on such matters as achieving fiscal balance. By referring to Axelrod (1984), they emphasise that "the enforceability of co-operation depends heavily on the repeated-play aspects of decision making" (Roubini and Sachs 1989a, p. 925) and because rapid turnover reduces the time horizon for repeated play among the parties, coalition governments have difficulties in making binding commitments, including commitments to fiscal discipline (see also Alesina and Tabellini 1990; Grilli, Masciandaro and Tabellini 1991).

Alesina and Drazen (1991) put forth a *war of attrition model* of budgeting, which regards decisions about the distribution of burdens of fiscal adjustments as involving a conflict between socio-economic groups. Alesina and Drazen suggest that even if there is an agreement on the need for fiscal consolidation, delays in stabilisation result from political stalemate over how to distribute the burden of increased taxes or expenditure cuts. When socio-economic groups consider it possible to shift the burden to other group(s), the rational strategy would be to "wait others out", despite the fact that waiting is costly (e.g., in the form of increasing debt service requirements, which have to be financed from distortionary taxation). Thus, according to the model, fiscal adjustment only occurs when one group concedes and, as a result, has to bear a disproportionate share of the resulting fiscal burden. (p. 1170) This model has been used to suggest that coalition governments with parties representing different socio-economic groups would wait significantly longer than unified governments to balance their budget (despite the principled agreement of the coalition partners on the need to consolidate the budget), contributing to an increase in deficits and accumulation of debt. Although, eventually, one party accepts paying a larger share of the costs of fiscal adjustment, the delay comes about, because the parties in the coalition hope that the other party (or parties) will give in first and bear the burden of fiscal adjustment, which would allow them to "export" the costs of fiscal adjustment to supporter groups of other parties in the coalition.[153] Thus, every party in the coalition has incentives to block fiscal retrenchment measures as long as the marginal benefit from waiting is higher than the marginal cost of distortions associated with the accumulation of debt and the political costs of fighting. The decision to curb deficits is delayed until the costs of delay become too high for (at least) one of the parties in the coalition. An important element in the model is the uncertainty with regard to the utility loss of the other parties from delaying the fiscal adjustment. If the parties knew what the costs of delaying would be for the other parties, they could predict the time each of them would be induced to give in; hence, the party for whom the delay is the costliest would have incentives to give in immediately rather than to engage in costly waiting.

A problem that arises with regard to the applicability of the war of attrition model proposed by Alesina and Drazen (1991) to real-life decision-making is: Why would coalition parties not attempt to externalise the costs of adjustment to non-coalition parties instead of trying to reach an agreement on how to divide the burden of adjustment between themselves? Franzese (2002b) has sought to address this question by arguing that even if part of the costs can be shifted to opposition parties, some of the burden has to be borne by coalition parties *themselves*. And, as he emphasises, in the context of multiparty governments, it is more difficult – compared with a single-party government – to devise corrective fiscal measures that would distribute the costs evenly between participants involved. Another problem with regard to the applicability of the war of attrition model to real-world coalition governments is the question of whether the assumption of uncertainty and asymmetric information with regard to utility losses resulting from a delay of fiscal retrenchment by other parties actually character-

153 As Eslava (2006) points out, the war of attrition models imply that fiscal consolidation should be prompter, the higher is the initial level of debt, since higher indebtedness moves the costs of further delay closer to the point where waiting becomes too costly.

ises the situation coalition parties are in when facing the need for fiscal consolidation. Why such informational asymmetry and uncertainty would exist and persist over time has not been sufficiently addressed in the war of attrition models of budgeting. The persistence of uncertainty with regard to the losses that another party has to bear is especially unlikely given the face-to-face interaction of the representatives of the parties in the cabinet on every-day basis.

Altogether, it appears that the budgetary commons models analysing the effects of coalition governments on budgetary outcomes have more plausibility when describing "good times", whereas the veto players models do a better job in explaining the decision-making obstacles that hinder the adoption of corrective fiscal measures in "difficult times". In other words, increasing the number of parties in the government contribute to increases of budget expenditures in good times, while posing obstacles for cutting expenditures or increasing taxes in difficult times. For maintaining analytical clarity, it is important to link the explanatory power of different models with the specific situations that the governments can face. This distinction, however, is often neglected in the existing literature.

5.3.1.2.3. Fractionalisation of Partisan Veto Players

As mentioned in 5.3.1.1.3., counting the parties in government or legislature in absolute numbers may present a flawed picture of the actual power constellations and bargaining positions. Therefore, a number of veto players approaches have called for analysing the effect of government fractionalisation on expenditure and deficits (see, for example, Kontopoulos and Perotti 1999; Volkerink and de Haan 2001).

Huber, Kocher and Sutter (2003, p. 336) argue that coalitions with *equally* strong partners run significantly higher deficits than coalitions with one dominating party. They suggest that the dispersion of power within a coalition plays an important role when it has to decide on how to distribute the burden of fiscal adjustment. In coalition governments with one strong party, the dominating party can put pressure on the relatively weaker party (or parties), who would have to bear a significant portion of the adjustment costs in stabilising the budget.

Padovano and Venturi (2001) suggest a modified version of the war of attrition model that takes into account the fractionalisation of both government and opposition. As Padovano and Venturi (2001, p. 17) point out, the fragmentation of the opposition – in addition to the fragmentation of the governing coalition – may significantly affect the costs of fiscal consolidation that the governing coalition has to bear. They argue that it would be more difficult for a government coalition to stabilise the budget when it has to surpass the opposition of a single cohesive party than when it faces resistance from a larger effective number of opposition parties (subject to coordination problems between themselves). Thus, although the common-pool models exploring the impacts of the effective number of parties in the parliament (including opposition parties) would predict that a larger number of parties in the opposition leads to higher expenditures and emergence of deficits, the war of attrition models would predict that when a legislature is faced with a need to curb the deficit and undertake fiscal consolidation, a larger effective number of parties in the opposition facilitates the adoption of corrective fiscal measures, because the opposition parties face coordination problems in putting up resistance to the plans of the governing coalition.

The effects of government fractionalisation on tax policies have been taken up by Steinmo and Tolbert (1998). Although the existing literature predicts that there is a linear relationship between the effective number of parties and the level of taxation, since polities with many small political parties tend to engage in tax-and-spend bidding wars (and thus have the highest average tax burdens), Steinmo and Tolbert (1998) emphasise that this relationship should be reconsidered. They distinguish between *majoritarian* polities, *dominant coalition* polities and *shifting coalition* polities. They argue that the more the political institutions entail incentives to compromise, the higher are spending and taxes. As Steinmo and Tolbert (1998, pp. 175, 180) elucidate, in *majoritarian* governments, where a single party controls a majority of seats in parliament, the dominant party can push through legislation on its own; therefore, it has fewer incentives to buy off other parties by increasing targeted public spending to their respective constituents. Instead, the governing party is likely to have incentives to shift tax burdens away from its supporters. On the other hand, there would be incentives to hold the general tax levels down, because the dominant party knows that a relatively small shift in the popular vote can lead to a complete change in who controls the offices of government. In *dominant coalition* governments (where one party tends to control close to 50 percent of the seats in the legislature but rarely achieves a majority and hence has to enter into coalitions with smaller parties), there are likely to be incentives to cut deals with coalition partners about taxes and spending. Further, as Steinmo and Tolbert emphasise, "Because the dominant party is dominant, the coalition parties can have a reasonable expectation that if they agree to passing tax increases, they (or their constituents) will specifically benefit from the increases in public spending." (p. 180) In *shifting coalition* governments with no dominant party (and where the largest political party may realistically be toppled from office), there are more likely to be incentives to defect from compromises. Given that no party has enough power to sanction defectors, there is an increased incentive to defect from compromise and shirk their share of the tax burden. Thus, because it is more difficult to hold coalitions together in such a setting, policies of persistent tax increases would be less likely. Taken together, Steinmo and Tolbert predict that dominant coalition polities have the electoral stability to engage in long-term tax commitments resulting in higher tax burdens, whereas shifting coalition governments tend to engage in short-term tax policy negotiations, leading to more moderate tax burdens. In majoritarian polities, they expect political and economic interests to demand short-term public policies, which would lead to lower overall taxation.

5.3.1.2.4. Minority Governments

In the case of minority governments, partisan veto actors may also be found outside the governing party (or coalition), as the opposition party (or parties) have the power to block policy proposals of the governing party (or parties). Therefore, minority governments are expected to have greater difficulties in restoring fiscal balances than governments that have a solid legislative majority. As Sakamoto (2001, p. 531) explains, curbing fiscal deficits requires unpopular decisions like cutting expenditures or increasing taxes, and minority governments have difficulties in getting such unpopular decisions adopted in the parliament, since they do not have a sufficient majority. In addition, minority governments are seen as being prone to the emergence of higher deficits, since they have to make side-payments to the opposition parties, in order to get the budgets passed (see Blais, Blake and Dion 1993).

Considering the effects of minority governments on budgeting is, however, more complicated than appears at first sight. The models considering the effects of minority governments are faced with the dilemma of how to accommodate the *budgetary commons* aspects and *veto players* aspects in describing budgetary decision-making. On the one hand, minority governments can be seen as having fewer parties "grazing" the budgetary commons – often only one party (see Strom 1990; Woldendorp, Keman and Budge 1993) – implying fewer incentives to "overgraze" the commons and fewer veto points in cutting expenditures or increasing taxes. On the other hand, since opposition parties can play a significant role in the decision-making of a minority government, the number of players – the n – is likely to encompass the effective number of parties in the opposition as well. Here, in turn, the number of opposition parties can have diverging effects. On the one hand, the "law of $1/n$" would predict that when the number of parties in budgetary decision-making process increases, expenditures would increase and, once the deficits have already been incurred, it would be more difficult to achieve cooperative agreements for undertaking corrective fiscal measures. On the other hand, when a minority government is faced with a large number of small parties in the opposition, the side-payments it may have to make, in order to get the budgets or tax increases passed, are likely to be smaller than when the minority government is faced with a unified opposition front (e.g., one strong opposition party). In the case of fractionalised opposition, procuring the support of a small opposition party may be sufficient to get the policies adopted. Thus, fragmentation of the opposition is likely to have implications on the ability of a minority government to maintain fiscal prudence.

5.3.1.3. Accountability in Different Governing Arrangements

As sections 5.3.1.1. and 5.3.1.3. have already indicated, in analyses of the number and kinds of participants in budgetary process, accountability mechanisms are closely intertwined with coordination mechanisms. In general, the larger the number of actors involved in a decision-making process, the more diluted the accountability of each actor becomes. Hence, the more parties there are in the parliament or in the government, the more ministers there are in the cabinet, the more members there are in the legislature, the weaker the individual or partisan accountability should become, because a particular decision cannot be easily attributed to a particular actor. Weaker accountability, in turn, would imply that the choices of elected representatives may be removed from the policy preferences of the electorate.

There are, however, disagreements over whether this inverse relationship between the number of actors and the level of institutional, partisan and individual accountability in the polity actually holds and what the implications of weaker accountability would be. Different authors have offered different conceptions of accountability mechanisms in the case of coalition governments, for example. Most authors assume that voters hold parties in coalition governments *collectively* responsible for the decisions taken. Persson and Tabellini (2004b), for example, argue that under coalition government, the incentives of individual parties to be responsive to the needs of the public might be diluted, since the votes lost for poor performance of the government would be born collectively by the coalition partners. Some other authors (e.g., Bawn and Rosenbluth 2006) conceive of voters as usually making a particular coalition party responsible for a specific policy decision. Hence, there is still a basic disagreement about how voters attribute responsibility to the parties in coalition governments; this makes explanations and predictions about the number of partisan actors in government on policy choices in public finance more complicated.

As already discussed in sections 4.4. and 5.1., the implications of stronger accountability of policy actors for public finance may also not be straightforward. While stronger accountability mechanisms may be conducive to prudent fiscal policy during good times, the concentration of blame may augment the reluctance of policy actors to take painful corrective fiscal measures in the face of a fiscal crisis. Hence, actor constellations subject to weaker accountability – like multiparty governments or minority governments – may have an advantage in pursuing fiscal consolidation. As Sakamoto (2001, p. 533) notes, minority governments may be *more willing* to undertake unpopular policies of fiscal consolidation, since the negative effects of expenditure cuts or tax increases are less clearly attributable to the government alone (with opposition parties sharing in the responsibility), whereas majority governments are faced with more clearly attributable accountability for painful policy decisions. On the other hand, in polities where inability to achieve fiscal consolidation is punished by voters (and the policy actors anticipate that correctly), stronger accountability would lead to prompter fiscal consolidation. Within a coalition government, stronger accountability of each coalition party to a particular constituency, as portrayed by Bawn and Rosenbluth (2006), may aggravate common-pool problems: when policy decisions are primarily influenced by one particular coalition partner, external costs of policy decisions are likely to be higher.

5.3.2. Empirical Evidence

There are a large number of studies that have explored the effects of the characteristics of governing arrangements (in terms of the number and kinds of participants involved in decision-making) on budgeting and taxation. The overview below considers first the effects of the margin of government majority, followed by weak governments (i.e., coalition and minority governments as opposed to single-majority governments), the number of parties in governing coalition and the number of spending ministers in the cabinet. Finally, the impacts of fractionalisation of governments and legislatures and the duration of cabinets are outlined. Although in principle, one could structure the overview of the empirical studies according to analytical structure (proceeding from different kinds of theoretical models) presented in section 5.3.1., this would be too cumbersome and duplicative, which is why the overview is structured according to the logic that the existing empirical studies themselves have followed when exploring the different elements (or combinations thereof). Also, since most of the empirical studies exploring the effects of the size of the legislature on fiscal outcomes have simultaneously addressed the issues of bicameralism and unicameralism, an overview of the effects of legislature size on budgeting and taxation will be presented together with empirical evidence on the cameral structure of the legislature in section 5.4.2.

5.3.2.1. Size of Governing Majority

Although simple budgetary commons models would predict that the larger the number of participants on the commons, the more severe the common-pool problems of budgeting, the studies exploring the effects of the size of governing majority have demonstrated contrary results. Volkerink and de Haan (2001) find that the larger the excess number of seats that the government had in parliament, the lower the deficit was in the OECD countries in 1970s. Elgie and McMenamin (2008) ascertain with a larger sample of OECD countries that a larger number of excess seats is associated with higher budget surplus, but this effect disappears when a larger sample of countries (including non-OECD countries) is considered. Lavigne (2006) finds that the margin of majority (the percentage of the legislature controlled by the government) is the *only* political variable found to have a significant effect on the fiscal status of developing countries: the larger the margin of majority, the more likely is a successful fiscal consolidation effort. Employing panel data on 110 countries from 1980 to 1996, Mukherjee (2003) finds confirmation for the conjectured *cube* relationship between the margin of majority held by the government and the level of expenditures, outlined in section 5.3.1.1.2.: the expenditures decrease when the margin of majority grows from 50 to 56 percent, increase between 56 and 68 percent, and fall again beyond the majority of 68 percent. Lagona and Padovano (2007) find that the size of the government majority is generally associated with greater fiscal discipline (smaller expenditures and lower budget deficits). Altogether, these results indicate that when the margin of majority increases, the increased bargaining power of the governing majority *vis-à-vis* the opposition (which is likely to reduce the need to make side-payments to the members of the opposition) would play a more important role than the "law of 1/*n*" within the governing majority itself.

Some other studies, however, have found the size of the majority to have only insignificant effects. Huber, Kocher and Sutter (2003) conclude, in their study of 21 OECD countries from 1970 to 1999, that government strength (i.e., the legislative power of the government *vis-à-vis* the opposition, measured with the Banzhaf index) is insignificant for budget deficit. Leachman *et al.* (2007) infer, based on their study of 15 industrialised countries, that the level of parliamentary support for the government is a poor predictor of fiscal performance. Mireau, Jong-A-Pin and de Haan (2007) also find that the margin of majority has not influenced the probability of fiscal adjustment in 20 OECD countries.

Under margin of majority, one can also explore the effects that the minority status of the government has on fiscal outcomes. Although a number of studies have collapsed the features of coalition governments and minority governments into a single index (see Roubini and Sachs 1989a,b, and other studies discussed in section 5.3.2.2.), the minority status of the government on its own would warrant closer inspection. Empirical evidence on the impacts of minority governments on fiscal discipline points to clearly diverging results. Edin and Ohlsson (1991) find that minority governments are associated with higher deficits and are less able to undertake fiscal adjustments. Grilli, Masciandro and Tabellini (1991) and Freitag and Sciarini (2001), on the other hand, find no effects of whether the government is a majority or minority government on budget deficit. Borrelli and Royed (1995) even claim that minority governments run smaller deficits than majority governments. Similarly, Sakamoto (2001) finds that there is evidence for deficits being lower under minority governments. With regard to taxation, Ganghof (2007) argues that the maintenance of high income tax burden in Denmark can be explained by a centripetal political dynamics created by a multiparty political setting where the right-wing minority governments needed the legislative support of centrist or leftist parties in the legislature and therefore refrained from undertaking extensive tax cuts.

5.3.2.2. Weak Government

The seminal studies systematically studying the effects of coalition governments on budget deficit were conduced by Roubini and Sachs (1989a,b). In order to assess the effect of the type of government on budget deficit in OECD countries (from 1975 to 1985), Roubini and Sachs constructed an index of "government weakness", assigning progressively higher scores to single-party majority, small coalition, large coalition and minority governments. They found that "there is a clear tendency for larger deficits in weaker governments" (p. 931). Roubini and Sachs also find that the relationship between governing arrangements and budgetary outcomes depends on economic circumstances: weak governments are able to maintain reasonable budget balance when economy is doing fine, but are much less able to do so under adverse economic conditions. As Roubini and Sachs (1989a, p. 925) explain it, "Individual coalition members may have the power to veto spending cuts, but not have the power to push through spending increases without the support of the other coalition members."

Several further studies have confirmed the Roubini-Sachs hypothesis (the so-called "weak government hypothesis"). Corsetti and Roubini (1993) endorse the empirical findings of Roubini and Sachs (1989a,b). Alesina and Perotti (1995) differentiate between single-party, coalition and minority governments in their study of 20 OECD countries over the period 1960–1992. They show that compared with single-party governments, coalition governments are less able to undertake budget consolidations: "They often try but systematically fail." (p. 210) Persson, Roland and Tabellini (2007) consider 50 parliamentary democracies and find that coalition governments spend more than single-party governments.[154]

There have been, however, a number of studies that have found contrary evidence to the weak government hypothesis put forth by Roubini and Sachs. Edin and Ohlsson (1991) replicate the study of Roubini and Sachs and ascertain, by disaggregating the index of government cohesion, that the coalition effect was entirely due to minority governments. Edin and Ohlson argue that the political power dispersion index used by Roubini and Sachs captures the effects of minority governments rather than majority coalition governments; hence, single-party governments can only be judged to have lower deficits in comparison to minority governments, but not to coalition governments in general. De Haan and Sturm (1994, 1997),[155] de Haan, Sturm and Beekhuis (1999), Borelli and Royed

154 In addition, their results indicate that higher spending under proportional elections seems to be entirely due to a higher incidence of coalition governments in proportional electoral systems (rather than by direct effects on policymaking incentives).

155 De Haan and Sturm (1994) consider the effects on debt accumulation and public sector size in 12 EC member countries between 1981 and 1989. They use a power dispersion index that is similar to the one proposed by Sachs and Roubini (1989a,b) and find that power dispersion has no effects on debt growth and expenditure. De Haan and Sturm

(1995),[156] Hahm, Kamlet and Mowery (1996), Sakamoto (2001) and Woo (2003) also dismiss the Roubini-Sachs hypothesis. Sakamoto (2001), by examining data from 18 OECD countries between 1961 and 1994, shows that there is some evidence to suggest that deficits are *lower* under "weak" governments, such as minority governments or coalition governments. Further, he does not find evidence for the argument that weak governments are less capable of reducing deficits, once the deficits have been created or economic conditions worsen.[157] Tujula and Wolswijk (2004), in their study of 22 OECD countries between 1970 and 2002, also find that weaker governments (e.g., caretaker governments or minority governments) had positive impacts on budget balances.

5.3.2.3. Number of Parties in the Coalition, Number of Spending Ministers

While the studies employing the Roubini-Sachs government weakness index collapse the coalition characteristics and minority characteristics into a single index, Kontopoulos and Perotti (1999, 2002) advocate using the actual number of parties in the coalition in empirical studies exploring the effects of size fragmentation. Kontopoulos and Perotti (1999) show, in their study of 20 OECD countries, that the number of spending ministers and, to a lesser extent, the number of political parties in a coalition influence spending growth and budget deficits, but that the effects have been diverging in different periods. They find that the size of the coalition had significant effects on deficits between 1984 and 1995 (but not between 1960 and 1984). The number of spending ministers had significant effects between 1974 and 1984, but not in the periods 1960–1973 and 1984–1995. Kontopoulos and Perotti (1999, p. 91) explain this dynamics by referring to the distinct nature that the fiscal shocks had in these different periods. The shocks in the 1970s were primarily external and the containment of expenditure growth depended on the decision-making processes within the executive; therefore, the number of spending ministers became a relevant factor. The fiscal shocks in the 1980s were more of internal nature; hence, fiscal consolidation depended on how cohesive the governments were in adopting political decisions. In disaggregating the effects, Kontopoulos and Perotti (1999) show that the

(1997) investigate cross-country differences in debt accumulation and the level of government spending in 21 OECD countries over the period 1982–1992. Again, they find that neither the growth of government debt nor the level of government spending is related to the corrected Roubini–Sachs power dispersion index.

156 Borelli and Royed (1995) consider 16 OECD countries (from 1959 to 1990) and find that while structural differences between governments may have little impact on deficits during good economic times, they may become noticeable and influential during periods when governments struggle to cope with severe economic problems. In other words, weaker governments lead to rises in deficits only in times of low GDP growth.

157 As Sakamoto notes (p. 550), the only indication supportive of the hypothesis observed in the data is that, from 1980 to 1994, minority governments had more difficulty reducing deficits than majority governments when faced with low economic growth.

number of spending ministers in the cabinet significantly increases the deficit and that this effect is mostly due to the effect on expenditures: a larger number of participants in budgetary policy-making leads to higher expenditures while leaving revenues unaffected. At the same time, they show that the effect of the number of parties in the coalition is more "balanced" for revenues and expenditures: although the number of parties has an effect on the level of expenditures, this effect is counterbalanced by an effect on revenues. In a later study, Perotti and Kontopoulos (2002) once more explore the influence of the coalition size and cabinet size on expenditures and deficits in 19 OECD countries between 1970 and 1995. They find clear and robust evidence that larger cabinets are associated with higher expenditures and higher deficits; the effect of the cabinet size is especially noteworthy at times of economic difficulties and fiscal stress. In their 2002 study, Perotti and Kontopoulos find that when the deficit is disaggregated into expenditures and revenues, virtually all the effect of type of governments on the deficit is due to revenues. They view it as evidence for the inability of more fragmented governments to increase taxes to fill the budget gap.

The findings of Perotti and Kontopoulos have been endorsed by a number of subsequent studies. De Haan, Sturm and Beekhuis (1999) find that the number of parties in government had a significant effect on central government debt growth in 21 OECD countries (in the period 1979–1995). Balassone and Giordano (2001) show, using data from a sample of eight EC countries in the period 1971–1990, that the larger the number of parties in the coalition, the higher are the deficits. Mulas-Granados (2003) examines the political and economic determinants of the composition of fiscal consolidations in the European Union between 1970 and 2001 and denotes that the number of parties in the coalition influences fiscal outcomes: coalition governments spend more, especially on transfers, and if forced to adjust, follow revenue-based strategies. Bawn and Rosenbluth (2006) ascertain, in their study of 17 European countries between 1970 and 1998, that the number of parties in government increases the fraction of GDP accounted for by government spending. Harrinvirta and Mattila (2001) find, in their study of 17 OECD countries between 1960 and 1995, that governments with more parties are not more inclined to have higher deficits, but they are more likely to raise both public expenditure and revenues. They also observe that in achieving deficit reductions, one-party governments emphasise expenditure cuts, while multiparty governments raise taxes; as a consequence, the highest tax rates can be found in countries where labour market centralisation is combined with multiparty governments.

Illera and Mulas-Granados (2008) ascertain, in their study of duration of fiscal consolidations in 15 EU countries (from 1960 to 2004), that both the number of parties in the government and the number of spending ministers helped to explain the probability of ending a fiscal consolidation. Further, they find that the relative importance of these variables weakened in the run-up to EMU; during this period, the countries were obliged to consolidate, irrespective of the composition of the government. Franzese (2002b) finds, in his study of 21 OECD countries between 1956 and 1990, that the number of parties in government is associated with debt-adjustment, but the relationship is not linear. A larger number of parties in the government slows debt-adjustment, but only when the debt level is already high (over 30 percent of GDP). When the debt level is lower than this threshold, a higher number of parties in government tends to reduce deficit. The higher the debt level, the stronger the effect of the number of parties in the coalition becomes. Franzese considers it as a confirmation for the war of attrition of model of fiscal adjustment in difficult times (when the debt level is already very high). During the "good times" (when the debt level is low), however, the "inaction effect", associated with a larger number of parties in the coalition, prevents introduction of new programmes. Franzese concludes that the number of partisan veto-actors "is a critical determinant of debt-adjustment paths and thereby plays a large role in any explanation of postwar OECD debt experiences" (p. 55).

The influence of the number of spending ministers on budget deficits has been endorsed by Volkerink and de Haan (2001), Woo (2003) and Ricciuti (2004a). Further, Schaltegger and Feld (2008) find, in their panel study of fiscal policy outcomes of 26 Swiss cantons, that larger cabinets favour both higher expenditures and higher revenues, while the size of the coalition does not have such robust effects. Brosens and Wierts (2007) observe, in their study of OECD countries, that fewer spending ministers in cabinet coincide with budgetary surpluses. Elgie and McMenamin (2008) confirm, with a sample of OECD countries, that a larger number of spending ministers is associated with lower surpluses; however, when ten non-OECD countries were added to the sample, the effect disappeared.[158]

There have been a number of studies that have found the number of parties in the coalition or the number of spending ministers to have no effects on fiscal policies. Freitag and Sciarini (2001) denote, in their study of EU member states (from 1978 to 1997), that the number of parties in the government does not matter for budgetary performance. Leachman *et al.* (2007) find that the number of parties in government coalition is a poor predictor of fiscal performance. Mireau, Jong-A-Pin and de Haan (2007) ascertain, in their study of 20 OECD countries for the period 1970–2003, that neither the number of parties in government nor the number of spending ministers played a role in influencing the likelihood of fiscal adjustment.

Some studies have considered the effects of coalition governments on more specific features of tax policies. Ashworth and Heyndels (2001) find a significant correlation between the persistence of tax structures and the number of parties in the coalition. Their study also indicates that the correlation between the

158 Elgie and McMenamin (2008) suggest that political fragmentation would have effects on budgetary outcomes only in older democracies with high level of institutionalisation.

number of parties in the legislature and the persistence of tax structure is more significant than the correlation for the number of parties in the government. Hallerberg and Basinger (1998) find a moderate but significant effect of the number of veto players (including the number of parties in the coalition) on the percentage reduction in the top personal income tax rate: the more parties there are in the coalition, the smaller the reduction.

5.3.2.4. Fractionalisation of Government and Legislature

In addition to the absolute number of parties in the government, the effects of party fractionalisation or power dispersion within the cabinet and legislature have been examined in a number of empirical studies. Most of the studies have found that fractionalisation of the government or the legislature or both play a role in shaping public finances.

The effective number of parties in the legislature has been found to be associated with higher expenditures. Crepaz (1998) demonstrates, in his study of 18 industralised countries (from 1965 to 1986), that the effective number of parties in the legislature is associated with a higher level of welfare expenditures. Scartascini and Crain (2002) show that the number of effective parties represented in the legislature is positively correlated with total spending for a panel of OECD countries 1970 and 1990 and for a larger sample of world countries between 1980 and 1996. Crepaz and Moser (2004) conclude, in their study of 15 OECD countries (1960–1996), that the larger the number of effective parties in the legislature, the higher the current government disbursements, civilian government consumption and social transfer payments. Further, they show that an increase in the effective number of parties leads to higher levels of spending on subsidies and transfers, but to lower level of spending appropriated for public goods.

Fractionalisation of government and legislature has also been examined with regard to their effects on deficits. Volkerink and de Haan (2001) conclude, in their study of OECD countries (between 1971 and 1996), that more fragmented governments have higher deficits.[159] In addition, they show that the more fragmented the whole parliament is, the larger the central government's budget deficit. Elgie and McMenamin (2008) endorse these findings with a OECD sample, but find that when ten non-OECD countries are added to the sample, the effects of fractionalisation become insignificant. Huber, Kocher and Sutter (2003) infer, from their study of 21 OECD countries from 1970 to 1999, that the power dispersion within the government (measured by Banzhaf index) is a significant predictor of deficit levels: coalitions with equally strong partners run significantly higher deficits than coalitions with one dominating party. Eslava (2006) ascertains, for a large set of developed and developing countries, that less frag-

159 They show, however, that the impact of effective number of parties in the government was negligible in the 1970s.

mented governments (measured by a Herfindahl type index for the fraction of seats held by the different parties represented in the legislature) are associated with lower deficits. Padovano and Venturi (2001) show that more fractionalised governments in Italy are associated with higher deficits, while more fractionalised oppositions are correlated with lower deficits.[160] In addition, their results indicate that fragmentation of the opposition played a relatively more important role in *deficit* decisions than in *spending* decisions: the opposition parties were more concerned about the choice between taxes and debt to finance public expenditures than about setting their level. Galli and Padovano (2002) endorse the findings of Padovano and Venturi (2001): they find that government fragmentation (as measured by the Herfindhal index of the parliamentary seats of the parties that did not vote against the government in the initial confidence debate) explains a significant part of the dynamics of the Italian public deficits between 1951 and 1991, compared with the determinants suggested by alternative theories. They show that more fragmented coalitions are associated with higher deficits. They also consider the effects of the fragmentation of the opposition (measured by the Herfindhal index of the parliamentary seats of the parties that voted against the government in the initial confidence) and find that lower fragmentation of opposition is associated with higher deficits. Lagona and Padovano (2007) find that fractionalisation of government and legislature have effects on budget deficit (the higher the fractionalisation, the higher the deficits) but no effects on levels of expenditure. Fabrizio and Mody (2006) find, for a sample of ten CEE countries (new and potential members of the EU), that more fragmented government coalitions tend to have higher deficits (but only when juxtaposed with ideological orientation). Elgie and McMenamin (2008) replicate the study by Volkerink and de Haan (2001) and confirm their results with an OECD sample.

Concerning tax policy, the effect of the fractionalisation of legislature has been explored by Ashworth and Heyndels (2001). They concentrate on tax structures in OECD countries and detect a significant correlation between the persistence of tax structures and the effective number of parties in the legislature. They show that it will take a government longer to return to its ideal tax structure if the effective number of parties in parliament is higher. Further, their study indicates that the correlation between the number of parties in the parliament and the persistence of tax structure is more significant and also higher than the correlation between the number of parties in the government and the persistence of tax structure. The effect of the fractionalisation of government on taxation has been examined by Steinmo and Tolbert (1998). They find that tax burdens are lowest in majoritarian governments, moderate in shifting coalition governments (with no party that would be substantially more powerful than other

160 Therefore, Padovano and Venturi (2001) conclude that the data provides support for their version of war of attrition model (see section 5.3.1.2.2.).

parties) and highest in dominant coalition governments (where the dominant party controls consistently less than 50 percent of the seats).

There have been some studies, however, indicating that fractionalisation of government or parliament has insignificant effects on public finances. Ricciuti (2004a) concludes that fractionalisation of government played only a marginal role in explaining the budget surpluses or deficits. In addition, Ricciuti (2004a) considers the effects of fractionalisation of the opposition and the parliament as a whole, and finds only marginal effects on fiscal outcomes. Woo (2003), in his study of 57 countries (between 1970 and 1990), ascertains that government fractionalisation (measured by Rae index) had no significant effects on deficits. Tujula and Wolswijk (2004) find that the effective number of parties in the parliament had no effect on budget balances in 22 OECD countries (in the period 1970–2002).

5.3.2.5. Duration of Governments

In addition to the effects of the composition and fractionalisation of the government, the impacts of government duration on budget discipline have been explored in a number of empirical studies.[161] Several studies have shown that shorter-lived governments tend to run larger deficits. Grilli, Masciandro and Tabellini (1991) show, in a sample of 18 OECD countries, that lack of fiscal discipline is almost exclusively limited to proportional electoral systems and that the one feature that appears to be responsible is the short duration of governments: the shorter the tenure of government, the larger the deficits. De Haan and Sturm (1994) demonstrate that the stability of governments had significant effects on the level of debt. Freitag and Sciarini (2001) find, for 14 EU member states between 1978 and 1997, that among a number of political and institutional variables only the political instability of a country (measured by the rate of government turnover) has had a consistent impact on the budget: the more frequently the government changed, the higher the deficits.

A number of studies have pointed to opposite results. Borrelli and Royed (1995) find no effects of the duration of governments on the level of deficit. Ricciuti (2004a) finds, for a panel of 19 OECD countries from 1975 to 1995, no evidence that a faster turnaround in government leads to a lack of fiscal disci-

161 The number of parties in government and parliament is one of the factors that is likely to influence the duration of governments. Warwick (1979, 1994) found that government durability is inversely related to the number of parties in the government. Lijphart (1984) shows that there is a clear negative correlation between the effective number of parties in the parliament and the duration of cabinets in a parliamentary system. As Mueller (1997, p. 137) underlines, however, the instability of government in multiparty systems cannot be attributed solely to the number of parties that gain representation but rather to the combination of multiparty system with confidence requirement and the use of majority vote.

pline and higher government expenditure. The same has been found by Leachman *et al.* (2007). Sakamoto (2001) even shows that governments with a shorter tenure run smaller deficits than durable governments.

5.3.3. Summary

The results of empirical studies exploring the effects of the number and kinds of participants in the budgetary process on public finance are summarised in Table 5.3. Altogether, the empirical evidence presents a complicated, even confusing, picture. Although many studies have found patterns between budgetary outcomes and the number of parties in the legislature or in the parliament, the minority status of the government or fractionalisation of the government and parliament, other studies exploring these relationships have found either contrary or insignificant effects. The effects of minority governments on budget deficits, for example, illustrate the diverging results of empirical studies very clearly. The contradictory conclusions of the studies reviewed above can be at least partly explained by the following factors. First, most of the studies have not distinguished between public finance choices in fiscally "good" times and "difficult" times. As discussed above, however, the effects of the institutional variables can be different: the characteristics that can hinder increases in spending may not be the same that are conducive to the adoption of painful corrective fiscal measures in the face of exogenous shock. Second, most of the studies have not explored the possibility for non-linear effects between institutional features and public finance outcomes. Third, the studies focusing on size fragmentation have neglected the countervailing effects that more centralised budgetary procedures (discussed in chapter 6) can have on common-pool resource problems in budgeting. Fourth, the characteristics of size fragmentation have not been juxtaposed with specific elements of electoral systems, which are likely to either reinforce or counteract the problems arising from size fragmentation. Fifth, the studies have not taken into account the different nature of size fragmentation problems in parliamentary and presidential systems.

For example, the application of the law of $1/n$ to the size of governing majority is complicated by a number of factors. Although simple budgetary commons models predict that the larger the number of graziers on the commons, the more severe the common-pool problems of budgeting, one needs to account for additional factors that may result in a significantly different decision-making dynamics than the basic budgetary commons models would foresee. As discussed in section 5.3.1.1.2., the effects of the "law of $1/n$" may be counteracted by the reduced possibilities to externalise the tax costs of adopted expenditure to the opposition and by the stronger bargaining power that the governing majority has *vis-à-vis* the opposition. Even these explanations, however, may present an overly simplified picture. In order to account for the effects of the size of the governing majority on budgeting, one should take into account the general form of government and the features of the electoral systems that are likely to influence the level of party discipline. If the level of party discipline is high, needing a "hedge" against defections may not be as important as in systems with lower party discipline. In parliamentary systems with closed lists, for example, the number of excess seats is likely to play a smaller role than in presidential systems or in parliamentary systems with open lists. Also, the specific electoral incentives provided by the electoral systems are likely to mediate the effects that the size of governing majority may have on budgetary decision-making. In electoral systems where the cultivation of personal vote and pursuit of particularistic spending are prevalent, the increasing size of the governing majority may increase the particularistic tendencies of the spending mix, whereas in systems with a low level of personal vote, the effects of the law of $1/n$ are less likely to be prevalent. Since the existing studies exploring the effects of the size of governing majority have not taken into account these interaction effects, it may help to explain why the empirical results studies point to contradictory conclusions.

There are, however, some patterns between governing arrangements and public finances that tend to be somewhat clearer than others – or what have not been refuted so far, at least. These include, for example, the association between larger effective number of parties in the legislature and higher expenditures, larger number of parties in the government and higher expenditures, larger number of cabinet ministers and higher expenditures. When juxtaposing these results with the empirical studies on electoral systems, they seem to point to converging evidence: more proportional electoral systems are also associated with higher expenditures. This is also intuitively plausible, since more proportional systems are associated with more parties in the government and the legislature. So far, however, there have been only few studies that have attempted to separate the direct and indirect effects of electoral systems (see, e.g., Persson, Roland and Tabellini 2007).

On the whole, the effects of the number and kinds of participants on budget *deficits* appear to be less consistent than the impacts on *spending levels*. The effects on government revenues and taxation have received relatively less attention compared with expenditure levels and deficits; therefore, further studies should certainly explore the fiscal results in a more disaggregated way than most of the studies have done so far. The effects of institutional variables on revenues may play an important role in explaining why higher expenditures do not always translate to higher deficits.

Another recurring problem in common-pool models of budgeting is the failure to take into account the transaction costs involved in forming the coalitions for adopting packages of particularistic expenditure. In principle, as the number of decision-makers increases, the higher become the transaction costs for finding a viable majority of votes for each proposed programme; hence, higher transaction costs should exercise countervailing effects to the law of $1/n$. This aspect, however, has been ignored by most studies that proceed from the common-pool models of budgeting.

Also, the models focusing only on *either* common-pool aspects *or* veto players are likely to present only a partial picture. More elaborate models – combining the elements of both common-pool and veto player models, while accounting for their potentially contradictory predictions – would do a better job of explaining the dynamics of decision-making in different kinds of fiscal situations. Although, at first sight, the *budgetary commons* and the *veto players* models give rise to diverging predictions with regard to the level of expenditures in coalition governments, a more elaborate model would regard these theoretical perspectives as complementary. For example, the more the veto players have incentives and possibilities to demand side-payments and the more they have opportunities to externalise the costs of increased expenditures to constituencies of other players, the more similar would be the effect of the number of veto players to the effect of *n* graziers on budgetary commons.

Table 5.3.: Effects of governing arrangements on public finances

	Spending	**Taxation**	**Deficit, surplus, fiscal adjustment**
Larger size of governing Majority	Lower spending: Lagona and Padovano (2007) Cube relationship: Mukherjee (2003)	Higher revenues: Lagona and Padovano (2007)	Lower deficit: Volkerink and de Haan (2001) Lagona and Padovano (2007) Higher surplus: Elgie and McMenamin (2008) No effect: Huber, Kocher and Sutter (2003) Leachman *et al.* (2007) Positive effect on fiscal adjustment: Lavigne (2006) No effect on fiscal adjustment: Mireau, Jong-A-Pin and de Haan (2007)

	Spending	Taxation	Deficit, surplus, fiscal adjustment
Minority government (vs majority government)	No effect: de Haan and Sturm (1994, 1997)	Lower revenues: Perotti and Kontopoulos (2002)	Higher deficit: Edin and Ohlsson (1991) Lower deficit: Sakamoto (2001) Borelli and Royed (2001) No effect on deficit: Grilli, Masciandaro and Tabellini (1991) Freitag and Sciarini (2001) Negative effect on fiscal adjustment: Edin and Ohlsson (1991)
Larger number of parties in the legislature	Higher spending: Scartascini and Crain (2002) Crepaz and Moser (2004) Mukherjee (2003)		No effect on deficit: Tujula and Wolswijk (2004)

	Spending	Taxation	Deficit, surplus, fiscal adjustment
Coalition governments (vs single-party governments); weak governments (coalition governments and minority governments)	Higher spending: Persson, Roland and Tabellini (2007) No effect: de Haan and Sturm (1994, 1997)	Higher revenues: Steinmo and Tolbert (1998)	Higher deficit: Roubini and Sachs (1989a, 1989b) Corsetti and Roubini (1993) Alesina and Perotti (1995) Lower deficit: Sakamoto (2001) Tujula and Wolswijk (2004) No effect: de Haan and Sturm (1994, 1997) de Haan, Sturm and Beekhuis (1999) Hahm, Kamlet and Mowery (1996) Sakamoto (2001) Woo (2003)
Larger number of parties in the government	Higher spending: Kontopoulos and Perotti (1999) Perotti and Kontopoulos (2002) Harrinvirta and Mattila (2001) Mulas-Granados (2003) Bawn and Rosenbluth (2006)	Higher revenues: Harrinvirta and Mattila (2001)	Higher deficit: Kontopoulos and Perotti (1999) Perotti and Kontopoulos (2002) Balassone and Giordano (2001) Franzese (2002b) No effect on deficits: Freitag and Sciarini (2001) Leachman et al. (2007) Shorter fiscal consolidation: Illera and Mulas-Granados (2008)

	Spending	Taxation	Deficit, surplus, fiscal adjustment
			Revenue-based adjustment: Mulas-Granados (2003) Harrinvirta and Mattila (2001) No effect on fiscal adjustment: Mireau, Jong-A-Pin and de Haan (2007)
More fractionalised government	Higher spending: Padovano and Venturi (2003) No effect: Lagona and Padovano (2007)	Lower revenues: Steinmo and Tolbert (1998)	Higher deficit: Volkerink and de Haan (2001) Huber, Kocher and Sutter (2003) Eslava (2006) Galli and Padovano (1998) Padovano and Venturi (2003) Fabrizio and Mody (2006) No effects: Ricciuti (2004a) Woo (2003) Elgie and McMenamin (2008)
More fractionalised legislature	Lower proportion of public goods: Crepaz and Moser (2004)		Higher deficit: Volkerink and de Haan (2001) Elgie and McMenamin (2008) No effect: Ricciutti (2004a) Elgie and McMenamin (2008)

	Spending	Taxation	Deficit, surplus, fiscal adjustment
More fraction-alised opposition			Lower deficit: Padovano and Venturi (2003) No effect: Ricciuti (2004a)
Larger number of spending ministers	Higher spending: Kontopoulos and Perotti (1999) Perotti and Kon-topoulos (2002)		Higher deficit: Perotti and Kon-topoulos (2002) Woo (2003) Ricciuti (2004a) Volkerink and de Haan (2001) Lower surplus: Brosens and Wierts (2007) Elgie and McMenamin (2008) No effect: Elgie and McMenamin (2008) Shorter fiscal con-solidation: Illera and Mulas-Granados (2008)
Short duration of government			Higher deficit: Grilli, Masciandaro and Tabellini (1991) De Haan and Sturm (1994) Freitag and Sciarini (2001) Lower deficit: Sakamoto (2001) No effect: Borelli and Royed (1995) Leachman et al. (2007)

5.4. Bicameral versus Unicameral Legislatures

5.4.1. Theoretical Propositions

Analogously to the organisation of the executive, the effects that the institutional structure of the legislature can have on fiscal outcomes can be explored by using *common-pool* and *veto players* models.

Veto players models view the second chamber in a bicameral legislature as constituting an additional veto point in the budgeting system.[162] As discussed in previous sections, a larger number of veto points is seen as contributing to reduced decisiveness of a polity (leading to status quo bias in policy-making) while at the same time enhancing its resoluteness, expressed in credible commitments to chosen policy paths (Tsebelis and Money 1997; Cox and McCubbins 2001). Hence, one can expect that in bicameral systems there are pressures to hinder increases in expenditures and taxes. Riker (1992) emphasises that the likelihood of legislative cycling between different majorities is lower in bicameral legislatures than in unicameral ones; therefore, bicameralism can be expected to lead to more stable expenditure levels (see also Hammond and Miller 1987; Brennan and Hamlin 1992; Tsebelis and Money 1997; Levmore 1992).[163]

Crepaz (1998) and Crepaz and Moser (2004) argue that the chambers in bicameral legislatures constitute *competitive* veto points, for whom the use of vetoes is less costly than for *collective* veto points (see also section 5.3.1.2.1.). Since the vetoes used by the chambers are institutionalised and "faceless", they can be used more often without bringing about a negative public backlash. Hence, Crepaz (1998) predicts that bicameral systems with symmetrical chambers would have lower levels of welfare expenditures. Crepaz and Moser (2004) predict that bicameralism exercises constraining effects on budget expenditures.

At the same time, once deficits have already occurred (e.g., as a result of an exogenous shock), bicameral systems, because of their lower level of decisiveness, can be expected to have difficulties in reacting promptly by taking corrective fiscal measures. Once a bicameral system manages to undertake fiscal consolidation, however, the consolidation is likely to be more credible and sustained longer than in unicameral systems.

162 Even if the upper chamber has only suspensive powers, it can be viewed as playing an important role in policy-making because of its power to delay legislation and to demand concessions from the impatient lower chamber (Tsebelis and Money 1997).

163 As Riker (1992) explains, because of frequent turnovers, current majorities in unicameral legislatures have incentives to extract more benefits from public spending, in order to compensate for future losses of transfers, which, in turn, can lead to increased demand for transfers and spending. For critical discussions on whether cyclical majorities in fact characterise decision-making in real-life legislative settings, see, for example, Tullock (1981) and Stratman (1997).

To what extent the second chamber would act as a veto point, depends, *inter alia*, on its party composition. If both chambers are dominated by the same party (or a coalition of parties), fiscal consolidation may be easier, since the costs of expenditure cuts or tax increases can be shifted to supporters of the opposition party (or parties). When the two chambers are dominated by different parties, externalisation of the costs of corrective fiscal measures is not as easy anymore and the preferences of opposition parties have to be taken into account when compiling the fiscal package.

Drawing on Alezina and Drazen (1991), Schwarz (2006) argues that bicameralism can give rise to *a war of attrition* in reducing budget deficits. He suggests that the delay in fiscal stabilisation can result from two different mechanisms. First, the two chambers may become engaged in a war of attrition game when there is uncertainty with regard to the voting outcome in the upper chamber. Second, the persistence of deficits can arise from ideological divisions between the two chambers, if the opposition parties have motives to vote strategically. Schwarz (2006, pp. 91–92) points out that the model proposed by Alezina and Drazen (1991) assumes that parties in the coalition benefit from cooperation; however, the incentive structure may be different when the game involves a governing coalition in the lower chamber and a dominating opposition in the upper chamber. In such a case, even if there is no uncertainty with regard to voting outcomes in the upper chamber, deficits may persist, because the opposition parties may gain from making the governing coalition "look bad" (i.e., unable to curb deficits). Hence, even if the opposition parties would gain from reduced deficits, these benefits may be outweighed by the advantages of increasing their chances to form the government after next elections (in the hope that the voters would make the incumbent coalition responsible for poor budgetary outcomes). However, if opposition parties are certain of the favourable electoral outcome of the next elections, they may be more willing to agree to the reduction of deficits; otherwise, they would have to undertake painful budgetary cuts themselves in the future.

In the *budgetary commons* models, both the number of chambers and the total number of legislators have been conceptualised as constituting the *n* actors. As discussed in section 5.3.1.1.1., the first common-pool models of budgeting (starting with Weingast, Shepsle and Johnsen 1981) focused on the number of legislators and predicted that the larger the number of legislators, the more severe the common-pool problems in budgeting would be. Heller (1997) argues that the number of chambers increases the number of graziers on the commons and access points for interest groups outside the legislature; an increase in the number of decision-makers who can influence the content of the budget implies a greater number of deals that have to be cut to get the budget adopted. Since it is easier to cut deals to raise spending than to raise taxes, bicameral legislatures would lead to higher spending and higher deficits. Persson, Roland and Tabellini (1997, pp. 1176–1179) demonstrate that if both chambers in a bicameral system can adopt independent budgetary decisions, common-pool problems of budgeting become more severe, compared with a unicameral system.

Tullock (1959), in contrast, argues that bicameral legislatures where the chambers have different electoral bases can mitigate the problem of overgrazing the fiscal commons. The constraining effect, however, presumes that both chambers have to reach an agreement on budgetary decisions and can block each other's decisions. Buchanan and Tullock (1962, ch. 16) suggest that although bicameral legislatures entail higher decision costs, they are likely to bring about smaller external costs, since they increase the effective majority required for passing a policy (especially if the basis of representation in the two chambers is significantly different). That, in turn, may imply lower levels of particularistic expenditures and more broad-based policies. Also, if representatives in the upper chamber have been elected by larger districts than those in the lower chamber, the problems of the "law of $1/n$" should be mitigated: the dilution of the geographic concentration of interests is likely to encourage programmes that encompass larger areas.

Bradbury and Crain (2001) call for integrating the *common-pool* and *veto player* approaches in analysing the effects of bicameral legislatures on fiscal outcomes. They emphasise the importance of distinguishing between chambers as n players and legislators as n players; they suggest conceptualising the two chambers as veto players and the number of legislators in each chamber as the n graziers. Bradbury and Crain emphasise that the existence of two chambers can mitigate common-pool resource problems in legislative budgeting; they predict that the "law of $1/n$" is less severe in bicameral legislatures; when reaching an agreement between the chambers requires unanimity, legislative trades would be significantly costlier *between* the chambers than *within* the chambers (pp. 312–313).

Further, in conceptualising the two chambers as veto players, Bradbury and Crain (2001) remind us that the chambers often have asymmetric bargaining powers; that, in turn, means that the size of the weaker chamber may have smaller effects on resulting policy outcomes than the size of the stronger chamber (p. 313). Altogether, they predict that the effect of the "law of $1/n$" on spending (in the form of higher expenditure associated with an additional legislator) would be larger in unicameral legislatures than in bicameral legislatures.

Again, conceptualising the number of legislators as the n graziers in budgetary decision-making can be criticised on the grounds pointed out in section 5.3.1.1. above. In a parliamentary setting (where parties have a strong control over their members), the role of each legislator in budgetary bargains might be significantly smaller than in a presidential system. Also, when members of legislature adhere to party discipline, the norm of universalism (or reciprocity) in compiling the budget is less likely to emerge among individual legislators. Further, in proportional electoral systems with closed lists, where the pressures to cater to the needs of home-districts are smaller, the model adopted by Bradbury and Crain (2001) may present a flawed picture.

5.4.2. Empirical Evidence

The empirical studies exploring the effects of bicameralism, unicameralism and the size of legislature on budgetary indicators point to diverging results: some find negative, some positive effects, and some no effects.

Bradbury and Crain (2002) analyse a panel of U.S. states and ascertain that the greater the difference in the interests represented by the chambers of a bicameral legislature, the smaller the per capita expenditures tend to be. In addition, their results suggest that legislatures with dissimilar chambers are more willing to spend on broad-based public goods (e.g., education) than on narrowly targeted programmes. Crepaz and Moser (2004) investigate the effects of bicameralism on current disbursements and civilian government consumption in 15 OECD countries (between 1960 and 1996) and find a negative effect on both.[164] Vatter (2005) examines the effect of bicameralism in OECD countries (from 1971 to 1996) and denotes that bicameral structures have significantly constrained the development of the welfare state. Similar results were found by Crepaz (1998). In contrast, Heller (1997), based on data from 17 countries (between 1965 and 1990), shows that bicameral legislatures in parliamentary systems are associated with higher spending and deficits. In a time-series study of Germany (from 1950 to 2000), Schwarz (2006) shows that different majorities in the two chambers induce higher central government deficits. In addition, he shows that the persistence of deficits arises from strategic voting by opposition parties in the upper chamber rather than from the uncertainty of voting outcomes (related to scarce majorities) in the upper chamber.[165] As he puts it, there is a misfit between a party system that is characterised by ideological polarisation (and intensive competition) and the institutional design of the decision-making process that requires cooperative decision-making (p. 91).

Bradbury and Crain (2001) explore the effects of bicameralism and the size of the legislature(s), using cross-country evidence from 36 countries, and observe that the partition of legislative power into two chambers exerts a considerable impact on fiscal policy: bicameral legislatures are associated with lower public expenditures in comparison with unicameral legislatures. In addition, Bradbury and Crain (2001) find a positive relationship between legislature size and spending (the "law of $1/n$") across countries, but the effect is far greater in unicameral legislatures than in bicameral legislatures. They view it as evidence for

164 At the same time, they find that bicameralism has no effects on social transfer payments.

165 As Schwartz (2006, p. 97) explains, even if the upper chamber is characterised by scarce majorities, parties seek to reduce the uncertainty with regard to voting outcomes in the upper chamber already when preparing the policy proposal by offering compromises or transfers.

the dampening effect of bicameralism on the "law of $1/n$" in budgeting. When checking the validity of the "law of $1/n$" separately in the different chambers in bicameral systems, Bradbury and Crain find support for it in the lower chambers but ambiguous results in upper chambers; they conjecture that such a result is caused by asymmetric distribution of powers between the chambers, biased towards greater power of the lower chamber. When the upper chamber has less impact on final outcomes, an additional member in the chamber would have a smaller effect on budgeting than an additional member in the lower chamber. (pp. 318–319) Ricciuti (2003) observes, in a panel of OECD countries, that the overall number of seats in the legislature(s) has an indefinite effect on expenditure levels, but when upper and lower chambers are distinguished, the number of seats in lower houses is positively linked to higher expenditure, while the number of seats in upper houses has negative impacts. In another study, however, Ricciuti (2004b), considering the effects of legislature size and structure on general government and welfare spending in 75 countries between 1990 and 1998, finds that neither legislature size nor bicameralism had a significant effect.

With regard to the effects of the "law of $1/n$", most of the empirical studies of the U.S. states have found that while the law has the predicted effect in upper chambers, it has insignificant or even opposite effects in lower chambers. The only study confirming the "law of $1/n$" in the lower chambers of the U.S. legislatures is by Shughart and Tollison (1986), who found the total size of Congress to be positively related to the number of bills passed and the level of government spending. All other studies, however, have found contrary results. Gilligan and Matsusaka (1995, 2001) examine the relationship between legislature size and spending, using the data of the U.S. states in the first and the second half of the 20th century, and find that in both time periods, spending increased with the size of state upper chambers but not with the size of state lower chambers. De Figueiredo (2003) examines the size of legislatures in the U.S. states (over the period 1865–1994) and ascertains that the legislature size has negative effects in lower chambers and insignificant effects in upper chambers. Primo (2006) analyses the U.S. states from 1969 to 2000 and shows that while the size of the upper chamber has significant positive effects on the level of spending, the size of the lower chamber has significant negative effects.

As Table 5.4. indicates, there have been no empirical studies that would have analysed the impacts of bicameralism or legislature size on revenues, spending mix or features of tax systems. With regard to the effects of bicameralism and legislature size (either the total size or the sizes of the respective chambers) on spending, the empirical studies point to clearly diverging evidence. While some studies have found positive effects of bicameralism on spending, others have found either negative or insignificant effects. The size of both chambers has also been found to have positive, negative and insignificant effects. In sum, it appears to be difficult to find clear associations between the cameral structure (and size) of the legislature and public finance when focusing on this particular institutional feature alone, without counting for the party system of the country and party-composition of the chamber(s).

Table 5.4.: Effects of cameral structure and legislature size on spending and deficit

	Spending	Deficit
Larger legislature size (total)	Higher spending: Bradbury and Crain (2001) No effect: Ricciuti (2003, 2004b)	
Bicameralism (versus unicameralism)	Higher spending: Heller (1997) Lower spending: Crepaz and Moser (2004) Vatter (2005) Bradbury and Crain (2001, 2002) No effect: Ricciuti (2004b)	Higher deficit: Heller (1997) Schwarz (2006)
Larger lower chamber	Higher spending: Ricciuti (2003) Shugart and Tollison (1986) Lower spending: De Figueiredo (2003) Primo (2006) No effect: Gilligan and Matsusaka (1995, 2001)	
Larger upper chamber	Higher spending: Gilligan and Matsusaka (1995, 2001) Lower spending: Ricciuti (2003) No effect: De Figueiredo (2003)	

Given the role that parties play in political systems (especially in parliamentary systems with proportional electoral rules), it would be analytically more fruitful to juxtapose the effects of bicameralism and the sizes of the different chambers with the electoral systems and other party-institutional variables. The interactions between the party system, party composition of the chambers and the cameral structure found by Schwarz (2006), in his case study of Germany, are certainly indicative in that regard. Further, an important shortcoming of the existing empirical studies is that they have not taken into account institutional differences between bicameral structures with regard to procedures for resolving the inter-cameral differences,[166] which can be expected to exercise a relevant impact on policy decisions (see Tsebelis and Money 1997). The existing studies have not distinguished between different bases of representation embodied in the upper chambers (territorial, sectoral, ethnic), which are also likely to shape the outcomes of legislative decision-making.

5.5. Direct Democracy Mechanisms

The two main mechanisms of direct democracy are referendum and popular initiative. Referenda, in turn, can be obligatory or optional. In the case of obligatory referenda the constitution prescribes the use of referenda for passing certain types of legislation. In the case of optional referenda, it is up to the legislature to decide whether an issue should be put on referendum.[167] Such optional referenda may be either binding or advisory. While in the case of referenda, the legislature is the "agenda-setter", popular initiatives allow citizens to become either agenda-setters or veto-setters. As agenda-setters, citizens can propose a piece of legislation that will be decided by ballot, provided that they manage to secure a certain number of signatures in favour of the initiative. As veto-setters, citizens can initiate a ballot on an issue adopted by the legislature and have it overturned, if it fails to gather a required number of votes. (Mueller 1996, ch. 12) Constitutions differ with regard to whether they limit the issue areas in which referenda or initiatives can be used and whether on some issues referenda are required. The constitution may require a referendum for enacting a range of budgetary decisions (e.g., for incurring debt or increasing taxes) or it may explicitly ban the use of referenda in budgeting and taxation. Also, referenda and initiatives may differ with regard to implementation procedures: Are there quorum requirements? Does the legislature have to adopt a measure itself before putting it on referendum? Can measures adopted in a referendum be amended only by another initiative or by the legislature itself? (Matsusaka 2005b)

---

166 For a detailed discussion on the different kinds of procedures, including the navette system and conference committees, see Tsebelis and Money (1997).

167 For a further discussion on different kinds of referenda, see Suksi (1993) and Hug (2005).

5.5.1. Theoretical Propositions

When viewing the referenda through the lens of *budgetary commons* models, then, at first sight, one may expect substantial common-pool resource problems, since the number of budgetary graziers is extended from the number of legislators to the number of voters. On the other hand, one has to keep in mind that common-pool resource problems of budgeting are likely to more severe when the graziers can engage in logrolls in order to gain support for each other's (inefficient) projects and are able to externalise the project costs to non-coalition members. Since referenda usually present choices in an unbundled way, logrolling is clearly inhibited (Besley and Coate 2000; Bails and Tieslau 2000). Even if referenda included bundled issues, transaction costs for vote-trading would be too high and the use of secret ballots would render it impossible to identify defectors (Tullock 1959, p. 571). Thus, referenda is considered to reduce decision-externalities of spending choices. As Feld (2002, p. 8) puts it, "The citizens in one district cannot easily coalesce with those of another district in order to exploit the resources of a third district." Also, given high transaction costs, it would be difficult for voters from different districts to negotiate logrolls over a series of issues presented to them in different referenda. Thus, as Matsusaka (2005a, p. 169) notes, "To the extent that inefficient logrolls are prevented or undone, external costs are lower under direct democracy than representative democracy." Altogether, direct democracy mechanisms are likely to work as a counterbalance to the incentives of elected representatives to "overgraze" the fiscal commons.

From the *veto players* perspective, the use of referenda in fiscal decisions can be viewed as bringing in an additional veto-point to the decision-making process – the public (Moser 1996; Feld 2002; Brunetti and Straubhaar 1996; Steunenberg 1992). General predictions of veto players approaches would thus be that the use of referenda is likely to bias policy decisions towards status quo (and constrain budgetary expansion, for example) but may at the same time prevent the making of necessary adjustments.

While the veto players and budgetary commons models have received some attention in theoretical discussions conceptualising the links between direct democracy mechanisms and public finance, the main theoretical point of departure has been the principal-agent problem and issues of *accountability* (see Matsusaka 1995, 2005a,b; Feld and Matsusaka 2003; Gerber 1996; Romer and Rosenthal 1978, 1979; Feld and Savioz 1997; Feld and Kirchgässner 2001a,b; Hug 2004). Referenda and initiatives are viewed as mechanisms for mitigating principal-agent problems between voters and politicians by providing voters as principals additional instruments for controlling and sanctioning their representatives. Direct democracy mechanisms are often conceived of as a way of bringing budgetary decisions closer to the preferences of the median voter. Although in principle, voters could enact their preferences by rewarding the candidates who have been responsive with re-election and punishing the dismissive ones by not re-electing them, political accountability in a representative system can be jeopardised by a number of factors. Frey (1994) has argued that the Schumpeter-Downs model is only valid in election years, whereas in non-election years, parties and politicians have great discretionary powers in their disposal with regard to policy decisions, since voters do not possess instruments that would enable them to effectively sanction politicians for passing decisions that are detrimental to voters' interests.[168] Further, Frey emphasises that voters discount heavily earlier decisions, which further increases the discretionary freedom of elected representatives. Informational problems have been underlined by Feld (2002, p. 8), who argues that high marginal private costs and low marginal private benefits of gathering pertinent information by voters and free-riding problems in monitoring the elected representatives impair correct evaluations of the incumbent parties or representatives, which, in turn, weakens the accountability-enforcing role of elections (see also Kessler 2005; Kau and Rubin 1979; Peltzman 1984). Frey (1994), Bohnet and Frey (1994) and Frey and Kirchgässner (1994) underline the communication-enhancing role of referenda, owing to public discussions taking place in the pre-referendum phase, which provide both citizens and their representatives with additional information on policy choices. Matsusaka (1992) suggests that the institution of popular initiative can mitigate the information problems by informing the representatives about voters' policy preferences that have not reached the legislative agenda through the representative process. Hence, referenda and initiatives can enhance accountability by providing an additional check on policy choices proposed or adopted by politicians. Initiatives can have a direct impact on policy by overriding undesired policy choices and an indirect impact by posing a threat that gives political representatives stronger incentives to ensure that chosen policies are in compliance with the will of the electorate (Matsusaka 2005b, p. 192).

Altogether, the mechanisms of direct democracy can curb politicians' tendencies to pursue their personal interests and constrain logrolling, vote-trading, political cartels and problems arising from agenda-control (see Shubik and van der Heyden 1978; Romer and Rosenthal 1978, 1979; Frey 1994). As Anderson (2002, p. 82) points out, the availability of institutions of direct democracy to voters reduces the lucrativeness of rent-seeking by rendering pork-laden legislation less secure (and hence less attractive for concentrated interest groups). In addition to the preventive role, "Initiatives provide the possibility of correcting logrolling at the parliamentary stage ex post facto by issue unbundling." (Feld 2002, p. 8) Referenda and popular initiatives can be viewed as valuable mechanisms for correcting political failures of representative democracy in public fi-

168 As an alternative to the Schumpeterian-Downsian model of representative democracy, Frey (1994) puts forth a model of the "classe politique", according to which a coalition of established parties and politicians acts against voters and taxpayers.

nance. By creating a "contestable decision market" (Zimmermann and Just 2000), these institutions "allow the citizens to interfere in taxation and spending decisions of representative bodies of the democratic system when decisions deviate too strongly from their own interests" (Feld 2002, p. 7).

Given that referenda are viewed as a remedy for several kinds of problems arising from principal-agent relations, one would expect that the use of referenda moves policy choices in public finance closer to the preferences of the public. Pommerehne (1983, 1990) argues that referenda and initiatives render the supply of public goods more demand-oriented and less supply-driven, approximating the level and mix of public goods to the preferences of the electorate. Whether moving policy choices closer to the preferences of the median voter leads to higher or lower expenditures, taxes and deficits, in turn, depends on the fiscal preferences of the voters. If voters are assumed to be fiscal conservatives (see Peltzman 1992; Moak 1982; Alesina, Perotti and Tavares 1998; Skilling and Zeckhauser 2002, among others),[169] extensive use of direct democracy mechanisms would lead to more constrained expenditure levels, lower taxes and lower budget deficits. Proceeding from such an assumption, Romer and Rosenthal (1979) conjecture that referenda will refrain public agencies from overspending. Pommerehne (1978) predicts that tax rates are lower when taxpayers can decide themselves on the bundle of public goods supplied. Feld and Kirchgässner (1999) suggest that voters would be more reluctant to increase public debt when given the right to voice their opinion in a fiscal referendum. In contrast, if one subscribes to Buchanan's (1958, 1987) notion that voters favour expansion of current expenditures but without corresponding increase in taxes, one would expect higher expenditures, lower tax revenues and higher deficits in jurisdictions with more widely used elements of direct democracy.

Although most of the recent literature on the effects of direct democracy mechanisms on policy-making has viewed it as a possibility for correcting the failures of political markets and moving policy choices closer to the median voter, a number of warnings have been put forth by some authors. The main perils of direct democracy are considered to emerge from the role interest groups play in agenda-setting and discussion of ballots. Brunetti and Straubhaar (1996),

169 Peltzman (1992) analyses the voting behaviour in the U.S. presidential, senatorial and gubernatorial elections in 1955–1988 and finds that voters "penalise" federal and state spending growth. Peltzman notes that the voters' basic objection appears to be to spending, not just to the part financed by taxes. In other words, "voters are not pacified by deficit finance" (p. 329). Alesina, Perotti and Tavares (1998) also find in their analysis of election outcomes and opinion polls for 19 OECD countries that governments that committed themselves to tight fiscal policies are no more likely to be thrown out of office than others, nor do their popularity ratings go down. Rather, they find evidence for the contrary: undertaking fiscal adjustments that focus on current spending cuts, the incumbent government can increase the probability of remaining in power. Skilling and Zeckhauser (2002) claim that voters favour small debt levels over large debt levels and are especially inclined to do so when the debt levels are already large.

for example, argue that well-organised interest groups may take advantage of the institutions of direct democracy for the purpose extracting rents. Anderson (2002) draws on Miller (1999, p. 2) and points to the "undemocratic" side of direct democracy by drawing attention to the fact that power in initiative campaigns is often focused in the hands of a small group of people who are not accountable to the general public. The costliness of initiative process imposes barriers of entry and clearly circumscribes the circle of citizen-legislators who can make use of this instrument (Anderson 2002, p. 87). Matsusaka (2005b, p. 192) points to the possibility that referenda might not necessarily move policy choices closer to the preferences of the median voter: for example, if the ballot boils down to two choices, one proposed by the legislature and another by an interest group, the limited choice presented to the voters might not include the ideal policy preferred by the median voter. Moreover, threats of starting a popular initiative by extreme interest groups can move a policy choice further away from the preferences of the median voter, when the relations between representatives and voters are characterised by asymmetric information: because of prevailing uncertainty about voter preferences, elected representatives may opt for meeting an extreme interest group half-way rather than taking the risk that voters support the policy proposed by the extreme group in a referendum (see also Gerber and Lupia 1995; Matsusaka and McCarty 2001). Anderson (2002) argues that the instruments of direct democracy can be utilised by special interest groups for obtaining more durable rearrangements in the tax burden (e.g., in the form of tax exemptions) to their own benefit.

5.5.2. Empirical Evidence

There have been several empirical studies testing the effects of direct democracy on public finances. For most part, the empirical studies have focused on subnational differences in the United States and Switzerland. Voigt, Müller and Blume (2007), however, have also conducted a study on cross-country basis.

A number of studies have demonstrated that elements of direct democracy have constraining effects on *spending* and *revenue* levels. Bails and Tieslau (2000) show that the initiative procedure has significant impact on expenditure levels: U.S. states that provide their citizens with the initiative process have lower levels of per capita spending. Pommerehne and Schneider (1982) find, in their study of Swiss municipalities, that the budgets were the smallest in municipalities with direct democracy, followed by those that combined representative and direct democracy, and the budgets were the largest in municipalities with only representative democratic mechanisms. Schneider and Pommerehne (1983, cited in Kirchgässner 2001, p. 13) find, in a sample of 110 Swiss cities, that cities with direct democracy (where obligatory or optional referendum is provided for passing fiscal legislation like tax rates, the budget draft or budget deficits) had, *ceteris paribus*, almost 3 percentage points lower expenditure growth between 1965 and 1975 than cities with only representative democracy. Feld and Matsusaka (2003) show, in their panel study of 26 Swiss cantons from 1986 to 1997, that spending in cantons with a fiscal referendum (i.e., where new spending programmes must be approved by referendum) was 19 percent lower than for the median canton. Schaltegger (2001) observes, in his analysis of the consolidated sum of cantonal and local spending between 1980 and 1998, that the higher the direct democracy index characterising the canton, the lower was the cantonal and local spending. Merrifield (1991) infers, from a study of 49 U.S. states, that states allowing citizens to legislate directly or indirectly through the petition and initiative process had lower tax revenues. Matsusaka (1995, 2004) demonstrates, drawing upon extensive data from the 50 states of the United States between 1960 and 1990, that states where the constitution allows voter initiative have lower expenditures and lower revenues than states where the agenda-setting for referenda lies exclusively with the legislature.[170] Feld and Kirchgässner (2001a), in a study covering 26 Swiss cantons between 1986 and 1997, look at the effects of a mandatory fiscal referendum and find that both expenditures and revenues in cantons with the mandatory referendum are lower (by about 7 and 11 percent, respectively) compared to cantons without mandatory referenda. In their study on 134 large Swiss cities, Feld and Kirchgässner (2001b) ascertain that in cities where a budget deficit has to be approved by the citizenry, expenditure and revenue are 20 percent lower on average. Schaltegger and Feld (2008) find, in their panel study of 26 Swiss cantons, that cantons with fiscal referenda have lower levels of expenditures and revenues.

Some studies, however, have found that direct democracy increases government spending or has no effect on it. For the period before the Second World War, Matsusaka (2000) observes higher public spending in states allowing initiatives than in those that do not allow it. In an analysis of 50 U.S. states and 1305 local communities (for the year 1980), Zax (1989) denotes that communities with initiatives have higher public expenditure. Farnham (1990) finds that the availability of initiative has insignificant effects on spending in a sample of U.S. cities. Bodmer (2006) has argued that during the 1990s, direct democracy had no effect on spending in Swiss cantons. Feld and Kirchgässner (2001a) conclude that an easier use of initiatives (with regard to signature requirements) restricts cantonal spending per capita only in the case of cantons without fiscal referenda, while initiatives appear to be used to expand public spending in cantons with fiscal referenda. Voigt, Müller and Blume (2007) find, in their cross-country study of 30 countries, that a higher level of direct democracy does not translate into significantly lower central government expenditure and/or central

170 In addition, Matsusaka (2004) shows, using data from opinion surveys, that these patterns coincided with the direction favoured by a majority of voters. He interprets it as evidence against the "special interest subversion" perspective of the effects of direct democracy.

government revenue. Rather, they find evidence that countries with a higher level of direct democracy have higher government revenues.

With regard to the effects on budget *deficits*, most of the intra-country studies of Switzerland have found that the elements of direct democracy have either no effect on budget deficits or that they tend to increase budget deficits. Feld and Kirchgässner (2001a) find that there is no significant difference in public debt between cantons with and without fiscal referenda, while budget deficits of the cantons with fiscal referenda are significantly higher than those of cantons without fiscal referenda.[171] Feld and Kirchgässner (2001b) report that there is no statistically significant impact of fiscal referenda on budget deficits of Swiss cities. Bodmer (2006) shows that direct democracy had no effect on deficits among the Swiss cantons. Intra-country studies of the U.S. and the cross-country study, however, found direct democracy to have constraining effects on debts and deficits. Voigt, Müller and Blume (2007) find that a higher degree of direct democracy leads to lower central government budget deficits. Kiewiet and Szakaly (1996) show, for a panel of the U.S. states from 1961 to 1990, that referendum approval of guaranteed debt constrains state borrowing. They find that those U.S. states that required a referendum on new bonds had 33 percent lower guaranteed debt per capita than with states with no such requirement. Bohn and Inman (1996) find that rules requiring debt approval by referendum reduce public debt, but this reduction comes at the expense of capital investment rather than general spending.

In addition to the aggregate levels of revenues, spending and deficits, some studies have explored the effects of direct democracy on the composition of revenues. Matsusaka (1995, 2004) shows that the initiative-states in the U.S. rely less on taxes and more on user-fees and charges for services than non-initiative states. Similar results have been found by Feld and Matsusaka (2003) for Switzerland: in the budgets of the cantons with fiscal referenda, user-charges make up a larger proportion than in cantons with more limited popular rights. With regard to the tax mix and characteristics of tax systems, Anderson (2002) shows that initiatives in the U.S. have often been used reallocate the tax burden (e.g., increasing sales taxes while decreasing property taxes, or introducing deductions and exemptions).

171 As Feld (2002, p. 11) explains it: "Since fiscal referenda appear to restrict revenue to a greater extent than spending at the cantonal level, it is no surprise that budget deficits of the cantons with fiscal referenda are significantly higher than those of cantons without fiscal referenda."

Table 5.5.: Effects of direct democracy on public finances

	Spending	Revenues	Deficit
Initiative	Higher spending: Matsusaka (2000) Zax (1989) Lower spending: Bails and Tieslau (2000) Matsusaka (1995, 2004) No effect: Franham (1990)	Lower revenues: Merrifield (1991) Matsusaka (1995, 2004)	
Fiscal referenda	Lower spending: Schneider and Pommerehne (1983) Feld and Matsusaka (2003) Feld and Kirchgässner (2001a,b) Schaltegger and Feld (2008)	Lower revenue: Feld and Kirchgässner (2001a,b) Schaltegger and Feld (2008) Higher proportion of user-charges: Matsusaka (1994, 2004) Feld and Matsusaka (2003)	Higher deficit: Feld and Kirchgässner (2001a) Lower deficit: Kiewiet and Szakaly (1996) Bohn and Inman (1996) No effect: Feld and Kirchgässner (2001b) Bodmer (2006)
Level of direct democracy	Lower spending: Pommerehne and Schneider (1982) Schaltegger (2001) No effect: Bodmer (2006) Voigt, Müller and Blume (2007)	No effect: Voigt, Müller and Blume (2007)	Lower deficits: Voigt and Blume (2006)

Table 5.5. summarises the results of the empirical studies exploring the effects of direct democracy on public finances. Altogether, the empirical evidence shows that allowing the use of initiative procedure is associated with lower revenues but can lead to lower or higher spending, depending on voter preferences. Fiscal referenda have been uniformly found to lead to lower spending and lower revenues, with ambiguous effects on deficit levels. The overall degree of direct democracy is associated with lower deficits, while the effect on spending and revenues is ambiguous. As the empirical studies show, it is analytically useful to distinguish between the initiative and fiscal referenda in considering the effects of direct democracy, since these two mechanisms can have different effects on public finance. Further studies should explore closer the effects of direct democracy mechanisms on the proportions of particularistic as opposed to broad-based expenditures in the budget and tax structure.

5.6. Judiciary and Constitutional Courts

The role of the judicial branch (especially constitutional courts) in influencing budgeting and taxation has received relatively little systematic attention so far.[172] Drawing on the analytical framework outlined in section 4.4., the impact of the judiciary can be analysed by focusing on its effects on accountability and coordination mechanisms characterising decision-making in public finance.

There have been a number of theoretical studies attempting to model the effects of judiciary on the *accountability* of other branches of government and on the quality of public policies resulting from their interaction and "division of work". Padovano, Sgarra and Fiorino (2003) provide a theoretical model of how an independent judiciary improves the accountability of the executive and legislature by inducing them to maximise the provision of public goods and preventing them from diverting public resources for their private use. Maskin and Tirole (2004) demonstrate that decision-making by the judiciary results in higher social welfare in situations where the majority would impose large losses upon the minority or where pork-barrel bargains lead to excessive power of minorities. Thus, because of its role in enhancing the accountability of the other two branches in policy-making process, an independent judiciary can enhance the public-regardedness of policies in public finance. Tridimas (2005) focuses on the accountability-enhancing function of the judiciary and its role in mitigating principal-agent problems between voters and their representatives by protecting individual rights from abuses of power. He investigates how judicial review and judicial independence affect the relative share of tax revenues in GDP. Tridimas predicts that the relative share of tax revenues decrease as the judicial independ-

172 There is, however, a host of studies looking at the effects of the characteristics of judiciary (primarily independence) on several other economic indicators like economic growth; see Henisz (2000) and Feld and Voigt (2003, 2006).

ence and powers of judicial review increase, since an independent judiciary can overturn policy measures like redistributive tax measures. He tests these predictions in a cross-section sample of 52 countries. While controlling for the effects of real income, age dependency, openness of the economy, the legal origins of a country and other socio-political variables, Tridimas shows that more extensive judicial review is associated with a smaller relative share of taxes in the economy.[173]

Veto players models would view a strong judiciary and especially a strong constitutional court with the power to invalidate laws and regulations as an additional veto-point in the policy-making process (Cox and McCubbins 2001, p. 33). An additional veto point embodied by the constitutional court can be expected to lower the level of decisiveness that characterises the polity and weaken its ability to deal with fiscal shocks. Drawing on some cases from Latin America where the decisions of constitutional courts have played an important role in hindering fiscal adjustment, Eslava (2006) conjectures that the stronger the involvement of the constitutional court in policy-making, the harder it is for the government to undertake fiscal adjustment to reduce budget deficit. As she explains, undertaking lasting fiscal adjustments usually requires spending cuts on items such as transfers, social security contributions and wage payments; thus, fiscal adjustments often impose costs that fall disproportionately on specific groups of the population. When these transfers are viewed as having acquired the nature of rights of the corresponding recipients, the constitutional courts are likely to interpret such cuts as unconstitutional. Eslava tests the hypothesis that greater judicial activism of courts in determination of the fiscal policy will lead to larger deficits and/or delayed reform on a sample of 23 Latin American and Caribbean countries (from 1996 to 2003). She finds that the degree of involvement of the courts in fiscal policy is "a key determinant of the level of deficit" (p. 29). She notes that though these results should be viewed as exploratory (due to data limitations), they indicate that analysing the role of the judiciary in fiscal policy choices would be a potentially fruitful avenue for future research.

Thus, on the one hand, strong constitutional courts may constrain the increasing of taxes; on the other hand, they may protect the entitlements to transfers, which, in turn, may translate into deficits, given constraints on taxes. Still, further studies on the effects of courts and the interaction on the effects on spending, taxes and deficits are warranted. A more elaborate framework for exploring the effects of constitutional review on framework laws in budgeting and taxation is presented in chapter 8.

---

173 As for judicial independence, Tridimas (2005) finds that it has a negative effect on the tax burden, but it is only significant at 10 percent level.

5.7. Summary and Discussion

The goal of this chapter was to give an overview of the recent literature examining the effects of political institutions on public finance: it focussed on how the position and boundary rules characterising a political setting influence the mechanisms of accountability and coordination in budgeting and taxation and, through these mechanisms, the resulting outcomes.

In exploring the impacts of political institutions on public finance, the existing literature has focused on a host of different aspects. Most commonly, the studies explore the effects of political institutions on levels of spending, revenue, debt and deficit. Some studies have also focused on the delays and duration of fiscal adjustments and the strategies adopted for fiscal consolidation. Only a small number of studies have explored the effects of political institutions on the spending mix and characteristics of tax systems.

Based on the existing empirical studies, one can point to a number of patterns between constitutional rules and public finance outcomes:

1. Presidential systems tend to have lower expenditure and revenue levels and higher proportion of parochial goods in the spending mix than parliamentary systems. Although the case studies indicate that presidential systems have disadvantages in maintaining fiscal discipline and undertaking fiscal adjustments, the large-n cross-country studies find no systematic effects of presidentialism on these aspects.
2. Proportional electoral systems are associated with higher expenditures, taxes, deficits and higher proportions of public goods and broad-based transfers in the budget than majoritarian systems. The more proportional the system is and the higher the level of personal vote, the higher are expenditures and deficits.
3. The empirical evidence on governing arrangements – the number and kinds of participants in executive and legislature – presents a complicated picture. Although many studies have found correlations between budgetary outcomes and the number of parties in the legislature or in the parliament, the minority status of the government or fractionalisation of the government and parliament, other studies exploring these relationships have found either contrary or insignificant effects. There are, however, some tendencies that tend to be somewhat clearer than others (or what have not been refuted so far). These include, for example, the association between larger effective number of parties in the legislature and higher expenditures, larger number of parties in the government and higher expenditures, larger number of cabinet ministers and higher expenditures.
4. The empirical studies on the effects of bicameralism and legislature size (either the total size or the sizes of the respective chambers) on spending point to clearly diverging evidence. While some studies have found positive effects

of bicameralism on spending, others have found either negative or insignificant effects. The size of both chambers has also been found to have positive, negative and insignificant effects.

5. The overall degree of direct democracy is associated with lower deficits, while the effect on spending and revenues is ambiguous. The use of popular initiative procedure is associated with lower revenues but can lead to lower or higher spending, depending on voter preferences. Fiscal referenda have been uniformly found to lead to lower spending and lower revenues, with ambiguous effects on deficit levels.
6. Strong (constitutional) courts protect entitlements to transfers; when combined with constraints of increasing taxes, this can translate into higher deficits.

As pointed out in sections 5.1.–5.6., the studies exploring the effects of political institutions on public finances are subject to a host of theoretical and empirical problems. In order to avoid repetition, only the cross-cutting problems are discussed here; for specific problems in the different strands of research, the reader is referred to the critiques in the previous sections. Also, the critique of the prevalent discourse in the emerging orthodoxy of constitutional public finance is put forth together with the critique of fiscal constitutionalist literature in section 6.5.2. In the current section, the critique remains "within the prevailing discourse".

As the discussions above show, the issues of accountability and coordination, arising from a particular political institution, can be closely intertwined and subject to *trade-offs*. While presidential systems may enhance fiscal accountability of the executive, the coordination of budgetary policy-making between the legislature and executive may be subject to difficulties. Further, weaker accountability of an individual legislator to the party in a presidential system may give rise to coordination problems within the legislature. While majoritarian systems (and proportional systems encouraging the cultivation of personal vote) enhance the accountability of individual legislators to their home-district, the coordination of budgeting *within* the legislature may become more complicated because of lower party discipline and the parochial imperative that the representatives are driven by, making the provision of public goods and maintaining efficient level of particularistic expenditures more complicated. Although a strong judiciary with extensive constitutional review powers may enhance the accountability of the other branches, having an additional veto point in the decision-making process on budgetary issues may hinder the adoption of potentially necessary but painful fiscal measures.

To what extent these interconnections and trade-offs come to the fore in theoretical models, depends on whether the models view individual legislators or parties or institutions as the main units of analysis. Looking at an *individual* level, for example, accountability mechanisms may be stronger in majoritarian systems than in proportional systems, but the coordination mechanisms between individual legislators in the legislative body may be significantly weaker. Since majoritarian systems result in fewer parties in the legislature, however, the coordination between *parties* might be easier than in proportional systems. Also, the accountability and coordination problems associated with a particular constitutional institution may differ, depending on whether one looks at the *legislative* or *executive* level. While majoritarian systems may lead to coordination problems between individual legislators, coordination on executive level might be a lot easier (than in proportional systems), owing to single-party governments that majoritarian systems usually lead to. An important shortcoming of many existing studies is that they confine themselves to a particular unit of analysis (be it individual, party or institution) and neglect the *interactions* between the individual, partisan and institutional incentives.

With regard to coordination problems in the policy arena of public finance, the existing literature employs primarily the *budgetary commons* and *veto players* approaches for exploring the effects of different political institutions. Although attractive because of their parsimony and intuitive appeal, these two approaches, in their simplest forms, may conceal more than they can reveal. The existing models may do a convincing job in explaining a particular phase in the decision-making process, but when other institutional aspects are brought up as well, a host of puzzles emerge. For instance, a model picturing the number of parties in the governing majority as the n graziers on budgetary commons appears straightforward at first sight. When additional questions – even about the simplest institutional arrangements – are asked, the "scene" on the commons becomes significantly more complicated. For example, in the case of a single-party majority government, one might indeed view the n to be equal to one. However, when the incentives provided by the electoral system are considered at the same time, then in a majoritarian system (and also in a proportional system with open lists), which provides stronger incentives for individual legislators to graze the budgetary commons in order to provide particularistic projects for their home-district, it would be more accurate to conceive of the individual legislators as making up the number of n. When some of the legislators have been elected by individual ballot and some by district ballot (like it is the case in Germany, Japan, Mexico, Croatia, among others),[174] the question of the size of n becomes even more complicated.

Juxtaposing the elements of presidentialism and parliamentarism with electoral systems is likely to complicate the counting of the graziers further. In a parliamentary system with majoritarian electoral rules, counting the number of graziers would be different than in a parliamentary system with a proportional system. Similarly, the fiscal commons in a presidential system with a proportionally elected legislature looks different from a presidential system combined

174 For an overview of mixed electoral systems, see Massicotte and Blais (1999).

with a majoritarian electoral system. The disciplining effects of a party on its members arise from two sources: the vote of confidence requirement and the role that the party plays in influencing the electoral chances of an individual legislator (which is larger in proportional system with party-lists but smaller in majoritarian systems and proportional systems with open lists). Thus, in a presidential system combined with a proportional electoral system with party-lists, the number of graziers can be better captured by the president plus the number of parties in the parliament, whereas in a presidential system with majoritarian electoral rules, the number of graziers may be significantly larger, since, given their greater independence from the party, individual legislators can be counted as graziers.

Further puzzles arise when the following questions are asked: Should one just count the number of parties in the governing coalition as the *n* or should one also include the number of opposition parties? Should coalition parties and opposition parties have equal weights when one counts them as graziers? On the one hand, as Mukherjee (2003) points out, the inherent instability of multiparty coalitions and the norm of universalism between the parties (arising from the prevailing uncertainties) should lead us to count the opposition parties as graziers. On the other hand, as Bawn and Rosenbluth (2006) have pointed out, the dividing lines between governing coalition and opposition are often clearly delineated (which would render coalition partners less willing to engage in logrolls and bargains with opposition parties) and coalition agreements can play an important role in guaranteeing the certainty of intra-coalition bargains and inhibit defection by coalition parties; from this perspective, one should count only the coalition partners rather than all the parties in the legislature as the *n* graziers. Thus, the enumeration of *n* graziers on the budgetary commons may become rather complicated, because such exercise is conditioned by several factors. For example, one can count the number of parties in the coalition as the *n* when the coalition has a solid majority and the political culture supports adherence to coalition agreement. When party discipline is weaker and adherence to coalition agreements is not a revered norm, counting the number of parties in the legislature as the *n* may be more justified. Counting all the parties in the legislature may appear particularly plausible in the case of minority governments, but even here, the situation may be more complex: if the minority government has one silent and solid supporter in the opposition, counting all other parties in the opposition would not be accurate either.

The view of political parties in the *coalition* as constituting *n* graziers on budgetary commons may also be problematic because of the different support bases and bargaining powers the parties have. The studies of Steinmo and Tolbert (1998) and a number of studies exploring the effects of fractionalisation of government point to an important direction in that regard. Coordination would be easier in a coalition government consisting of one large partner and one or more small partners than in a government where all coalition partners have equal powers in terms of parliamentary support base. As some theoretical and empirical studies have shown, while coalition governments are more likely to increase expenditures, a party constellation with one dominant party would be able to match this tendency with higher tax revenues. Moreover, once deficits have already been incurred, a constellation of coalition partners where one party is clearly dominant can facilitate swifter fiscal adjustment. Further studies should therefore take into account the power constellations of the parties in the coalition rather than just *counting* the number of parties in the coalition.

Though both budgetary commons models and veto players models appear plausible on their own, then the predictions they make (about the number of participants on budgetary commons) may sound contradictory, unless concrete conditions are specified and different kinds of veto players distinguished. More comprehensive political economy models of budgeting should address simultaneously the common-pool resource issues (including the "law of $1/n$" problem) and veto players aspects – and their potentially countervailing and reinforcing effects in different circumstances. An important link between veto players models and budgetary commons models has been brought out by Cox and McCubbins (2001, p. 46), who point to the tendency of systems with many veto points, prone to indecision, to trade private goods (at the expense of the fiscal commons) in order to attain the passage of decisions. Thus, an important puzzle that the studies in constitutional public finance have to address is: When do veto players become graziers and when do they remain constrainers? Do different veto players follow different patterns in this regard? On the whole, one can conjecture that the more the veto players have incentives and possibilities to demand side-payments and the more they have opportunities to externalise the costs of increased expenditures to constituencies of non-veto-players, the more similar would be the effect of the number of veto players to the effect of the n graziers on budgetary commons. In coalition governments, for example, the smaller the parties are and the narrower their support base, the more likely they are to behave as graziers.

The study by Crepaz and Moser (2004), discussed in section 5.3.1.2.1., certainly points to a right direction in addressing the aforementioned puzzle – the contradictory predictions that common-pool models and veto players models make – by distinguishing between collective and institutional veto players and by explicating how collective veto players can be enablers (in other words, behaving like graziers) in decisions concerning budget expenditures. Still, a host of unresolved issues remain. For example, the approach of Crepaz and Moser (2004) does not consider the behaviour of collective veto points in times of fiscal stress and fails to examine the costliness of exercising the veto in such a context. A further shortcoming of the approach put forth by Crepaz and Moser (2004) is that it is not entirely clear why competitive veto points (e.g., the second chamber in the bicameral parliament) would be more motivated to act as a *constrainer* rather than *enabler*: Why would the institutional veto point use its power as a constrainer instead of using the bargaining power it has for demanding side-payments and additional expenditures in the budget? Different kinds of second chambers may have very different incentives here and a simplified view of the second chamber as a constrainer might again conceal too much.

Another set of issues that the approach distinguishing between competitive and collective veto points approach has to address is: How should one categorise the institution of the president? Should the categorisation depend on whether the government is divided or unified? Under what conditions is the presidential institution likely to behave as a constrainer and under what conditions as a grazier? Like with other institutional elements, the effects of the president as a grazier or as a constrainer should be explored in different fiscal situations. While the constraining role of the president can facilitate the maintenance of fiscal balances during good times, it may act as a break on fiscal consolidation during a fiscal crisis.

As a number of studies have indicated, the effects of the number of graziers or veto players are conditional on whether the decision-makers are faced with fiscally "good times" or "difficult times". Common-pool resource models have more plausibility in explaining why budget deficits emerge in the first place, while veto players models are more applicable in explaining why fiscal consolidations are delayed and deficits, once they have occurred, persist. Further models and studies should certainly take the pertinent fiscal situation into account more explicitly and differentiate the explanations and predictions in this regard. An underlying normative assumption of the existing studies often is that budget deficits are necessarily negative and no attention is paid to their role in cyclical adjustments. In other words, the level of fiscal prudence may not necessarily be captured by simple deficit measures, since deficits may be employed purposefully as counter-cyclical measures. Therefore, cyclically adjusted balances would be a more appropriate focus of analysis. Also, in existing studies, only limited attention is paid to the question of which institutional features encourage counter-cyclical use of deficits, and which ones promote pro-cyclical use of deficits.

Discerning the effects of the number of participants on policy choices in public finance is complicated by *non-linear* effects, indicated by a number of empirical studies. As discussed in sections 5.3.1.1.2. and 5.3.2.1., an increasing number of legislators in governing majority is associated with additional expenditures, but up to a certain threshold, beyond which expenditures start decreasing (see Mukherjee 2003). While the "law of $1/n$" appears to be valid in legislatures up to a certain size, then in legislatures that exceed a certain size threshold, an additional legislator would result in lower total expenditures adopted by the legislature, resulting in a "reverse law of $1/n$" (Primo and Snyder 2008). As Steinmo and Tolbert (1998) demonstrate, while single-party majoritarian governments collect the lowest revenues, the highest revenues are not collected by coalition governments with a large number of parties but by those that have a limited number of partners and one dominating party. Gould (2001) also demonstrates that proportional countries with at least one large party collected more tax revenues than did proportional countries with only small parties. With regard to electoral systems, a very proportional electoral system with many small parties may be more similar in its spending mix (with regard to the level of targeted expenditures) to a majoritarian system than to another (but somewhat less) proportional system that has fewer parties. Further studies should focus more explicitly on the possibilities of such non-linear effects and integrate the different explanatory factors behind them.

The non-linearity of the effects of institutional factors like the number of partisan or individual participants in the budget process is likely to be influenced by the following aspects: How high are the transaction costs involved in inter-actor bargaining (and would the costs be higher for benefit-cutting interactions than for benefit-increasing interactions)? How extensive are the possibilities for externalising the costs associated with adopted expenditures? How fractionalised are the partisan actors? These aspects are often interrelated and reinforce each other. For example, the level of fractionalisation of partisan actors influences the bargaining power each of them has; the symmetries or asymmetries they have in bargaining powers, in turn, are likely to influence the transaction costs involved in budgetary negotiations. In addition, the level of transaction costs in budgetary decision-making would depend on whether the decision concerns adopting or cutting expenditures and on the extent to which the costs of additional expenditure can be externalised to other partisan actors or district representatives. An important shortcoming of the legislative fiscal commons approaches discussed in this chapter is that most of them ignore the transaction costs involved in building coalitions for adopting packages of particularistic spending.

A more serious shortcoming of the studies reviewed in this chapter is that they have, for most part, confined themselves to partial analyses of the different political institutions and try to find out how a particular institution influences policy choices in public finance. The main caveat of such partial analyses is that, in reality, the effects of political institutions on policy choices are likely to be *configurational* rather than *additive*: a particular institutional element might have an opposite effect depending on the values of other institutional elements or on a particular combination of these elements (see Scharpf 1997). Ostrom (1986, p. 8) also emphasises that it is the *configurations* of rules, rather than single rules, that jointly affect the structure of situations subject to analysis. The following examples demonstrate the relevance of taking into account the *configurations* of constitutional elements when exploring their effects on public finance.

- The fractionalisation of the opposition may have a positive effect on budget expenditures when the government is a minority government but may have a negative effect when the government is a majority government.
- Common-pool resource problems of budgeting may become more severe when a large district magnitude in proportional systems is combined with open lists but may be less severe with large district magnitude and closed lists. Further, the mutually reinforcing effects of an open list and a large district magnitude may be alleviated by particular electoral formulas (e.g., the D'Hondt formula, which treats the dominant parties more favourably and is hence likely to lead to less fractionalised parliaments and governments) but may be aggravated by electoral formulas that are strictly "more proportionate" (like the LR-Hare formula).
- The tendency of the presidential systems to increase the complexity of the tax system may be significant in a system where the legislature has been elected according to a majoritarian system or open-list proportional system, but may be less relevant in a proportional system with closed lists.
- In parliamentary systems with closed lists, the number of excess seats that the governing majority has in the legislature is likely to play a smaller role than in presidential systems or in parliamentary systems with open lists. In electoral systems where the cultivation of personal vote and pursuit of particularistic spending are prevalent, the increasing size of the governing majority may increase the particularistic tendencies of the spending mix and the tax system, whereas in systems with a low level of personal vote, the increase in the number of seats that the governing majority has in the legislature is less likely to translate into more particularistic spending and taxation.
- A larger number of parties in the legislature may have more important effects on public finances in presidential systems than in parliamentary systems where the vote of confidence requirement secures a stronger dividing line between governing and opposition parties.
- Constitutional courts may have stronger de facto decision-making powers in issues of public finance when policy-making is biased towards status quo (because of a large number of veto points) than in polities with lesser status quo bias (see Tsebelis 2000).

Furthermore, the effects of specific configurations of distinct institutional elements would be different depending on the general fiscal situation. A particular configuration may have strong effects on budgetary expansion in good times but may have weak effects on the governmental ability to deal with fiscal shocks. Since the effects of different arrangements are likely to be asymmetrical in good times and difficult times, the empirical studies looking at the *aggregate* effects may conceal too much.

Given the configurational effects of constitutional rules and governing arrangements, further studies exploring the institutional arrangements could experiment with the Boolean approach suggested by Ragin (1997, 2000, 2008) and attempt to use the Boolean algebra and truth tables in ascertaining the effects of different configurations. Even such an analysis, however, is likely to be complicated by the fact that the number of relevant elements and the different combinations arising thereof is very large, while the number of countries is relatively small. If one wished to incorporate the most basic constitutional elements that are likely to play a role in budgetary decision-making, the list would become rather long:

- Is the system presidential or parliamentary or a hybrid?
- Is the electoral system proportional or majoritarian? If proportional, then how proportional and what elements make it more proportional (district magnitude, list votes) and what elements reduce proportionality (e.g., thresholds, formula)?
- To what extent does the electoral system encourage personal vote?
- How many legislators are there in the legislature?
- What is the effective number of parties in the legislature?
- Is the legislature bicameral or unicameral?
- What is the ratio of seats in lower and upper chamber?
- How many parties make up the government?
- How large margin of majority does the government have?
- How fractionalised is the government?
- How fractionalised is the opposition?
- How many (spending) ministers are there in the cabinet?
- Does the constitution provide for popular initiatives?
- Are there obligatory referenda on public finance issues?
- Are referenda allowed on public finance issues?
- Does the constitutional court have extensive powers?

This list can be complemented by more specific institutional details, like the conflict-resolution mechanisms in bicameral systems or rules governing the interaction between parliaments and presidents.

Although studies looking at local governments could overcome the small sample problem to a certain extent, budgetary decision-making on the central and local level have significant differences and the institutional arrangements are too different to consider them as equivalents, meaning that the results obtained at sub-national levels are not easily translatable to explain the dynamics of institutional constellations at the national level.

Given the configurational rather than additive effects of the different institutional elements, the development of specific typologies and ideal types of political settings may be better able to capture the interactions between the different institutional aspects than partial studies. The typology offered, for example, by Gerring, Thacker and Moreno (2005), which distinguishes between "centripetal" and "centrifugal" polities goes in the direction of integrating specific institutional features into configurations or typologies.[175] Such typologies can certainly go a longer way than partial analyses in illuminating the interactive effects (reinforcing or countervailing) of the different institutional elements and providing a better grasp of the interplay of causal mechanisms.[176] Hence, constitutional public finance would benefit from making a better use of recent developments in small-n comparative studies and "building-block" approaches (see Bennett and Elman 2006) employed in coming up with more accurate typologies of different kinds of polities. Further, the "process-tracing" techniques put forth by recent developments in case-study research (see Bennett and Elman 2006; George and Bennett 2005; George and McKeown 1985; McKeown 2004) can be employed as a complementary venue for elaborating on the underlying causal mechanisms that can influence the translation of constitutional rules into specific features of political setting, which in turn shape interactions between political actors and the outcomes of their interactions.

Further, one should consider the interactive effects of political institutions (entailed in constitutions) and fiscal constitutions (i.e., fiscal rules and budgetary procedures). In particular, it is important to juxtapose the effects of *size* fragmentation (reflected in a number of graziers on budgetary commons) with *procedural* fragmentation of budgetary decision-making. The effects of the number of legislators, ministers and parties on budgetary outcomes are likely to be mediated through the budgetary institutions. If budgetary institutions are fragmented, the translation of *potential* common-pool problems into *actual* problems in budgeting is more likely. When budgetary institutions provide for centralised coordination mechanisms, the common-pool problems arising from size fragmentation are likely to be mitigated. This is topic of the next chapter.

---

175 A centripetal polity is characterised by a strong cabinet, medium-strength legislative committees, strong party cohesion, the power to dissolve parliament, no limits on tenure in office, few elective offices, congruent election cycles, closed procedures of candidate selection, voting according to the party labels of the candidates, party-centred political campaigns, multiparty competition, centralised and cohesive party organisations, popular referenda only at the initiative of the legislature (or not at all), a restrained (non-activist) judiciary, and a neutral and relatively centralised bureaucracy (Gerring, Thacker and Moreno 2005, p. 570).

176 See also Lijphart and Crepaz (1991), for elements of the kind of polity that they call "consensus" democracy.

Chapter 6: Fiscal Constitutions as *Explanantia* in Public Finance

6.1. Outline of Terminology

In the literature, one can meet a host of different terms that pertain to the constitutional and institutional framework for budgeting and taxation: fiscal constitutions, fiscal governance institutions, fiscal rules, fiscal contracts, budgetary institutions (or budgeting institutions), organic budget laws, budget procedures, tax constitutions and organic tax laws. Although different categorisations can be offered for explaining the inter-relations between these terms, this section proposes a following conceptualisation as a basis for further discussion.

The most encompassing of these terms is *fiscal governance institutions*, which refers to the general rules of the game that govern the policy arena of public finance. The term *fiscal constitution* can be understood in a broad and in a narrow sense. In a *narrow* sense, *fiscal constitution* refers to provisions pertaining to budgeting, taxation and other aspects of public finance that are expressly contained in the formal constitution. In a *broad* sense, it is equivalent with the concept of fiscal governance institutions; here, the term "constitution" does not only refer to the actual formal constitution, but to the general rules of the game in the polity, regardless of where exactly they have been stipulated. In order to distinguish between the broad and narrow conceptions of fiscal constitution, *extended fiscal constitution* is used here as the term for capturing the broad notion.

Fiscal rules refer to output-based limitations: to substantive constraints on spending, taxation, deficit and debt. Fiscal rules can be contained either in the fiscal constitution in a narrow sense (when they are constitutionally stipulated) or in the extended fiscal constitution (when they can be found in lower level acts). *Fiscal contracts* refer to shorter-term agreements expressing the commitment of the government to certain fiscal goals (e.g., with regard to expenditure and deficit levels) that are not expressed in a statutory form but are established by "softer" instruments like coalition agreements.

Budgetary institutions or *budgeting institutions* entail procedural aspects of budgeting: the competencies of the various actors and the procedures that govern the preparation, adoption and implementation of the budget. Budgetary institutions can also include fiscal rules, but for the purposes of this chapter, they are taken to refer primarily to *procedural* constraints (as opposed to *substantive* output-related constraints like fiscal rules). Budgetary institutions can in part be outlined in formal constitutions (e.g., in the form of constitutional articles referring to the general competencies of the various branches in budget-making process) but are usually more extensively established in *organic budget laws* (also called framework laws for budgeting) or other (organic) laws concerned with procedural aspects of budgeting (e.g., rules of procedure for the legislature).

Tax constitutions refer to the general rules of the game that govern the preparation and adoption of tax laws (e.g., supermajority requirements for tax increases) and to substantive limitations for tax laws (e.g., requirements concerning the generality and non-discriminatory nature of taxation).[177] Tax constitutions can be entailed either in the formal constitution or on a statutory level in organic tax laws or other organic laws. *Organic tax laws* refer to laws that govern the preparation and adoption of tax laws. Part of the fiscal rules can also be seen as falling under tax constitutions (e.g., limitations on tax increases).

Figure 6.1. depicts how these different concepts are related to each other. Most simply put, fiscal governance institutions (or extended fiscal constitutions) encompass budgetary institutions, tax constitutions and fiscal rules.[178] Organic budget laws and fiscal contracts are part of budgetary institutions, organic tax laws are part of tax constitutions, and fiscal rules can fall under both budgetary institutions and tax constitutions.

Figure 6.1.: Fiscal constitution: terminological relations

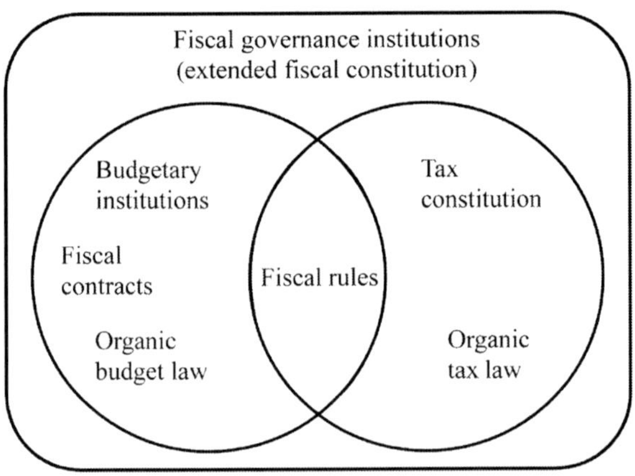

177 Although Buchanan and his colleagues (see, e.g. Buchanan and Wagner 1977, Buchanan 1997b) have argued that such a requirement should not be viewed as a *substantive* constraint but a *procedural* constraint, then, in comparison with the procedure foreseen for adopting tax laws, it would be analytically clearer to categorise such requirement as falling under substantive rules.

178 In the existing literature, the terms *fiscal governance* institutions and *fiscal constitutions* are sometimes used to refer only to the budgetary institutions (see Hallerberg 2004; Helland 2000), but it would be more accurate to view them as encompassing tax constitutions as well.

In this chapter, the analytical framework that was outlined in section 4.4. (and was used for giving an overview of the role of political institutions in public finance in chapter 5) is used for discussing the role of extended fiscal constitution (or fiscal governance institutions) in shaping budgeting and taxation. Different institutions of fiscal governance are analysed with a view to how they influence the *accountability* of elected representatives and the *coordination* of decision-making between political actors. Section 6.2. deals with the *substantive* (or output-oriented) aspects of the fiscal constitution: with rules that establish clear numerical targets or ceilings for fiscal indicators (i.e., budget balance rules, deficit and debt ceilings, tax and expenditure limits).[179] Section 6.3. considers the *procedural* aspects of budgeting, and section 6.4. covers the *procedural* aspects of tax constitutions. Section 6.5.1 discusses critically the existing literature on fiscal governance institutions; it takes a closer look at the use of the "budgetary commons" metaphor, explores analogies between the governance of fiscal commons and natural commons, and juxtaposes the recent fiscal governance literature with classical works of budgeting by Wildavsky. Section 6.5.2. puts forth a number of critical remarks on the discourse employed by constitutional public finance.

6.2. Fiscal Rules

Output-oriented or substantive fiscal rules, also called numerical fiscal rules, are rules that pertain directly to particular aggregate parameters of the budget. Kopits and Symansky (1998, p. 2) have defined a fiscal rule as "a permanent constraint on fiscal policy, expressed in terms of a summary indicator of fiscal performance". The four main types of fiscal rules are deficit rules (e.g., balanced budget requirements or deficit limits), debt rules (e.g., debt ceilings), expenditure rules (e.g., ceilings on general public expenditure growth or on certain types of government spending) and tax revenue rules (e.g., limits on the increase in the overall tax burden) (Corbacho and Schwartz 2007; European Commission 2006). What exactly the term "permanent" means in the definition of fiscal rules has been conceived differently by various authors. Most of the literature on fiscal rules assumes that this means establishing a fiscal rule either in a constitution or in a statute. More recent discussions on fiscal rules, especially in the EU context, however, view fiscal rules as also encompassing fiscal targets established in political agreements, multi-annual budgetary frameworks or coalition agreements. Using the distinction made by Schick (2003), this chapter views fiscal rules as encompassing the "hard constraints", established in constitutions or

179 Although the more normative strand of constitutional political economy (represented among others by Buchanan and his co-authors) would argue that a balanced budget rule is not a *substantive* rule but a *procedural* rule, then in comparison with the rules governing *budget procedure*, it should still be viewed as belonging to the substantive sphere, which is why it is covered under the substantive rules in this chapter.

statutes, whereas the "soft constraints" are viewed as "fiscal contracts" that constitute an institutional element in budget procedures (discussed in section 6.3.). Because fiscal contracts entailed in medium-term fiscal frameworks, coalition agreements and other informal political agreements can be renegotiated on an annual basis, it would be misleading to call them "permanent" constraints (see Debrun, Hauner and Kumar 2007, p. 16).

Balanced budget rules and deficit constraints have received most extensive attention in the literature on fiscal rules so far (von Hagen 2007, p. 32). The general category "balanced budget requirement", however, may involve rather different rules in terms of scope and content. Strauch and von Hagen (2001, p. 12) differentiate between balanced budget rules in three different aspects. First, the rules vary with respect to the *stage* of the budget process they apply to: the executive may be required to submit a balanced budget, the legislature may be required to approve a balanced budget or the government can be required to balance the budget at the end of the year. Second, balanced budget rules may vary in terms of the *type of funds* they cover: the rule may apply only to general funds but may also cover capital funds or special revenue funds. Inasmuch as the balanced budget rule applies only to the current budget, it is equivalent to the "golden rule", which requires that deficits may only be run in order to fund investment. Third, balanced budget requirements can vary with regard to when and how the legislature can *override or suspend* the requirement: the provisions can entail specific circumstances and special majority requirements. Balanced budget requirement can also be set for a number of years; in that case, the rule deals with a structural (i.e., cyclically-adjusted) balance.[180] Deficit and debt limits cap the allowed deficit or debt at a certain percentage of GDP. Here, too, exceptions may be provided for fiscal shocks.

Fiscal rules pertaining to tax and expenditure limits have received relatively less attention compared to debt and deficit rules so far, and most of the literature until recently was primarily concerned with the tax and expenditure limits (TELs) adopted in the U.S. states during the "tax revolt" of the 1970s. Since the beginning of 1990s, a number of European countries have adopted expenditure rules, bringing about resurgence in the interest of such rules and their impacts (von Hagen 2008, pp. 103–104).[181] Tax and expenditure ceilings can be established either in nominal or real terms, and limits can be tied to growth in personal income, inflation or population. Expenditures can also be limited to a percentage of projected revenues, with rest of revenues channelled to a rainy-day fund. (Musso, Graddy and Grizard 2008, p. 262) In terms of coverage, expendi-

180 For overviews of different taxonomies of balanced budget rules see, for example, Poterba (1995), and Hou and Smith (2006).

181 For overviews of fiscal rules in different countries and their historical development, see Kopits (2001), Kennedy and Robbins (2001), Schneider and Hedbavny (2003), Sutherland, Price and Joumard (2005) and von Hagen (2006, 2008).

ture limits can set a limit on primary expenditure, wage (and pension) expenditure, interest payments and debt service (Schneider and Hedbavny 2003).

Most broadly put, fiscal rules can be divided into two categories. The first category entails rules that are directed to general indicators of fiscal discipline: budget balance, deficit and debt rules. The second category entails rules that are concerned with fiscal scale – expenditures and tax revenues. This division is taken as a basis for the discussion on the empirical effects of the various kinds of rules in section 6.2.2. Before, however, an overview of the theoretical propositions of the existing literature with regard to how fiscal rules are expected to influence public finances is given in section 6.2.1., with a focus on how fiscal rules influence the *accountability* of elected officials and *coordination* mechanisms between governmental actors, and how the incentive structure of the setting, established by these mechanisms, shapes policy choices in the policy arena of public finance.

6.2.1. Theoretical Propositions

On the one hand, since fiscal rules establish clear benchmarks with which actual policies can be compared, they can be viewed as enhancing the *accountability* of elected representatives to the public (von Hagen 2007; Debrun and Kumar 2007). If, for example, the allowed budget deficit is fixed at a certain percent of the GDP, voters can use this indicator as a yardstick: as a basis for evaluating the prudence of policy choices undertaken by their representatives (Schuknecht 2005; Morris, Ongena and Schuknecht 2006; von Hagen 2007). Further, fiscal rules can heighten attention to budgeting and attract closer monitoring by interested voters and interest groups (Gordon 2008, p. 285). As Debrun and Kumar (2007, p. 23) put it, "To the extent that a fiscal rule crystallizes social consensus on what constitutes 'optimal policy', it will be used by voters to assess fiscal performance."

To what extent the fiscal rules can be used as yardsticks by voters depends, however, on a host of factors, including how visible, clear and simple the rules are. For example, when a balanced budget rule is established on a statutory (rather than constitutional) level and entails a number of technical specifications of what exactly is meant by the required balance, monitoring the correspondence of actual policies with the fiscal rule by voters is significantly more complicated (Schuknecht 2005). Thus, while more detailed and technical provisions allow the government to be more flexible in its fiscal choices (e.g., to use relevant counter-cyclical measures when the fiscal situation requires that or to engage in tax-smoothing policies in order to preventing sub-optimal volatility of tax rates), the role of such fiscal rules as accountability-enhancing mechanisms may be weakened (see Alesina and Perotti 1999; Schuknecht 2005; Hou and Smith 2006; Kopits and Symansky 1998; Morris, Ongena and Schuknecht 2006). For example, rules that allow the impact of the cycle to be taken into account may be more difficult to monitor, since the estimates of cyclically adjusted budget balance may undergo significant *ex post* revisions, which may make it more difficult to judge whether the fiscal rule has been complied with or not (Morris, Ongena and Schuknecht 2006, p. 9). In other words, there is a potential trade-off between complex rules with a fine-tuned economic rationale and simple rules that allow easy monitoring.

From another perspective, fiscal rules establishing numerical fiscal targets can reduce the *accountability* of the elected officials to their voters – if accountability is conceived as *responsiveness*. If, for example, voters prefer higher expenditures or higher taxes than fixed in the tax and expenditure limits, fiscal rules will restrict the ability of politicians to react to the wishes of their constituencies. To what extent such reduced responsiveness is problematic, depends on one's assumptions about the biases, illusions and irrationalities haunting policy-making in the policy arena of public finance. In other words, fiscal rules may be designed exactly with the goal to reduce the "too eager" short-term responsiveness of elected political actors to voters' preferences. For example, balanced budget rules or expenditure limits may help to prevent exaggerated pre-election spending (electoral cycles) or other forms of potentially pro-cyclical spending increases as a reaction to prevailing moods in the electorate (see Cukierman and Meltzer 1986; Nordhaus 1975; Tufte 1978). Also, when one assumes that a significant part of the electorate is subject to fiscal illusions – reflected in inaccurate perceptions of the cost-benefit ratios of spending programmes, inconsistent preferences of desiring simultaneously higher spending and lower taxes, and deficit biases resulting from inappropriate discount rates or from not fully grasping the mechanics of the inter-temporal budget constraint (see e.g., Buchanan and Wagner 1977; Hansen 1998; Debrun, Hauner and Kumar 2007)[182] – reducing the "overly eager" responsiveness of elected officials to the demands of the electorate can be seen as contributing to prudent policy-making in public finance. Thus, those approaches that view voters as fiscally prudent would view fiscal rules as imposing undue limitations on the government and restraining the responsiveness of elected officials to their constituencies in an unnecessary way. Those approaches, however, that assume fiscal profligacy and inconsistent preferences of voters would argue that limitations on the responsiveness of elected officials can counteract the biases and irrationalities that prevail in political decision-making on issues of public finance (see Schuknecht 2005; Abrams and Dougan 1986).

182 Hansen (1998, pp. 526–527) notes, in a review of the empirical evidence on public preferences over public finance in the United States, that though on the whole, individual preferences over trade-offs involved in public finance are remarkably well-structured, consistent and coherent, the public "underestimates the hazard to the future of financing current consumption with borrowed money". Stronger inconsistencies in the public preferences with regard to spending, taxes and deficit have been pointed out by Citrin (1979).

Often, those who advocate the constraints fiscal rules impose on the responsiveness of elected officials to their constituencies and supporter groups argue that such rules can mitigate the *common-pool problems* involved in budgeting and taxation. Fiscal rules are considered to enhance the coordination of budgetary and tax policy making by providing the actors involved with a clear focal point that can facilitate the internalisation of decision externalities entailed in spending or borrowing. Since common-pool resource problems of budgeting are considered to become more intensive in good times – because of the voracity effects, pointed out by Tornell and Lane (1999) – fiscal rules constraining expenditures or revenues (e.g., revenue rules that require windfall revenues to be channelled into rainy-day funds) can be viewed as instruments for countering the tendencies of pro-cyclicality and dissipation of budgetary windfalls during good times (European Commission 2006; Balassone and Kumar 2007).

An important criticism of fiscal rules is, however, that political decision-makers would deviate from these rules when it is politically profitable to do so (Schick 2003). In other words, the attempt of *current* principals to lock in the budgetary decision of *future* agents is marred by principal-agent problems, since the future agents may have diverging goals from the current principals (Kousser, McCubbins and Rozga 2008, p. 291). To what extent political decision-makers would adhere to fiscal rules depends, importantly, on how the rules are enforced and what the sanctions for violating the rules are. Fiscal rules can be enforced by voters, who punish the incumbent government for side-stepping the fiscal rules and reward adherence to the rules by re-election. As Debrun and Kumar (2007, p. 4) stress, however, the electoral mechanism may remain a weak enforcement mechanism when the deficit bias originates from political institutions themselves rather than from electoral incentives. Further, Frey's (1994) critique of mechanisms of representative democracy (see section 5.5.1.) would imply that voters do not have sufficient instruments to sanction politicians in non-election years, giving the elected representatives extensive discretionary freedom in those periods. Another enforcement mechanism would be to give a right to impose sanctions to a constitutional court or to an outside agency, like it is – at least in principle – the case with the fiscal rules entailed in the Stability and Growth Pact (SGP) of the EU. With stricter enforcement mechanisms in place, however, political actors may have motives to engage in accounting gimmicks, which can reduce the transparency of the budgeting process and reduce the ability of voters to monitor other substantive aspects of budgets. Milesi-Ferretti (2003) demonstrates that when a government has possibilities to employ "creative accounting", a fiscal rule may lead to a trade-off between expensive "window-dressing" and real fiscal adjustment. Von Hagen (2003) has emphasised that such reduced transparency can altogether lead to lower accountability of political agents to their principals in budgetary decision-making.

Kopits and Symansky (1998) emphasise that if fiscal rules were to be effective, they should be well-defined (with regard to the indicator to be constrained, the institutional coverage and specific escape clauses), transparent, simple, flexible (to accommodate exogenous shocks), adequate (with respect to the specified goal), enforceable, consistent (both internally and with other policies) and efficient. They point out, though, that no fiscal rule can fully combine all these features. Hence, there are usually significant trade-offs that have to be made in establishing fiscal rules, which may underline their overall effectiveness.

Altogether, the theoretical literature predicts that fiscal rules can enhance fiscal prudence, if they are well-designed and backed up by democratic accountability mechanisms, but may also lead to undesired effects of pro-cyclical fiscal policies and creative accounting (especially when balanced budget rules or deficit limits do not leave sufficient space for counter-cyclical policies).

6.2.2. Empirical Evidence

6.2.2.1. Balanced Budget Requirements, Deficit and Debt Limits

Most of the empirical studies exploring the effects of balanced budget rules on public deficits and debts have been conducted on the sub-federal jurisdictions in the United States and Switzerland. More recent studies on fiscal rules have also looked at the effects of deficit and debt limits on the member states of the European Union. Overviews of the empirical studies on the effects of balanced budget rules and rules constraining budget deficit and debt have been given by Krol (1997), Kirchgässner (2001), Strauch and von Hagen (2001), von Hagen (2002, 2003) and Kennedy and Robbins (2001). This section draws on these overviews and adds the results of more recent studies. The overview below does first present evidence on the impacts of balanced budget and debt rules on deficit and debt, then on their effects on spending, creative accounting and cyclical features of fiscal policies.

Kirchgässner (2001, p. 4) concludes, on the basis of empirical research on deficit and debt rules in the United States, that although some of the first studies (e.g., von Hagen 1991; Alt and Lowry 1994) found no significant impacts, later studies mostly presented evidence of significant constraining effects. Since almost all states in the United States have some form of balanced budget rules, this has been used to ascertain whether *different kinds* of balanced budget rules have different effects. Von Hagen (1991) investigated whether the *stringency* of balanced budget rules has played a role in fiscal outcomes in the U.S. states. He found that average debt per capita was significantly lower in states with highly stringent balanced budget rules than in those with low stringency; at the same time, there was no statistical difference between states where the balanced budget rules had medium and high stringency. These findings have been endorsed by Eichengreen (1994) and Eichengreen and Bayoumi (1994). The most comprehensive study regarding the effects of different kinds of balanced budget constraints in the United States has been conducted by Bohn and Inman (1996). Using a panel of 47 states between 1970 and 1991, they conclude that in order to constrain deficits, the budget balance rules have to be grounded in the state's constitution (rather than being established on a statutory level), should require end-of-the-year budget balance (rather than only prospective balance) and have to be enforced by supreme courts made up of justices who are elected directly by the citizens (rather than political appointments). Alesina and Bayoumi (1996) also find that stricter balanced budget rules are correlated with larger average budget surpluses.

In their studies of Swiss cantons, Feld and Kirchgässner (2006) and Schaltegger (2002) conclude that fiscal rules have led to smaller budget deficits. Krogstrup and Wälti (2008) examine the effects of fiscal rules in Swiss cantons and find that the rules exercise significant impacts on budget balances, even when voter preferences are taken into account. At the same time, Feld and Kirchgässner (2001b) found that fiscal rules did not have significant effects on debt and deficit levels.

The Maastricht Treaty (1992) established fiscal rules for the EU member states in the Excessive Deficit Procedure (EDP), which was further elaborated in the Stability and Growth Pact (SGP) adopted in 1997 and reformed in 2005.[183] The numerical fiscal targets entailed in these frameworks establish that a member state's annual budget deficit should not exceed 3 percent of the GDP and the overall government debt should remain under 60 percent of the GDP. The SGP added the requirement that the member states should strive for their budgets to be "close to balance or in surplus" (CBS) in a medium-term, which has been interpreted as postulating cyclically-adjusted balance (CAB) (Annett 2006).[184] In evaluating the effects of the Maastricht rules and the SGP, empirical studies generally conclude that although the Maastricht rules had constraining effects on deficits, marking clear structural breaks in the policy regimes and bringing about an average improvement in the cyclically-adjusted primary balances (especially in the immediate run-up to the EMU), the experience under the SGP has been more mixed, as demonstrated by deteriorating cyclically-adjusted primary balances and excessive deficits incurred by some of the member states (Briotti 2004; Annett 2006; Strauch and von Hagen 2001; Fatas *et al.* 2003; von Hagen 2006a, 2008). Von Hagen (2008, p. 116) notes that as long as EMU membership was not secured, voters rewarded governments for measures strengthening fiscal discipline, but once the membership was secured, the familiar pattern of political

183 For a more detailed overview of the EDP and the SGP see, for example, von Hagen (2008).

184 Although the CBS is not associated with a specific numerical target, it has been interpreted as ruling out deficits that are "systematically larger then 0.5 percent of GDP over the cycle" (Annett 2006, p. 7). In addition, the SGP requires the member states to submit annual Stability Programmes outlining how the intended fiscal policies enable to achieve the medium-term objective of CBS.

budget-cycles returned. While smaller EU countries have generally adhered to the fiscal framework of the SGP, a number of larger countries have deviated from the rules (von Hagen 2006a; Annett and Jaeger 2004; Buti and Pench 2004; Annett 2006).[185] Annett (2006) also points out that most of the countries have not followed the medium-term CBS dictum. Briotti (2004) notes that most of the progress made in fiscal consolidations took the form of revenue-based adjustment, with insufficient attention paid to primary expenditure restraint. Morris, Ongena and Schuknecht (2006, p. 16) find that the fiscal consolidation achieved in the 1990s can be attributed to increases in revenue-to-GDP ratio; two-thirds of this increase, however, was reversed in later years, while primary expenditures started increasing after 1999. Hallerberg (2004), von Hagen (2006a) and Annett (2006) show that the EU fiscal rules have contributed to improving budgetary institutions in those countries where the political environment is appropriate for a rules-based approach to fiscal discipline (i.e., who have adopted the contracts approach to fiscal governance).[186] Annett (2006) also ascertains that the delegation approach to fiscal governance was conducive to fiscal discipline before the adoption of the SGP, but not in the aftermath.

In addition to the fiscal framework provided by the Maastricht Treaty and the SGP, a number of EU countries have adopted national level fiscal rules since 1990s.[187] Ayuso-i-Casals *et al.* (2007, p. 209) remark that the EU fiscal framework has acted as a catalyst for the introduction of numerical fiscal rules by the member states. Von Hagen (2005) examines the effects of numerical fiscal rules and concludes that these rules (when designed in an effective way) have had constraining effects on deficits and debts. This finding has been further endorsed by the European Commission (2006) and Ayuso-i-Casals *et al.* (2007, p. 195).[188] In particular, the study by the European Commission (2006) points out that the link between numerical fiscal rules and deficits (or surpluses) is stronger, the larger the share of government finances covered by the rules and the stronger the rules. "Stronger" rules are rules that have been established in a constitution or a

185 Annett (2006) argues that one of the reasons behind that pattern is that small countries are more used to external constraints on domestic policies (exerted through international organisations, for example) and they perceive the loss of reputation from deviating from the fiscal rules to be greater because of their generally lower bargaining power. In addition, Annett points out, drawing on Rogowski (1987), Hallerberg (2004) and von Hagen (2006b), that smaller countries tend to adopt a commitment or contracts approach to fiscal governance, because they have proportional electoral systems, leading to prevalence of coalition governments, which is functionally more compatible with fiscal rules.

186 See section 6.3. for a discussion of the different modes of fiscal governance.

187 For overviews of these rules, see von Hagen (2006a), European Commission (2006), Ayuso-i-Casals *et al.* (2007).

188 Both von Hagen (2006b) and Ayuso-i-Casals *et al.* (2007) include fiscal targets that have been expressed in political agreements (e.g., coalition governments or multi-annual budgetary frameworks) under the notion of "fiscal rules".

statute (rather than in informal political agreements) and prescribe automatic enforcement mechanisms.

Alesina *et al.* (1999) demonstrate, by looking at Latin American countries, that properly constructed borrowing constraints have played a significant role in curbing deficits. Eslava (2006) also considers the effects of numerical targets for deficit in 23 Latin American and Caribbean countries (between 1996 and 2003) and finds that the rules play an important rule in constraining deficits.

As noted above, an oft-mentioned counter-argument to fiscal rules is that they invite cosmetic changes, manipulation of the budgetary data and accounting gimmicks. Empirical evidence on that points to diverging directions. Poterba (1995) argues that the experience of the U.S. states suggests that while cosmetic changes are occasionally used to secure compliance with the balanced budget requirements, these modifications are less important in their scale than tax increases and spending cuts. The study by Bohn and Inman (1996) concludes that there is little evidence to claim that balanced budget rules shift deficits into other accounts. On the other hand, von Hagen (1991) argues that the U.S. states with more stringent balanced budget requirements simply have a higher share of non-guaranteed debt compared to the states with no such limits. While Kiewiet and Szakaly (1996) could not find any evidence that states evade debt limits by issuing non-guaranteed debt, their findings indicate that restrictive provisions at the state level result in the shift of debt issuance to the municipal level. Conversely, von Hagen and Eichengreen (1996) find that countries where sub-national governments are subject to more stringent statutory borrowing constraints tend to have higher central government debt ratios. Von Hagen and Wolff (2006) find that the EDP and the SGP have induced creative accounting in the form of stock-flow adjustments. Koen and van den Noord (2006) confirm an increased recourse to gimmicks (e.g., using one-off measures and creative accounting) in the EU countries. Buti, Martins and Turrini (2007) also conclude that the fiscal rules underpinning EMU have led to more extensive use of "fiscal engineering" and "accounting gimmicks" (e.g., stock-flow adjustments expressed in the discrepancy between the accounting value of deficit and the change in debt).

In addition to the effects of budget balance and debt rules on budget *deficits* or *surpluses*, several studies have also looked at the effects of these rules on *expenditure* and *revenue* levels in the United States and have mostly found constraining effects. Crain and Miller (1990) find that constitutional balanced budget requirements have constraining effects on spending. Bohn and Inman (1996) ascertain that in states with more stringent anti-deficit laws, spending tends to be lower over time. Bails and Tieslau (2000) show that a balanced budget rule in combination with expenditure limits (and a balanced budget rule together with a supermajority requirement for tax increases) have had a significant negative impact on public expenditures. As for the impact on *tax revenues*, Merrifield (1991) finds that balanced budget requirements are associated with higher levels of tax revenues. Nelson (1986) finds that borrowing limitations have had constraining effects on taxes per capita and on taxes as percent of personal income.

What has also been of interest in connection with balanced budget rules, deficit rules and borrowing restrictions is how they influence *reactions* to adverse shocks and the *cyclical* nature of fiscal policies. As Manasse (2005, p. 3) has succinctly put it, the main dilemma that fiscal rules face is how to get rid of the "dirty water" of excessive deficits "without sacrificing the 'baby' of fiscal stabilisation". Again, different authors point to diverging evidence. Fatas and Mihov (2003) find, in their study of 91 countries from 1960 to 2000, that *ex ante* rules have helped to contain output volatility by constraining governments in pursuit of discretionary policies. Poterba (1994) showed that the U.S. states with "tighter fiscal constitutions" (i.e., with relatively tight constitutional or statutory rules that make it more difficult to run deficits) undertook prompter fiscal adjustments when revenues fell short of expectations or spending exceeded projections. Alesina and Bayoumi (1996) conclude that in the U.S. states, balanced budget rules have not brought about costs in terms of increased output variability. In contrast, Levinson (1998) concludes that strict balanced budget provisions have exacerbated business cycles in the U.S. states.

As for the cyclical effects of fiscal policies in EU countries under the EMU fiscal framework, once again, the empirical studies point to mixed evidence. A number of studies conclude that fiscal policies were predominantly pro-cyclical before the Maastricht Treaty, acyclical between the Maastricht Treaty and the SGP, and pro-cyclical after the adoption of the SGP (Annett 2006; Gali and Perotti 2003; Fatas *et al.* 2003).[189] Briotti (2004) finds that fiscal policies in EU member states showed a clear pro-cyclical bias between 1991 and 2002, and that fiscal policies were more pro-cyclical in high-deficit countries than in low-deficit countries. She suggests that the risk of exceeding the fiscal reference values in difficult times might have prompted pro-cyclical consolidation in countries with serious fiscal imbalances. In a similar vein, Beetsma and Giuliodori (2008) show that the EU countries have responded to an unexpected worsening of the business cycle by undertaking pro-cyclical fiscal policies, while not undertaking any systematic fiscal policies during an improvement of the business cycle. A study by the European Commission (2006) indicates that while during the run-up to the EMU, pro-cyclicality was prevalent during bad times, then after the completion of EMU, pro-cyclical policies re-emerged in good times and the frequency of pro-cyclical episodes in bad times dropped. Buti and Pench (2004) conclude that the fiscal framework of the SGP has not provided sufficient incentives for discontinuing expansionary policies and undertaking consolidations in good times. To what extent the reform of the SGP undertaken in 2005 is

189 At the same time, however, Annett (2006) finds that the deficit bias generated by the electoral cycle has been lower in the post-SGP period than in the pre-SGP period.

likely to improve those results, is yet to be seen (see Morris, Ongena and Schuknecht 2006; Buti 2007). With regard to the effects of *national* fiscal rules on the cyclicality of fiscal policies in EU countries, the study by the European Commission (2006) finds that in countries with strong fiscal rules, the percentage of pro-cyclical fiscal policy episodes was slightly higher (both in good and bad times) than in countries with weak rules.

6.2.2.2. Tax and Expenditure Limits

Most of the empirical studies examining the effects of tax and expenditure limits have focused on the U.S. states. First the effects on spending are reviewed, followed by revenues and fiscal adjustments.

Poulson (2004) and Krol (2007) review the empirical studies on the impacts of tax and expenditure limits (TELs) in the United States and conclude that the results diverge widely.[190] They suggest that the divergence reflects the use of different methodologies and data sets. Cross-section studies by Bails (1982, 1990), Abrams and Dougan (1996) and Cox and Lowery (1990) found TELs to be ineffective in constraining state spending. Time-series studies have found mixed results for the impact of TELs on state spending. Kenyon and Baker (1984) did not find significant differences in the growth of state spending relative to personal income in states with TELs and states without TELs. Dougan (1988), however, examined time-series data from 1960 to 1984 for sixteen states and ascertained that in seven of these states the TELs *had* a significant negative impact on government spending. King-Meadows and Lowery (2003) point to some (although weak) evidence that TELs have reduced the level of expenditures. Similar results have been reported by Bails and Tieslau (2000). Stansel (1994) concludes that the relative growth rate of spending in states that adopted tax and expenditure limits fell considerably within five years of the implementation of the limits. Strauch (1998) shows that constitutional expenditure limits have induced a shift from the (constrained) current budget to the (unconstrained) investment budget. Shadbegian (1996) observes that TELs reduce government spending growth in states with low income growth, but they increase government spending growth in states with high income growth. New (2001) finds that TELs that were adopted by the initiative process significantly reduced state and local spending, while TELs enacted by state legislatures were associated with higher subsequent spending. Poterba (1994) points out that TELs that have limited spending most are constitutional, written by voters and limit spending rather than revenues. Poulson (2004) concludes, based on the large-n studies and case studies from the United States, that tax and spending limits can significantly re-

190 For other overviews on tax and expenditure limitations and their impacts, see Knight and Levinson (1999a), Strauch and von Hagen (2001), Mullins and Wallin (2004) and Gordon (2008).

duce state spending.[191] Bails and Tieslau (2000) find that while the imposition of a balanced budget requirement by itself has not been an effective instrument for decreasing government expenditures, it has been effective in constraining spending when combined with tax and expenditure limitations. Kousser, McCubbins and Rozga (2008) examine the effects of TELs in four U.S. states and conclude that TELs have failed to constrain the size of government.

With regard to the effects of TELs on *revenues*, the empirical studies also point to mixed evidence. Crain and Miller (1990) observe that taxes grew less between 1979 and 1986 in states with tax limits than in states without such limits. Joyce and Mullins (1991), however, ascertain that TELs led to lower state revenues in the short run, but not the long run. Elder (1992) finds that while expenditure limitations have led to lower tax burdens and constrained the growth of taxes, fiscal rules limiting revenues have not been effective in limiting the growth and levels of tax burdens.[192] Stansel (1994) concludes that the relative decline in the growth of state taxes was still significant in five years after the TEL had been enacted. Drawing on Poterba (1994), Poulson (2004) points out that states with TELs undertake lower tax increases in periods of recession than states without TELs. Besley and Case (2003) ascertain that while non-binding TELs have no effects on revenues, states with (potentially) binding TELs have *higher* tax revenues.[193]

Concerning the effects of TELs on *fiscal adjustments*, Poterba (1994) concludes that the states that had TELs in place adjusted more promptly. He also finds that states with TELs are more likely to run a deficit than to increase taxes as a reaction to a negative budget shock. In their study of fiscal consolidation efforts in OECD countries, Guichard *et al.* (2007) conclude that fiscal rules that, alongside with deficit levels, set expenditure targets, have led to more extensive and longer-lasting fiscal adjustments. Most of the studies looking at the effects of rainy day fund rules (i.e., revenue rules that require windfall surpluses to be accumulated to a special fund that can be used during downturns) in the United States have found positive impacts on fiscal performance (both in terms of total balances and reduced volatility of expenditures), especially in states where the rules are strong (e.g., are based on a mathematical formula) (see Knight and Levinson 1999; Sobel and Holcombe 1996; Wagner and Elder 2005).

---

191 Poulson (2004) concludes that in order to be effective, TELs should be constitutional (rather than statutory), limit the growth of government spending to inflation and population growth (rather than other aggregate indicators), require immediate refunds of surplus revenue above the foreseen limit, and they should be linked to other fiscal rules, like balanced budget requirements.

192 Elder (1992, p. 60) notes that one of the reasons behind this result is that the fiscal rules imposing revenue limitations have rather lax control and enforcement mechanisms.

193 As Besley and Case (2003) point out, this might refer to the endogeneity of such institutions.

While most of the TELs in the U.S. states can be considered to be *fiscal rules* proper, since they have been established either on constitutional or statutory level, the expenditure rules adopted in several European countries since the beginning of 1990s have been established in political agreements: that is, taking the form of fiscal contracts rather than fiscal rules.[194] The *fiscal contracts* approach as one mode of fiscal governance (entailing a configuration of specific budgetary institutions, of which agreed-upon fiscal target is one element) will be discussed in section 6.3., but for the purposes of comparison with the TELs in place in the United States, it is worth bringing out the effects of the expenditure rules adopted in European countries on aggregate budgetary indicators already here. Brosens and Wierts (2007) find that countries experiencing larger surpluses had stronger expenditure rules. Ayuso-i-Casals *et al.* (2007) find that expenditure rules have exercised constraining effects on expenditures.

A study by the European Commission (2006) shows that the decline in the ratio of cyclically adjusted primary government expenditure has been larger (compared with the average change) after the introduction of expenditure rules. The larger the proportion of government finances covered by expenditure rules and the stronger the rules, the larger the reduction has been. Further, this study ascertains that episodes of pro-cyclicality in good times have been less frequent in countries where strong expenditure rules are in place.

Wierts (2008) finds, when considering the effects of expenditure rules on responses to fiscal shocks, that countries with strong expenditure rules have undertaken a counter-cyclical response in the face of revenue shortfalls, while countries with weak expenditure rules have opted for pro-cyclical responses.

6.2.3. Summary

Table 6.1. summarises the results of empirical studies on fiscal rules. Altogether, the empirical studies exploring the effects of fiscal rules point to diverging results. Even the literature reviews conducted so far have come to discrepant conclusions. Krogstrup and Wälti (2008, p. 134) state that the empirical literature on fiscal rules "finds relative unambiguously that fiscal rules are associated with improved budget balances". In a similar vein, Kirchgässner (2001, p. 21) concludes that "Balanced-budget rules and limitations of expenditure, taxes, and deficits, have in most cases proved to be effective in cutting down public expenditure, revenue, and debt." Von Hagen (2002), however, notes that "the effectiveness of fiscal rules is limited at best, because politicians are likely to find ways to circumvent them". Kennedy and Robbins (2001, pp. 1, 14) conclude that fiscal rules *can* have an impact on fiscal policy outcomes, such rules may be

194 A number of authors (e.g., Ayuso-i-Casals *et al.* 2007) consider such rules to fall under the term "fiscal rules".

helpful in achieving fiscal success and *may* even be necessary in certain countries, but they are clearly *not necessary* in all countries.

Table 6.1.: Effects of fiscal rules

	Balanced budget rules, deficit and debt limits	**Tax and expenditure limitations**
Expenditures	Lower spending: Crain and Miller (1990) Bohn and Inman (1996) Bails and Tieslau (2000)	Lower spending: Dougan (1988) King-Meadows and Lowery (2003) Bails and Tieslau (2000) Stansel (1994) Ayuso-i-Casals et al. (2007) European Commission (2006) Contingent effects in lowering spending: Shadbegian (1996) New (2001) Poterba (1994) Bails and Tieslau (2000) No effects on spending: Bails (1982, 1990) Abrams and Dougan (1996) Cox and Lowery (1990) Kenyon and Baker (1984) Kousser, McCubbins and Rozga (2008)
Tax revenues	Higher tax revenues: Merrifield (1991) Lower tax revenues: Nelson (1986)	Lower tax revenues: Crain and Miller (1991) Stansel (1994) Short-run negative effects on revenues: Joyce and Mullins (1991) Higher tax revenues: Besley and Case (2003) Lower tax increases during recession: Poterba (1994) Poulson (2004)

	Balanced budget rules, deficit and debt limits	Tax and expenditure limitations
Deficit and debt levels	Lower debts and deficits: Ayso-i-Casals et al. (2007) von Hagen (2006a) Alesina et al. (1999) Eslava (2006) Impact of more stringent rules on deficits: von Hagen (1991) Eichengreen (1994) Eichengreen and Bayoumi (1994) Bohn and Inman (1996) Alesina and Bayoumi (1996) Feld and Kirchgässner (2006) Schaltegger (2002) Krogstrup and Wälti (2008) European Commission (2006) Limited effect on deficits: Briotti (2004) Annett (2006) Strauch and von Hagen (2001) Fatas et al. (2003) von Hagen (2006a, 2008) Annett and Jaeger (2004) Buti and Pench (2004) No effect: Alt and Lowry Feld and Kirchgässner (2001b)	Lower deficits: Knight and Levinson (1999) Sobel and Holcombe (1996) Wagner and Elder (2005) Higher surpluses: Brosens and Wierts (2007)
Fiscal adjustment	Prompter fiscal adjustment: Poterba (1993) Revenue-based adjustment: Briotti (2004) Morris, Ongena and Schuknecht (2006) Shifts into other accounts: Von Hagen (1991) No shifts into other accounts: Bohn and Inman (1996) Kiewet and Szakaly (1996) von Hagen and Eichengreen (1996)	Shift of expenditure from current budget to investment budget: Strauch (1998) Prompter adjustment: Poterba (1994) More extensive, longer-lasting adjustment: Guichard et al. (2007)

	Balanced budget rules, deficit and debt limits	Tax and expenditure limitations
	Increased creative accounting: von Hagen and Wolff (2006) Koen and van den Noord (2006) Buti et al. (2007)	
Cyclical effects, effects on output volatility	Constrained volatility: Fatas and Mihov (1993) Alesina and Bayoumi (1996) Exacerbated business cycle: Levinson (1998) Higher pro-cyclicality: Annett (2006) Gali and Perotti (2003) Fatas et al. (2003) Briotti (2004) Beetsma and Guiliodori (2008) European Commission (2006)	Counter-cyclical response to fiscal shock: Wierts (2008)

A common concern that remains with the studies exploring the effects of fiscal rules on fiscal outcomes is that while the institutional variation in fiscal rules is assumed to be exogenous, it may in fact be endogenous. A number of authors have referred to the possibility that both the adoption of the fiscal rules and the fiscal outcomes may be driven by political preferences, implying that the association found between fiscal rules and outcomes may be spurious (Poterba 1996; Inman 1996; Debrun and Kumar 2007; Gordon 2008). Debrun and Kumar (2007), for example, argue that fiscal rules are adopted by government to signal competence; therefore, governments that are more disciplined would be more likely to use stringent fiscal rules. Further, Debrun and Kumar (2007) show, in their study of 14 EU countries (between 1990 and 2004), that when taking into account potential endogeneity, the restrictiveness of fiscal rules and their coverage had no meaningful effect on the cyclically adjusted budget balance. Therefore, they conclude that "One should not dismiss a priori the possibility of a serious endogeneity problem when estimating the impact of fiscal rules on fiscal behaviour." (p. 37) Fiscal rules are likely to be effective when the deficit bias is low to start with, and low deficit countries may be more likely to set up such institutions.

The dissatisfaction with the ineffectiveness or perverse effects of substantive fiscal rules led both normative and positive streams of fiscal governance literature to focus their attention to the *procedural* aspects of budgeting, with the hope that budgeting procedures can provide better explanations (and for the normative side, also more effective solutions) for budgetary policies.

6.3. Budgetary Institutions

Budgetary institutions and their influence on budgetary outcomes (especially on budget deficits and debt levels) have received increasing attention in the political economy literature since the beginning of 1990s, starting with von Hagen (1992).[195] Budgetary institutions are a set of rules that guide the decision-making process in formulating, approving and implementing the budget. Chapter 5 discussed how political institutions – by establishing position and boundary rules – influence the number of participants who can potentially take part in budgetary decision-making process. Using Ostrom's (1986) terminology, budgetary institutions, embedded in the general institutional framework provided by the political institutions, entail position, authority, aggregation, information and payoff rules that guide and constrain the behaviour and decisions of political actors in the action arena of budgeting. Succinctly put, budgetary institutions can be seen as the "rules of the game" that shape the interaction of the participants involved in budget-making process by distributing strategic influence among them and regulating the flow of information (Stein, Talvi and Grisanti 1999, p. 118; von Hagen 2006a, p. 47).

While political institutionalists (represented most clearly by the adherents of "political economics", like Persson and Tabellini) seek to ascertain how budgetary outcomes differ in parliamentary as opposed to presidential systems, budgetary institutionalists (represented most clearly by von Hagen and his followers) assume that budgetary outcomes can be very different *among* parliamentary systems, depending on budgetary institutions that govern decision-making within cabinet and legislature (and modes of interaction that are foreseen for the two branches in budgeting).

This section first gives an overview of the emerging orthodoxy in budgetary institutionalist literature (section 6.3.1.), then considers the empirical evidence

195 There were, however, already earlier studies concentrating on the design effects of different parts of the budget process (rather than viewing all the phases of the budget process together). Ferejohn and Krehbiel (1987) analysed the effects of the new congressional budget process in the United States (i.e., voting first on the budget size and then on its components, rather than voting on different components that residually add up to the total budget) on the size of the budget. They found that, in line with theoretical hypotheses, such process may sometimes lead to larger budgets. Crain and Muris (1995) investigated the effect of legislative organisation on fiscal policy in the U.S. states. In particular, they compared the effects of different committee structures and find that when only one legislative committee has the authority to spend, spending is restrained; when spending authority is "balkanized" (i.e., spread across multiple committees), the spending constraint is difficult to maintain.

for the main theoretical propositions of this stream of literature (section 6.3.2.) and, finally, presents a "within-discourse" critique of it in section 6.3.3.

6.3.1. Theoretical Propositions

Most of the literature on budgetary institutions deals with the question of how different budget procedures address the common-pool problems inherent in an action arena where the "general" tax fund is grazed by political decision-makers for the purposes of providing "less general" expenditures (see, among others, von Hagen and Harden 1994, 1995, 1996; Hallerberg and von Hagen 1997, 1999; von Hagen 1992, 2002, 2006a,b; Strauch and von Hagen 2001). As discussed in section 4.4. (and also in sections 5.1.–5.6.), the core problem of budgetary commons is that constituencies who benefit from a particular programme have to bear only a fraction of the costs involved in providing this programme. Given the divergence between the perceived costs and benefits involved in targeted spending, the elected officials (representing geographically or socially defined constituencies) either in the legislature or executive have incentives to demand excessive levels of expenditures on targeted programmes. The budgetary institutionalist literature assumes that certain kinds of budgetary procedures can address the common-pool problems of budgeting more effectively than others, and can thus influence aggregate fiscal outcomes, especially deficits. It is suggested that "properly" designed budgetary rules can lead the participants in the budgeting process to internalise the costs of spending decisions and the budget deficit.

While the political institutionalist literature discussed in section 5.3. dealt with the issue of *size fragmentation* (referring to the number of participants) in budgetary decision-making, the budgetary institutionalist literature is primarily concerned with the questions of *procedural fragmentation* in budgeting. In analyses of the likely effects of different kinds of budgetary institutions, a *centralised* budget process is often contrasted with a *fragmented* budget process.[196] A fragmented process is seen as more likely to give rise to excessive spending and deficits, while a centralised process is considered to be conducive to fiscal discipline.

As von Hagen (2002) emphasises, the institutional elements of centralisation can be relevant at all different stages of the budget process: the planning and drafting of the budget by the executive, the adoption of the budget by the parliament and the implementation of the budget.[197] The executive phase can be

196 Some authors formulate the distinction as *hierarchical* versus *collegial* budget process (e.g., Alesina and Perotti 1996, 1999; Stein, Talvi and Grisanti 1999) or *centralised* versus *decentralised* process (e.g., Haggard, Kaufman and Shugart 2001).

197 Von Hagen (2002, p. 271) also points to the "*ex post* accountability stage", which involves a review of the final budget documents by a court of auditors or a similar institution checking the consistency of the actual spending and revenues with the legal authori-

characterised as centralised, when it promotes the setting of spending and deficit (or surplus) targets at the outset; conversely, it can be designated as fragmented, when the resulting budget is merely a sum of uncoordinated bids from individual ministries. At the legislative approval stage, the process can be described as fragmented when the following elements are present: the parliament can make unlimited amendments to the draft budget submitted by the executive, spending decisions can be made by legislative committees with narrow and dispersed authorities, and there is little guidance of the parliamentary process either by the executive or by the speaker.[198] Elements of centralisation at the adoption stage give the executive or the budget committee an important role in setting the agenda of budget proceedings in the legislature, limit legislative amendments to the budget, require amendments to be offsetting, postulate the legislature to vote on the total budget size before the approbation of single provisions and raise the political stakes of rejecting the executive's budget (e.g., by making this equivalent to a vote of non-confidence).[199] At the implementation stage, elements of centralisation assure that the adopted budget would actually be the basis for the spending decisions of the executive. Thus, implementation can be regarded as centralised when it is difficult to change the existing budget document or to adopt supplementary budgets during the fiscal year, when transfers of funds between chapters are forbidden or limited, and when unused funds cannot be carried over to the next year's budget. Further elements of centralisation in the implementation stage include: extensive powers of the finance minister to monitor and control spending flows during the fiscal year (e.g., by blocking expenditures and imposing cash limits on spending ministers) and sanctioning the disbursement of funds by a central unit in the ministry of finance. (von Hagen 2002, 2003; Hallerberg, Strauch and von Hagen 2007)

Hallerberg and von Hagen (1999) distinguish between two modes of fiscal governance that help to resolve the common-pool problems of budgeting by inducing decision-makers to internalise the budgeting externalities: the *delegation* approach and the *fiscal contracts* (also called the *commitment*) approach.

The *delegation* approach involves lending significant strategic powers to the finance minister, who can be assumed to take a more comprehensive view of the budget than other actors and who would have incentives to internalise the costs

sation, but he notes that the institutional elements of centralisation primarily concern the first three stages.

198 As von Hagen (2002, p. 271) notes, "Because of the much larger number of decision makers involved, the common pool problem is even larger in the legislature than in the executive."

199 For models on the effects of centralised versus decentralised budgetary decision-making in a legislature, see, for example, Cogan (1994), Dixit (1996), Crain and Muris (1995) and Dharmapala (2003).

of public spending programmes.[200] In the delegation approach, the preparation phase of the budget procedure is characterised by strong agenda-setting powers of the finance minister *vis-à-vis* the spending ministers: the finance minister makes binding proposals for broad budgetary categories, negotiates directly with the individual ministries, approves the bids submitted to the final cabinet meeting and can act as a veto player over budgetary issues in the cabinet. In the legislative approval phase of the process, the delegation approach limits the rights of the legislature to amend the budget (in order to avoid major changes in the executive's budget proposal) and gives the executive strong agenda-setting powers *vis-à-vis* the legislature. In the implementation phase, the minister of finance has strong monitoring powers regarding the actual use of budget appropriations by the spending ministers and the authority to prevent and correct any deviations from the budget plan. (von Hagen 1992, 2002, 2006a,b, 2008; von Hagen and Harden 1994, 1995; Alesina *et al.* 1999; Hahm, Kamlet and Mowery 1996; Alesina and Perotti 1996, 1999)

Under the *fiscal contracts* approach, at the beginning of the annual budget cycle, all members of government negotiate multilaterally and commit themselves to a key set of budgetary parameters or fiscal targets (usually spending targets for each ministry) that are considered to be binding for the rest of the budget cycle. It is assumed that the process of collective negotiations would lead the different actors involved to understand and take into account the externalities entailed in budgetary decisions. During the rest of the budget preparation process, the minister of finance has the responsibility to evaluate the consistency of the budget proposals submitted by the spending ministers with the agreed targets. At the legislative stage, the fiscal contracts approach puts less emphasis on constraining legislative budgetary amendments and more emphasis on the legislature's role in monitoring the compliance of the executive's budget with the fiscal targets, by giving the legislature significant rights to demand budgetary information from the executive. In the implementation phase, the minister of finance would have strong monitoring and control rights to prevent and correct deviations from the adopted budget; while the delegation approach emphasises the need for managerial discretion by the minister of finance, allowing him to react flexibly to changing budgetary circumstances, the contracts approach is characterised by contingent rules for dealing with unforeseen events. (von Ha-

200 As Alesina and Perotti (1999, p. 23) explain, while the constituencies of spending ministers are groups and industries who benefit from certain spending programmes, the constituency of the minister of finance, at least in principle, is the "average" taxpayer. Wildavsky (1986, p. 13) also underlines that the finance minister has – compared with the other ministers – the strongest incentives for expenditure limitation and his "power motive can rarely by satisfied by advocating more expenditure", since "People do not complain about surplus, but if there is a large deficit leading to increased taxes or inflation, the ministry of finance will take the blame."

gen 1992, 2002, 2006a,b, 2007, 2008; von Hagen and Harden 1994, 1995; Hallerberg and von Hagen 1999)

These two ideal types of fiscal governance are usually contrasted with the *fiefdom* approach to budgeting (Hallerberg 2004), which is characterised by fragmented, uncoordinated and ad hoc decision-making in all phases of the budgetary process. Under the fiefdom approach, the budgetary decision-making is expected to be plagued by common-pool problems, leading to lower levels of fiscal discipline than the delegation or contracts approach. In addition, Hallerberg (2004) has pointed to a *mixed* type of fiscal governance, which employs elements of delegation in the preparation phase but is followed by a contract-like adoption phase, with the parliament playing an equally strong role in the passage of the budget alongside the executive.

A typical question raised in the budgetary institutionalist literature is: Which of the fiscal governance mechanisms is more effective in solving the common-pool problems of budgeting? Hallerberg and von Hagen (1999) conjecture that the delegation approach is likely to be more successful in safeguarding fiscal discipline because enforcement and punishment mechanisms are more credible under the delegation approach. They argue that under the delegation approach, the defecting minister can be punished by dismissal – which is a harsh punishment for an individual but does not bring about severe consequences for the government as a whole. Under the contracts approach, however, the defecting minister cannot usually be dismissed so easily, since the distribution of portfolios is decided in the coalition agreement; thus, ousting a minister from another party could be regarded as an interference with the internal issues of the other parties in the coalition. Hallerberg and von Hagen (1999) note that the main sanction under the contracts approach – when a minister deviates from the agreed budget targets – is the break-up of the coalition. That, however, would be a harsh punishment for the government as a whole. Further, this "punishment" would only be credible if there are other parties in the parliament with whom alternative coalitions could be formed by the party who seeks to penalise the coalition partner(s) for reneging on the agreement. Thus, given that the parties do not always have incentives to monitor and punish each other, it is more difficult to uphold successfully the negotiated targets than it is to maintain a strong finance minister.

Besides distinguishing between the different ideal types of fiscal governance, the budgetary institutionalist literature has been concerned with factors that influence the polity's choice between the different modes. While the fiefdom approach could in principle be chosen by any kind of government (Hallerberg 2000a), the choice between delegation and contracts approach is likely to be influenced by the government type. Most broadly put, in parliamentary systems, single-party governments can be expected to opt for the delegation approach, and coalition governments for the contracts approach (Hallerberg and von Hagen 1999). Specifications of the general idea note that delegation approach could also be adopted by coalition governments that consist of a large party and a smaller one without an obvious alternative coalition partner (Hallerberg 2000b; von Hagen 2006a) or coalition parties that plan to run together in the next elections (Hallerberg 2000a; von Hagen 2007, 2008; Hallerberg, Strauch and von Hagen 2007).[201] The main explanatory factor behind this conjecture is the degree of similarity in spending preferences among the members of the government. In single-party governments, the ministers come from the same party and are likely to have similar views with respect to the distribution of funds between different groups of recipients. Thus, the finance minister would be trusted to use his authority to solve the common-pool resource problems within the framework of the overall spending preferences shared by the whole cabinet.[202] In a coalition government, however, the ministers may have divergent views on the basic spending needs. Hence, the coalition partners can be expected to be reluctant to lend strong powers to the finance minister: they are likely to suspect that the finance minister would unduly promote the budgetary interests of his own party at the expense of other parties. Ensuing from the desire to assure that the priorities of one's own party are taken into account in the agenda-setting stage of the budget process, the parties in the coalition government would be more likely to prefer the contracts approach, where the negotiations on fiscal targets involve all cabinet ministers.

As Hallerberg and von Hagen (1999) underline, another factor that plays a role in influencing the choice of fiscal governance mode is a set of enforcement and punishment mechanisms available under the different approaches and their functional fit with the party constellation in the government. If the minister of finance were to secure the adoption of his proposals regarding the budget, he would need a strong backing from the prime minister. While in single-party governments, the prime minister can lend unquestioned support to the finance minister, this may not be the case in coalition governments. Thus, the delegation approach would run into difficulties here. In single-party governments, on the other hand, the "contracts alone" approach is conjectured to be seen as too weak a mechanism compared with a strong finance minister: if the finance minister lacks mechanisms for enforcement and there is no effective threat against reneging on the targets (e.g., the fall of the government, as it could be in the case of coalition government), the spending ministers could be easily tempted to deviate from the agreed-upon targets. Hallerberg (2000b) adds, drawing on Laver

201 With regard to the *mixed* type of fiscal governance, Hallerberg (2004) notes that this is likely to be chosen by minority governments, which need to have a consent of the opposition to pass the budget in the legislature.

202 Hallerberg (2000a, p. 10) notes, however, that if the parties in the coalition plan to run together in the next elections, it would also be feasible to delegate power to a finance minister: "Any attempt on the finance minister's part to undermine a particular minister or party of a minister will, in the end, undermine her own chances of winning the next election."

and Shepsle (1996), that if the party constellation includes a strong party that cannot be excluded from a possible coalition because of the combination of its electoral strength and its position in the middle of the political spectrum of the party landscape, fiscal contracts are unlikely to work, because the strong party cannot be punished by other coalition parties. Therefore, countries with a track record of strong parties are especially likely to opt for fiefdom arrangements in budgetary decision-making.[203] Yläoutinen (2004a,b) suggests that fiefdom would be especially likely in a political system that is undergoing constant changes and these changes translate into instability in terms of government types. Also, he argues that if the party system is so unstable that party discipline in the legislature is undermined, credible fiscal commitments cannot be enforced, because the political parties within the executive would be reluctant to make commitments that may be impaired by unreliable voting behaviour of the coalition partners' parliament members at the legislative stage.

Although most of the literature discussing the delegation and contracts approaches to budgeting deal with parliamentary systems, some remarks have been made with regard to the application of these two models in a presidential system. Von Hagen (2003, 2007) notes that while the delegation approach can be conceivable in the budget preparation phase (since the president usually appoints the members of his administration), then given the separation of powers between the legislature and the executive in presidential systems, a contracts approach rather than delegation approach would be operable in the legislative-executive interactions in budgetary decision-making. Hence, in Hallerberg's (2004) terminology, presidential systems would be most likely to adopt a mixed type of fiscal governance (if they were to centralise their budgetary procedures).

While the discussions on the delegation and contracts modes of fiscal governance are primarily concerned with common-pool problems of budgeting, a stream of literature within the budgetary institutionalism focuses on the question of what kind of institutional elements are likely to enhance the *accountability* of budgeting and mitigate the principal-agent relations between voters and elected officials in the budgetary arena. An emerging consensus is that accountability of budgeting can be strongly facilitated by institutional elements that enhance the transparency of both the budget process and the budget document itself (see Stein, Talvi and Grisanti 1999; Poterba and von Hagen 1999; von Hagen 2002; Alt and Lassen 2006; Garrett and Vermeule 2008). The transparency of the budget refers to the extent to which the "budget document provides an accurate representation of projected expenditures, revenues, and deficits" (Stein, Talvi and Grisanti 1999, p. 119) and is accessible to the public and participants in the decision-making process (Poterba and von Hagen 1999, p. 4). The more trans-

203 This is a contrary prediction that the literature on political institutions would make. As argued in section 5.3.1.2.3., it is the more fractionalised governments that are predicted to have difficulties with fiscal discipline rather than the ones with a dominant party.

parent the budget process and the resulting documents are, the lower are the monitoring costs that voters would have to incur; hence, the slack in the principal-agent relations would be reduced. There is a common agreement that transparency of the budget is reduced by the existence of extra-budgetary items, special accounts, hidden liabilities and contingent liabilities. Thus, budgetary rules that curtail the use of these elements are likely to enhance the transparency of the budget process and hence the accountability of political actors. Further, transparency of the budget and the resulting accountability of political actors is considered to be strongly facilitated by the existence of independent bodies (like state audit offices) in charge of evaluating the transparency and verifying the accuracy of the budget process and documents (Alesina and Perotti 1999; Alt and Lassen 2006).

6.3.2. Empirical Evidence

A fast-growing empirical literature starting from the beginning of 1990s has examined the effects of budgetary institutions on public finances. The studies have primarily explored the following questions: How do different budgetary institutions (the degree of centralisation, delegation as opposed to contracts approach, particular elements of the budget process) influence budgetary outcomes (especially debts and deficits)? What have been the factors behind the institutional choices for particular types of fiscal government? How has the functional fit between political institutions and budgetary institutions influenced budgetary outcomes?

The first studies analysing the impacts of budget institutions on fiscal performance using cross-country data were conducted by von Hagen (1992) and von Hagen and Harden (1994, 1995). They constructed a set of indices capturing the most important institutional features of the budget process in 12 EU countries and found that budget institutions have had a significant impact on debt ratios and budget deficits. They showed that there is a strong and negative association between the indices capturing the degree of centralisation of the budget process and general government expenditures, deficits and debts relative to GDP. Their studies conclude that budgetary institutions that give the finance minister more extensive powers *vis-à-vis* the spending ministers, constrain the amendment powers of legislature and leave little space for additional changes during the implementation phase are strongly conducive to fiscal discipline. These indices and the methodology of compiling an index measuring the centralisation of the budget process suggested by von Hagen (1992) and von Hagen and Harden (1994) have been used in a number of subsequent studies for several samples of developed and developing countries. The most comprehensive study in terms of sample size has been conducted by Woo (2003); he examined the effects of economic, institutional and political variables on budget deficit in 57 developed and developing countries between 1970 and 1990, and found that centralisation of authority in budgetary decisions is one of the variables that is significant and robust in explaining public deficits. Since the empirical studies have predominantly focused on specific regions, the overview below follows the regional logic as well: first, the studies concerning old member states of the EU and OECD countries will be considered, followed by Latin American countries and Central and Eastern European countries.

The European Union countries (especially the old member states) have received most extensive attention in the empirical literature on budgetary institutions so far. The results found in the seminal studies by von Hagen (1992) and von Hagen and Harden (1994), indicating a negative correlation between the degree of centralisation of the budget process and budget deficit, have been confirmed by several subsequent studies. De Haan and Sturm (1994) and de Haan, Moessen and Volkerink (1999) show that the result holds even when a number of political factors such as the composition and stability of governments are controlled for. Hallerberg and von Hagen (1999), in their panel study of 15 EU countries, confirm the relationship even when controlling for a number of economic and political variables. These findings have been endorsed by Leachman *et al.* (2007), Helland (2000) and Lagona and Padovano (2007). In addition to looking at the general level of centralisation in budgetary decision-making, a number of studies have sought to disentangle the impacts of different forms of fiscal governance and the effects of specific institutional elements in the budget procedure. Hallerberg and von Hagen (1999) confirm, in their study of 15 EU countries (from 1981 to 1994), that the use of *either* delegation to a strong finance minister *or* commitment to negotiated budget targets can have a significant impact on the budget deficit, but a strong finance minister is more effective in keeping the deficit lower than the contracts approach, *ceteris paribus*. De Haan, Moessen and Volkerink (1999) analyse the effects of different components of the centralisation index in a sample of European countries and conclude that the position of the minister of finance is especially important. Lagona and Padovano (2007) ascertain for 12 EU countries (from 1980 to 2003) that the effects of different elements of budgetary institutions are different for financial variables (i.e., debts and deficits) and for public expenditures. For example, the elements concerning long-term budget plans, including the level of commitment to multi-annual fiscal targets, appear to play the most important role in constraining the stock of public debt. Primary deficits and expenditures appear to be best constrained by limiting changes to the budget in the execution phase. Further, Lagona and Padovano emphasise that the disciplining effect on fiscal outcomes is exerted by the budgetary institutions *conjointly,* that is, by a configuration of rules rather than by single rules in isolation (p. 413).

Alongside with examining the effects of different forms of fiscal governance on budget discipline, a number of studies have explored factors behind the institutional choices and how these factors might in turn influence the impacts of budgetary institutions on budgetary outcomes. Hallerberg and von Hagen (1999) establish a link between the number of parties in the government and the choice between delegation and fiscal contracts: one-party governments are likely to opt for delegation, while coalition governments tend to choose the contracts approach. Hallerberg, Strauch and von Hagen (2007) consider 15 EU member states from 1985 to 2004 and confirm the result of Hallerberg and von Hagen (1999) by showing that the contracts approach has been chosen by countries with ideologically dispersed coalition governments, while single-party governments or coalitions with closely aligned party constellations have opted for a delegation approach. Also, when taking steps to *further* centralise the budget processes, the contract states tended to tighten the stringency of their fiscal rules, while delegation states moved towards empowering the minister of finance.[204] Hallerberg, Strauch and von Hagen (2007) point out that the impact of further centralisation of the budget process varies according to the initial form of fiscal governance. For the delegation states, strengthening the elements of "delegation" (especially increasing the power of the finance minister) has contributed to lower debt growth, but adding "contracts" elements has not. Conversely, in the contract states, strengthening delegation elements has contributed less to fiscal sustainability than substantiating the "contracts" elements.

Besides the interaction between domestic political institutions and budgetary institutions, the interaction between the EU fiscal framework (established by the Maastricht Treaty and the SGP) and domestic budgetary institutions has been explored. A number of studies have found that the EU fiscal rules have been more effective in contract states than in delegation states, owing to functional complementarities between the contracts approach and fiscal rules (Hallerberg 2004; Annett 2006; von Hagen 2008).[205] Hallerberg (2004, p. 194) notes that the domestic fiscal targets and the EU rules can be mutually reinforcing: the SGP can enhance the commitment of coalition partners to fiscal targets, and the institutions that contract states use for monitoring the adherence to the fiscal contract by coalition partners foster compliance with the SGP. Annett (2006) shows that delegation was beneficial for fiscal discipline before the SGP was signed,

204 Debrun and Kumar (2007) show, however, in their study of 14 European Union countries from 1990 to 2004, that delegation countries have tightened fiscal rules more than commitment countries. A study by the European Commission (2006) also shows that the total number of fiscal rules (and fiscal targets) is similar in both contract and delegation states; rather, they can be differentiated according to the *type* of rules that have been adopted. While the contracts states have more fiscal rules that apply to the *central* government, the delegation states have fiscal rules that apply predominantly to *regional* and *local* levels.

205 As Annett (2006, p. 15) puts it, "With its emphasis on multi-annual targets and a regular review procedure, the SGP fits snugly with the numerical contracts approach associated with commitment states."

but not thereafter; the commitment approach did better than fiefdom in both periods, but to a greater extent after the SGP was signed.[206]

While the studies on EU countries have found significant effects of budgetary institutions on deficits, the two studies that have explored a larger sample of OECD countries, have found only insignificant effects. Perotti and Kontopoulos (2002), in their study of 19 OECD countries between 1970 and 1995, examine the effects of two elements of centralisation in the preparation phase of the budget process: whether the budgetary negotiations are bilateral (as opposed to multilateral) and whether aggregate spending limits are imposed (either on the entire budget size as a whole or in the form of spending limits for individual ministries). They find that neither of these elements plays a role in explaining expenditures, revenues or budget deficits. In a similar vein, Tujula and Wolswijk (2004), in their study of 22 OECD countries, find no effects of the form of fiscal governance (delegation, contracts, mixed, fiefdom) on budget balances.

Several studies have analysed the impact of budgetary institutions in Latin America. Alesina *et al.* (1999) study 20 Latin American and Caribbean countries from 1980 to 1993 and find that budgetary institutions have had an important effect on primary deficits. They use indices of budget procedures capturing the degree of centralisation and budget transparency and find that more centralised and transparent procedures are associated with lower deficits, after controlling for several economic determinants. They find that the most influential aspects of the budget process are a binding macroeconomic programme and limits on the legislature to amend the budget. Filc and Scartascini (2005), using a more comprehensive index of budgetary institutions, endorse the findings of Alesina *et al.* (1999). Similar results have been found by Stein, Talvi and Grisanti (1999), who use a cross-section with 26 Latin American countries. They also look at the interaction between the budget institutions and electoral system and conclude that "There is no evidence that centralised budgetary arrangements can neutralise the potentially adverse impact on fiscal deficits of a larger degree of proportionality of the electoral system." (p. 132) Thus, their findings suggest that *both* budgetary institutions and electoral institutions are significant determinants of fiscal performance in Latin America. Hallerberg and Marier (2004) also consider interactions between political and budgetary institutions in shaping fiscal outcomes in Latin-American countries. They find that strengthening the authority of the finance minister at the preparation phase improves budget discipline in both parliamentary and presidential systems with one-party governments found in Latin American and Caribbean countries. The effect of strengthening the power of the executive *vis-à-vis* the legislature in the adoption phase is, however, dependent on the features of the electoral system: budget discipline is in-

206 Hodson (2007), however, points out that not all delegation states have incurred excessive deficits, and both contracts and delegation states have failed to comply fully with the medium-term rules of the SGP.

creased only in countries where the electoral system encourages the cultivation of personal vote by elected representatives (see also section 5.2.1.). As Hallerberg and Marier (2004) argue, in such systems, a stronger executive has been able, by reducing the amount of particularistic spending projects, to contribute to tighter fiscal discipline. Conversely, they find that countries with electoral systems where the level of personal vote is low (and hence the tendency for particularistic spending is also lower), strengthening the executive in the adoption phase has not significantly influenced fiscal discipline.

Of particular interests for this book, given its focus on transition, are the studies exploring budgetary institutions in the CEE region. Brusis and Dimitrov (2001) examine the relationship between the changing configuration of executive institutions and corresponding aggregate fiscal discipline in four CEE countries (Hungary, Poland, the Czech Republic and Bulgaria) from 1989 to 1999. The main conclusion of their study is that a greater degree of centralisation of executive institutions leads to better fiscal performance (in terms of deficit levels and predictability of the budget, expressed in the number of supplementary budgets adopted). They show that the relatively weak positions of the prime minister and the finance minister in the cabinet coincided with deteriorating fiscal performance in all four countries and that those two countries (Hungary and Poland) that augmented the institutional positions of the prime minister and finance minister achieved improvements in fiscal performance. Dimitrov (2005) endorses these findings. Gleich (2002, 2003) conducted a study of the budget processes in ten Central and East European countries (candidates for accession to the EU at the time). He shows that there is a strong correlation between the degree of centralisation of the budget process and public sector deficits and debts that emerged between 1994 and 1998.[207] Moreover, he points out that the institutional qualities of the budget *preparation* stage in particular appear to have a strong explanatory power. The rules governing the budget implementation, however, do not seem to have a significant effect. Yläoutinen (2004a) finds, in his study of ten CEE countries, that countries with more centralised fiscal procedures have enjoyed better fiscal discipline. He also points out that strong finance ministers have enhanced fiscal discipline by complementing the commitments imposed by jointly negotiated targets and that all phases of the budget process have been important in ensuring fiscal rigour. Yläoutinen (2004a) notes, however, that these results are clear only for the later part of the transition period (from 1999 to 2002), while for the early period (from 1994 to 1998), the indices of centralisation of budget procedures can not explain the differences in fiscal performance in the CEE countries. Fabrizio and Mody (2006)

207 As Yläoutinen (2004a) notes, however, the association between the debt-to-GDP ratio and budgetary institutions is primarily due to the fact that Estonia and Latvia have both low accumulated debt levels (since these countries inherited very little debt from the Soviet era, as the debts of the Soviet Union were taken over by Russia) and have high index values for budgetary institutions.

examine the effects of different economic, political and institutional variables on the resulting budget deficits in the ten new and potential member states of the EU (over the period 1997–2003). One of their main findings is that budgetary institutions matter strongly in determining fiscal outcomes: the higher the index capturing the centralisation of the budget process, the higher the fiscal discipline. Fabrizio and Mody (2006) also examine whether the three components of the budget institutions index (referring, respectively, to the preparation, authorisation and implementation stage) have a differential impact on budgetary performance. They find that while each component appears to have a strong and independent impact, the index capturing the elements of the *implementation* stage appears to be the most relevant (p. 23). In addition, their results suggest that the phases are not substitutes: if any of the phases has weaknesses, this can hurt fiscal discipline and cannot be compensated by higher level of centralisation in another phase of the process. There has been one study, though, that has found budgetary institutions to have weak explanatory power in CEE countries. Berger, Kopits and Szekely (2007) find, in their study of eight CEE countries (that joined the EU in 2004) that the indicators of fiscal centralisation and transparency are not significant in explaining the fiscal performance of these countries.[208]

A number of studies have also explored the factors behind the choices of budgetary institutions in CEE countries. Gleich (2002) finds that countries with a larger degree of political fragmentation (reflected in a larger number of parties in the parliament) and social polarisation (gauged by the degree of ethnic fragmentation or the degree of income inequality) have been more likely to adopt centralised budget institutions. Gleich (2002, p. 193) considers it as evidence for the tendency of decision-makers to "choose strong institutional mechanisms supportive of coordinated decision-making when they perceive that the individuals in the budget process have very different interests and thus might have low incentives to follow cooperative strategies voluntarily". In addition, he finds that countries that experienced large budget deficits in the early stage of transition opted for more centralised budget institutions.[209] Yläoutinen (2004a) investigates budget institutions in ten CEE countries and finds that the governments in the CEE countries use jointly negotiated agreements to commit themselves to fiscal targets, rather than only delegating significant fiscal powers to the finance

---

208 Berger, Kopits and Szekely (2007) find that the large Central European countries progressively relaxed their fiscal stance upon securing NATO membership in 1999. Being a member of NATO increased the perceived bargaining strength of these countries in EU accession negotiations, which in turn, could have played a role in relaxing the fiscal discipline.

209 Gleich (2002, p. 193) also finds that political instability has not had significant effects on the design of budget institutions, the level of initial debt is not significantly correlated with the index of budget institutions, and countries that have relied more heavily on IMF's financial support have established less centralised budget institutions.

minister. Gregor (2004) examines whether the modes of fiscal governance in the ten new member states of EU conform to what could be expected according to Hallerberg and von Hagen (1999). He finds that, in most cases, the fiscal governance structure is *not* what could be expected. He points out, for example, that Latvia, Slovakia and Poland look like the delegation type but would politically need a commitment framework. Further, Gregor notes that Lithuania, Estonia and Slovenia remain the most puzzling cases, since they exhibit excessively strong finance ministers. Dimitrov (2005) examines the budgetary institutions adopted in four CEE countries (Poland, Hungary, the Czech Republic and Bulgaria) and confirms the hypotheses put forth by Hallerberg (2000b): the delegation approach has been adopted by one-party governments or coalition blocks in which parties expect to run together in future elections, while multi-party coalition governments in which the parties do not expect to run together have led to the adoption of decentralised budgeting institutions.[210] Fabrizio and Mody (2006) also indicate, contrary to the findings in Hallerberg and von Hagen (1999), that *both* delegation approach and fiscal contracts approach have been adopted by coalition governments in CEE countries. Further, they show that both contracts elements and delegation elements have improved fiscal discipline, irrespective of the prevailing mode of fiscal governance.

While budgetary institutions have been extensively explored in the empirical literature, the effects of transparency in budgeting have received somewhat less attention. Von Hagen (1992) and de Haan, Moessen and Volkerink (1999) find only a weak association between fiscal transparency and fiscal performance in European countries. Alesina and Perotti (1999) demonstrate that transparency has played a positive role in fiscal performance in Latin American countries. Alt and Lassen (2006) focus on the effect of fiscal transparency on the level of gross debt (and spending) and average change of debt in 19 OECD countries between 1990 and 1999, while controlling for several economic and political variables. Their results suggest that a higher degree of fiscal transparency is associated with lower public debt and deficits.

6.3.3. Summary

Altogether, the existing studies point to strong evidence that budgetary institutions matter and that they matter in a predictable manner. Table 6.2. summarises the results of the empirical studies. More centralised budgetary procedures are associated with stronger budget discipline. In contrast to the fiefdom approach, both delegation and contracts approach to fiscal governance can improve fiscal discipline. With regard to the differential relevance of the distinct phases of

210 As Dimitrov (2005, p. 61) notes, although such governments could have theoretically opted for the commitment approach, it was unfeasible in practice since the parties lacked "clear programmatic identity" and, hence, were not willing to commit themselves to clearly articulated policy goals.

budget procedure, the empirical literature points to diverging results: some point to the preparation phase as playing a particularly substantial role, others underline the elements of the adoption phase and implementation phase.

Table 6.2.: Effects of budgetary institutions

	Effects on deficit and debt
Overall degree of centralisation of budgetary institutions	Constraining effect: von Hagen (1992) von Hagen and Harden (1994, 1995) Woo (2003) de Haan and Sturm (1994) de Haan, Moessen and Volkerink (1999) Hallerberg and von Hagen (1999) Leachman et al. (2007) Helland (2000) Lagona and Padovano (2007) Alesina et al. (1999) Brusis and Dimitrov (2001) Dimitrov (2005) Gleich (2002, 2003) Yläoutinen (2004a) Fabrizio and Mody (2006) Filc and Scartascini (2005) No effect: Tujula and Wolswjik (2004) Berger, Kopits and Szekely (2007)
Strong minister of finance	Constraining effect: Hallerberg and Marier (2004) Most important constraining effect compared to other elements: de Haan, Moessen and Volkerink (1999)
Centralised preparation phase	Most important constraining effect compared to other elements: Fabrizio and Mody (2006) Gleich (2002. 2003) Constraining effect: Yläoutinen (2004a) No effect: Perotti and Kontopoulos (2002)

	Effects on deficit and debt
Centralised adoption phase	Constraining effect: Fabrizio and Mody (2006) Yläoutinen (2004a) Contingent effects: Hallerberg and Marier (2004) – significant effects only when level of personal vote high
Centralised implementation phase	Constraining effect: Yläoutinen (2004a) Most important constraining effect compared with other variables: Lagona and Padovano (2007) Fabrizio and Mody (2006)
Higher degree of transparency	Constraining effect: Alesina et al. (1999) Alesina and Perotti (1999) Alt and Lassen (2006) Weak effect: Von Hagen (1992) de Haan, Moessen and Volkerink (1999)

The choice of the fiscal governance mode appears to follow a clearer pattern in Western Europe than in Central and Eastern Europe. While in Western Europe, delegation approach has been chosen by single-party governments or coalition governments with closely aligned partners, the institutional choices in CEE region are more puzzling: in a number of cases, the delegation approach has been chosen by countries for which the "logical" choice would have been the contracts approach. Studies exploring the interaction effects between the transnational fiscal framework and domestic fiscal governance institutions also point to the importance of the functional fit between political and budgetary institutions in influencing budgetary outcomes: the countries that employ the contracts approach have a better compliance record with the EU fiscal rules than delegation countries.

The budgetary institutionalist literature has taken significant steps towards providing a better understanding of how extended fiscal constitutions influence policy choices in public finance. The development of the theoretical literature on this topic has been closely intertwined with empirical research, with a focus on specific institutional elements that make up the overall framework of fiscal governance in a polity. While the literature exploring the effects of political institutions on budgetary choices is primarily concerned with size fragmentation in budgetary decision-making (i.e., the number and kinds of participants, as discussed in chapter 5), the budgetary institutionalist literature takes a closer look at the participants in the budget process and how their interaction is structured. The attention to institutional details in the budgetary institutionalist literature certainly helps to explain why the empirical studies have pointed to more consistent results than the studies on the effects of political institutions reviewed in chapter 5.

There are, however, several aspects that have been neglected by the existing budgetary institutionalist literature, which should be taken up in further studies. As could be seen from the overview in section 6.3.2., hitherto, most of the studies exploring the effects of budgetary institutions have focused on deficit and debt levels, while paying less attention to other aspects of public finance, like expenditure and revenue levels, spending mix, tax mix and so forth. Hence, future studies on budgetary institutions should dedicate more attention to these aspects. Also, the existing literature on budgetary institutions has not paid sufficient attention to the question of which institutional aspects would be conducive to *maintaining* fiscal discipline and which aspects would be conducive to undertaking *fiscal adjustments* in the face of fiscal shocks. One can expect that because of the discretion granted to the minister of finance in delegation systems, such systems would have advantages in undertaking prompt fiscal measures, compared with contracts systems. Further studies should also explore the effects of different modes of fiscal governance on pro-cyclical tendencies, both in "good" times and "difficult" times. Contracts systems that employ spending targets in multi-annual frameworks might be better equipped to deal with pro-cyclical pressures during good times (compared with delegation systems), while potentially running into difficulties when counter-cyclical (but unplanned) measures are needed during difficult times. In other words, the flexibility of the minister of finance in delegation systems might be an asset during difficult times but pose problems in good times, whereas the opposite is true for the contracts system, where the fiscal targets may be an asset in good times but create obstacles in difficult times.

The existing studies of the "von Hagen group" can also be criticised for not addressing sufficiently the *incentive mechanisms* involved in the different modes of fiscal governance and the links between incentives and policy choices. The problem of incentives is somewhat better addressed in theoretical discussions on the delegation approach (than in theoretical propositions concerning the contracts approach). The minister of finance in the delegation approach is assumed to have incentives to internalise the costs of all spending programmes in the budget, since his "performance" as a minister is usually evaluated according to the level of fiscal discipline he manages to maintain. However, even the minister of finance may be subject to countervailing pressures, arising either from the ideological preferences of his party or from the demands of the electorate, which may make the a priori assumption of "fiscally conservative" orientation of the minister of finance difficult to maintain.[211] Even more questions arise, however, with regard to the incentives to internalise the fiscal externalities in the contracts mode. Most of the theoretical discussions by von Hagen, Hallerberg and their colleagues underline how agreeing on common targets at the beginning of the budgetary process helps to overcome the *information* problems regarding the common-pool resource, as if the individual ministers were – without collective negotiations – unable to realise that individual large bids may add up to an excessively large budget. As von Hagen (2007, pp. 42–43) argues, the goal of the contracts approach is "to *reveal* the externalities involved in budget decisions" (emphasis added). The question that arises here is how addressing the *information* problems can simultaneously address the *incentive* problems.[212] It may well be that the individual ministers are aware and informed about the common-pool problems in budgeting and that the general tax fund is a limited resource, but they do not have *incentives* to reduce their budget proposals accordingly. The theoretical discussions on the contracts approach should address more thoroughly the question of *how exactly* the process of coming together and discussing the overall targets is able to mitigate the potentially adverse incentives.

Alongside the incentives provided by budgetary institutions, further studies should focus more explicitly on the interaction between the institutional incentives and the actual *capacities* of the institutional actors. In particular, the analytical competence to forecast accurately the revenues and expenditures can be expected to influence the ability of the budgetary institutions to deal with arising problems. Molander (2000, p. 198) emphasises that accurate forecasting can mitigate the risk of acute conflicts that can put even well-designed budgetary institutions under strong pressures. As mentioned above, the ability of the legislature to monitor the budgetary decisions of the executive is expected to play an important role in ensuring the effectiveness of the contracts approach. Therefore, information gathering and analytical capacities of parliamentary committees (see Wehner 2006) are likely to influence the functionality of the monitoring element in the contracts approach, warranting closer attention in future studies.[213]

Further, juxtaposing the effects of political institutions with budgetary institutions would strongly complement the existing literature on extended fiscal

211 As Schick (2003, pp. 12–13) describes it, "It is not only that spenders want more; government leaders and a phalanx of interest groups want to give them more. Little opprobrium attaches to a government that tables a budget with spending increases; this is a normal occurrence, built into the expectations of budgeting and the behaviour of participants. Government leaders often point to spending increases as evidence of the good they are doing. It is the budget that cuts which stirs political unrest and analytical curiosity, not the one that adds this year's increases to last year's and to those of the years before that."

212 For a discussion on the distinction between the information problems and incentives problems involved on budgetary commons, see Jakee and Turner (2002).

213 Some steps in that direction have been taken by Hallerberg (2000b).

constitutions. In addition to the link made between the electoral systems and the mode of fiscal governance (indicating that proportional electoral rules give rise to multiparty coalition governments, which are likely to opt for the contracts mode), the electoral incentives offered by the electoral rules to individual legislators and cabinet ministers should be explored closer. The study by Hallerberg and Marier (2004) – indicating that strengthening the elements of delegation have effects on budgetary decision-making in the parliament only when the electoral system encourages the cultivation of personal vote – clearly points to an important direction in this regard. Alongside with accounting for more detailed elements of electoral systems, juxtaposing the fractionalisation of the government (and legislature) with a particular mode of fiscal governance would help to explain why the effects of budgetary institutions can vary in strength. For example, in electoral systems with d'Hondt formula (giving rise to less fractionalised governments than more proportional formulas), the effects of centralising the decision-making in the preparation phase may have *weaker* effects on budget discipline than in electoral systems with more proportional formulas (like the LR-Hare formula), giving rise to more fractionalised coalition governments. As discussed in section 5.3., coalition governments with one dominant party are considered to face fewer common-pool problems in budgeting than coalition governments with equally-sized partners.

The existing literature on budgetary institutions, though explicitly addressing the *common-pool problems* of budgeting, have concentrated only on one "pathology" – excessive deficits – while not addressing other potential "pathologies" pointed out by the "fiscal commons" literature, like the inefficiency of particularistic spending programmes (with marginal costs exceeding marginal benefits) or the "exploitation" problem arising from the ability of decision-making majorities to externalise the tax costs of spending programmes to the minorities (who were not part of the decision-making coalition). Although the institutional solutions offered by the "von Hagen group" may help to internalise the costs of expenditure programmes to a larger extent than a fiefdom approach would do, these solutions are not necessarily able to address the problem of shifting the tax costs of new spending programmes to the supporter groups of opposition parties. In other words, although a fiscal contract or a strong minister of finance enables decision-makers to take a more comprehensive view of the costs involved in expenditure programmes, the question is whether they would have incentives to internalise those tax costs that can be shifted to the supporter groups of opposition parties. Although related, these different "pathologies" are analytically separate problems and might therefore warrant different institutional solutions if they were to be mitigated. While super-majority requirements or fiscal referenda can be offered as solutions for mitigating the problem of "decision externalities", a supermajority requirement for increasing taxes, for example, may undermine fiscal discipline, by forcing the decision-makers to resort to deficit-financing instead of tax-financing the increased expenditures. These distinctions, however, are often neglected in the existing studies.

What has not received sufficient attention in the literature so far is the question of what kind of budgetary institutions would be more conducive to public-regardedness of the spending mix and to what extent budget procedures can aggravate or mitigate the particularistic tendencies inherent in particular constellations of political institutions. It can be conjectured that extensive rights of the parliament to amend the budget in a decentralised legislature in a presidential system with little party discipline, where the legislators have been elected according to an electoral system that promotes personal vote, would be likely to give rise to a budget that is biased towards particularistic spending at the expense of public goods and broad-based programmes. In parliamentary systems, also, especially with majoritarian electoral systems or open-list proportional systems, the limits on the right of the parliament to amend the budget are likely to constrain the particularistic tendencies. The budgetary institutionalist literature should explore these issues further, by examining, for example, whether limited amendment rights of the parliament in the budget process have stronger effects on spending mix in parliamentary systems with open-list electoral procedures (that encourage personal vote) compared with closed-list procedures.

6.4. Tax Constitutions

Compared with budgetary institutions, the procedural aspects of tax constitutions have received relatively less attention in the "positively oriented" literature so far, although it has been a prominent question in the more normatively oriented constitutional public finance, represented most prominently by Buchanan and his co-authors.[214] The main aspect of tax constitutions that has been discussed both in positive and normative theoretical literature is the supermajority requirement for tax increases.[215] Such a requirement is expected to enhance the accountability of the legislature as *a collective body* to a larger portion of the electorate (rather than just the supporters of the majority) in tax decisions.[216] Supermajority requirement is also expected to alleviate the common-pool problems of public finance arising from the ability of a majority coalition of decision-makers to externalise the costs of additional spending to a minority. The main theoretical prediction is that such a requirement would exert constraining effects on tax burdens. Constraints on tax revenues can be expected to lead to lower expenditures, but can, in principle, also give rise to higher deficits when tax con-

214 See, for example, Buchanan (1979), Brennan and Buchanan (1980) and Wagner (2002).

215 In the discussions of normative constitutional political economy, the supermajority requirements for tax decisions go back to Wicksell (1896).

216 On the other hand, it can be argued that such a requirement can curtail the accountability of the legislature to the majority of the electorate by giving a minority the right to block decisions.

straints prevent tax financing of increasing expenditures. Hence, the constraining effects of supermajority requirements for tax increases on the size of government can be expected to be stronger when such requirements are combined with stringent balanced budget rules (Knight 2000).

The list of empirical literature on supermajority requirements, however, is pretty short and is confined to the U.S. states.[217] Knight (2000) demonstrates that supermajority requirements have a large, negative impact on state taxes. In addition, he examines the interaction between supermajority requirements and balanced budget rules but finds little evidence for such an interactive effect. Bails and Tieslau (2000) conclude that while supermajority requirement by itself is ineffective in reducing state-level spending, it does exert a significant negative influence when combined with balanced budget rules. Besley and Case (2003) find that supermajority requirements have large, negative and significant effects on total taxes collected per capita. Further, they find that supermajority requirement has a similarly large, negative effect on state spending (but its effect is not significant when other rules are included in the model). Musso, Grady and Grizard (2008, p. 259) conclude that "Little empirical evidence is available on the impact of supermajority voting requirements, presumably because of the difficulty for controlling for the joint effects of endogeneity and interaction with other fiscal institutions."

Altogether, the positive literature exploring the procedural aspects of tax constitutions and organic tax laws is still in an embryonic phase of development, with many questions still unexplored. Although the procedural issues here are often not as straightforward as it is in the case of budgetary institutions, the tax institutionalist literature could draw on the budgetary institutionalist literature, for example, by exploring the effects of specific powers given to minister of finance in the area of taxation, the agenda-setting powers of the executive (e.g., whether tax laws can be bound to an issue of confidence) and the initiation and amendment rights of the parliament in the issue area of taxation.

6.5. Discussion

The discussion in this section addresses the dominant metaphor in the emerging orthodoxy of constitutional public finance – "the budgetary commons". Section 6.5.1. points to the lessons that the "budgetary commons" literature can learn from "governing the natural commons" literature, which appears to have advanced further than the budgetary commons literature in conceptualising the problem-structures involved in managing common-pool resources. Section 6.5.2. criticises the hidden normative assumptions of the budgetary commons models employed by existing studies and brings out the problematic implica-

217 Supermajority requirements for tax increases have been enacted in 13 states of the United States, most of them as part of the "tax revolt" of the 1970s (Knight 2000).

tions these assumptions have for conducting research in constitutional public finance.

6.5.1. Insights from Governing the Natural Commons

As already mentioned, both political institutionalists (including electoral institutionalists) and budgetary institutionalists assume budgeting to be subject to common-pool resource problems. As Elgie and McMenamin (2008, p. 257) put it, "Much of the contemporary work on deficits relies explicitly or implicitly on assumptions consistent with a common-pool resource approach." Despite the fact that "budgetary commons" has become a standard starting point for analysing fiscal governance, surprisingly little reference has been made to the literature pertaining to the governance of *natural* common-pool resources. If the literature on budgetary institutions wanted to maintain adherence to the common-pool metaphor of budgeting, it could learn more from the literature on natural common-pool resources for elaborating its theoretical underpinnings and practical solutions. The goal of this section is to bring out aspects from the "governing the commons" literature (represented most prominently by Elinor Ostrom) that can help to illuminate, clarify and criticise the problems and governance solutions pertaining to "budgetary commons".

As it appears, "the natural commons" literature could be of guidance for "the budgetary commons" literature already with regard to the most basic issues. Budgetary commons literature often seems to assume that budgetary decision-making (either in the cabinet or in the legislature) is subject to the *tragedy of the commons*, arising from prisoner's dilemma type problems, where the players would have an incentive to stick to the overgrazing strategy, no matter what the others do. Dixit (1996, p. 21), for example, has characterised budgetary decision-making in a legislature with decentralised committees as following, "No one committee in a decentralized structure will internalize the overall budget constraint, and the result will be a Prisoners' Dilemma of overspending." Hallerberg and von Hagen (1999, p. 215) also refer to "the prisoner's dilemma game being played in the cabinet". In other words, it is Hardin's (1968) "tragedy of the commons" that has become the favourite "commons" metaphor employed by budgetary institutionalists, rather than any alternative conception of the commons. As Ostrom (1990, ch. 1) warns, however, relying on metaphors like "the tragedy of the commons" or "prisoner's dilemma" as over-simplified conceptions of the problem-arenas can lead to false policy prescriptions.

The problem with using the prisoner's dilemma as a model of budgetary decision-making is that the *very* literature on natural common-pool resources has shown that such an assumption may not often hold. Dasgupta and Heal (1979, p. 59) note that "Contrary to what is often claimed, the problem of 'the commons' and the resulting suboptimality of the market equilibrium are *not* formally identical to an N-person version of the prisoners' dilemma game." (emphasis in the original) The same standpoint has been endorsed by Gardner, Ostrom and Walker (1990, p. 337). A strand of literature on common-pool natural resources has shown that it would be more accurate to view the common-pool resource as subject to coordination problems rather than to prisoner's dilemma type cooperation problems. Runge (1981) has emphasised that "Properly formulated, the commons problem involves the interdependence of agents, such that it is in the interest of each to restrict output if that is the only way to get other agents to do likewise." Therefore, Runge (1981) has suggested that a more accurate conception of common-pool problems would be offered by the assurance game (see Sen 1967).[218] As he explains, in an assurance game, if each individual expects everyone else on the commons to stint, that individual will stint, too. If each expects others to graze exploitatively, then each will have a reason to do so. In other words, there is no dominant strategy for each individual cattle-holder: no individual can decide on the preferred grazing strategy until it is known whether or not the others will stint. Thus, Runge argues, the major motivating force in overexploitation of common property resources is uncertainty; hence, the preservation of commons can be achieved through devising institutional rules that facilitate coordination by offering assurance on the intended actions of others. (p. 602) Runge (1981, p. 603) adds that as the number of graziers on the commons become larger, it becomes more difficult for an individual grazier to estimate the actions of the others and, therefore, the need for coordinating institutions that provide the assurance also grows.

A number of problems on the budgetary commons are also likely to be primarily assurance problems. The voracity effect leading to pro-cyclicality in good times (see Tornell and Lane 1999; Lane 2003), for example, could be viewed as resulting from an assurance problem: the appropriators would have incentives to act prudently if they were sure that others would do the same. Further, the problems of a cabinet facing the need of fiscal adjustment may also be primarily assurance problems: the ministers might be willing to undertake cuts when they are sure that other ministers cut their budgets as well.

Thus, the budgetary commons literature should pay closer attention to the issue of whether *the tragedy of the commons* and *prisoner's dilemma* metaphors really convey an accurate conception of the problems involved on fiscal commons. As Ostrom (1990, p. 48) and Runge (1981, p. 596) have pointed out, prisoner's dilemma is likely to characterise common-pool resources with *open access*: when there are no limits on who can appropriate and no possibilities for communication. Given that the access to budgetary commons is limited – by constitutional structures outlining the position, boundary and authority rules – it would be misleading to conceive of the budgetary commons as open-access resource. Further, as Ostrom (1990, p. 39) underlines, the herders in the tragedy of

218 For overviews of different models that can be used to for conceptualising CPRs, see Ostrom, Gardner and Walker (1994) and Faysse (2005).

commons model by Hardin act independently: the decision on how many animals to take to the meadow is taken without a concern for how that will affect others' actions. Since budgetary decision-making is *collective* decision-making, the assumption of the ability to act independently, inherent in Hardin's model, would not apply to budgetary commons. Furthermore, the repeated interaction among the appropriators on the budgetary commons (foreseen by fiscal constitutional rules) further reduces the applicability of the prisoner's dilemma and the tragedy of the commons metaphors.

Constitutionally prescribed collective decision-making on budgetary commons also calls into question another favourite metaphor employed by studies on budgetary commons – the "law of $1/n$". The following explanation of the common-pool problems in budgeting is typical for the budgetary commons literature: "Each group and their representatives fully internalize the benefits of the expenditures they propose; however, they internalize only a fraction $1/n$ of the costs the associated revenues impose on the whole economy." (Perotti and Kontopoulos 2002, p. 195) As already referred to in chapter 5, the "law of $1/n$" metaphor, despite its intuitive plausibility at first sight, can convey a misleading picture of the appropriation taking place on actual budgetary commons. The "law of $1/n$" metaphor, in its simplest form, implies that the budget is simply a sum of appropriations requested by the participants, which would emerge without the need to take collective decisions (be it majority vote or consensus). Given that both in the cabinet and the legislature, the budget is adopted as a result of a collective decision, the appropriators proposing a specific assignment for themselves have to secure support of other appropriators, which, in turn, implies that they would – in proposing their bids – also take into account the costs that their constituencies would have to bear as a result of the overall package. In other words, while graziers on "Hardin's commons" may be able to take their cattle to the meadows without the consent of others, the herders on budgetary commons do need the consent of the rest of the "grazing community".[219]

Another important insight of the "governing the commons" literature represented by Elinor Ostrom and her co-authors is that there is not simply *a* common-pool resource problem or *one particular* structure underlying a common-pool resource, but "appropriators relying on any CPR face *a variety of problems* to be solved" (Ostrom 1990, p. 47, emphasis added). The shortcoming of the existing budgetary commons literature is that the "common-pool resource problem of budgeting" is simply stated, without exploring closer the different kinds of problems involved. As Ostrom (1990) notes, in discussing the problems involved in any common-pool resource, one should distinguish between *appro-*

219 Thus, as discussed in section 5.3.1.1., the law of $1/n$ can be expected to operate in collective decision-making setting, if there are opportunities to externalise the tax costs of expenditure programmes to actors outside the coalition involved in the "package deal" of particularistic expenditures and if there is a divergence between the "political" and "economic" costs of the targeted programmes.

priation problems and *provision* problems, pertaining to flow and stock aspects of the resource, respectively (see also Blomquist and Ostrom 1985; Ostrom, Gardner and Walker 1994). These problems have different underlying structures, resulting in different kinds of externalities, and call for different institutional solutions. The literature on budgetary commons could, in this respect, draw on the natural CPR literature, by making an explicit distinction between appropriation and provision problems and by exploring whether specific kinds of appropriation and provision problems can also be encountered on budgetary commons.

An important appropriation problem that the natural CPR literature deals with is "rent dissipation". Dissipated rents characterise an outcome where the marginal costs of appropriation process are higher than the marginal returns (Ostrom 1990, p. 48; Gardner, Ostrom and Walker 1990, p. 341). As Ostrom (1990, p. 48) explains, rent dissipation can result when too many individuals appropriate from the resource, when they are allowed to withdraw economically sub-optimal quantities of resource units and when appropriators over-invest in appropriation equipment. The solutions to appropriation problems hence seek to avoid rent dissipation and reduce uncertainty and conflict over the assignment of appropriation rights, by proposing and adopting agreements on the level of appropriation, the method of appropriation and the allocation of output (Ostrom, Gardner and Walker 1994, p. 9; Ostrom 1990, p. 48).

Thus, one could ask whether there are equivalent appropriation problems on budgetary commons and how these could be addressed through institutional solutions. For example, do appropriation externalities (occurring in a situation where increased appropriation by one user reduces the yield that other users can obtain) that result in over-investment in the appropriation process (Ostrom, Gardner and Walker 1994, p. 10) also have their analogues on budgetary commons? At the most obvious level, the appropriation costs on fiscal commons are the costs of collecting taxes; thus, appropriation problems may be reflected in properties of taxes that render tax collection excessively expensive. When analysing the appropriation process at the phase when the "fiscal resource" has already been created (i.e., when the general tax fund is already there), further appropriation problems may arise. Extensive possibilities for budgetary amendments in the legislature – giving the districts and interest groups ample possibilities to be engaged in the appropriation process – are likely to be associated with higher "appropriation costs" of rent-seeking.[220] Even on the cabinet and legislative level, however, appropriation problems might be reflected in high political transaction costs incurred in conflicts over budgetary appropriations. In that light, the incremental approach to budgeting, although much criticised,

220 For analogous discussions on taxation, referring to the idea that the easier it is to change the tax system, the higher are political transaction costs, including the rent-seeking costs, see Buchanan (1967), Holcombe (1998) and Poterba (1998).

might have served as one solution for keeping budgetary conflicts within limits (see Wildavsky 1986).

The provision problems in natural CPRs are related to creating a resource, maintaining and improving the resource and avoiding the destruction of it (Ostrom, Gardner and Walker 1994, p. 9; Ostrom 1990, p. 49). Most simply put, provision problems can be divided into two kinds of problems: supply-side and demand-side problems (Ostrom, Gardner and Walker 1994, p. 12). Supply-side problems can result from individual incentives to free-ride on the efforts of others in creating and improving the resource, while demand-side problems result from excessive appropriation activities, which undermine the productive capacity of the resource in the future (e.g., reduce its replenishment rate) (Ostrom, Gardner and Walker 1994, pp. 13–14). On budgetary commons, the supply-side provision problems might be expressed in the reluctance of a party to agree on a tax increase that would fall on its supporters. What makes the budgetary commons special compared with most natural CPRs is that here the provision costs can be *imposed* by a circle of appropriators (i.e., the governing majority) on other parties, in the form of increasing taxes that fall on the constituencies of opposition parties, making the free-riding temptation even stronger. The demand-side provision problems on budgetary commons can refer to two different issues. First, the replenishment rate of fiscal commons might be reduced when appropriation activities (i.e., the taxes imposed) become too excessive and induce the flight of the tax base either to abroad or to shadow economy. Second, unlike on natural commons, participants on budgetary commons can use part of the future flow already today (in t_0), without influencing the current replenishment rate – by incurring debt that will have to be paid back at the expense of the *future* flow in t_1. As a result of the need to pay back the debt in t_1, the appropriation rates in t_1 *may* reduce the amount of flow units available in t_2. If the borrowed funds, however, have been used for productive purposes that increase the replenishment rate of the tax fund, the incurred debt would *not* translate into provision problems. Although most of budgetary commons literature is concerned with deficits, it is interesting that the discussions have not pointed out the rather special nature of budgetary commons compared with natural commons. The natural CPR literature has repeatedly emphasised the complexities involved in evaluating the feedback mechanisms between current appropriations and future level of stock, and the implications it has for devising appropriate institutional solutions. The complexities involved in the feedback mechanisms on budgetary commons, however, appear to be even greater, which makes the design of institutions for governing budgetary commons even more challenging than is the case with natural commons.[221]

An important insight from governing the commons literature is that those CPR systems that have managed to self-govern the common resource over time

221 For an analogous argument, see Jakee and Turner (2002).

are characterised by the *enduring* nature of the appropriators community. As Ostrom (1990, pp. 35, 88) has underlined, a stable community of appropriators (with a common past and a common future) that is dependent on the resource has longer time-horizons and lower discount rates, which facilitates the attainment of solutions for provision problems. On budgetary commons, however, the membership of the appropriating community (the parties or ministers in the cabinet or members of the legislature) is often limited to relatively short time periods, owing to turnovers that result from elections. The inherent instability of "the community of appropriators" with decision-making powers on budgetary commons, in turn, can shorten the time horizons, increase discount rates and hence aggravate the provision problems. If members of the appropriating community in t_0 are not sure that they will be the community governing the budgetary commons in t_1 and t_2, they can externalise at least some of the costs of the debt to "future governing communities".[222]

One should keep in mind, however, that while on the highest level of budgetary decision-making (i.e., the cabinet or the parliament), the turnover of appropriators may be frequent, then on lower or intermediary levels (e.g., officials involved in budgetary negotiations in the ministry of finance and spending ministries), the membership and relations between the members may be more enduring, which can facilitate the emergence of norms and role-definitions that are conducive to maintaining the fiscal commons. Wildavsky (1986, p. 36) elucidates the relations between the advocates and the guardians in a following way:

> The most powerful coordinating mechanisms in budgeting undoubtedly are the various roles adopted by major participants in the budgetary process. Because the roles fit with one another and set up a stable pattern of mutual expectations, they do a great deal to reduce the burden of calculations for individual participants.

Thus, while reliance on "self-governance" mechanisms can encounter problems on the level of cabinet or legislature, informal conventions can be important coordination mechanisms on the lower levels of budgetary negotiations.[223]

Another relevant insight from governing the commons literature is that successful governing arrangements are those that address the underlying structure of the appropriation and provision problems and take into account *local conditions* and *prevailing norms* (Ostrom 1990, pp. 89–91). The same can be ex-

---

222 As Krogstrup and Wyplosz (2007, p. 2) have underlined, the incumbent governments fail to internalise the full costs of incurring deficits, since at least some of the debt will be serviced by future governments. Debrun and Kumar (2007, p. 6) also note that "deficit bias arises because uncertainty about re-election increases the discount rate of partisan policy-makers".

223 Even here, however, the informal coordination mechanism may run into difficulties when the polity is faced with extensive fiscal shock(s), which may disturb the functionality of existing elements of governance.

pected to apply for the budgetary institutions. For example, although assurance problems are likely to be greater in coalition governments than in single-party governments, calling, in principle, for a leader who can provide certainty about the behaviour of other ministers (see e.g., Calvert 1992), a strong finance minister may face problems in providing assurance (e.g., about demanding other ministers to engage in spending cuts in difficult times or curbing voracity in good times) in coalition governments, since the ministers may have doubts about his "neutrality". This is a result that has been repeatedly pointed out by the budgetary institutionalist literature as well (see Hallerberg and von Hagen 1999).

Besides the functional fit with the existing political institutions, budgetary institutions, in order to be successful, should fit with the prevailing *norms* in the budgeting process. Therefore, the literature on budgetary institutions should also pay attention to the different kinds of budgeting norms and budgeting styles that have been extensively explored in qualitative studies of budgeting by Wildavsky.

Wildavsky (1986) has underlined that in addition to the institutional structure of budgeting (reflecting both the number of institutions or institutional levels involved in budgeting and their relative powers), the budgeting process would be affected by prevailing norms of conduct among political actors. In particular, he has pointed to three kinds of norms that are likely to play an important role in budgeting: the level of personal trust among the higher civil servants and politicians, preferences for face-to-face as opposed to formalistic courtroom-style dispute resolution modes and the degree of disposition towards proportionality (or parity) in decision-making (p. 21). The norms pertaining to trust, arbitration and proportionality, in turn, are likely to influence the kinds of fiscal governance institutions that are proposed and adopted and how the adopted governance modes shape budgetary outcomes. Further, Wildavsky has pointed to different *styles* of solving conflicts in budgetary decision-making, resulting from the prevalent norms and the number of institutional levels involved in budgetary decision-making. The *diversionary* style (characteristic to the United States) combines a large number of different institutional levels with codes of conduct conducive to high levels of trust, arbitration and proportionality. The *containment* style (characteristic to France) is characterised by formalism and many levels of hierarchy. The *avoidance* style (typical for Japan) combines a small number of different levels with extensive preferences for proportionality. The *absorption style* (represented by the Great Britain) is a constellation of few levels and high level of trust.

The informal norms prevalent on the policy arena of budgeting and the style of budgeting can be expected to influence how well exogenously imposed elements of fiscal governance (e.g., fiscal rules) or institutional solutions adopted as a result of policy transfer function in practice. For example, stringent fiscal rules might suit for polities with diversionary style but encounter difficulties in polities with the absorption style of budgeting, where it might disturb the trustful relations and the coordinating function played by the different roles. Delegation approach would be likely to run into difficulties in the avoidance style of budgeting, while contracts approach, with its focus on collective agreements, would face obstacles when combined with containment style. Exploring the functional fit between different norms and styles of budgeting with the formal modes of fiscal governance would certainly complement the existing literature in constitutional public finance.

6.5.2. Critical Remarks on the Discourse

As already mentioned, "the tragedy of budgetary commons" has become *the* favourite metaphor of the recent literature in constitutional public finance. A large number of studies considering the effects of constitutions on public finance start with the allegation that "budgeting is subject to common-pool problems that leads to overgrazing the fiscal commons". As discussed in section 6.5.1., one important problem in the recent literature is that the "common-pool resource problem" is simply mentioned, without elaborating on the exact problem structure and the different dynamics of various kinds of problems potentially involved in administering common-pool resources. Thus, conceptually, the budgetary commons metaphor faces the danger of becoming "a catch-all term" that is simply taken as a starting point, without giving detailed attention to the fit between the metaphor and the actual situation. If stretched too far, this metaphor may end up being used for explaining "everything" in budgeting, without actually being able to explain anything. While the governing of natural commons literature has already moved away from over-simplified notions of the common-pool resource problem, the literature of constitutional public finance still subscribes to the over-simplified version of the metaphor.

Alongside the problems of over-simplification, the constitutional public finance literature appears to be overly obsessed with one particular problematic outcome of budgeting – budget deficits. Such "obsession" with deficits in constitutional public finance has a number of roots. First, the concern for deficits has been inspired by the "founding fathers" of constitutional political economy, who followed a very specific normative agenda; somehow, the cynicism with regard to deficits by the pioneers of normative constitutional political economy has been carried over to the positive strands of constitutional public finance as well. Second, the concern with excessive deficits has been motivated by strains such deficits impose on the budget by taking away substantial resources for interest payments. Third, the "fascination" with deficits has also been inspired by the fact that this indicator is easily "measurable" and hence readily available for regression analyses, which, as discussed in previous sections, is the preferred empirical method in the recent studies. As mentioned in section 6.7., an important shortcoming of many recent studies in constitutional public finance is that all budget deficits are treated "equally" (and are generally viewed in a negative light), without paying sufficient attention to deficits that have been incurred for counter-cyclical purposes or for funding long-term investment.

It is also noteworthy that although the earlier models of "budgetary commons" (like the one put forth by Weingast, Shepsle and Johnsen 1981) were primarily concerned with the inefficient level of expenditures allocated for *particularistic* projects (whereby the inefficiency was conceived in welfare economic terms), the more recent literature appears to consider *any* increase in expenditure as a problem, irrespective of the specific content and welfare economic value. In other words, the recent studies in constitutional public finance have paid disproportionate attention to the *level* of expenditure, at the expense of paying closer attention to the *spending mix*.

When one takes a step further in the critique of the "budgetary commons" metaphor, even deeper problems come to the fore. The notion of budgetary commons, though presented in "neutral terms" in the recent literature, is in fact value-laden and carries in it rather specific connotations: it presents a very particular view of the nature of the polity, the role of the state and the goals it has. Indeed, although conceptually attractive at first sight, because of its simplicity and intuitive appeal, employing the budgetary commons metaphor for representing the policy arena of budgetary decision-making leaves one with the impression that the policy-makers are grazing the commons only for their own selfish purposes and by "grazing" the commons, they simply *take resources away* from the common-pool, without adding to it or expanding it. Such "static" view, however, neglects the possibility that by using the common-pool resources – the general tax fund – prudently, the grazing community (the policy-makers) may be able to *expand* the very common-pool resource by employing the funds for purposes that are conducive for the development of the economy: by investing in education, encouraging innovation, enhancing the legal framework for the functioning of the market and providing goods that would otherwise be subject to market failures. Thus, the commitment to the common-pool metaphor in its most simplified and primitive form in constitutional public finance confines the analyst to a very narrow (and conceptually misleading) perspective of public budgeting. When the notion of the "tragedy of budgetary commons" is combined with other ideologically coloured terms like "exploitation", "logrolling", "side-payments", "expansionary pressures", "collusive decision-making", "excessive spending" and so forth, one certainly cannot claim to be doing "merely positive" or "agenda-less" research anymore.

Furthermore, by utilising the metaphor of "budgetary commons", the studies in constitutional public finance implicitly problematise the *very nature* of public budgeting: it is the *essence* of public budgeting that the "general" tax fund is used for financing "less general" expenditure programmes. The reason the general tax fund has been created in the first place is that, otherwise, certain aspects of social life – considered valuable by the community – would not be adequately provided for. Thus, the statement that using the *general* fund for financing *particular* purposes is "a problem" leaves an impression that the analyst has completely forgotten why *public* finance has come about in the first place. By stating that the "very nature" of public budgeting is problematic, one cannot claim to be conducting a "neutral inquiry" anymore; rather, one should admit that such an inquiry is biased towards a particular understanding of the role of the state.

Chapter 7: Constitution as *Explanans* for Budgetary Discipline in Estonia?

While chapters 5 and 6 focused on the effects of particular constitutional features (either political institutions or fiscal constitutions) on a range of policy choices in public finance, this chapter adopts a different perspective and asks: To what extent can the constitutional elements outlined in chapters 5 and 6 explain and provide insights for understanding of a particular case – the commitment to fiscal discipline in Estonia from 1992 to 2007?

Among the CEE countries, Estonia has hitherto stood out as an "exemplary" case of fiscal discipline, with the lowest level of debt and the best indicators for budget balances. The question that arises for constitutional public finance is, "To what extent has the commitment to budgetary discipline been driven by institutional factors, like particular features of political institutions, fiscal rules and budgetary institutions?" With the Estonian case study, this chapter attempts to test the usefulness of the emerging orthodoxy in positive constitutional public finance in offering explanations for choices made in a particular political reality.

Section 7.1. considers the impacts of political institutions, section 7.2. explores the fiscal rules and section 7.3. takes up the budgetary institutions. Section 7.4. complements the constitutional explanations by bringing out other factors that have fostered the adherence to fiscal discipline and discusses how these elements have interacted with the constitutional aspects. The case study in this chapter draws on parliamentary discussions on the main framework acts for budgeting, legislative budgetary proceedings, media discussions and, importantly, on in-depth qualitative studies of budgeting in Estonia undertaken by Ostrow (2000) and Martinez-Vazquez (1997).

Given the positive orientation of this book, the discussion below consciously refrains from passing a normative judgement on the "soundness" of fiscal policy choices in Estonia and discussing the problems (like social costs and procyclical effects), such budgetary choices have implied. The "commitment to fiscal discipline" is in this chapter regarded as a phenomenon to be *explained* (rather than condemned or praised).

7.1. The Role of Political Institutions in Fiscal Discipline

As brought out in chapter 2, the 1992 Constitution of Estonia provides for a political system that is parliamentary (with a figurehead president), with a unicameral legislature elected in a proportional two-tier electoral system (which combines both closed-list and open-list elements).[224] Throughout the period of

224 The first tier is made up of 11 multi-member constituencies, with average district magnitude of 9.2. On the district level, each candidate who receives a full (Hare) district quota obtains a seat. After the allocation of "personal" seats, the remainders are summed

1992–2007, Estonia has been governed by coalition governments (comprising usually of three different parties), subject to frequent turnovers, and fractionalised legislatures.[225] The use of referenda is constrained and issues pertaining to budgeting and taxation cannot be put on referendum in Estonia. Further, the Constitution foresees an independent constitutional review mechanism by the Supreme Court and provides strong guarantees of autonomy for the judiciary. When looking at this constitutional constellation at a most general level, then, based on the discussions in chapter 5, one would expect Estonia to have problems with commitment to fiscal discipline, especially if one subscribes to the "presidentialist" position (see section 5.1.). The budgetary indicators, however, provide a different picture. Among the EU countries, Estonia has the lowest level of government debt. In 2007, for example, the ratio of debt to GDP was 3.5 percent for the general government and 1.1 percent for the central government (Eurostat). As figure 7.1. indicates, the levels of general government debt have been significantly lower in Estonia between 1995 and 2007 than in the ten new member states (NMS) that joined the EU in 2004.

Figure 7.1.: General government debt in 10 NMS and Estonia, 1995–2007, as % of GDP

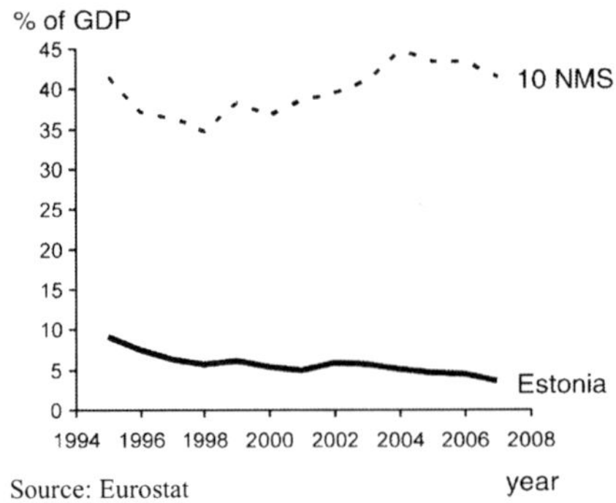

Source: Eurostat

up for each party and those parties for whom the remainders add up to additional quota(s) receive additional seat(s), which are allocated to the vote-winners in the district. For the third round – taking place in the second tier – the district remainders are added up and the mandates are distributed through the nationwide party lists according to a modified D'Hondt formula (with divisors 1, $2^{0.9}$, $3^{0.9}$ and so forth). All voters have one vote that they cast for a specific candidate. On the district level, the voters can influence the order of candidates in the "district list", but on a national level, closed lists are employed. For a discussion of similar two-tier systems, see Eklit and Roberts (1996).

225 The average effective number of parties represented in the parliament from 1992 to 1999, for example, was 5.18; this was the second highest among the CEE countries that have joined the EU, topped only by Latvia (Yläoutinen 2004b, p. 11). For more detailed descriptions of the Estonian political system, including the electoral system, party system and political development, see Grofman, Mikkel and Taagepera (2000), Mikkel and Pettai (2004), Pettai (2003), Sikk (2004) and Smith (2001).

Figure 7.2.: General government primary balances in 10 NMS and Estonia, 1995–2007, as % of GDP

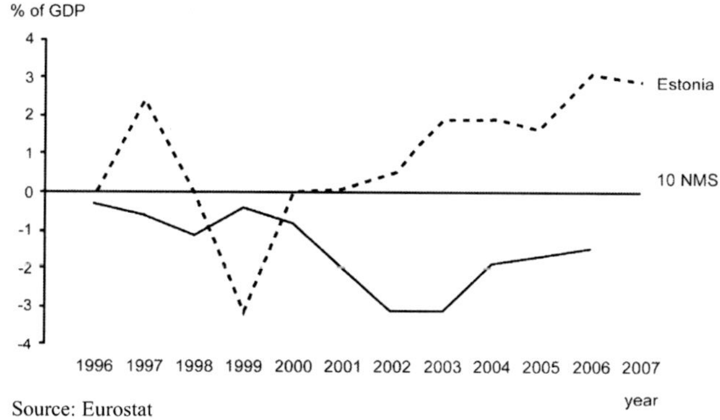

Source: Eurostat

Also, as figure 7.2. demonstrates, the primary balances in Estonia have been positive for most of the period from 1996 to 2007, whereas the primary balances in 10 new member states have been negative. Table 7.1. brings out fiscal indicators for different groups of EU countries in 2007. As can be seen, there is an especially stark contrast between the ratio of government debt to GDP in different groups of EU countries and Estonia: the general government consolidated gross debt amounted to 3.5 percent of GDP in Estonia, while reaching 58.7 percent in EU 27 (all member states), 60.4 percent in EU 15 (old member states) and 41.4 percent in 10 new member states that joined the EU in 2004.

Table 7.1.: Fiscal indicators for groups of EU countries in 2007, % of GDP

	EU 27	EU 25	EU 15	10 NMS	Estonia
General government debt	58.7	59.3	60.4	41.4	3.5
Central government debt	50.7	51.2	51.8	40.5	1.1
General government primary balance	1.9	1.9	2.0	0.4	2.9
General government net lending (+) / net borrowing (-) under the EDP	-0.9	-0.8	-0.8	-1.8	2.7

Source: Eurostat

Table 7.2. provides the general indicators of fiscal discipline in 2007 for the CEE countries that are members of the EU. As can be seen, again Estonia stands out for having the lowest level of debt and deficit among the CEE countries.

Table 7.2.: Fiscal indicators of CEE countries in 2007, % of GDP

	General government consolidated gross debt	General government deficit (-) / surplus (+)	Central government net borrowing (+) / net lending (-) under EDP	Central government debt
Bulgaria	18.2	3.4	0.0	17.8
Czech Republic	28.7	-1.6	-2.0	26.5
Estonia	3.4	2.8	2.6	1.1
Latvia	9.7	0.0	-2.3	13.3
Lithuania	17.3	-1.2	-0.8	16.1
Hungary	66.0	-5.5	-5.7	63.4
Poland	45.2	-2.0	-3.2	43.1
Romania	13.0	-2.5	-3.4	14.1
Slovenia	24.1	-0.1	0.4	23.2
Slovakia	29.4	-2.2	-1.9	28.4

Source: Eurostat

Furthermore, the budgets *adopted* by the legislature in Estonia have been balanced or in surplus, with the exception of the 2003 budget: this budget was adopted with a prospective deficit, due to the introduction of the second pillar of the pension system, undertaken in 2002, which transferred part of the contributions from the first pillar to the second pillar (Raudla 2007).[226]

Thus, the question that arises is – are there some elements in the political institutions of Estonia that have facilitated the adherence to fiscal discipline or has such a commitment been achieved *despite* the unfavourable constitutional conditions? Looking more closely, an important configuration of constitutional elements that can be considered to have been conducive to such fiscal choices is the parliamentary form of government, combined with an electoral system that entails closed-list elements (alongside the open-list elements), used a 5 percent threshold and employs an electoral formula – a modified D'Hondt formula – which awards a disproportionately high number of seats to the winning party. Such a constitutional configuration promotes party discipline, mitigates the tendencies towards fractionalisation and allows the coalitions formed to have one partner that is more dominant than the others.

Owing to the co-existence of open-list and closed-list elements in the electoral rules, individual candidates face mixed motives and "play a dual game" (Pettai 2005a, p. 465) in choosing their electoral strategies. Although the open-list elements reflected in the employment of district-level mandates offer incentives for cultivating a personal vote and following the parochial imperative in the service of the home district, adherence to the party line and securing a high

226 The-end-of-the-year balance, however, was positive in 2003.

position in the party list is likely to have appeared as a safer strategy for securing electoral success (given uncertainties involved in voter behaviour) – at least until 2003, when changes were made to the electoral rules that strengthened the "open list" personal elements and decreased the number of seats allocated through nationwide party lists.[227] As Pettai (2005a) shows, on the basis of survey data, the Estonian legislators do indeed view their primary duties to lie with the party and not with their home district and voters. Further, he finds that the party structures are relatively autocratic, with the ranks in the party lists decided by primarily by the party leaders (p. 470), which is likely to encourage voting according to party lines, at least on vital issues, like the budget. As Yläoutinen (2004b, p. 34) notes, in Estonia the degree of party discipline in budget votes has been high and there are usually no defecting MPs.[228]

Owing to the fusion of the legislature and the executive in Estonia and increasing party discipline, the Government has been able – to a large extent – to dictate the terms of budgetary policy and to undertake painful expenditure cuts (in 1992–1993 and in 1999) (see, e.g., Ostrow 2000, ch. 7). Alongside party discipline, the agenda-setting powers of the executive in the budget process, discussed in more detail in section 7.2., has been facilitated by the constitutional provision requiring the legislative amendments to the budget to be offsetting (see also chapter 3). This has provided a further constraint for the legislators to pursue particularistic spending strategies beyond the level of rhetoric and has allowed the Government to harness the aggregate parameters of the budget. Indeed, the only Government that lost control over the parliament in the budgetary process – resulting in extensive legislative amendments that increased the budgetary expenditures by 3.5 percent (Raju 2003) – was the minority government in 1997. Owing to the modified D'Hondt formula that awards the winning party of the elections disproportionately more seats than other parties, the coalition governments (though still fractionalised) have usually had a dominant party, with stronger bargaining powers than the others, which has been able to coordinate budgetary decision-making and set the terms for budgetary debates.

Altogether, the configuration of the parliamentary system with the particular elements of the electoral system has provided at least some coordinating mecha-

227 The amendment states that those party lists that receive at least 0.75 of quota in excess after allocation of mandates on the district level receive an additional quota. As a result of these changes, the mandates distributed through the nationwide lists declined significantly: while until 2003, about half of the mandates were allocated on the basis of nationwide lists, then in 2003 elections, only one-third were awarded through the lists. (Sikk 2003, pp. 5–6)

228 As Pettai and Madise (2006) note, though there were problems with party discipline in the early phase of transition (see also Kask 1996), party discipline has become tighter over time.

nisms for counteracting the common-pool problems of budgeting in Estonia.[229] Alongside the most general supportive features, however, one should inquire how the coordination and accountability mechanisms of budgeting look like on a more detailed level and how they are shaped by fiscal rules and budgetary institutions. Indeed, the same configuration of political institutions might well have led to different fiscal choices, had they not been supported by particular features of the extended fiscal constitution.

7.2. Fiscal Rules

The 1992 Constitution of Estonia itself does not contain balanced budget requirements or substantive debt, expenditure or tax limits. The only procedural constraints on borrowing are established in Articles 65 and 104, requiring, respectively, that loans taken by the state have to be approved by the *Riigikogu* (and cannot, hence, be subject to the discretion of the Government) and that Acts pertaining to foreign and domestic borrowing and to proprietary obligations of the state can only be passed and amended by a majority of the membership of the *Riigikogu*.

The organic budget law adopted in 1994 stipulated a balanced budget requirement, but, in terms of content, the notion of budget balance in the act was merely "formalistic". Since the loans were listed among "revenues", the resulting budget would always be "balanced", even if deficits (in the conventional sense of the term) were incurred. The following examples from legislative debates demonstrate clearly the prevailing understanding of the budget "balance" among political actors in the early phase of transition. When discussing the draft organic budget law (that was, however, rejected) in November 1992, the presenter of the draft Kalle Kulbok stated, "We consider it correct that the requirement of balanced budget should be stipulated in the organic act. If there appears a need for deficit, then a loan can be included in the budget, or, if the revenues are larger than expenditures, a reserve fund could be foreseen." (*Riigikogu* Verbatim Record, 11 November 1992) Even the Minister of Finance Madis Üürike, when presenting the draft organic budget law in May 1993, argued that "In order to balance the budget, the organic budget law provides for different possibilities, including borrowing." (*Riigikogu* Verbatim Record, 12 May 1993) The formalistic conception of budget balance was, at least in part, a residue from the Soviet period. As Bönker (2007, p. 40) notes, in the Soviet budgeting, financing items such as treasury bonds were routinely counted as revenues rather than financial transactions. The "formalistic" balanced budget requirement remained in the organic budget law of Estonia until 2002. Only with the changes made to the law

229 Owing to the changes made to the electoral system in 2003, which make the cultivation of personal vote more attractive, party discipline as a coordinating mechanism might be somewhat weakened in the future.

in 2002, the balanced budget requirement was abolished and the notion of budget deficit and the concept of "financial transactions" introduced. Despite the formalistic conception of budget balance, however, the actual budgets proposed by the Government and adopted by the *Riigikogu* sought to adhere to budget balance in its substantive sense. Also, after the abolition of the "balanced budget" requirement in the organic budget law, balanced budget was still considered to be the main guiding line of budgetary policy.

With regard to the fiscal rules pertaining to borrowing, the framework laws for budgeting went through several changes. While the 1994 State Budget Act (i.e., the organic budget law) simply stated that if in the course of implementing the budget, revenues were less than needed to cover expenditures, the Government could propose the parliament to take a loan, the reformed 1999 Act stipulated that the maximum amount of loan allowed to be taken by the *Government* would be established by the state budget, with the limitation that it should not be larger than the amounts foreseen for investment (thus establishing the "golden" rule) and should not exceed 10 percent of the revenues of the state budget for that year. Besides the State Budget Act, another organic law regulated the taking of loans until 2002. The Foreign Borrowing by the Republic of Estonia and State Guarantees for Foreign Loan Agreements Act (shortly, the Foreign Borrowing Act), which came into force in 1995, stipulated that: 1) the total amount of foreign loans taken by the Republic of Estonia in a current budget year can not exceed 15 percent of the state budget revenue approved by the *Riigikogu*; 2) the total amount of all foreign loans cannot exceed 75 percent of the budget revenue for the current budget year; 3) the total amount of loans in a current budget year shall not exceed 15 percent of the budget revenue. In 2002, together with passing the new organic budget law, the Foreign Borrowing Act was abolished, but the debt limits were not transferred to the new organic budget law. The amendments made to the organic budget law in 2003 (and enacted in 2004) abolished the 10 percent limit in the organic budget law. Since then, the Maastricht criteria for deficit and debt limits have been regarded as the fiscal rules that the government has to conform to.

Altogether, one could argue that although the conception of balanced budget was formalistic (on a statutory level) until 2002, the golden rule established in 1999 and the debt limits established by the Foreign Borrowing Act constituted formal fiscal rules that can be expected to have facilitated the maintenance of fiscal discipline, at least until 2004. At the same time, it is important to note that the amount of taken loans did not even come close to the established limits.[230] The notion of fiscal discipline that the governments in reality sought to adhere to was significantly stricter than these fiscal rules entailed. Thus, it would be diffi-

230 The ratio of the total central government debt to budget revenues was 24 percent in 1995 and has been steadily falling since then, reaching 9 percent in 2000, 5 percent in 2005 and 1.2 percent in 2007.

cult to argue that the commitment to fiscal discipline *ensued* from these formal fiscal rules. One should also note that in the public discussion (in the media, for example), these borrowing limits were hardly mentioned at all. Rather, the main "fiscal rule" that dominated the public discussions was the "balanced budget" requirement established in the organic budget law.

What makes the Estonian case especially interesting is that, as can be observed from several debates on the budget document or on other laws with budgetary implications, several members of the legislature and the cabinet were of the opinion that the Constitution itself establishes a balanced budget requirement.[231] It is noteworthy that even Jüri Adams, the author of the draft constitution that became the basis for debates in the Constitutional Assembly (see chapters 2 and 3) and who later became a prominent politician and member of parliament, underlined in one parliamentary debate that the Estonian Constitution requires a balanced budget (*Riigikogu* Verbatim Record, 20 May 1997). Thus, the *informal* fiscal constitution requiring substantive budget balance appears to have been more important than the formal fiscal rules in Estonia. How the emergence of such an informal fiscal constitutional norm can be explained, is discussed in section 7.4.

7.3. Budgetary Institutions

In the recent literature exploring fiscal policies in transition, a significant part of variation in budgetary performance between CEE countries has been attributed to differences in budgetary institutions. In explaining Estonia's commitment to budget discipline, the highly centralised budgetary institutions are usually pointed out as the main factor. (Gleich 2003; Yläoutinen 2004a; Fabrizio and Mody 2006) What has *not* been discussed in these comparative and cross-sectional studies is that the organic budget law in Estonia has undergone a number of changes during the transition. Section 7.3.1. therefore gives an overview of the development of the budgetary institutions in Estonia and section 7.3.2. discusses these developments in the light of theoretical predictions put forth by the budgetary institutionalist literature discussed in section 6.3.

7.3.1. Development of the Organic Budget Law in Estonia

As Haggard and Kaufman (2001, p. 4) have emphasised, the budget processes had been very opaque during the communist rule; therefore, at the wake of the

231 For example, at the first reading of the organic budget law in 1992, Kalev Kukk (Centre Party) raised the question of whether it is reasonable to simply require budget balance in the organic budget law and whether it would not be better to set a specific maximum limit for budget deficit. To this, the Minister of Finance Madis Üürike answered that the budget has to be balanced "because the Constitution requires so". (*Riigikogu* Verbatim Record, 14 April 1993)

transition, a fundamental reform of the whole budget process was necessary.[232] The development of the organic budget law in Estonia since 1992 can be divided into following phases. First, the making of the State Budget Act of 1994. Second, the legislative proceedings of the State Budget Act of 1999, taking place from 1997 to 1999. Third, a number of significant amendments made to the 1999 State Budget Act in 2002, with the debates on these changes having lasted one year. Some additional changes have been made to the Act in 2003 and 2004 as well.

The first State Budget Act (the organic budget law or the framework law for budgeting) of the independent period in Estonia was passed in June 1993 and came into force in January 1994. Until then the budget process was governed by the State Budget Act of the Soviet Republic of Estonia adopted in 1989. The 1989 Act, however, set out only very general guidelines (e.g., that the executive prepares the budget and the legislature approves it) and left many aspects of the process open. Such "open framework" enabled both the *Riigikogu* and the Government to gain experiences with the budgeting process; many discussions of the state budgets in 1992 and 1993 already referred to the main points of contention that would come up in the discussions over the organic budget law later on: for example, how detailed the classification of the revenues and expenditures in the budget should be and how extensive changes the parliament should be allowed to make to the budget.[233]

Shortly after the State Budget Act of 1994 had come into force, the preparations for amending it started in the Ministry of Finance. Based on experiences of other countries (especially Germany and Finland) and recommendations made by the international financial institutions (especially the IMF and the World Bank), changes were constantly made to the draft, which in turn prolonged the drafting process. In June 1996, a new draft organic budget law was initiated by the Government. The draft State Budget Act was then discussed at six different sessions of the parliament and was eventually passed on 27 January 1999. The President did not promulgate it, however, on the grounds that some provisions in the Act violated the Constitution. After the *Riigikogu* made some of the recommended changes to the Act, the President promulgated it. In June 2001, substantial amendments to the Act were initiated, but when put on final vote in Decem-

232 Tanzi and Tsibouris (2000, p. 4) note, for example, that the communist countries usually lacked a budget office in its conventional sense, since budgetary allocations were made through the plan.

233 In particular, there were extensive debates on the implications of Article 115 of the Constitution (stipulating that "The *Riigikogu* shall pass as a law the budget of all state revenue and expenditure for each year") for the budget. Throughout all the readings of the 1993 budget, the members of the opposition argued that the budget was unconstitutional since a number of state revenues (e.g., privatisation yields, planned foreign loans and the revenues of extra-budgetary funds) were not included in the budget. (*Riigikogu* Verbatim Record, 22 December 1992, 20 January 1993, 26 January 1993, 9 February 1993)

ber 2001, they did not get enough votes. In February 2002, for most part the same amendments were proposed again and were passed in April 2002. The President did not promulgate the amended Act, on the grounds of unconstitutionality. After the *Riigikogu* had made changes to the Act, it did not receive enough votes (falling short of one vote). In June 2002, the amendment Act was initiated again (accommodating some of the arguments of the President); it was passed on 20 June 2002 and this time the President promulgated it.[234]

In the following, the changes made to the main phases of the budget process – the preparation, adoption and implementation – are outlined.

7.3.1.1. Changes in Preparation Phase

The budgetary institutionalist literature has pointed to the particularly strong powers that the minister of finance has in Estonia (Gleich 2003, p. 17). It should be noted, however, that as a result of the changes made to the State Budget Act in 1999 and 2002, the role of the minister of finance in the preparation phase of the budget process has been weakened. While according to the 1994 Act, the minister of finance *established* the expenditure ceilings (to be used as the basis for preparing the budget requests) for all line ministries, the 1999 Act stipulated that the minister of finance *would make proposals* regarding the ceilings for operating expenses to the Cabinet, who would pass a decision on them. Furthermore, according to the 1999 Act, no prior expenditure ceilings would be established for the so-called "constitutional institutions" (i.e., the *Riigikogu*, the President, the Chancellor of Justice, the Supreme Court and the State Audit Office).[235] According to the changes made to the Act in 2002, the line ministries would have to proceed from the general state budget strategy as the starting point for preparing their budget requests. The state budget strategy is a multiannual planning document (encompassing four years), which establishes the overall targets for spending, revenues, deficits or surpluses and indicates the spending and revenue targets for individual ministries.

The changes made to the Act in 1999 and 2002 also lessened the power of the minister of finance in the budget negotiations held with the line ministries and constitutional institutions *after* the submission of budget requests. According to the 1994 Act, the minister of finance had the right to *delete* or *change* the sums agreed upon during the negotiations between the representatives of the Ministry of Finance and the line ministries (or constitutional institutions). Pursuant to the 1999 Act, although the minister of finance could still delete or change the sums in the case of ministries, he or she would not be allowed to do that with the budget requests of the constitutional institutions (i.e., the president,

234 The constitutional debates between the *Riigikogu* and the President are discussed in more detail in chapter 9.

235 These institutions are called "constitutional institutions" because they have been explicitly mentioned in the Constitution.

the parliament, the Supreme Court, the State Audit Office, the Legal Chancellor), unless these changes had been agreed upon in the negotiations between the representatives of the constitutional institutions and the officials of the Ministry of Finance. The 2002 Act further weakened the power of the minister of finance by stating that the minister of finance has the right to *make a proposal* to another minister for the amendment or omission of amounts set in the minutes of the negotiations between the representatives of the two ministries.

The role of the Cabinet as a whole in the budget process was clearly increased as a result of the changes made to the organic budget law. The amendments to the 1994 Act retained the role of the Cabinet in resolving the disagreements arising from budget negotiations between the minister of finance and the spending ministers. In addition, the role of the Cabinet in reviewing the draft state budget was specified. While according to the 1994 Act, the Cabinet was just to *review* the draft state budget compiled by the Ministry of Finance, the 1999 Act established that the Cabinet has the right to *change or delete* the sums in the draft state budget submitted by the minister of finance (with the qualification, however, that in the case of changing the draft budgets of constitutional institutions, the Cabinet would have to add justification for that in the explanatory memorandum to the draft state budget submitted to the parliament). The introduction of the concept of the state budget strategy by the 2002 Act could also be seen as increasing the role of the Cabinet as a whole in the budget preparation phase. The state budget strategy has to be *approved* by the cabinet, on the proposal of the minister of finance. Thus, the Cabinet obtained a stronger role in the budget process as a result of the changes made to the organic budget law.

7.3.1.2. Changes in Adoption Phase

Between 1994 and 2007, the legislative phase of the budget process became more specified and the freedom of the parliament to make changes to the draft state budget submitted by the Cabinet more constrained. The only limitation on the motions to amend the draft state budget (during the legislative proceedings of the budget) in the 1994 organic budget law was Article 116 taken from the Constitution, stipulating the requirement to append financial calculations and indicating a source of revenue if the amendment to the draft state budget decrease estimated revenue or increase or reallocate expenditure (shortly put, requiring the budget amendments to be offsetting). During the debates on the state budgets from 1992 onward, discussions arose in the parliament, with regard to how active role the parliament should play in the budget process. Some members of the parliament argued, from early on, for a more limited role of the parliament in making amendments to the budget,[236] while others advocated an active role of

236 During the readings of the 1995 budget, for example, the Chairman of the Finance Committee Valve Kirsipuu noted that the role of the *Riigikogu* should be to fix the general

the *Riigikogu*.[237] The representatives of the Government usually stated that the parliament should trust the executive with regard to the budget.

The 1999 Act added another provision taken from the Constitution, stipulating that the *Riigikogu* is not allowed to eliminate or reduce expenditure in a draft state budget if the expenditure is prescribed by other acts or arises from international agreements ratified by the *Riigikogu*. In addition, the 1999 Act introduced a limitation stating that motions to amend that are submitted after the suspension of the second reading of the draft state budget can not be put to a vote if they are not supported by the Government and not accepted by the Finance Committee of the *Riigikogu*. In 1999, an important provision was added to the *Riigikogu* Rules of Procedure Act, which had a clear bearing on the budget process as well. While the Rules of Procedure had hitherto forbidden binding the draft state budget to an issue of confidence, in June 1999, this exception was abolished. The 2002 Act established a further limitation on the *Riigikogu*, stating that a motion to amend the draft state budget is not allowed to cause budget deficit, increase the deficit or reduce the surplus.

In a nutshell, the changes made to the organic budget law gradually constrained the budgetary amendment rights of the parliament. Also, by allowing the Government to bind the passage of the budget to an issue of confidence, the potential power of the Government *vis-à-vis* the parliament in the budget process was increased. If the Government wanted to, this provision would allow it to bypass the detailed discussion of the state budget in the parliament altogether.

Besides the changes made to the organic budget law, one should also note that the enforcement of the constitutional requirement of offsetting amendments by the Finance Committee of the *Riigikogu* has become stricter. While in the early years of transition, the Finance Committee was fairly lenient with the offsetting calculations proposed by the MPs, then, over time, the Finance Committee has established higher "standards" for the calculations and has rejected amendment proposals in which the offsets are not well-founded.

7.3.1.3. Changes in Implementation Phase

On the whole, the Finance Ministry's control over the implementation of the budget has become more centralised. According to the 1994 Act, the state institutions had their own bank accounts, but the changes made in 1996 repealed that provision and the 2002 Act stipulated explicitly that the institutions would not

---

proportions of expenditures and not to analyse all the specific sums or to reallocate them. (*Riigikogu* Verbatim Record, 12 October 1994)

237 At the reading of the state budget for year 1996, for example, Eiki Nestor (Moderates) pointed out that there is only one country in Europe where the parliament has merely the right to approve or to disapprove the budget submitted by the government, without the right to make changes, and that is France; in other countries, the parliaments can be actively engaged in changing the budget. (*Riigikogu* Verbatim Record, 8 November 1995)

be allowed to have their own separate accounts. While the 1994 Act simply stated that the Ministry of Finance would transfer the funds to the accounts of the line ministries, the 1999 Act stipulated that the execution of the state budget payments would be performed by the Treasury Department, which has the right to verify that a document that is the basis for a payment conforms to legislation and, in the event that it does not conform, to refuse making the payment. An amendment made in 2003 added that in the event of lower receipts of revenue than planned in the course of implementing the state budget, the minister of finance has the right to place a temporary restriction on the incurrence of expenditure prescribed in the budget.

The role of the Government in controlling the implementation of the state budget has increased as well. The 1999 Act stated that when the spending minister classifies the budget appropriations additionally, he has to inform the minister of finance about it (otherwise the classification would not be valid). The 2002 Act, however, established that ministers have to classify the expenditure, pursuant to the procedure established by the Government.

The role of the *Riigikogu* in controlling the implementation of the budget also went through some changes. The 1999 Act introduced a provision according to which a committee of the *Riigikogu* could ask a ministry to submit reports on how the budget has been implemented. In 2002, this provision was abolished. In 2003, changes were made to the State Audit Office Act, according to which a select committee of the *Riigikogu* is established that would deliberate the audit results of the implementation of the budget. The select committee has the right to summon officials, obtain oral and written explanations from them and demand relevant documents. In addition, it was stated that as a result of the deliberation of audit results, the select committee may submit inquiries to the Cabinet, which has to respond to the inquiries within one month. These provisions gave the parliament a *potentially* greater role in the control over the implementation of the state budget.

With regard to the authority of the Government and the *Riigikogu* to take loans in the course of the budget implementation process, the changes made to the organic budget law gradually increased the discretion of the Government and decreased the functions of the parliament. The 1994 Act stated that if in the course of implementing the budget, revenues were less than needed to cover expenditures, the Government could propose the parliament to take a loan. The 1999 Act gave the Government the right to decide on the need and size of the loan within the limits established by the state budget. The formal role of the *Riigikogu* in controlling the purposes of loans has diminished as a result of the changes made to the framework laws. According to the 1995 Foreign Borrowing Act, the parliament had to pass a separate decision on each foreign loan (with the foreign financing department of the Ministry of Finance acting as a strict gate-keeper with regard to what proposals reached the parliament at all). With the amendments made to the organic budget law in 2002, taking loans has become significantly easier for the Government: no separate decision by the *Riigikogu* is needed for each foreign loan, no separate permission is needed for a domestic loan in the middle of the budget year, the maximum amount of allowed borrowing is established with the annual state budget, and within this limit it would be in the discretion of the Government (on the proposal of the minister of finance) to decide on taking a loan.

7.3.2. Discussion

Altogether, the development of the budgetary institutions in Estonia between 1992 and 2007 can be summed up as following. The delegation approach employed in the *preparation* phase has been gradually replaced by contracts approach and, on the whole, the preparation process has become less centralised and the formal powers of the minister of finance have been gradually curtailed.[238] At the same time, the *adoption* phase has been complemented by an increasing number of elements characteristic to the delegation approach, emphasising the constraints on parliamentary amendments to the state budget.[239] The *implementation* phase has become more centralised and a number of delegation elements have been added, alongside with some contracts elements (like the establishment of select committee on public accounts). A number of questions arise in the face of such dynamics. First, how to explain the initial choice of the delegation approach in 1994? Second, how explicate the replacement of delegation approach by contracts approach in the preparation phase and increasing the elements of the delegation approach in the adoption phase? Third, have the alterations in the budgetary institutions led to changes in fiscal discipline? Fourth, have the configuration of changes made to the formal budgetary institutions, according to which the preparation phase has moved closer to the contracts approach, while the adoption (and partly the implementation) phases have moved closer to the delegation mode, caused any problems?

One of the main puzzles in the development of the budgetary institutions in Estonia pertains to the initial choice of adopting extremely centralised budgetary institutions, which clearly correspond to the delegation approach described by

---

238 For explanations of the characteristics of the delegation approach and contracts approach of fiscal governance, see section 6.3.1.

239 As pointed out by the budgetary institutionalist literature, discussed in section 6.3.1., the adoption phase in the delegation mode of fiscal governance emphasises strong agenda-setting powers of the executive *vis-à-vis* the parliament and extensive constraints on the legislature to make amendments to the budget, while the contracts mode puts less emphasis on constraining legislative budgetary amendments and more emphasis on the legislature's role in monitoring the compliance of the executive's budget with the fiscal targets, by giving the legislature significant rights to demand budgetary information from the executive. (von Hagen 2002, 2006b, 2007, 2008; Hallerberg and von Hagen 1999)

Hallerberg and von Hagen (1999). Hallerberg and von Hagen posit that such an approach would only be chosen by single-party governments or by multiparty governments where the coalition parties expect to run together in the next elections. The first government of the independent Estonia in 1992 does not conform to either of these conditions. The coalition consisted of three parties from different parts of the political spectrum. Notwithstanding the ideological differences, the development of the party system in Estonia at that point was in an embryonic phase, which made it next to impossible for the parties in the coalition to say whether they would be running together in the next elections as well: there was large uncertainty with regard to how the coalition partners would behave and what other parties would emerge in the political scene (who might be more appropriate coalition partners in the future). Still, in the context of a multiparty coalition government and strategic uncertainty with regard to future political partners, the first government opted for formal budgetary institutions that came very close to the delegation model.

How to explain such an institutional choice in Estonia? In a situation of high political uncertainty, where the notions of what it means to have a coalition government and how coalition partners are supposed to behave were still developing, combined with a pressure to adopt a large umber of laws in a relatively short time, the policy-makers decided to draw on the existing and past budgetary institutions. The provisions pertaining to the preparation of the budget (especially the role of the minister of finance) in the 1994 State Budget Act were taken over from the State Budget Act of 1938, which had been compiled and passed in a very different political system, emphasising the power of the executive and the president. In addition, the authors of the organic budget law drew on the existing institutional arrangements, which also gave the minister of finance extensive powers in the budget process. The State Budget Act of 1989 itself was very vague on what the exact tasks of the minister of finance would be, leaving it to be established by the minister of finance himself (who, not surprisingly, established procedures that gave him a central role in the budget process). Given the newness of the political system and limited experiences with democratic government, the authors of the first organic budget law in Estonia could have hardly foreseen the implications such an arrangement would have for coalition governments. It is also noteworthy that the fact that the organic budget law proposed in 1993 drew heavily on the 1938 organic budget law was not contested or questioned by the members of the *Riigikogu* during the legislative proceedings. Like it was the case with many other laws in Estonia during the first years of transition, the argument of historical lesson-drawing and taking over legal acts from the inter-war period were even seen as adding weight and legitimacy to the draft law in question.

Given that all the governments in Estonia so far have been coalition governments, there was a pressure to increase the power of the whole cabinet *vis-à-vis* the minister of finance. Through the changes made to the organic budget law

– moving from the right of the minister of finance to delete and change the sums in the budget requests of the spending ministers to the concept of budget strategy, which would set fiscal targets (approved by the Government) at the beginning of the budget process – there was a clear movement from the delegation approach towards the fiscal contracts (or commitment) approach (see Hallerberg and von Hagen 1999). The movement towards the contracts approach was also encouraged by the European Union: in order to profit from the structural funds already in the pre-accession phase, the Government had to submit multi-annual plans covering the use of the funds.

It should be noted, however, that even before the passing of the new organic budget law in 1999, the power of the minister of finance was not *as* strong as could be inferred from the State Budget Act but was constrained by *informal* agreements. Martinez-Vazquez (1997, p. 9) notes that the minister of finance did not have the "authority" to change budget shares across line ministries by more than 10 percent. In addition, at least for 1997, the political agreement within the governing coalition was that changes in budget shares would not exceed plus-minus 3 percent of the previous year's allocations. Ostrow (2000, ch. 7), in his analysis of the informal side of the Estonian budget process during the first two legislative periods, has also noted that although the minister of finance dominated the budget process, then in the budget preparation phase, an important role was also played by the leaders of the coalition factions, who negotiated, together with the prime minister and other selected ministers, what the budget priorities would be and which changes should be made to the initial plans. The cooperation between the leaders of the factions of the coalition parties and the most important ministers was necessary in order to hold the coalition – and hence the Government – together. Since the prevailing opinion in the *Riigikogu* (although it was not stipulated in the Constitution or in the organic budget law) was that if the parliament were to reject the budget, this would imply the fall of the government, it was important for the Government members to ensure that the draft budget would be acceptable to the *Riigikogu* (Ostrow 2000, p. 221). Thus, although according to the *formal* rules in the organic budget law, one might gain the impression of the minister of finance as almost a single player in the budget preparation process, in reality, he was constrained by the proposals of the leaders of the coalition. Thus, when taking into account the informal side of the budget procedure, one can argue that the formal changes in the organic budget law that increased the role of the cabinet as a whole in the budget process reflected and simply formalised in the law what the prevailing practices were – at least what regards the role of the Cabinet in the budget process (the meetings between the heads of the factions of coalition parties with the key ministers were not formalised).

In explaining why an increasing number of elements of the delegation approach were added to the adoption phase of the budget (which constrained the role of the parliament in the budgetary process), a number of factors can be brought out. First, as is discussed more extensively in chapter 9, an important source of inspiration for these restrictions were the experiences gained in making the 1998 budget, when the minority government lost control over the legislative budgetary amendments. Second, the provision allowing the government to bind the draft budget to an issue of confidence was adopted after the opposition had resorted to filibustering tactics during the discussions of the negative supplementary budget in summer 1999. Third, the constraints on the legislative budgetary amendments were also motivated by the wish of the executive and the Finance Committee of the *Riigikogu* to make the legislative budgetary proceedings "smoother" and swifter. At the same time, one should note that the role of the legislative amendments in the budget process had de facto been relatively constrained – even without the *formal* constraints. Ostrow (2000, p. 222) points out that the only legislative amendments that passed were those with the "blessing of the government and the coalition", whereas the amendments made by the opposition were usually rejected or were not even put on vote. Ostrow (2000, p. 221) notes that the amendments proposed during the legislative proceedings of the budget often reflected the desire of the factions (especially the opposition factions) to be seen and heard. As he puts it, "the game is not about getting these amendments adopted" but rather about having "the opportunity for the amendment author to rise on the floor and make a speech in defence of the particular sector for which he or she is proclaiming support" (p. 221).

The third question posed at the beginning of this section was whether changes in budgetary institutions found an expression in changes in fiscal discipline in Estonia. Although the cross-sectional studies have emphasised the importance of centralised budgetary institutions and especially the strong role of the minister of finance as an explanatory factor, the overview of the developments of budgetary institutions in Estonia indicates that the institutions have evolved over the years towards a more collegial system of budgetary decisions-making, where more important decisions would be made by the cabinet as a whole (and the leaders of the coalition party factions) rather than single-handedly by the minister of finance. For most part, at least in the period under consideration, the weakened role of the minister of finance in the preparation phase has not translated into reduced fiscal discipline. At the same time, one should note that the contracts mode of fiscal governance in Estonia suffers a number of shortcomings, which may pose problems for the future. In particular, though the multi-annual budgetary strategy should serve the role of establishing a fiscal contract by committing the government to a set of fiscal targets, the targets established so far have suffered from inaccurate forecasts and have, therefore, been not adhered to in practice. As was emphasised in section 6.3., the capacities of institutional actors to analyse and forecast the developments in revenues and expenditures is likely to play an important role in whether the contracts mode of fiscal governance can function or not (see Molander 2000; Wehner 2006).

The fourth question concerned the problems involved in the mismatch between the different phases of budgeting. The advancement of the monitoring capacities of the parliament, required by the contracts mode, has been insufficiently addressed so far. Though the establishment of the public accounts committee could be seen as serving the purpose of enhancing the parliament's monitoring powers over the government, the primary goal of the select committee is to provide opportunities for the opposition to uncover abuse (or inefficient use) of budgetary allocations by the executive, rather than offering a forum for the members of the coalition parties to monitor the adherence to the fiscal contracts by the executive. Further, the ability of the legislators to monitor whether the preparation and implementation of the budget takes place according to the agreed-upon targets would require additional legislative resources for analysis and research, which have been insufficient so far. Combined with the increasing flexibility given to the ministries in making specific budgetary appropriations, this may lead to a situation where the *Riigikogu* has only very limited control over the budget. Though the mismatch between the contracts mode in the preparation phase and the delegation mode in the adoption phase has not led to problems so far, it is likely to give rise to tensions in the face of fiscal difficulties.

7.4. Going beyond Constitutional Explanations

Confining the analysis of fiscal discipline in Estonia to the constitutional aspects brought up in chapter 5 and 6, however, would leave an important part of the overall picture unexplained. Drawing on secondary literature, parliamentary debates, autobiographical books published by the prominent politicians and discussions in the media, one can say that the following factors appear to have played an important role in the emergence of the informal fiscal constitutional norm of balanced budget and in maintaining fiscal discipline in Estonia.

First, given the choice of currency board system in Estonia, the commitment to fiscal discipline by government was seen as very important for maintaining the stability of the currency. Because of the traumatic experiences with the hyperinflation at the beginning of the 1990s, during which many people lost their savings, having one's own currency was seen as a "saviour" from the perils of the high inflation. In this background, maintaining the stability of Estonia's own currency was seen as one of the "cornerstones" or "holy cows" in the Estonian politics (see, for example, Korhonen 2000). The need to maintain budget balance because of the currency board arrangements was consistently pointed out in the debates over the annual budgets and other public finance acts. The Argentine experience with the currency board arrangements, indicating the problems that can arise if fiscal discipline is not maintained, only endorsed the prevailing convictions among the dominant political actors in Estonia.[240]

Second, the need to maintain budget balance (*inter alia*, because of the currency board system) was repeatedly pointed by the IMF, which had an important influence on the public finance discourse in Estonia. Very often, the argument "We have to do it, because the IMF says so" was the end of discussion and the prescriptions of the IMF were taken as "givens" that could not be challenged. From the beginning of transition in Estonia, the IMF officials and their advice were well received and almost "blindly trusted" by the local political leaders (see, e.g., Knöbl and Haas 2003). Indeed, one could speak of "elective affinity" between the reformers in Estonia and the IMF advisors (see Bönker, Müller and Pickel 2002, p. 6). One of the important reasons behind such an extensive influence of the IMF over Estonian budgeting was the fact that the Estonian economy was highly dependent on foreign sources of investment and the politicians reckoned that the IMF's opinions on a country play an important role in influencing the international rating agencies, which, in turn, would shape the decisions of foreign investors. This argument was openly used both in the parliamentary discussions and in the media.

Third, given the successful economic development of Estonia in the 1990s, certain policy choices came to be seen as important guarantors of success – almost as "talismans" that cannot be neglected because this would bring bad luck. It was repeatedly argued by the politicians in the second half of the transition that the currency board, the balanced budget and the proportional income tax are the three "holy pillars" of the Estonian politics, which cannot be challenged since "they are the bases for Estonian economic success". Thus, the norm of balanced budget became a quasi-constitutional norm or the central norm of the informal fiscal constitution in Estonia, which could not be challenged without incurring significant political costs. Indeed, this norm has been considered to be important by all governments, irrespective of their ideological orientation (see, e.g., Lagerspetz and Vogt 1998).

Alongside the incentives provided by the informal fiscal constitutional norm of balanced budget, one should take into account a number of economic, political and societal aspects that *facilitated* the adherence to this norm.

First, Estonia had a more advantageous financial starting point, compared with most of the other CEE countries: the newly independent Estonia entered the transition without an existing debt burden and without corresponding debt service costs.[241]

---

240 For a discussion over the role of currency board in the maintenance of fiscal discipline in Estonia, see also Hansson and Sachs (1994), Knöbl and Haas (2003), and Knöbl, Sutt and Zavoiko (2002).

241 For a discussion of the "inherited" debt burdens in other CEE countries, see Campbell (1996).

Second, Estonia, like many other countries in the region, faced objective constraints on the possibility to borrow during early years of transition (Lavigne 1999, p. 140). External finance for covering budget deficits was hardly available, given the newness of the country and not-yet-established credibility. Further, borrowing on domestic financial markets was next to impossible due to underdeveloped financial markets.

Third, as Norgaard *et al.* (1999, p. 145) have noted, the period of "extraordinary politics" lasted longer in the Estonia (and also other Baltic countries) than in most other post-communist systems, increasing the threshold for what the population could endure. Faced with a feeble civil society and weak party system, fiscal reforms could be undertaken by market-oriented reform teams in relative insulation from more broad-based party political demands. Thus, compared with the other CEE countries, the first government of the independent period in Estonia was able to go further in cutting, *inter alia*, social expenditures and subsidies.[242] The Government that came to power in 1992 cut the expenditures planned for 1993 by one-fourth. In the area of pensions, for instance, the Estonian government suspended the implementation of a pension law that would have provided for relatively generous pensions and implemented flat-rate allowances from 1992 onwards (replaced by slightly differentiated pensions, according to the number of years of worked, in 1994) (Leppik and Võrk 2006). Only with the pension reform undertaken in 1999 was a system of earnings-related pensions introduced. Throughout the 1990s, the pension levels in Estonia were among the lowest in the CEE region and this factor played an important role in easing the pressures on the budget (see Müller 2002; Lipsmeyer 2002). For the entire 1990s, the pension system in Estonia was "defined contribution" on a macro-level, implying that the size of the pensions paid out to the current pensioners was determined by the amount of contributions flowing into the social insurance budget from the current workers (Leppik and Võrk 2006). Indexation of the pensions, which, in principle, should have untied the size of the current pension benefits from current contributions, was only introduced in 2000 (Raudla and Staehr 2003).

Fourth, as Norgaard *et al.* (1999, p. 145) note, the pursuit of very conservative fiscal policy in Estonia at the beginning of transition was made easier by the fact that the Russian-speaking minority – of whom many had worked in the large state-owned factories and who were, consequently, among those most significantly affected by economic reforms – was largely excluded from political influence since they, in the absence of Estonian citizenship, had no right to vote at national elections.

Fifth, for the most part of the 1990s, the trade unions were weak, their membership shrinking and they had very limited influence on the policy-

242 For a discussion on the difficulties faced by other CEE countries in their attempts to impose such cuts, see Campbell (1996).

making. The special functions of trade unions during the communist period contributed to their isolation after the regime change. (Steen 1999, p. 134)

Sixth, one should also account for the dominant influence of specific individuals who played a role in the policy choices adopted by the successive governments. In particular, the personal influence of Ardo Hansson, who was the economic advisor of the governments between 1992 and 1999, was an important factor. Drawing on his experiences as an advisor of economic reforms (together with Jeffrey Sachs, who had been Hansson's PhD supervisor) in several CEE countries, he strongly influenced the course of budgetary policies and called for conservative fiscal stance. Combined with a lack of qualified experts of budgetary policy in the early years of the transition, the small size of Estonia was certainly conducive to the dominant influence of single individual experts.

It is also important to note that the different phases of transition require different explanations for how Estonia managed to maintain fiscal discipline. In the early phase of transition, the benefit of crisis, the extraordinary politics, the militant type of leaders, willing to undertake policies with "politically suicidal" consequences, the objective constraints on borrowing and strong external pressures (from the IMF) played an important role. In the later phases, other explanations for the continuation of fiscal discipline are more relevant. In particular, the development of political discourse – that viewed the general stance of fiscal conservatism as a guarantor of economic success and international recognition – started to replace the more "tangible" constraints, which had prevailed at the beginning of transition, facilitated by continuing dependence on foreign investments and thus, by the perceived need to maintain friendly and deferential terms with the IFIs. From 2004 onwards, joining the euro has been a dominating goal in the budgetary discourse in Estonia, turning the Maastricht criteria for debt and deficit levels into a focal point of budgetary decision-making in Estonia.

Thus, it would be insufficient to attribute the fiscal discipline in Estonia only to the constitutional factors: the objective economic constraints on borrowing, favourable economic developments, ideological factors, the idiosyncratic features of the political leaders and their advisors, the specific political and societal features have certainly played some role. Some of these aspects are more tangible and more easily measurable than others, but the difficulty of measuring a variable does not necessarily mean that it has been less influential than the more tangible factors. Thus, as the Estonian case shows, the choices made and results obtained in budgeting are influenced by a large number of factors, which can interact with each other in complex ways. That, in turn, should make one especially cautious in passing simplified judgements in the context of explaining policy choices in transition countries.

7.5. Summary

Altogether, the conjectures offered by the recent literature in positive constitutional public finance provide *some* explanations for the budgetary developments in Estonia, but do not tell the entire story. In particular, if one confined the analysis to the most general features of constitutional arrangements, Estonia, with its commitment to fiscal discipline, would appear as an outlier that has somehow been able – "despite" the parliamentary system, proportional electoral rules and coalition governments, the lack of fiscal rules in the formal constitution – to maintain fiscal discipline. The case study in this chapter indicates, however, that one needs to dig deeper into institutional details in order to get a more accurate picture of the constitutional setting. In particular, the specific elements of the electoral system that are conducive to party discipline and reduce the fractionalisation of governments can be considered to have exercised countervailing effects to common-pool problems of budgeting.

Alongside the constitutional arrangements conducive to achieving coordinated policy-making on the policy-arena of public finance, the coordinating function played by the budgetary institutions can be considered to have played an *enabling* role for the commitment to fiscal discipline in Estonia. At the same time, one should note that despite the initial mismatch between the form of government and the mode of fiscal governance, the emerging mismatch between contracts elements in the preparation phase and delegation elements in the adoption phase, the discrepancy between forecasting capacities and the contracts mode in preparing the budget did not, at least until 2007, translate into problems with fiscal discipline, which would weaken the "budgetary institutions matter" argument.

Further, the constitutional elements and the centralised budgetary institutions conducive to coordination of budgetary policy would leave up the question, "What incentives do the political actors have to use the party discipline and coordinating arrangements in order to achieve budget discipline?" As discussed in section 6.3.3., the solutions to the *information* problems involved in budgetary decision-making do not necessarily simultaneously address the *incentive* problems. In Estonia's case as well, the incentives to adhere to fiscal discipline did not *arise* from the organic budget law but originated elsewhere. The incentives to maintain fiscal discipline arose from the currency board arrangements, the guidelines of the IMF (the adherence to which was driven by the desire to secure good ratings, necessary for foreign investments), and, in a later phase, from the Maastricht criteria, the importance of which was driven by the desire to join the euro. Driven by these incentives, the informal fiscal constitutional norm of budget balance emerged, which provided the overriding focal point for policy actors in budgetary decision-making. This informal fiscal constitutional norm acquired almost a "mythic" nature, because of the prevailing beliefs that this had been a guarantor of Estonia's economic success and abandoning this norm would amount to throwing away a valued talisman. As Lieberman (2002, p. 700) has aptly put it, drawing on Orren and Skowronek (1994, 1996), "Any political moment or episode or outcome is situated within a *variety* of ordered institutional and ideological patterns, each with its own origins and history and each with its own logic and pace." (emphasis in original) Metaphorically speaking, these patterns can "take on lives of their own": "they come to structure and delimit political interests, understandings, and behavior independently of other factors that might also be important." (Lieberman 2002, p. 700)

Altogether, a detailed explanation of the commitment to fiscal discipline in Estonia would have to take into account the interaction between the formal institutional elements, the informal fiscal constitutional norms, the incentives and beliefs of the political actors and the objective economic constraints and possibilities.

PART III: The Role of Constitutions in Shaping Public Finance Laws

Chapter 8: Theoretical Framework for Analysing the Role of Constitution in the Development of Public Finance Laws

8.1. Introduction

While part II of this book was concerned with the "emerging orthodoxy" of constitutional public finance and its shortcomings, part III of this book (chapters 8–10) offers an alternative way of approaching the question "How do constitutions influence public finance?" As discussed in part II, the recent literature on constitutional public finance is primarily concerned with exploring the associations between particular constitutional features and aggregate fiscal indicators. Confining the analysis to such an exercise, however, would present only a very limited picture of the role of constitutions in the policy arena of public finance.

As mentioned in chapter 4, the studies in the emerging orthodoxy usually employ the "calculus approach" in explaining how a constitution (as a particular type of institution) shapes the behaviour of political actors, while neglecting the insights from the "cultural approach". The goal of this chapter is to offer an analytical framework that integrates both the calculus approach and cultural approach in exploring the role of constitutions in public finance. This chapter assumes that since "politics is a place for discovering, elaborating, and expressing meanings" constitutional law can serve as an essential "instrument of interpretive order" (Burgess 1993, p. 447). Therefore, alongside strategic calculations of policy actors one needs to account for the "transformative power" (Burgess 1993, p. 450) that constitutional discourse can entail.

In particular, this chapter is concerned with the question of how constitutions shape public finance laws: the organic budget law, organic tax law and specific tax laws. Curiously, this link has not been brought up by the studies of constitutional public finance so far. Figure 8.1. presents an analytical framework for approaching this question.

First, the constitution can have a straightforward impact, when the constitutional provisions pertaining to the budget process are integrated in the organic budget law and the provisions on taxation are incorporated in tax laws. The constitutional provisions on budget process or taxation, however, are rarely precise enough to provide a full content for the public finance acts. Therefore, the constitutional provisions have to be specified and further aspects added when public finance laws are drafted.

Second, as discussed in chapter 6, the choice of budgetary institutions is likely to be influenced by the form of government: whether it is a single-party majority government or a multiparty coalition government (Hallerberg and von Hagen 1999). Hallerberg and von Hagen (1999) argue that if a more coordinated budget process is sought for, single-party governments are more likely to opt for a "delegation approach", where the minister of finance is given extensive powers in coordinating the preparation of the budget, whereas multiparty coalition governments are likely to choose a "fiscal contracts" (also called a "commitment") approach, where the fiscal goals for the budget are established collectively by the cabinet. The form of government, in turn, as discussed in chapter 5, is influenced by the electoral system (see Duverger 1954; Rae 1967; Taagepera and Shugart 1989, 1993). Thus, the electoral system outlined in the constitution can indirectly influence the basic choices made with regard to the organic budget law

Figure 8.1.: The role of constitution in shaping public finance laws

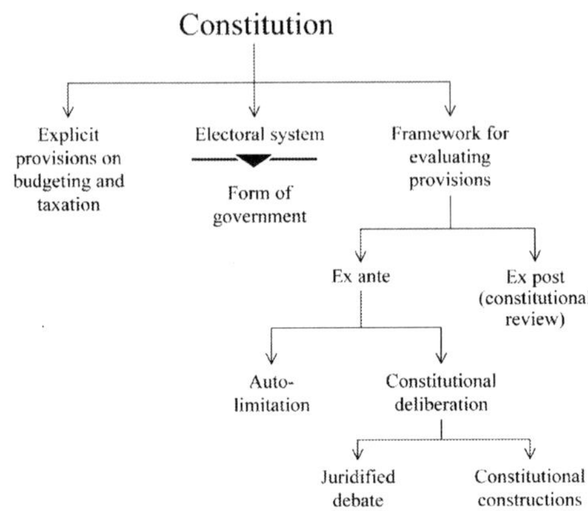

Third, the constitution can shape public finance laws by providing a framework for *evaluating* the enacted or proposed provisions in these laws on the grounds of constitutionality. Even if the constitution is silent on the exact role of the cabinet or the minister of finance in the budget procedure, for example, the respective provisions in the organic budget law can be viewed and assessed in the light of the constitution. In addition to the constitutional provisions pertaining directly to the issues of budgeting and taxation, other constitutional articles can be evoked for evaluating, contesting and defending the provisions in the organic budget law, framework law for taxation and tax acts.

The rest of this chapter elaborates on the third mode of influence and outlines how to analyse the role of the constitution as a framework of evaluation that different political institutions and policy actors employ in drafting, amending and abolishing public finance laws.

8.2. Constitution as Framework for Evaluating Public Finance Laws

As depicted in Figure 8.1., the constitution – as a framework for evaluating the public finance laws – can exert influence through *ex post* and *ex ante* constitutional review. The *ex ante* constitutional review can take the form of auto-limitation and constitutional deliberation. Constitutional deliberation, in turn, can take two different forms: juridified debate and constitutional construction. The subsections below explain these different mechanisms of influence in detail. Section 8.2.1. discusses the role of *ex post* constitutional review and 8.2.2. takes up the different forms of *ex ante* constitutional review.

8.2.1. *Ex Post* Constitutional Review

The constitution can shape the public finance laws (or any other law, for that matter) through the official process of constitutional review,[243] in which the constitutional court (or an equivalent) assesses the constitutionality of the contested provisions, strikes down unconstitutional legislation and indicates how the law should be changed in order to be in compliance with the constitution. This effect – called the "downstream" or "remedial" effect by Favoreu (1988, p. 103) and "immediate, direct, or formal" effect by Stone Sweet (2000, p. 63) – is often considered as the most obvious one and has received the most extensive scholarly attention.

The distinction between the American model and the European model is the usual point of departure for analysing constitutional review mechanisms (Stone Sweet 2000, p. 63; Romeu 2006, p. 105). The American model attributes the power of review of legislation to all ordinary courts, whereas the European model (also called the Austrian or the Kelsenian model) assigns the exclusive power of constitutional review to a special constitutional court. While in the American model, the courts can only exercise concrete review, then in the European model, the constitutional court can also exercise abstract review (or only that, as is the case with the French Constitutional Council). Abstract review procedure enables the court to examine the constitutionality of a law without reference to any specific case, while concrete review proceeds from a concrete lawsuit, originating in the judiciary. Abstract review can take place either before the promulgation of the law (also called *a priori* review) or after the promulgation of the law (*a posteriori* review) or both. These institutional elements can, in reality, be combined in different ways.[244]

To what extent the *potential* effects of constitutional review are translated into *actual* effects – that is, whether the legislature defers to the court and revises the law according to the court's interpretation – has received increasing

243 Though earlier literature used to distinguish between "judicial review" (which characterised the American model) and "constitutional review" (which referred to the European model), then, by now, these terms are used interchangeably (McWhinney 1986).

244 For elaborations on the different forms of constitutional review and the combinations of the different institutional choices involved, see von Brünneck (1988), McWhinney (1986), Stone (1992a), Stone Sweet (1999), Romeu (2006), Ferejohn (2002), Harutyunyan and Mavcic (1999) and Sadurski (ed.) (2002).

attention in the literature. Among other factors, the willingness of the legislature to comply with the decisions of the court is influenced by public support for constitutional "rules of the game" in general and for constitutional courts in particular (see Caldeira 1986; Murphy and Tanenhaus 1990; Weingast 1997). As Vanberg (2001, p. 347) emphasises, in democracies where the constitutional court enjoys a high degree of public support, "a legislative decision not to comply with judicial rulings may result in a negative public backlash and the fear of such a backlash may be a powerful inducement for legislative majorities to respect judicial decisions". The prevailing assessment of the scholars investigating the relations between legislatures and constitutional courts in Western democracies is that, on the whole, legislatures follow the decisions of the constitutional court and open confrontations are rare (see Rubio Llorente 1988; von Brünneck 1988). Still, reversals and more subtle modifications of the constitutional review decisions by legislature can take place and have been discussed in a number of studies. Fisher (1990), for example, has shown that in the U.S. case, the Court's rulings have "hardly been the last word". Congress has repeatedly attempted to override the Supreme Court decisions and often succeeded.[245]

To what extent the potential *threat of an override*, in turn, influences the decision of the constitutional court, has also received extensive attention in the literature, especially by scholars focusing on the U.S. Supreme Court. A strand of research following the rational choice tradition has emphasised strategic interactions between the legislature and the judiciary, implying that the court might be subject to stronger external constraints than the attitudinal model (Segal 1997) postulates.[246] Pickerill summarises the assumptions of this approach as following: "Justices make decisions to maximise their policy preferences while minimising the likelihood that Congress will enact legislation to 'override' the judicial decision" (2004, pp. 18–19). Drawing on the existing theoretical literature, Hansford and Damore (2000) emphasise the necessity to combine the attitudinal and rational choice models into more elaborated models that would bring out under what conditions the constitutional court would be constrained by legislative preferences.[247] They argue that justices would be constrained by con-

245 Meernik and Ignagni (1997, p. 463) find that between 1954 and 1990, the Congress attempted to reverse the judgement of the Supreme Court in 22 percent of the cases and succeeded in 33 percent of the attempts. For the discussion of factors behind the U.S. Congress's attempts to reverse the decisions of the Supreme Court, see Ignani and Meernik (1994, 1997), Eskridge (1991), Rogers (2001) and Segal (1997), among others.

246 See, for example, Spiller and Gely (1992), Gely and Spiller (1992), Epstein and Knight (1998), Epstein and Walker (1995). An overview of the literature taking the rational choice perspective for analysing the Supreme Court-Congress interactions has been given by Pickerill (2004).

247 As Hansford and Damore (2000, p. 491) underline, the rational choice models postulate unrealistically high levels of external constraint, whereas the attitudinal model underestimates the extent to which judicial behaviour can be influenced by other political actors.

gressional preferences only when the legislature "poses a credible threat". Hansford and Damore hypothesise that previous legislative overrides in an issue area and case-level interest group activity are likely to be important factors in influencing whether the court perceives the potential override as a credible threat. They explain that the number of recent overrides in a specific issue area (e.g., in taxation) offer a clear cue about willingness of legislature to override legislation in that specific area (p. 495). Further, interest group participation can make the congressional threat more credible, because interest groups are important conduits of information between the court and the legislature: interest groups that are unhappy with the court's decision are likely to lobby for legislative response. Epstein, Knight and Shvetsova (2001) predict, based on a game-theoretic model involving the court, executive and a bicameral legislature, that a court that wishes to strengthen itself (which is especially the case with the courts in CEE countries), both in short-term and in long-term perspective, has to take decisions that lie in the overlap of the other players' tolerance interval concerning the particular case; otherwise, the other players will override the decision of the court.[248] In addition, they argue that the court would be motivated to abstain from intense political conflict and contentious political issues – especially with regard to the controversies concerning institutional prerogatives of the other branches.

Subscribing to the interactive perspective, Vanberg (2005) discusses how the anticipated legislative reactions to constitutional review decisions influence decision-making in the court. Vanberg (2005, pp. 169–170) argues that although most of the literature on constitutional courts views the courts as "unconstrained actors that are capable to impose their preferences on other policy-makers", the courts' decisions are in fact shaped by the political environment. Vanberg concurs that the courts must usually rely on the majority of the legislature to implement their decision (by revising the statutes) and the main "enforcement mechanism" the courts have in such a situation is public support for the constitutional court and the fear – by the members of parliament – of public disdain (with its possible electoral consequences), were the legislature not to follow the rulings of the court.[249] (pp. 14, 170) Given the importance of public support as a venue for ensuring compliance – thus constituting an important "judicial resource" – judges are likely to be concerned with the public support for their decisions, assuming that "specific support" for concrete decisions can be transformed into "diffuse support" for the court as a whole, over time (pp. 14, 51–52).[250] Along-

248 Epstein, Knight and Shvetsova (2001) demonstrate the applicability of this model in the case of Russia.

249 The importance of public support in guaranteeing compliance has also been discussed by Canon and Johnson (1999), Gibson, Caldeira, Baird (1998), Murphy and Tanenhaus (1990) and Caldeira (1986).

250 Vanberg borrows the distinction between "diffused" and "specific" support from Easton (1975). Vanberg (2005, pp. 50–51) points to several studies concluding that specific sup-

side the satisfaction of the public with the specific substance of the decisions, "Public support for courts is likely to be a function of courts' ability to convey the image of impartial, apolitical legal body." (p. 52)[251]

As an important corollary to existing theoretical propositions, Vanberg adds that the effectiveness of the enforcement mechanism based on public support depends on how easily the legislature's failure to defer to the court can be detected; in order to "activate" the public backlash against the non-complying legislature, the public must be aware of the infringement (p. 21). Vanberg conjectures that possibilities for detection are higher, if the political environment fosters transparent decision-making (e.g., if the political system fosters more extensive scrutiny by opposition groups by allowing them to initiate public hearings or to shape the agenda of committee hearing or floor debate) (pp. 22, 46). Further, the possibilities for detection vary across different cases. The likelihood of detection is higher in cases that have received intensive attention from well-organised interest groups (pp. 22, 46). However, for cases that are more complicated and technical (Vanberg brings the example of tax codes), it is harder to establish that the legislator has violated the ruling (pp. 22, 47). Inherent complexity of the policy area or provision under review does not only make it harder to discover the evasion, it also makes it harder for the monitoring interest groups to persuade the general public that the infringement of the ruling has indeed taken place (p. 47). Drawing on the two main dimensions – public support and transparency of the environment – Vanberg conjectures that the Court would be in a strong position when the public support for the court is high and when the environment of decision-making is transparent. If these two conditions are not satisfied, the court is likely to be in a weaker position than the legislature in the inter-institutional confrontation. (p. 25) Vanberg proposes that in issue areas with lower transparency, the court anticipates the evasion by the legislature, were the court to annul the law, and, therefore, it is likely to uphold the statute, in order to "circumvent the confrontation that has the potential damage to its institutional standing", especially if it places higher importance on avoiding the evasion than on the issue under consideration (pp. 32, 42).[252] In addition, the court would become more deferential as the political importance of the issue under review increases for legislative majorities (p. 42).

---

port influences diffuse support for a court in the sense that "substantive evaluations of particular court decisions do affect the level of public support for a court" (e.g., Grosskopf and Mondak 1998; Caldeira and Gibson 1992; Franklin and Kosaki 1995; Marshall 1989). See also Durr, Martin and Wolbrecht (2000) and Mondak and Smithey (1997).

251 See also Capelletti (1989), Gibson (1989, 1991), Schwartz (2000), Shapiro (1981), and Tyler and Raskinski (1991).

252 This is probably one of the weakest elements in Vanberg's (2005) model since he does not explain why and how exactly would a confrontation where the legislature prevails damage the institutional standing of the constitutional court.

Based on these considerations, Vanberg (2005, p. 57) puts forth a list of hypotheses:

> Hypothesis 1: *Ceteris paribus*, a constitutional court will be more aggressive in using its powers of review as transparency increases.
> Hypothesis 2: Judges are motivated by a concern to maintain public support and are sensitive to prevailing public opinion.
> Hypothesis 3: Judges are sensitive to the interests of governing majorities.
> Hypothesis 4: The potential for a public backlash is an important consideration for legislators in deciding how to respond to a judicial ruling.
> Hypothesis 5: When evading a decision, legislators will try to hide evasion by reducing transparency. When anticipating evasion, judges will try to increase transparency in their decisions.

Further, Vanberg notes that cases arising under abstract judicial review tend to be the most transparent (pp. 89–90). He also argues that since legislative majorities are inclined to resist a ruling that imposes financial costs, the courts (anticipating the likely evasion) would be more deferential to the parliament in cases where the judicial decision would have budgetary impacts, in terms of demanding additional expenditures or reducing available revenues (pp. 130–132).[253]

With regard to the question of whether the courts in CEE countries are likely to impose costs on the legislature, the prediction could go both ways. On the one hand, given tighter financial constraints in these countries, the constitutional court could anticipate the difficulties that the parliaments would have with such decisions and would hence be unwilling to impose large costs with its decisions. On the other hand, since the public support for the court depends on its reputation of being an impartial mediator, the court should be willing to take decisions that impose costs on the legislature, when the merits of the case require so. Further, given the need to build up the support of the general public, a constitutional court in a CEE country would have incentives to favour the rights and positions of taxpayers *vis-à-vis* the state in constitutional disputes.

Drawing on the hypotheses offered by Vanberg, one can put forth a number of competing conjectures about the behaviour of political actors in the context of extensive political and economic transition (like the transition process in CEE countries):

Conjecture 1: Given the need to build up public support, constitutional courts in transition countries will favour taxpayers in their decisions (even if these decisions would have budgetary implications).

253 The German case study conducted by Vanberg confirmed this conjecture (pp. 131–137). The interviews indicated that "There was a unanimous agreement that a ruling is likely to be ignored or compliance with it delayed if it imposes considerable additional expenses or leads to a shortfall in revenue" (p. 131) and that the court will be more deferential in such cases.

Conjecture 2: Given the need to build up the reputation as a neutral arbiter, constitutional courts in transition countries will adopt decisions that bring about high budgetary costs (if the merits of the case require so).
Conjecture 3: Given the need to build up support of other political institutions, the constitutional courts will not adopt decisions that have costly budgetary consequences.
Conjecture 4: Given stringent fiscal constraints faced by the governments in the countries in transition, constitutional courts will not adopt decisions that would imply high budgetary costs.

With regard to the behaviour of the legislatures, the competing pressures and incentives would lead to competing conjectures as well:

Conjecture 5: Given stringent fiscal constraints, parliaments in transition countries will not defer to the constitutional court in cases with costly budgetary implications.
Conjecture 6: Given the need to build up public support for the institution, parliaments in countries of transition will be deferential to the court's decisions in cases which favour taxpayers' rights (even if they have costly budgetary implications).

Which of these configurations of incentives would dominate and which of the outcomes would prevail in transitional contexts, is difficult to say a priori and would have to be tested empirically.

In addition to constitutional review exercised by courts, the analytical framework that is concerned with the effects of a constitution on legislation should consider the role of other "constitutional watchdogs" or "guardians of the constitution" that may play an important role in supervising the constitutionality of laws and initiating constitutional review proceedings.[254] The functions of a constitutional watchdog can be performed by a president in promulgation of laws (e.g., when the president has the right to refuse promulgation on the grounds of unconstitutionality and send the law back to the parliament), an ombudsman or a legal chancellor or some other body that is *formally independent* of the parliament (e.g., local governments and state governments in federal systems).[255] The roles of the president and the legal chancellor (or public defender

254 Although the term "constitutional review" usually refers to the review exercised by the constitutional court, the term has also a broader meaning, referring, in addition, to the review of the constitution undertaken by bodies or persons with the right to refer bills to the court.

255 Although in several countries a certain number of members of the parliament can initiate the proceedings of constitutional review, the fluid constellations of opposition parties cannot be assumed to have the level of institutionalisation that a constitutional watchdog is expected to have. As discussed below, however, the right of the members of the legis-

or an equivalent institution) can be considered to be of particular importance, provided that these bodies have been specifically entrusted with the task of constitutional supervision. The extent to which the presidential veto (on the grounds of unconstitutionality) can influence legislative decisions depends on a number of factors, including: a) the majority needed for overriding the presidential veto; b) the follow-up mechanisms for the override (especially whether the president can take issue to the constitutional court); c) the assessment of the likelihood that the president would pursue the issue further after the legislative override. Similar factors should be in play in the case of other watchdogs as well. In addition, the specific content of the arguments given by the watchdog is likely to have a varying impact on how willing the legislature is to incorporate the proposed changed into the vetoed act.

8.2.2. *Ex Ante* Constitutional Review

Alongside the official, "institutionalised" venues of constitutional review or the "first face" of constitutional power (Whittington 2005) where the constitution can shape the legislation *ex post*, the constitution can shape a law already *before* the adoption of the law by the legislature, *ex ante*. Here, the constitution can play a role by framing legislative debates on the law and by providing a source of arguments for the proponents and opponents of particular provisions. As Stone Sweet emphasises, "Such debates can alter legislative outcomes, sometimes profoundly." (2000, p. 73) Such *ex ante* influence of the constitution can be observed "by tracing legislation through the policy process to determine how and why it is altered as a result of constitutional argument" (Stone 1994, p. 447). Here, again, it would be analytically fruitful to divide this kind of influence of the constitution into two different forms: auto-limitation and constitutional deliberation.

8.2.2.1. Auto-Limitation

First, *ex ante* constitutional review can take the form of "indirect" authority of the constitutional court – what Stone Sweet calls "pedagogical, indirect, or feedback effect" (2000, p. 63) or "auto-limitation" (2000, p. 76), Favoreu (1988, p. 104) terms "upstream or preventative effect", and Whittington (2005) views as the "second face" of power[256] of the constitutional system. "Auto-limitation" is "the exercise of self-restraint on the part of the government and its parliamentary majority in anticipation of an annulment by the constitutional court" (Stone

lature to file a complaint of unconstitutionality of an act can play an important role in influencing the extent to which the issues of constitutionality play a role in legislative debates.

256 For the original formulation of the concept of "second face of power", see Bachrach and Baratz (1962, 1963).

Sweet 2002, p. 94). Auto-limitation can be observed when the government and parliament take decisions during the legislative process that "sacrifice initially held policy objectives" with the aim to "reduce the probability that a bill will either be referred to the court, or be judged unconstitutional" (p. 94). To what extent the legislature engages in auto-limitation depends, *inter alia*, on how extensive court's constitutional review powers are, and, in particular, whether its powers are confined to concrete review or whether it can undertake abstract review. Vanberg (1998) suggests that abstract review results in more moderate legislative proposals than would be expected in its absence. Stone Sweet even considers the opportunity for the abstract review as one of the main causes of "judicialisation of law-making" (2000, p. 195) and "coordinate construction" (1994, p. 443).[257] In addition, the extent of auto-limitation is likely to depend on existing precedents of constitutional review: how many decisions there are in that particular sector (in other words, how "thick" the constitutional law is or how "constitutionalised" the sector is),[258] how they were made (e.g., the level of detail), and how easily analogies can be drawn between the existing decisions and the issue at hand. The number of bills that are referred to the constitutional court (and hence, the number of constitutional review decisions), in turn, depends on the kinds of bodies that have the right of referral. In countries where the legislative minority (a certain number of legislators) can initiate proceedings of constitutional review, the number of abstract review decisions is likely to be larger than in the absence of such a right. Opposition parties often provoke a constitutional debate in order to win, in constitutional review process, what they could never win in "normal" legislative processes" (Stone Sweet 1999, p. 23). Altogether, the easier it is for a bill to end up in the constitutional court, the more likely the legislature is to engage in auto-limitation. In addition, Stone Sweet (2000, p. 52) argues that the more radical a piece of legislation adopted by the parliament is (the more extensive departure from the status quo it foresees), the more likely it is going to be referred to the constitutional court. Thus, political systems that give rise to more frequent radical reforms are more likely to have more constitutionalised sectors and "thicker" constitutional law. The proneness of the political system to produce more radical reforms depends, importantly, on the degree of centralisation and the number of veto points in the system (pp. 52–53).

The mechanisms of "auto-limitation" or the "power of anticipation" or the "second face of power" can also come into play in parliament's relations with other institutions of constitutional review (see Cameron 2000; Pickerill 2004, pp. 23–24). The president, for example, can also use the threat of a veto or a refusal to promulgate a law in order to shape the content of the law or get policy

257 Stone Sweet (1994, p. 443) has defined "coordinate construction" as "a condition in which both public policy and constitutional law are the products of sustained and intimate judicial-political interaction".

258 See Stone Sweet (2000, 2002).

concessions from the parliament during the proceedings of a law. The extent to which constitutional supervision by the president (the threat of the veto) can lead to auto-limitation by the legislators is likely to depend on a number of factors, including: a) the assessment of the probability that the president will actually exercise the veto; b) the extent to which the presidential veto would damage the reputation of the legislature (or the governing coalition) in the eyes of the electorate; c) perceived reputation loss of the president, were it to lose the case in the constitutional court. The same considerations should apply with regard to other constitutional watchdogs as well.

8.2.2.2. Constitutional Deliberation

In addition to the possible "threat" of the constitutional court (or other channels of constitutional review that, in the last instance, can refer the issue to the court), a constitution can have subtler effects, arising from the intrinsic value accorded to the constitution. For a lack of better definition, this form of influence is termed "constitutional deliberation". Pickerill (2004, p. 28) has defined "constitutional deliberation" as "reflection and debate over constitutional issues that rise in the context of specific legislation", which encompasses "interpretation, construction, and other forms of discourse and reflection over the meaning of constitutional provisions and powers". Constitutional arguments can shape deliberations on legislation and make certain options more or less feasible depending on how they appear to fit with the constitutional provisions – *independently* of the threat of referral and the anticipation of what the court's decision would be. Interpreting the constitution and pointing to possible unconstitutionality of certain provisions can add weight and legitimacy to the arguments (presented in the parliamentary discussions) about why they should be removed or changed. Of course, on occasion, the constitutional deliberations can be merely rhetorical, but they can also play an important role in increasing "constitutional consciousness" and leading to "more carefully drafted statutory language" (Pickerill 2004, p. 29). The literature pertaining to legislative constitutional deliberation is still in its infancy, but, based on the existing works, two stylised modes of legislative constitutional deliberation can be taken as a starting point: juridified debate and constitutional constructions.[259]

---

259 Legislative constitutional interpretation in the U.S. context has been discussed by Katyal (2001), Peabody (1999, 2004), Fisher (1985), Whittington (1999, 2002), Tushnet (1999), Devins (1996) and Pickerill (2004). For most part, these studies have been carried by normative rather than positive considerations. The main questions addressed in these works have been the following: *Should* the legislature be involved in constitutional interpretation? *How* should it do that? What are the *advantages* of legislative constitutional interpretation? Still, some authors have sought to take a more positive stance, by looking at how frequently constitutional deliberations take place, what factors are conducive to it and how it can be characterised. In the European context, the literature concerned with

8.2.2.2.1. Juridified Constitutional Deliberation

First, there is a mode of legislative deliberation that can be called "juridified" (or "juridicised") constitutional deliberation (Landfried 1988a, p. 8; Favoreu 1988, p. 105; von Brünneck 1988, p. 254; Stone 1992b, p. 49) or "legalistic interpretation" (Whittington 1999; see also Pickerill 2004, pp. 29). In the juridified mode of legislative debate on the constitutionality of proposed legislation, legislators follow closely the decisions of the constitutional court and the constitutional interpretations offered by the legislators are worded similarly to court decisions and imitate the styles of interpretation adopted by the courts.

Although connected to auto-limitation, this mode of constitutional influence should still be considered analytically separate from auto-limitation per se, given that here the debates are not confined to threatening the majority with the court referral or guessing what the court decisions would be. Rather, references to the previous court decisions and legal style of reasoning are viewed as rhetorical means for conveying the authoritative interpretation of the constitution, valued also for *intrinsic* reasons.

As Pickerill (2004, p. 26) puts it, legislators can "turn to Court opinions to help them articulate their position", "latch on to judicial doctrine as a means of justifying their opposition to popular legislation" and "analyze constitutional issues through judicial prism because they perceive constitutional issues to be primarily legal matters that are most properly with in the province of courts". Boulanger (2000, drawing on Füzer 2001 and Nelken 1996), has worded it very aptly, when stating that the decisions of constitutional courts are likely to develop into "legal-constitutional discourses", that, although formulated by constitutional judges, "develop their own lives" and "create a 'constitutional language' with its own rationality, which competes with other discourses in the public realm for recognition". The larger the existing number of constitutional court decisions in the particular sector, the more juridified the legislative constitutional debates are likely to be (Rubio Llorente 1988; Favoreu 1988; Landfried 1984, 1988b; Stone Sweet 1999, 2000).

8.2.2.2.2. Constitutional Construction

Second, constitutional deliberation can take the form of "constitutional construction". Fisher (1988, p. 6) has noted that it would be "misleading to treat constitutional interpretation as simply the interactions between the judiciary and the other branches" since the "government operates within a political culture

---

judicial politics and judicialisation of politics has also discussed the effects of the constitution on legislative debates (Landfried 1984; contributions in Landfried ed. (1988); Stone Sweet 2000, 2002).

that presses its own brand of constitutional law".[260] In a similar vein, Whittington argues that "Although the history and practice of judicial review have obviously influenced the effect of the Constitution on politics, the Constitution also operates more directly on political actors, without the mediation of the courts or the creation of amendments." (1999, p. 2) As he puts it, "The Constitution penetrates politics, shaping it from the inside and altering the outcomes." (p. 1) Whittington puts forth and elaborates on the concept of "constitutional construction", which supplements other methods of determining the meaning of the constitution and plays an important role in the political (especially legislative) arena.[261] For him, "constitutional construction" refers to the "method of elaborating constitutional meaning in this political realm" (p. 1). Whittington argues that actors on the political arena "can be expected to bring a different set of concerns and interests to bear on the Constitution, leading to a much more contested and rather different process of constitutional deliberation than a simple reliance on judicial interpretation would allow." (p. ix) Whittington emphasises that "constitutional constructions are often made in the context of political debate" (p. 6) and "by altering the discursive space of politics, a successful construction makes certain policy options more difficult to realize" (p. 219). In addition, constitutional constructions acquire their authority more from their capability to give practical content to constitutional provisions than from their "unassailable derivation from textual imperatives" (p. 8). Indeed, constructions can help to fill an important void when the conventional tools of interpretation are unable to translate constitutional principles into specific guides of action. In other words, constitutional constructions aid in transforming "constitutional theory into constitutional practice" (p. 9).[262] Whittington underlines that though constitutional constructions function from the inside of politics, they also accomplish the task that constitutions are expected to fulfil: "They structure and constrain future political debate and government action." (p. 219) Thus, analysing such mechanisms of constitutional order enables one to gain a more comprehensive picture of constitutional constraints that "operate beyond judicial review" (p. 219). Constitutional constructions can achieve their lasting effect through different modes:

260 The "constitutional dialogues" research conducted by Fisher and Devins in the United States has also shown how the institutions outside the Supreme Court (in particular the Congress and the President) offer independent interpretations of the Constitution and, through these, influence the development of constitutional law (see Devins 1996; Fisher 1988; Fisher 1985; Fisher and Devins 2001).

261 The concept of "constitutional construction" should not be confused with "coordinate construction" of the constitution. Meernik and Ignani (1997) used the term coordinate construction for labelling the efforts of the Congress to re-interpret and override the Supreme Court's constitutional decisions.

262 Whittington (1999, p. 9) notes, for example, that the concept of legislature's power of purse "depends on a myriad of specific practices that are intimately connected with the founding document but that cannot be completely subsumed by it".

ideological persuasion, structuring of political support and creation of new institutional structures (pp. 219–221).

Whittington (1999) has, based on the analysis of debates in the U.S. Congress, put forth a list of features that are likely to characterise constitutional construction by the legislature:

- While constitutional construction also draws on technical and traditional interpretive instruments, its main orientation is to expound the meaning of a constitutional provision by mixing the document with external interests and principles (p. 1). Although assuming allegiance to the existing text, constitutional constructions "do not pursue a pre-existing if deeply hidden meaning in the founding document", but offer definitive guidelines for political action where the text is broad and under-determined, by bringing in political principles, policy concerns, social interests and partisan considerations. (pp. 5–6, 209)
- Those who advocate a given construction expect to benefit from it. Self-interest is an inherent part of the arguments compiled by various government actors seeking to construe the constitution so as to favour their own institutional position. (pp. 210–212)
- Those defending a construction consonant with the status quo seek to depict that understanding as required by a legalistic constitution. Those who argue for changes stress the contingent nature of constitutional provisions. Still, both sides seek to identify themselves with the true and required meaning of the constitution. (p. 212)
- The advocates of constructions employ rational and legal arguments, but also metaphorical logic, emotional rhetoric, appeal to political power and deliberate vagueness (regarding the boundaries of the new construction) (p. 210).

In a similar vein, Peabody (2004) has advocated going beyond the conventional legal interpretive modalities when analysing constitutional interpretation in a parliamentary setting and adopting a broader view of what counts as constitutional analysis, including an explicitly political form of legislative constitutional interpretation. Peabody (2004, p. 167) suggests, based on his study of constitutional interpretation in the U.S. Congress, that interpretation in the legislature is flexible, informed by constituent interests and policy concerns, expansive and open-ended. Pickerill (2004, p. 66) adds that constitutional arguments in legislative deliberation can either serve the purpose of "a principled argument against legislation" or provide "political cover" for a legislator to vote against legislation that appears popular with the public.

8.2.2.3. When Are Constitutional Issues Likely to Emerge in Legislative Debates?

In addition to different forms of constitutional debate, the frequency and saliency of constitutional issues in legislative debates has been discussed. The empirical studies of the United States and European countries point to diverging evidence. In the Continental European countries, constitutional issues come up frequently in the legislative debates (see contributions to Landfried ed. 1988),[263] as a result of abstract constitutional review by the court and the right of a legislative minority to refer legislation to court. Stone Sweet (1999, p. 24) underlines that constitutional deliberation is very often triggered by the possibility of an abstract review referral by the opposition. He adds, drawing on the experiences of Germany, Spain and France that "The more important the bill being discussed, the greater the chance that debates will become exercises in constitutional decisionmaking." (p. 25) In France, for example, since 1981, one-third of all legislation adopted has been referred to the Constitutional Council, including all major pieces of legislation and every budget (Stone Sweet 2000, p. 63). This, in turn, has made constitutional debates prevalent in the French legislature. Drawing on the Hungarian case, Seitzer (1999, p. 45) notes that legislative minorities often view the threat of referring an act to the constitutional court as an effective legislative tactic for gaining concessions from majorities; the desire to avoid adverse rulings in the constitutional court, in turn, gives parties in the majority incentives to engage in constitutional debates with the opposition.

In the context of the U.S. Congress, Pickerill (2004, p. 22) conjectures that "It is not so clear that we should expect members [of the Congress] to routinely add constitutional issues to the list of factors routinely considered during the legislative process." Furthermore, he argues that "the incentives of the institution and democratic lawmaking are not favourable for encouraging routine constitutional deliberation" (p. 64) and presents empirical evidence confirming that constitutional issues come up only rarely in congressional debates.[264] He argues, however, that under certain circumstances, legislators are more likely to be attentive to constitutional issues and engage in constitutional deliberation (pp. 64–66). First, issues of constitutionality are likely to come to the forefront when the law is controversial and has a strong opposition: the opponents of the draft law may use arguments of unconstitutionality as a reason for voting against it. Second, constitutional issues are likely to be taken up during the debates when the act concerns some "pet issue" of a particular legislator (p. 144). Third, con-

263 Some contributors note even that it has become "excessive" (see Rubio Llorente 1988, p. 145; Landfried 1988b, p. 161).

264 Here, however, Whittington (1999, p. 226) is of different opinion. He argues that "The outcomes of constitutional debates are too significant to political actors' own concerns to leave such decisions exclusively to the judiciary." In addition, "Judicial decrees are unlikely to be able to resolve many of the issues at stake in these disputes."

stitutional issues are more likely to surface in legislative debates when the Supreme Court has acted recently or frequently on the issue under discussion (p. 66). In addition, Pickerill notes that most of the constitutional deliberations in the Congress have been "legalistic" (or juridified), rather than resembling the constitutional constructions outlined by Whittington (p. 59). Peabody (2004) also discusses factors that make the issues of constitutionality salient for legislators. He argues that legislative awareness of constitutional issues is highest when they bear on the benefits of their constituencies and concern the relations of the legislature to other branches of government (p. 138). In other words, legislators are likely to give greatest attention to constitutional areas close to their constituent or institutional interests. With regard to the U.S. case, one should also note that the prevalence of constitutional debates in the legislature has changed over time. As Curried (2005, p. 21) notes, "In the early Congress virtually everything became a constitutional question."

8.3. Outline of Conjectures

With regard to making predictions about the influences of the constitution on public finance laws in CEE in general and Estonia in particular, a number of conjectures can be advanced, drawing on the theoretical and empirical literature discussed in the previous sections of this chapter.

Concerning the decisions of the constitutional court in the area of public finance and the reactions of the legislature to these decisions, both the court and the legislature are likely to be subject to competing pressures in deciding whether to defer to the other institution and whether to adopt decisions that favour the rights of taxpayers, even if they are costly for the budget. As already outlined above, a number of competing conjectures can be put forth for analysing these competing pressures more systematically:

Conjecture 1: Given the need to build up public support, constitutional courts in transition countries will favour taxpayers in their decisions (even if these decisions would have budgetary implications).
Conjecture 2: Given the need to build up the reputation as a neutral arbiter, constitutional courts in transition countries will adopt decisions that bring about high budgetary costs (if the merits of the case require so).
Conjecture 3: Given the need to build up support of the other political institutions, constitutional courts will not adopt decisions that have costly budgetary consequences.
Conjecture 4: Given stringent fiscal constraints faced by the governments in the countries in transition, constitutional courts will not adopt decisions that imply high budgetary costs.

Conjecture 5: Stringent fiscal constraints in countries in transition will make parliaments less deferential to the constitutional courts in cases with costly budgetary implications.
Conjecture 6: Given the need to build up public support for the institution, parliaments in countries of transition will be deferential to the court's decisions in cases that favour taxpayers' rights (even if they have costly budgetary implications).
Conjecture 7: The constitutional courts are likely to be deferential to the preferences of the legislature in cases that concern the institutional prerogatives of different branches. (Epstein, Knight and Shvetsova 2001)

With regard to the prevalence and content of constitutional deliberations on framework laws of public finance, a number of conjectures can be put forth as well:

Conjecture 8: Because of the importance of the organic budget law in hammering out the institutional powers of the different branches of government, its implications for the "division of powers" between the legislative majorities and minorities and the significance of the budget for the constituents of the legislators, constitutional arguments are likely to play an important role in legislative discussion over the organic budget law.
Conjecture 9: Given the importance of issues of taxation for constituents of legislators, one would expect constitutional arguments to play an important role in legislative discussions over the framework law for taxation and specific tax acts.
Conjecture 10: Given that the constitutional courts have been functioning for a relatively short time in the CEE countries, legislators are likely to face greater uncertainty with regard to how the court would view the organic budget law, the framework law for taxation and tax acts, were they to be submitted for constitutional review.[265] This, in turn, should lead to attempts of legislators to interpret the constitution themselves, rather than just guessing the possible decision of the court. Also, in a CEE country, like Estonia, one would expect constitutional deliberations to be dominated by "constitutional constructions" rather than by juridified constitutional arguments.

Since the organic budget law can be considered to be a part of the "extended" constitution, some questions that are usually asked of constitution-making processes (see chapter 1) can be asked in the context of the making of organic budget law as well. Drawing on the existing body of research in consti-

265 This statement, however, should be qualified with regard to some countries in CEE. In Hungary, for example, the constitutional court reviewed more than 600 laws and struck down about one-third of them in 1990–1995 (Bond 2006).

tutional political economy addressing that issue (in particular the works of Elster 1992, 1995a,b, 1996a,b 1998a), important questions in this context would be: 1) To what extent has the making of the organic budget law been driven by institutional self-interest of the political actors involved? 2) To what extent have the different institutions involved in the making of the organic budget law been willing to engage in self-binding? 3) To what extent have the changes reflected partisan interests? As Molander (2001, p. 29) has noted, "The choices associated with the design of budgetary institutions reflect classical, or even existential, dilemmas of self-binding." At the same time, he reminds us, "Binding others rather than oneself is perhaps the overarching goal in the context of practical constitutional politics."

The analytical framework developed in this section and the conjectures just outlined are taken as the structure for analysing the Estonian case in chapters 9 and 10. In particular, the following chapters are concerned with the question of how the constitution – as a framework of evaluation employed by political actors – has influenced the content and development of the most important public finance laws in Estonia: the organic budget law, the organic tax law and three most important tax acts (income tax act, social tax act and value added tax act).

Chapter 9: The Role of the Constitution in the Development of the Organic Budget Law in Estonia

The goal of this chapter is to employ the analytical framework outlined in chapter 8 for exploring how the 1992 Constitution has shaped the development of the organic budget law in Estonia between 1992 and 2007. In particular, this chapter is concerned with the following questions: Has the Constitution been relevant in the evolvement of the organic budget law? What role have the different institutions of constitutional review played? Has the legislature engaged in autolimitation when drafting the organic budget law? Has the organic budget law given rise to legislative constitutional deliberations and what form have such deliberations taken? What were the motives behind the constitutional interpretations offered by different participants in the constitutional debates? In what directions have the constitutional review mechanisms and constitutional deliberations changed the organic budget law? Before analysing the constitutional controversies that arose during the debates on the organic budget law (in section 9.2.), a brief overview will be given of the mechanisms of constitutional review in Estonia (section 9.1.).

9.1. Mechanisms of Constitutional Review in Estonia

The Estonian 1992 Constitution provides for four different venues of constitutional review: 1) the president when proclaiming laws; 2) the Legal Chancellor when reviewing the consistency of legislation with the Constitution; 3) the courts that review the constitutionality of legislation when applying it to the adjudication of specific cases; 4) the Supreme Court when resolving constitutional review decisions of the president, the legal chancellor and courts.[266] Roosma (1998, p. 36) has noted that although in a narrow sense the exercise of "constitutional review" refers to the authoritative determination of whether a legal act contradicts the Constitution or not – which is only carried out by the Supreme Court – then, in a broader sense, one can say that the president, the legal chancellor and lower courts also exercise "constitutional review" when they evaluate the conformity of legal acts with the Constitution and undertake certain steps when they find a conflict between the Constitution and other legal acts.

The Constitution of Estonia accords the president the powers of a priori (or pre-emptive) constitutional review of pending legislation. The president may refuse to proclaim a law passed by the *Riigikogu* and return the law to the parliament for a new debate and decision. If the *Riigikogu* passes the law unamended, the president can either proclaim the law or propose to the Supreme Court to de-

266 For more detailed discussions on constitutional review in Estonia, see Maruste and Schneider (1996, 1998), Roosma (1998, 2001) and Pettai (2000).

clare the law unconstitutional. If the Supreme Court declares the law constitutional, the president has to proclaim the law.

The second avenue for constitutional appeal is the Legal Chancellor, who can exercise abstract review. The Legal Chancellor is an independent institution and is elected by the parliament for a seven-year term. As stipulated in the Constitution, if the Legal Chancellor finds that legislation passed by the legislative or executive powers or by a local government is in conflict with the Constitution, he or she shall propose to the body that passed the legislation to bring the legislation into conformity with the Constitution within 20 days. If the body does not comply, the Legal Chancellor will propose to the Supreme Court to declare the legislation invalid.[267] In addition, the Legal Chancellor can be engaged in constitutional review through consultative review during the proceedings of legislation in parliament. The members of the parliament can turn to the Legal Chancellor with interpellations. Pettai (2005b, p. 94) has noted that among the institutions that can appeal cases to the Constitutional Review Chamber of the Supreme Court, "the Legal Chancellor is the most unconventional within constitutional law".

According to the Estonian Constitution, all ordinary courts can exercise constitutional review when hearing a case. Articles 15 and 152 provide that the courts shall declare unconstitutional any legislation that conflicts with "the provisions and spirit" of the Constitution and shall not apply it. It should be noted, however, that although the ordinary courts can declare a law to be *unconstitutional*, only the Supreme Court has the power to declare a law *invalid*. When an ordinary court finds that legislation is in conflict with the Constitution, it has to file an appeal to the Supreme Court to initiate the procedure of constitutional review.[268]

What makes constitutional review in Estonia special compared to other countries in CEE and in Western Europe is that Estonia does not have a *separate* constitutional court (see, *inter alia*, Salzberger and Voigt 2002, p. 37; Sadurski 2002b, p. 163; Maruste 2007, p. 12). As Maruste (2007, p. 12) puts it, the Estonian system "is a unique mixture of the American model and the Continental/Kelsenian model".[269] Thus, the highest court of general jurisdiction – the final appellate court – also fulfils the functions of a constitutional court in Estonia.

---

267 The office of Legal Chancellor in Estonia has also received attention in the academic literature (see Järvelaid 2001 for an overview). The relationship between the Legal Chancellor and the Supreme Court has been discussed by Maveety and Pettai (2005); they show that, in most cases, the Constitutional Review Chamber has agreed with position taken by the Legal Chancellor.

268 The appeal is made on behalf of the lower court and not in the name of the original petitioners: the arguments referring to the unconstitutionality are made by the court and not by the participants in the case.

269 Maruste (2007, p. 12) adds that "The whole solution was justified in the context of its time by the limited means of a small state."

The issues of constitutional review would usually be decided by the Constitutional Review Chamber (CRC), which consists of nine judges who serve as members of Supreme Court (and at the same time are members of other specialised chambers as well) and are elected by the Supreme Court *en banc* for the term of five years. The issues are usually reviewed by a panel of five judges. If at least one judge of the Review Chamber dissents, the issue would be decided by the Supreme Court *en banc*. The justices of the Supreme Court of Estonia are appointed to office by the *Riigikogu* on the proposal of the Chief Justice and the Chief Justice is proposed to the *Riigikogu* by the president.

As a result of the changes made to the Constitutional Review Court Procedure Act since 2002, the powers of the Supreme Court in constitutional review have increased. With the new Constitutional Review Court Procedure Act adopted in 2002, the Court was authorised to adjudicate complaints and protests against decisions and acts of electoral committees. After the changes made in 2004, the Court is explicitly allowed to verify "the conformity of the refusal to issue an instrument of legislation of general application with the Constitution" and adjudicate requests for opinion on the interpretation of the Constitution in conjunction with the European Union law. In addition, the circle of subjects who have a right to submit an application to the CRC has been extended.

For most part, the mechanisms of constitutional review in Estonia are similar to the "model" adopted by most other CEE countries. Sadurski (2005, p. 5) has summarised the CEE "model" as follows: it is "a 'centralised' or 'concentrated' constitutional review, conducted by a court composed of judges appointed for limited tenure by the political branches of government, exercising abstract, *ex post* and final review of the constitutional of statutes and other infra-constitutional acts".[270] In some aspects, however, Estonia departs from this "model". First, as already noted, Estonia does not have a separate constitutional court like all other CEE countries: constitutional review is conducted by a special chamber of the Supreme Court.[271] Second, the range of actors who can initiate abstract review is more limited in Estonia than in most CEE countries; Sadurski (2005, p. 6) has even termed it as "a very restrictive system".[272] Al-

270 Only in the Ukraine is the constitutional court limited to concrete review (Sadurski 2002b, p. 163). In half of the CEE countries, there is a possibility of constitutional complaint initiated by citizens (Sadurski 2005, p. 8). Only in Romania can the verdict of the constitutional court be overridden by a qualified majority of the parliament; this applies to decisions resulting from abstract review, conducted prior to promulgation. This possibility existed also in Poland – but only until 1997, when the "big" Constitution was adopted. (Sadurski 2005, p. 13)

271 As Sadurski (2005, p. 5) notes, however, this does not affect the position of the Constitutional Review Chamber in the overall constitutional system and, "For all practical purposes, the Estonian Chamber can be viewed as a separate constitutional court."

272 At the other end of the spectrum is the constitutional review system in Hungary, where each individual citizen has a right to initiate abstract review regardless of his or her specific legal interest in the case under consideration – the so-called *actio popularis* (Sadur-

though like in most countries in the region, the president has a right to initiate abstract review, this right is not extended to members of parliament (or groups of parliamentarians) in Estonia, setting it apart from most CEE countries (Bartole 2002, p. 413). Third, while the members of the Supreme Court in Estonia are appointed by the legislature (like in other countries in the region), they are not appointed for a limited tenure but remain in office until retirement. Also, since the members of the CRC are appointed by the Supreme Court *en banc*, the *Riigikogu* cannot determine directly, who of the judges would belong to the Chamber and who not. Fourth, a priori abstract review (i.e., before the promulgation of the act) can only be exercised in Hungary, Poland and Estonia, but only when the president initiates the review before promulgating the act (Sadurski 2002b, p. 163).[273]

Hence, the Estonian Constitutional Court is likely to have a smaller workload than many of its CEE counterparts (especially the Hungarian Constitutional Court) but has, at the same time, stronger guarantees of independence. Indeed, when one compares the caseload of the Estonian CRC with the Hungarian Constitutional Court, the differences are stark. Between 1992 and 2007, the Supreme Court of Estonia issued 192 constitutional judgements,[274] of which in 79 cases an act was declared contrary to the Constitution; between 1990 and 1995, the Hungarian Constitutional Court passed 1326 judgements, 905 of those reviewed national law, of which 273 laws were found unconstitutional (Scheppele 2003, p. 224).[275] In assessing whether the Estonian Supreme Court has been activist in its constitutional review decisions, Aaviksoo (2007, p. 69) concludes that the Supreme Court "has not shown particularly activist stance in shaping the life of the polity". As she puts it, the Court has tended to hide "behind procedural justifications in cases concerning sensitive issues". For discussions over how the constitutional review and the CRC have influenced policy developments in Estonia, see Annus (2007), Maveety and Grosskopf (2004), Pettai (2003, 2005b).

In addition to the Constitutional Review Chamber, constitutional review in a broader sense has been exercised also by the Legal Chancellor and the president. Between 1992 and 2007, the President refused to proclaim a law passed by the *Riigikogu* 51 times and proposed the Supreme Court to declare the law (left unamended by the *Riigikogu*) unconstitutional 12 times. In three cases, the Su-

---

ski 2005, p. 6). In addition, the Hungarian Constitutional Court can even act *sua sponte*: that is, to activate the constitutional review proceedings itself (p. 9).

273 For discussions and overviews of the different systems of constitutional review in CEE countries, see Sadurski (2002b), Sajo (1995), Sadurski (2005), Scheppele (2003, 2002), Schwartz (2000) and Hausmaninger (1995).

274 Of these decisions, about 70 concerned complaints and protests against the decisions and acts of electoral committees.

275 At the same time, the Hungarian legislature was able to "retaliate" and, in 1999, replaced the justices in the Court with appointments who were less activist and more supportive of the legislature (Scheppele 2003).

preme Court did not agree with the President and he had to promulgate the contested law. On three occasions, although the *Riigikogu* passed the law unamended, the President did not turn to the Supreme Court.

From 1993 to 2007, the Legal Chancellor made 386 proposals to the issuers of various legal acts to bring these acts into compliance with the Constitution. In 21 of these cases, the legislation was not corrected and the Legal Chancellor turned to the Supreme Court and the Court agreed with the Chancellor in all but two cases. (Jõks 2007)

Table 9.1.: Constitutional review in Estonia, 1992–2007: Overview

CRC decisions	Invalidated acts	Review initiated by President	Review initiated by Legal Chancellor	Review initiated by lower courts
192	79	12	21	67

Source: Author's calculations

Table 9.2.: Constitutional review in Estonia, 1992–2007: Types of decisions

CRC decisions total	Decisions concerning laws	Decisions concerning Government decrees	Decisions concerning Ministerial Decrees	Appeals concerning decisions of electoral committees*	Other
192	70	18	8	66	30

* The appeals concerning decisions of electoral committees could only be made from 2002 onwards; hence, the number reflects decisions from between 2002 and 2007.
Source: Author's calculations

9.2. The Impact of the Constitution on the Development of the Organic Budget Law

The aim of this section is to analyse how the Constitution has shaped the organic budget law of Estonia through the mechanisms of constitutional review and constitutional deliberations. The analysis is presented by taking up the issues of the organic budget law that have dominated the constitutional debates in the parliament. Table 9.3. gives an overview of the number of times constitutional issues came up in the legislative discussions or were raised by the institutions of constitutional review.

Table 9.3.: Constitution and the organic budget law in Estonia, 1992–2007

	Number of acts concerning the organic budget law adopted	Number of acts concerning organic budget law rejected	Number of constitutional issues concerning organic budget act discussed in the *Riigikogu*	Constitutional review decisions on organic budget law by President, Legal Chancellor or CRC
7th *Riigikogu* (1992–1995)	2	1	3	-
8th *Riigikogu* (1995–1999)	2	2	4	1 (President)
9th *Riigikogu* (1999–2003)	4	4	8	2 (President) 1 (Legal Chancellor)
10th *Riigikogu* (2003–2007)	1	3	-	-
11th *Riigikogu* (2007– …)	-	-	-	-

Source: Author's calculations

9.2.1. Increasing Budgetary Autonomy of Constitutional Institutions

One of the most important constitutional debates on the organic budget law concerned increasing the budgetary autonomy of constitutional institutions (i.e., the *Riigikogu*, the Supreme Court, the President, the Legal Chancellor, the State Audit Office) by reducing the powers of the Minister of Finance and the Government in budgetary negotiations with these institutions.

The question of establishing different kinds of budget procedures for different state institutions came up first in a draft act amending the organic budget law, initiated by a member of parliament Arvo Junti (Centre Party, Development Party) in November 1995, and it was discussed by the *Riigikogu* from October 1996 until June 1997.[276] The draft foresaw that a different procedure for compiling the budget proposal would be applied for the *Riigikogu* and the Supreme Court (compared with the procedure applied to other state institutions) and it would have significantly increased the budgetary autonomy of these two institutions. It was proposed that 1) the Minister of Finance would not establish ceilings for budget proposals to be submitted by the *Riigikogu* and the Supreme Court; 2) the budget proposals of these two institutions would be included in the

276 In November 1995, the coalition between the Coalition Party, the Country People's Party and the Centre Party had split and had been replaced by a coalition of the Coalition Party, the Country People's Party and Reform Party.

draft state budget as a result of negotiations between the representatives of the Ministry of Finance, after the Minister of Finance has approved them; 3) if no agreement is achieved or the Minister of Finance does not approve the budget proposals, the proposals would be submitted to the Finance Committee of the *Riigikogu*, which would decide on the size of these budgets (but subject to the constraint that it can not *increase* the sum that was stipulated in the original budget proposal submitted); 4) the Government has no right to leave out sums foreseen for the *Riigikogu* and the Supreme Court in the state draft budget. If it does not consider the sums foreseen for these institutions in the budget to be reasonable, it will make a suggestion to change them together with the draft budget submitted to the *Riigikogu*.

In the explanatory note to this draft act and in his presentation to the plenary assembly of the parliament, Junti explained that the budget procedure outlined by the organic budget law violated the constitutional principle of separation of powers by giving the executive too extensive powers and thereby subjecting the legislature and the judiciary to the executive in compiling the budget. Thus, he emphasised that the proposed changes would allow a more complete realization of the principle of separation of powers stipulated in the Constitution, by giving the parliament and the judiciary the right to decide more autonomously over their own budgets. Both the initiator of the draft act and the Chairman of the Finance Committee Jürgen Ligi (Reform Party) referred to specific examples from the preceding years, when the officials from the Ministry of Finance had unilaterally changed the sums in the budget proposal of the *Riigikogu* and sometimes even the Minister of Finance had not been informed about them. Junti also stated that in preparing the draft law he had drawn upon the examples of other countries – for example, Germany, Sweden, Finland and Hungary. He added that in Spain, such a specific procedure had even been established by the constitution. (*Riigikogu* Verbatim Record, 8 October 1996, 22 October 1996) As he emphasised, "The question is not that the *Riigikogu* or the Supreme Court would want to get more money. Rather the issue is that our constitutional basis, the institutional system has to be tidied up." (*Riigikogu* Verbatim Record, 22 October 1996) Ligi also agreed that the existing arrangements put the Minister of Finance higher than the parliament, and such an arrangement would enable the executive to impose political pressure on the legislative and judicial powers if it wanted to. (*Riigikogu* Verbatim Record, 8 October 1996)

At the second reading of the act, Rait Maruste, the Chairman of the Supreme Court, was also invited to give his opinion. Maruste emphasised the importance of the principle of the separation of powers and pointed out that the Estonian Constitution is one of few constitutions where this principle is clearly spelled out. Thus, he stated, the legislative, executive and judicial powers should be separated (though he noted that the president, the Legal Chancellor and other similar institutions are not independent "powers"). Maruste pointed out that Article 4 of the Constitution is in the most important part of the Constitution – in the Chapter called "General Provisions", which can only be changed by a referendum – and, therefore, the provision of Article 87 point 5 stipulating that the budget is prepared by the Government should be subjected to the more privileged Article 4. Thus, he emphasised, the Government should play the role of *coordinating* the preparation of the budget but should not be able to *dictate* the conditions for the *Riigikogu* and the Supreme Court. Maruste added that such specific procedure presumes that the parliament and the judiciary are modest in their budget requests and this, in turn, can be checked through the public's control of these institutions. Maruste also noted that such a change in the organic budget law was necessary for facilitating the development of democratic institutions in Estonia and for overcoming the tendency (prevalent in transition countries) of the continuation of an excessively strong executive, a relict of the totalitarian regime. He warned that if the proportions of the budget were fixed only by the Government, then the development of the legislative and judicial branches might be curtailed. He also noted that even if the *Riigikogu* and the Supreme Court were to ask somewhat larger sums of money from the budget than hitherto, then these would still constitute a negligible proportion of the overall budget.[277] (*Riigikogu* Verbatim Record, 22 October 1996)

Interestingly, several members of the parliament argued *against* increasing the budgetary autonomy of the parliament and the Supreme Court. Liia Hänni (Moderates), for example, referred to the existing organic budget law, which required a balanced budget and argued that if the judiciary and the legislature submit their budget proposals independently, then, in order to balance the overall budget, the executive might have to cut its own expenditures, which, in turn, would imply a clear weakening of the executive in the budget process. Jüri Adams (Pro Patria Union), who had been the author of the draft Constitution that had become the basis for discussions in the Constitutional Assembly in 1991–1992, noted that such amendments could bring about the tendency that all state institutions would start requiring separate budget procedures; this would endanger adherence to the principle of budget balance, which in turn could undermine the success of Estonia.[278] Lauri Vahtre (Pro Patria Union) stated that there should be one budget; otherwise, the budget process would tear the state and the state budget apart. He admitted that the parliament and the Government were not at the best terms at the time, but such a situation would be temporary and it would be unwise to solve it by such changes in the budget procedure. (*Riigikogu* Verbatim Record, 22 October 1996) At the discussion of the same act in May 1997, Adams again noted that the Constitution requires a balanced

277 He pointed out that the *Riigikogu*'s budget constitutes 0.7 percent and the Supreme Court's budget 0.06 percent of the overall state budget.

278 Adams noted, with irony, that perhaps the budget department of the Ministry of Finance should be abolished altogether. He also argued that by agreeing to such changes, the parliament would overreact to some recent misgivings in the work of the Ministry of Finance. (*Riigikogu* Verbatim Record, 22 October 1996)

budget and argued that the Government would be in a difficult situation when the budget requests of the *Riigikogu* and the Supreme Court unbalance the budget (*Riigikogu* Verbatim Record, 20 May 1997).

The amendments that would have increased the budgetary autonomy of the *Riigikogu* and the Supreme Court were not passed, since in June 1997, the Government submitted a new draft organic budget law to the parliament and the initiator of the draft act decided to withdraw the proposal from the proceedings, arguing that these issues should be solved together with the new organic budget law. In addition, it became clear during the proceedings of the Act that the Government was opposed to these changes. (*Riigikogu* Verbatim Record, 20 May 1997) Although, not surprisingly, this proposal had been initiated by a member of the opposition, the most vocal opponents of this provision were also members of the opposition. One would have expected the opposition members to argue *in favour* of such a provision, given that it would have enabled the parliament to have more control over its own budget, but the opposition members considered the overall budget balance to be more important than the budgetary autonomy of the parliament and they were therefore willing to maintain the extensive budgetary powers of the executive *vis-à-vis* the legislature.

The provisions proposed by Junti were not included in the first version of the new organic budget law passed on 27 January 1999, but the same issue – although in an extended form – was taken up by the President. President Lennart Meri decided not to promulgate the State Budget Act on the grounds that several provisions in it were unconstitutional (Resolution No. 507, from 17 February 1999). For most part, the objections of the President concerned the provisions that gave the Government (and the Minister of Finance) too extensive powers *vis-à-vis* the constitutional institutions in the budget process. His main objection was that the same procedure for drafting, implementing and reporting on the budget that applies to the ministries applies to the constitutional institutions (i.e., the *Riigikogu*, the President, the State Audit Office, the Legal Chancellor and the Supreme Court) as well. The procedure in the adopted act foresaw that: 1) the Government would set (based on the proposal from the Minister of Finance) upper ceilings for the budget requests of the constitutional institutions; 2) the Minister of Finance has the right to change or delete the sums in the budget proposals; 3) in the case of disagreement between the Minister of Finance and a constitutional institution the dispute is solved by the Government; 4) the Government has a right to change or delete the expenditures in the budget requests of the constitutional institutions. The President argued that such a procedure would violate the principle of separation and balance of powers stipulated in Article 4 of the Constitution. He argued that the Act would make the constitutional institutions dependent on the Government and the Minister of Finance and hence violate the principle of the rule of law. Further, the President claimed that such a procedure would endanger the realisation of constitutionally stipulated rights and duties of the constitutional institutions, since by assessing the expediency of expenditures, the content of the *decisions* of these institutions could be indirectly evaluated. With regard to the relations *between* the constitutional institutions, the President sought to protect the other constitutional institutions from too much interference from the *Riigikogu*. He found that the right given to the committees of the *Riigikogu* to demand reviews of the implementation of the budget from other constitutional institutions also violated the principle of separation and balance of powers.

The resolution of the President was discussed both in the Constitutional Committee and the Finance Committee of the *Riigikogu*, and the opinions were presented in the plenary session of the parliament. The Constitutional Committee agreed with the President's argument that it would be unconstitutional to have the same procedures for constitutional institutions as for ministries. As the Chairman of the Constitutional Committee Tiit Käbin (Reform Party) explained at the plenary session, especially the Finance Minister's right to change or delete the sums in the budget requests of the constitutional institutions could be seen as going against the principle of the separation of powers. He added, "As we know, in practice, these sums are not changed or eliminated by the Minister of Finance himself but by some officials from the Ministry of Finance." The Finance Committee, however, remained ambiguous on the issue. The Chairman of the Finance Committee Kalle Jürgenson (Pro Patria Union), when presenting the opinion of the Committee at the plenary session, stated that it was debatable whether the Government can influence the decisions of the constitutional institutions by influencing the budget. (*Riigikogu* Verbatim Record, 14 April 1999)

Still, by the next reading of the Act, the Finance Committee suggested special arrangements for the constitutional institutions (which were also incorporated into the new version of the act): if during the budget negotiations between the Minister of Finance and the constitutional institution no agreement is reached, only the Government (and not the Minister of Finance) has the right to change the sums in the budget request and it has to motivate the decision in the explanatory note to the draft state budget submitted to the *Riigikogu*. At this reading, the Minister of Finance Siim Kallas (Reform Party) addressed the issue as well,

> I understand that the constitutional institutions have been irritated by bureaucratic treatment, when they have received a letter from the Ministry of Finance saying that these are the wages for your officials and that is it. … But the question is, who bears the responsibility for the budget as a whole. It is the Government, and the Government has to submit a budget with balanced expenditures and revenues." The Minister agreed, however, that the constitutional institutions have to be treated somewhat differently and it is justified that the budget requests the institutions *themselves* have applied for should be reflected in the draft budget, so that the parliament can decide which of the appropriations to prefer. (*Riigikogu* Verbatim Record, 19 May 1999)

Thus, it can be argued that the Constitution played an important role in increasing the budgetary autonomy of the "constitutional institutions". Appealing to the special role attributed to the constitutional institutions by the Constitution and evoking the constitutionally stipulated (though a very vague) notion of the separation and balance of powers allowed the President to achieve the respective changes in the organic budget law. The arguments of the President were eventually accepted by the *Riigikogu* and, as a result, changes were made to the law that would have otherwise not been included in it. This controversy is a clear example of auto-limitation by the Estonian parliament. If the *Riigikogu* had not made the changes to the organic budget law, the President would have taken the Act to the Supreme Court. Fighting for the budgetary autonomy of the constitutional institutions was one among the several battles that the President undertook in protecting his institution from the *Riigikogu* and the Government; the previous decisions of the Supreme Court regarding the powers of the President had agreed with the President. In addition, if the issue had reached the Supreme Court, there would have been clear incentives for the Court to the support the President, since the Court itself was one of the constitutional institutions whose budgetary autonomy was in question. The remarks by the Chief Justice of the Supreme Court during the discussion on a similar issue in 1996 also indicated that the Court would have been likely to find the organic budget law unconstitutional. Thus, the mechanism of auto-limitation played a significant role here: the *Riigikogu* could anticipate that it would lose the case in the Supreme Court, were it to pass the law unamended. Although some of the members of the parliament (especially from the Finance Committee) sought to contest the constitutional interpretation of the President, the majority of the legislature agreed with his interpretation and did not seek to offer alternative constructions of the notion of the separation and balance of powers.

It is also appropriate to ask here to what extent the debate – framed in constitutional terms – was motivated by institutional self-interest. In many ways, the decision of the President could be seen as having been motivated by the desire to increase the autonomy of his institution in compiling the budget. In his decision, the President pointed to a list of other contradictions between the organic budget law and the Constitution, but the *Riigikogu* did not change most of these other aspects (or did so in a purely formal way). Given that the President still promulgated the law, one can guess that his main goal was to have the budget procedure for the constitutional institutions changed and the other arguments were added to give some length and weight to the resolution.

It is interesting to note that the issue of giving more autonomy in compiling the budget proposal had already had been considered by the *Riigikogu* itself in 1995 (inspired by problematic relations between the Government and the parliament). But, as could be seen from the discussions on the organic budget law in October 1996, several members of the parliament did not support such changes, since they were afraid of the implications that such changes would have for budget balance and the unity of the budget. Thus, when the President took the question up, it was not an entirely new issue on the agenda. It might have well been the discussions on granting the *Riigikogu* and the Supreme Court more extensive budgetary autonomy in 1996–1997 that inspired the President to proceed with this issue in 1999.

9.2.2. Parliament versus Cabinet in Budget Process

In most of the readings of the organic budget law, the issues of constitutionality pertaining to the relations between the government and parliament in the budget process were taken up. The main issues were: limiting the amendment power of the parliament in the budget process, binding the draft state budget to an issue of confidence and how detailed the classification of the budget should be.

9.2.2.1. Limiting the Amendment Power of the Parliament

As pointed out in chapter 7, the amendment power of the parliament in Estonia has been constrained as a result of the changes made to the organic budget law. The constraints that were *actually* incorporated to the Act, however, were relatively mild compared to several *proposals* that were made either in the draft laws or in the course of the legislative debates. The provisions that sought to constrain the role of the parliament in the budget process more extensively, however, were rejected by members of the parliament on the grounds of alleged unconstitutionality.

One of the main issues that was debated during the readings of the State Budget Act in 1997–1999 was a question that had been brought up in the discussions of the Estonian Constitutional Assembly in 1991–1992 as well: To what extent should the *Riigikogu* have the right to make changes to the draft budget and should Government consent be received before making the amendments?[279] In February 1998, a motion to amend the organic budget law was made by a member of opposition Heiki Kranich (Reform Party),[280] according to which the *Riigikogu* could only make amendments to the draft budget after receiving consent from the Government. This proposal gave rise to heated discussions in the *Riigikogu* and the MPs held widely diverging opinions on whether this provision would be constitutional or not.

There were several members of the *Riigikogu* who clearly supported this proposal and viewed it as conforming to the Constitution. If in the initial phases of the debate the supporters came primarily from an opposition party (Reform Party), then in the later phases, members of the coalition parties started sup-

279 The Constitutional Assembly decided to leave out a proposed provision that would have required Government consent on the amendments to the draft budget (see chapter 3).

280 Kranich had also been minister of finance for six months in 1994.

porting it as well. At the first debate on the issue, Kalev Kukk (Reform Party) argued, referring to the Constitution, that the task of the Government is to *prepare* the budget and the task of the *Riigikogu* is to *pass* the budget, and the way *Riigikogu* had made changes to the budget in the previous years had amounted to interference with the executive authority. Valve Kirsipuu (Reform Party) pointed out that the Constitution does not say anywhere that the *Riigikogu* can *make changes* to the budget; to the contrary, Article 65 Section 6 says that the *Riigikogu* shall pass the state budget and approve the report on its implementation. She added that preparing the budget requires thorough preparations by the Ministry of Finance, which could easily be rendered meaningless by the motions to amend the draft budget by the *Riigikogu*. She argued that the way the *Riigikogu* had dealt with the state budget in 1997, for example, was not normal for a democratic state.[281] (*Riigikogu* Verbatim Record, 11 February 1998)

Another member of the parliament, Liia Hänni (Moderates), who had been the chairman of the redaction committee in the Constitutional Assembly, argued that although the Constitution does not give an answer to the question of how exactly the budget procedure should look like, there are still some footholds. She emphasised that it has to be analysed what the general constitutional principle of the separation and balance of powers means in the particular context of Estonia. She suggested that when the state has a strong parliament and developed democracy, it would be conceivable to employ the model used in Germany, where the Government puts together the budget and the parliament simply agrees or disagrees with it. She emphasised that a strong parliament, where the governing coalition is able to control the government, can afford the luxury of not changing the budget submitted by the Government. She argued, however, that the *Riigikogu* was not yet strong enough to give the Government so much freedom and doing that would endanger the Estonian democracy. Eiki Nestor (Moderates) pointed out that giving the parliament the right to say only "yes" or "no" to the budget submitted by the Government is characteristic to presidential systems. To this, Kukk answered that Germany, which is even less presidential than Estonia, also uses a system that limits the rights of the parliament to make amendments to the budget submitted by the government. The Chairman of the Finance Committee Olev Raju (Coalition Party) stated that the general position of the Committee was that although this provision would not directly violate any article in the Constitution, it could go against the *context and ideology* of the Constitution. (*Riigikogu* Verbatim Record, 11 February 1998)

By the next reading (8 April 1998), the disputed amendment proposal was modified by Kranich, and the role of the *Riigikogu* Finance Committee was

281 At the reading of the state budget for the year 1998, altogether 915 motions to amend were made by the *Riigikogu*, of which 193 were accepted. As a result of the amendments made by the *Riigikogu*, the volume of the state budget was increased by 3.5 percent. Such extensive amendments were possible because the majority coalition had collapsed and the existing government was a minority government. (Raju 2003)

added. Thus, the proposed provision stated that those amendment proposals to the draft budget that the Government has not agreed with *and* the Finance Committee has not consented to, can not be put on vote. The Finance Committee of the *Riigikogu* supported this provision. The Minister of Finance Mart Opmann (Coalition Party), when presenting the draft act in the *Riigikogu*, argued that this amendment would enable the Government to fulfil the goals it has set. He pointed out that the experience of the previous years had shown that during the passage of the budget in the parliament, not only the structure but also the size of the expenditures had been changed; this meant that the Government's plan of economic policy was changed without thorough prior analysis. He emphasised that the provision that would limit the right of the parliament to make amendments to the draft budget would preclude such situations. He added that in putting together the draft State Budget Act, the organic budget acts of Germany and Finland had been used as examples, and if such a restriction of parliamentary amendments were included in the Estonian organic budget law, Estonia would take "a big step towards countries with progressive economic development". (*Riigikogu* Verbatim Record, 8 April 1998)

This proposal, again, gave rise to debates over constitutionality. Liina Tõnisson (Centre Party) asked the Minister of Finance, "What kind of a principle of democracy is this proposal based on?" In his answer, the Minister noted that the approach so far had been "unrestrictedly democratic" and referred to year 1993, when one particular MP had made 102 amendment proposals to the draft budget during one reading. The Minister also brought out that the experience with the amendments made to the draft budget in the past showed that the amendments had often not been justified and the Government had had to revert these amendments. As an answer to the question by Siiri Oviir (Centre Party) – "What constitutional provision is this amendment in compliance with?" – the Minister of Finance admitted that he did not know. The question of constitutionality was also taken up by Raju. He stated that he had consulted with the Supreme Court judges (he admitted though that he did not know whether they were members of the Constitutional Review Chamber). Although the judges could not issue written opinions on draft legislation, they had been willing to give him their opinion unofficially (since they had been together at university). The judges he had consulted thought unanimously that such a restriction was in compliance with the Constitution, since the Constitution stipulates that the proceeding of the budget in the parliament is a special procedure and a special procedure can be made different from the general procedure. (*Riigikogu* Verbatim Record, 8 April 1998)

Kranich, who had made the proposal to limit the amendment powers of the *Riigikogu*, addressed the question of whether the procedure for the budget should be different than for other acts. He pointed out although the Constitution says that the budget is passed as a law, the budget has a different nature compared to other laws: it is a financial document that is the basis for implementing the Government's programmes and plans, which, given its importance, is passed as a law. He pointed out that such a restriction would be especially significant in a situation where there is a minority government (as it was at the time of the debates). In such a situation, he argued, it would be very easy for the parliament to change the budget and thus nullify the will of the Government. As a result, the Government could get a budget with which it does not want to govern. Kranich emphasised that the budget should be seen as the plan of the government, which it submits to the *Riigikogu*, presents it thoroughly, answers exhaustively to all questions and asks whether *Riigikogu* thinks it is a financial document, on the basis of which the Government can govern. He also emphasised,

> In deciding over this issue, we should not think of the current situation and belonging to opposition. All members might belong to a governing coalition in the future, and for such a situation, one would want to have a strong backing and the ability to govern based on the budget that was planned. Therefore, we have to look further into the future. (*Riigikogu* Verbatim Record, 8 April 1998)

Still, when put on vote, this provision was not supported. Instead, a "softer" version of the legislative constraint was adopted, stating that motions to amend, which are submitted after the suspension of the second reading of the draft state budget shall not be put to a vote if they are not supported by the Government and not accepted by the Finance Committee of the *Riigikogu*.

During the debates on the organic budget law in 2001–2002, it was proposed to limit the right of the *Riigikogu* to *increase the budget revenues* if the Government or the Finance Committee does not agree with it. This proposal was supported by the Government and by the Finance Committee. Again, this was seen by some MPs from the opposition as violating the Constitution. Arvo Sirendi (Coalition Party) argued that this limitation would violate the Constitution, since the Constitution does not restrict the powers of the *Riigikogu* in such a way. Jürgen Ligi (Reform Party), the Chairman of the Finance Committee, answered that the Finance Committee thought the *Riigikogu* can certainly establish such a restriction; he emphasised that it was *not* the role of the *Riigikogu* to correct the revenue prognoses made by the executive authority. He added, "Life has shown that voluntary self-binding has become more effective during the recent years, compared to the early years of the *Riigikogu*; however, in the proceedings of the budget, there have still been pressures to include unfounded revenues." (*Riigikogu* Verbatim Record, 19 March 2002) When put on vote, the *Riigikogu* did not support the provision.

It is noteworthy that the first proposal for restricting the amendment rights of the parliament in 1998 was not brought up by the Government or by MPs from the governing coalition but by a member of opposition. At first, the members of the governing coalition were even sceptical of it (see comments by Raju at the first debate on the issue), although they did, indeed, support it at the next reading. Thus, it can be argued that the proposal made by Kranich (and supported by a number of members) did reflect a will of institutional self-binding. The proposal of self-binding was certainly facilitated by the personal experience of Kranich in the executive, the antecedent experiences of the *Riigikogu* with budgeting, and the examples from Germany and Finland. Other participants in the debate, however, were driven by institutional self-interests: the Government eventually supported the proposal, and the Finance Committee supported the proposal only after it had been included as a veto power alongside the Government, and the majority of the parliament was against it (at least in 1998). Still, in 2002, the majority of the legislature supported the constraint according to which motions to amend the draft state budget can not cause a state budget deficit, an increase in the deficit or a reduction in the surplus, partly reflecting the desire of institutional self-binding by the parliament, partly the institutional self-interest of the Government, partly the partisan interests of the Reform Party to maintain fiscal discipline and follow conservative fiscal policies. Vocal objections to these proposals came in particular from the MPs who were in the opposition. The interest of the opposition in maintaining the amendment rights of the parliament is particularly strong, since the amendments (or amendment proposals) to the budget is an important way of signalling to the constituents the work done for them. Indeed, in the light of the actual importance of the amendments made to the budget during the legislative proceedings, the fight for the right to make amendments was rather a fight for maintaining the symbolic process (see Ostrow 2000, ch. 7).

These debates are an interesting example of an attempt to use the reverse of "auto-limitation". The arguments by Raju show that the anticipated decision of the Supreme Court can also be used to *facilitate* the adoption of a provision that is suspected to be unconstitutional by other members of the legislature. The unofficial opinion of the Supreme Court judges served as rhetorical means to persuade other legislators of the constitutionality of the contested provision.

Constitutional arguments were used by all actors in the debate to corroborate their viewpoints. Given that the Constitution is very vague on the division of work between the legislature and the executive with regard to the budget, both proponents and opponents of the provision limiting the amendment rights of the parliament could evoke arguments of constitutionality. Although it can be argued that it was not necessarily the alleged unconstitutionality of the proposed provision *itself* that led to leaving it out from the Act in 1998 (but the institutional self-interest of the legislators), the arguments of unconstitutionality provided rhetorical ammunition to its opponents and made the decision to appear more legitimate.

Although Whittington (1999) argues that those desiring the maintenance of the status quo resort to literal interpretation of the constitution, this example from Estonia shows that when the constitution is still very young, also those advocating the change of the status quo can engage in literal interpretation of the text of the constitution. Those desiring the maintenance of status quo, however, used a contingent interpretation of the Constitution (or constitutional construction) arguing that the current state of development of the democracy in Estonia calls for a particular interpretation of the Constitution. It is also noteworthy that those opposing the proposals to limit the budgetary powers of the parliament did not use interpretive arguments endorsing the original intent of the framers. The verbatim reports of the Constitutional Assembly of 1991–1992 show that the Assembly had explicitly rejected the constitutional provision giving the Government a budgetary veto power (see chapter 3).

9.2.2.2. Binding the Draft State Budget to Issue of Confidence

In addition to the organic budget law, some aspects of the budget procedure are stipulated in the *Riigikogu* Rules of Procedure Act. Shortly before the adoption of the negative supplementary budget in June 1999, a significant change was made to the Rules of Procedure Act, allowing the Government to bind the draft state budget to an issue of confidence. The 1994 Rules of Procedure Act had hitherto explicitly forbidden the use of that procedure in the budget process. This provision came about a result of constitutional review. After the opposition had submitted more the 500 motions to amend during the debates on the negative supplementary budget in June 1999 (signalling the intended use of obstructionism, which did indeed take place some days later), the Legal Chancellor notified the *Riigikogu* that the provision in the Rules of Procedure Act forbidding the binding of the draft state budget to an issue of confidence was unconstitutional, since the Constitution provided no limitations with regard to what kind of draft acts can be bound to an issue of confidence. As a result, an amendment to the Rules of Procedure was passed less than a fortnight later, allowing *all* draft acts to be bound to an issue of confidence. Given that the amendment was enacted very fast, it would have allowed the coalition to bind the draft negative supplementary budget (under discussion) to an issue of confidence; this would have meant that those motions to amend the draft act not supported by the Government would not have been put on vote in the parliament. In anticipation of that, the opposition stopped filibustering and the supplementary budget was passed.

During the parliamentary deliberations on the proposed provision, the members of opposition argued that the timing of the letter of the Legal Chancellor was obviously advantageous to the governing coalition and was clearly addressed to the proceedings of the negative supplementary budget in the parliament. It was pointed out that this provision in the Rules of Procedure had been in force for five years and it was suspicious that its unconstitutionality was only brought up then. In defending the provision, Liia Hänni (Reform Party), the Chairman of the Constitutional Committee, stated that the fact that the Rules of Procedure violated the Constitution only became evident because of the obstructionist tactics of the opposition, which made it impossible to proceed with the draft supplementary budget in a normal way. She emphasised that it was an important role of the Legal Chancellor to bring up issues of unconstitutionality that have risen from the *actual context*. She admitted that although the goal of Article 98 in the Constitution (allowing the government to bind a draft act to an issue of confidence) was not to provide a solution to the problem of parliamentary obstructionism but was meant as a possibility for the Government to control whether it still has the support of the majority, the existing situation showed that there was a need for a counterbalance against the behaviour of the opposition. (*Riigikogu* Verbatim Record, 15 June 1999)

Several opposition members argued that allowing the Government to bind the draft state budget to an issue of confidence would be unconstitutional. Edgar Savisaar (Centre Party) argued that the same logic that is expressed in the Constitution concerning acts that cannot be submitted to a referendum should apply to binding the draft acts to an issue of confidence. He stated that since the list of acts that cannot be put on referendum includes acts pertaining to the state budget, the Government should not be allowed to bind the passage of the budget to an issue of confidence. Savisaar also pointed out that by binding the draft budget to an issue of confidence, the Government would assume the role of a legislature and this would violate the principle of the balance of powers, which would be dangerous to development of democracy in Estonia.[282] (*Riigikogu* Verbatim Record, 15 June 1999) The opposition also criticised the fact that the governing coalition wanted to change the rules of the game in the middle of the game: to use the amended procedure to continue the proceedings of the draft supplementary budget. Changing the procedure for the purpose of passing one particular act was seen as undemocratic (*Riigikogu* Verbatim Record, 15 June 1999). Despite the objections of the opposition, the amendment was passed.

Introducing a provision that allow the Government to bind the passage of the state budget to issue of confidence is a clear example of how the Constitution was evoked to serve the pressing political needs of the governing coalition. If the coalition parties had initiated the change of the Rules of Procedure Act themselves, they would have had a lower leverage in justifying the change, because it was clearly connected to the desire to pass the supplementary budget. Since the proposal came from the Legal Chancellor, who is considered to be a neutral guardian of the Constitution, the proposal had more weight and legitimacy. Introducing this provision reflected clearly a partisan interest rather than

282 Similarly, Sven Mikser (Centre Party) noted in a media article that since the state budget can not be submitted to a referendum, giving the right to the Government to push the budget through the parliament would further reduce the voice of the people in budgetary deliberations (Mikser 1999). Mikser also argued that Article 117 of the Constitution, stating that the procedures for the drafting and passage of the state budget shall be provided by law, indicates that the Constitution allows restrictions to be made to the budget procedure (including the restriction that an issue of confidence can not be used).

the institutional self-interest of the parliament. The coalition parties in the parliament were willing to *increase* the power of the Government and *reduce* the power of the parliament in budget process in order to achieve pertinent partisan policy goals.

9.2.2.3. The Concept of "Government Budget": How Detailed Should the Budget Be?

An important constitutional issue that came up in the proceedings of the organic budget law in 1999 and 2001 was the question of how detailed the classification of expenditures in the state budget should be.

The question of who should establish the budget classification and how detailed it should be was not a new issue; it had been discussed already during the readings of the organic budget law in 1992–1994 and was repeatedly brought up during the legislative proceedings of the budget itself. The general development of the level of detail in the budget has been curvilinear. While the first budgets of the independent period were very general (for example, the budget for 1993 was only six pages long and contained nine articles), the budgets became more detailed until 2001; from then on, the level of detail has decreased and the budgets have become less detailed. In part, the increasing level of detail came about as a result of the complaints of the members of parliament (see *Riigikogu* Verbatim Record, 22 December 1992, 20 January 1993, 26 January 1993).[283] In addition, the level of detail in the budget was increased as a result of drawing on the example of Finland. Ostrow (2000, pp. 208–212) argues, based on the interviews with the members of the Finance Committee and Government officials, that the Estonian Ministry of Finance had transformed the structure of the budget to mirror the budget in Finland and the advice on the classification of budget items "came directly from representatives of the Finnish Ministry of Fi-

283 Kalle Kulbok (Royalist Party) remarked, for example, that the budget should be like it was in the inter-war period; he pointed to years 1934–1935, when the budget had been 270 pages long (*Riigikogu* Verbatim Record, 9 February 1993). Heido Vitsur (Free Democrats), the Vice Chairman of the Budget and Tax Committee, argued that, in his personal opinion, the budget should be as detailed as it is for example in Germany, where the budget is divided into 6000 expenditure lines and 1000 revenue lines; it should be possible to see how many computers would be bought by the Ministry of Finance and how much the cleaning ladies would be paid (*Riigikogu* Verbatim Record, 14 April 1993). Valve Kirsipuu expressed the fear that a too general budget document would give the executive possibilities to make many changes in the expenditure articles. She added, "The money coming from the state budget has to be strictly controlled. This is like that in most states and it would be naïve to think that the abuse of power is only a socialist or post-socialist phenomenon. So, given the current situation, the budget should be as detailed as possible." (*Riigikogu* Verbatim Record, 9 February 1993)

nance" (p. 211).[284] Though the early discussions on the level of detail in the budget were not framed in terms of constitutionality, the debates from 1999 onwards viewed these issues primarily through the constitutional lens.

During the debates on the organic budget law in 1999, the President contested the provisions that gave the Government the right to establish – prior to the submission of the draft state budget to the parliament – on what level of detail revenues and expenditures should be classified (Resolution No. 507, from 17 February 1999). The President argued that this would give the executive branch excessive powers to determine the scope of the budget, while not enabling the *Riigikogu* to have a full overview of the state revenues and expenditures in the budget. He argued that this would violate Article 4 (stipulating the balance of powers), Article 65 sub-point 6 and Article 115 of the Constitution (stipulating that *Riigikogu* passes as a *law* the budget of *all* state revenue and expenditures). In discussing the President's decision, the Constitutional Committee found it difficult to say whether it was unconstitutional. The Finance Committee did not see a violation of the Constitution and did not change the provision. (*Riigikogu* Verbatim Record, 14 April 1999) The organic budget law passed in June 1999 contained similar provisions and the President promulgated it nevertheless; as mentioned above, his main concern with the law had to do with the budgetary autonomy of the constitutional institutions.

During the debates on the organic budget law in 2001, the issue of classification came up again. The draft acts amending the organic budget law initiated in 2001 and 2002 sought to introduce the concept of "Government budget", which would be adopted *after* the *Riigikogu* passes the annual state budget and which would additionally classify the categories of expenditures in the budgets of individual ministries. The "Government budget" implied that the budget submitted to the parliament would contain more general classifications, which would be additionally sub-divided by the Government itself after the adoption of the budget in the parliament. As pointed out in the explanatory note to the draft act, the purpose of this amendment was to change the level of decision-making: to "give more authority to the level that has the most information" and to stop the practice that the *Riigikogu* decides on the internal structure of the operating expenses.

Again, this proposal gave rise to extensive debates in the parliament. While it was supported by the majority of the Finance Committee and the members of the coalition parties, it was considered to be unconstitutional by the opposition and the President. The main argument of the opponents was that the "Government budget" violates the constitutional principle of the balance of powers by

284 The level of detail became so high that some legislators even felt that the budget was too detailed; furthermore, given the limited resources of the Finance Committee, there was no sufficient analytical capacity to deal with all the specific details of the budget (Ostrow 2000, p. 211).

reducing the transparency of the budget and by giving excessive powers to the Government.

Jaanus Männik (People's Union), Vice Chairman of the Finance Committee, the most vocal opponent of the concept of Government budget, asked from the Minister of Finance, "Which articles in the Constitution allow that the state budget contains only general contours and aggregate sums, and the actual expenditures are determined by regulations of the Government?" The Minister of Finance Siim Kallas (Reform Party) answered that the Constitution does not say how the budget classification should look like. (*Riigikogu* Verbatim Record, 5 December 2001) When asked the same question at the next reading of the draft, Kallas argued that the draft act had been discussed with legal experts and the Constitutional Committee of the *Riigikogu*, and no violation of the Constitution had been found (*Riigikogu* Verbatim Record, 19 December 2001). In his speech at the first reading of the draft act, Männik stated that this provision would clearly violate the Constitution, since the Constitution says nothing of a "Government budget" but says that *all* state revenues and expenditures are enacted as a law by the parliament. (*Riigikogu* Verbatim Record, 5 December 2001) At the second reading, Männik added that the "Government budget" violates the Constitution and the principle of parliamentary democracy, since it is the constitutional *obligation* of the *Riigikogu* to decide on the expenditures and enact them as a law; therefore, it should not delegate these decisions to the executive (*Riigikogu* Verbatim Record, 19 December 2001). At a reading of the re-initiated draft act in 2002, Männik argued:

> We have a good Constitution and the Constitution stipulates fairly well how the taxpayers' money should be used. ... We can certainly discuss what the role of the executive authority should be in preparing the budget and whether that role should be increased, but the final decisions should be up to us and the decision has to be in a form of a law. ... We can not allow decisions on the use of taxpayers' money to be taken outside this hall. Our Constitution does not allow it. (*Riigikogu* Verbatim Record, 9 April 2002)

Tiit Toomsalu (United People's Party of Estonia) also brought up the issue of constitutionality in his speeches and argued that the Estonian Constitution foresees a parliamentary system, but the concept of "Government budget" would lead towards a state where the executive power dominates (*Riigikogu* Verbatim Record, 5 December 2001). At a later reading of the re-initiated act, he argued that the Government budget would take away authority from the legislature, would violate Article 115 of the Constitution and would therefore be unconstitutional. To this, Raju, the initiator of the draft, answered that according to the Constitution, the constitutional institutions have their own revenues and since the Government is also a "constitutional institution", it should also have its own budget. (*Riigikogu* Verbatim Record, 9 April 2002)

Article 115 of the Constitution ("The *Riigikogu* shall pass as a law of all state revenue and expenditure for each year") was brought up several times during the debates. The word "all" was interpreted as an affirmation of the extensive role of the *Riigikogu* by the Constitution, in the sense that the parliament should have a complete overview of the revenues and expenditures, which in turn means that the Government should not have the right to additionally classify the expenditures after the parliament has passed the budget. The Chairman of the Finance Committee Olev Raju criticised the article several times. He conjectured that by including the word "all", the Constitution-makers had been influenced by the Soviet regime: "In a socialist budget, all state revenues belonged to the state budget, since all revenues were state revenues." As he put it, "Only in the Soviet Union were the state budget revenues and state revenues regarded to be the same thing, but no other state has it like that." Raju argued that it is in fact impossible to fulfil the requirement of including "all state revenue and expenditure" in the budget, since this provision is nonsensical: it would mean, for example, that all the local government revenues also have to be included in the state budget. He argued that this provision in the Constitution should be changed. (*Riigikogu* Verbatim Record, 17 April 2002)

Similar arguments as those pointed out by the members of the opposition against the notion of "Government budget" were also brought up by President Arnold Rüütel in his resolution not to promulgate the State Budget Act (Resolution No. 153, from 6 May 2002). The President argued that the introduction of the Government budget would give the Government a right to structure most of the budget and reduce the control that the *Riigikogu* would have over the necessity and functionality of the expenditures, and he considered it to be in conflict with Articles 4, Article 65 sub-point 6 and Article 115 of the Constitution (that is, the same articles that had been evoked by the previous President and by the opposition), since only the *Riigikogu* can pass the budget of all state revenues and expenditures. Further, he argued that according to Article 110 of the Constitution, the President has no right to change the state budget with its decrees, and such a ban also excludes delegating such a right to the Government.

The Constitutional Committee of the *Riigikogu* agreed for most part with the arguments of the President, while the Finance Committee did not agree. The Chairman of the Finance Committee Meelis Atonen pointed out that the Constitution says nothing on the extent of the classification of revenues and expenditures. (*Riigikogu* Verbatim Record, 14 May 2002) Still, the organic budget law adopted in June 2002 did *not* include the concept of the Government budget anymore. Instead, a more ambiguous version was proposed (and eventually adopted), stipulating that more detailed classification of expenditure in the state budget (according to the economic content) can be done *either* in the state budget *or* by the Government after the budget has been passed, and that on the basis of a reasoned proposal made by the Minister of Finance, the Government of the Republic may further classify expenditure incurred by the ministries.

At the readings of the re-initiated organic budget law in June 2002, the main issue debated was the question of whether the changes made to the Act removed the alleged conflicts with the Constitution that the President had pointed out. Atonen (the initiator of the draft) asserted that the problems the President had pointed out had been removed from the draft (*Riigikogu* Verbatim Record, 18 June 2002). The Chairman of the Finance Committee Jürgen Ligi even argued that the previous draft had not been unconstitutional either; the governing coalition had not considered the arguments of the President very convincing but had still been willing to come half the way and to make some changes as a compromise (*Riigikogu* Verbatim Record, 20 June 2002). The members of the opposition who had opposed the idea of "Government budget" asserted that the new draft law had just made cosmetic changes but had not the changed the content of the Act with regard to the Government's authority to further classify the expenditures. Jaanus Männik, the main opponent of the Act, argued that the new draft act still violated the Constitution (*Riigikogu* Verbatim Record, 18 June 2002, 20 June 2002). Janno Reiljan (People's Union) pointed out that this Act would give an absolute power to the governing coalition and to prevent the control by the opposition: the opposition would know what is in the budget only after the Government has classified it, but then it would be too late for any changes by the *Riigikogu*. (*Riigikogu* Verbatim Record, 18 June 2002) Arvo Sirendi (People's Union) argued that the "unavoidable condition of democracy is that the supreme authority knows in detail what is going on in the state", and that the Constitution says clearly that the Government *prepares* the budget and the *Riigikogu adopts* it. In his opinion, the draft law would lead to a situation where many appropritations have to be approved blindly. (*Riigikogu* Verbatim Record, 20 June 2002) Ligi argued that the Act was not in conflict with the Constitution and that the *Riigikogu* could still decide on what level of detail the expenditures have to be written in the budget. He emphasised, however, that from the point of view of the users of the money, flexibility would allow greater efficiency. (*Riigikogu* Verbatim Record, 18 June 2002) Männik pointed out that half of the members of the parliament had a different understanding of the Constitution and that this conception should be assessed by the Supreme Court. Despite the contentions by the opposition, the provision allowing additional classification of items was included in the Act that was passed on 20 June 2002. This time, the President did not contest these provisions.

In summary, as a result of the alleged unconstitutionality, the concept of "Government budget" as such was abandoned and a more ambiguously worded version (in essence still allowing the classification to be done by the Government, but also mentioning the opportunity for the parliament to do it) was adopted. On the whole, these debates indicate that since the Constitution contains only very general provisions on what the roles of the *Riigikogu* and the Government in the budget process are, it was easy – by both sides of the dispute – to appeal to the same constitutional provisions. It is interesting to note that the parliamentary majority was willing to increase the budgetary powers of the Government and to reduce the powers of the parliament. In part, this attempt of self-binding (against future interference with the details of the budget) was driven by the desire to make the execution of the budget more flexible. On the whole, however, the high level of detail had been advantageous to the members of the *Riigikogu*, since an extensive break-down of the expenditures allowed them to make very specific amendment proposals during the legislative proceedings of the budget and, in that way, demonstrate to their constituents that they had at least *attempted* to stand up for them. Another question is, why was the President so concerned with protecting the power of the *Riigikogu* against that of the Government? In part, this may have to do with the fact that the President had been a member of the party (People's Union) that was in opposition and whose members were the most vocal opponents of the concept. It is also noteworthy that while during the debates in 2001, the People's Union and the Centre Party were against increasing the power of the Government (and thus the governing coalition) in the budget-making, then after the shift in the coalition, as a result of which the Centre Party became part of the governing coalition in January 2002, the members of this party started supporting the concept of the Government budget.

With regard to constitutional interpretation, in this case, those advocating the status quo sought to evoke a literal interpretation of the Constitution (by pointing to the word "all" in Article 115, for example) and those supporting a reform used a contingent interpretation. There was even an attempt to claim that the original intent of the framers had been influenced by a different type of regime, which was not valid anymore. These debates also demonstrate a prevailing confusion about the nature of the Constitution among the political actors with regard to how the principles "everything that is not forbidden, is allowed" versus "everything that is not allowed, is forbidden" apply in the case of inter-branch division of powers. On the one hand, it was argued that since the Constitution is silent on the issue of how budget classification should look like, no restrictions regarding that could be derived from the Constitution. On the other hand, it was argued that since the Government budget is not mentioned in the Constitution, such a concept should not be allowed.

Altogether, the debates on the budgetary roles of the Government *vis-à-vis* the legislature law can be summarised as following: the Government sought repeatedly to increase the power of the executive in the budget process and the parliamentary opposition endeavoured (together with the President) to prevent the reduction of the parliament's role in the budget process by evoking constitutional arguments. At the same time, there were also clear exceptions to this pattern: the proposal introducing Government veto on legislative budgetary amendments came from a member of opposition and the Legal Chancellor supported increasing the authority of the budgetary powers of the executive *vis-à-vis* the legislature.

9.2.3. What Does "All" State Revenues Mean?

Article 115 Section 1 of the Constitution (stating that "The *Riigikogu* shall pass as a law the budget of all state revenue and expenditure for each year.") played an important role already at the readings of the very first budget of the independent period. The discussions on the 1993 budget repeatedly brought up the problem that the draft budget did not in fact include *all* the revenues (and expenditures), as required by the Constitution. In particular, the legislators were concerned with the fact that the revenues from selling state property and the foreign loans were not included in the budget, though the Constitution required the inclusion of all revenues. (see *Riigikogu* Verbatim Record, 20 January 1993, 26 January 1993) The Minister of Finance Madis Üürike sought to rebut these accusations of unconstitutionality by arguing that the Constitution can be interpreted in different ways. In addition, he argued that if it was indeed the will of *Riigikogu* to have all state revenues and expenditures included in the state budget, this should be established in the new organic budget law. The Chairman of the Finance Committee of the *Riigikogu* argued, "If we interpret the Constitution literally, then there could indeed be a contradiction, but I guess there is no person in this hall who would not find discrepancies in the Constitution." (*Riigikogu* Verbatim Record, 26 January 1993) Similar discussions arose again at the readings of the 1994 and 1995 budgets. In particular, not including the foreign loans and extra-budgetary funds in the revenues was viewed as problematic by several members of the parliament (*Riigikogu* Verbatim Record, 10 November 1993, 12 October 1994).

The question of what the word "all" means in terms of budget revenues came up again in debates on the organic budget law in 2001–2002. The question was whether fees and fines should also be included among the revenues of the state budget. Although both the 1994 and 1999 organic budget laws had included them, the draft initiated in 2001 did not include fees and fines among the categories of budget revenues anymore. Several MPs from the opposition viewed leaving out fees and fines from the list of revenues as unconstitutional. Tiit Toomsalu argued that since Article 113 of the Constitution requires that state taxes, duties, fees, fines and compulsory insurance payments shall be provided by law and the Article 115 requires that the *Riigikogu* shall pass as a law the budget of all state revenue and expenditure for each year, fees and fines should be included in the budget revenues and thus brought out accordingly in the State Budget Act. The initiator of the Act Olev Raju answered that "All economists would agree that according to macroeconomics, fees and fines are not a gain for the state or the society, they are just a mechanism for redistribution." Jaanus Männik pointed out that he was puzzled by this answer and asked: "If state fines and fees are not state revenues, why are they written in the Constitution?" Raju answered again that, macro-economically speaking, fines cannot be seen as revenues since they are not a net gain. In an answer to that, Mihkel

Pärnoja pointed out that "what is written in the Constitution has to be followed, even if the macroeconomic principles say something else", to which the counter-argument by Raju was that perhaps the Constitution should be changed. In his speech, Toomsalu argued,

> When we talk about macroeconomic questions, then the issue is very simple: the state budget needs revenues and the more clearly they are expressed the better. If already the Constitution lays down what the budget revenues should be, then it should be followed, it is a social contract. ... I am sure that if the Act is passed in such a form, the President would face a difficult dilemma again. (*Riigikogu* Verbatim Record, 17 April 2002)

In his Resolution No. 153 (from 6 May 2002), the President did not promulgate the Act and argued that not enlisting fines and fees among the state budget revenues would violate Article 115 of the Constitution, which establishes the principle of universality, unity and transparency of the budget. He alleged that such an omission would limit the right of the *Riigikogu* to gain information and decide over the allocation of the revenues and receipts. Although the Finance Committee did not agree with the President, fines and fees were added to the categories of revenues in the Act that was passed in June 2002.

It is interesting to note here that although the Constitution does not define fines and fees as state revenues, in the course of the debates, the opinion emerged among several legislators as if the Constitution defined them as a source of state revenue (as a result of repeating the stipulations of Articles 113 and 115 together). The President's interpretation of Article 115 certainly went further than the literal interpretation of the article would allow – pointing to generally well accepted principles of budgeting, which, while compatible with the Constitution, do not arise from the wording of it. On the other hand, some members of the parliament called for the literal following of the Constitution, no matter whether this would be compatible with general economic principles or not.

9.2.4. Budget Balance, Budget Deficit and Borrowing

Given the commitment to fiscal discipline in Estonia, it is often assumed (both internationally and also by domestic actors) that the Estonian Constitution requires a balanced budget. In fact, the Constitution does not have any provisions stipulating such a requirement. Despite the fact that the Constitution is silent on budget balance and deficit, the question of the constitutionality of budget deficit was discussed during the debates of the 1994 organic budget law. At the first reading of the organic budget law (14 April 1993), Kalev Kukk raised the question of whether it is reasonable to simply require budget balance in the organic budget law and whether it would not be better to set a specific maximum limit for budget deficit. To this, the Minister of Finance Madis Üürike answered that the budget has to be balanced "because the Constitution requires so". He added that in order to balance the budget, the organic budget law provides for different possibilities, including borrowing. (*Riigikogu* Verbatim Record, 14 April 1993) As mentioned in chapter 7, the conception of budget balance in the 1994 Act was entirely formalistic, implying that budget can be considered to be "balanced" – even when the expenditures that exceed revenues are financed from loans.

As mentioned in chapter 3, although the Constitution does not establish any substantive fiscal rules, it does impose some procedural constraints on borrowing (by requiring the parliament's consent to the loans and proprietary obligations of the state). During the debates on the State Budget Act in spring 1999, discussion arose over a provision in the draft act giving the Government greater freedom to take a loan, up to a certain ceiling. Kranich suggested leaving out this provision, because, according to the Constitution, it is the *Riigikogu* that decides over the proprietary obligations of the state. He even stated, "If we passed this Act with these paragraphs, the Supreme Court will declare it unconstitutional." (*Riigikogu* Verbatim Record, 8 April 1998) When put on vote, this provision was voted out of the draft.[285]

9.2.5. The State Budget in the Constitutional Review Chamber

Although the organic budget law itself has not been considered by the Constitutional Review Chamber of the Supreme Court, the Chamber has decided on two cases pertaining to the state budget.

The first case, called the "supplementary budget case" (Judgement No. 3-4-1-1-00 of the Supreme Court *en banc*, of 17 March 2000) was initiated by the Legal Chancellor, who questioned the constitutionality of two provisions in the supplementary budget of 1999: one provision eliminated allocations for the implementation of Dwelling Act and another decreased the surplus of State Forest Management Centre. The Legal Chancellor argued that these provisions violate Article 116 of the Constitution (stating that the *Riigikogu* shall not eliminate or reduce expenditure in the state budget or in its draft that is prescribed by other laws). The Supreme Court did not find that the entries in the supplementary budget were unconstitutional. The Court argued that since the Dwelling Act did not provide for exact amounts to be allocated for the construction and purchasing of residential space but depended on applications from local government bodies, it could not assess whether the elimination of the funds had *de facto* stopped the implementation of the contested provision in the Dwelling Act for 1999. Still, the Court was of the opinion that the state has to fulfil its obligations arising from the provision, regardless of whether the pertinent resources are pro-

285 As discussed in chapter 7, however, the restrictions on the Government to take a loan were still eased with the changes made to the organic budget law in 2002 and 2004.

vided for in the state budget or not. The Court also found that reducing the surplus of State Forest Management Centre in the supplementary budget was constitutional.

Three dissenting judges, however, did not agree with the statement that since the Dwelling Act does not provide for the exact sums for the construction or purchasing of residential space, it is not possible to tell whether the passage of supplementary budget *de facto* stopped the implementation of the provision. They were of the opinion that Article 116 of the Constitution has to be taken into consideration in case of all laws without any exceptions and irrespective of whether the Dwelling Act provided for concrete sums or not. They also emphasised that provision of concrete sums in laws is not typical.

Another interesting dispute that arose during this case was whether the Legal Chancellor was actually competent to review the legality and constitutionality of the state budget or supplementary state budget. The Minister of Justice held the view that the Legal Chancellor had no competence to exercise review over supplementary budget, since the disputed entries involved individual precepts, while the Legal Chancellor can only review legislation of general application. The Supreme Court decided that the Legal Chancellor had this competence, since the budget and supplementary budget amount to legislation, despite the fact that they also contain individual precepts.

This case can have several implications for the future. One of the important implications is that the Legal Chancellor has the competence to question the constitutionality of the state budget (or supplementary budgets), which, if used actively, could be an important weapon in the hands of the Legal Chancellor. On the other hand, with this case, the Court created an important precedent: by saying that it could not judge whether the implementation of an act was hindered because of the removed funds, given that no exact sum was expressed in the law and the court had no information of the actual requirements or applications of those needing the funds. As pointed out by dissenting judges, legislative acts do not usually provide for exact funds. Thus, such a precedent would seem to weaken the capacity of the Court itself to enforce Article 116 of the Constitution in the future.

The second case where the State Budget came up (Judgement No. 3-3-1-46-03 of the Supreme Court *en banc*, of 19 April 2004) can be considered to be of lesser importance; although contested as an act, the Court decided that the state budget was not the right act to dispute.

9.3. Summary and Discussion

As previous sections indicate, the Constitution has played an important role in shaping the organic budget law in Estonia. In addition to constitutional articles pertaining to budgeting that have been incorporated in the organic budget law, the Constitution has influenced the development of the law through mechanisms of constitutional review and by framing legislative discussions on the law. As a result of the constitutional review by the President and constitutional deliberations in the parliament, the budgetary autonomy of constitutional institutions was increased. Ensuing from the constitutional review by the Legal Chancellor, the budgetary powers of the Government were increased by giving it the right to bind the passage of the state budget to an issue of confidence. At the same time, constitutional deliberations circumscribed the extent to which the budgetary powers of the Government were increased and it did not go as far as the Government had desired: the concept of Government budget was abandoned (and a more ambiguous version of it adopted) and the Government was not given the right to veto parliamentary amendments at the first readings of the state budget. The role of the parliament in the budget process has also been influenced by the interpretations and constructions of the pertinent articles. As a result of constitutional deliberations and constitutional review, the budgetary amendment rights of the parliament were constrained (although not to the extent desired by some actors). The constraints imposed could be viewed as constitutional, given the very vague wording of the budgetary powers of the parliament in the Constitution. Altogether, still, the Constitution has played a balancing role by not allowing the budgetary powers of the executive to become excessive or the powers of the legislature too constrained.[286]

The analysis above indicates that the most important mechanism of constitutional review in the development of the organic budget law so far has been that of the President. Although the Legal Chancellor has generally been very active in Estonia, his role in the development of the organic budget law was limited to bringing up binding the passage of the state budget to an issue of confidence. The Supreme Court has not played a substantive role in the development of the organic budget law so far, although through its ruling in the "supplementary budget" case, it certainly increased the power of the Legal Chancellor, by regarding it constitutional to allow the Chancellor to contest specific provisions in the state budget. In addition, the Court confirmed the duty of the state to provide for funds if these have been foreseen by laws, irrespective of whether they have been stipulated in the state budget or not.

Although the organic budget law itself has not been discussed in the Constitutional Review Chamber of the Supreme Court, auto-limitation by the *Riigikogu* – the guesses of how the Court would decide, were the President to take the contested laws to the Court – played a role in the *Riigikogu*'s reaction to the Presidents' protests and influenced its willingness to make the amendments sug-

286 With regard to the changes made to the position of the Minister of Finance *vis-à-vis* the Cabinet (decreasing the power of the Minister and increasing the power of the Cabinet) in the budget preparation phase, however, no constitutional controversies arose. In fact, these changes were not even subject to debates in the legislature. Augmenting the centralisation of the implementation of the budget by the Minister of Finance was also not subject to constitutional controversies.

gested by the President. As Hänni (2002b) notes, in its decisions, the Supreme Court has, in general, protected the right of the President to carry out its constitutional functions without excessive interference from the parliament. In addition, the Supreme Court has usually given the right in constitutional cases to the President.[287] Also, by evoking the argument of protecting the budgetary autonomy of the constitutional institutions, the President could appeal (at the same time as protecting its own institution) to safeguarding the budgetary autonomy of the Supreme Court itself. Also, the remarks of the Chief Justice of the Supreme Court in an earlier debate on the same issue indicated that the Court was dissatisfied with the excessive budgetary powers of the executive. In that way it is understandable that the members of the *Riigikogu* were – during the disputes in 1999 – fairly convinced that they would lose the case if it were referred to the Supreme Court.

Even though in Estonia the parliamentary opposition does not have the right to refer a bill for constitutional review in the Supreme Court, on several occasions, the opposition used the explicitly worded call for auto-limitation: for example, when arguing against increasing the borrowing autonomy of the Government and against the provisions concerning budget classification by the Government. Several times, the members of opposition "threatened" the majority with the claim that the President would not promulgate the Act because of unconstitutionality. This shows that "auto-limitation" can take place not only in reference to the constitutional review by the Court but also by other institutions of constitutional review. Further, it demonstrates that even in countries where the opposition does not have referral rights to the constitutional court, it can use other institutions of constitutional review to sustain their calls for auto-limitation. Although Sadurski (2005, p. 90), in his review of how constitutional courts have influenced legislation in the post-communist CEE countries, argues, with reference to auto-limitation, that "it is very hard to find evidence that such anticipatory behaviour has occurred in CEE legislature/court interactions", the Estonian case shows that even in a relative small area – the budget procedure – auto-limitation has in fact taken place.

The bargaining over issues of constitutionality between the *Riigikogu* and the President followed different dynamics in different cases. At the first debate, in 1999, the parliament was willing to come a longer way in accommodating the arguments of the President in changing the organic budget law (especially with regard to the constitutional institutions). Still, not all issues pointed out by the President were included in the new version of the act; it appears that the parliament was willing to change those aspects that were likely to be of overriding importance for the President. At the 2002 debate between the *Riigikogu* and the

287 Between 1992 and 2001, for example, the Court agreed with the President in seven cases out of the eight cases that the President took to the Supreme Court.

President, the parliament was less willing to accommodate the proposed changes of the President and the changes made were rather ambiguous.

As conjectured in chapter 8, constitutional issues came up frequently at the parliamentary discussions over the organic budget law, providing support for Conjecture 8. Indeed, a large portion of the debates over the organic budget law was dominated by constitutional deliberations. Constitutional deliberations in the parliament took the form of "constitutional construction" rather than "juridified" debate, providing corroboration for Conjecture 10. Given the limited number of constitutional review decisions by the Supreme Court and the fact that the organic budget law had not been referred to the Court, the constitutionalisation of this sector was low and the constitutional law "thin". The participants in constitutional deliberations did not refer to any existing court decisions.

Most of the elements of constitutional construction that Whittington (1999) brought out (based on the U.S. experience) played a role in the constitutional debates on the organic budget law in Estonia as well. The political actors – the members of the parliament, the cabinet members, the President – used the text of the Constitution to support their own political and institutional interests. The plea to increase the budgetary autonomy of constitutional institutions certainly reflected the institutional self-interest of the President to have more budgetary autonomy for his institution.[288] The proposals to significantly constrain the right of the parliament to make amendments to the draft budget were rejected by the majority of the parliament (during the discussions in 1998–1999), reflecting the desire of the parliament not to cede its budgetary powers. The Finance Committee agreed to support the constraints on parliamentary amendment rights after it had been included as a gatekeeper alongside the Cabinet.

In addition to institutional self-interests, partisan interests were reflected in most of the constitutional disputes. As could be seen in the discussions during 2001–2002 over the different proposals that sought to constrain the role of the legislature and to increase the role of the executive, the members of the opposition sought to demonstrate unconstitutionality of the proposed provisions. In addition, in 2002, the President sought to protect the role of the parliament (and in particular the role of the opposition) *vis-à-vis* the Government in the budget process. The President's concern with protecting the role of the parliament and the opposition is likely to have been related to the fact that he had been a presidential candidate of one of the parties in the opposition. The partisan interests were also reflected in the fact that the Centre Party, which had been against the

288 This also indicates the need to pay attention to the institutional details in an analysis of a political setting. Although the powers of the president with regard to the budget are explicitly constrained by the Constitution (see chapter 3), the right of the president to undertake constitutional review has enabled the president to advance the budgetary autonomy of his own institution (alongside other constitutional institutions). Thus, the rights of constitutional review granted to particular institutions enable these institutions to advance their budgetary interests.

concept of "Government budget" when it was in the opposition, started supporting it once it was in the governing coalition. The dispute over the right of the Government to bind the passage of the budget to an issue of confidence was perhaps the clearest example of how alleged unconstitutionality was used as a means for serving short-term partisan interests (the adoption of the supplementary budget) in the face of the obstructionist tactics of the opposition.

There were some proposals, however, that went beyond institutional and partisan self-interest and reflected the will of "self-binding". The proposals to constrain the parliament's right to amend the organic budget law in 1998 were made by a member of the opposition (and supported by some other members of the opposition), appealing to the desire to improve the rationality of the budget process. The proposal of parliamentary "self-binding" was certainly facilitated by the personal experience of the proponents of this proposal in the executive branch. In addition, these proposals were inspired by specific experiences of budgeting in 1997, when the parliament had lost "self-control" and increased the volume of the budget by a significant amount. Also, self-binding concerns came to the fore in the discussions in 1995–1996 over granting more budgetary autonomy to the *Riigikogu* in the preparation phase of the budget process. Motivated by the concerns of maintaining budget balance, a number of opposition MPs called for not granting the parliament (and the Supreme Court) more extensive freedom in compiling its own budget proposal. In other cases, however, the "self-binding" provisions of the parliament (e.g., the provisions allowing the Government to have a more important role in classifying the expenditures, introduced in 2002) came about as a decision of the coalition parties, reflecting – in addition to the desire to increase the efficiency and flexibility of the budget process – the wish to increase the power of the coalition at the expense of the opposition parties. The parties in the coalition are usually able to pursue their goals through the cabinet, which can explain their readiness to limit the role of the parliament to a certain extent.

With regard to the techniques of constitutional construction, as could be seen in some debates, contrary to what Whittington proposed, those advocating a change sought to engage in literal interpretation of the text and those advocating the status quo pointed to a contingent interpretation of the text. In other situations, the reverse was the case. On several occasions, it was argued that if the Constitution says nothing on the issue, then "it should be allowed". For example, during the debates on the Government budget it was argued that since the Constitution is silent on how the classification should take place, no restrictions pertaining to classification can be derived from the Constitution. Surprisingly few arguments in the constitutional debates pointed to original intent. Once evoked, it was said that the original intent had been substantively wrong and unduly influenced by the Soviet setting. Had the constitutional interpretations sought to look for original intent, it would have clearly favoured maintaining extensive rights of the parliament in the budget process, since that had been the prevailing view in the debates of the Constitutional Assembly (1991–1992). The Assembly had rejected, for example, the Government veto on budgetary amendments and other constitutional provisions that would have given the Government large budgetary powers *vis-à-vis* the parliament (see chapter 3).

The constitutional constructions offered by participants in legislative debates often went beyond the text of the Constitution and evoked external elements, like the experiences of other countries (e.g., when discussing whether in a parliamentary democracy the parliament plays an extensive role in budgetary discussions), pointing to the fact that Estonia was still not a mature democracy, which should be taken into account when interpreting the Constitution, or referring to very recent experiences in the Estonian politics. The generality of the Constitution allowed the interpretation of how the budget procedure should look like to shift according to the experiences with what works and what does not.

In addition to the genuine attempts to assess the constitutionality of controversial provisions, in some cases, the references to the Constitution served purely rhetorical purposes. The generality of the constitutional provisions allowed the participants in the debate simply to refer to the Constitution and to claim congruence or incongruence on the level of assertion and without in-depth explanation. The Estonian experience also provides evidence for how just one word can create a lot of confusion: the word "all" in Article 115 ("*Riigikogu* shall pass as a law the budget of all state revenues and expenditures") gave rise to lengthy parliamentary constitutional deliberations and even constitutional review by the President.

Altogether, the case study of Estonia shows that the constitution can indeed shape the organic budget law through constitutional review and legislative constitutional deliberation. Hence, constitutional public finance should pay a closer attention to this kind of analysis and take more advantage of in-depth case studies that are able to bring to the fore the more subtle interactions between the Constitution and the policy arena of public finance. In the next chapter, the analytical framework outlined in chapter 8 is used for exploring the role of the Constitution in the development of tax legislation in Estonia.

Chapter 10: The Role of the Constitution in the Development of Tax Laws in Estonia

10.1. Introduction

This chapter focuses on the impacts that the 1992 Constitution of Estonia has had – through constitutional review and constitutional deliberations – on the development of the Taxation Act (which is the main framework law for taxation), Income Tax Act, Social Tax Act and Value Added Tax Act. Income tax, social tax and value added tax have been chosen for analysis since they constitute the most important taxes in Estonia, both in terms of the revenue proceeds, making up over 70 percent of the total tax revenues in all years from 1994 to 2007 (see Table 10.2.), but also because of their visibility and standing as the three main pillars of the Estonian tax system.[289] Broadly speaking, the tax system in Estonia is similar to that of Western European countries: most tax revenues come from taxing labour and consumption (see Table 10.2.). The structure of the tax system established in the early years of transition has remained essentially the same and the tax burden – as percentage of GDP – has been stable (see Table 10.1.).[290]

Table 10.1.: Tax revenues as % of GDP in Estonia, 1995–2007

	'95	'96	'97	'98	'99	'00	'01	'02	'03	'04	'05	'06	'07
Tax burden	38	36	36	36	35	31	31	31	31	31	31	31	32

Source: Ministry of Finance of the Republic of Estonia

Table 10.2.: Revenues of personal income tax, corporate income tax, social tax and value added tax, as % of total tax revenues, 1995–2007

	'95	'96	'97	'98	'99	'00	'01	'02	'03	'04	'05	'06	'07
PIT	11	10	9	10	10	10	10	9	9	9	6	6	6
CIT	6	4	5	7	6	3	2	4	5	5	5	5	5
Social tax	35	34	32	33	36	35	35	35	34	34	33	33	34
VAT	26	27	27	23	23	27	27	27	27	25	28	30	29
Sum	78	75	73	73	75	75	74	75	75	73	72	74	74

Source: Ministry of Finance of the Republic of Estonia

289 For an overview of the Estonian tax system and the reforms that have been undertaken during the transition, see Purju (2004); for a detailed description of the various taxes in Estonia, see Kuldkepp (2005).

290 The drop in 2000 resulted from the abolition of corporate income tax (on reinvested profits).

A discussion of the role of the Constitution in the development of tax legislation in Estonia also has to consider the specific features of the transition period and the challenges the countries in the CEE region had to overcome in building up their new tax systems after the collapse of the planned economy. The constraints and difficulties faced by CEE countries at the wake of transition have been explained in detail by Martinez-Vazquez and McNab (2000), Tanzi and Tsibouris (2000) and Campbell (1996), among others. A short summary of these discussions would therefore suffice here.

Martinez-Vazquez and McNab (2000) have taken together the characteristics of the tax systems inherited from the Soviet regime as follows: the Soviet tax system was interventionist, with highly "customised" taxes (with liabilities resulting from negotiations between the authorities and the firms),[291] there was no tradition of voluntary compliance (the population at large was not even aware that they were paying taxes), and the tax administration was underdeveloped. In sum, the tax system was largely "implicit and uncodified" (McKinnon 1992, p. 110); taxes were not collected according to specific and codified tax laws that defined tax bases and parametric tax rates[292] (Tanzi and Tsibouris 2000, p. 14) and the notion of "taxpayers' rights" was essentially an empty concept. Therefore, as Tanzi and Tsibouris (2000, p. 15) put it, it became clear to the reforming governments that the inherited tax systems "could not simply reformed on the margin", but totally new systems were needed.

The collection of taxes in the centrally planned system had been relatively easy, since the authorities could use the information from the plan to ascertain how much the small number of large state enterprises produced and what prices they charged (Tanzi and Tsibouris 2000, p. 13). In addition, all the payments of the state enterprises were processed through the monobank, in which they had to have their account, and this made transactions easy to monitor. As Campbell (1996, p. 50) has described it, "Since the monobank kept the accounts for all state enterprises, tax collection was simply a matter of the bank deducting taxes due to the budget from the enterprise accounts." There was, in fact, little need for tax administration, in the conventional sense of the word.[293]

Hence, after the collapse of the planned system, the tax offices faced immense challenges, given the loss of centralised information from the plan and the monobank, and the increasing decentralisation of the structure of the econ-

291 As Tanzi and Tsibouris (2000, p. 14) put it: "When an enterprise was in difficulty, the taxes were negotiated downward; when the government needed extra revenue the taxes were negotiated upward."

292 For example, the rates of turnover taxes were not even published.

293 Indeed, these "countries did not need market-type tax systems to raise public revenue because the government could simply appropriate the share of total, and mostly public, production for its own needs. Given that it owned practically everything, the government would decide how it wanted to divide and use the total output." (Tanzi and Tsibouris 2000, p. 4)

omy through the creation of a large number of small and medium-sized enterprises. It could be expected that the generally hostile attitude towards having to start paying explicit taxes (due to the underdeveloped tax consciousness caused by the hidden taxes in the previous system) combined with the need to guarantee tax revenues for the state budget would make the question of taxpayers' rights *vis-à-vis* the revenue needs of the state an important issue on the agenda of the tax system reform.

Estonia undertook a swift overhaul of the tax system already at the end of 1980s and established a modern tax system patterned according to the tax systems of developed market economies in Western Europe and North-America, including personal and corporate income tax, value added tax and excise taxes. Ebrill and Havrylyshyn (1999), in their assessment of progress in tax policy reform in the Baltics, Russia and other countries from the FSU from 1992 through mid-1998, awarded Estonia with the highest index of progress in tax reform.[294]

In the following sections, the framework outlined in chapter 8 is used for analysing the development of the Taxation Act (the organic tax law) and specific tax acts – Income Tax Act, Social Tax Act and Value Added Tax Act – in Estonia. The main questions that the analysis will look at are: Have constitutional debates played a role in the development of these acts? In what direction have constitutional debates changed these acts? What have been the dominating avenues for constitutional review – abstract review or concrete review? Have the decisions of the Constitutional Court (and other constitutional review institutions) favoured the rights of the taxpayers or the state? Have the decisions of the Constitutional Court implied costs for the state budget? Has the legislature deferred to the Court even if the decisions imposed budgetary costs? How have constitutional debates in the parliament shaped the tax acts? What form have the legislative constitutional deliberations taken? Has the parliament been active or passive when engaging in constitutional deliberations on tax laws? In answering these questions, the analysis seeks to find out whether the conjectures put forth in chapter 8 are corroborated or contradicted and in what way they should be elaborated and specified. Section 10.2. focuses on the organic tax law (the Taxation Act) and section 10.3. considers the most important tax acts and section 10.4. concludes.

10.2. The Impacts of the Constitution on the Development of the Taxation Act

The Taxation Act is the framework law for taxation (i.e., the "organic tax law"), which sets out the main principles of taxation in Estonia: it defines the concept

294 The index captured, *inter alia*, whether the country had adopted a comprehensive tax code, established the VAT, implemented modern profit taxes and eliminated pervasive exemptions and preferences.

of tax, outlines the general features of the tax system, specifies the rights, obligations and liability of tax authorities and taxable persons, and establishes the procedure for tax proceedings and the procedure for the resolution of tax disputes. The first Taxation Act of the transition period in Estonia was adopted in 1989 and enacted in 1990. It provided the framework for establishing a modern Western style tax system that was to be separate from the existing Soviet tax system. The 1990 Taxation Act outlined the kind of taxes that would constitute the tax system (personal income tax, corporate income tax, value added tax, excise taxes, social tax, pollution tax, land tax, natural resources tax, activity license tax, vehicle tax, performance tax and investment tax) and which governmental institutions would be responsible for establishing the different kinds of taxes (with the general principle being that the executive would establish taxes that concern firms, while the legislature would establish taxes that concern individual persons). In sum, the 1990 Taxation Act gave to the state the right and duty to impose and collect taxes and made tax evasion a violation of the law (Tang and Nilgo 1995, p. 94). With the changes made to the Taxation Act in 1991, the number of taxes that were to be established by the executive was reduced (and included customs duties, pollution charges, natural resource charges and state fees; that is, taxes that took the form of absolute and not percentage values).[295] The Vice Minister of Finance Enn Roose explained that although in Western countries the prevailing principle was that all issues related to taxes are established by laws, in the Estonian context, there was still need to give the right to establish some taxes to the executive, because of the necessity to react flexibly to changing circumstances: in order to increase the tax levels according to the rate of inflation, for example (Verbatim Record of the Supreme Council, 18–21 February 1991, p. 133). With the changes made to the Taxation Act in 1991, criminal liability for tax evasion was introduced, in addition to administrative liability. A new Taxation Act was adopted in 1993 and enacted in 1994. Compared with the previous versions of the Act, the 1994 Act deprived the Government of the right to establish taxes and outlined detailed procedures for collecting taxes by tax authorities.

In addition to the Taxation Act, which can be considered to be the organic tax law for Estonia, there was a proposal, submitted by the Government in May 1992 and discussed in the Supreme Council on 10 August 1992, to adopt an additional organic tax law – an "organic tax laws act" – which would have regulated the preparation and adoption of tax laws in Estonia (i.e., establishing a specific procedure for these acts, analogous to the organic budget law that outlined the procedure for the preparation, adoption and implementation of the state budget). Enn Roose noted, when presenting the draft act, that it was important to establish such a procedure with a law, since "this is how the neighbouring coun-

295 Vehicle tax, investment tax and performance tax were excluded from the list of state taxes with the changes made in 1991.

tries and 'civilised' countries do it" (Verbatim Record of the Supreme Council, 10–13 August 1992, p. 10).

A noteworthy aspect of this draft "organic tax laws act" was that it sought to fix the total tax burden at the existing level and to forbid further increases. This would have implied that if the government and the parliament sought to increase one tax, they would simultaneously have to reduce another tax, so that the general tax burden would remain the same. The draft act also stipulated that if tax burden were reduced, the initiators would have to indicate which expenditures are reduced correspondingly. In addition, it foresaw that the preparation of tax laws had to be more thorough than for ordinary laws: it stipulated the obligation of the Ministry of Finance to be involved in the preparation of these laws and in the assessment their impacts. Thus, if a member of the parliament were to initiate a change in a tax law, the Ministry of Finance would prepare an economic analysis of this amendment. Roose argued that the members of the parliament were usually not able to provide such analysis themselves. (pp. 5–6) In the preparation process of this draft organic law, there was a proposal for a provision according to which the tax burden could only be increased with a two-thirds majority of the legislature. But, as Roose pointed out, this provision would violate the Constitution, which requires that laws should be passed with a simple majority, unless the Constitution stipulates otherwise and tax laws were not included in the list of acts for which a qualified majority was required (p. 5).

Most of the legislators participating in the debate on the draft "organic tax laws act", however, were sceptical of the need for such a law. Liia Hänni (who had also been a member of the Constitutional Assembly) pointed out that procedural aspects for passing laws and specific provisions for particular kinds of laws should be adopted all together in the Rules of Procedure Act for the parliament (p. 18). While the participants agreed in general with the idea that the tax burden should not be increased, there was a prevailing uncertainty as to what exactly the status quo was (pp. 9–10, 14–15).[296] Also, as Hänni commented, passing such an act just three months before the elections of the new *Riigikogu* would send a distrustful signal to the future parliament (p. 14). The Supreme Council decided to reject the draft act and in the subsequent legislative history of Estonia, no other acts like that – regulating specifically the preparation and adoption of tax laws – have been proposed.

Table 10.3. gives an overview of the number of acts concerning the Taxation Act (either the Act as a whole, or Acts amending the Taxation Act) adopted and rejected by the different *Riigikogu*s from 1992 to 2007, the number of constitutional issues raised in the debates of the *Riigikogu* and the number of cases per-

296 Together with the currency reform, a package of tax laws increasing the tax rates was adopted. Since the currency reform committee had no authority to increase taxes, it was still argued in August 1992, whether these changes to the tax laws continued to have a legal force or not. Before the currency reform, the tax burden had been 38.2 percent of GDP and after the currency reform, it was 44.2 percent of GDP.

taining to Taxation Act decided by the Constitutional Review Chamber of the Supreme Court. Table 10.3. indicates that constitutional debates within the *Riigikogu* and between the *Riigikogu* and the institutions of constitutional review have played at least some role in the development of the Taxation Act. Constitutional issues pertaining to the Taxation Act are reviewed in a chronological order in the following sections, in order to make it easier to follow the development of the constitutional conceptions over time.

Table 10.3.: Constitution and Taxation Act in Estonia, 1992–2007

	Number of acts concerning Taxation Act adopted	Number of acts concerning Taxation Act rejected	Number of constitutional issues discussed in the *Riigikogu*	Number of cases concerning Taxation Act in the CRC
7th *Riigikogu* (1992–1995)	9	3	4	1
8th *Riigikogu* (1995–1999)	12	6	1	1
9th *Riigikogu* (1999–2003)	13	2	1	1
10th *Riigikogu* (2003–2007)	7	3	-	-
11th *Riigikogu* (2007– …)	0	-	-	-

Source: Author's calculations

10.2.1. The 1994 Taxation Act

Already the first Taxation Act of the independent period (passed by the *Riigikogu* on 25 August 1993, enacted on 1 January 1994)[297] gave rise to extensive discussions pertaining to constitutionality of several provisions. It is noteworthy though that during the debates on the first version of the 1994 Act in the *Riigikogu*, no constitutional issues were raised – it was only the constitutional review by the President that set going the constitutional debates on the Act. The lack of constitutional debates in the first round of the parliamentary debates is especially remarkable, since the changes introduced with the 1994 Taxation Act were clearly of "fiscal constitutional" nature. While the previous versions of the Act had only outlined the duties of taxpayers, then the 1994 Act provided explicitly for the rights of taxpayers. As the presenter of the draft, the Minister of Finance Madis Üürike noted, the goal of the new Act, compared with the previous ones, was to offer a balanced set of rights and duties for both taxpayers and tax authorities. He pointed out that the taxpayers have a right and duty to pay

297 Until then the 1990 Taxation Act (called the Taxation Act of the Soviet Republic of Estonia) had been used as a framework law for taxation.

taxes only according to tax acts, which, according to him, should prevent situations where the tax authorities proceed from other legal acts that do not directly pertain to taxes (*Riigikogu* Verbatim Record, 9 June 1993). In addition, the 1994 Act extended the rights of the Tax Office, and established explicitly and in detail the procedures, control mechanisms and sanctions for tax collection, which had so far been stipulated only in very general terms. These aspects, however, did not call for any questions, remarks or comments by members of parliament in the plenary sessions of the readings of this Act.[298] The Act was, after brief discussions, swiftly passed on 25 August 1993.

The President, however, refused to promulgate the Taxation Act on the grounds of unconstitutionality and returned it to the *Riigikogu* for a new reading and decision (Resolution No. 177, from 8 September 1993). The President pointed to four aspects of the Taxation Act that did not conform with the Constitution. First, he argued that giving the Minister of Finance the authority to establish the nature of local taxes and to approve those taxes violated the autonomy of local governments, protected by the Constitution. Second, the rules included in the Taxation Act did not provide a taxpayer with the constitutional right to turn directly to the court, without first exhausting pre-trial procedures. Third, he stated that the authority vested in judges by the Act to permit tax inspectors to control tax evasions was unconstitutional, since the Constitution provides that the sole jurisdiction of courts is the administration of justice and not the conduct of a pre-trial procedure. Fourth, he argued that the use of special means by tax inspectors should be regulated by law and can not be left to the discretion of the tax inspectors, as the Act essentially did. When the President's resolution was discussed in the *Riigikogu*, the participants in the debate – in particular the chairmen of the Constitutional Committee and Finance Committee – argued that all these aspects pointed out by the President could be interpreted differently and there was no violation of constitutional norms; thus, there was no reason to change the Taxation Act (*Riigikogu* Verbatim Record, 28 September 1993). On 28 September 1993, the *Riigikogu* passed the Taxation Act unamended, and President requested the Supreme Court to declare the law unconstitutional.

In its Judgement No. III-4/A-4 (of 4 November 1993) the Constitutional Review Chamber agreed with the President (and with the Legal Chancellor who had also given his opinion about the case) and declared the Taxation Act unconstitutional. First, the CRC pointed out that the authority delegated to the Minister of Finance to establish the nature of local taxes and the requirement to have the local taxes approved and registered by the Minister of Finance before they could be enacted by the local councils was unconstitutional, since it violated the right of the local governments to levy and collect taxes (Article 157 of the Constitu-

298 In general, the debates on the Act were very brief; most of the questions concerned the list of local taxes (*Riigikogu* Verbatim Record, 9 June 1993, 25 August 1993).

tion). According to the CRC, since, under the Constitution, local governments conduct their activities in accordance with the *laws*, the *Riigikogu* had no authority to *delegate* its legislative powers regarding the regulation of the activities of local governments. Authorising the Minister of Finance to determine the nature of local taxes and to establish the rules for their approval and registration, however, meant delegating the legislative authority to the executive and was, hence, unconstitutional. In the Court's opinion, the Taxation Act gave the Minister of Finance an opportunity to interfere directly with the establishment of local taxes. Second, the Court argued that the provisions in the Taxation Act according to which a tax inspector was authorised to inspect the property and buildings of enterprises without a prior warning or special authorisation, to set up measurements on containers, storage areas and equipment and to place cameras were unconstitutional, since all those activities required entry into another's property and the provisions in the Act did not require the owner's or possessor's consent, which went against the constitutional principles governing the inviolability of ownership. In addition, the Court pointed out that giving a tax inspector the right to conduct a needed inspection on a court order, if he has a reason to believe that a delay in inspection would lead to tax evasion was unconstitutional, since the inviolability of living spaces, possessions or places of business as provided by Article 33 of the Constitution may not be restricted on the basis of the tax inspector's *belief* that a delay in inspection would result in tax evasion. Third, the Court stated that the Taxation Act did not specify whether the placement of surveillance cameras mentioned in the Act also included the use of cameras for secret surveillance. The Court added that when cameras are intended for secret surveillance, they are so-called "special means", but according to existing laws, tax inspectors did not belong to the group of persons who can use "special means". Fourth, the CRC stated that the requirement to exhaust an administrative procedure before gaining access to the courts violated Article 15 of the Constitution, which establishes that every person whose rights have been violated has access to the courts.[299]

As a result of the Court's decision, the *Riigikogu* changed the controversial provisions in the Taxation Act. The discussions on the Taxation Act (after it had been returned to the parliament) indicated that the legislators were primarily interested in getting the Taxation Act passed as fast as possible (before the end of the year 1993), since many tax laws were to come into force at the beginning of 1994; having the Taxation Act (which was the framework law for the other tax laws) suspended would have complicated the implementation of these laws (*Riigikogu* Verbatim Record, 7 December 1993). Thus, the *Riigikogu* sought to

299 Further, the CRC argued that the pre-trial procedure outlined in the Taxation Act did not meet the requirement of Article 13 Section 2 of the Constitution (according to which everyone must be protected by law against arbitrary treatment by government), since the jurisdiction to decide a dispute had been given to an administrative agency whose action was being complained of.

remove the contradictions with the Constitution indicated by the Constitutional Review Chamber. The new version of the Taxation Act stipulated that local taxes would be established by law (and would by implication not be controlled and registered by the Minister of Finance). Although the first draft of the new Act stipulated that the use of cameras would be foreseen for collecting the gambling tax, then, by the second reading, the Finance Committee of the *Riigikogu* decided to leave it out, arguing that the revenues from gambling tax were so small that it would not be worth fighting another constitutional debate for that issue (*Riigikogu* Verbatim Record, 16 December 1993). In addition, the new version of the Act established that tax inspectors can only enter the premises after receiving consent from the owner of the territory or building. Also, the new version stipulated that in any phase of a tax dispute, the taxpayer has a right to turn to the court.

Thus, as a result of the constitutional review disputes, the Taxation Act was significantly changed: it constrained the rights of local governments and taxpayers considerably less than the original version of the Taxation Act would have done.

10.2.2. Amending the Taxation Act in 1996 and 1998

In 1996, an amendment was introduced to the Taxation Act, giving tax administrators the right to determine a fine for alleged tax evasion. It was stipulated that if an individual does not pay the tax due by the set deadline or if they pay a sum that is smaller than the established sum, the tax administrator can stipulate additional tax, which could be up to 50 percent of the unpaid sum. Some members of the opposition considered this amendment to be unconstitutional and argued that it would violate the principle of separation of powers by giving tax inspectors a function that actually belong to the judiciary (*Riigikogu* Verbatim Record, 19 September 1996). The amendment, however, was still introduced. In this case, no constitutional review was initiated by the Legal Chancellor or the President. In 1998, the Centre Party faction, which had been against the provision, abolished this provision on the grounds of unconstitutionality. Liina Tõnisson (Centre Party), who presented the amending Act, argued that such a provision had essentially given the tax administrator the right to determine the tax, which violated the constitutional norms, since the Constitution stipulates that taxes can only be established by laws and according to laws. (*Riigikogu* Verbatim Record, 17 March 1998)

10.2.3. The Timber Case

The Judgement No. 3-4-1-5-98 of the Constitutional Review Chamber (of 17 June 1998), which became known as the "timber case", had important implications for the interpretation of the Taxation Act and for the Estonian tax system as a whole. The case concerned a regulation of the Government of the Republic entitled "Instructions for transactions carried out with timber" (adopted by the Government on 18 December 1992) and it came to the Constitutional Review Chamber through concrete review. The court case was initiated by a firm that had been required by the Tax Board to pay unpaid income tax and interests, because in deducting expenditure from income, the firm had failed to meet some of the requirements of the "Instructions for transactions carried out with timber" (the "Instructions"). The Constitutional Review Chamber (like the Circuit Court that had initiated constitutional review) found that the "Instructions" were unconstitutional, since they had not been issued on the basis of a delegation norm previously provided for by the legislature; thus, it violated Article 87 sub-point 6 of the Constitution (stipulating that the Government shall issue regulations on the basis of and for the implementation of law). The CRC found that the fact that the amended Forest Act adopted in May 1995 included a delegation norm regarding the issue of "Instructions" by the Government, did not make the previously passed "Instructions" valid, and there was no provision in the new wording of the Forest Act to the effect that the former instructions for transactions with timber would remain in force. The CRC stated that a delegation norm has to be *directed to the future*; otherwise, the principle of legal certainty would be violated. As an important corollary, the CRC noted that the Taxation Act establishes that taxpayers are required to pay *only* such state taxes as are prescribed by *law*, at the rates and pursuant to the procedure provided for in tax Acts. The CRC underlined that this provision gives taxpayers the grounds to expect that their liability to pay state taxes proceeds from a tax Act and this liability may be specified on the basis of regulations issued pursuant to a tax Act. As the CRC remarked, the Forest Act is not a tax Act; therefore, a regulation of the Government issued pursuant to the Forest Act can not affect the tax liability of taxpayers. The Court emphasised that the system of legal acts has to be comprehensible to the addressees of law and it should be taken into account that the taxpayer may not be able to find a single norm affecting his or her tax liability outside the limits prescribed by a tax Act.

This decision of the Constitutional Review Chamber can certainly be considered to have important implications for guaranteeing the transparency of the tax system as a whole: it purports that taxpayers can rely on the regulations pointed out by the tax Acts and do not have to search for all other possible acts they might have to conform with when paying taxes. Although this principle had been established by the 1994 Taxation Act itself, it had not been strictly adhered to in practice. The Court's decision turned this provision into a focal point and facilitated the emergence of this requirement as one of the underlying constitutional principles of the tax system in Estonia.

10.2.4. The Interest Rates Case

The biggest constitutional controversy regarding the Taxation Act took place in 2002–2003, following the Judgement No. 3-4-1-8-02 of the Constitutional Review Chamber (of 5 November 2002). It concerned the question of whether establishing the interest rate on tax arrears can be delegated to the executive power (the Minister of Finance) or not. Since this case turned out to be one of the paradigmatic cases in the Estonian constitutional discourse, it is worth looking at the decision, the arguments presented, the parliament's reaction and the legislative constitutional constructions offered, in detail.[300]

The 1994 Taxation Act had delegated the right to establish the interest rates charged on tax arrears to the Minister of Finance, and only with changes made to the Act coming into force 1 July 2002 were the interest rates established in the Taxation Act itself.[301] Constitutional review in this issue was initiated by the Administrative Court (on the basis of a taxation dispute), which argued that since the interests paid on the tax debt are in nature similar to taxes, the interest rate should be stipulated by law (since Article 113 of the Constitution states that "State taxes, duties, fees, fines and compulsory insurance payments shall be provided by law"); otherwise, the principles of legal certainty and separation of powers would be violated.

At the discussion of the case in the Constitutional Review Chamber, the views of the judiciary (and the Legal Chancellor) on the one hand and the executive and the legislature on the other hand clearly clashed. The Legal Chancellor, who had been invited to voice his opinion on the case, argued that although the interest paid on tax arrears cannot be regarded as a tax, it still belongs to the sphere of protection of Article 113, since this article should be interpreted broadly. The legislature and the executive sought to argue for the constitutionality of the delegation provision in the Taxation Act in their statements submitted to the Court. The Finance Committee of the Parliament explained that the delegation of the right to establish interest rates had been motivated by the desire to give the Minister of Finance a simpler possibility to *lower* the interest rates. It pointed out that the Minister of Finance had repeatedly lowered the interest rate and had not abused the power vested in him. The Finance Committee also found that an interest was not a tax but an obligation accessory to a tax, and the conditions for imposing a tax and an interest need not be the same. The Minister of Finance also argued that the imposition of interest had not been *delegated* to the executive power: the obligation to pay interests on tax arrears had been estab-

300 As the Chairman of the Constitutional Committee of the *Riigikogu* noted, "This is not an ordinary constitutional debate, its dimension and meaning is unique for the Estonian public law." (Protocol of the Constitutional Committee of the *Riigikogu*, 17 April 2003)

301 The interest rates on tax arrears had been 0.15 percent per day until the end of 1996, 0.07 percent in 1997, 0.035 percent in 1998, 0.07 percent from the beginning of 1999 to June 2002, and 0.06 percent from July 2002 onwards.

lished by law; it was only the right to establish a rate for interest that had been delegated. Besides, the Minister of Finance pointed out that the financial obligations in public law, referred to in Article 113 of the Constitution, are unilateral (in the sense that the state imposes an obligation and persons have to fulfil it), whereas the contested article did not establish an obligation only to taxable persons but also to the state: the interest was also calculated for the benefit of the taxpayer, when the taxpayer had paid a greater amount of tax than was actually due. Therefore, the Minister of Finance noted, the interest on arrears cannot be regarded as a tax; otherwise, one could come to the conclusion that there are also "taxes" that the state pays to the taxpayer. In a similar vein, the Minister of Justice found that an interest is not a tax, but an accessory obligation to a financial obligation and the obligation to pay interest is reciprocal – whereas in case of a tax the entitled subject should always be either the state or a local government. In addition, the Minister of Justice stated that an interest is not an element of any tax law relationship and it is not a penalty fine but a coercive measure. He also noted that although the regulation was in formal conflict with the Constitution, the provisions in the regulation constituted norms that had been in force for a long time and declaring them invalid because of a mere formal error would prejudice several constitutional values and would bring about new injustice: it would be in conflict with the principle of legal certainty, prejudice the stability of legal order and violate the principle of equal treatment of these persons who had been paying interests without any dispute. The Minister of Justice argued that when weighing different constitutional values – legality, legal certainty, equal treatment – the latter two have to be considered as most important.

Notwithstanding the explanations offered by the legislature and the executive, the Constitutional Review Chamber of the Supreme Court decided that such delegation was unconstitutional and that interest rates on tax arrears should be established by law and not by regulation. The Court argued that although Article 113 of the Constitution does not refer to an interest or a fine for delay, the protected area of the provision is broader and does not include only the financial obligations listed therein but "all financial obligations in public law". The judgement stated that the purpose of Article 113 of the Constitution is to achieve a situation where "all financial obligations in public law" are established solely by the Acts passed by the *Riigikogu* (like it had been outlined in the Judgement No. 3-4-1-10-2000 of the Supreme Court *en banc*, of 22 December 2000).[302] The

302 The case concerned unreturnable participation fees charged from participants of an auction of land, established by a Government regulation. The Supreme Court *en banc* stated in its decision that since such fees are in essence taxes (since they are not used only for covering the costs of a specific auction), these fees should be established by law, as required by Article 113 of the Constitution. According to the Court, the sphere of protection of Article 113 is much wider than the literal interpretation would allow: the listing of state taxes, duties, fees, fines and compulsory insurance payments indicates that this provision attempts to enumerate all financial obligations of public law. Thus, the Court

Court emphasised that interest on a tax as an accessory obligation to tax liability constitutes a financial obligation in public law which, pursuant to Article 113 of the Constitution, should be provided by law.[303] Thus, the CRC decided that a delegation norm authorising the Minister of Finance to establish interest rates on tax arrears and the regulations issued on the basis thereof were in conflict with Article 113 of the Constitution.

This judgement provoked an extensive debate between the political institutions, involving the Court, the *Riigikogu*, the Legal Chancellor, the Tax Board, the Ministry of Finance, the Taxpayers Association, the Chamber of Commerce and tax lawyers. In particular, it was discussed what the budgetary implications of the judgement would be. The costs for the budget could arise from three main sources. First, the Tax Board had to annul the precepts pertaining to charges of interest on tax arrears (accumulated between 1 January 1994 and 1 July 2002) for which there were pending court cases or for which the deadline for dispute had not yet lapsed. The Tax Board assessed the sum of annulled interests to be around 2.5 billion kroons (about 160 million euros) (Reinap 2002b).[304] Second, tax offices could not, in their *further* work, issue precepts that would charge interests on tax arrears accumulated before 1 July 2002. Third, budgetary costs could arise from future court cases where the taxpayers who had already paid the interests on tax arrears would demand them back. According to the Tax Board, the sum of interests that the taxpayers had paid between 1994 and 2002 was 970 million kroons (about 62 million euros) (Reinap 2002b). Different actors had different conceptions of the conditions under which persons would be entitled to demanding back the paid interests. The head of the Supreme Court stated that, in his opinion, the judgement of the CRC would not bring about a large number of cases, claiming back the paid interest, because this had been a formal violation (Reinap 2002a). The Legal Chancellor pointed out in his opin-

---

underlined that "all financial obligations of public law, irrespective of how these are named in different pieces of legislation are within the sphere of protection of Article 113" and this article "is aimed at achieving a situation where all financial obligations of public law are imposed by legislation adopted only by the *Riigikogu* in the form of parliamentary Acts". In other words, the aim of Article 113 is "to allow only the legislator to restrict fundamental rights of person by imposing an obligation to pay state taxes". The Court decided that the Government had, by establishing such a fee, exceeded the delegation norm, since the Land Reform Act had not provided for a participation fee.

303 The Court admitted that under certain conditions it would be possible to establish the minimum and maximum levels of interest on a tax by law and to delegate the right to establish a concrete interest rate to the executive (like had been pointed out in Judgement No. 3-4-1-2-98 of the Constitutional Review Chamber of the Supreme Court (from 23 March 1998), but, in the case at hand, the legislator had left the interest rate in its entirety to be imposed by the executive power.

304 The head of the Tax Board Aivar Sõerd noted, however, that 90 percent of the cases were anyway hopeless, implying that the actual direct costs of the judgement would be lower than the potential costs (Reinap 2002b).

ion to the CRC that this judgement implies that only those taxpayers who had disputed the calculation and demand of interests or in regard of whose complaints a judgement of an administrative court had not yet already entered into force could demand the paid interests back (Reinap 2002c). Some tax lawyers, however, argued that the implication of this judgement was that those taxpayers who had paid the unconstitutionally stipulated interests in 1994–2002 and had contested the tax payment in the court on *some grounds* had a right to claim them back from the state (Reinap 2002c; Mereste 2003). The Tax Board conjectured, however, that those taxpayers who had already paid the interests and who had not disputed the payments had no grounds to claim them back. The worst case scenario (suggested by some members of the parliament) was that *all* taxpayers who had paid interests on tax arrears until July 2002 would have a right to demand the paid interests back.

Against the background of these discussions, the *Riigikogu* introduced a provision in the Taxation Act in December 2002, according to which interest could still be demanded from the tax arrears accumulated before 30 June 2002. The provision stipulated retrospectively the different interest rates that would be charged for different time periods in the past; these rates were the same that had been established by the Minister of Finance with his regulations. Already during the debates on this amendment in the parliament, a majority of the discussions focused on the question of whether such a provision would be constitutional. The Minister of Finance Harri Õunapuu, when presenting the Act in the parliament, explained that the amendment allowing the charging of interest for the tax arrears accumulated before 1 July 2002 was necessary in order to ensure equality before the law. He stated that the obligation to pay interest on arrears had existed since 1989 and the taxpayers had never had the grounds to say that they do not have to pay the interest. He argued that if such a provision were not introduced, it would imply the declaration of tax amnesty. This position was endorsed by the Chairman of the Finance Committee Meelis Atonen, who stated that the Finance Committee also considered this provision necessary for guaranteeing equality and justice: if the interest on arrears were not demanded from those who had not yet paid them, it would mean that those who had paid the interests would be treated unequally. That would mean, in his opinion, that those who had paid the interests already would have the right to demand them back, and this sum would be very large. Olev Raju argued that if one were to interpret the judgement of the Supreme Court literally, it would mean the bankruptcy for the Estonian state, since all the interests on tax arrears that had been paid to the state would have to be paid back. He stated,

> The judgement of the Supreme Court is strange: they say that it is legal to demand the interest but it is established in the wrong act. Thus, we do not change anything retrospectively, we would just take the elements that had been established in the regulation of the Minister of Finance and shift them

> to the Taxation Act; by doing that, we would follow word by word the judgement of the Supreme Court. Yes, it is likely that this will be disputed and taken to the Court. And let us see what the Supreme Court does then. In order to protest these particular provisions in the Taxation Act, the Supreme Court then has to admit that its previous judgement was wrongful. (*Riigikogu* Verbatim Record, 11 December 2002)

Uno Mereste also argued that the Finance Committee had found a good solution to the situation that could otherwise endanger the economy of Estonia. He pointed out that the Article 113 of the Constitution is a comprehensive list and it does not mention interest on arrears; thus, interest rates on arrears can be established with a lower level act. (*Riigikogu* Verbatim Record, 11 December 2002)

There were, however, some MPs who warned against the implications of overriding the Supreme Court's ruling. Kalle Jürgenson noted that the judgement of the Supreme Court "is a phenomenon on its own and has put the parliament and the state on the whole in an embarrassing situation" but he emphasised that by retrospectively establishing the interest rates in the Taxation Act, the parliament would go against the decision of the Supreme Court – this would establish a dangerous precedent and undermine the principle of the balance of powers. He argued that the judgement of the Supreme Court was very unpleasant for the state, but the damage the parliament would do by overriding the decision of the Court would be even greater than the cost of the Court's judgement. Mihkel Pärnoja pointed out that the interest rate that had been charged on the basis of the regulation had meant an annual interest of 21.9 percent, which was clearly higher than the market interest rate; thus, the arrears did have a punitive nature (rather than being just a measure of coercion) and retroactive imposition of a punishment would be problematic. (*Riigikogu* Verbatim Record, 11 December 2002) Notwithstanding these warnings, the Parliament passed the amendment and stipulated the interest rates charged on tax arrears retrospectively.

Immediately, the Taxpayers Association criticised this provision. In their opinion, this amendment made the Supreme Court's decision meaningless and by doing that the *Riigikogu* had abused its powers, since the judgement of the Supreme Court on constitutionality of an act should be finite. Further, the Association considered this provision to be retroactive, hence violating the most basic values of the Constitution (ETA 2002; Protocol of the meeting of the Constitutional Committee of the *Riigikogu*, 17 April 2003). Similar arguments – appealing to the principle of legal certainty and to the principle of separation of powers – were pointed out by the Chamber of Commerce. The Taxpayers Association turned to the President with a request not to promulgate the amended Taxation Act on the grounds of unconstitutionality. The President still promulgated it. In the media, both the *Riigikogu*'s amendment and the resolution of the President to promulgate it had predominantly negative repercussions. The Taxpayers Association viewed the legislative override as a tyranny of the parliament, turning the administration of justice into a "farce" (ETA 2002). The secretary general of the Taxpayers Association stated that for the Estonian constitutional order, the actions of the parliament and the President were equivalent to a "murder" (Mereste 2003). In justifying the decision of the *Riigikogu* in the media, Uno Mereste stated that with the interest rates judgement, the Supreme Court had gone beyond the task of interpreting the Constitution and laws and assumed the legislative task of creating norms; it had created a concept of "obligation accessory to a tax" and used it as if it was a concept that had been established by some law. Mereste emphasised that the Court's arguments about such a principle did not come from the Constitution but from a previous judgement of the Court itself. According to Mereste, by starting to create norms, the Supreme Court had violated the principle of separation of powers. (Mereste 2003)

After the promulgation of the Act, the Taxpayers Association turned to the Legal Chancellor with a plea to initiate constitutional review of the retrospective provisions introduced to the Taxation Act. The Legal Chancellor Allar Jõks initiated a constitutional review procedure and argued in his plea to the *Riigikogu* that the amendment passed by the *Riigikogu* had disregarded the ruling of the Supreme Court. He stated that the provision establishing interest on tax arrears retroactively was unconstitutional: it violated the right to property (Article 32 of the Constitution) and the principle of legal certainty (expressed in Article 10 of the Constitution). He emphasised that the state cannot change the rules of the game retrospectively in a way that is disadvantageous to persons. He admitted that in extreme cases, retrospective provisions are allowed but there have to be very weighty grounds for that; since the Constitution forbids absolutely the imposition of punishments retroactively, it would be hard to find cogent enough arguments for retroactive imposition of interest. In his opinion, securing the finances of the state could certainly not be one such ground. He emphasised that if the contested provision in the Taxation Act remained, it would strongly undermine the principle of the rule of law and send a very negative signal about Estonia. (*Riigikogu* Verbatim Record, 30 April 2003) At the meeting of the Constitutional Committee, the Legal Chancellor noted that the state does not have an obligation to pay back the interest to those who had not disputed it. The sum that the state would lose as a result of not getting the interest on arrears from those who had disputed it would be between 225 and 300 million kroons (i.e., between 14 and 19 million euros) and this would not be enough to justify establishing a retroactive provision. When Siiri Oviir asked how large a sum would then justify demanding the interests, Jõks noted that the Constitution does not set a limit on that, but he would have not made the proposal, had it meant the bankruptcy of the state. Maret Ambur (the head of the legal department of the Tax Board) noted that, based on the State Liability Act, those taxpayers who had already paid the interest and disputed it would have the right to demand the paid interest back and the sum would be around 1 billion kroons (about 64 million euros). (Protocol of the Constitutional Committee of the *Riigikogu*, 17 April 2003)

The debate that took place between the Legal Chancellor and the members of the parliament at the plenary session focused again on the costs of the Court's judgement, in terms of financial costs (this time the sum mentioned was 970 million kroons, about 62 million euros) and also in terms of creating disincentives to pay taxes by treating dishonest taxpayers favourably (see questions and speeches by Männik, Opmann and Kallas). Several MPs contested the argument that the parliament had established the interests retroactively, since in essence they had existed already before (*Riigikogu* Verbatim Record, 30 April 2003). The Finance Committee and the Constitutional Committee as a whole, however, supported the plea of the Legal Chancellor. Siim Kallas (the chairman of the Reform Party faction) argued that the misbehaving taxpayers had created an impression in the public discussion that this was a case where on the one side was the evil state and on the other side the poor taxpayer. He added that the state was correct in demanding interest on tax arrears and thus, the solution to claim this activity invalid is clearly disproportional, inadequate and unfair. Further, he noted that it was the parliament who eventually had to find the money for paying back the arrears and this would have to come at the expense of reducing expenditure on other needs. "Thus, it would perhaps even be reasonable to let the Legal Chancellor go to the Supreme Court and see what comes out of it." (*Riigikogu* Verbatim Record 30 April 2003) Despite many arguments to the contrary, the *Riigikogu* decided to agree with the Legal Chancellor and annulled the amendment made to the Taxation Act.

10.2.5. Discussion

The development of the Taxation Act has, in important aspects, been influenced by the constitutional review by the Legal Chancellor, the President and the Supreme Court. Most of the constitutional debates on the Taxation Act concerned the rights of taxpayers. On the whole, the President, the Legal Chancellor and the Constitutional Review Chamber of the Supreme Court have repeatedly sought to affirm and extend the rights of the taxpayers. As a result of the CRC's judgement in 1993, significant constraints were placed on the means that could be used by tax inspectors in their attempts to detect tax evasion, compared with the authority granted to tax inspectors in the initial act. The "timber case" ruling in 1998 also extended taxpayers' rights by requiring the tax system to be transparent and comprehensible for the taxpayers, in the sense that all the necessary rules pertaining to tax obligations should be outlined only by tax laws (and regulations adopted on the basis of delegation norms in tax laws) and not by other laws. The "interest rates" judgement passed in 2002 further extended the taxpayers' rights by establishing that "all financial obligations in public law" have to be established by law (and cannot be established by regulation). Thus, the institutions of constitutional review in Estonia have repeatedly sought to curtail the powers and discretion of the executive branch in taxation, and emphasised the need to establish important aspects of taxation by law (i.e., by the legislature) and not have them delegated to the executive. These judgements offer corroboration for Conjecture 1 in chapter 8.

All the constitutional review judgements on the organic tax law in Estonia have implied costs for the state budget. As a result of the 1993 judgement, tax inspectors were more constrained in the methods they could use for detecting tax evasion, which in turn might have led to smaller tax revenues than would have been the case with the original provisions in the Taxation Act. The "timber case" judgement implied that the existing regulations that were not issued on the basis of tax acts could not be used for increasing the required tax payments from taxpayers. The ensuing costs were the clearest and most tangible in the case of the "interest rates" judgement. It was also the only case among the three for which the costs were estimated in actual numbers and brought out in the public discussion immediately after the Court's judgement.

The willingness of the CRC to impose significant budgetary costs appears to go against Conjectures 3 and 4, and the hypotheses proposed by Vanberg (2005), Epstein, Knight and Shvetsova (2001) and Hansford and Damore (2000), discussed in chapter 8, which stated that a constitutional court would be unwilling to go against the preferences of the other branches and pass judgements with significant budgetary costs. Rather, the judgements of the CRC offer corroboration for Conjecture 2, which put forth that in transition countries, constitutional courts are willing to impose budgetary costs. Indeed, in the Estonian case, the need to build up public support (by favouring taxpayers) and the aspiration to appear as a neutral arbiter dominated over the considerations of fiscal constraints and over the goal to secure the support of other branches of government. In addition to the considerations pointed out in the theoretical discussion in chapter 8, the "interest rates" case indicates that a strong motivation behind the willingness to impose budgetary costs on the legislature can be the Court's desire to be consistent in its judgements and follow the precedents established by itself. The judgements of the Estonian CRC offer contrary evidence to the proposition of Epstein, Knight and Shvetsova (2001), according to which constitutional courts in CEE countries would be deferential to the parliamentary preferences in judgements that concern institutional prerogatives of the other branches. In the interest rates case, the CRC decided that the legislature cannot delegate its institutional prerogative to establish financial obligations in public law to the executive, even if the legislature itself wanted that.

With regard to the legislature's reactions to these "costly" judgements, the three cases point to diverging evidence. In the case of the first constitutional dispute on the organic tax law between the parliament and the Constitutional Court, in 1993, the parliament was pragmatic: despite possible financial implications of the CRC's judgement, the legislators were willing to go ahead with the changes considered necessary by the CRC without longer discussions, because of the need to have the amended Taxation Act passed as fast as possible. The debates in the *Riigikogu* hinted at a kind of a "cost-benefit" analysis of following the ruling of the court, which indicated that the benefits of parliamentary override (more gambling tax revenues) would not be outweighed by the costs of another court dispute. It is noteworthy that, for most part, the parliamentary discussion here did not even focus on the potential costs of the court judgement; the desire to secure public support of the taxpayers was more prevalent, thus offering corroboration for Conjecture 6 (see chapter 8), suggesting that, in the context of transition, the legislatures would be deferential to the court's decisions in cases that favour taxpayers' rights.

In the "interest rates" case, however, the costs of the Court's judgement became the main focus of the parliamentary reaction and the potential budgetary implications emerged as the main argument to justify the override of the Court's ruling. What makes the interest rates case interesting in the light of the hypotheses put forth by Vanberg (2005) is that despite the environment of high transparency – there were organised interest groups monitoring the process (the Taxpayers Association, for example) and the content of the court's decision was not so technical – the parliament still took the risk and chose to go against the court's decision. Taking this risk was especially noteworthy given that the judgement was passed just some months before general elections. On the other hand, one should take into account that this decision was taken on the very day the parliament adopted the state budget for year 2003 and this was the first budget of the independent period that was with a planned (prospective) deficit.[305] This indicates that, in some cases, the possible public backlash for ignoring the court's decision can be outweighed by budgetary considerations and these considerations can be especially weighty when the legislature is faced with a budget deficit. In addition, the Estonian legislators hoped that they could persuade the public with independent constitutional constructions, appealing to the unfairness of the Court's decision for honest taxpayers. The override decision by the *Riigikogu* thus offers corroboration for Conjecture 5 (which is a competing conjecture for Conjecture 6) and is line with the Vanberg's (2005) hypothesis that a legislature is likely to evade the constitutional court's judgement, if the judgement would bring about significant budgetary costs. The willingness of the legislature to *annul* the retroactive interest rates only some months after the override, however, goes against Conjecture 5.

These dynamics illustrate well the competing pressures that legislatures are subject to when having to decide on deferral or override. It appears, however, that the final decision of the parliament to reverse the override had more to do with the symbolic meaning of the override itself (seen as a dangerous precedent that could send a signal about the legal order and legal certainty in Estonia) than with the concern for taxpayers' rights (or the popularity of the Court's decision). The Legal Chancellor and the involved interest groups viewed the override as a

305 See section 7.1. for a more detailed discussion on that issue.

paradigmatic case, violating the rule of law and the balance of powers, and they managed to make these arguments dominant in the constitutional discourse that ensued the override. The balancing role of the Legal Chancellor played an important "cooling down" effect here, allowing additional consideration of whether going against the Court's decision and possibly violating the rule of law would be worthwhile and whether this would be justified by the financial costs that could be saved by overriding the Court's decision. Thus, further models of interactions between the legislature and the constitutional court should take note of such additional veto points in the constitutional system that could have dampening effects on the determination of the legislature to evade the court's decision. In Vanberg's terminology, such specific institutions entrusted with constitutional review can significantly increase the transparency – both of the court's decision and of the legislative override.

An implication of the constitutional discourse that emerged after the override in 2002–2003 and led to the annulment of the override is that it certainly makes it more difficult for the parliament to override the Court's ruling in the future because of the established "precedent" (by the parliament itself) that the parliament has to defer to the court if the constitutional order is to be protected, even if it brings about significant budgetary costs. This, in turn, can make the Constitutional Court more willing to impose costs on the parliament in the future. Thus, although Vanberg (2005) presents the models regarding the interaction between the court and the legislature as equilibria, it might be more fruitful – especially in a transitional context – to take a more evolutionary viewpoint and account for possibilities of path-dependencies that paradigmatic constitutional disputes can create.

Another aspect worth discussion in the interest rates case is the question of whether the CRC could foresee that the *Riigikogu* would – as a first reaction – choose to override the Court's decision. An important element in the models of Vanberg (2005), Hansford and Damore (2000), and Epstein, Knight and Shvetsova (2001) is a proposition that in issue areas where the court anticipates evasion by the legislature, it is likely to uphold the statute. In the Estonian case, although the CRC could foresee that its decision would bring about budgetary costs and a clear monetary value could be attached to this decision, it did not anticipate the evasive reaction by the parliament; the *Riigikogu* had deferred to the Supreme Court in all previous cases until that point, even in cases that had brought about significant budgetary costs. Thus, the interactions between the constitutional court and the legislature should be viewed in a dynamic perspective, taking into account that mutual anticipations of the institutions come about as a result of an evolutionary process. While in the German case discussed by Vanberg (2005), the anticipations of the institutions concerning each other's reactions are likely to be solid, institutional actors in transitional contexts have to act on less certain assumptions. Also, as the Estonian case indicated, the constitutional court's need (as a relatively new institution) to build up the public support can be stronger than the need to build up the support of other political institutions.

As for the willingness of the President and the Legal Chancellor to pass constitutional review decisions that would be costly for the parliament, both the President's 1993 decision and the Legal Chancellor's 2003 decision indicated that they were apt to go ahead with "costly" decisions. On the other hand, the fact that the President promulgated the 2002 amendments establishing the interest rates on tax arrears retroactively and that neither the President nor the Legal Chancellor started constitutional review in 1996, can be interpreted as signs of sensitivity to cost considerations.

While constitutional issues have played an important role in the development of the Taxation Act (the organic tax law) in Estonia, the comparison with the constitutional debates on the organic budget law indicates that the legislature has been in a more passive role in the constitutional debates on the organic tax law than in the debates on the organic budget law. For most part, constitutional debates on the organic tax law in the parliament took place as a result of the constitutional review decisions of the CRC, and the constitutional arguments presented took the form of a reaction to the court decisions rather than being initiated by the members of the parliament themselves.

Although the parliament did not play an extensive role in *initiating* the constitutional debates on the organic tax law, once it was compelled into constitutional deliberations by the constitutional review decisions of the other institutions, the parliament sought to offer independent constitutional constructions of the disputed norms. In particular, the arguments presented at the dispute of the interest rates case in the Constitutional Review Chamber and in the subsequent parliamentary debates point to very clear examples of constitutional constructions (in the sense conceived by Whittington 1999), which differ from traditional legal constitutional interpretations. Constructions offered with regard to whether interests on tax arrears can be seen as equivalent to tax (and therefore subject to the same legal regulation) were creative, emphasising that the constitutional provision pertaining to taxes and other financial obligations covers only *unilateral* financial obligations, while the interest charged on arrears is a *bilateral* obligation, making it substantively different. As the Minister of Finance put it, "If interest is a tax, then there are also taxes that the state pays to the taxpayer." The Finance Committee of the *Riigikogu* also offered pragmatic and functional arguments, referring to the reason behind delegating the establishment of interest rates on tax arrears to the executive, and pointing to the fact the Minister had not abused its power in stipulating these rates. Also, arguments presented at the parliamentary debates on establishing the interest rates retroactively offer good illustrations of constitutional constructions: the constructions sought to employ symbolic appeals by playing two groups of taxpayers (the cheating and the honest) against each other and emphasising the need not to demotivate the honest taxpayers. These constructions were strongly rhetorical, metaphorical and symbolic, with a strong emphasis on consequentialist arguments and managed to shape the discursive space for political action – making it appear legitimate, at least for some time, to establish interest rates on tax arrears retroactively.

10.3. The Impacts of the Constitution on Tax Acts

While the previous section focused on the effects of the 1992 Constitution on the development of organic tax law in Estonia, the subsequent sections would analyse the role of the Constitution in shaping the three main tax laws – the Income Tax Act, Social Tax Act and Value Added Tax Act.

10.3.1. The Constitution and the Income Tax Act

The Personal Income Tax Act came into force on 1 January 1991, and the Corporate Income Tax Act on 1 January 1992.[306] The main controversies at the discussions of the 1991 and 1992 Acts concerned the general ideology of the tax system, how progressive it should be and what the tax bases and rates should be. The Vice Minister of Finance Enn Roose, who is considered to be "the father" of the tax system of pre-independent Estonia (1989–1991), noted, when presenting the draft Income Tax Act (which was eight pages long) in the Supreme Council in summer 1990, that the main principles that had been followed when putting together the draft act were the following: all sources of income have to be taxed, the number of exemptions should be kept at minimum, the number of different tax rates has to be small, the tax burden has to be internationally competitive, so that foreign capital would come to Estonia, and the revenues from personal income tax would go to local governments (Verbatim Record of the Supreme Council, 22 August 1990, p. 92). When asked why the tax rates were foreseen to be so high, Roose answered that in calculating the rates, the Government had proceeded from the level of expenditures needed. He also added that in choosing the brackets and the rates he had copied them from the U.S. tax system. (p. 111).

The discussions of the tax laws of the pre-independent period could not have been expected to be influenced by the existing Soviet Constitution, but broadly speaking, of course, these debates were of fiscal constitutional nature, outlining the basic features of the income tax system. At the same time, however, none of these general principles, which could be seen as a basis for a fiscal constitution, were included in the actual Constitution of 1992.

In December 1993, the *Riigikogu* adopted a unified Income Tax Act that regulated the income taxation of both persons and corporations, and the Act came into force on 1 January 1994. The Personal Income Tax Act of 1991 had

306 Although the Corporate Income Tax Act was enacted in 1992, the tax had already been collected since January 1991, according to the regulation adopted by the Government.

established a progressive schedule, with rates ranging from 16 to 33 percent, but the 1994 Income Tax Act replaced it with a flat rate of 26 percent. With the 1994 Income Tax Act, the corporate income tax rate was lowered from 35 percent to 26 percent. At the same time, the 1994 Act broadened the tax base by abolishing a number of existing tax exemptions (Kuldkepp 2005, p. 5).

Although one could have expected constitutional debates during the proceedings of the 1994 Income Tax Act, given the visibility and importance of the Act for both legislators and their constituents, no constitutional issues were raised. The debates concentrated on the size of the income tax free minimum, whether the income tax should be progressive or proportional, whether the same tax rates should apply for corporate and personal income tax, what the tax rates should be, how large sums of charitable donations could be deducted and what kind of incomes would be exempted (e.g., scholarships, pensions, lotteries) (*Riigikogu* Verbatim Record, 10 November 1993; 8 December 1993), but none of these issues were framed in terms of constitutional controversies. It is also noteworthy that the introduction of the most noteworthy features of the Estonian tax system – the flat rate income tax – was not viewed through constitutional prism; that is, no arguments were presented offered in constitutional terms, like by appealing to the "equality of treatment of taxpayers".[307]

Over the subsequent years, the Income Tax Act was changed about 55 times and there were even more attempts to introduce changes that were eventually not adopted. The most important changes to the Income Tax Act since 1994 have been the exemption of undistributed profits from corporate income tax and the lowering of the income tax rates gradually to 21 percent between 2005 and 2008. The main debates over the acts concerning income tax in the *Riigikogu* focused on introducing further deductibles, exempting some types of incomes from income tax and offering other tax advantages. Some issues of constitutionality were indeed raised in the debates over the Income Tax Act.

307 Estonia was essentially the first country in the world to introduce a flat tax; this set off the wave of adopting such tax in the rest of CEE (Baturo and Gray 2007).

Table 10.4.: Constitution and income tax in Estonia, 1992–2007

	Number of acts concerning income tax adopted	Number of acts concerning income tax rejected	Number of constitutional issues discussed in the *Riigikogu*	Number of cases concerning income tax in the CRC
7th *Riigikogu* (1992–1995)	5	12	2	1
8th *Riigikogu* (1995–1999)	27	35	4	1
9th *Riigikogu* (1999–2003)	10	19	4	1
10th *Riigikogu* (2003–2007)	13	36	1	-
11th *Riigikogu* (2007–…)	1	4	-	-

Source: Author's calculations

On the whole, however, as can be seen from Table 10.4., the number of constitutional issues raised was small, in relation to the number of acts concerning the Income Tax Act discussed in the parliament. For example, during the tenth *Riigikogu*, despite the fact that 36 draft acts proposing changes to the Income Tax Act were rejected and 13 were adopted, the Constitution was mentioned only once in the proceedings of proposed amendments to the Income Tax Act. Also, another paradigmatic change to the Estonian tax system – the exemption of retained profits from corporate income tax in 2000 – was not viewed through constitutional prism and did not invite any constitutional debates. In the following, an overview of the constitutional issues raised in the parliamentary debates and CRC's decisions concerning the Income Tax Act is given.

10.3.1.1. Equality of Treatment of Taxpayers

On a number of occasions, the principle of equal treatment of taxpayers arose at the debates on the Income Tax Act. During the debates on amending the Income Tax Act in spring 1995, one of the amendment proposals suggested to exempt the producers of farm products from paying income tax. Valve Kirsipuu, the Chairman of the Finance Committee argued, however, that this would violate the principle of equality stipulated by the Constitution. To this, Vambo Kaal argued that such an amendment would actually restore equal treatment. (*Riigikogu* Verbatim Record, 4 May 1995) Special provisions for producers of farm products were, however, not introduced.

At a reading of the amending act of the Income Tax Act in November 1995, some members of the opposition argued that unequal treatment of self-employed entrepreneurs and corporate enterprises (foreseen by the amendment proposals) would violate the constitutional norm of equal treatment (*Riigikogu* Verbatim

Record, 22 November 1995). Nevertheless, this did not suffice as a basis for rejecting these proposals.

The question of equal treatment of taxpayers also came up during the discussions on the Income Tax Act in the ninth *Riigikogu*. The 2000 Act included a provision according to which pensions that are larger than four times the income tax free minimum (implying primarily the special pensions of the members of the parliament and higher officials) would be taxed on the amount that exceed the limit. At the debates on this provision, Toomas Varek (Centre Party) asked whether a differential treatment of pensions would not violate the provision in the Constitution according to which all citizens are treated equally. The Minister of Finance Siim Kallas answered that the Constitution does not forbid such a provision. (*Riigikogu* Verbatim Record, 10 November 1999) Jürgen Ligi, the Chairman of the Finance Committee, pointed out that taxing the special pensions might go against the principle of lawful expectations of those who have the right to receive the special pension. Toivo Tootsen (Centre Party) pointed out that in most other countries, the special pensions of the president and other higher officials are not taxed. Kallas answered, however, that taxing these large pensions would be just. (*Riigikogu* Verbatim Record, 24 November 1999) In the end, the Income Tax Act included the provision for taxing higher pensions.

Another provision contested on the grounds of constitutionality was the requirement according to which taxpayers need to open a bank account. Jaanus Männik considered it unconstitutional, but the Chairman of the Finance Committee Jürgen Ligi answered that it was safer to keep money in a bank account than in a drawer. (*Riigikogu* Verbatim Record, 24 November 1999)

During the discussions on the Income Tax Act in October 2001, Georg Pelisaar pointed out that not taxing the interests received from banks but taxing the interests from mutual loan associations violated the principle of equal treatment stipulated by the Constitution. The Minister of Finance agreed that both should be taxed and such a provision was stipulated. (*Riigikogu* Verbatim Record, 24 October 2001)

10.3.1.2. Central Government versus Local Governments

Given that an important proportion of the local government revenues comes from income tax, fiscal relations between the central government and local government came up on several occasions during debates on the Income Tax Act. In particular, Article 154 (stating that "Expenditure related to duties of the state imposed by law on a local government shall be funded from the state budget") and Article 157 (stating that "A local government shall have an independent budget for which the bases and procedure for drafting shall be provided by law") were repeatedly mentioned in the legislative debates on the formula according to which the revenues from income tax are divided between the different levels of government. (See, e.g., *Riigikogu* Verbatim Record, 11 December 2003, 12 December 2003)

There was also a case in Constitutional Review Chamber pertaining to implementation of the Income Tax Act that concerned the revenues of local governments. The case concerned the authority of the Minister of Finance to establish the implementing regulation of the Income Tax Act, and the constitutional review was initiated by the Legal Chancellor.[308] The 1993 Income Tax Act stipulated that the Minister of Finance were to formulate the implementing regulation of the Act. The regulation approved by the Minister of Finance stipulated that 48 percent of the income tax revenue would be transferred into state budget and 52 percent to the budgets of local governments.[309] The Constitutional Review Chamber pointed out in its Judgement No. III-4/A-9/94 (of 7 December 1994) that a provision for such a division of income tax revenues between budgets of the state and local governments had no legal ground. There was no delegation norm in the Income Tax Act or other laws commissioning the Minister to decide on the division of the revenues between state and local governments. As a result of the Court's ruling, the division of the income tax revenues was established in the Income Tax Act itself.

10.3.1.3. Lacking Calculations

On several occasions during the debates on the Income Tax Act in the parliament, the opponents of the proposed changes pointed out that the initiators of the draft act had not followed Article 116 of the Constitution which requires that "If a proposed amendment to the state budget or to its draft has the effect of decreasing estimated revenue, or increasing expenditure or reallocating expenditure, the proponent of the amendment shall append financial calculations to the proposed amendment which demonstrate the sources of revenue necessary to cover the expenditure."

During the debates on amending the Corporate Income Tax Act in December 1992, the Government proposed to make the taxable base narrower (by allowing larger deductions of expenditures made to capital assets and donations to charity). Arvo Junti pointed to Article 116 of the Constitution and asked why such calculations had not been presented by the Minister of Finance together with the draft act. The Minister of Finance Madis Üürike answered that the Constitution requires such calculations only in the case of amending the budget, but the Corporate Income Tax was not a budget. (*Riigikogu* Verbatim Record, 28

308 The Legal Chancellor had turned to the Minister of Finance in April 1994 and pointed to contradictions between the regulation and the Constitution, but the Minister satisfied the proposal of the Legal Chancellor only in part.

309 According to the Individual Income Tax Act (which was effective until 31 December 1993), the revenues from personal income tax had been exclusively paid into the budgets of local governments.

December 1992) In a similar vein, when discussing an amending act of the Income Tax Act in 1995, Andres Lipstok argued that although the Act would imply reduced revenues for the state budget, the initiators of the draft had not indicated how to deal with this shortfall, required by the Constitution. Jaanus Männik, however, argued that this constitutional provision pertained to discussions over the budget but not over other draft acts. (*Riigikogu* Verbatim Record, 4 May 1995)

10.3.1.4. The "Personal Automobiles" Case

The Judgement No. 3-4-1-5-2000 of the Constitutional Review Chamber (of 12 May 2000) – the "personal automobiles" case – played a further role, alongside with the "timber" case (discussed in section 10.2.3.), in offering constitutional interpretations about how the system of rules governing the tax system should be structured, what the obligations of the different political institutions are and what the implications of the shortcomings in the formal framework of tax laws and regulations should be for taxpayers. The judgement of the CRC concerned Regulation No. 161 of the Government, entitled "Reimbursement of expenses for the use of personal automobiles for business travel" (dated 27 May 1993). The goal of the Regulation was to establish the procedure that would govern the payment of such reimbursements and fix the sum, in the excess of what the reimbursements would constitute fringe benefits and be therefore subject to taxation. The CRC found that the Regulation No. 161 was unconstitutional because this regulation had been issued under the under the 1991 Personal Income Tax Act, which had lost effect when the 1994 Income Tax Act was enacted.[310] Although the Regulation was unconstitutional, the CRC emphasised the principle that "If the regulation was to grant benefits to taxpayers, it should be applied, in the interests of the protection of trust of taxpayers". Further, the CRC stated that "In regard to taxation it is in principle impossible to accept a regulation of the executive power, which imposes financial burdens on a taxpayer, which has not been issued within the scope of the provision delegating authority to issue regulations." Thus, the CRC concluded that in order to enforce the 1993 Income Tax Act, the Government had to establish the limit of reimbursement so that income tax could be imposed on the sums exceeding that limit and as there was no such regulation, there were no legal grounds to impose income tax on payments of reimbursement for the expenses related to the use of a personal automobile for business travel.

---

310 The CRC underlined that although the new Income Tax Act provided for a delegation norm, according to which the Minister of Finance (and with the 1995 amendments, the Government) was authorised to establish the procedure for the reimbursements and the tax exempted sum, the Minister of Finance and the Government had not fulfilled the obligation imposed by law since no such regulations were adopted and the Regulation No. 161 was continued to be applied.

By the time of the Court's judgement (May 2000), the Government had already declared its regulation No. 161 invalid (in March 2000). The CRC noted that its judgement had *ex nunc* effect in time, and that this judgement gave "no ground to get refund of the income tax paid on fringe benefits to those taxpayers who had not disputed the tax or in respect of whose complaints a decision of an administrative court has become effective". By stating that, the CRC helped to guarantee that the decision would not bring about extensive budgetary costs for the state, in the form of having to pay back the income taxes that had been charged on the basis of invalid regulation. Only those who had pending court disputes concerning the payment of income tax on these particular reimbursements had, in principle, the right to demand the tax payments back. The decision, however, clearly advanced taxpayers' rights: they could expect to benefit from invalid regulations and they had a right to expect that the regulations they have to follow when paying taxes are issued on the basis of the law that is valid at the time of paying the taxes.

As the overview presented above indicates, constitutional review and constitutional debates did not play a *major* role in the development of the Income Tax Act itself. The three judgements of the CRC concerning income tax (the timber case, the local governments' case and the personal automobiles' case) pertained to the *implementation* of the Act rather than to the *substance* of the Act itself. They did, however, have implications for the taxpayers' rights and established that the rules making up the tax system have to be clear, comprehensible and adhere to the principles of legal certainty. None of the judgements provoked constitutional controversies between the different political institutions (comparable to debates on the organic tax law) and the legislature and the Government followed the Court's decisions (or corrected the mistakes already before the Court decision). The parliament did not contest any of these Court's decisions and no arguments concerning budgetary implications were raised. The constitutional arguments put forth in the legislative debates did not play a decisive role in getting the proposed provisions adopted or rejected.

10.3.2. The Constitution and the Social Tax Act

The Social Tax Act, adopted in 1990 and enacted in 1991, introduced a payroll tax of 33 percent of gross wage, from which 20 percent was earmarked for social insurance and 13 percent for health insurance. The social tax rate was established according to the existing expenditures for pensions and health care. In the subsequent years, the formal rates of the social tax were not changed. The pension reform adopted in 2002, however, implied *de facto* lowering of the social tax since for those who have joined the second pillar, 4 percentage points of the social tax is transferred to private retirement accounts (see Raudla and Staehr 2003).

Table 10.5.: Constitution and social tax in Estonia, 1992–2007

	Number of acts concerning social tax adopted	Number of acts concerning social tax rejected	Number of constitutional issues concerning social tax discussed in the *Riigikogu*	Number of cases concerning social tax in the CRC
7th *Riigikogu* (1992–1995)	4	1	1	-
8th *Riigikogu* (1995–1999)	7	3	-	1
9th *Riigikogu* (1999–2003)	10	3	-	2
10th *Riigikogu* (2003–2007)	6	8	-	-
11th *Riigikogu* (2007–...)	-	-	-	-

Source: Author's calculations

The issue of constitutionality was raised only once during the debates of the Social Tax Act in the *Riigikogu*. At the second reading of the Social Tax Act in June 1993, Valve Kirsipuu, the Chairman of the Budget and Tax Committee, noted that the Constitution requires that all taxes, fees and so forth have to be reflected in the state budget, while the Social Tax Act foresaw that the revenues would go to the Social Tax Fund, which was a separate fund from the state budget. She stated that in discussing this issue, those who proceeded from the Constitution, had one opinion, while the Ministry of Social Affairs had another opinion, and it was a question that needed further discussion. (*Riigikogu* Verbatim Record, 22 June 1993) Social tax revenues were included in the state budget starting from year 2000.

There were, however, three cases in the Constitutional Review Chamber that concerned the social tax. In all three cases, the disputes did not concern the substance of the Social Tax Act and its constitutional interpretation but focused on formal problems of lacking or inappropriate delegation norms.

10.3.2.1. The Sub-Delegation Case

The Judgement No. 3-4-1-8-98 of the Constitutional Review Chamber (of 23 November 1998) concerned the instructions for the implementation of the Social Tax Act, approved by the Minister of Finance in 1993. The lower court initiated constitutional review since it found that the instructions were not issued under a delegation norm proceeding from law; consequently, the instructions were in conflict with the Constitution. The Constitutional Review Chamber found that the regulation was unconstitutional because there was no delegation norm according to which the instructions could be issued by the Minister of Finance. The Social Tax Act established that the procedure for the implementation of the Act would be established by the Government without giving the right to delegate it further. The CRC argued that in issuing the instructions, the Minister of Finance had exceeded his competence and this was in conflict with Article 94 Section 2 of the Constitution, according to which a minister shall issue regulations *on the basis of* and for the implementation of law.

10.3.2.2. The Personal Automobiles Cases

The second judgement of the CRC concerning the social tax, Judgement No. 3-4-1-5-2000 (from 12 May 2000), also pertained to a delegation norm: in this case, the Government had exceeded the delegation norm and imposed restrictions that the delegation norm in the law had not foreseen. The review was initiated by a lower court and concerned the Government regulation No. 161 of 27 May 1993 entitled "Reimbursement of expenses for the use of personal automobiles for business travel".[311] The CRC argued that the 1990 Social Tax Act that contained the delegation norm for the regulation in question, only referred to "personal" automobiles of employees; therefore, it was irrelevant whether the user of a vehicle was the owner thereof or a possessor on the basis of a contract or an authorisation document.[312] The case arose from a tax dispute where an employer had paid compensation to employees who had used personal automobiles for official trips but where the employees had not been the *owners* of the cars; thus, according to the regulation (which added the criterion of "ownership"), these compensations were subject taxation. The CRC underlined that the authorisation to establish the procedure for the implementation of the Act did not include the right to establish conditions or grounds *in addition* to those specified by law. Since the Social Tax Act did not refer to a vehicle "in the ownership of an employee", but to "a personal vehicle", the Government had – by stipulating the requirement of "ownership" of the car – exceeded the limits of the provision of the Social Tax Act delegating authority to issue a regulation. The CRC found that the Government had violated Section 6 of Article 87 of the Constitution, according to which the Government of the Republic shall issue regulations and orders on the basis of and for the implementation of law. The CRC also noted that although the 1990 Social Tax Act had been replaced by a new Social Tax Act adopted in 1998, no new regulation concerning the imposition of social tax on reimbursements had been adopted.

---

311 The same judgement was discussed in the section 10.3.1.4. as well – but only to the extent that it pertained to the Income Tax Act.

312 The Regulation constituted, in principle, a valid basis for imposing social tax on the reimbursements since the law on the basis of which it had been adopted was still in force in 1996 and 1997.

The CRC Judgement No. 3-4-1-3-01 (of 22 February 2001) also concerned the regulation "Reimbursement of expenses for the use of personal automobiles for business travel". Based on a tax dispute, the lower level court started the constitutional review procedure, arguing that the regulation in question was not based on an existing and valid delegation norm. The new Social Tax Act that came into force on 1 January 1999 stipulated that the rules for reimbursement of expenses for the use of personal automobiles for business travel would be subject to social tax according to the rates and procedure stipulated by the Government.

The Government had to stipulate an upper limit above which the reimbursement for using a personal vehicle would be taxed. The Government did not pass such a regulation in 1999 and the upper limits stipulated by the regulation of 1993 (based on the 1990 Social Tax Act that had become invalid as of 1 January 1999) were used by tax offices.[313] The Constitutional Court found that the application of the regulation, the delegation norm of which had become invalid, was unconstitutional: it was in conflict with Section 6 of Article 87 of the Constitution. The Chamber pointed out that the validity of the Regulation of 1993 would enable the Government of the Republic to ignore the changes brought about by the new Act. In addition, the CRC underlined that the validity of the regulation of 1993 after the invalidation of the Act containing pertinent delegation norm was in conflict with the principle of legal certainty.[314] Further, the CRC stated,

> The fact that the regulation of 1993 was unconstitutional or that the necessary regulation was not issued can not give rise to the conclusion that full amount of every compensation paid for the use of a personal automobile during the period when the regulation of 1993 was declared unconstitutional or when there was no pertinent regulation should be subjected to taxation with social tax. Such a conclusion would be in conflict with the principle of legal certainty. Upon imposition of social tax one has to recognise the right of a taxpayer, upon paying social tax, to proceed from the limit of 500 kroons per month, established by the invalid regulation of 1993.

Here, again, the CRC sought to interpret the implication of its decision favourably for the taxpayers.

Like in the case of the income tax, the Constitution has not played a significant role in the development of the substance Social Tax Act itself but has

313 A new regulation on the reimbursement of expenses for the use of personal automobiles for business travel (which established the new procedure and re-established the same limits and declared the regulation of 1993 invalid) had been adopted in 2000 but it was issued under Income Tax Act, and not under the 1998 Social Tax Act.

314 The same principle – stating that application of a regulation issued prior to a pertinent delegation norm violates legal certainty – had already been explained in a previous ruling of the CRC, in Judgement No. 3-4-1-5-98 (of 17 June 1998).

steered the development of the system of implementation of tax laws towards greater legal certainty and transparency. In addition, the CRC sought to protect the taxpayers from excessive inference from the executive and to restore the will of the legislature in implementing the social tax legislation.

10.3.3. The Constitution and the Value Added Tax Act

The Value Added Tax Act, adopted in 1991 and enacted in 1992, established a tax rate of 10 percent, which was increased to 18 percent in 1993.[315] In preparing the Act, the VAT directives of the European Communities were taken as a basis (see presentation by Enn Roose, Minister of Finance, Verbatim Record of the Supreme Council, 9–12 September 1991, pp. 168–169). On the whole, the value added tax system in Estonia can be characterised as having a broad tax base and only few exemptions (Purju 2004, p. 168). Compared with most EU countries, significantly fewer types of goods qualify for a lower rate. Over the course of the time, the main changes made to the VAT Act concerned the list of goods and services that would be exempted from VAT or taxed at a lower rate than the standard 18 percent.

For most part, constitutional issues played only a minor role in the debates on the VAT Act. As can be seen from Table 10.6., during the debates on VAT Act in the seventh *Riigikogu*, the Constitution was not mentioned at all. In the eighth and ninth *Riigikogu*, the Constitution was mentioned only once or twice and it took the form of a rhetorical statement (i.e., the reference to the Constitution was used as an additional rhetorical tool when arguing for or against a particular provision in the act) rather than a full-fledged constitutional deliberation. In 2007, however, the VAT Act became subject to more extensive constitutional debates.

315 From 1 January to 31 December 1991, the collection of value added tax took place according to a Government regulation.

Table 10.6.: Constitution and value added tax in Estonia, 1992–2007

	Number of laws on Value Added Tax Act adopted	Number of laws on Value Added Tax Act rejected	Number of constitutional issues discussed in the *Riigikogu*	Number of cases pertaining to value added tax in the CRC
7th *Riigikogu* (1992–1995)	6	4	-	-
8th *Riigikogu* (1995–1999)	19	15	1	-
9th *Riigikogu* (1999–2003)	14	14	2	2
10th *Riigikogu* (2003–2007)	7	8	1	-
11th *Riigikogu* (2007– …)	0	3	1	1

Source: Author's calculations

10.3.3.1. Rhetorical Arguments

When discussing the changes made to the Value Added Tax Act in 1996, Mihkel Pärnoja pointed to Article 116 of the Constitution and asked whether calculations have been made with regard to how the proposed changes to the VAT Act would decrease the budget revenues. The Chairman of the Finance Committee Jürgen Ligi noted that although no exact calculations had been made, the implications of the changes for the budget would be very small compared to some previous changes made to the VAT Act. (*Riigikogu* Verbatim Record, 15 October 1996) In October 1999, it was proposed to tax water and canalisation services provided to households and to the non-profit sector with a lower VAT (5 percent instead of 18 percent). The Chairman of the Finance Committee Jürgen Ligi criticised this proposal and noted that it was not expedient to confuse the voters just before upcoming local government elections with tax policy proposals, since the ordinary voters might have difficulties comprehending them. When criticised for using the term "ordinary voters" he added, "Tax policy is not an issue area that is grasped by the majority of the population; therefore, also the Constitution says that tax issues should not be put on referendum, since it might lead to an unreasonable result." He emphasised that the nuances of tax policy are not understandable to people without specific professional preparation. (*Riigikogu* Verbatim Record, 19 October 1999) In November 2000, the Centre Party Faction proposed to exempt heating provided to households from VAT. In justifying that proposal, Raju argued that it was motivated by the constitutional obligation of the state to provide help in the case of need (Article 28) and that in a situation of increasing heating prices, this would provide relief for poorer parts of the society. (*Riigikogu* Verbatim Record, 15 November 2000). The proposal was, however, not passed by the parliament.

10.3.3.2. The 50 000 Kroons Judgements

The two judgements passed by CRC on VAT Act in 2002 – Judgement No. 3-4-1-1-02 (of 6 March 2002) and Judgement No. 3-4-1-6-02 (of 12 June 2002) – were of relatively minor importance and did not give rise to considerable constitutional debates. Both cases concerned the question of whether the deduction of VAT should depend on whether the transaction was made in cash or not. An amendment to the VAT Act (passed on 17 November 1999 and enacted on 1 January 2000) stipulated that if the taxable value of goods or services purchased for money in Estonia exceeds 50 000 kroons (ca 3200 euros) per transaction, deduction was permitted in the case the payment for the goods or services had been carried out in full through a credit institution either by a bank transfer or a cash payment had been made to the bank account of the seller. The CRC found in both cases that such interference with the freedom to engage in enterprise was not a proportionate measure for the prevention of tax fraud.

10.3.3.3. Value Added Tax and Cultural Events

Only in the tenth and eleventh *Riigikogu* did the Value Added Tax Act become subject to extensive constitutional debates, involving the Legal Chancellor and the Constitutional Review Chamber. The most significant constitutional debate concerning the VAT concerned the issue of the VAT rates applying to cultural events. The main controversy focused on the question of whether cultural events should be taxed with a lower VAT rate (than the usual rate of 18 percent) and to what kind of cultural events the lower rate would apply.

According to the Value Added Tax Act adopted on 10 December 2003 and enacted on 1 May 2004, a reduced rate of value added tax (5 percent) was to be applied to "organisation of performances or concerts by a state, municipal or private performing arts institution or the national opera on the condition that the funds received by the organiser of the performance or concert from the state, rural municipality or city budget or the Cultural Endowment of Estonia amount to at least 10 percent of its budget revenue for the calendar year".[316] In October 2005, the Legal Chancellor sent a memorandum to the *Riigikogu*, pointing out that this provision allowed unequal treatment and was therefore unconstitutional. During the discussions following the memorandum, the Finance Committee and the Cultural Affairs Committee of the *Riigikogu* did not manage to agree on how to bring the contested provision of the VAT Act into conformity with the Con-

316 Similar provision existed also in the 2002 VAT Act.

stitution. In April 2006, the Finance Committee proposed to the Ministry of Finance to analyse the created legal situation and to find a solution for this conflict. The Ministry of Finance supported the abolition of this particular tax incentive altogether but did not introduce a relevant draft Act. Since 2005, there were three draft Acts in the legislative proceedings of the Finance Committee of the *Riigikogu* that were aimed at substantial extension of the value added tax incentive on cultural services, but the Committee decided not to support these draft Acts. The Finance Committee argued that the extension of the tax incentive to the events of mass and commercial culture would bring about a disproportional, unjustified and undesired pressure on the budget, and support persons who would not in fact need it. Despite the fact that the legislature had not managed to solve the constitutional problems in the VAT Act, the Legal Chancellor did not appeal to the Constitutional Review Chamber. The very issue, however, reached the Chamber through concrete review procedure and this provision was declared unconstitutional by the Supreme Court.[317]

The Constitutional Review Chamber stated in its Judgement No. 3-4-1-12-07 (of 29 September 2007) that laws should treat equally all persons who are in a similar situation but that unequal treatment of equals can be justified when there is a reasonable and appropriate ground for it. The CRC argued that although the *Riigikogu* had pursued a reasonable aim – promoting high culture – when enacting this norm, the norm was not appropriate because it failed to achieve the desired aim. The Chamber noted that this provision in the VAT Act enables the performing arts institutions that meet the requirement of having at least 10 percent of their financing coming from public law funds to apply the 5 percent value added tax rate to *all* their performances and concerts, irrespective of whether these are high culture performances and concerts or not. The Chamber was not convinced that the circle of private performing arts institutions offering high culture events is confined to those institutions in whose annual budgets the public funds make up at least 10 percent. Therefore, the Chamber noted that the provision of the VAT Act provided for arbitrary discrimination and was not in conformity with the principle of equal treatment, arising from Article 12 Section 2 of the Constitution.

As a result of the Court's judgement, those organisers of performances who had paid a higher VAT rate in the time period 2005–2007 could demand back the 13 percentage points they had paid extra. The estimations of these costs for the budget reached 10 million kroons (about 640 000 euros) (Linnamäe 2007). Also, as a result of the Court's judgement, the 5 percent rate applied to *all* performances or concerts organised by a state, municipal or private performing arts

317 The case arose from a tax dispute between the Tax Office and a musical theatre who had used the 5 percent VAT rate, although the public funds constituted less than 10 percent of its annual revenues.

institution – leading to a wider circle of beneficiaries from the lower VAT rate, which also implied lower revenues for the state budget.

After the Court's judgement, there were discussions in the *Riigikogu* pertaining to the application of VAT to culture. The leading party in the coalition government (the Reform Party) suggested increasing the VAT rate for all concerts and performances to 18 percent; such an amendment to the Value Added Tax Act was adopted in December 2008 and enacted on 1 January 2009.

There were also two draft acts (with exactly the same content) initiated by the Centre Party (one in March 2008 and one in October 2007) to change the Value Added Tax Act and to *extend* the 5 percent rate to admissions to shows, theatres, circuses, fairs, amusement parks, concerts, museums, zoos, cinemas, exhibitions and similar cultural events and facilitates.[318] As argued in the explanatory note to these draft acts and the presenter of the draft act in the *Riigikogu*, Evelin Sepp, this change would be required in order to make the VAT Act compatible with the Constitution, according to the judgement by the CRC. Though the judgement of the CRC did not imply an extension of the reduced rate to *all other* cultural services, the proponents of the draft act sought to use the arguments of the CRC in the service of extending the lower tax rate to a larger number of areas related to culture. Sepp emphasised that the Supreme Court had said very clearly that it was not possible to distinguish between "culture" and "no culture". In addition, she argued that the main conclusion of the judgement of the Supreme Court was that the list of services provided for by Appendix H of the Sixth Directive should not be applied selectively; it cannot be justified that all theatre performances are taxed with 5 percent rate and all museum entrances with 18 percent. She underlined that in order to prevent constitutional debates in the future, the entire list provided for by Annex H should be included in the Estonian VATA (*Riigikogu* Verbatim Record, 5 June 2008). This proposal was not adopted by the parliament, however.

10.3.4. Discussion

In sum, the Constitution has played *some* role in the development of the tax acts in Estonia. In particular, the constitutional review decisions of the Supreme Court have consistently steered the development of the system of tax laws towards greater clarity and transparency. The Court has emphasised the need for unequivocal, valid, up-do-date delegation norms and the adherence of the executive power to the content of the delegation norms issued by the legislature. As a result of the Court's decisions, the rules making up the tax system are more comprehensible and accessible for the taxpayers; for example, taxpayers can

318 This list is a copy of the list provided for by Article 12(3)c) and Annex H of the Sixth Council Directive of the EU, which establishes that member states are *allowed* to apply a reduced rate, which was not to be less than 5 percent, to these categories.

only rely on regulations that have been adopted after the enactment of a specific tax act and do not have to go back in time to search for possible regulations that have to be complied with. In addition, the Court has sought to protect taxpayers from excessive interference from the executive, by declaring regulations that exceeded the delegation norms stipulated in legislative acts to be unconstitutional. The Constitutional Court has also sought to protect the local governments from interference from the executive, by requiring that the percentage of income tax revenues that is transferred to the budgets of local governments has to be established by the legislature. While in the social tax and income tax cases, the CRC sought to protect the taxpayers from excessive interference from the executive, then in the value added tax decisions, the Chamber also judged upon the constitutionality of the constraints imposed by the legislature (see the 50 000 kroons requirement cases) and on the constitutionality of differential tax treatment.

In all cases where the rules concerning income tax, social tax and value added tax were subject to constitutional review, the Constitutional Review Chamber found the contested rules to be unconstitutional; it ruled in favour of the taxpayers, who, because of the invalidity of the regulations, were partially freed from tax payments. Most of the tax decisions by the CRC brought about at least some budgetary costs – offering corroboration for Conjectures 1 and 2 and contrary evidence for Conjectures 3 and 4, outlined in chapter 8. It is noteworthy, however, that in most cases the budgetary implications were not brought up in the subsequent public discussion. The most notable exception here is the decision concerning the VAT and cultural events: here, the costs of the Court's decision were evaluated in clear monetary terms (the estimated sum was about 10 million kroons; that is, about 640 000 euros). Unlike in the interest rates case (see section 10.2.4.), however, the parliament did not attempt to override the Court's decision, contrary to Conjecture 5. In principle, it could have done so by re-introducing the provision that had been struck down by the court. Still, the costs of this judgement were mitigated by an amendment made to the VAT Act that abolished the preferential value added tax rate for cultural events, enacted in January 2009.

It is also worth noting that the President has not refused to promulgate any of the tax acts passed by the *Riigikogu*, and the Legal Chancellor has initiated only two constitutional reviews with regard to tax acts. The first one concerned fiscal relations between the local governments and the central government: after the *Riigikogu* failed to introduce appropriate changes, the Legal Chancellor took the issue to the Supreme Court. The Legal Chancellor also initiated constitutional review on the differential tax treatment of cultural events, but despite the failures of the legislature to solve the problematic situation, the Legal Chancellor did not turn to the Supreme Court. A main explanation behind the reluctance of the President and the Legal Chancellor to initiate constitutional review concerning tax issues is that the substantive issues of taxation were seen as inherently political, belonging to the sphere of ideology rather than to legal discourse.

Since both the President and the Legal Chancellor are institutions that are concerned with establishing and maintaining an image of neutrality, interfering in such an explicitly political and potentially very sensitive issue area could have easily damaged these pursuits.

As for the parliamentary debates on the tax acts, then compared with the organic tax law, the legislators have been somewhat more active here in pointing to constitutional issues *themselves* (without waiting first for the constitutional review decisions of other institutions). At the same time, however, the legislative constitutional discussions on the tax acts were significantly briefer than those on the organic tax law. Given the visibility of tax laws and their importance for constituents, one could have expected more constitutional deliberations on tax laws. The number of constitutional issues discussed at legislative debates was rather small in relation to the total number of times the tax acts were discussed in the parliament. Constitutional interpretations and rhetorical arguments referring to the articles of the Constitution (especially references to the constitutional principle of equal treatment) did provide additional support for changing some provisions (more so for the Income Tax Act than for the other tax acts), but none of the legislative debates on tax acts took the form of a full-fledged constitutional deliberation (that would have been comparable with discussions on the organic budget law) and constitutional arguments did not play a decisive role in getting the provisions in the Act adopted or rejected.[319] With the exception of the readings of the Value Added Tax Act in June 2008 (see section 10.2.3.3.), there were no explicit calls for auto-limitation in the discussions of tax acts.

Relatively minor role of the Constitution in debates on the tax laws in the parliament can also be explained by the very small number of constitutional provisions on taxation. Thus, there were fewer constitutional "focal points" that could have been easily taken up by the political actors, without risking the creation of an impression that they are just trying to use the Constitution for rhetorical purposes. The main constitutional provision that came up in the debates was Article 12, stating that "Everyone is equal before the law." Although the Constitutional Court had, in its decisions, set examples of how to interpret that particular provision (e.g., that unequal treatment of unequals is justified and that unequal treatment of equals can be justified on weighty grounds), such interpretive approaches were not taken up by the members of parliament in legislative debates. The interpretations of the principle of equal treatment remained on the level of assertions: the members of the parliament repeatedly stated that any unequal treatment – be it farmers versus non-farmers, interests received from banks versus interests from mutual loan associations, self-employed versus cor-

319 It is noteworthy that one of the most controversial changes made to the income tax system – the exemption of undistributed profits from corporate income tax, which took effect in January 2000 – was not at all discussed in constitutional terms.

porate enterprises, taxpayers with bank accounts versus taxpayers without bank accounts, lower pensions versus higher pensions – is simply unconstitutional.

10.4. Summary

On the whole, the Constitution has played a noteworthy role in the development of the main pieces of tax legislation in Estonia. As Table 10.7. indicates, the Constitutional Review Chamber has passed three decisions pertaining to each major act under consideration, altogether ten decisions (two decisions had implications for two different acts) and, all in all, 23 constitutional issues were raised in the parliamentary debates on these acts.

Table 10.7.: Constitution and tax legislation in Estonia, 1992–2007

	Number of constitutional issues discussed in the *Riigikogu*	Number of CRC decisions	Number of constitutional review decisions by the President	Number of constitutional review decisions by the Legal Chancellor
Organic tax law	6	3	1	-
Income tax	11	3	-	1
Social tax	1	3	-	-
Value added tax	5	3	-	1

Source: Author's calculations

While in the budget cases, the Constitutional Court did not find a violation of the Constitution (see section 9.3.5.), then in all taxation cases the Constitutional Review Chamber found that the tax norms (that were unfavourable to the taxpayers) violated the Constitution. Although the decisions of the CRC for most part concerned the *implementation* of the tax laws (six decisions out of ten) rather than amounting to *substantive* evaluation of the constitutionality of these acts themselves, these decisions had significant implications for the development of the rules governing the tax system in Estonia. In seven cases, the norms concerning taxation were declared unconstitutional because of delegation norms: they either lacked a valid delegation norm in the law (in three cases), exceeded the authority provided for in the existing delegation norm (one case) or the authority to issue a regulation should have not been delegated to the Minister of Finance (three cases). The general position of the CRC has been that: 1) regulations pertaining to taxation have to be based on valid delegation norms in laws; 2) the Government cannot delegate its authority to adopt tax regulations further (e.g., to the Minister of Finance), unless the tax laws explicitly provide so; 3) the Government, when adopting tax regulations, has to adhere strictly to the delegation norm in the law and is not allowed to impose additional financial obligations on the taxpayers.

As a result of the decisions of the CRC, the system of rules pertaining to taxation has become more comprehensible, accessible and transparent for the taxpayers: the taxpayers have a right to rely *only* on existing tax laws and regulations based on the delegation norms stipulated by these laws (with the delegation norms directed to the future and not retroactively), which follow exactly the delegation norms and do not exceed them. In fact, for the general development of the legal system in Estonia, the CRC's judgements on taxation have been paradigmatic, since they have clarified the implications of the principle of legal certainty for a system of laws and regulations. Also, as a result of the Court's decisions, an important fiscal constitutional principle has emerged, stating that all financial obligations in public law – irrespective of how exactly they are called – have to be established by laws (that is, by the legislature and not by the executive).

In four decisions pertaining to taxation – the decision on the 1994 Taxation Act, the 2002 decisions on the VAT Act and the 2007 decision on the VAT Act – the Constitutional Review Chamber evaluated the constitutionality of the *content* of the tax laws themselves (and not only the implementation thereof). Here, too, in all cases, the CRC ruled in favour of taxpayers. As result of the Court's decision on the 1994 Taxation Act, the tax authorities were significantly more constrained in their investigations for detecting tax evasion, compared with the original version of the Act. The differential treatment of organisers of performances and concerts (on the basis of their sources of revenues) with regard to the value added tax rate applied was declared unconstitutional, extending the circle of beneficiaries of reduced VAT rate considerably, compared with the original formulation.

The decisions of the CRC in Estonia offer corroboration for Conjecture 1 put forth in chapter 8, suggesting that because of the need of the constitutional courts in transition countries to build up public support, the courts are more likely to favour taxpayers. Most of the CRC's decisions pertaining to taxation have imposed budgetary costs on the state. Budgetary implications were especially clear for the interest rates case of 2002 and the value added tax case of 2007. The willingness of the Constitutional Review Chamber to adopt decisions that impose budgetary costs corroborates Conjecture 2 put forth in chapter 8, suggesting that – because of the need to build up the reputation as a neutral arbiter – constitutional courts in transition countries are willing to adopt decisions that bring about high budgetary costs. Conversely, the Estonian case provides contrary evidence to Conjectures 3 and 4. The readiness of the Estonian Constitutional Court to be aggressive in using its powers in the Taxation Act case, the interest rates case and the value added taxation of performances case offer support for Vanberg's (2005) hypothesis that a constitutional court will be more aggressive in using its powers of review as transparency increases. All these three cases were closely scrutinised by specific interest groups, which guaranteed a high degree of transparency in tracing the legislature's actions following the decision of the Court. Further, as the interest rates case shows, constitutional review institutions like the Legal Chancellor in Estonia can play an important role in increasing the transparency of the court's decisions, since it is the specific task of the Legal Chancellor to examine whether laws (including laws that are changed as a result of the decisions of the constitutional court) are in compliance with the constitution.

A constitutional court's readiness to issue rulings that impose budgetary costs should be viewed in a dynamic perspective: if the legislature continuously defers to the constitutional court's costly decisions over time, the court also becomes more willing to adopt costly decisions. Drawing an analogy with the hypothesis employed by Hansford and Damore (2000), one can conjecture that the court, when deciding whether to issue a costly ruling or not, will take into account how many times the legislature has recently overridden the costly decisions of the court. The Estonian case illustrates this dynamics very well. The legislature had until 2002 always deferred to the decisions of the Constitutional Court and the Court became continuously more inclined to adopt costly decisions. After the legislature had been forced into reversing the override, the Constitutional Review Chamber demonstrated continued (and even increased) willingness to pass costly rulings (e.g., the 2007 VAT decision), since the "finality" of the constitutional court's decisions was even more firmly established after the retreat of the *Riigikogu* in the interest rates case.

In the light of the repeatedly demonstrated readiness to issue rulings with impacts on the budget, it is interesting that the CRC itself has voiced reservations about the Court's role in budgetary policies and did, in Judgement No. 3-4-1-7-03 (of 21 January 2004), call for a self-restraint in that regard. The case concerned social assistance and the CRC had to decide whether the legislature had unconstitutionally constrained the circle of persons who qualify for social assistance (by linking the grant of subsistence benefits to cover living costs to particular kinds of dwellings, excluding, for example, student hostels). Although the Court declared such constraints unconstitutional, it noted in its decision that "A court of constitutional review must avoid a situation where the development of budgetary policies goes, to a large extent, into the hands of court. That is why in implementing social policies the court can not replace the legislative or executive powers."

When comparing the Estonian constitutional court with other transition countries, it appears that the willingness of the CRC to impose budgetary costs is by no means unique. As Sadurski (2002a, p. 4) has noted, some of the decisions of the constitutional courts in CEE countries "have had enormous budgetary implications"; this offers contrary evidence to Conjectures 3 and 4 in chapter 8. The readiness of the constitutional courts in CEE to go repeatedly against the prevailing majority preferences in the legislatures by adopting "costly" decisions also appears to go against the Hypothesis 3 put forth by Vanberg (2005) (see section 8.2.1.). Indeed, in transitional context, where young constitutional courts have to build up their reputation and garner political capital in the form of public support, the strategy of visible deference to other government branches may backfire. As Bond (2006) has demonstrated with the case studies of Hungarian and Polish constitutional courts, it was *not* through the decisions where these courts deferred to other branches (or refrained from adjudicating controversial cases) that they built up the diffuse support. Rather, it was "precisely in their moments of well-calculated boldness that they achieved the most" (Bond 2006, p. 18). Indeed, when the courts were too deferential, they were seen as "bow[ing] to political expedience at the expense of constitutional coherence" (Brzezinski 2000, p. 175).

Although Epstein, Knight and Shvetsova (2001) conjecture that CEE courts would be motivated to abstain from intense political conflict and contentious political issues, especially with regard to controversies concerning institutional prerogatives of the other branches, Bond (2006, p. 18) concludes that constitutional courts in CEE countries have not adopted a strategy of hiding from serious conflicts. The Estonian Constitutional Court has repeatedly ruled on the institutional prerogatives of the president versus the parliament (for an overview, see Pettai 2005b). In the tax decisions, the CRC repeatedly delineated the aspects that have to be established by the legislature: it forced the legislature into establishing certain rules by law, even if the legislature itself had considered it expedient to delegate the stipulation of these rules to the executive. Thus, in a transition country, where the court still has to build up the reputation of being impartial, the wish to appear as a neutral arbiter may make the court more willing to pass rulings on the institutional prerogatives of other branches with regard to budgeting and taxation. In transition countries, the Court's aspiration to prove adherence to the separation of powers principle might have taken the form of not deferring to the preferences of other powers, in order to provide a clear contrast to the Soviet practices where the boundaries between the different powers were blurred. Since the constitutional courts in transition countries are particularly dependent on the public support for the enforcement of the court's decisions, they appear to be especially motivated to pass decisions that favour taxpayers, even if these impose additional costs (in terms of foregone revenues) for the state. It seems that those CEE constitutional courts that have been willing to adopt "costly decisions" (e.g., in Hungary, Poland, Slovenia, Estonia), are also the ones that have garnered "deep legitimacy among the public" and have become "permanent features of the new political landscape" (Scheppele 2003, p. 221, drawing on Schwartz 2000).[320]

---

320 There is little evidence that the CRC in Estonia and constitutional courts in CEE would attempt to systematically estimate the financial implications of their decisions. This stands in a stark contrast to the practice of constitutional courts in some Western European countries. Rolla and Groppi (2002, p. 157), for example, have referred to the practice of the Italian Constitutional Court to issue evidence-gathering orders about the costs of possible judgements that strike down laws; it has even created a specific office with a

Although there is still little systematic evidence on the differences between the constitutional courts in Western Europe and Eastern Europe with regard to the readiness to impose budgetary costs with their decisions, the preliminary evidence points to the tendency of the CEE constitutional courts to be more willing – than their Western counterparts – to pass decisions with significant budgetary implications. In some ways, this tendency is paradoxical. One would expect more self-restraint by constitutional courts, with regard to the "costliness" of its decisions, in countries that face more stringent budgetary constraints, as it has been the case in most CEE countries during transition. Further inquiry into the comparison of the decisions of the constitutional courts in Western and Eastern Europe would certainly constitute a fruitful avenue of research for understanding better the incentives of the constitutional courts and the strategies they adopt in different contexts.[321] One aspect such comparative analysis should look into is the question of whether the reasons for divergence in the courts' strategies lie in the different political norms. It can be conjectured that through an evolutionary process of continued interaction between the legislature and the constitutional court, an unwritten consensus may emerge, to the effect that budgetary issues do not belong to the realm of the constitutional court and it should therefore exercise self-restraint in that regard. Also, it would be interesting to investigate whether the willingness of the constitutional courts to impose budgetary costs changes over time: whether it is larger in the early phase of the transition compared with the later phases, and whether the willingness has changed in response to the legislature's reactions to the previous decisions. Another element the comparative model should entail is the question of how the budgetary situation of the country (balance, surplus and deficit) influences the willingness of the constitutional court to pass rulings with costly budgetary implications.

Coming back to the tax decisions of the Estonian Constitutional Review Chamber, it can be observed that in nine decisions out of ten, there was no attempt by the Legislature to override the Court's decisions or to contest the decisions in public discussion.[322] Only on one occasion – after the interest rates deci-

---

purpose to quantify the financial burdens of the constitutional review decisions before they are adopted. Further, in order to avoid the creation of budgetary burdens with its decisions, the Constitutional Court in Italy has sought to develop innovative decision techniques, which, while aiming at the recognition of rights, leave it up to the legislature to choose the means for implementing them and to decide on the necessary budgetary appropriations.

321 Useful insights could also be gained by comparing the constitutional courts in CEE with those in Latin-America. Eslava (2006) has argued that constitutional courts in Latin-America have played an increasing role in fiscal policies.

322 In fact, most of the decisions did not require active steps to be taken by the legislature. When the decisions concerned regulations that were adopted on the basis of invalid delegation norms or exceeded the delegation norms, it was the Government who had to take steps to ameliorate the situation by adopting new regulations.

sion – did the *Riigikogu* choose to go against the decisions of the Constitutional Court. This provides corroboration for Conjecture 5 put forth in chapter 8 – at first sight – but taking into account the fact that the *Riigikogu* itself annulled the override, offers contrary evidence to that. The decision of the *Riigikogu* to override the Court's decision, at least as a first step, is especially noteworthy since it took place in a very transparent environment, with the Taxpayers Association and tax lawyers closely observing the steps of the legislature; this goes against the predictions of the model put forth by Vanberg (2005).

The interest rates case and the legislative reaction to that provides a very clear illustration of the competing pressures that a legislature is subject to when deciding how to react to a court's decision that has high budgetary costs. On the one hand, saving budgetary costs make an override more attractive; at the same time, the expected negative public backlash following an override makes it a less attractive choice for the legislature. As the interest rates case shows, the legislature can be so split between these two forces that it can choose to override first and then annul the override. Further, the interest rates case illuminates the importance of intermediary institutions of constitutional review – like that of the Legal Chancellor – in facilitating the "cooling down" of the legislative bravado and offering a window of opportunity for reconsideration. As the Estonian case exemplifies, whether the legislature chooses to override the Constitutional Court's decision and stick to that override, depends clearly on the symbolic role attached to the override. The parliamentary override was clearly dramatised in the public discourse: it was viewed as undermining the constitutional order and sending a negative signal about Estonia to abroad; this, in turn, led to the annulment of the override. In further models concerning parliament's reaction, the interactions between the considerations of the budgetary costs and negative public backlash following an override should be spelled out more clearly, with an understanding that idiosyncratic features of a country can play an important role.[323]

An important element in Vanberg's (2005) model is that if the constitutional court anticipates that the legislature would override its decision, it will choose to be deferential to the preferences of the legislative majority. It is difficult to ascertain whether in the interest rates case the Estonian Constitutional Review Chamber anticipated the override of the parliament. But, it can be conjectured that even if it had anticipated it, it would have still passed the decision in the form it did. What is lacking explanation in Vanberg's model and other similar models of interaction between the constitutional court and the legislature is the question of why a constitutional court would be *so* concerned with a potential legislative override. As the Estonian case shows, the legislative override would

323 In Hungary, for example, the legislature deferred to the constitutional court in the "Bokros package" case, where the decision of the court imposed substantial costs to the budget (Boulanger 2006).

reflect more negatively on the parliament *itself* rather than putting the constitutional court in a negative light. Even if the legislature overrides the court's decision, the court can claim that it made a clear statement of affirming certain rights, complied with the prevalent international principles for interpreting constitutional norms and was consistent with its own previous decisions. Since it is the public's support that forms most of the constitutional court's political capital, constitutional courts are more likely to be concerned with the general public opinion than with the opinion of the existing majority in the parliament.

Compared with the organic budget law, the President was less active in exercising his constitutional review powers in promulgating tax laws. The only tax law that he sent back to the parliament was the 1994 Taxation Act. Even though the Taxpayers Association clearly called for a presidential veto after the *Riigikogu* established interest rates on tax arrears retroactively, the President promulgated the law. The Legal Chancellor exercised the power of constitutional review three times: with Income Tax Act in 1994, with the Taxation Act in 2003 (after *Riigikogu* had overridden the interest rates decision of the CRC) and with the Value Added Tax Act in 2005. In 1994, the Legal Chancellor was not successful in persuading the *Riigikogu* and had to turn to the CRC; in 2003, the Legal Chancellor was successful; and in 2005, although the parliament did not respond to the memorandum by the Legal Chancellor with changing the VAT Act, the Legal Chancellor did not pursue the issue further.

As for constitutional deliberations on the organic tax law and specific tax laws in the Estonian legislature, Conjecture 9 put forth in chapter 8 suggested that given the importance of the issue of taxation for constituents, constitutional arguments would play an important role in legislative debates. As Peabody (2004, p. 138) argues, legislative constitutional awareness would be highest in issues that bear on the benefits of their constituencies. The analysis in previous sections indicates, however, that in relation to the number of times the tax laws were discussed in the *Riigikogu*, the number of constitutional issues raised was small. Especially noteworthy is the fact that during the discussions on Social Tax Act throughout the 15-year period, the Constitution was mentioned only once during the legislative debates. While the discussions on the *organic budget law* were predominantly constitutional deliberations, the legislative debates on the *organic tax law* paid attention to constitutional issues only after the constitutional review decisions of the Constitutional Court, the President or the Legal Chancellor. Although the legislature was itself more active in bringing up constitutional issues during discussions of specific tax laws (especially the income tax act) than during deliberations on the organic tax law, the constitutional discussions on specific tax laws, for most part, remained incidental, serving the goals of rhetorical support for particular arguments rather than being geared to genuine constitutional interpretations or constructions. While the division of powers between the main branches of government in budgetary procedures (regulated by the organic budget law) were seen as *intrinsically* constitutional issues, calling for active constitutional debates by the legislators, issues of taxation were not viewed as *a priori* constitutional issues, necessarily calling for analysis through constitutional prism. Thus, the Estonian case offers contrary evidence to Conjecture 9 put forth in chapter 8. Explanations for the lack of constitutional debates on tax issues can be following. First, the number of constitutional articles pertaining to taxation is very small. Second, tax issues were seen as predominantly ideological (for broader decisions) or technical (for specific regulations) rather than legal or constitutional. Third, given the very comprehensive reforms undertaken and the large number of laws passed, constitutional analysis was focused on other areas that were more "obviously" of constitutional nature (including electoral laws, ownership reform and minority rights). Fourth, tax laws were not subject to systematic scrutiny by the Constitutional Committee of the *Riigikogu*. The tax laws were thoroughly discussed only by the Finance Committee; the Constitutional Committee only became involved when constitutional review was initiated by the President, Legal Chancellor or the CRC.

Debates on the organic tax law – especially after the interest rates decision – however, took a form of a full-fledged constitutional debate, with extensive efforts to construe the meaning of particular constitutional articles and offer competing interpretations to the court's. The constitutional article most often referred to in the legislative constitutional arguments concerning taxation was Section 1 of Article 12 stating that "Everyone is equal before the law." The overviews of the constitutional discussions indicate, however, that the use of this article usually took the form of stating that a particular differential tax treatment violates the principle of equal treatment, without more detailed discussion. According to Conjecture 10, it was expected that constitutional discussions in a CEE parliament would not take the form of juridified deliberation, given the small number of constitutional court decisions. In the Estonian case, indeed, the constitutional arguments on tax laws, for most part, took the form of either assertion or constitutional construction. Despite the accumulating number of CRC's decisions, more juridified modes of argumentation did not make its way to the parliament, at least in the first 15 years of transition.

Auto-limitation by the parliament – that is, changing certain provisions in the fear that the constitutional court might otherwise declare them unconstitutional – was less predominant in the legislative proceedings of tax laws compared with the organic budget law. During the discussions on the 1994 Taxation Act, for example, despite the fact that the Act concerned important constitutional issues, no constitutional arguments were raised before the adoption of the Act. Even after the President had sent the organic tax law back to the *Riigikogu*, the legislators did not consider it necessary to engage in auto-limitation. Further, despite the warnings (although not through official review) given by the Legal Chancellor in 1994 about possible unconstitutionality of delegating the authority to establish interest rates on tax arrears to the Government, the corresponding provisions in the organic tax law were not changed. Debates on the Value Added Tax Act in 2008 show, however, that the legislators have started using the threat of a further ruling of unconstitutionality by the CRC as an argument for getting certain changes adopted. The decision of the CRC on the VAT Act in 2007 was used for portraying the differential treatment of different cultural events as a potential constitutional problem. The very fact that the Court had ruled on the issue was used for drawing much broader conclusions than the content of the Court decision itself would have allowed.

Altogether, the Estonian case study elucidates that the Constitution can indeed play a relevant role in the development of tax laws, both through the mechanisms *ex post* and *ex ante* constitutional review. Indeed, although the Constitution did play a more essential role in the evolvement of the organic budget law, understanding the unfolding of the tax system in Estonia would be incomplete without accounting for the constitutional review decisions of the Constitutional Review Chamber and constitutional debates in the parliament.

Chapter 11: Conclusions

Writing this book (and no doubt reading it) has been a lengthy journey, haunted by centrifugal forces tempting one to explore numerous side-paths on the way. Still, there are a number of converging conclusions that have emerged from the different chapters and this final chapter endeavours to pull the various threads together in answering the two guiding questions of this book: How do constitutional provisions that concern public finance come about? How do constitutions shape policy choices in public finances?

11.1. Constitution as *Explanandum*

The first part of the book was concerned with the stream of constitutional political economy that analyses constitutions as *explananda*. Chapter 1 gave an overview of the hypotheses regarding the effects that different kinds of framers (and the constraints they face) have on the resulting constitution. Although most of the theoretical discussions on constitutions as *explananda* focus on the strategic calculations of the framers who are motivated by institutional or partisan interests, some authors exploring constitution-making during the transition in Central and Eastern Europe have emphasised the potential importance that the historical constitutions of these countries can play, because of their symbolic importance for the framers.

The Estonian case study in chapter 2 was employed for testing the different hypotheses outlined in chapter 1. The Estonian case can be regarded as a crucial case, since the 1992 Constitution was prepared by a separate assembly (convened for the specific purpose of drafting the constitution), which worked in the knowledge that the final document would be put on referendum. Thus, if institutional self-interest were found to play a significant role in the constitution-making of the Estonian case, it can be expected to have been even more prevalent in the constitutional design of other CEE countries. On the one hand, indeed, even in the Estonian case of constitution-making, institutional self-interest of the framers strongly drove the drafting of certain parts of the Constitution – the chapter on the institution of the president, in particular. On the other hand, however, attributing the institutional choices merely to strategic considerations inspired by institutional or partisan self-interest would present a very distorted picture of constitution-making in Estonia. On a number of issues, the framers were above all motivated by symbolic considerations. The symbolic importance of the inter-war constitutions – representing the "golden past" (Offe 1997, p. 212) – led to extensive lesson-drawing over time, expressed in a large number of constitutional provisions that were taken over from the historical constitutions: the 1920 Constitution and the 1938 Constitution. The symbolic significance of the inter-war constitutions was enhanced by the aspiration of the Estonian framers to affirm the continuity of the Estonian statehood. Thus, in explicating the role of the historical constitutions in the making of the new constitution, it would be insufficient to say that they just happened to provide a convenient "focal point" for the framers, who were faced with an infinite number of possible institutional choices and tight time constraints. As the discussions in the Estonian Constitutional Assembly demonstrate, the previous constitutions were more than just "focal points": they were carriers of identity, provided interpretive frames and were a major source of constitutional theories. A number of institutional choices (e.g., with regard to the guarantees of autonomy granted to the judiciary) were also inspired by the desire to indicate a clear break with the communist past – a pursuit carried by strong emotional and symbolic motivations.[324]

An important lesson that can be drawn from the in-depth case study of constitution-making in Estonia is that the causal mechanisms put forth by cross-sectional studies (when accounting theoretically for links between particular features of the constitution-making process and the resulting institutional choices) are often different from the *actual* mechanisms. For example, although the Estonian case supports the hypothesis stating that the framers will design a strong and independent judiciary (with extensive powers of constitutional review), if they are faced with electoral uncertainties, the causal mechanisms behind this institutional choice are different than conjectured by Ginsburg (2002), Smithey and Ishiyama (2000) and Romeu (2006), who focused on the strategic calculations of the members of the constituent body. The proposals to increase the constitutional powers of the judiciary in Estonia came primarily from constitutional experts (both foreign and local); altogether, the strategic considerations with regard to the design of the judiciary played only a minor role compared to the "constitutional theories" and symbolic motivations pointing to the need to break with the Soviet heritage and to establish a European-type judicial system.

In sum, it was usually the *interaction* between the strategic calculations of the framers and the symbolic meanings attached to particular alternatives that shaped the final institutional choices. The symbol-driven constitutional discourse often influenced the perceived payoffs attached to particular institutional choices and forced the framers to make trade-offs between strategic calculations

324 Understanding the role of experts in Estonian constitution-making also calls for looking beyond the strategic calculations of the framers. The proposals put forth by local constitutional experts were viewed with a priori scepticism by many members of the Assembly – as if the affiliation with the existing government had "tainted" the proposals, irrespective of their specific content. Another aspect that the "calculus" perspective of constitution-making would leave unexplained is the fact that the Constitutional Assembly of Estonia decided to go against the most loudly voiced objections of the public concerning particular constitutional choices: although a large majority of the public supported direct elections of the president, the Assembly opted for indirect elections. Also, the scepticism of the framers with regard to the participation of the public in constitution-making had a lot to do with the connotation that the "public discussion" had had during the Soviet times.

and symbolic motivations. At the same time, the actor constellations and their bargaining powers influenced *whose* symbolic commitments came to the fore.

Drawing on the hypotheses outlined in chapter 1, chapter 3 provided a list of conjectures for analysing the making of constitutional provisions pertaining to budgeting and taxation and tested these conjectures with the Estonian case. Again, the design of the fiscal constitutional provisions was significantly influenced by institutional self-interest of the framers. The framers who were members of the existing legislative body or expected to become members of the legislature in the post-constitutional phase were reluctant to impose constitutional limitations on the legislature in budgeting, while the representatives of the existing executive branch sought to curtail legislative budgetary powers and to increase the powers of the Government. Given the dominance of more "legislatively oriented" framers in the Assembly, proposed constraints on the *Riigikogu* – like the Government veto on legislative budgetary amendments – were rejected.[325] At the same time, the Estonian case provides confirmation for the conjectures predicting that framers would present their arguments in the form of constitutional *theories* rather than in the form of constitutional *interests*. Also, as hypothesised, most of the constitutional solutions were targeted to existing problems in budgeting. In the light of the pressing problems in budgetary proceedings (especially the difficulties with adopting budgets on time), even the representatives of legislative interests were willing to make compromises and accepted constitutional provisions that render it "costly" for the legislature not to pass the budget on time.

Attributing the content of the provisions pertaining to budgeting and taxation in the 1992 Constitution only to the institutional self-interest of the framers and their desire to solve existing problems, however, would again neglect an important part of the explanation. The analysis of the origins of the budgetary provisions in the Constitution indicates that most of them were taken over (almost word by word) from the inter-war constitutions. Such an extensive lesson-drawing – including provisions that went against the institutional self-interest of the majority of framers (like the requirement that the legislative budgetary amendments have to be offsetting) – was facilitated by the time-constraints that the Constitutional Assembly faced and the symbolic importance that the inter-war constitutions had for the framers.

The Estonian case of drafting fiscal constitutional provisions does not support the theoretical conjectures concerning the role of the general public. Given the extensive reforms of the tax system – moving from the "invisible" Soviet tax system towards a more "visible" Western type tax system – that took place in parallel to constitutional discussions, one would have expected the general pub-

325 Further, a majority of the framers were reluctant to include a provision according to which the initiators of legislation should indicate the budgetary implications of the draft act and show the sources of finance, since such a constraint was perceived as increasing the power of the executive *vis-à-vis* the legislature.

lic in Estonia to be concerned with fiscal provisions and use the opportunities for participation to submit proposals concerning taxation. However, no constitutional concerns were expressed by the public with regard to taxation and no proposals concerning substantive or procedural constraints on taxation were put forth. The framers themselves also showed no interest in including any further provisions on taxation beyond the most general stipulation that taxes have to be established by laws. Altogether, both the general public and the framers appeared to regard the issue of taxation as belonging to the realm of either technical economic policy or political ideology, with little repercussions for the Constitution. Though the constitution-making and extensive economic reforms were taking place in parallel, there was very little substantive interaction between the two processes. Limited attention to public finance aspects is characteristic to most of the constitutions adopted in the CEE countries (with the 1997 Polish Constitution being the only exception). For the framers in these transition countries, the question of "citizens" appeared indeed to be more important than the question of "taxpayers".

11.2. Constitution as *Explanans*

The goal of part II of the book was to give an overview and criticise the existing studies in positive constitutional public finance and explore whether the insights provided by the emerging orthodoxy can help to explain a particular case – the adherence to fiscal discipline in Estonia. Chapter 4 outlined an analytical framework for summarising, synthesising and criticising the existing literature on constitutional public finance and chapters 5 and 6 employed the analytical framework for reviewing and discussing the existing literature in constitutional public finance.

Chapter 5 focused on the effects of different political institutions (either outlined in the constitutions or emerging from them) – presidentialism versus parliamentarism, electoral rules and governing arrangements (the size of the legislature and cabinet, the number of parties in the legislature and the cabinet, unicameral versus bicameral legislatures), direct democracy mechanisms and judicial institutions – on public finance. It considered how the different constitutional rules (and governing arrangements) influence accountability and coordination mechanisms and through that policy choices in public finance. Although the existing literature takes an interesting step forward, it is subject to a host of empirical and theoretical problems. Among the problems put forth in chapter 5, the following issues are especially important.

First, the *budgetary commons* and *veto players* approaches employed by the existing literature – though attractive because of their parsimony and prima facie intuitive appeal – may conceal more than they can reveal. These models may do a convincing job in explaining a particular phase in the decision-making process, but when other institutional aspects are brought up as well, a host of puzzles emerge. For instance, a model picturing the number of parties in the governing majority as the n graziers on budgetary commons appears straightforward at first sight. When additional questions – even about the simplest institutional arrangements – are asked, the "scene" on the commons becomes significantly more complicated.[326]

Second, though both budgetary commons models and veto players models appear plausible on their own, then juxtaposing the predictions they make (about the number of participants in budgetary decision-making) may give rise to contradictory predictions, unless concrete conditions are specified and different kinds of veto players distinguished. More comprehensive constitutional public finance models should simultaneously address the common-pool resource issues (including the "law of $1/n$" problem) and veto players aspects – and their potentially countervailing and reinforcing effects in different circumstances. Important issues in this regard are the following: When do veto players become graziers and when do they remain constrainers? Do different veto players follow different patterns in this regard? One can conjecture that the more the veto players have incentives and possibilities to demand side-payments and the more they have opportunities to externalise the costs of increased expenditures to constituencies of non-veto-players, the more similar would be the effect of the number of veto players to the effect of n graziers on budgetary commons. As a number of studies have indicated, the effects of the number of graziers or veto players are conditional on whether the decision-makers are faced with fiscally "good times" or "difficult times". Common-pool resource models have more plausibility in explaining why budget deficits emerge in the first place, while veto players models are more applicable in explaining why fiscal consolidations are delayed and deficits, once they have occurred, persist. Further models and studies should certainly take the pertinent fiscal situation into account more explicitly and differentiate the explanations and predictions in this regard.

Third, the most serious shortcoming of the studies reviewed in chapter 5 is that they have, for most part, confined themselves to partial analyses of the different political institutions and try to find out how a particular institution influences policy choices in public finance. The main caveat of such partial analyses is that, in reality, the effects of political institutions on policy choices are likely to be *configurational* rather than *additive*: a particular institutional element might have an opposite effect depending on the values of other institutional ele-

326 For example, in the case of a single-party majority government, one might indeed view the n to be equal to one. However, when the incentives provided by the electoral system are considered at the same time, then, in a majoritarian system (and also in a proportional system with open lists), which provides stronger incentives for individual legislators to graze the budgetary commons in order to provide particularistic projects for their home-district, it would be more accurate to conceive of the individual legislators as making up the number of n. Juxtaposing the elements of presidentialism and parliamentarism with electoral systems is likely to complicate the counting of the graziers further.

ments or on a particular combination of these elements (see Scharpf 1997). Ostrom (1986, p. 8) also emphasises that it is the *configurations* of rules, rather than single rules, that jointly affect the structure of situations subject to analysis. Just to name some examples, common-pool resource problems of budgeting may become more severe when a large district magnitude in proportional systems is combined with open lists but may be less severe with a large district magnitude and closed lists. The mutually reinforcing effects of an open list and a large district magnitude may be alleviated by particular electoral formulas (e.g., the D'Hondt formula, which favours the dominant parties) but may be aggravated by electoral formulas that are strictly "more proportionate" (like the LR-Hare formula). The tendency of the presidential systems to increase the complexity of the tax system may be significant in a system where the legislature has been elected according to a majoritarian system or open-list proportional system, but may be less relevant in a proportional system with closed lists.

Given the configurational rather than additive effects of the different institutional elements, the development of typologies and ideal types of political settings would be better able to capture the interactions between the different institutional aspects, illuminate their interactive effects and provide a more profound grasp of the interplay of causal mechanisms.[327] Hence, constitutional public finance should make a more extensive use of recent developments in small-n comparative studies and "building-block" approaches (see Bennett and Elman 2006) employed in coming up with more accurate typologies of different kinds of polities. Further, the "process-tracing" techniques put forth by recent developments in case-study research (George and Bennett 2005; George and McKeown 1985; McKeown 2004) should be employed as a complementary venue for elaborating on the underlying causal mechanisms that influence the translation of constitutional rules into specific features of political setting, which in turn shape interactions between political actors and the outcomes of their interactions.

Chapter 6 explored the effects of fiscal rules and budgetary institutions (i.e., the extended fiscal constitution) on public finance. While fiscal rules have been found to have ambiguous impacts on public finances, budgetary institutions appear to have more consistent and significant effects. The budgetary institutionalist literature, in particular, has taken substantial steps towards providing a better understanding of how fiscal constitutions influence policy choices in public finance. The development of the theoretical literature on this topic has been closely intertwined with empirical research, with a focus on specific institutional elements that make up the overall framework of fiscal governance in a polity. While the literature exploring the effects of political institutions on budgetary

327 The typology offered, for example, by Gerring, Thacker and Moreno (2005), which distinguishes between "centripetal" and "centrifugal" polities, goes in a fruitful direction of integrating specific institutional features into configurations or typologies.

choices is primarily concerned with size fragmentation in budgetary decision-making (i.e., the number and kinds of participants, discussed in chapter 5), the budgetary institutionalist literature takes a closer look at the participants in the budget process and how their interaction is structured.[328] Attention to institutional details in the budgetary institutionalist literature certainly helps to explain why the empirical results have pointed to more consistent results than the studies on the effects of political institutions reviewed in chapter 5. There is, however, a list of issues that have not been sufficiently addressed by the budgetary institutionalist literature. Among the problems brought up in chapter 6, the following ones are particularly relevant.

First, the existing studies on budgetary institutions have not paid sufficient attention to the question of which institutional aspects would be conducive to *maintaining* fiscal discipline and which aspects would be conducive to undertaking *fiscal adjustments* in the face of fiscal shocks. One can expect that because of the discretion granted to the minister of finance in the delegation mode, such systems would have advantages in undertaking prompt fiscal measures, compared with contracts systems. Further studies could also explore the effects of different modes of fiscal governance on pro-cyclical tendencies, both in "good" times and "difficult" times. Contracts systems that employ spending targets in multi-annual frameworks might be better equipped to deal with pro-cyclical pressures during good times (compared with delegation systems), while potentially running into problems when counter-cyclical (but unplanned) measures are needed during difficult times. In other words, the flexibility of the minister of finance in delegation systems might be an asset during difficult times, but pose problems in good times, whereas the opposite is true for the contracts system, where the fiscal targets may be an asset in good times but create obstacles in difficult times.

Second, the existing studies of the "von Hagen group" can also be criticised for not addressing sufficiently the *incentive mechanisms* involved in different modes of fiscal governance. In particular, questions arise with regard to the incentives to internalise the fiscal externalities in the contracts mode. Most of the theoretical discussions by von Hagen, Hallerberg and their colleagues underline

328 In particular, it is important to juxtapose the effects of size fragmentation (reflected in a large number of graziers on budgetary commons) with procedural fragmentation of budgetary decision-making. The effects of the number of legislators, ministers and parties on budgetary outcomes are likely to be mediated through budgetary institutions. If budgetary institutions are fragmented, the translation of *potential* common-pool problems into *actual* problems in budgeting is more likely. When budgetary institutions provide for centralised coordination mechanisms, the common-pool problems arising from size fragmentation are likely to be mitigated. For example, whether the "law of $1/n$" in a legislative setting will translate into excessive deficits, depends clearly on the role ascribed to the legislature by the rules of budget procedure. If the legislature has very limited powers to amend the budget, the "law of $1/n$" may not have the conjectured impacts.

how agreeing on common targets at the beginning of the budgetary process helps to overcome the *information* problems regarding the common-pool resource, as if the individual ministers were – without collective negotiations – unable to realise that individual large bids may add up to an excessively large budget. The question that arises here is how addressing *information* problems can simultaneously address *incentive* problems. It may well be that the individual ministers are aware about the common-pool problems in budgeting and understand that the general tax fund is a limited resource, but they do not have *incentives* to reduce their budget proposals accordingly.

Third, juxtaposing the effects of political institutions with budgetary institutions would strongly complement the existing literature on fiscal constitutions. In addition to the link made between the electoral systems and the mode of fiscal governance (indicating that proportional electoral rules lead to multiparty coalition governments, which are likely to opt for the contracts mode), the electoral incentives offered by the electoral rules to individual legislators and cabinet ministers should be explored closer. Alongside with accounting for more detailed elements of electoral systems, juxtaposing the fractionalisation of the government (and the legislature) with a particular mode of fiscal governance would help to explain why the effects of budgetary institutions can vary in strength.[329]

Fourth, the existing literature on governing the *budgetary* commons should draw on insights offered by the literature discussing the governance of *natural* commons. As the literature on the governance of natural commons has elucidated, it is important to scrutinise the underlying problem structure on the commons and not just resort to simplified metaphors. The literature on budgetary commons should also make an explicit distinction between appropriation and provision problems and explore whether specific kinds of appropriation and provision problems can also be encountered on budgetary commons. The suggestions that the natural commons literature has offered about successful governance mechanisms can proffer ideas for the fiscal governance literature as well.

Chapter 7 explored whether the constitutional elements discussed in chapters 5 and 6 – political institutions and extended fiscal constitution – can provide insights for understanding one particular aspect of public finances in Estonia: the commitment to fiscal discipline between 1992 and 2007. Altogether, the conjectures offered by the recent literature in constitutional public finance provide some explanations for the budgetary developments in Estonia, but tell only a small part of the story. In particular, if one confined the analysis to the most general features of constitutional arrangements, Estonia, with its commitment to

329 For example, in electoral systems with D'Hondt formula (giving rise to less fractionalised governments than more proportional formulas), the effects of centralising the decision-making in the preparation phase may have weaker effects on budget discipline than in electoral systems with more proportional formulas, which give rise to more fractionalised coalition governments.

fiscal discipline, would appear as an outlier that has somehow been able – "despite" the parliamentary system, proportional electoral rules and coalition governments, not subject to formal fiscal constitutional rules – to maintain fiscal discipline. The discussions in chapter 7 indicate, however, that one needs to dig deeper into institutional details in order to get a more accurate picture of the constitutional setting. In particular, the specific elements of the electoral system that are conducive to party discipline and reduce the fractionalisation of governments have exercised countervailing effects to common-pool problems of budgeting. The coordinating function performed by the centralised budgetary institutions has also played an "enabling" role for the commitment to fiscal discipline in Estonia.

Further, after admitting that particular constitutional elements and centralised budgetary institutions have been *conducive* to fiscal discipline, one is left with the question – what incentives have the political actors had to use the party discipline and other coordinating arrangements to maintain budget discipline? The solution to the *information* problems involved in budgetary decision-making does not necessarily simultaneously address the *incentive* problems. In Estonia's case as well, the incentives to stick to fiscal discipline did not *emanate* from the budgetary institutionalist arrangements but originated elsewhere: they arose from the currency board arrangements, the guidelines of the IMF (the adherence to which was driven by the desire to secure good international ratings, necessary for attracting foreign investment), and, in a later phase, from the Maastricht criteria, the salience of which was enhanced by the aspiration to join the euro.

Driven by these incentives, an *informal* norm of balanced budget emerged, which acquired almost a mythic nature, because of the prevailing beliefs that the balanced budget had been a guarantor of Estonia's economic success and abandoning this norm would amount to throwing away a valued "talisman". Altogether, the explanation of the commitment to fiscal discipline in Estonia would have to take into account the interaction between the formal institutional elements, the informal fiscal constitutional norms, the incentives and (even irrational) beliefs of the political actors, and the objective economic constraints and possibilities.

11.3. The Role of Constitution in Shaping Public Finance Laws

While part II of this book was concerned with the "emerging orthodoxy" of constitutional public finance and its shortcomings, then part III of this book (chapters 8–10) offered an alternative way of approaching the question "How do constitutions influence public finance?" The recent literature of constitutional public finance is primarily concerned with exploring the associations between particular constitutional features and aggregate fiscal indicators. Confining inquiry to such an exercise, however, would present only a very limited picture of the role of constitutions in the policy arena of public finance. Chapter 8 outlined an analytical framework for exploring how constitutions can shape public finance laws through constitutional review, auto-limitation and constitutional deliberation. The case studies on Estonia, presented in chapters 9 and 10, indicate that a constitution can *indeed* play an important role in the development of public finance laws.

Though the emerging orthodoxy has paid only scant attention to the role of *constitutional courts* and *judicial review* in public finance (see section 5.6.), the Estonian case study (especially chapter 10) indicates that the constitutional court can play a significant role in shaping the policy arena of public finance. The Constitutional Review Chamber in Estonia has emphasised the need for clear, valid, up-do-date delegation norms and the adherence of the executive power to the content of the delegation norms issued by the legislature. As a result of the CRC's decisions, the rules making up the tax system are more comprehensible and accessible for taxpayers: for example, in calculating their tax obligations, taxpayers can rely only on tax laws (and regulations that have been adopted according to the tax laws) and do not have to search for pertinent rules in other acts. The President, the Legal Chancellor and the Constitutional Review Chamber have sought repeatedly to affirm and extend the rights of the taxpayers, curtail the powers and discretion of the executive and forbid arbitrary discrimination in taxation.

The rulings of the Constitutional Review Chamber have implied significant costs for the state budget. Although the "strategic interaction" model of the courts and legislatures (see, *inter alia*, Vanberg 2005; Epstein, Knight and Shvetsova 2001; Hansford and Damore 2000; Epstein and Knight 1998; Epstein and Walker 1995) would predict that courts would be reluctant to pass rulings with costly budgetary implications, the Constitutional Review Chamber in Estonia has been repeatedly willing to go ahead with costly decisions. In the Estonian case, the Court's aspiration to build up public support, to appear as a neutral arbiter and to demonstrate commitment to the principle of separation of powers (and, by doing that, provide a contrast to the Soviet practices of blurred boundaries between the different branches) were more important than the considerations of fiscal constraints and the goal to secure the support of other branches of government.

With regard to legislature's reactions to such costly decisions, although the existing theoretical models predict that the parliament would overrule them, the Estonian case provides evidence to the contrary. The *Riigikogu* attempted to override the Court's decision only on one occasion (in the so-called interest rates case) but a result of constitutional review by the Legal Chancellor, it reversed the override. The Legal Chancellor and the involved interest groups viewed the override as a paradigmatic case, violating the rule of law and the balance of powers, and sending a negative signal about Estonia to abroad; they managed to make these symbolic arguments dominant in the constitutional discourse ensuing the override and persuaded the legislature to annul the provisions that had gone against the ruling of the CRC.

The Estonian case also demonstrates that alongside the usually considered venue of constitutional review – the Constitutional Court – other institutions of constitutional review (the President and the Legal Chancellor) can play a significant role in initiating constitutional discussions over public finance acts and in persuading the parliament to change the acts. The development of the organic budget law, in particular, was affected by the constitutional review decisions of the President; for example, the budgetary autonomy of the constitutional institutions was clearly increased and the extension of the budgetary powers of the Government (*vis-à-vis* the parliament) did not go as far as the executive would have wished.

Besides *ex post* constitutional review, which is the most obvious and straightforward way the constitution can shape public finance laws, the Estonian case demonstrates that *ex ante* constitutional review – the anticipations of the legislators that the constitutional court or the President or the Legal Chancellor may find the law under discussion to be unconstitutional – steered the legislature towards changing a number of provisions in the acts. Although Sadurski (2005, p. 90) has claimed that it is hard to find evidence for auto-limitation in interactions between constitutional courts and legislatures in CEE countries, the Estonian case provides clear evidence to the contrary.[330]

While in the case of tax laws, constitutional review by other institutions was more salient than constitutional deliberations in the parliament (initiated by legislators themselves), the debates on the organic budget law in the *Riigikogu* were full-fledged constitutional debates. Indeed, most of the readings on the organic budget law were constitutional deliberations, and the issues pertaining to budget procedure were perceived by the legislators as *inherently* constitutional issues, which needed to be interpreted and discussed in the light of the Constitution. As a result of the constitutional deliberations on the organic budget law, the amendment rights of the parliament in the budget process became increasingly constrained (although not going as far as the executive would have wished), extra-budgetary funds were integrated with the budget and the parliament retained some authority over the classification of articles in the budget. While constitutional deliberations in the parliament were most intensive when constitutional problems had been brought up either by the President or the Legal Chancellor, the legislators themselves also initiated the constitutional discussions.[331] On a

330 Because of the anticipated decisions of the constitutional court, the budgetary autonomy of constitutional institutions was increased, fees and fines were listed among state revenues, the Government was not given extensive freedom for borrowing and the parliament retained at least some power over budget classification.

331 In particular, the members of the opposition evoked constitutional arguments whenever the executive and the governing coalition sought to curtail the budgetary powers of the parliament.

number of occasions, the constitutional arguments pointed out during legislative debates were taken up and pursued further by the President or the Legal Chancellor; in other words, the agenda-setting of constitutional discussions was also influenced by the legislators themselves and not only by the institutions of constitutional review.

Most of the elements of constitutional construction that Whittington (1999) brought out (based on the U.S. experience) played a role in the constitutional debates on the organic budget law in Estonia as well. The political actors – the members of the parliament, the cabinet members, the President – used the text of the Constitution to support their own partisan and institutional interests.[332] There were, however, some proposals that went beyond institutional and partisan self-interest and reflected the will of "self-binding". The motion to constrain the parliament's right to amend the organic budget law in 1998 was put forth and supported by members of the opposition who wished to improve the rationality of the budget process. Also, the symbolic importance attached to some notions (the inherent right of the parliament to have power over the purse, for example) did not allow the Government to go too far in constraining the budgetary amendment rights of the parliament.

Altogether, the case studies of Estonia demonstrate that constitutional discourse – the interpretations and constructions put forth by the different participants involved – can play an important role in shaping the policy arena of public finance.[333] The constitutional law and meanings attached to particular choices as a result of constitutional discourse did indeed have a "transformative" power (Burgess 1993): in part, the symbolic role of the constitution was employed by political actors in their strategic arguments (to add weight and legitimacy to their arguments); in part, the symbolic meaning of ideas and notions that emerged

---

332 The plea to increase the budgetary autonomy of constitutional institutions certainly reflected the institutional self-interest of the President to have more budgetary autonomy for his own institution. The proposals to significantly constrain the right of the parliament to make amendments to the draft budget were rejected by the majority of the parliament (during the discussions in 1998–1999), reflecting the desire of the parliament not to cede its budgetary powers. The Finance Committee agreed to support the constraints on parliamentary amendment rights after it had been included as a gatekeeper alongside with the Cabinet.

333 A number of constitutional constructions offered by participants in the constitutional deliberations gave rise to the emergence of certain notions that came to dominate the subsequent constitutional discourse. For example, despite the fact that Estonia has a parliamentary system of government, implying fused legislative and executive powers, the constitutional article prescribing separation and balance of powers was interpreted as applying for the parliament and Government as well. As a result of the Court's decisions, an important fiscal constitutional principle has emerged, stating that all financial obligations in public law – irrespective of how exactly they are called – have to be established by laws (that is, by the legislature and not by the executive with regulations).

from the constitutional discourse changed the perceived payoffs attached to different choices and were able to transform the strategies of the actors involved.

11.4. Constitutional Public Finance in Transition

While the term "transition" in the heading of this book refers primarily to regime transitions in the region of Central and Eastern Europe, it is also clear that positive constitutional public finance is *itself* also in "transition". In order to provide more meaningful insights about the role of constitutions in public finance, a number of challenges have to be overcome on this transitional path.

Methodologically, the challenge is how to deal with the configurational effects of different constitutional elements and idiosyncratic features of polities' constitutional settings. As the in-depth case studies in this book indicate, the causal mechanisms underlying particular constitutional choices or post-constitutional policy choices are often different from those assumed by theoretical and cross-sectional studies. Although the emerging orthodoxy strongly favours large-n studies and regression analyses, the case study approach should play a strong complementary role here in exploring the causal mechanisms and explaining the performance of outliers.

Conceptually, the challenge is to go beyond simplified metaphors and to explain what one really means by "common-pool problems of budgeting" or "budgetary commons", for example; otherwise, there is a danger that these notions become catch-all phrases that, while appearing to explain everything, do not actually explain anything. Proceeding from over-simplified models may render policy prescriptions meaningless or even counterproductive. Furthermore, an analysis that employs the metaphor of "budgetary commons" should admit that this is not a "normatively neutral" metaphor but proceeds from a very particular view of a polity and the role of the state.

Theoretically, constitutional public finance should expand its horizons. Most of the existing studies in constitutional public finance confine themselves to the "calculus approach" of institutionalism and ignore insights from the "cultural approach". As the case studies in this book demonstrate, integrating the "calculus" approach and "cultural" approach in explaining the emergence of fiscal constitutional norms and elucidating the influence of constitutions on public finance provides a more complete picture of the reality. Since politics is indeed a place for discovering and creating ideas, symbols and meanings, constitutional discourse can play an important part in shaping the policy arena of public finance; neglecting such a role of constitutions would leave an analyst puzzled by many things going on in the political reality.

References

Aaskivi, Ü. (2002). "Mälestused Põhiseaduse Assambleest." [Memories from the Constitutional Assembly] In E. Pärnaste (ed.), *Põhiseaduse Tulek. Kogumik.* [The Coming of the Constitution] Tallinn: Justiitsministeerium, Kirjastus SE&JS.

Aaskivi, Ü. and E. Pärnaste. (2002). "Kronoloogia: EV Ülemnõukogu. Eesti Kongress, Põhiseaduse Assemblee." [Chronology: The Supreme Council, the Estonian Congress, the Constitutional Assembly] In E. Pärnaste (ed.), *Põhiseaduse Tulek. Kogumik.* [The Coming of the Constitution] Tallinn: Justiitsministeerium, Kirjastus SE&JS.

Aaviksoo, B. (2007). "Judicial Activism in Constitutional Review Decisions of the Supreme Court of Estonia." *Juridica International* 13(2): 60–69.

Abrams, B. A. and W. R. Dougan. (1986). "The Effects of Constitutional Constraints on Government Spending." *Public Choice* 49(2): 101–116.

Acemoglu, D. (2005). "Constitutions, Politics, and Economics: A Review Essay on Persson and Tabellini's *The Economic Effects of Constitutions.*" *Journal of Economic Literature* 43(4): 1025–1048.

Ackerman, B. A. (1984). "The Storrs Lectures: Discovering the Constitution." *Yale Law Journal* 93: 1013–1072.

Ackerman, B. A. (1991). *We the People, Vol. 1: Foundations.* Cambridge: Belknap.

Ackerman, B. A. (1992). *The Future of Liberal Revolution.* New Haven: Yale University Press.

Adamovich, I. B. (2004). *Enstehung von Verfassungen. Ökonomishce Theorie und Anwendung auf Mittel- und Osteuropa nach 1989.* Tübingen: Mohr Siebeck.

Adams, J. (2002). "Eelnõu sünd ja saatus." [The Birth and the Fate of the Draft] In E. Pärnaste (ed.), *Põhiseaduse Tulek. Kogumik.* [The Coming of the Constitution] Tallinn: Justiitsministeerium, Kirjastus SE&JS.

Aghion, P. and P. Bolton. (1990). "Government Domestic Debt and the Risk of Default in a Political Economic Model of the Strategic Role of Debt." In R. Dornbusch and M. Draghi (eds.), *Public Debt Management: Theory and History.* Cambridge: Cambridge University Press.

Alesina, A. and T. Bayoumi. (1996). "The Costs and Benefits of Fiscal Rules: Evidence from the US States." National Bureau of Economic Research, Working Paper No. 5614.

Alesina, A. and A. Drazen. (1991). "Why are Stabilizations Delayed?" *The American Economic Review* 81(5): 1170–1188.

Alesina, A., R. Hausmann, R. Hommes and E. Stein. (1999). "Budget Institutions and Fiscal Performance in Latin America." *Journal of Development Economics* 59(2): 253–273.

Alesina, A. and R. Perotti. (1995). "The Political Economy of Budget Deficits." *IMF Staff Papers* 42(1): 1–31.

Alesina, A. and R. Perotti. (1996). "Fiscal Discipline and the Budget Process." *The American Economic Review* 86(2): 401–407.

Alesina, A. and R. Perotti. (1999). "Budget Deficits and Budget Institutions." In J. M. Poterba and J. von Hagen (eds.), *Fiscal Institutions and Fiscal Performance.* Chicago: University of Chicago Press.

Alesina, A., R. Perotti and J. Tavares. (1998). "The Political Economy of Fiscal Adjustments." *Brookings Papers on Economic Activity* 1: 197–248.

Alesina, A. and N. Roubini. (1997). *Political Cycles and the Macroeconomy.* Cambridge: MIT Press.

Alesina, A. and G. Tabellini. (1990). "A Positive Theory of Fiscal Deficits and Government Debt." *Review of Economic Studies* 57(3): 403–414.

Alesina, A. and G. Tabellini. (2005). "Why is Fiscal Policy Often Procyclical?" CESifo Working Paper No. 1556. Available at: http://www.cesifogroup.de/DocCIDL/cesifo1_wp 1556.pdf [Last retrieved January 2009]

Alt, J. E. and D. D. Lassen. (2006). "Fiscal Transparency, Political Parties and Debt in OECD Countries." *European Economic Review* 50(6): 1403–1439.

Alt, J. E. and R. C. Lowry. (1994). "Divided Government and Budget Deficits: Evidence from the States." *American Political Science Review* 88(4): 811–828.

Amorim Neto, O. and H. Borsani. (2004). "Presidents and Cabinets: The Political Determinants of Fiscal Behavior in Latin America." *Studies in Comparative International Development* 39(1): 3–27.

Amorim Neto, O. and G. Cox. (1997). "Electoral Institutions, Cleavage Structures and the Number of Parties." *American Journal of Political Science* 41(1): 149–174.

Anderson, G. M. (2002). "Referendum, Redistribution, and Tax Exemption: A Rent-Seeking Theory of Direct Democracy." In D. P. Racheter and R. E. Wagner (eds.), *Politics, Taxation, and the Rule of Law: The Power to Tax in Constitutional Perspective*. Boston: Kluwer Academic Publishers.

Andrikopoulos, A., I. Loizides and K. Prodromidis. (2004). "Fiscal Policy and Political Business Cycles in the EU." *European Journal of Political Economy* 20(1): 125–152.

Aninat, C., J. Landregan, P. Navia and J. Vial. (2006). "Political Institutions, Policymaking Processes and Policy Outcomes in Chile." Inter-American Development Bank, Latin American Research Network, Working Paper No. R-521. Available at: http://cdi.mecon.gov.ar/biblio/doc/bid/R521.pdf [Last retrieved January 2009]

Annett, A. (2006). "Enforcement and the Stability and Growth Pact: How Fiscal Policy Did and Did Not Change Under Europe's Fiscal Framework?" IMF Working Paper No. 06/116. Available at: http://www.imf.org/external/pubs/ft/wp/2006/wp06116.pdf [Last retrieved January 2009]

Annett, A. and A. Jaeger. (2004). "Europe's Quest for Fiscal Discipline." *Finance and Development* 41: 22–25.

Annus, T. (2007). "Courts as Political Institutions." *Juridica International* 13: 22–30.

Arjakas, K. (2002). "Eesti Vabariigi põhiseadustest." [The Constitutions of the Republic of Estonia] In E. Pärnaste (ed.), *Põhiseaduse Tulek. Kogumik*. [The Coming of the Constitution] Tallinn: Justiitsministeerium, Kirjastus SE&JS.

Arnold, R. D. (1990). *The Logic of Congressional Action*. New Haven: Yale University Press.

Ashworth, J. and B. Heyndels. (2001). "Political Fragmentation and the Evolution of National Tax Structures in the OECD." *International Tax and Public Finance* 8(4): 377–393.

Austen-Smith, D. (2000). "Redistributing Income under Proportional Representation." *Journal of Political Economy* 108(6): 1235–1269.

Axelrod, R. (1984). *The Evolution of Cooperation*. New York: Basic Books.

Ayuso-i-Casals, J., D. Gonzalez Hernandez, L. Moulin and A. Turrini. (2007). "Beyond the SGP: Features and Effects of National Level Fiscal Rules." *European Economy Economic Papers* 275: 191–242.

Bachrach, P. and M. S. Baratz. (1962). "Two Faces of Power." *American Political Science Review* 56(4): 947–952.

Bachrach, P. and M. S. Baratz. (1963). "Decisions and Nondecisions: An Analytical Framework." *American Political Science Review* 57(3): 632–642.

Backhaus, J. G. (1996). "Stackelberg's Concept of the Post-War Economic Order." *Journal of Economic Studies* 23(5–6): 141–148.

Backhaus, J. G. (1998). "Book Review: Constitutional Law and Economics of the European Union." *European Journal of Law and Economics* 6(1): 83–85.

Backhaus, J. G. (2002a). "Old or New Public Finance? A Plea for the Tried and True." *Public Finance Review* 30(6): 612–645.

Backhaus, J. G. (2002b). "Fiscal Sociology: What For?" *American Journal of Economics and Sociology* 61(1): 55–77.

Backhaus, J. G. (2004). "Joseph A. Schumpeter's Contributions in the Area of Fiscal Sociology: A First Approximation." *Journal of Evolutionary Economics* 14(2): 143–151.

Backhaus, J. G. and J. J. Krabbe. (1991). "Henry George's Contribution to Modern Environmental Policy: Part I, Theoretical Postulates." *American Journal of Economics and Sociology* 50(4): 485–501.

Backhaus, J. G. and R. E. Wagner. (2004). "Chapter 1: Society, State, and Public Finance: Setting the Analytical Stage." In J. G. Backhaus and R. E. Wagner (eds.), *Handbook of Public Finance*. Boston: Kluwer Academic Publishers.

Backhaus, J. G. and R. E. Wagner. (2005). "From Continental Public Finance to Public Choice: Mapping Continuity." *History of Political Economy* 37: 314–332.

Bails, D. G. (1982). "A Critique on the Effectiveness of Tax-Expenditure Limitations." *Public Choice* 38(2): 129–138.

Bails, D. G. (1990). "The Effectiveness of Tax-Expenditure Limitations: A Reevaluation." *American Journal of Economics and Sociology* 49(2): 223–238.

Bails, D. G. and M. A. Tieslau. (2000). "The Impact of Fiscal Constitutions on State and Local Expenditures." *Cato Journal* 20(2): 255–277.

Balassone, F. and R. Giordano. (2001). "Budget Deficits and Coalition Governments." *Public Choice* 106(3–4): 327–349.

Balassone, F. and M. S. Kumar. (2007). "Addressing the Procyclical Bias." In M. S. Kumar and T. Ter-Minassian (eds.), *Promoting Fiscal Discipline*. Washington, DC: IMF.

Baldini, A. (2000). "Parliamentary Dynamics, Government Stability and Fiscal Policy." In R. R. Strauch and J. von Hagen (eds.), *Institutions, Politics and Fiscal Policy*. Boston: Kluwer Academic Publishers.

Banzhaf, J. F. (1965). "Weighted Voting Doesn't Work: A Mathematical Analysis." *Rutgers Law Review* 19(2): 317–343.

Baron, D. P. (1991). "Majoritarian Incentives, Pork Barrel Programs, and Procedural Control." *American Journal of Political Science* 35(1): 57–90.

Baron, D. P. and J. A. Ferejohn. (1989). "Bargaining in Legislatures." *American Political Science Review* 83(4): 1181–1206.

Barro, R. (1979). "On the Determination of the Public Debt." *Journal of Political Economy* 87(5): 940–971.

Bartole, S. (2002). "Conclusions: Legitimacy of Constitutional Courts: Between Policy Making and Legal Science." In W. Sadurski (ed.), *Constitutional Justice, East and West, Democratic Legitimacy and Constitutional Courts in Post-Communist Europe in a Comparative Perspective.* The Hague: Kluwer Law International.

Baturo, A. and J. Gray. (2007). "Flatliners: Ideology and Rational Learning in the Diffusion of the Flat Tax." Institute for International Integration Studies, Discussion Paper No. 210. Available at: http://www.tcd.ie/iiis/documents/discussion/pdfs/iiisdp210.pdf [Last retrieved January 2009]

Bawn, K. (1999). "Money and Majorities in the Federal Republic of Germany: Evidence for a Veto Players Model of Government Spending." *American Journal of Political Science* 43(3): 707–736.

Bawn, K. and F. Rosenbluth. (2006). "Short versus Long Coalitions: Electoral Accountability and the Size of the Public Sector." *American Journal of Political Science* 50(2): 251–265.

Beetsma, R. and M. Giuliodori. (2008). "Fiscal Adjustment to Cyclical Developments in the OECD: An Empirical Analysis based on Real-Time Data." CEPR Discussion Paper No. 6692. Available at: http://www.cepr.org/pubs/dps/DP6692.asp [Last retrieved January 2009]

Bennett, A. and C. Elman. (2006). "Qualitative Research: Recent Developments in Case Study Methods." *Annual Review of Political Science* 9: 455–576.

Berger, H., G. Kopits and Szekely. (2007). "Fiscal Indulgence in Central Europe: Loss of External Anchor." *Scottish Journal of Political Economy* 54(1): 116–135.

Berger, P. L. and T. Luckmann. (1967). *The Social Construction of Reality*. New York: Doubleday.

Berggren, N. and N. Karlson. (2003). "Constitutionalism, Division of Power and Transaction Costs." *Public Choice* 117(1–2): 99–124.

Berggren, N. and P. Kurrild-Klitgaard. (2002). "Economic Effects of Political Institutions, With Special Reference to Constitutions." In N. Berggren, N. Karlson and J. Nergelius (eds.), *Why Constitutions Matter*. New Brunswick: Transaction Publishers.

Besley, T. and A. Case. (2003). "Political Institutions and Policy Choices: Evidence from the United States." *Journal of Economic Literature* 7(1): 7–73.

Blais, A., D. Blake and S. Dion. (1993). "Do Parties Make a Difference? Parties and the Size of Government in Liberal Democracies." *American Journal of Political Science* 37(1): 40–62.

Blais, A. and L. Massicotte. (1996). "Electoral Systems." In L. LeDuc, R. Niemei and P. Norris (eds.), *Comparing Democracies: Elections and Voting*. Thousand Oaks: Sage.

Blankart, C. B. and G. B. Koester. (2006). "Political Economics versus Public Choice: Two Views of Political Economy in Competition." *Kyklos* 59(2): 171–200.

Blankart, C. B. and G. B. Koester. (2007). "The Economic Analysis of Constitutions: Fatalism Versus Vitalism." *Econ Journal Watch* 4(2): 169–183.

Blatter, J. and T. Blume. (2008). "In Search of Co-Variance, Causal Mechanisms or Congruence? Towards Plural Understanding of Case Studies." *Swiss Political Science Review* 14(2): 315–356.

Blom-Hansen, J. (2002). "Budget Procedures and the Size of the Budget: Evidence from Danish Local Government." *Scandinavian Political Studies* 25(1): 85–106.

Blomquist, W. and E. Ostrom. (1985). "Institutional Capacity and the Resolution of a Commons Dilemma." *Review of Policy Research* 5(2): 383–393

Bodmer, F. (2006). "Warum die Direkte Demokratie den Anstieg der Staatsaquote in der Schweiz nicht verhindern konnte." University of Basle, Centre for Business and Economics, Discussion Paper.

Bohman, J. (2004). "Constitution Making and Democratic Innovation." *European Journal of Political Theory* 3(3): 315–337.

Bohn, H. and R. P. Inman. (1996). "Balanced-Budget Rules and Public Deficits: Evidence from the U.S. States." *Carnegie-Rochester Conference Series on Public Policy* 45: 13–76.

Bohnet, I. and B. S. Frey. (1994). "Direct-Democratic Rules: The Role of Discussion." *Kyklos* 47(3): 341–354.

Boix, C. (2001). "Democracy, Development and the Public Sector." *American Journal of Political Science* 45(1): 1–17.

Bond, J. (2006). "Concerning Constitutional Courts in Central and Eastern Europe." *International Public Policy Review* 2(2): 5–25.

Bönker, F. (2006). *The Political Economy of Fiscal Reform in Central-Eastern Europe*. Cheltenham: Edward Elgar.

Bönker, F., K, Müller and A. Pickel. (2002). "Cross-Disciplinary Approaches to Postcommunist Transformation: Context and Agenda." In F. Bönker, K. Müller and A. Pickel (eds.), *Postcommunist Transformation and the Social Sciences*. Lanham: Rowman and Littlefield Publishers.

Borge, L.-E. and J. Rattso. (2002). "Spending Growth with Vertical Fiscal Imbalance: Decentralized Government Spending in Norway 1880–1990." *Economics and Politics* 14(3): 351–373.

Borrelli, S. A. and T. J. Royed. (1995). "Government 'Strength' and Budget Deficits in Advanced Democracies." *European Journal of Political Research* 28(2): 225–260.

Boulanger, C. (1999). "Constitutionalism in East Central Europe? The Case of Slovakia under Meciar." *East European Quarterly* 33(1): 21–50.

Boulanger, C. (2000). "Charisma, Rationality, and Legitimacy: A Weberian Analysis of Post-Communist Legal Transformation." Paper presented at Conference on Law and Social Theory, Wolfson College, University of Oxford, December 14–15, 2000. Available at: http://www.panyasan.de/publications/texts/Boulanger2000ab.pdf. [Last retrieved January 2009]

Boulanger, C. (2006). "Europeanization Through Judicial Activism? The Hungarian Constitutional Court's Legitimacy and the 'Return to Europe'." In W. Sadurski, A. W. Czarnota and M. Krygier (eds.), *Spreading Democracy and the Rule of Law*. Dordrecht: Springer.

Bradbury, J. C. and W. M. Crain. (2001). "Legislative Organization and Government Spending: Cross-Country Evidence." *Journal of Public Economics* 82(3): 309–325.

Bradbury, J. C. and W. M. Crain. (2002). "Bicameral Legislatures and Fiscal Policy." *Southern Economic Journal* 68(3): 646–659.

Brady, H. E. and D. Collier. (eds.) (2004). *Rethinking Social Inquiry*. Lanham: Rowan and Littlefield.

Bräuninger, T. (2005). "A Partisan Model of Government Expenditure." *Public Choice* 125(3–4): 409–429.

Brender, A. and A. Drazen. (2005). "Political Budget Cycles in New Versus Established Democracies." *Journal of Monetary Economics* 52(7): 1271–1295.

Brennan, G. and J. M. Buchanan. (1980). *The Power to Tax. Analytical Foundations of a Fiscal Constitution*. Cambridge: Cambridge University Press.

Brennan, G. and G. Eusepi. (2004). "Fiscal Constitutionalism." In J. G. Backhaus and R. E. Wagner (eds.), *Handbook of Public Finance*. Boston: Kluwer Academic Publishers.

Brennan, G. and A. Hamlin. (1992). "Bicameralism and Majoritarian Equilibrium." *Public Choice* 74(2): 169–179.

Brennan, G. and A. Hamlin. (2002). "Expressive Constitutionalism." *Constitutional Political Economy* 13(4): 299–311.

Brennan, G. and J. C. Pardo. (1991). "A Reading of the Spanish Constitution (1978)." *Constitutional Political Economy* 2(1): 53–79.

Briffault, R. (2008). "Courts, Constitutions, and Public Finance: Some Recent Experiences from the States." In E. Garrett, A. Graddy and H. E. Jackson (eds.), *Fiscal Challenges: An Interdisciplinary Approach to Budget Policy*. Cambridge: Cambridge University Press.

Briotti, M. G. (2004). "Fiscal Adjustment between 1991–2002: Stylised Facts and Policy Implications." European Central Bank, Occasional Paper Series No. 9. Available at: http://www.ecb.europa.eu/pub/pdf/scpops/ecbocp9.pdf [Last retrieved January 2009]

Brosens, T. and P. Wierts. (2007). "The Surplus Factor." *European Economy Economic Papers* 275: 73–104.

Brower, R. S., M. Y. Abolafia and J. B. Carr. (2000). "On Improving Qualitative Methods in Public Administration Research." *Administration and Society* 32(4): 363–397.
Brubaker, E. R. (1997). "The Tragedy of the Public Budgetary Commons." *Independent Review* 1(3): 353–370.
Brunetti, A. and T. Straubhaar. (1996). "Direkte Demokratie – "Bessere Demokratie"? Was lehrt uns das Schweizer Beispiel?" *Zeitschrift für Politikwissenschaft* 6(1): 7–26.
Brünneck, A. von. (1988). "Constitutional Review and Legislation in Western Democracies." In C. Landfried (ed.), *Constitutional Review and Legislation.* Baden-Baden: Nomos Verlagsgesellschaft.
Brusis, M. and V. Dimitrov. (2001). "Executive Configuration and Fiscal Performance in Post-Communist Central and Eastern Europe." *Journal of European Public Policy* 8(6): 888–910.
Bruszt, L. (2002). "Market-Making as State-Making. Constitutions and Economic Development in Post-Communist Eastern Europe." *Constitutional Political Economy* 13(1): 53–72.
Brzezinski, M. (2000). *The Struggle for Constitutionalism in Poland.* London: Macmillan.
Buchanan, J. M. (1958). *Public Principles of Public Debt.* Homewood: Irwin.
Buchanan, J. M. (1967). *Public Finance in Democratic Process: Fiscal Institutions and Individual Choice.* Chapel Hill: University of North Carolina Press.
Buchanan, J. M. (1975). *The Limits of Liberty – Between Anarchy and Leviathan.* Chicago: University of Chicago Press.
Buchanan, J. M. (1987). "Constitutional Economics." In J. Eatwell, M. Milgate and P. Newman (eds.), *The New Palgrave – A Dictionary of Economics. Vol 1.* London: Macmillan.
Buchanan, J. M. (1990). "The Domain of Constitutional Economics." *Constitutional Political Economy* 1(1): 3–20.
Buchanan, J. M. (1991). *The Economics and the Ethics of Constitutional Order.* Ann Arbor: The University of Michigan Press.
Buchanan, J. M. (1997a). *Post-Socialist Political Economy. Selected Essays.* Cheltenham: Edward Elgar.
Buchanan, J. M. (1997b). "The Balanced Budget Amendment: Clarifying the Arguments." *Public Choice* 90(1–4): 117–138.
Buchanan. J. M. (2002). "Why Do Constitutions Matter?" In N. Berggren, N. Karlson and J. Nergelius (eds.), *Why Constitutions Matter.* New Brunswick: Transaction Publishers.
Buchanan, J. M. and G. Tullock. (1962). *The Calculus of Consent.* Ann Arbor: University of Michigan Press.
Buchanan, J. M. and R. E. Wagner. (1977). *Democracy in Deficit.* London: Academic Press.
Buchanan, J. M. and Y. J. Yoon. (2001). "Majoritarian Management of the Commons." *Economic Inquiry* 39(3): 396–405.
Buchanan, J. M. and Y. J. Yoon. (2002). "Universalism through Common Access: An Alternative Model of Distributive Majoritarian Politics." *Political Research Quarterly* 55(3): 503–519.
Buiter, W. H. and C. Grafe. (2002). "Patching up the Pact: Some Suggestions for Enhancing Fiscal Sustainability and Macroeconomic Stability in an Enlarged European Union." CEPR Discussion Paper No. 3496. Available at: www.cepr.org/pubs/dps/DP3496.asp. [Last retrieved January 2009]
Burgess, S. R. (1993). "Beyond Instrumental Politics: The New Institutionalism, Legal Rhetoric, and Judicial Supremacy." *Polity* 25(3): 445–459.

Buti, M. (2007). "Will the New Stability and Growth Pact Succeed? An Economic and Political Perspective." In F. Breuss (ed.), *The Stability and Growth Pact: Experiences and Future Aspects.* Vienna: Springer.

Buti, M., J. N. Martins and A. A. Turrini. (2007). "From Deficits to Debt and Back: Political Incentives under Numerical Fiscal Rules." *CESifo Economic Studies* 53(1): 115–152.

Buti, M. and L. R. Pench. (2004). "Why Do Large Countries Flout the Stability Pact? And What Can Be Done About It?" *Journal of Common Market Studies* 42(5): 1025–1032.

Cain, B. E., J. Ferejohn and M. P. Fiorina. (1987). *The Personal Vote: Constituency Service and Electoral Independence.* Cambridge: Cambridge University Press.

Cain, B. E. and W. T. Jones. (1989). "Madison's Theory of Representation." In B. Grofman and D. Wittman (eds.), *The Federalist Papers and the New Institutionalism.* New York: Agathon Press.

Caldeira, G. (1986). "Neither the Purse nor the Sword: Dynamics of Public Confidence in the Supreme Court." *American Political Science Review* 80(4): 1209–1226.

Calvert, R. L. (1992). "Leadership and Its Basis in Problems of Social Coordination." *International Political Science Review* 13(1): 7–24.

Calvert, R. L. and J. Johnson. (1998). "Interpretation and Coordination in Constitutional Politics." W. Allen Wallis Institute of Political Economy, University of Rochester, Working Paper No. 15. Available at: http://www.wallis.rochester.edu/WallisPapers/wallis_15.pdf [Last retrieved January 2009]

Cameron, C. M. (2000). *Veto Bargaining. Presidents and the Politics of Negative Power.* Cambridge: Cambridge University Press.

Cameron, D. (1985). "Does Government Cause Inflation? Taxes, Spending, and Deficits." In L. Lindberg and C. Maier (eds.), *The Politics of Inflation and Economic Stagnation.* Washington, DC: Brookings Institution.

Campbell, J. L. (1996). "An Institutional Analysis of Fiscal Reform in Postcommunist Europe." *Theory and Society* 25(1): 45–84.

Canon, B. and C. Johnson. (1999). *Judicial Policies: Implementation and Impact.* Washington, DC: Congressional Quarterly Press.

Capelletti, M. (1989). *The Judicial Process in Comparative Perspective.* Oxford: Clarendon Press.

Carey, J. M. and M. S. Shugart. (1995). "Incentives to Cultivate a Personal Vote: A Rank Ordering of Personal Formulas." *Electoral Studies* 14(4): 417–439.

Carlsen, F. (1997). "Counterfiscal Policies and Partisan politics: Evidence from Industrialized Countries." *Applied Economics* 29(2): 145–151.

Carter, J. R. and D. Schap. (1987). "Executive Veto, Legislative Override, and Structure Induced Equilibrium." *Public Choice* 52(2): 227–244.

Chambers, S. (2005). "Measuring Publicity's Effect: Reconciling Empirical Research and Normative Theory." *Acta Politica* 40(2): 255–266.

Chaney, B. A., P. A. Copley and M. S. Stone. (2002). "The Effect of Fiscal Stress and Balanced Budget Requirements on the Funding and Measurement of State Pension Obligations." *Journal of Accounting and Public Policy* 21(4–5): 287–313.

Chen, J. and N. Malhotra. (2007). "The Law of k/n: The Effect of Chamber Size on Spending in Bicameral Legislatures." *American Political Science Review* 101(4): 657–676.

Christensen, J. G. (1992). "Hierarchical and Contractual Approaches to Budgetary Reform." *Journal of Theoretical Politics* 4(1): 67–91.

Citrin, J. (1979). "Do People Want Something for Nothing: Public Opinion on Taxes and Government Spending." *National Tax Journal* 32(2): 113–130.

Cogan, J. F. (1994). "The Dispersion of Spending Authority and Federal Budget Deficits." In J. F. Cogan, T. J. Muris and A. Schick (eds.), *The Budget Puzzle: Understanding Federal Spending*. Stanford: Stanford University Press.

Cohen, M. D., J. G. March and J. P. Olsen. (1972). "A Garbage Can Model of Organizational Choice." *Administrative Science Quarterly* 17(1): 1–25.

Collie, M. P. (1988). "The Legislature and Distributive Policy Making in Formal Perspective." *Legislative Studies Quarterly* 13(4): 427–458.

Congleton, R. D. and B. Swedenborg. (2006). "Introduction: Rational Choice Politics and Political Institutions." In R. D. Congleton and B. Swedenborg (eds.), *Democratic Constitutional Design and Public Policy, Analysis and Evidence*. Cambridge: MIT Press.

Cooter, R. D. (2000). *The Strategic Constitution*. Princeton: Princeton University Press.

Corbacho, A. and G. Schwartz. (2007). "Fiscal Responsibility Laws." In M. S. Kumar and T. Ter-Minassian (eds.), *Promoting Fiscal Discipline*. Washington, DC: IMF.

Corsetti, G. and N. Roubini. (1993). "The Design of Optimal Fiscal Rules in Europe after 1992." In F. Torres and F. Giavazzi (eds.), *Adjustment and Growth in the European Monetary System*. Cambridge: Cambridge University Press.

Cowart, A. T. (1978). "The Economic Policies of European Governments, Part II: Fiscal Policy." *British Journal of Political Science* 8(4): 425–439.

Cox, G. W. (1997). *Making Votes Count: Strategic Coordination in the World's Electoral Systems*. Cambridge: Cambridge University Press.

Cox, G. W. and M. D. McCubbins. (1991). "Divided Control of Fiscal Policy." In G. W. Cox and S. Kernell (eds.), *The Politics of Divided Government*. Boulder: Westview.

Cox, G. W. and M. D. McCubbins. (1993). *Legislative Leviathan*. Berkeley: University of California Press.

Cox, G. W. and M. D. McCubbins. (2001). "The Institutional Determinants of Economic Policy Outcomes." In S. Haggard and M. D. McCubbins (eds.), *Presidents, Parliaments and Policy*. Cambridge: Cambridge University Press.

Cox, G. W. and F. Rosenbluth. (1993). "The Electoral Fortunes of Legislative Factions in Japan." *American Political Science Review* 87(3): 577–589.

Cox, J. and D. Lowery. (1990). "The Impact of the Tax Revolt Era State Fiscal Caps." *Social Science Quarterly* 71(3): 492–509.

Crain, W. M. (1979). "Cost and Output in the Legislative Firm." *Journal of Legal Studies* 8(3): 607–622.

Crain, W. M. and J. C. Miller III. (1990). "Budget Process and Spending Growth." *William and Mary Law Review* 31(4): 1021–1046.

Crain, W. M. and T. J. Muris. (1995). "Legislative Organization of Fiscal Policy." *Journal of Law and Economics* 38(2): 311–333.

Crepaz, M. M. L. (1996). "Consensus Versus Majoritarian Democracy. Political Institutions and Their Impact on Macroeconomic Performance and Industrial Disputes." *Comparative Political Studies* 29(1): 4–26

Crepaz, M. M. L. (1998). "Inclusion versus Exclusion: Political Institutions and Welfare Expenditures." *Comparative Politics* 31(1): 61–80.

Crepaz, M. M. L. and A. W. Moser. (2004). "The Impact of Collective and Competitive Veto Points on Public Expenditures in the Global Age." *Comparative Political Studies* 37(3): 259–285.

Crum, B. (2004). "Politics and Power in the European Convention." *Politics* 24(1): 1–11.

Cukierman, A. and A. H. Meltzer. (1986). "A Positive Theory of Discretionary Policy, the Cost of Democratic Government and the Benefits of a Constitution." *Economic Inquiry* 24(3): 367–388.

Cukierman, A. and A. H. Meltzer. (1989). "A Political Theory of Government Debt and Deficits in a Neo-Ricardian Framework." *American Economic Review* 79(4): 713–732.

Curried, D. P. (2005). "Prolegomena for a Sampler. Extrajudicial Interpretation of the Constitution, 1789–1861." In N. Devins and K. E. Whittington (eds.), *Congress and the Constitution*. Durham: Duke University Press.

Cusack, T. R. (1997). "Partisan Politics and Public Finance: Changes in Public Spending in the Industrialized Democracies, 1955–1989." *Public Choice* 91(3–4): 375–395.

Cusack, T. R. (1999). "Partisan Politics and Fiscal Policy." *Comparative Political Studies* 32(4): 464–486.

Dahl, R. A. (1956). *A Preface to Democratic Theory*. Chicago: University of Chicago Press.

Dalen, H. R. van and O. H. Swank. (1996). "Government Spending Cycles: Ideological or Opportunistic." *Public Choice* 89(1–2): 183–200.

Dasgupta, P. S. and G. M. Heal. (1979). *Economic Theory and Exhaustible Resources*. Cambridge: Cambridge University Press.

Davidson, J. (1984). "The Limits of Constitutional Determinism." In R. B. McKenzie (ed.), *Constitutional Economics – Containing the Economic Power of Government*. Lexington: Lexington Books.

Dearden, J. A. and T. Husted. (1990). "Executive Budget Proposal, Executive Veto, Legislative Override, and Uncertainty." *Public Choice* 65(1): 1–19.

Debrun, X., D. Hauner and M. S. Kumar. (2007). "Discretion, Institutions, and Fiscal Discipline." In M. S. Kumar and T. Ter-Minassian (eds.), *Promoting Fiscal Discipline*. Washington, DC: IMF.

Debrun, X. and M. S. Kumar. (2007). "The Discipline-Enhancing Role of Fiscal Institutions: Theory and Empirical Evidence." IMF Working Paper No. 07/171. Available at: http://www.imf.org/external/pubs/ft/wp/2007/wp07171.pdf [Last retrieved January 2009]

Debrun, X., L. Moulin, A. Turrini, J. Ayuso-i-Casals and M. S. Kumar. (2008). "Tied to the Mast? National Fiscal Rules in the European Union." *Economic Policy* 23(54): 297–362.

De Figueiredo, R. J. P. Jr. (2003). "Budget Institutions and Political Insulation: Why States Adopt the Item Veto." *Journal of Public Economics* 87(12): 2677–2701.

De Haan, J., W. Moessen and B. Volkerink. (1999). "Budgetary Procedures – Aspects and Changes: New Evidence for Some European Countries." In J. M. Poterba and J. von Hagen (eds.), *Fiscal Institutions and Fiscal Performance*. Chicago: University of Chicago Press.

De Haan, J. and J.-E. Sturm. (1994). "Political and Institutional Determinants of Fiscal Policy in the European Community." *Public Choice* 80(1–2): 157–172.

De Haan, J. and J.-E. Sturm. (1997). "Political and Economic Determinants of OECD Budget Deficits and Government Expenditures: A Reinvestigation." *European Journal of Political Economy* 13(4): 739–750.

De Haan, J. and J.-E. Sturm. (2000). "Do Financial Markets and the Maastricht Treaty Discipline Governments? New Evidence." *Applied Financial Economics* 10(2): 221–226.

De Haan, J., J.-E. Sturm and G. Beekhuis. (1999). "The Weak Government Thesis: Some New Evidence." *Public Choice* 101(3–4): 163–176.

Denemark, D. (2003). "Partisan Pork Barrel in Parliamentary Systems: Australian Constituency-Level Grants." *Journal of Politics* 62(3): 896–915.

Devins, N. (1996). *Shaping Constitutional Values: Elected Government, the Supreme Court and the Abortion Debate*. Baltimore: Johns Hopkins University Press.

Dharmapala, D. (2003). "Budgetary Policy with Unified and Decentralized Appropriations Authority." *Public Choice* 115(3–4): 347–367.

Diermeier, D. and T. Feddersen. (1998). "Cohesion in Legislatures and the Vote of Confidence Procedure." *American Political Science Review* 92(3): 611–622.
Diermeier, D. and K. Krehbiel. (2003). "Institutionalism as Methodology." *Journal of Theoretical Politics* 15(2): 123–144.
Dimitrov, V. (2005). "Ready for European Economic and Monetary Union? Party Composition of Government, Budgeting Institutions and Fiscal Deficit in Central and Eastern Europe." *International Journal of Organization Theory and Behavior* 8(1): 40–66.
Dixit, A. K. (1996). *The Making of Economic Policy: A Transaction Cost Politics Perspective.* Cambridge: MIT Press.
Dodd, L. C. (1976). *Coalitions in Parliamentary Government.* Princeton: Princeton University Press.
Dougan, W. (1988). "The Effects of Tax or Expenditure Limits on State Government." Center for the Study of the Economy and the State, Working Paper No. 54.
Drazen, A. (2000). *Political Economy in Macroeconomics.* Princeton: Princeton University Press.
Drechsler, W. (2001). "On the Viability of the Concept of Staatswissenschaften." *European Journal of Law and Economics* 12(2): 105–111.
Durr, R., A. Martin and C. Wolbrecht. (2000). "Ideological Divergence and Public Support for the Supreme Court." *American Journal of Political Science* 44(4): 768–776.
Duverger, M. (1954). *Political Parties, Their Organization, and Activity in the Modern State.* New York: Wiley.
Easton, D. (1975). "A Re-Assessment of the Concept of Political Support." *British Journal of Political Science* 5(4): 435–457.
Ebrill, L. and O. Havrylyshyn. (1999). *Tax Reform in the Baltics, Russia, and Other Countries of the Former Soviet Union.* Washington, DC: International Monetary Fund.
Eckstein, H. (1975). "Case Studies in Political Science." In F. Greenstein and N. Polsby (eds.), *Handbook of Political Science.* Reading: Addison-Wesley.
Edin, P. A. and H. Ohlsson. (1991). "Political Determinants of Budget Deficits: Coalition Effects vs. Minority Effects." *European Economic Review* 35(8): 1597–1603.
Edwards, M. S. and F. C. Thames. (2007). "District Magnitude, Personal Votes, and Government Expenditures." *Electoral Studies* 26(2): 338–345.
Eggertsson, T. (1997). "The Old Theory of Economic Policy and the New Institutionalism." *World Development* 25(8): 1187–1203.
Eichengreen, B. (1994). "Fiscal Policy and EMU." In B. Eichengreen and J. Frieden (eds.), *The Political Economy of European Monetary Unification.* Boulder: Westview Press.
Eichengreen, B. and T. Bayoumi. (1994). "The Political Economy of Fiscal Restrictions: Implications for Europe from the United States." *European Economic Review* 38(3–4): 783–791.
Eklit, J. and N. S. Roberts. (1996). "A Category of Its Own? Four PR Two-tier Compensatory Member Electoral Systems in 1994." *European Journal of Political Research* 30(2): 217–240.
Elder, H. W. (1992). "Exploring the Tax Revolt: An Analysis of the Effectiveness of State Tax and Expenditure Limitation Laws." *Public Finance Quarterly* 20(1): 47–63.
Elgie, R. and I. McMenamin. (2008). "Political Fragmentation, Fiscal Deficits, and Political Institutionalisation." *Public Choice* 136(3–4): 255–267.
Elgie, R. and J. Zielonka, J. (2001). "Constitutions and Constitution-Building: A Comparative Perspective." In J. Zielonka (ed.), *Democratic Consolidation in Eastern Europe. Vol 1. Institutional Engineering.* Oxford: Oxford University Press.

Elster, J. (1991). "Arguing and Bargaining in the Federal Convention and the Assemblée Constituante." Center for the Study of Constitutionalism in Eastern Europe, Working Paper No. 4.

Elster, J. (1992). "Making Sense of Constitution-Making." *East European Constitutional Review* 1(1): 15–17.

Elster, J. (1993). "Constitution-Making in Eastern Europe: Rebuilding the Boat in the Open Sea." *Public Administration* 71(1–2): 169–217.

Elster, J. (1995a). "Strategic Uses of Argument." In K. Arrow, R. H. Mnookin, L. Ross, A. Tversky and R. Wilson (eds.), *Barriers to Conflict Resolution.* New York: W.W. Norton & Company.

Elster, J. (1995b). "Forces and Mechanisms in the Constitution-Making Process." *Duke Law Journal* 45(2): 354–396.

Elster, J. (1996a). "The Role of Institutional Interest in East European Constitution-Making." *East European Constitutional Review* 5(1): 63–65.

Elster, J. (1996b). "The Constitution-Making Process." In J. C. Pardo and F. Schneider (eds.), *Current Issues in Public Choice*. Cheltenham: Edward Elgar.

Elster, J. (1997a). "Ways of Constitution-Making." In A. Hadenius (ed.), *Democracy's Victory and Crisis.* Cambridge: Cambridge University Press.

Elster, J. (1997b). "Afterword: The Making of Postcommunist Presidencies." In R. Taras (ed.), *Postcommunist Presidents*. Cambridge: Cambridge University Press.

Elster, J. (1998a). "Deliberation and Constitution Making." In J. Elster (ed.), *Deliberative Democracy*. Cambridge: Cambridge University Press.

Elster, J. (1998b). "A Plea for Mechanisms." In P. Hedstrom and R. Swedberg (eds.), *Social Mechanisms: An Analytical Approach to Social Theory*. Cambridge: Cambridge University Press.

Elster, J. (2000). *Ulysses Unbound.* Cambridge: Cambridge University Press.

Elster, J., C. Offe and U. K. Preuss. (1998). *Institutional Design in Post-Communist Societies: Rebuilding the Ship at Sea.* Cambridge: Cambridge University Press.

Epstein, L. and J. Knight. (1998). *The Choices Justices Make*. Washington, DC: CQ Press.

Epstein, L., J. Knight and O. Shvetsova. (2001). "The Role of Constitutional Courts in the Establishment and Maintenance of Democratic Systems of Government." *Law and Society Review* 35(1): 117–174.

Epstein, L. and T. G. Walker. (1995). "The Role of the Supreme Court in American Society: Playing the Reconstruction Game." In L. Epstein (ed.), *Contemplating Courts.* Washington, DC: CQ Press.

Ernits, M. (1999). "Põhiseaduse Riigikogu peatüki probleemid." [The Problems with the Riigikogu Chapter in the Constitution] *Juridica* 10: 472–479.

Eskridge, W. N. Jr. (1991). "Overriding Supreme Court Statutory Interpretation Decisions." *Yale Law Review* 101(2): 331–455.

Eslava, M. (2006). "The Political Economy of Fiscal Policy: Survey." Inter-American Development Bank, Research Department, Working Paper No. 583. Available at: http://www.mdb-egp.com/res/publications/pubfiles/pubWP-583.pdf [Last retrieved January 2009]

ETA. (2002). "President kuulutas välja maksuintresse puudutava seaduse." [The President Promulgated the Act Pertaining to Tax Interests] 30 December 2002. Available at: http://www.aktiva.ee/index.php?book=0&chapter=00&news=2002N3103&mainpage=1 [Last retrieved January 2009]

European Commission. (2006). "National Numerical Fiscal Rules and Institutions for Sound Public Finance." *Public Finances in EMU*, No. 3.

Fabrizio, S. and A. Mody. (2006). "Can Budget Institutions Counteract Political Indiscipline?" *Economic Policy* 21(48): 689–739.
Farnham, P. G. (1990). "The Impact of Citizen Influence on Local Government Expenditures." *Public Choice* 64(3): 201–211.
Farr, W. K., R. A. Lord and J. L. Wolfenbarger. (1998). "Economic Freedom, Political Freedom and Economic Well-Being: A Causality Analysis." *Cato Journal* 18(2): 247–262.
Farrell, D. M. (2001). *Electoral Systems: A Comparative Introduction*. New York: Palgrave.
Fatas, A., A. H. Hallett, A. Sibert, R. Strauch and J. von Hagen. (2003). *Stability and Growth in Europe: Towards a Better Pact*. London: CEPR.
Fatas, A. and I. Mihov. (2003). "The Case for Restricting Fiscal Policy Discretion." *Quarterly Journal of Economics* 118(4): 1419–1448.
Favoreu, L. (1988). "The Constitutional Council and Parliament in France." In C. Landfried (ed.), *Constitutional Review and Legislation. An International Comparison*. Baden-Baden: Nomos Verlagsgesellschaft.
Faysse, N. (2005). "Coping with the Tragedy of the Commons: Game Structure and Design of Rules." *Journal of Economic Surveys* 19(2): 239–261.
Feld, L. P. (2002). "Budgetary Procedures and Public Finance or: Quis Custodiet Ipsos Custodes?" *Journal for Institutional Innovation, Development and Transition* 6: 4–17.
Feld, L. P. and G. Kirchgässner. (2000). "Direct Democracy, Political Culture, and the Outcome of Economic Policy: A Report on Swiss Experience." *European Journal of Political Economy* 16(2): 287–306.
Feld, L. P. and G. Kirchgässner. (2001a). "The Political Economy of Direct Legislation: Direct Democracy and Local Decision-Making." *Economic Policy* 16(33): 329–363.
Feld, L. P. and G. Kirchgässner. (2001b). "Does Direct Democracy Reduce Public Debt? Evidence from Swiss Municipalities." *Public Choice* 109(3–4): 347–370.
Feld, L. P. and G. Kirchgässner. (2006). "On the Effectiveness of Debt Brakes: The Swiss Experience." CREMA Working Paper No. 2006/21. Available at: http://www.crema-research.ch/papers/2006-21.pdf [Last retrieved January 2009]
Feld, L. P. and J. Matsusaka. (2003). "Budget Referendums and Government Spending: Evidence from Swiss Cantons." *Journal of Public Economics* 87(12): 2703–2724.
Feld, L. P. and M. R. Savioz. (1997). "Direct Democracy Matters for Economic Performance: An Empirical Investigation." *Kyklos* 50(4): 507–538.
Feld, L. P. and S. Voigt. (2003). "Economic Growth and Judicial Independence: Cross Country Evidence Using a New Set Of Indicators." *European Journal of Political Economy* 19(3): 497–527.
Feld, L. P. and S. Voigt. (2006). "Judicial Independence and Economic Growth: Some Proposals Regarding the Judiciary." In R. D. Congleton and B. Swedenborg (eds.), *Democratic Constitutional Design and Public Policy, Analysis and Evidence*. Cambridge: MIT Press.
Fenno, R. (1978). *Home Style: House Members in the Their Districts*. Boston: Little, Brown.
Ferejohn, J. A. (1974). *Pork Barrel Politics: Rivers and Harbors Legislation, 1947-1968*. Stanford: Stanford University Press.
Ferejohn, J. A. and K. Krehbiel. (1987). "The Budget Process and the Size of the Budget." *American Journal of Political Science* 31(2): 296–320.
Ferejohn, J. E. (2002). "Constitutional Review in the Global Context." *Legislation and Public Policy* 6(1): 49–59.
Figueiredo, R. de. (2003). "Budget Institutions and Political Insulation: Why States Adopt the Item Veto." *Journal of Public Economics* 87(12): 2677–2701.

Filc, G. and C. Scartascini. (2005). "Budget Institutions and Fiscal Outcomes." *International Journal of Public Budget* 59: 81–138.
Fiorina, M. P. (1981). "Universalism, Reciprocity, and Distributive Policymaking in Majority Rule Institutions." In J. P. Crecine (ed.), *Research in Public Policy Analysis and Management, Vol. I.* Greenwich: JAI Press.
Fiorina, M. P. (1992). *Divided Government*. New York: Macmillan.
Fiorina, M. P. and R. Noll. (1979). "Majority Rule Models and Legislative Elections." *Journal of Politics* 41(4): 1081–1104.
Fiorino, N. and R. Ricciuti. (2007). "Legislature Size and Government Spending in Italian Regions: Forecasting the Effects of a Reform." *Public Choice* 131(1–2): 117–125.
Fisher, L. (1985). "Constitutional Interpretation by Members of Congress." *North Carolina Law Review* 63(4): 707 747.
Fisher, L. (1988). *Constitutional Dialogues: Interpretation as Political Process.* Princeton: Princeton University Press.
Fisher, L. (1990). "Separation of Powers: Interpretation Outside the Courts." *Pepperdine Law Review* 18(1): 57–93.
Fisher, L. (1997). *Constitutional Conflicts between Congress and the President.* 4th ed. Lawrence: University Press of Kansas.
Fisher, L. and N. Devins. (2001). *The Political Dynamics of Constitutional Law.* 3rd ed. St Paul: West.
Fitts, M. and R. Inman. (1992). "Controlling Congress: Presidential Influence in Domestic Fiscal Policy." *Georgetown Law Review* 80(5): 1737–1785.
Forte, F. (1985). "Competitive Democracy and Fiscal Constitution." *Atlantic Economic Journal* 13(3): 1–11.
Franklin, C. and L. C. Kosaki. (1995). "Media, Knowledge, and Public Evaluations of the Supreme Court." In L. J. Epstein (ed.), *Contemplating Courts*. Washington, DC: Congressional Quarterly Press.
Franzese, R. J. (2000). "Electoral and Partisan Manipulation of Public Debt in Developed Democracies, 1956–90." In R. Strauch and J. Von Hagen (eds.), *Institutions, Politics and Fiscal Policy.* Boston: Kluwer Academic Press.
Franzese, R. J. (2002a). *Macroeconomic Policies of Developed Democracies.* Cambridge: Cambridge University Press.
Franzese, R. J. (2002b). "The Positive Political Economy of Public Debt: An Empirical Examination of the OECD Postwar Experience." Mimeo.
Available at: http://www-personal.umich.edu/~franzese/rjf.debt.paper.pdf
Franzese, R. J. (2002c). "Electoral and Partisan Cycles in Economic Policies and Outcomes." *Annual Review of Political Science* 5(4): 369–421
Fredriksson, P. G. and D. L. Millimet. (2004). "Comparative Politics and Environmental Taxation." *Journal of Environmental Economics* 48(1): 705–722.
Freitag, M. (1999). *Politik und Währung. Ein internationaler Vergleich.* Bern: Paul Haupt.
Freitag, M. and P. Sciarini. (2001). "The Political Economy of Budget Deficits in the European Union: The Role of International Constraints and Domestic Structure." *European Union Politics* 2(2): 163–189.
Frey, B. S. (1994). "Direct Democracy: Politico-Economic Lessons from Swiss Experience." *American Economic Review* 84(2): 338–342.
Frey, B. S. (1997). "A Constitution for Knaves Crowds Out Civic Virtues." *Economic Journal* 107(443): 1043–1053.
Frey, B. S. and L. Lau. (1968). "Towards a Mathematical Model of Government Behaviour." *Zeitschrift für Nationalökonomie* 28: 355–380.

Frey, B. S. and F. Schneider. (1978a). "An Empirical Study of Politico-Economic Interaction in the United States." *Review of Economics and Statistics* 60(2): 174–183.
Frey, B. S. and F. Schneider. (1978b). "A Politico-Economic Model of the United Kingdom." *Economic Journal* 88: 243–253.
Frohlich, N. and J. A. Oppenheimer. (1978). *Modern Political Economy*. Englewood Cliffs: Prentice-Hall.
Frye, T. (1997). "A Politics of Institutional Choice: Post-Communist Presidencies." *Comparative Political Studies* 30(5): 523–552.
Furuboth, E. G. and F. Richter. (1997). *Institutions and Economic Theory: The Contribution of the New Institutional Economics*. Ann Arbor: University of Michigan Press.
Füzer, K. (1997). "The Invisible Constitution: The Construction of Constitutional Reality in Hungary." *International Journal of Sociology* 26(4): 48–65.
Gali, J. and R. Perotti. (2003). "Fiscal Policy and Monetary Integration in Europe." *Economic Policy* 18(37): 533–572.
Gallagher, M. (1991). "Proportionality, Disproportionality and Electoral Systems." *Electoral Studies* 10(1): 33–51.
Galli, E. and F. Padovano. (2002). "A Comparative Test of Alternative Theories of the Determinants of Italian Public Deficits (1950–1998)." *Public Choice* 113(1–2): 37–58.
Ganghof, S. (2002). "Promises and Pitfalls of Veto Player Analysis." *Swiss Political Science Review* 9(2): 1–25.
Ganghof, S. (2006). *The Politics of Income Taxation*. Colchester: European Consortium for Political Research Press.
Ganghof, S. (2007). "The Political Economy of High Income Taxation: Capital Taxation, Path Dependence, and Political Institutions in Denmark." *Comparative Political Studies* 40(9): 1059–1084.
Gardner, R., E. Ostrom and J. M. Walker. (1990). "The Nature of Common-Pool Resource Problems." *Rationality and Society* 2(3): 335–358.
Garrett, E. and A. Vermeule. (2008). "Transparency in the U.S. Budget Process." In E. Garrett, E. A, Graddy and H. E. Jackson (eds.), *Fiscal Challenges: An Interdisciplinary Approach to Budget Policy*. Cambridge: Cambridge University Press.
Garrett, G. (1998). *Partisan Politics in the Global Economy*. Cambridge: Cambridge University Press.
Garrett, G. and P. Lange. (1991). "Political Responses to Interdependence: What's 'Left' for the Left?" *International Organization* 45(4): 539–564.
Gärtner, M. (2000). "Political Macroeconomics: A Survey of Recent Developments." *Journal of Economic Surveys* 14(5): 527–561.
Geddes, B. (1996). "Initiation of New Democratic Institutions in Eastern Europe and Latin America." In A. Lijphart and C. Waisman (eds.), *Institutional Design in New Democracies: Eastern Europe and Latin America*. Boulder: Westview Press.
Gelazis, N. (2001). "Institutional Engineering in Lithuania: Stability through Compromise." In J. Zielonka (ed.), *Democratic Consolidation in Eastern Europe. Vol 1. Institutional Engineering.* Oxford: Oxford University Press.
Gely, R. and P. T. Spiller. (1992). "The Political Economy of Supreme Court Constitutional Decisions: The Case of Roosevelt's Court-packing Plan." *International Review of Law and Economics* 12(1): 45–67.
George, A. K. and A. Bennett. (2005). *Case Studies and Theory Development in Social Sciences.* Cambridge: MIT Press.
George, A. K. and T. J. McKeown. (1985). "Case Studies and Theories of Organizational Decision Making." *Advances in Information Processing in Organizations* 2(1): 21–58.

Gerber, E. R. (1996). “Legislative Response to the Threat of Popular Initiatives.” *American Journal of Political Science* 40(1): 99–128.
Gerber, E. R. and A. Lupia. (1995). “Campaign Competition and Policy Responsiveness in Direct Legislation Elections.” *Political Behavior* 17(2): 287–306.
Gerring, J. (2004). “What Is a Case Study and What Is It Good For?” *American Political Science Review* 98(2): 341–354.
Gerring, J. (2007). *Case Study Research: Principles and Practices.* Cambridge: Cambridge University Press.
Gerring, J., S. C. Thacker and C. Moreno. (2005). “Centripetal Democratic Governance.” *American Political Science Review* 99(4): 567–581.
Gersl, A. (2007). “Political Economy of Public Deficit: Perspectives for Constitutional Reform.” *Czech Economic Review* 1(1): 67 86.
Gibson, J. (1989). “Understandings of Justice: Institutional Legitimacy, Procedural Justice, and Political Tolerance.” *Law and Society Review* 23(3): 469–496.
Gibson, J. (1991). “Institutional Legitimacy, Procedural Justice, and Compliance with Supreme Court Decisions: A Question of Causality.” *Law and Society Review* 25(3): 631–636.
Gibson, J., G. Caldeira and V. Baird. (1998). “On the Legitimacy of National High Courts.” *American Political Science Review* 92(2): 343–358.
Gilligan, T. W. and J. G. Matsusaka. (1995). “Deviations from Constituent Interests: The Role of Legislative Structure and Political Parties in the States.” *Economic Inquiry* 33(3): 383–401.
Gilligan, T. W. and J. G. Matsusaka. (2001). “Fiscal Policy, Legislature Size, and Political Parties: Evidence from State and Local Governments in the First Half of the 20th Century.” *National Tax Journal* 54(1): 57–82.
Ginsburg, T. (2002). "Economic Analysis and the Design of Constitutional Courts.” *Theoretical Inquiries in Law* 3(1): 49–86.
Gleich, H. (2002). *The Evolution of Budget Institutions in Central and Eastern European Countries.* Ph.D. Thesis. Bonn: University of Bonn.
Gleich, H. (2003). “Budget Institutions and Fiscal Performance in Central and Eastern European Countries.” European Central Bank Working Paper Series, Working Paper No. 215. Available at: http://www.ecb.int/pub/pdf/scpwps/ecbwp215.pdf [Last retrieved January 2009]
Gomm, R., M. Hammersley and P. Foster. (eds.) (2000). *Case Study Method: Key Issues, Key Texts*. London: Sage Publications.
Goodhart, C. A. E. and R. I. Bhansali. (1970). “Political Economy.” *Political Studies* 18(1): 43–106.
Gordon, T. M. (2008). “The Calculus of Constraint: A Critical Review of State Fiscal Institutions.” In E. Garrett, E. A. Graddy and H. E. Jackson (eds.), *Fiscal Challenges: An Interdisciplinary Approach to Budget Policy*. Cambridge: Cambridge University Press.
Gould A. C. (2001). “Party Size and Policy Outcomes: An Empirical Analysis of Taxation in Democracies.” *Studies in Comparative International Development* 36(2): 3–26.
Gould, A. C. and P. J. Baker. (2002). “Democracy and Taxation.” *Annual Review of Political Science* 5(1): 87–110.
Gregor, M. (2004). "Governing Fiscal Commons in the Enlarged EU.” Charles University Prague, Faculty of Social Sciences, Institute of Economic Studies, Working Paper No. 56. Available at: http://ies.fsv.cuni.cz/default/file/download/id/1277 [Last retrieved January 2009]

Grilli, V., D. Masciandaro and G. Tabellini. (1991). "Political and Monetary Institutions and Public Financial Policies in the Industrial Countries." *Economic Policy* 13(2): 341–392.

Grofman, B. N., E. Mikkel and R. Taagepera. (2000). "Fission and Fusion of Parties in Estonia, 1987–1999." *Journal of Baltic Studies* 31(4): 329–357.

Grofman, B. N. and A. Reynolds. (2001). "Electoral Systems and the Art of Constitutional Engineering: An Inventory of the Main Findings." In R. Mudabi, P. Navarra and G. Sobbrio (eds.), *Rules and Reason: Perspectives on Constitutional Political Economy.* Cambridge: Cambridge University Press.

Grosskopf, A. and J. Mondak. (1998). "Do Attitudes Toward Specific Court Decisions Matter? The Impact of Webster and *Texas vs Johnson* on Public Confidence in the Supreme Court." *Political Research Quarterly* 51(3): 633–654.

Grubel, H. G. (1998). "Economic Freedom and Human Welfare: Some Empirical Findings." *Cato Journal* 18(2): 287–304.

Guichard, S., M. Kennedy, E. Wurzel and C. André. (2007). "What Promotes Fiscal Consolidation: OECD Country Experiences." OECD Economics Department, Working Paper No. 553. Available at: http://www.sourceoecd.org/10.1787/180833424370 [last retrieved January 2009]

Gwartney, J. D. and R. Lawson. (2000). *Economic Freedom of the World: 2000 Annual Report.* Vancouver: Fraser Institute.

Hagen, J. von. (1991). "A Note on the Empirical Effectiveness of Formal Fiscal Restraints." *Journal of Public Economics* 44(2): 99–110.

Hagen, J. von. (1992). "Budgeting Procedures and Fiscal Performance in the European Communities." Commission of the European Communities, DG ECFIN, European Economy Economic Paper No. 96.

Hagen, J. von. (2002). "Fiscal Rules, Fiscal Institutions, and Fiscal Performance." *The Economic and Social Review* 33(3): 263–284.

Hagen, J. von. (2003). "Budgeting Institutions and Public Spending." In A. Shah (ed.), *Ensuring Accountability When There Is No Bottom Line. Handbook on Public Sector Performance Reviews, Vol 1.* Washington, DC: The World Bank.

Hagen, J. von. (2006a). "Fiscal Rules and Fiscal Performance in the European Union and Japan." *Monetary and Economic Studies* 14(1): 25–60.

Hagen, J. von. (2006b). "Political Economy of Fiscal Institutions." In B. Weingast and D. Wittman (eds.), *Oxford Handbook of Political Economy*. Oxford: Oxford University Press.

Hagen, J. von. (2007). "Budgeting Institutions for Better Fiscal Performance." In A. Shah (ed.), *Budgeting and Budgetary Institutions*. Washington, DC: The World Bank.

Hagen, J. von. (2008). "European Experiences with Fiscal Rules and Institutions." In E. Garrett, E. A. Graddy and H. E. Jackson (eds.), *Fiscal Challenges: An Interdisciplinary Approach to Budget Policy*. Cambridge: Cambridge University Press.

Hagen, J. von and B. Eichengreen. (1996). "Federalism, Fiscal Restraints, and European Monetary Union." *American Economic Review* 86(2): 134–38.

Hagen, J. von and I. Harden. (1994). "National Budget Processes and Fiscal Performance." *European Economy: Reports and Studies* 3: 311–418.

Hagen, J. von and I. Harden. (1995). "Budget Processes and Commitment to Fiscal Discipline." *European Economic Review* 39(3–4): 771–779.

Hagen, J. von and I. Harden. (1996). "Budget Processes and Commitment to Fiscal Discipline." IMF Working Paper No. 96/78.

Hagen, J. von. and G. B. Wolff. (2006). "What Do Deficits Tell us about Debt?" *Journal of Banking and Finance* 30(12): 3259–3279.

Haggard, S. and R. R. Kaufman. (2001). "Introduction." In J. Kornai, S. Haggard and R. R. Kaufman (eds.), *Reforming the State: Fiscal and Welfare Reform in Post-Socialist Countries*. Cambridge: Cambridge University Press.

Haggard, S., R. R. Kaufman and M. S. Shugart. (2001). "Politics, Institutions and Macroeconomic Adjustment: Hungarian Fiscal Policy Making in Comparative Perspective." In J. Kornai, S. Haggard and R. R. Kaufman (eds.), *Reforming the State. Fiscal and Welfare Reform in Post-Socialist Countries*. Cambridge: Cambridge University Press.

Hahm, S. D., M. S. Kamlet and D. C. Mowery. (1996). "The Political Economy of Deficit Spending in Nine Industrialized Parliamentary Democracies: The Role of Fiscal Institutions." *Comparative Political Studies* 29(1): 52–77.

Hall, P. A. (1986). *Governing the Economy*. New York: Oxford University Press.

Hall, P. A and R. C. R. Taylor. (1996). "Political Science and the Three New Institutionalisms." *Political Studies* 44(5): 936–957.

Hallaste, I. (1996). "Eesti Vabariigi põhiseaduse sünd." [The Birth of the Constitution of the Republic of Estonia] *Juridica* 9: 438–442.

Hallerberg, M. (2000a). "The Importance of Domestic Political Institutions: Why and How Belgium and Italy Qualified for EMU." Center for European Integration Studies, Working Paper No. B10/2000. Available at: http://www.zei.de/download/zei_wp/B00-10.pdf [Last retrieved January 2009]

Hallerberg, M. (2000b). "A Theory for the Structure of Parliamentary Monitoring of the Government." Mimeo. Available at: http://www.essex.ac.uk/ECPR/events/jointsessions/paperarchive/copenhagen/ws10/hallerberg.pdf [Last retrieved January 2009]

Hallerberg, M. (2004). *Domestic Budgets in a United Europe: Fiscal Governance from the End of Bretton Woods to EMU*. Ithaca: Cornell University Press.

Hallerberg, M. and S. Basinger. (1998). "Internationalization and Changes in Tax Policy in OECD Countries: The Importance of Domestic Veto Players." *Comparative Political Studies* 31(3): 321–352.

Hallerberg, M. and S. Basinger. (1999). "Globalization and Tax Reform: An Updated Case for the Importance of Veto Players." *Politische Vierteljahresschrift* 40: 618–627.

Hallerberg, M. and J. von Hagen. (1999). "Electoral Institutions, Cabinet Negotiations, and Budget Deficits in the European Union." In J. M. Poterba and J. von Hagen (eds.), *Fiscal Institutions and Fiscal Performance*. Chicago: University of Chicago Press.

Hallerberg, M. and P. Marier. (2004). "Executive Authority, the Personal Vote, and Budget Discipline in Latin American and Caribbean Countries." *American Journal of Political Science* 48(3): 571–587.

Hallerberg, M., L. V. de Souza and W. R. Clark. (2002). "Political Business Cycles in EU Accession Countries." *European Union Politics* 3(2): 231–250.

Hallerberg, M., R. Strauch and J. von Hagen. (2007). "The Design of Fiscal Rules and Forms of Governance in European Union Countries." *European Journal of Political Economy* 23(2): 338–359.

Hammond, T. H. and G. J. Miller. (1987). "The Core of the Constitution." *American Political Science Review* 81(4): 1155–1174.

Hänni, L. (2002a). "Põhiseaduse sünd redaktsioonitoimkonnast nähtuna." [The Birth of the Constitution Seen from the Side of Redaction Committee] In E. Pärnaste (ed.), *Põhiseaduse Tulek. Kogumik.* [The Coming of the Constitution] Tallinn: Justiitsministeerium, Kirjastus SE&JS.

Hänni, L. (2002b). "Põhiseaduse mõju poliitilisele otsustusprotsessile." [The Effects of the Constitution on Political Decision Process] *Riigikogu toimetised* 5: 82–87.

Hansen, J. M. (1998). "Individuals, Institutions, and Public Preferences over Public Finance." *The American Political Science Review* 92(3): 513–531.

Hansford, T. G. and D. F. Damore. (2000). "Congressional Preferences, Perceptions of Threat, and Supreme Court Decision Making." *American Politics Research* 28(4): 490–510.

Hansson, A. and J. Sachs. (1994). "Monetary Institutions and Credible Stabilisation: A Comparison of Experience in the Baltics." Paper presented at conference on Central Banks in Eastern Europe and the Newly Independent States, University of Chicago Law School, 22–23 April 1994.

Hardin, G. (1968). "The Tragedy of the Commons." *Science* 162: 1243–1248.

Hardin, R. (1989). "Why a Constitution?" In B. Grofman and B. Wittman (eds.), *The Federalist Papers and New Institutionalism*. New York: Agathon Press.

Harriger, K. J. (1998). "Cues and Miscues in the Constitutional Dialogue." *The Review of Politics* 60(3): 497–524.

Harrinvirta, M. and M. Mattila. (2001). "The Hard Business of Balancing Budgets: A Study of Public Finances in Seventeen OECD Countries." *British Journal of Political Science* 31(3): 497–521.

Harutyunyan, G., and A. Mavcic. (1999). *Constitutional Review and Its Development in the Modern World. A Comparative Constitutional Analysis*. Yerevan- Ljubljana.

Hattam, V. C. (1992). "Ideas and the Politics of Bounded Innovation." In S. Steinmo, K. Thelen and F. Longstreth (eds.), *Structuring Politics: Historical Institutionalism in Comparative Analysis*. Cambridge: Cambridge University Press.

Hausmaninger, H. (1995). "Towards a 'New' Russian Constitutional Court." *Cornell International Law Journal* 28: 349–386.

Helland, L. (2000). "Fiscal Constitutions, Fiscal Preferences, Information and Deficits: An Evaluation of 13 West-European Countries 1978–1995." In R. R. Strauch and J. von Hagen (eds.), *Institutions, Politics and Fiscal Policy*. Dordrecht: Kluwer Academic Publishers.

Heller, W. B. (1997). "Bicameralism and Budget Deficits: The Effect of Parliamentary Structure on Government Spending." *Legislative Studies Quarterly* 22(4): 485–516.

Henisz, W. (2000). "The Institutional Environment for Economic Growth." *Economics and Politics* 12(1): 1–31.

Hettich, W. and S. L. Winer. (1999). *Democratic Choice and Taxation. A Theoretical and Empirical Analysis*. Cambridge: Cambridge University Press.

Hibbs, D. A. (1977). "Political Parties and Macroeconomic Policy." *American Political Science Review* 71(4): 1467–1487.

Hodgson, G. M. (2006). "What Are Institutions?" *Journal of Economic Issues* 40(1): 1–25.

Hodson, D. (2007). "National Fiscal Governance and the Stability and Growth Pact: Are Delegation States at a Disadvantage." *European Economy Economic Papers* 275: 143–169.

Holcombe, R. G. (1998). "Tax Policy from a Public Choice Perspective." *National Tax Journal* 51(2): 359–371.

Holmes, S. and C. Lucky. (1994). "Storm over Compatibility." *East European Constitutional Review* 3(1): 120–122.

Holzinger, K. (2004). "Bargaining Through Arguing: An Empirical Analysis Based on Speech Act Theory." *Political Communication* 21(2): 195–222.

Horowitz, D. (1985). *Ethnic Groups in Conflict*. Berkeley: University of California Press.

Hou, Y. and D. L. Smith. (2006). "A Framework for Understanding State Balanced Budget Requirement Systems: Reexamining Distinctive Features and an Operational Definition." *Public Budgeting and Finance* 26(3): 22–45.

Huber, E., C. Ragin and J. D. Stephens. (1993). "Social Democracy, Christian Democracy, Constitutional Structure, and the Welfare State." *American Journal of Sociology* 99(3): 711–749.

Huber, G., M. Kocher and M. Sutter. (2003). "Government Strength, Power Dispersion in Governments and Budget Deficits in OECD-countries. A Voting Power Approach." *Public Choice* 116(3–4): 333–350.

Huber, J. D, (1996). "The Vote of Confidence in Parliamentary Democracies." *American Political Science Review* 90(2): 269–282.

Hug, S. (2004). "Occurrence and Policy Consequences of Referendums: A Theoretical Model and Empirical Evidence." *Journal of Theoretical Politics* 16(3): 321–356.

Hug, S. (2005). "The Political Effects of Referendums: An Analysis of Institutional Innovations in Eastern and Central Europe." *Communist and Post-Communist Studies* 38(4): 475–499.

Ignagni, J. and J. Meernik (1994). "Explaining Congressional Attempts to Reverse Supreme Court Decisions." *Political Research Quarterly* 47(2): 353–371.

Illera, M. R. and C. Mulas-Granados. (2008). "What Makes Fiscal Consolidations Last? A Survival Analysis of Budget Cuts in Europe (1960–2004)." *Public Choice* 134(3–4): 147–161

Imbeau, L. M. and K. Chenard. (2002). "The Political Economy of Public Deficits: A Review Essay." Paper presented at the Conference of European Public Choice Society, Belgirate, Italy, April, 2002. Available at: http://www.capp.ulaval.ca/publication/cahier/Imbeau-Chenard2002.pdf [Last retrieved January 2009]

Immergut, E. M. (1992). "The Rules of the Game: The Logic of Health Policy-Making in France, Switzerland, and Sweden." In S. Steinmo, K. Thelen and F. Longstreth (eds.), *Structuring Politics: Historical Institutionalism in Comparative Analysis*. New York: Cambridge University Press.

Immergut, E. M. (1998). "The Theoretical Core of the New Institutionalism." *Politics and Society* 26(1): 5–34.

Inman, R. P. (1988). "Federal Assistance and Local Services in the United States: The Evolution of a New Federalist Fiscal Order." In H. Rosen (ed.), *Fiscal Federalism: Quantitative Studies*. Chicago: University of Chicago Press.

Inman, R. P. (1998). "Do Balanced Budget Rules Work? U.S. Experience and Possible Lesson for the EMU." NBER Working Paper Series No. 5838. Available at: http://www.nber.org/papers/w5838.pdf [Last retrieved January 2009]

Inman, R. P. and M. A. Fitts. (1990). "Political Institutions and Fiscal Policy: Evidence from the U.S. Historical Record." *Journal of Law, Economics and Organization* 6: 79–132.

Jakee, K. and S. Turner. (2002). "The Welfare State as a Fiscal Commons: Problems of Incentives Versus Problems of Cognition." *Public Finance Review* 30(6): 481–508.

Jarne, A. (2002). "Põhiseaduse Assemblee ajakirjanduses 1991–1992." [Constitutional Assembly in the Press] In E. Pärnaste (ed.), *Põhiseaduse Tulek. Kogumik.* [The Coming of the Constitution] Tallinn: Justiitsministeerium, Kirjastus SE&JS.

Järvelaid, P. (2001). "Das Institut des Justizkanzlers in Estland: Geschichte und Gegenwart." *Osteuropa Recht* 47(5): 365–374.

John, P. and H. Ward. (2002). "Political Manipulation in a Majoritarian Democracy: Central Government Targeting of Public Funds to English Subnational Government, In Space and Across Time." *British Journal of Politics and International Relations* 3(3): 308–339.

Jõks, A. (2007). "The Chancellor of Justice's Role in Protecting the Constitution and Balancing the Legislature's Activity: Is the Chancellor of Justice Only a Prosecutor of the Supreme Court?" *Juridical International* 13: 14–21.

Joyce, P. G. and D. R. Mullins. (1991). "The Changing Fiscal Structure of the State and Local Public Sector: The Impact of Tax and Expenditure Limitations." *Public Administration Review* 51(3): 240–253.

Jürgenson, K. (2000). "2000. Aasta eelarve, mis ja milleks." [The Budget of 2000: What and Why?] *Riigikogu Toimetised* 1: 55–58.

Kama, K. (2002). "Intervjuu Inge Rumessenile." [Interview with Inge Rumessen] In E. Pärnaste (ed.), *Põhiseaduse Tulek. Kogumik*. [The Coming of the Constitution] Tallinn: Justiitsministeerium, Kirjastus SE&JS.

Kask, P. (1996). "Institutional Development of the Parliament of Estonia." *The Journal of Legislative Studies* 2(1): 193–212.

Kask, P. (2002) "Järelmõtteid Põhiseaduse Assamblee tööst ja rollist." [Reflections on the Work and Role of the Constitutional Assembly] In E. Pärnaste (ed.), *Põhiseaduse Tulek. Kogumik*. [The Coming of the Constitution] Tallinn: Justiitsministeerium, Kirjastus SE&JS.

Katyal, N. K. (2001). "Legislative Constitutional Interpretation." *Duke Law Journal* 50(5): 1335–1394.

Katz, R. (1980). *A Theory of Parties and Electoral Systems*. Baltimore: The Johns Hopkins University Press.

Kau, J. B. and P. H. Rubin. (1979). "Selfinterest, Ideology, and Logrolling in Congressional Voting." *Journal of Law and Economics* 22(2): 365–384.

Keech, W. R. (1985). "A Theoretical Analysis of the Case for a Balanced Budget Amendment." *Policy Sciences* 18(2): 157–168.

Kennedy, S. and J. Robbins. (2001). "The Role of Fiscal Rules in Determining Fiscal Performance." Department of Finance, Canada, Working Paper No. 2001-16. Available at: http://www.fiscalreform.net/library/pdfs/the_role_of_fiscal_rules_in_determining_fiscal_performance.pdf [Last retrieved January 2009]

Kenyon, D. and K. M. Benker. (1984). "Fiscal Discipline: Lessons from the State Experiences." *National Tax Journal* 37(3): 437–446.

Kessler, A. S. (2005). "Representative versus Direct Democracy: The Role of Informational Asymmetries." *Public Choice* 122(1–2): 9–38.

Kiewiet. D. R. and M. D. McCubbins. (1991). *The Logic of Delegation: Congressional Parties and the Appropriations Decisions*. Chicago: University of Chicago Press.

Kiewiet, D. R. and K. Szakaly. (1996). "Constitutional Limitations on Borrowing: An Analysis of State Bonded Indebtedness." *Journal of Law, Economics and Organization* 12(1): 62–97.

King-Meadows, T. and D. Lowery. (2003). "The Impact of the Tax Revolt Era State Fiscal Caps: A Research Update." *Public Budgeting and Finance* 16(1): 102–112.

Kirchgässner, G. (2001). "The Effects of Fiscal Institutions on Public Finance: A Survey of the Empirical Evidence." CESifo Working Paper Series No. 2001-15. Available at: http://www.cesifo-group.de/DocCIDL/cesifo_wp617.PDF [Last retrieved January 2009]

Knight, B. G. (2000). "Supermajority Voting Requirements for Tax increases: Evidence from the States." *Journal of Public Economics* 76(1): 41–67.

Knight, B. G. and A. Levinson. (1999a). "Fiscal Institutions in the US States." In R. R. Strauch and J. von Hagen (eds.), *Institutions, Politics and Fiscal Policy*. Dordrecht: Kluwer Academic Publishers.

Knight, B. G. and A. Levinson. (1999b). "Rainy Day Funds and State Government Savings." *National Tax Journal* 52(3): 459–472.
Knöbl, A. and R. Haas. (2003). "IMF and the Baltics: A Decade of Cooperation." IMF Working Paper No. 03/241.
Knöbl, A., A. Sutt and B. Savoiko. (2002). "The Estonian Currency Board: Its Introduction and Role in the Early Success of Estonia's Transition to a Market Economy." IMF Working Paper No. 02/96. Available at: http://www.imf.org/external/pubs/ft/wp/2002/wp0296. pdf [Last retrieved January 2009]
Kodrzycki, Y. K. (1993). "Tax Reform in Newly Emerging Market Economies." *New England Economic Review* November: 3–17.
Koelble, T. A. (1995). "Review: The New Institutionalism in Political Science and Sociology." *Comparative Politics* 27(2): 231–243.
Koen, V. and P. van den Noord. (2006). "Fiscal Gimmickry in Europe: One-Off Measures and Creative Accounting." In P. Wierts, S. Deroose, E. Flores and A. Turrini (eds.), *Fiscal Policy Surveillance in Europe.* Basingtoke: Palgrave McMillan.
Kontopolous, Y. and R. Perotti. (1999). "Government Fragmentation and Fiscal Policy Outcomes: Evidence from the OECD Countries." In J. M. Poterba and J. von Hagen (eds.), *Fiscal Institutions and Fiscal Performance.* Chicago: University of Chicago Press.
Kopits, G. (1993). "Lessons in Fiscal Consolidation." In H. Siebert (ed.), *Overcoming the Transformation Crisis: Lessons for the Successor States of the Soviet Union.* Tübingen: Mohr Siebeck.
Kopits, G. (2001). "Fiscal Rules: Useful Policy Framework or Unnecessary Ornament?" IMF Working Paper No. 01/145. Available at: http://www.imf.org/external/pubs/ft/wp/2001/wp01145.pdf [Last retrieved January 2009]
Kopits, G. and S. Symansky. (1998). *Fiscal Policy Rules.* Washington, DC: IMF.
Korhonen, I. (2000). "Currency Boards in the Baltic Countries: What Have We Learned?" *Post-Communist Economies* 12(1): 25–46.
Kornai, J. (1997). *Struggle and Hope: Essays on Stabilization and Reform in a Post-Socialist Economy.* Northampton: Edward Elgar.
Kousser, T., M. D. McCubbins and K. Rozga. (2008). "When Does the Ballot Box Limit the Budget: Politics and Spending Limits in California, Colorado, Utah, and Washington." In E. Garrett, E. A. Graddy and H. E. Jackson (eds.), *Fiscal Challenges: An Interdisciplinary Approach to Budget Policy.* Cambridge: Cambridge University Press.
Kraan, D-J. (1996). *Budgetary Decisions. A Public Choice Approach.* Cambridge: Cambridge University Press.
Kramer, G. H. (1971). "Short-Term Fluctuations in U.S. Voting Behavior, 1986–1964." *American Political Science Review* 65(1): 131–143.
Krogstrup, S. (2008). "Do Fiscal Rules Cause Budgetary Outcomes?" *Public Choice* 136(1–2): 123–138.
Krogstrup, S. and C. Wyplosz. (2007). "A Common Pool Theory of Deficit Bias Correction." *European Economy Economic Papers* 275: 1–29.
Krol, R. (1997). "A Survey of the Impact of Budget Rules on State Taxation, Spending, and Debt." *Cato Journal* 16(3): 295–307.
Kuldkepp, A. (2005). "Tax Policy of Estonia in the Framework of the EU Integration." Phd Thesis. Erasmus University Rotterdam. Available at: http://publishing.eur.nl/ir/repub/ asset/6956/ProefschriftAikiKuldkepp290905.pdf [Last retrieved January 2009]
Laakso, M. and R. Taagepera. (1979). "Effective Number of Parties: A Measure with Applications to West Europe." *Comparative Political Studies* 12(1): 3–27.

Laar, M. (2002) "Assamblee." [Assembly] In E. Pärnaste (ed.), *Põhiseaduse Tulek. Kogumik.* [The Coming of the Constitution] Tallinn: Justiitsministeerium, Kirjastus SE&JS.

Lagerspetz, M. and H. Vogt. (1998). "Estonia." In S. Berglund, T. Hellen and F. H. Aarebrot (eds.), *The Handbook of Political Change in Europe.* Cheltenham: Edward Elgar.

Lagona, F. and F. Padovano. (2007). "A Nonlinear Principal Component Analysis of the Relationship between Budget Rules and Fiscal Performance in the European Union." *Public Choice* 130(3–4): 401–436.

Lancaster, T. D. and W. D. Patterson. (1990). "Comparative Pork Barrel Politics: Perceptions from the West German Bundestag." *Comparative Political Studies* 22(4): 458–477.

Landfried, C. (1984). *Bundesverfarsungsgericht und Gesetrgeber.* Baden-Baden: Nomos Verlagsgesellschaft..

Landfried, C. (1988a). "Introduction." In C. Landfried (ed.), *Constitutional Review and Legislation. An International Comparison.* Baden-Baden: Nomos Verlagsgesellschaft.

Landfried, C. (1988b). "Constitutional Review and Legislation in the Federal Republic of Germany." In C. Landfried (ed.), *Constitutional Review and Legislation. An International Comparison.* Baden-Baden: Nomos Verlagsgesellschaft.

Lane, J. E. (1996). *Constitutions and Political Theory.* Manchester: Manchester University Press.

Lane, R. P. (2003). "The Cyclical Behaviour of Fiscal Policy: Evidence from the OECD." *Journal of Public Economics* 87(12): 2661–2675.

Lang, R. (2002). "Mõned mõtted seoses põhiseadusega." [Some Thoughts on the Constitution] In E. Pärnaste (ed.), *Põhiseaduse Tulek. Kogumik.* [The Coming of the Constitution] Tallinn: Justiitsministeerium, Kirjastus SE&JS.

La Porta, R., F. Lopez-de-Silanes, C. Pop-Eleches and A. Shleifer. (2004). "Judicial Checks and Balances." *Journal of Political Economy* 112(2): 445–470.

Lascher, E. L. Jr. (1996). "Legislative Deliberation: A Preface to Empirical Analysis." *Legislative Studies Quarterly* 21(4): 501–519.

Lauristin, M. and P. Vihalemm. (1997). "Recent Historical Developments in Estonia (1987–1997)." In M. Lauristin and P. Vihalemm (eds.), *Return to the Western World. Cultural and Political Perspectives on the Estonian Post-Communist Transition.* Tartu: Tartu University Press.

Laver, M. and K. A. Shepsle. (1996). *Making and Breaking Governments.* Cambridge: Cambridge University Press.

Lavigne, M. (1999). *The Economics of Transition. From Socialist Economy to Market Economy.* 2nd edition. Palgrave.

Lavigne, R. (2006). "The Institutional and Political Determinants of Fiscal Adjustment." Bank of Canada Working Paper No. 2006-1. Available at: http://www.bank-banquecanada.ca/ en/res/wp/2006/wp06-1.pdf [Last retrieved January 2009]

Leachman, L. L., G. Rosas, P. Lange and A. Bester. (2007). "The Political Economy of Budget Deficits." *Economics and Politics* 19(3): 369–420.

Lehis, L. (2002). "VII Peatükk. Rahandus ja Riigieelarve." [Chapter VII. Finance and the State Budget] In J. Truuväli (ed.), *Põhiseaduse kommenteeritud väljaanne.* [Commented Edition of the Constitution] Tallinn: Juura, Õigusteabe AS.

Lehne, J. (2004). *Constitutional Compliance. A Game-Theoretic Analysis.* Berne: Staempfli.

LeLoup L. T., B. Ferfila and C. Herzog. (2000). "Budgeting in Slovenia During the Democratic Transition." *Public Budgeting and Finance* 20(3): 51–79.

Leppik, L. and G. Männik. (2002). "Transformation of Old-Age Security in Estonia." In W. Schmähl and S. Horstmann (eds.), *Transformation of Pension Systems in Central and Eastern Europe.* London: Edward Elgar Publishing.

Leppik, L. and A. Võrk. (2006). "Pension Reform in Estonia." In E. Fultz (ed.), *Pension Reform in the Baltic States.* Budapest: International Labour Office.

Leston-Bandeira, C. (1999). "The Role of the Portuguese Parliament Based on a Case Study: The Discussion of the Budget, 1983–95." *Journal of Legislative Studies* 5(2): 46–73.

Levinson, A. (1998). "Balanced Budgets and Business Cycles: Evidence from the States." *National Tax Journal* 51(4): 715–732.

Levmore, S. (1992). "Bicameralism: When Are Two Decisions Better than One?" *International Review of Law and Economics* 12(2): 145–162.

Lieberman, R. C. (2002). "Ideas, Institutions, and Political Order: Explaining Political Change." *American Political Science Review* 96(4): 697–712.

Lienert, I. (2005). "Who Controls the Budget: The Legislature or the Executive?" IMF Working Paper No. 05/115. Available at: http://www.imf.org/external/pubs/ft/wp/2005/wp051 15.pdf [Last retrieved January 2009]

Lijphart, A. (1984). *Democracies*. New Haven: Yale University Press.

Lijphart, A. (1990). "The Political Consequences of Electoral Laws, 1945–85." *American Political Science Review* 84(2): 481–496.

Lijphart, A. (1992). "Democratization and Constitutional Choices in Czecho-Slovakia, Hungary and Poland, 1989–91." *Journal of Theoretical Politics* 4(2): 207–223.

Lijphart, A. (1994). *Electoral Systems and Party Systems*. Oxford: Oxford University Press.

Lijphart, A. (1999). *Patterns of Democracy. Government Forms and Performance in Thirty-Six Countries*. New Haven: Yale University Press.

Lijphart, A. and M. M. L. Crepaz. (1991). "Corporatism and Consensus Democracy in Eighteen Countries: Conceptual and Empirical Linkages." *British Journal of Political Science* 21(2): 235–246.

Linnamäe, L. (2007). "Riik tahab kaotada soodustused kontserdipiletite käibemaksule." [The State Wants to Abolish the VAT Tax Advantages for Concert Tickets] *Postimees* 28.09.2007. Available at: http://www.postimees.ee/280907/esileht/kultuur/ [Last retrieved January 2009]

Linz, J. J. (1994). "Presidentialism or Parliamentary Democracy: Does it Make a Difference?" In J. J. Linz and A. Valenzuela (eds.), *The Failure of Presidential Democracy*. Baltimore: The Johns Hopkins University Press.

Lipsmeyer, C. S. (2002). "Parties and Policy: Evaluating Economic and Partisan Influences on Welfare Policy Spending during the European Post-Communist Transition." *British Journal of Political Science* 32(4): 641–661.

Lizzeri, A. and N. Persico. (2001). "The Provision of Public Goods under Alternative Electoral Incentives." *American Economic Review* 91(1): 225–245.

Lizzeri, A. and N. Persico. (2005). "A Drawback of Electoral Competition." *Journal of the European Economic Association* 3(6): 1318–1348.

Lucas, R. and N. Stokey. (1983). "Optimal Fiscal and Monetary Policy in Economy without Capital." *Journal of Monetary Economics* 12(1): 55–94.

MacRae, C. (1977). "A Political Model of the Business Cycle." *Journal of Political Economy* 85(2): 239–263.

Magalhaes, P. C. (1999). "The Politics of Judicial Reform in Eastern Europe." *Comparative Politics* 32(1): 43–62.

Magalhaes, P. C. (2003). "The Limits to Judicialization: Legislative Politics and Constitutional Review in the Iberian Democracies." PhD Dissertation, The Ohio State University.

Magnette, P. and K. Nicolaidis. (2004). "The European Convention: Bargaining in the Shadow of Rhetoric." *West European Politics* 27(3): 381–404.

Malova, D. and T. Haughton. (2002). "Making Institutions in Central and Eastern Europe, and the Impact of Europe." *West European Politics* 24(2): 101–120.
Manasse, P. (2005). "Deficit Limits, Budget Rules, and Fiscal Policy." IMF Working Paper No. 05/120. Available at: http://www.imf.org/external/pubs/ft/wp/2005/wp05120.pdf [Last retrieved January 2009]
March, J. G. and J. P. Olsen. (1989). *Rediscovering Institutions*. New York: Free Press.
March, J. G. and J. P. Olsen. (2005). "Elaborating the 'New Institutionalism'." Centre for European Studies, University of Oslo, Working Paper No. 11. Available at: http://www.arena.uio.no/publications/workingpapers2005/papers/wp05_11.pdf [Last retrieved January 2009]
March, J. G. and J. P. Olsen. (2006). "The Logic of Appropriateness." M. Moran, M. Rein and R. E. Goodin (eds.), *Oxford Handbook of Public Policy*. Oxford: Oxford University Press.
Marshall, T. (1989). *Public Opinion and the Supreme Court.* Boston: Unwin Hyman.
Martinez-Vazquez, J. (1997). "Estonia: Fiscal Management and the Budget Process." Georgia State University, International Studies Program Working Paper No. 97-8. Available at: http://isp-aysps.gsu.edu/papers/ispwp9708.pdf [Last retrieved January 2009]
Martinez-Vazquez, J. and J. Boex. (2000). "Budgeting and Fiscal Management in Transitional Countries." Georgia State University, International Studies Program Working Paper No. 00-6. Available at: http://aysps.gsu.edu/isp/files/ispwp0006.pdf [Last retrieved January 2009]
Martinez-Vazquez, J. and R. McNab. (2000). "The Tax Reform Experiment in Transitional Countries." *National Tax Journal* 53(2): 273–298
Maruste, R. (2007). "The Role of the Constitutional Court in Democratic Society." *Juridica International* 13: 8–13.
Maruste, R. and H. Schneider. (1996). "Constitutional Review of Legislation in Estonia – Its Principal Scheme, Practice and Evaluation." In J. Engelbrecht (ed.), *Constitution as a Legal Base for a System and Functions of Organs of the State.* Tallinn: Estonian Academy of Sciences.
Maruste, R. and H. Schneider. (1998). "Constitutional Review in Estonia – Its Principal Scheme, Practice and Evaluation." In R. A. Müllerson, F. Fitzmaurice and M. Andenas (eds.), *Constitutional Reform and International Law in Central and Eastern Europe.* The Hague: Kluwer Law International.
Maskin, E. and J. Tirole. (2004). "The Politician and the Judge: Accountability in Government." *American Economic Review* 94(4): 1034–1054.
Massicote, L. and A. Blais. (1999). "Mixed Electoral Systems: A Conceptual and Empirical Survey." *Electoral Studies* 18(3): 341–366.
Matsusaka, J. G. (1992). "Economics of Direct Legislation." *Quarterly Journal of Economics* 107(2): 541–571.
Matsusaka, J. G. (1995). "Fiscal Effects of the Voter Initiative: Evidence from the Last 30 Years." *The Journal of Political Economy* 103(3): 587–623.
Matsusaka, J. G. (2000). "Fiscal Effects of the Voter Initiative in the First Half of the Twentieth Century." *Journal of Law and Economics* 43(2): 619–650.
Matsusaka, J. G. (2004). *For the Many or the Few: The Initiative, Public Policy, and American Democracy*. Chicago: University of Chicago Press.
Matsusaka, J. G. (2005a). "The Eclipse of Legislatures: Direct Democracy in the 21st century." *Public Choice* 124(1–2): 157–177.
Matsusaka, J. G. (2005b). "Direct Democracy Works." *Journal of Economic Perspectives* 19(2): 185–206.

Matsusaka, J. G. and N. M. McCarty. (2001). "Political Resource Allocation: Benefits and Costs of Voter Initiatives." *Journal of Law, Economics, and Organization* 17(2): 413–448.

Maveety, N. and A. Grosskopf. (2004). "Constrained Constitutional Courts as Conduits for Democratic Consolidation." *Law and Society Review* 38(3): 463–488.

Maveety, N. and V. Pettai. (2005). "Government Lawyers and Non-Judicial Constitutional Review in Estonia." *Europe-Asia Studies* 57(1): 93–115.

McCarty, N. M. (2000). "Presidential Pork: Executive Veto Power and Distributive Politics." *The American Political Science Review* 94(1): 117–129.

McCormick, R. E. and R. D. Tollison. (1981). *Politicians, Legislation, and the Economy*. Boston: Martinus Nijhoff.

McCubbins, M. D. (1991a). "Government on Lay-Away: Federal Spending and Deficits under Divided Party Control." In G.W. Cox and S. Kernell (eds.), *The Politics of Divided Government*. Boulder: Westview.

McCubbins, M. D. (1991b). "Party Governance and U.S. Budget Deficits: Divided Governments and Fiscal Stalemate." In A. Alesina and G. Carliner (eds.), *Politics and Economics in the Eighties*. Chicago: Chicago University Press.

McFaul, M. (1999). "Institutional Design, Uncertainty, and Path Dependency during Transitions: Cases from Russia." *Constitutional Political Economy* 10(1): 27–52.

McGregor, J. P. (1996). "Constitutional Factors in Politics in Central and Eastern Europe." *Communist and Post-Communist Studies* 29(2): 147–166.

McKenzie, K. J. (2001). "A Tragedy of the House of Commons: Political Institutions and Fiscal Policy Outcomes from a Canadian Perspective." C.D. Howe Institute Benefactors Lecture. Toronto, November 8, 2001. Available at: http://www.cdhowe.org/pdf/bene factor_lecture_2001.pdf [Last retrieved January 2009]

McKeown, T. J. (2004). "Case Studies and the Limits of the Quantitative Worldview." In H. E. Brady and D. Collier (eds.), *Rethinking Social Inquiry*. Lanham: Rowan and Littlefield.

McKinnon, R. (1992). "Taxation, Money, and Credit in a Liberalizing Socialist Economy." In C. Clague and G. C. Rausser (eds.), *The Emergence of Market Economies in Eastern Europe*. Cambridge: Blackwell.

McWhinney, E. (1981). *Constitution-Making: Principles, Process, Practice*. Toronto: University of Toronto Press.

McWhinney, E. (1986). *Supreme Courts and Judicial Law-Making: Constitutional Tribunals and Constitutional Review*. Dordrecht: Martinus Nijhoff.

Meernik, J. and J. Ignagni. (1997). "Judicial Review and Coordinate Construction of the Constitution." *American Journal of Political Science* 41(2): 447–467.

Mereste, U. (2003). "Advokaadifirmad ründavad rahva huve." [The Law Firms Attack the Public Interest) *Eesti Ekspress* 12 February 2003.

Merrifield, J. (1991). "The Institutional and Political Factors which Influence Taxation." *Public Choice* 69(3): 295–310.

Mezey, M. L. (1979). *Comparative Legislatures*. Durham: Duke University Press.

Mikkel, E. and V. Pettai. (2004). "The Baltics: Independence with Divergent Electoral Systems." In J. M. Colomer (ed.), *The Handbook of Electoral System Design*. New York: Palgrave Macmillan.

Mikser, S. (1999). "Libe tee. Teerull, demokraatia ja usaldus." [Slippery Road. Roadgrader, Democracy and Trust] *Postimees* 18 June 1999. Available at: http://arhiiv2.postimees.ee:8080/leht/99/06/18/arvamus.htm#kolmas [Last retrieved January 2009]

Milesi-Ferretti, G. M. (1995). "Do Good or Do Well? Public Debt Management in a Two-Party Economy." *Economics and Politics* 7(1): 121–140.
Milesi-Ferretti, G. M. (2003). "Good, Bad or Ugly? On the Effects of Fiscal Rules with Creative Accounting." *Journal of Public Economics* 88(1–2): 377–394.
Milesi-Feretti, G. M., R. Perotti and M. Rostagno. (2002). "Electoral Systems and the Composition of Government Spending." *Quarterly Journal of Economics* 117(2): 609–657.
Milesi-Ferretti, G. M. and E. Spolaore. (1994). "How Cynical Can An Incumbent Be? Strategic Policy in a Model of Government Spending." *Journal of Public Economics* 55(1): 121–140.
Mireau, J. O., R. Jong-A-Pin and J. de Haan. (2007). "Do Political Variables Affect Fiscal Policy Adjustment Decisions? New Empirical Evidence." *Public Choice* 133(3–4): 297–319.
Moak, L. (1982). *Municipal Bonds: Planning, Sale, and Administration*. Chicago: Municipal Finance Officers Association.
Moberg, E. (1998). "The Expanding Public Sector: A Threat to Democracy?" In G. Eliasson and N. Karlson (eds.), *The Limits of Government: Competence and Economic Growth*. Stockholm: City University Press.
Molander, P. (2000). "Reforming Budgetary Institutions: Swedish Experiences." In R. Strauch and J. von Hagen (eds.), *Institutions, Politics, and Fiscal Policy*. Dordrecht: Kluwer Academic Publishers.
Molander, P. (2001). "Budgeting Procedures and Democratic Ideals: An Evaluation of Swedish Reforms." *Journal of Public Policy* 21(1): 23–52.
Mondak, J. and S. I. Smithey. (1997). "The Dynamics of Public Support for the Supreme Court." *Journal of Politics* 59(4): 1114–1142.
Morris, R., H. Ongena and L. Schuknecht. (2006). "The Reform and Implementation of the Stability and Growth Pact." European Central Bank, Occasional Paper Series No. 47. Available at: http://www.ecb.europa.eu/pub/pdf/scpops/ecbocp47.pdf [Last retrieved January 2009]
Moser, P. (1996). "Why is Swiss Politics So Stable?" *Swiss Review of Economics and Statistics* 132(1): 31–60.
Mueller, D. C. (1996). *Constitutional Democracy*. Oxford: Oxford University Press.
Mueller, D. C. (1997). "Constitutional Public Choice." In D. C. Mueller (ed.), *Perspectives on Public Choice: A Handbook*. Cambridge: Cambridge University Press.
Mueller, D. C. (2002). "Interest Groups, Redistribution, and the Size of Government." In S. L. Winer and H. Shibata (eds.), *Political Economy of Public Finance*. Cheltenham: Edward Elgar.
Mueller, D. C. (2003). *Public Choice III*. Cambridge: Cambridge University Press.
Mueller, D. C. and T. Stratmann. (2003). "The Economic Effects of Democratic Participation." *Journal of Public Economics* 87(9–10): 2129–2155.
Mukherjee, B. (2003). "Political Parties and the Size of Government in Multiparty Legislatures." *Comparative Political Studies* 36(6): 699–728.
Mulas-Granados, C. (2003). "The Political and Economic Determinants of Budgetary Consolidation in Europe." *European Political Economy Review* 1(1): 15–39.
Müller, K. (2002). "Old-Age Security in the Baltics: Legacy, Early Reforms and Recent Trends." *Europe-Asia Studies* 54(5): 725–748.
Mullins, D. R. and B. A. Wallin. (2004). "Tax and Expenditure Limitations: Introduction and Overview." *Public Budgeting and Finance* 24(4): 2–15.
Murphy, W. and J. Tanenhaus. (1990). "Publicity, Public Opinion, and the Court." *Northwestern University Law Review* 84: 985–1023.

Musso, J. A., E. A. Graddy and J. B. Grizard. (2008). "Budgetary Arrangements in the 50 States: In Search of Model Practices." In E. Garrett, E. A. Graddy and H. E. Jackson (eds.), *Fiscal Challenges: An Interdisciplinary Approach to Budget Policy*. Cambridge: Cambridge University Press.

Myerson, R. B. (1993). "Effectiveness of Electoral Systems for Reducing Government Corruption: A Game Theoretic Analysis." *Games and Economic Behavior* 5(1): 118–132.

Myerson, R. B. (2000). "Economic Analysis of Constitutions." *The University of Chicago Law Review* 67(3): 925–940.

Nelson, M. A. (1986). "An Empirical Analysis of State and Local Government Tax Structures in the Context of the Leviathan Model of Government." *Public Choice* 49: 283–294.

Nelson, R. R. and B. N. Sampat. (2001). "Making Sense of Institutions as a Factor Shaping Economic Performance." *Journal of Economic Behaviour and Organization* 44(1): 31–54.

New, M. J. (2001). "Limiting Government Through Direct Democracy: The Case of State Tax and Expenditure Limitations." *Policy Analysis* 420: 1–17.

Niitsoo, V. (2002). *Müürimurdjad. MRP-AEG ja ERSP lugu.* [The Breakers of the Wall. The Story of MRP-AEG ja ERSP] Tallinn: Ortwil.

Niou, E. and P. Ordeshook. (1985). "Universalism in Congress." *American Journal of Political Science* 29(2): 246–258.

Nordhaus, W. D. (1975). "The Political Business Cycle." *The Review of Economic Studies* 42(1): 169–190.

Norgaard, O., L. Johannsen, M. Skak and R. Sorensen. (1999). *The Baltic States after Independence.* Cheltenham: Edward Elgar.

O'Donnell, G. and P. Schmitter. (1986). *Transitions from Authoritarian Rule: Tentative Conclusions about Uncertain Democracies.* Baltimore: Johns Hopkins University Press.

Offe, C. (1996). *Varieties of Transition: The East European and East German Experience.* Cambridge: Polity Press.

Offe, C. (1997). "Designing Institutions in East European Transitions." In R. E. Goodin (ed.), *The Theory of Institutional Design.* Cambridge: Cambridge University Press.

Olsen, J. P. (2003). "Coping with Conflict at Constitutional Moments." *Industrial and Corporate Change* 12(4): 815–842.

Oppenheimer, B. I. (1983). "How Legislatures Shape Policy and Budgets." *Legislative Studies Quarterly* 8(4): 551–597.

Ordeshook, P. C. (1990). "The Emerging Discipline of Political Economy." In J. Alt and K. Shepsle (eds.), *Perspectives on Positive Political Economy.* Cambridge: Cambridge University Press.

Ordeshook. P. C. (1992). "Constitutional Stability." *Constitutional Political Economy* 3(2): 137–175.

Ordeshook, P. C. (2002). "Are 'Western' Constitutions Relevant to Anything Other than the Countries they Serve?" *Constitutional Political Economy* 13(1): 3–24.

Ordeshook, P. C. and O. Shvetsova. (1984). "Ethnic Heterogeneity, District Magnitude, and the Number of Parties." *American Journal of Political Science* 38(1): 100–123.

Orren, K. and S. Skowronek. (1994). "Beyond the Iconography of Order: Notes for a 'New Institutionalism.'" In L. C. Dodd and C. Jillson (eds.), *The Dynamics of American Politics: Approaches and Interpretations*. Boulder: Westview Press.

Orren, K. and S. Skowronek. (1996). "Institutions and Intercurrence: Theory Building in the Fullness of Time." In I. Shaprio and R. Hardin (eds.), *Nomos XXXVIII: Political Order.* New York: New York University Press.

Orren, K. and S. Skowronek. (2004). *The Search for American Political Development*. Cambridge: Cambridge University Press.

Ostrom, E. (1986). "An Agenda for the Study of Institutions." *Public Choice* 48(1): 3–25.

Ostrom, E. (1990). *Governing the Commons: The Evolution of Institutions for Collective Action*. New York: Cambridge University Press.

Ostrom, E., R. Gardner and J. Walker. (1994). *Rules, Games and Common-Pool Resources*. Ann Arbor: University of Michigan Press.

Ostrom, E., J. Walker and R. Gardner. (1992). "Covenants With and Without a Sword: Self-Governance is Possible." *American Political Science Review* 86(2): 404–417.

Ostrow, J. M. (2000). *Comparing Post-Soviet Legislatures. A Theory of Institutional Design and Political Conflict*. Columbus: Ohio State University Press.

Padovano, F., G. Sgarra and N. Fiorino. (2003). "Judicial Branch, Checks and Balances and Political Accountability." *Constitutional Political Economy* 14(1): 47–70.

Padovano, F. and L. Venturi. (2001). "Wars of Attrition in Italian Government Coalitions and Fiscal Performance: 1948–1994." *Public Choice* 109(1–2): 15–54.

Paldam, P. (1997). "Political Business Cycles." In D. C. Mueller (ed.), *Perspectives on Public Choice: A Handbook*. Cambridge: Cambridge University Press.

Pärnaste, E. (2002) "Põhiseaduse istungitel kõige enam arutlusel olnud teemad." [The Most Discussed Topics in the Sessions of the Constitutional Assembly." In E. Pärnaste (ed.), *Põhiseaduse Tulek. Kogumik.* [The Coming of the Constitution] Tallinn: Justiitsministeerium, Kirjastus SE&JS.

Peabody, B. G. (1999). "Nonjudicial Constitutional Interpretation, Authoritative Settlement, and a New Agenda for Research." *Constitutional Commentary* 16(1): 63–90.

Peabody, B. G. (2004). "Congressional Constitutional Interpretation and the Courts: A Preliminary Inquiry into Legislative Attitudes, 1959–2001." *Law and Social Inquiry* 29(1): 127–175.

Peabody, B. G. (2005). "Congressional Attitudes toward Constitutional Interpretation." In N. Devins and K. E. Whittington (eds.), *Congress and the Constitution*. Durham: Duke University Press.

Peltzman, S. (1984). "Constituent Interest and Congressional Voting." *Journal of Law and Economics* 27(1): 181–210.

Peltzman, S. (1992). "Voters as Fiscal Conservatives." *Quarterly Journal of Economics* 107(2): 327–361.

Perotti, R. and Y. Kontopoulos. (2002). "Fragmented Fiscal Policy." *Journal of Public Economics* 86(2): 191–222.

Persson, T. (2002). "Do Political Institutions Shape Economic Policy?" *Econometrica* 70(3): 883–905.

Persson, T. (2003). "Consequences of Constitutions." NBER Working Paper No. W10170. Available at: http://www.nber.org/papers/w10170 [Last retrieved January 2009]

Persson, T. and L. Svensson (1989). "Why a Stubborn Conservative Would Run a Deficit: Policy with Time Inconsistent Preferences." *Quarterly Journal of Economics* 104(2): 325–346.

Persson, T. and G. E. Tabellini. (1999a). "Political Economics and Public Finance." In A. Auerbach and M. Feldstein (eds.), *Handbook of Public Finance*. Amsterdam: North Holland.

Persson, T. and G. E. Tabellini. (1999b). "The Size and Scope of Government: Comparative Politics with Rational Politicians." *European Economic Review* 43(4–6): 699–735.

Persson, T. and G. E. Tabellini. (2000). *Political Economics: Explaining Economic Policy*. Cambridge: MIT Press.

Persson, T. and G. E. Tabellini. (2003). *Economic Effects of Constitutions.* Cambridge: MIT Press.

Persson, T. and G. E. Tabellini. (2004a). "Constitutions and Economic Policy." *Journal of Economic Perspectives* 18(1): 75–98.

Persson, T. and G. E. Tabellini. (2004b). "Constitutional Rules and Fiscal Policy Outcomes." *American Economic Review* 94(1): 24–45.

Persson, T., G. Roland and G. E. Tabellini. (1997). "Separation of Powers and Political Accountability." *Quarterly Journal of Economics* 112(4): 1163–1202.

Persson, T, G. Roland, and G. E. Tabellini. (2000). "Comparative Politics and Public Finance." *Journal of Political Economy* 108(6): 1121–1161.

Persson, T, G. Roland and G. E. Tabellini. (2007). "Electoral Rules and Government Spending in Parliamentary Democracies." *Quarterly Journal of Political Science* 2(2): 155–188.

Peters, G. (1991). *The Politics of Taxation. A Comparative Perspective.* Cambridge: Blackwell.

Pettai, V. (2000). "Estonia's Constitutional Review Mechanisms: A Guarantor of Democratic Consolidation?" European University Institute, Roman Schuman Centre Working Paper No. 2000/59.

Pettai, V. (2001). "Estonia: Positive and Negative Institutional Engineering." In J. Zielonka (ed.), *Democratic Consolidation in Eastern Europe. Vol 1. Institutional Engineering.* Oxford: Oxford University Press.

Pettai, V. (2003). "Estonia." *European Journal of Political Research* 42(7): 935–359.

Pettai, V. (2005a). "Assessing Institutional Determinants of MP Behaviour: Survey Data from the Baltic States." *Czech Sociological Review* 41(3): 461–486.

Pettai, V. (2005b). "Democratic Norm Building and Constitutional Discourse Formation in Estonia." In A. Czarnota, M. Krygier and W. Sadurski (eds.), *Rethinking the Rule of Law After Communism.* Budapest: Central European University Press.

Pettai, V. and Ü. Madise. (2006). "The Baltic Parliaments: Legislative Performance from Independence to EU Accession." *Journal of Legislative Studies* 12(3–4): 291–310.

Pettersson-Lidbom, P. (2001). "An Empirical Investigation of the Strategic Use of Debt." *Journal of Political Economy* 109(3): 570–583.

Pickerill, J. M. (2004). *Constitutional Deliberation in Congress: The Impact of Judicial Review in a Separated System.* Durham: Duke University Press.

Pies, I. (1996). "Public Choice versus Constitutional Economics: A Methodological Interpretation of the Buchanan Research Program." *Constitutional Political Economy* 7(1): 21–34.

Pinho, M. M. (2004). "Political Models of Budget Deficits: A Literature Review." University of Porto, Faculty of Economics, Working Paper No. 138. Available at: http://www.fep.up.pt/investigacao/workingpapers/04.03.08_WP138_Maria%20Pinho.pdf [Last retrieved January 2009]

Põhiseadus ja Põhiseaduse Assamblee. Koguteos. [The Constitution and the Constitutional Assembly. Anthology] (1997). Tallinn: Juura, Õigusteabe Aktsiaselts.

Pommerehne, W. W. (1978). "Institutional Approaches to Public Expenditure." *Journal of Public Economics* 9(2): 255–280.

Pommerehne, W. W. (1983). "Private versus öffentliche Müllabfuhr – nochmals betrachtet." *Finanzarchiv* 41(2): 466–475.

Pommerehne, W. W. (1990). "The Empirical Relevance of Comparative Institutional Analysis." *European Economic Review* 34(2–3): 458–69.

Pommerehnne, W. W. and F. Schneider. (1982). "Unbalanced Growth Between Public and Private Sectors: An Empirical Investigation." In R. H. Haveman (ed.), *Public Finance and Public Employment*. Detroit: Wayne State University Press.

Posner, R. (1987). "The Constitution as An Economic Document." *George Washington Law Review* 56(1): 4–38.

Poterba, J. M. (1994). "State Responses to Fiscal Crises: The Effects of Budgetary Institutions and Politics." *Journal of Political Economy* 102(4): 799–821.

Poterba, J. M. (1995). "Balanced Budget Rules and Fiscal Policy: Evidence from the States." *National Tax Journal* 48(3): 329–337.

Poterba, J. M. (1996). "Budget Institutions and Fiscal Policy in the U.S. States." *The American Economic Review* 86(2): 395–400.

Poterba, J. M. (1998). "Public Finance and Public Choice." *National Tax Journal* 51(2): 391–396.

Poterba, J. M. and J. von Hagen. (1999). "Introduction." In J. M. Poterba and J. von Hagen (eds.), *Fiscal Institutions and Fiscal Performance*. Chicago: University of Chicago Press.

Poulson, B. W. (2004). "Tax and Spending Limits: Theory, Analysis and Policy." Independence Institute, Issue Paper No. 2. Available at: http://www.i2i.org/articles/2-2004.pdf [Last retrieved January 2009]

Poulson, B. W. and J. Kaplan. (1994). "A Rent Seeking Model of TELs." *Public Choice* 79(1–2): 117–134.

Powell, G. B. Jr. (1982). *Contemporary Democracies: Participation, Stability and Violence*. Cambridge: Cambridge University Press.

Powell, G. B. Jr. (2000). *Elections as Instruments of Democracy*. New Haven: Yale University Press.

Purju, A. (2004). "Tax Reforms in the Baltic States." In M. Dabrowski, B. Slay and J. Neneman (eds.), *Beyond Transition: Development Perspectives and Dilemmas*. Aldershot: Ashgate.

Primo, D. M. (2006). "Stop Us Before We Spend Again: Institutional Constraints on Government Spending." *Economics and Politics* 18(3): 269–297.

Primo, D. M. and J. M. Snyder, Jr. (2008). "Distributive Politics and the Law of 1/n." *The Journal of Politics* 70(2): 477–486.

Przeworski, A. (1991). *Democracy and the Market: Political and Economic Reforms in Latin America and Europe*. New York: Cambridge University Press.

Przeworski, A., S. Stokes and B. Manin. (1999). *Democracy, Accountability and Representation*. Cambridge: Cambridge University Press.

Rae, D. (1967). *The Political Consequences of Electoral Laws*. New Haven: Yale University Press.

Ragin, C. C. (1997). *The Comparative Method: Moving Beyond Quantitative and Qualitative Strategies*. Berkley: University of California Press.

Ragin, C. C. (2000). *Fuzzy-Set Social Science*. Chicago: University of Chicago Press.

Ragin, C. C. (2008). *Redesigning Social Inquiry: Fuzzy Sets and Beyond*. Chicago: Chicago University Press.

Raitviir, T. (1996). *Eesti Üleminekuperioodi valimiste (1989-1993) võrdlev uurimine*. [Elections in Estonia During the Transition Period. (1989-1993): A Comparative Study] Tallinn: Teaduste Akadeemia Kirjastus.

Raju, O. (2003). "Riigikogu roll riigieelarve kujundamisel." [The Role of the Riigikogu in Designing the Budget] *Riigikogu toimetised* 7: 113–118.

Rakove, J. (1997). *Original Meanings*. New York: Alfred Knopf.

Raudla, R. (2007). "Fiscal Sociological Analysis of the Estonian Pension Reform." In J. Backhaus (ed.), *Fiscal Sociology*. Frankfurt am Main: Peter Lang.
Raudla, R. and K. Staehr. (2003). "Pension Reforms and Taxation in Estonia." *Baltic Journal of Economics* 4(1): 64–92.
Razzolini, L. and W. F. Shugart II. (1997). "On the (Relative) Unimportance of a Balanced Budget." *Public Choice* 90(1–4): 215–233.
Reddick, C. (2003). "Testing Rival Theories of Budgeting Decision-Making in the US States." *Financial Accountability and Management* 19(4): 315–340.
Reed, S. R. (1994). "Democracy and the Personal Vote: A Cautionary Tale from Japan." *Electoral Studies* 13(1): 17–28.
Reinap, A. (2002a). "Maksuvõlglased võivad riigilt intressid tagasi küsida." [Tax Bearers Can Demand Back Interests from the State] *Postimees* 6 November 2002.
Reinap, A. (2002b). "Maksuamet tühistas 2,5 miljardi krooni eest intresse." [The Tax Board Annulled Interests for 2.5 Billion Kroons] *Postimees* 7 November 2002.
Reinap, A. (2002c). "Jurist soovitab ebaseaduslikud interessid riigilt tagasi küsida." [A Lawyer Recommends to Demand Back the Illegal Interests from the State] *Postimees* 7 November 2002.
Ricciuti, R. (2003). "Representing Interests: Legislature Size, Constituency Size and Government Spending in a Panel of Countries." Societa Italiana di Economia Pubblica, Working Paper No. 194. Available at: http://www-1.unipv.it/websiep/wp/194.pdf [Last retrieved January 2009]
Ricciuti, R. (2004a). "Political Fragmentation and Fiscal Outcomes." *Public Choice* 118(3–4): 365–388.
Ricciuti, R. (2004b). "Legislatures and Government Spending: Evidence from Democratic Countries." ICER Working Paper No. 20 Available at: http://polis.unipmn.it/seminari/Legislat.pdf [Last retrieved January 2009]
Riker, W. H. (1962). *The Theory of Political Coalitions*. New Haven: Yale University Press.
Riker, W. H. (1982). "Two Party Systems and Duverger's Law." *American Political Science Review* 76: 753–766.
Riker, W. H. (1992). "The Justification of Bicameralism." *International Political Science Review* 13(1): 101–116.
Riker, W. H. (1996). "The Experience of Creating Institutions: The Framing of the United States Constitution." In J. Knight and I. Sened (eds.), *Explaining Social Institutions*. Ann Arbor: University of Michigan Press.
Robertson, J. D. (1982). "Economic Policy and Election Cycles: Constraints in Nine OECD Countries." *Comparative Social Research* 5: 129–145.
Rogers, J. R. (2001). "Information and Judicial Review: A Signalling Game of Legislative-Judicial Interaction." *American Journal of Political Science* 45(1): 84–99.
Rogoff, K. (1990). "Equilibrium Political Budget Cycles." *The American Economic Review* 80(1): 21–36.
Rogoff, K. and A. Sibert (1988). "Elections and Macroeconomic Policy Cycles." *Review of Economic Studies* 55(1): 1–16.
Rogowski, R. (1987). "Trade and Variety of Democratic Institutions." *International Organization* 41(2): 203–223.
Rolla, G. and T. Groppi. (2002). "Between Politics and the Law: The Development of Constitutional Review in Italy." In W. Sadurski (ed.), *Constitutional Justice, East and West, Democratic Legitimacy and Constitutional Courts in Post-Communist Europe in a Comparative Perspective*. The Hague: Kluwer Law International.

Romer, T. and H. Rosenthal. (1978). "Political Resource Allocation, Controlled Agendas, and the Status Quo." *Public Choice* 33(4): 27–43.

Romer, T. and H. Rosenthal. (1979). "Bureaucrats versus Voters: On the Political Economy of Resource Allocation by Direct Democracy." *Quarterly Journal of Economics* 93(4): 563–587.

Romeu, F. R. (2006). "The Establishment of Constitutional Courts: A Study of 128 Democratic Constitutions." *Review of Law and Economics* 2(1): 103–135.

Roosma, P. (1998). "Constitutional Review under 1992 Constitution." *Juridica International* 3: 35–42.

Roosma, P. (2001). "Development of Constitutional Review in Estonia." *Revue de Justice Constitutionelle Est-Europeenne* 2: 283–323.

Rose, R. (1983). "Elections and Electoral Systems: Choices and Alternatives." In V. Bogdanor and D. Butler (eds.), *Democracy and Elections.* Cambridge: Cambridge University Press.

Rose, R. (1992). "Toward a Civil Economy." *Journal of Democracy* 3(2): 13–26.

Roubini, N. and J. D. Sachs. (1989a). "Political and Economic Determinants of Budget Deficits in the Industrial Democracies." *European Economic Review* 33(5): 903–938.

Roubini, N. and J. D. Sachs. (1989b). "Government Spending and Budget Deficits in the Industrial Countries." *Economic Policy* 8: 100–132.

Rubio Llorente, F. (1988). "Constitutional Review and Legislation in Spain." In C. Landfried (ed.), *Constitutional Review and Legislation. An International Comparison.* Baden-Baden: Nomos Verlagsgesellschaft.

Runge, C. F. (1981). "Common Property Externalities: Isolation, Assurance and Resource Depletion in Traditional Grazing Context." *American Journal of Agricultural Economics* 63(4): 595–606.

Ruutsoo, R. (2002a). "Tähelepanekuid riikluse ja riikliku mõtlemise sünnist." [Remarks on the Birth of the Stateness and Constitutional Thinking] In E. Pärnaste (ed.), *Põhiseaduse Tulek. Kogumik.* Tallinn: Justiitsministeerium, Kirjastus SE&JS.

Ruutsoo, R. (2000b). "Presidendi institutsiooni taustast ja kujundamisest 1992. aasta Põhiseaduses. Meenutusi ja arutlusi aastaist 1991–1992." [The Background and the Making of the Institution of President. Memories and Discussions from 1991–1992] In R. Toomla (ed.), *Presidendiraamat.* [The Book on President]. Tartu: Tartu Ülikooli Kirjastus.

Sadurski, W. (ed.). (2002). *Constitutional Justice, East and West: Democratic Legitimacy and Constitutional Courts in Post-Communist Europe in a Comparative Perspective.* The Hague: Kluwer Law International.

Sadurski, W. (2002a). "Introduction." In W. Sadurski (ed.), *Constitutional Justice, East and West: Democratic Legitimacy and Constitutional Courts in Post-Communist Europe in a Comparative Perspective.* The Hague: Kluwer Law International.

Sadurski, W. (2002b). "Legitimacy and Reasons for Constitutional Review After Communism." In W. Sadurski (ed.), *Constitutional Justice, East and West: Democratic Legitimacy and Constitutional Courts in Post-Communist Europe in a Comparative Perspective.* The Hague: Kluwer Law International.

Sadurski, W. (2005). *Rights Before Court: A Study of Constitutional Courts in Postcommunist States of Central and Eastern Europe.* Dordrecht: Springer.

Sajo, A. (1995). "Reading the Invisible Constitution: Judicial Review in Hungary." *Oxford Journal of Legal Studies* 15(2): 253–267.

Sakamoto, T. (2001). "Effects of Government Characteristics on Fiscal Deficits in 18 OECD Countries." *Comparative Political Studies* 34(5): 527–554.

Salinas, J. (1998). "The Constitutional Political Economy of Public Deficits: The Spanish Case." *Constitutional Political Economy* 9(3): 235–249.
Salzberger, E. and S. Voigt. (2002). "On the Delegation of Powers: With Special Emphasis on Central and Eastern Europe." *Constitutional Political Economy* 13(1): 25–52.
Sartori, G. (1968). "Political Development and Political Engineering." In J. D. Montgomery and A. O. Hirschman (eds.), *Public Policy*. Cambridge: Cambridge University Press.
Sartori, G. (1994). *Comparative Constitutional Engineering: An Inquiry into Structures, Incentives and Outcomes*. London: Macmillan.
Scartascini, C. G. and W. M. Crain. (2002). "The Size and Composition of Government Spending in Multi-Party Systems." George Mason University, Working Papers in Economics. Available at: http://economics.gmu.edu/working/WPE_02/02_23.pdf [Last retrieved January 2009]
Schaffer, M. E. and G. Turley. (2002). "Effective versus Statutory Taxation: Measuring Effective Tax Administration in Transition Economies." In M. Cuddy and R. Gekker (eds.), *Institutional Change in Transition Economies*. London: Ashgate.
Schaltegger, C. A. (2001). "The Effects of Federalism and Democracy on the Size of Government: Evidence from Swiss Sub-National Jurisdictions." *IFO Studien* 47: 145–162.
Schaltegger, C. A. (2002). "Budgetregeln und ihre Wirkung auf die öffentliche Haushalte: empirische Ergebnisse aus den US-Bundesstaaten und den Schweizer Kantonen." *Schmollers Jahrbuch* 122(3): 369–413.
Schaltegger, C. A. and L. Feld. (2008). "Do Large Cabinets Favor Large Governments? Evidence on the Fiscal Commons Problem for Swiss Cantons." *Journal of Public Economics* 93(1–2): 35–47.
Scharpf, F. W. (1989). "Decision Rules, Decision Styles and Policy Choices." *Journal of Theoretical Politics* 1(2): 149–176.
Scharpf, F. W. (1997). *Games Real Actors Play. Actor-Centered Institutionalism in Policy Research*. Boulder: Westview Press.
Scharpf, F. W. (2000). "Institutions in Comparative Policy Research." *Comparative Political Studies* 33(6–7): 762–790.
Schattschneider, E. E. (1960). *The Semi-Sovereign People*. New York: Holt, Rinehard & Winston.
Schauer, F. (1998) "The Causes and Consequences of Constitutional Form." CID (Center for International Development) Working Paper. Available at: http://siteresources.worldbank.org/INTLAWJUSTINST/Resources/ConstilReformSchauer.pdf [last retrieved January 2009]
Schauer, F. (2005). "On the Migration of Constitutional Ideas." *Connecticut Law Review* 37(4): 907–919.
Schelling, T. (1960). *The Strategy of Conflict*. Cambridge: Harvard University Press.
Scheppele, K. L. (2002). "Declarations of Independence: Judicial Reaction to Political Pressure." In S. Burbank and B. Friedman (eds.), *Judicial Independence at the Crossroads*. Thousand Oaks: Sage.
Scheppele, K. L. (2003). "Constitutional Negotiations: Political Contexts of Judicial Activism in Post-Soviet Europe." *International Sociology* 18(1): 219–238.
Schick, A. (1993). "Governments versus Budget Deficits." In K. Weaver and B. A. Rockman (eds.), *Do Institutions Matter? Government Capabilities in the United States and Abroad*. Washington, DC: Brookings Institution Press.
Schick, A. (2003). "The Role of Fiscal Rules in Budgeting." *OECD Journal of Budgeting* 3(3): 7–35.

Schmid, A. A. (2004). *Conflict and Cooperation: Institutional and Behavioural Economics*. Malden: Blackwell.

Schmidt, M. G. (1996). "When Parties Matter: A Review of the Possibilities and the Limits of Partisan Influence on Public Policy." *European Journal of Political Research* 30(2): 155–183.

Schneider, F. and W. W. Pommerehne. (1983). "Macroeconomia della crescita in disequilibrio e settore pubblico in espansione: il peso delle differenze istituzionali." *Rivista Internazionale di Scienze Economiche e Commerciali* 33: 306–420.

Schneider, H. (1999). "Kohus lahusvõimude süsteemis." [Courts in the System of Separation of Powers] *Juridica* 9: 414–424.

Schneider, H. (2002). "Eesti põhiseadused ja nende järelevalve." [The Constitutions of Estonia and the Story of its Supervision] *Riigikogu toimetised* 5: 193–207.

Schneider, O. and P. Hedbavny. (2003). "Fiscal Policy: Too Political?" UK FS-IES Working Paper No. 37.

Schnellenbach, J. (2004). "The Evolution of a Fiscal Constitution When Individuals are Theoretically Uncertain." *European Journal of Law and Economics* 17(1): 97–115.

Schotter, A. R. (1981). *The Economic Theory of Social Institutions*. Cambridge: Cambridge University Press.

Schuknecht, L. (2005). "Stability and Growth Pact: Issues and Lessons from Political Economy." *International Economics and Economic Policy* 2(1): 65–89.

Schuster, K., F. Pukelsheim, M. Drton and N. R. Draper. (2003). "Seat Biases of Apportionment Methods for Proportional Representation." *Electoral Studies* 22(4): 651–676.

Schwartz, H. (2000). *The Struggle for Constitutional Justice in Post-Communist Europe*. Chicago: University of Chicago Press.

Schwartz, T. (1994). "Representation as Agency and the Pork Barrel Paradox." *Public Choice* 78(1): 3–21.

Schwarz, P. (2006). "Deficits and Divided Governments: The Case of the German 'Bundesrat'." *Constitutional Political Economy* 17(2): 87–101.

Segal, J. A. (1997). "Separation-of-Powers Games in the Positive Theory of Congress and the Court." *American Political Science Review* 91(1): 28–44.

Seitzer, J. (1999). "Experimental Constitutionalism: A Comparative Analysis of the Institutional Bases of Rights Enforcement in Post-Communist Hungary." In S. J. Kenney, W. M. Reisinger and J. C. Reitz (eds.), *Constitutional Dialogues in Comparative Perspective*. London: Macmillan.

Sen, A. K. (1967). "Isolation, Assurance and the Social Rate of Discount." *Quarterly Journal of Economics* 81(1): 112–124.

Shadbegian, R. J. (1996). "Do Tax and Expenditure Limitations Affect the Size and Growth of State Government." *Contemporary Economic Policy* 14(1): 22–35.

Shapiro, M. (1981). *Courts: Comparative and Political Analysis*. Chicago: University of Chicago Press.

Shapiro, M. (1999). "The Success of Judicial Review." In S. J. Kenney, W. M. Reisinger and J. C. Reitz (eds.), *Constitutional Dialogues in Comparative Perspective*. New York: St. Martin's Press.

Shen, R. (1994). *Restructuring the Baltic Economies: Disengaging Fifty Years of Integration with the USSR*. Westport: Praeger.

Shepsle, K. A. (1986). "Institutional Equilibrium and Equilibrium Institutions." In H. Weisberg (ed.), *Political Science: The Science of Politics*. New York: Agathon.

Shepsle, K. A. (1989). "Studying Institutions: Some Lessons from the Rational Choice Approach." *Journal of Theoretical Politics* 1(2): 131–147.

Shepsle, K. A. and B. R. Weingast. (1981). "Political Preferences for the Pork Barrel." *American Journal of Political Science* 25(1): 96–111.
Shi, M. and J. Svensson. (2006). "Political Budget Cycles: Do They Differ Across Countries and Why?" *Journal of Public Economics* 90(8–9): 1367–1389.
Shubik, M. and L. Van der Heyden. (1978). "Logrolling and Budget Allocation Games." *International Journal of Game Theory* 7(3–4): 151–162.
Shugart, M. S. (1993). "Of Presidents and Parliaments." *East European Constitutional Review* 2: 30–32.
Shugart, M. S. and J. Carey. (1992). *Presidents and Assemblies: Constitutional Design and Electoral Dynamics*. Cambridge: Cambridge University Press.
Shugart, M. S. and S. Haggard. (2001). "Institutions and Public Policy in Presidential Systems." In Haggard S. and M. D. McCubbins (eds.), *Presidents, Parliaments and Policy*. Cambridge: Cambridge University Press.
Shughart, W. F. and R. D. Tollison. (1986). "The Political Economy of Legislation and the Growth of Government." *Research in Law and Economics* 9: 111–127.
Sibul, H. (2002). "Põhiseaduse sekretär." [The Secretary of the Constitution] In E. Pärnaste (ed.), *Põhiseaduse Tulek. Kogumik.* [The Coming of the Constitution] Tallinn: Justiitsministeerium, Kirjastus SE&JS.
Sikk, A. (2003). "Cartel Party System in a Post-Communist Country? The Case of Estonia." Paper Prepared for the ECPR General Conference, Marburg, 18–21 September 2003. Available at: http://www.essex.ac.uk/ecpr/events/generalconference/marburg/papers/16/3/Sikk.pdf [Last retrieved January 2009]
Sikk, A. (2004). "Estonia." In D. Nohlen (ed.), *Elections in Europe.* Oxford: Oxford University Press.
Skilling, D. and R. J. Zeckhauser. (2002). "Political Competition and Debt Trajectories in Japan and the OECD." *Japan and the World Economy* 14(2): 121–135.
Smith, D. J. (2001). *Estonia: Independence and European Integration.* London: Routledge.
Smith, R. M. (1988). "Political Jurisprudence, the 'New Institutionalism', and the Future of Public Law." *American Political Science Review* 82(1): 89–108.
Smithey, S. I. and J. Ishiyama. (2000). "Judicious Choices: Designing Courts in Postcommunist Politics." *Communist and Post-Communist Studies* 33(2): 163–182.
Sobel, R. S. and R. Holcombe. (1996). "The Impact of State Rainy Day Funds in Easing State Fiscal Crises During the 1990–1991 Recession." *Public Budgeting and Finance* 16(3): 28–48.
Spiller, P. T. and R. Gely. (1992). "Congressional Control or Judicial Independence: The Determinants of U.S. Supreme Court Labor-Relations Decisions, 1949–1988." *RAND Journal of Economics* 23(4): 463–492.
Spiller, P. T., E. Stein and M. Tommasi. (2003). "Political Institutions, Policymaking Processes, and Policy Outcomes. An Intertemporal Transactions Framework." Latin American Research Network–IADB, Design Paper No. 1. Available at: http://burbuja.udesa.edu.ar/departamentos/economia/mariano_tommasi/cedi/dts/dt81.pdf [Last retrieved January 2009]
Spiller, P. T. and M. Tommasi. (2003). "The Institutional Foundations of Public Policy: A Transactions Approach with Application to Argentina." *Journal of Law, Economics and Organization* 19(2): 281–306.
Sprudzs, A. (2001). "Rebuilding Democracy in Latvia: Overcoming a Dual Legacy." In J. Zielonka (ed.), *Democratic Consolidation in Eastern Europe. Volume I, Institutional Engineering*. Oxford: Oxford University Press.

Stansel, D. (1994). *Taming Leviathan: Are Tax and Spending Limits the Answer? Policy Analysis*. Washington, DC: CATO Institute.

Steen, A. (1997). *Between Past and Future: Elites, Democracy and State in Post-Communist Countries. A Comparison of Estonia, Latvia, Lithuania.* Aldershot: Ashgate.

Stein, E., E. Talvi and A. Grisanti. (1999). "Institutional Arrangements and Fiscal Performance: The Latin American Experience." In J. M. Poterba and J. von Hagen (eds.), *Fiscal Institutions and Fiscal Performance*. Chicago: University of Chicago Press.

Steiner, J., A. Bächtiger, M. Spörndli and M. R. Steenbergen. (2004). *Deliberative Politics in Action: Analyzing Parliamentary Discourse.* Cambridge: Cambridge University Press.

Steinmo, S. (1993). *Taxation and Democracy: Swedish, British and American Approaches to Financing the Modern State.* New Haven: Yale University Press.

Steinmo, S., K. Thelen and F. Longstreth. (eds.) (1992). *Structuring Politics. Historical Institutionalism in Comparative analysis*. Cambridge: Cambridge University Press.

Steinmo, S. and C. J. Tolbert. (1998). "Do Institutions Really Matter? Taxation in Industrialized Democracies." *Comparative Political Studies* 31(2): 165–187.

Steunenberg, B. (1992). "Referendum Initiative, and Veto Power: Budgetary Decision Making in Local Government." *Kyklos* 45(4): 501–529.

Stienlet, G. (2000). "Institutional Reforms and Belgian Fiscal Policies in the 90s." In R. Strauch and J. von Hagen (eds.), *Institutions, Politics, and Fiscal Policy.* Dordrecht: Kluwer Academic Publishers.

Stigler, G. J. (1979). "The Size of Legislatures." *Journal of Legal Studies* 5(1): 17–34.

Stone, A. (1992a). *The Birth of Judicial Politics in France. The Constitutional Council in Comparative Perspective.* New York: Oxford University Press.

Stone, A. (1992b). "Abstract Constitutional Review and Policy Making in Western Europe." In D. W. Jackson and C. N. Tate (eds.), *Comparative Judicial Review and Public Policy.* London: Greenwood Press.

Stone, A. (1994). "Judging Socialist Reform. The Politics of Coordinate Construction in France and Germany." *Comparative Political Studies* 26(4): 443–469.

Stone Sweet, A. (1999). "Constitutional Dialogues: Protecting Human Rights in France, Germany, Italy and Spain." In S. J. Kenney, W. M. Reisinger and J. C. Reitz (eds.), *Constitutional Dialogues in Comparative Perspective.* London: Macmillan.

Stone Sweet, A. (2000). *Governing with Judges*. Oxford: Oxford University Press.

Stone Sweet, A. (2002). "Constitutional Courts and Parliamentary Democracy." *West European Politics* 25(1): 77–100.

Stratman, T. (1997). "Logrolling." In D. C. Muller (ed.), *Perspectives on Public Choice: A Handbook.* Cambridge: Cambridge University Press.

Stratman, T. and M. Baur. (2002). "Plurality Rule, Proportional Representation, and the German Bundestag: How Incentives to Pork-Barrel Differ across Electoral Systems." *American Journal of Political Science* 46(3): 506–514.

Strauch, R. R. (1998). "Budget Processes and Fiscal Discipline: Evidence from the US States." Zentrum für Europäische Integrationsforschung, Working Paper.

Strauch, R. R. and J. von Hagen. (1999). "Tumbling Giant: Germany's Experience With the Maastricht Criteria." In D. Cobham and G. Zis (eds.), *From EMS to EMU.* London: MacMillan.

Strauch, R. R. and J. von Hagen. (2001). "Formal Fiscal Restraints and Budget Processes as Solutions to a Deficit and Spending Bias in Public Finance – US Experience and Possible Lessons for EMU." Zentrum für Europäische Integrationsforschung, Working Paper No. 14. Available at: http://www.zei.de/download/zei_wp/B01-14.pdf [Last retrieved January 2009]

Straussman, J. D. (1996). "Ideals and Reality in the Evolution of Fiscal Reform in Central and Eastern Europe." *Public Budgeting and Finance* 16(2): 79–95.

Strom, K. (1990). *Minority Governments and Majority Rule.* Cambridge: Cambridge University Press.

Suksi, M. (1993). *Bringing in the People: A Comparison of Constitutional Forms and Practices of the Referendum.* Dordrecht: Martinus Nijhoff.

Sutherland, D., R. Price and I. Joumard. (2005). "Fiscal Rules for Sub-Central Governments: Design and Impact." OECD Economics Department Working Paper No. 465. Available at: http://www.sourceoecd.org/10.1787/606015633336 [Last retrieved January 2009]

Sutter, D. (1997). "Enforcing Constitutional Constraints." *Constitutional Political Economy* 8(2): 139–150.

Sutter, M. (2003). "The Political Economy of Fiscal Policy: An Experimental Study on the Strategic Use of Deficits." *Public Choice* 116(4): 313–332.

Swank, D. and S. Steinmo. (2002). "The New Political Economy of Taxation in Advanced Capitalist Democracies." *American Journal of Political Science* 46(3): 642–655.

Swank, O. H. (2002). "Budgetary Devices for Curbing Spending Prone Ministers and Bureaucrats." *Public Choice* 111(3–4): 237–257.

Taagepera, R. (1991). "Building Democracy in Estonia." *PS: Political Science and Politics* 24(3): 478–481.

Taagepera, R. (1993). *Estonia: Return to Independence*. Boulder: Westview Press.

Taagepera, R. (1994). "Estonia's Constitutional Assembly, 1991–1992." *Journal of Baltic Studies* 25(3): 211–232.

Taagepera, R. and B. Grofman. (1985). "Rethinking Duverger's Law: Predicting the Effective Number of Parties in Plurality and PR Systems – Parties Minus Issues Equals One." *European Journal of Political Research* 13(4): 341–352.

Taagepera, R. and M. Laakso. (1980). "Proportionality Profiles of West European Electoral Systems." *European Journal of Political Research* 8(4): 423–446.

Taagepera, R. and M. S. Shugart. (1989). *Seats and Votes: The Effects and Determinants of Electoral Systems.* New Haven: Yale University Press.

Taagepera, R. and M. S. Shugart. (1993). "Predicting the Number of Parties: A Quantitative Model of Duverger's Mechanical Effect." *American Political Science Review* 87(2): 455–464.

Taaler, J. (1995). "Tax Reform." In O. Lugus and G. A. Hachey Jr. (eds.), *Transforming the Estonian Economy*. Tallinn: Estonian Academy of Sciences, Institute of Economics.

Tang, P. and H. Nilgo. (1995). "Budget Reform." In O. Lugus and G. A. Hachey Jr. (eds.), *Transforming the Estonian Economy*. Tallinn: Estonian Academy of Sciences, Institute of Economics.

Tang, S. (1991). "Fiscal Constitution, Income Distribution and the Basic Law of Hong Kong." *Economy and Society* 20(3): 283–305.

Tanzi, V. and G. Tsibouris. (2000). "Fiscal Reform Over Ten Years of Transition." IMF Working Paper No. 00/113. Available at: http://www.imf.org/external/pubs/ft/wp/2000/wp00113.pdf [Last retrieved January 2009]

Thornton, M. and M. Ulrich. (1999). "Constituency Size and Government Spending." *Public Finance Review* 27(6): 588–599.

Tornell, A. and P. R. Lane. (1999). "The Voracity Effect." *The American Economic Review* 89(1): 22–42.

Tridimas, G. (2005). "Judges and Taxes: Judicial Review, Judicial Independence and the Size of Government." *Constitutional Political Economy* 16(1): 5–30.

Tsebelis, G. (1990). *Nested Games: Rational Choice in Comparative Politics*. Berkeley: University of California Press.

Tsebelis, G. (1995a). "Decision-Making in Political Systems: Veto Players in Presidentialism, Parliamentarism, Multicameralism, and Multipartyism." *British Journal of Political Science* 25(3): 289–326.

Tsebelis G. (1995b). "Veto Players and Law Production in Parliamentary Democracies." In H. Döring (ed.), *Parliaments and Majority Rule in Western Europe*. Frankfurt am Main: Campus.

Tsebelis, G. (1999). "Veto Players and Law Production in Parliamentary Democracies: An Empirical Analysis." *American Political Science Review* 93(3): 591–608.

Tsebelis, G. (2000). "Veto Players and Institutional Analysis." *Governance* 13(4): 441–474.

Tsebelis, G. (2002). *Veto Players: How Political Institutions Work*. Princeton: Princeton University Press.

Tsebelis, G. and E. C. C. Chang. (2004). "Veto Players and the Structure of Budgets in Advanced Industrialized Countries." *European Journal of Political Research* 43(3): 449–476.

Tsebelis, G. and J. Money. (1997). *Bicameralism*. Cambridge: Cambridge University Press.

Tufte, E. R. (1978). *Political Control of the Economy*. Princeton: Princeton University Press.

Tujula, M. and G. Wolswijk. (2004). "What Determines Fiscal Balances? An Empirical Investigation in Determinants of Changes in OECD Fiscal Balances." European Central Bank Working Paper Series, No. 422. Available at: http://www.ecb.europa.eu/pub/pdf/scpwps/ ecbwp422.pdf [Last retrieved January 2009]

Tullock, G. (1959). "Some Problems of Majority Voting." *Journal of Political Economy* 67(6): 571–579.

Tullock, G. (1981). "Why so Much Stability?" *Public Choice* 37(2): 189–202.

Tullock, G. (1994). "Thoughts About Representative Government." *European Journal of Political Economy* 10(1): 27–39.

Tushnet, M. (1999). *Taking the Constitution Away from the Courts*. Princeton: Princeton University Press.

Tushnet, M. (2003). "Non-Judicial Review." *Harvard Journal on Legislation* 40(2): 453–492.

Tyler, T. and K. Rasinski. (1991). "Legitimacy and the Acceptance of Unpopular U.S. Supreme Court Decisions: A Reply to Gibson." *Law and Society Review* 25(3): 621–630.

Vahtre, L. (1996). *Vabanemine*. [Liberation] Tallinn: IM Meedia.

Vanagunas, S. (1995). "Problems of Budgeting During the Great Transformation." *Public Budgeting and Finance* 15(1): 84–95.

Vanberg, G. (1998). "Abstract Judicial Review, Legislative Bargaining, and Policy Compromise." *Journal of Theoretical Politics* 10(3): 299–236.

Vanberg, G. (2001). "Legislative-Judicial Relations: A Game-Theoretic Approach to Constitutional Review." *American Journal of Political Science* 45(2): 346–361.

Vanberg, G. (2005). *The Politics of Constitutional Review in Germany*. Cambridge: Cambridge University Press.

Vanberg, V. J. (1994). *Rules and Choice in Economics*. London: Routledge.

Vanberg, V. J. and J. M. Buchanan. (1989). "Interests and Theories in Constitutional Choice." *Journal of Theoretical Politics* 1(1): 49–63.

Vatter, A. (2005). "Bicameralism and Policy Performance: The Effects of Cameral Structure in Comparative Perspective." *The Journal of Legislative Studies* 11(2): 194–215.

Velasco, A. (1999). "A Model of Endogenous Fiscal Deficits and Delayed Fiscal Reforms." In J. M. Poterba and J. von Hagen (eds.), *Fiscal Institutions and Fiscal Performance*. Chicago: University of Chicago Press.

Velasco, A. (2000). "Debts and Deficits with Fragmented Fiscal Policymaking." *Journal of Public Economics* 76(1): 105–125.

Voigt, S. (1996). "Pure Eclecticism – The Tool Kit of the Constitutional Economist." *Constitutional Political Economy* 7(3): 177–196.

Voigt, S. (1997). "Positive Constitutional Economics: A Survey." *Public Choice* 90(1–4): 11–53.

Voigt, S. (1998). "Implicit Constitutional Change: Changing the Meaning of the Constitution without Changing the Text of the Document." *European Journal of Law and Economics* 7(3): 117–144.

Voigt, S. (1999). *Explaining Constitutional Change. A Positive Economics Approach.* Cheltenham: Edward Elgar.

Voigt. S. (2004). "The Consequences of Popular Participation in Constitutional Choice – Towards a Comparative Analysis." In A. van Aaken, C. List and C. Luetge (eds.), *Deliberation and Decision: Economics, Constitutional Theory and Deliberative Democracy.* Aldershot: Ashgate.

Voigt, S., J. Müller and L. Blume. (2007). "The Economic Effects of Direct Democracy – A First Global Assessment." CESifo Working Paper No. 2149. Available at: http://www.cesifo.de/DocCIDL/cesifo1_wp2149.pdf [Last retrieved January 2009]

Voigt, S. and H-J. Wagener. (2002). "Introduction." In S. Voigt and H-J. Wagener (eds.), *Constitutions, Markets and Law. Recent Experiences in Transition Economies.* Cheltenham: Edward Elgar.

Volkerink, B. and J. de Haan. (2001). "Fragmented Government Effects on Fiscal Policy: New Evidence." *Public Choice* 109(3–4): 221–242.

Wagner, G. A. and E. M. Elder. (2005). "The Role of Budget Stabilization Funds in Smoothing Government Expenditures over the Business Cycle." *Public Finance Review* 33(4): 439–465.

Wagner, R. E. (1976). "Revenue Structure, Fiscal Illusion and Budgetary Choice." *Public Choice* 25(1): 45–61.

Wagner, R. E. (1992). "Grazing the Federal Budgetary Commons: The Rational Politics of Budgetary Irresponsibility." *The Journal of Law and Politics* 9: 105–119.

Wagner, R. E. (2001). "Politics and the Macro Economy." In W. F. Shughart and L. Razzolini (eds.), *The Elgar Companion to Public Choice.* Cheltenham: Edward Elgar.

Wagner, R. E. (2002). "Property, Taxation, and the Budgetary Commons." In D. P. Racheter and R. E. Wagner (eds.), *Politics, Taxation, and the Rule of Law: The Power to Tax in Constitutional Perspective.* Boston: Kluwer Academic Publishers.

Wagschal, U. (1998). "Politische und institutionelle Determinanten der Staatsverschuldung." *Zeitschrift für Wirtschaftspolitik* 47: 220–243.

Warwick, P. V. (1979). "The Durability of Coalition Governments in Parliamentary Democracies." *Comparative Political Studies* 11(4): 465–498.

Warwick, P. V. (1994). *Government Survival in Parliamentary Democracies.* Cambridge: Cambridge University Press.

Weaver, R. K. and B. A. Rockman. (1993). "Assessing the Effects of Institutions." In R. K. Weaver and B. A. Rockman (eds.), *Do Institutions Matter? Government Capabilities in the United States and Abroad.* Washington, DC: The Brookings Institution.

Wehner, J. (2006). "Assessing the Power of the Purse: An Index of Legislative Budget Institutions." *Political Studies* 54(4): 767–785.

Weingast, B. R. (1979). "A Rational Choice Perspective on Congressional Norms." *American Journal of Political Science* 23(2): 245–262.

Weingast, B. R. (1997). "The Political Foundations of Democracy and the Rule of Law." *American Political Science Review* 91(2): 245–263.

Weingast, B. R. and W. J. Marshall. (1988). "The Industrial Organization of Congress; or, Why Legislatures, Like Firms, Are not Organized as Markets." *Journal of Political Economy* 96(1): 132–163.

Weingast, B. R., K. A. Shepsle and C. Johnsen. (1981). "The Political Economy of Benefits and Costs: A Neoclassical Approach to Distributive Politics." *Journal of Political Economy* 89(4): 642–664.

Welan, M. (1988). "Constitutional Review and Legislation in Austria." In C. Landfried (ed.), *Constitutional Review and Legislation. An International Comparison*. Baden-Baden: Nomos Verlagsgesellschaft.

Whittington, K. E. (1999). *Constitutional Construction. Divided Powers and Constitutional Meaning*. Cambridge: Harvard University Press

Whittington, K. E. (2002). "Extrajudicial Constitutional Interpretation: Three Objections and Responses." *North Carolina Law Review* 80(3): 773–851.

Whittington, K. E. (2005). "Constitutional Theory and the Faces of Power." In K. D. Ward and C. R. Castillo (eds.), *The Judiciary and American Democracy: Alexander Bickel and the Countermajoritarian Difficulty and Contemporary Constitutional Theory*. Albany: State University of New York Press.

Wicksell, K. (1896). *Finanztheoretische Untersuchungen*. Jena: Fischer.

Wierts, P. (2008). "How Do Expenditure Rules Affect Fiscal Behaviour?" Netherlands Central Bank, Working Paper No 166/2008. Available at: http://www.dnb.nl/en/binaries/Working%20Paper%20166-2008_tcm47-170648.pdf [Last retrieved January 2009]

Wildavsky, A. (1986). *Budgeting. A Comparative Theory of Budgetary Processes*. 2nd edition. Oxford: Transaction Books.

Wildavsky, A. (1992). *The New Politics of the Budgetary Process*. 2nd ed. New York: Harper Collins.

Wolczuk, K. (2001). "Ukraine: Tormented Constitution-Making." In J. Zielonka (ed.), *Democratic Consolidation in Eastern Europe. Volume I, Institutional Engineering*. Oxford: Oxford University Press.

Woldendorp, J., H. Keman and I. Budge. (1998). "Party Government in 20 Democracies: An Update (1990–1995)." *European Journal of Political Research* 33(1): 125–164.

Wolff, J. de. (1998). *The Political Economy of Fiscal Decisions*. Heidelberg: Physica-Verlag.

Woo, J. (2003). "Economic, Political, and Institutional Determinants of Public Deficits." *Journal of Public Economics* 87(3–4): 387–426.

Wyrzykowski, M. (2001). "Legitimacy: The Price of a Delayed Constitution." In J. Zielonka (ed.), *Democratic Consolidation in Eastern Europe. Vol 1. Institutional Engineering*. Oxford: Oxford University Press.

Yin, R. K. (2003). *Case Study Research: Design and Methods*. Thousand Oaks: Sage Publications.

Yläoutinen, S. (2004a). "Fiscal Frameworks in the Central and Eastern European Countries." Finnish Ministry of Finance, Economics Department Discussion Paper No. 72. Available at: http://www.vm.fi/vm/en/04_publications_and_documents/01_publications/08_other_publications/20040406Fiscal/Discussion_paper_72.pdf [Last retrieved January 2009]

Yläoutinen, S. (2004b). "The Role of Electoral and Party Systems in the Development of Fiscal Institutions in the Central and Eastern European Countries." Zentrum für Europäische Integrationsforschung, Working paper No. B13/2004. Available at: http://www.zei.de/download/zei_wp/B04-13.pdf [Last retrieved January 2009]

Zax, J. S. (1989). "Initiatives and Government Expenditures." *Public Choice* 63(3): 267–277.

Zielonka, J. (ed.). (2001). *Democratic Consolidation in Eastern Europe. Vol 1. Institutional Engineering*. Oxford: Oxford University Press.
Zimmermann, K. W. and T. Just. (2000). "Interest Groups, Referenda, and the Political Process: On the Efficiency of Direct Democracy." *Constitutional Political Economy* 11(2): 147–163.

Legal Acts of the Republic of Estonia

1992 Constitution of the Republic of Estonia. *State Gazette*, 06.07.1992, 26, 349. Available at: https://www.riigiteataja.ee/ert/act.jsp?id=24304&replstring=33 Available in English at: http://www.legaltext.ee/et/andmebaas/tekst.asp?loc=text&dok=X0000K1&keel=en&pg= 1&ptyyp=RT&tyyp=X&query=constitution [last retrieved January 2009]
1989 Budget Act of the Soviet Republic of Estonia. *State Gazette of the Soviet Republic of Estonia* 1989, 36, 555. Available at: https://www.riigiteataja.ee/ert/act.jsp?id=30678 [last retrieved January 2009]
1990 Taxation Act of the Soviet Republic of Estonia. *State Gazette of the Soviet Republic of Estonia* 1989, 41, 648. Available at: https://www.riigiteataja.ee/ert/act.jsp?id=30697 [last retrieved January 2009]
1991 Personal Income Tax Act. *State Gazette* 1990, 14, 151. Available at: https://www.riigi teataja.ee/ert/act.jsp?id=30512 [last retrieved January 2009]
1992 Corporate Income Tax Act. *State Gazette* 08.11.1991, 36, 446. Available at: https://www.riigiteataja.ee/ert/act.jsp?id=30536 [last retrieved January 2009]
1992 Value Added Tax Act. *State Gazette* 08.11.1991, 36, 447. Available at: https://www.riigiteataja.ee/ert/act.jsp?id=30538 [last retrieved January 2009]
1993 Constitutional Review Court Procedure Act. *State Gazette* I, 24.05.1993, 25, 435. Available at: https://www.riigiteataja.ee/ert/act.jsp?id=24452 [last retrieved January 2009]
1994 Taxation Act. *State Gazette* I, 06.01.1994, 1, 5. Available at: https://www.riigiteataja.ee/ert/act.jsp?id=28626 [last retrieved January 2009]
1994 Riigikogu Election Act. *State Gazette* I, 01.07.1994, 47, 784. Available at: https://www.riigiteataja.ee/ert/act.jsp?id=28675 [last retrieved January 2009]
1994 State Budget Act. *State Gazette* I, 09.07.1993, 42, 614. Available at: https://www.riigi teataja.ee/ert/act.jsp?id=28545 [last retrieved January 2009]
1994 Value Added Tax Act. *State Gazette* I, 14.09.1993, 60, 847. Available at: https://www.riigiteataja.ee/ert/act.jsp?id=28578 [last retrieved January 2009]
1994 Riigikogu Rules of Procedure Act. *State Gazette* I, 13.12.1994, 90, 1517. Available at: https://www.riigiteataja.ee/ert/act.jsp?id=28713 [last retrieved January 2009]
1994 Income Tax Act. *State Gazette* I, 29.12.1993, 79, 1184. Available at: https://www.riigi teataja.ee/ert/act.jsp?id=28610 [last retrieved January 2009]
1995 Foreign Borrowing by the Republic of Estonia and State Guarantees for Foreign Loan Agreements Act. *State Gazette* I, 22.03.1995, 31, 387. Available at: https://www.riigitea taja.ee/ert/act.jsp?id=31961 [last retrieved January 2009]
1996 Amending Act of Taxation Act. *State Gazette* I, 02.05.1996, 29, 577. Available at: https://www.riigiteataja.ee/ert/act.jsp?id=31189 [last retrieved January 2009]
1996 Amending Act of Income Tax Act. *State Gazette* I, 05.12.1995, 90, 1587. Available at: https://www.riigiteataja.ee/ert/act.jsp?id=30993 [last retrieved January 2009]
1998 Social Tax Act. *State Gazette* I, 13.05.1998, 40, 611. Available at: https://www.riigiteataja.ee/ert/act.jsp?id=75200 [last retrieved January 2009]

1999 Amending Act of § 104 of Riigikogu Rules of Procedure. *State Gazette* I, 17.06.1999, 53, 574. Available at: https://www.riigiteataja.ee/ert/act.jsp?id=77560 [last retrieved January 2009]

1999 State Budget Act. *State Gazette* I, 30.06.1999, 55, 584. Available at: https://www.riigi teataja.ee/ert/act.jsp?id=77570 [last retrieved January 2009]

1999 Amending Act of Taxation Act. *State Gazette* I, 08.10.1998, 86/87, 1409. Available at: https://www.riigiteataja.ee/ert/act.jsp?id=76188 [last retrieved January 2009]

2000 Income Tax Act. *State Gazette* I, 30.12.1999, 101, 903. Available at: https://www.riigiteataja.ee/ert/act.jsp?id=13122153 [last retrieved January 2009]

2001 Social Tax Act. *State Gazette* I, 28.12.2000, 102, 675. Available at: https://www.riigi teataja.ee/ert/act.jsp?id=72571 [last retrieved January 2009]

2002 Amending Act of Foreign Borrowing by the Republic of Estonia and State Guarantees for Foreign Loan Agreements Act. *State Gazette* I, 20.03.2002, 27, 152. Available at: https://www.riigiteataja.ee/ert/act.jsp?id=163039 [last retrieved January 2009]

2002 Constitutional Review Court Procedure Act. *State Gazette* I 25.03.2002, 29, 174. Available at: https://www.riigiteataja.ee/ert/act.jsp?id=12849846 [last retrieved January 2009]

2002 Value Added Tax Act. *State Gazette* I, 11.07.2001, 64, 368. Available at: https://www. riigiteataja.ee/ert/act.jsp?id=73049 [last retrieved January 2009]

2002 Amending Act of State Budget Act and other Related Acts. *State Gazette* I, 19.07.2002, 64, 393. Available at: https://www.riigiteataja.ee/ert/act.jsp?id=209462 [last retrieved January 2009]

2002 Amending Act of Income Tax Act. *State Gazette* I, 20.11.2001, 91, 544. Available at: https://www.riigiteataja.ee/ert/act.jsp?id=73248 [last retrieved January 2009]

2002 Taxation Act. *State Gazette* I, 19.03.2002, 26, 150. Available at: https://www.riigitea taja.ee/ert/act.jsp?id=13114422 [last retrieved January 2009]

2002 Riigikogu Election Act. *State Gazette* I, 08.07.2002, 57, 355. Available at: https://www.riigiteataja.ee/ert/act.jsp?id=13117287 [last retrieved January 2009]

2003 Amending Act of State Budget Act, Accounting Act, State Audit Act, Rural Municipality and City Budgets Act, Local Government Organisation Act, Act on the Use of Proceeds from Privatisation. *State Gazette* I, 29.12.2003, 88, 588. Available at: https://www.riigiteataja.ee/ert/act.jsp?id=690824 [last retrieved January 2009]

2003 Amending Act of Wages Act, Income Tax Act, Social Tax Act, Funded Pensions Act and Taxation Act. *State Gazette* I, 31.12.2002, 111, 662. Available at: https://www.riigiteataja.ee/ert/act.jsp?id=234610 [last retrieved January 2009]

2003 Amending Act of § 163 of Taxation Act. *State Gazette* I, 27.06.2003, 48, 341. Available at: https://www.riigiteataja.ee/ert/act.jsp?id=602367 [last retrieved January 2009]

2004 Value Added Tax Act. *State Gazette* I, 22.12.2003, 82, 554. Available at: https://www.riigiteataja.ee/ert/act.jsp?id=13114742 [last retrieved January 2009]

2005 Amending Act of Constitutional Review Court Procedure Act. *State Gazette* I, 22.12.2005, 68, 524. Available at: https://www.riigiteataja.ee/ert/act.jsp?id=969322 [last retrieved January 2009]

2009 Amending Act of Value Added Tax Act and Income Tax Act. *State Gazette* I, 30.12.2008, 58, 324. Available at: : https://riigiteataja.ee/ert/act.jsp?id=13096340

Judgements of the Constitutional Review Chamber of the Supreme Court of Estonia

Judgement of the Constitutional Review Chamber of 4 November 1993, No. III-4/A-4. Available at: http://www.nc.ee/?id=487 [last retrieved January 2009]

Judgement of the Constitutional Review Chamber of 7 December 1994, No. III-4/A-9/94. Available at: http://www.nc.ee/?id=478 [last retrieved January 2009]
Judgement of the Constitutional Review Chamber of 23 March 1998, No. 3-4-1-2-98. Available at: http://www.nc.ee/?id=463 [last retrieved January 2009]
Judgement of the Constitutional Review Chamber of 17 June 1998, No. 3-4-1-5-98. Available at: http://www.nc.ee/?id=460 [last retrieved January 2009]
Judgement of the Constitutional Review Chamber of 23 November 1998, No. 3-4-1-8-98. Available at: http://www.nc.ee/?id=457 [last retrieved January 2009]
Judgement of the Supreme Court *en banc* of 17 March 2000, No. 3-4-1-1-2000. Available at: http://www.nc.ee/?id=451 [last retrieved January 2009]
Judgement of the Constitutional Review Chamber of 12 May 2000,No. 3-4-1-5-2000. Available at: http://www.nc.ee/?id=448 [last retrieved January 2009]
Judgement of the Supreme Court *en banc* of 22 December 2000, No. 3-4-1-10-2000. Available at: http://www.nc.ee/?id=443 [last retrieved January 2009]
Judgement of the Constitutional Review Chamber of 22 February 2001, No. 3-4-1-3-01. Available at: http://www.nc.ee/?id=439 [last retrieved January 2009]
Judgement of the Constitutional Review Chamber of 6 March 2002, No. 3-4-1-1-02. Available at: http://www.nc.ee/?id=434 [last retrieved January 2009]
Judgement of the Constitutional Review Chamber of 12 June 2002, No. 3-4-1-6-02. Available at: http://www.nc.ee/?id=429 [last retrieved January 2009]
Judgement of the Constitutional Review Chamber of 5 November 2002, No. 3-4-1-8-02. Available at: http://www.nc.ee/?id=427 [last retrieved January 2009]
Judgement of the Constitutional Review Chamber of 21 January 2004, No. 3-4-1-7-03. Available at: http://www.nc.ee/?id=412 [last retrieved January 2009]
Judgement of the Supreme Court *en banc* of 19 April 2004, No. 3-3-1-46-03. Available at: http://www.nc.ee/?id=403 [last retrieved January 2009]
Judgement of the Constitutional Review Chamber of 29 September 2007, No. 3-4-1-12-07. Available at: http://www.riigikohus.ee/?id=849 [last retrieved January 2009]

Resolutions of the President of the Republic of Estonia

Resolution No. 507 of the President of the Republic of Estonia. (17 February 1999). Riigieelarve seaduse väljakuulutamata jätmine. [Resolution not to promulgate the State Budget Act] *State Gazette* 23.02.1999, 18, 297. Available at: https://www.riigiteataja.ee/ert/act.jsp?id=77128 [last retrieved January 2009]
Resolution No. 47 of the President of the Republic of Estonia (5 December 2001). Eesti Vabariigile välislaenude võtmise ja välislaenulepingutele riigigarantiide andmise seaduse muutmise seaduse väljakuulutamata jätmine *State Gazette* 13.12.2001, 130, 1891. [Resolution not to promulgate the Amending Act of the Foreign Borrowing by the Republic of Estonia and State Guarantees for Foreign Loan Agreements Act] Available at: https:/ /www.riigiteataja.ee/ert/act.jsp?id=86738 [last retrieved January 2009]
Resolution No. 153 of the President of the Republic of Estonia (6 May 2002). Riigieelarve seaduse muutmise ja sellest tulenevalt teiste seaduste muutmise seaduse» väljakuulutamata jätmine. State Gazette, 14.05.2002, 56, 840. [Resolution not to proclaim the Amending Act of the State Budget Act and other related acts] Available at: https://www.riigiteataja.ee/ert/act.jsp?id=95077 [last retrieved January 2009]

Riigikogu Verbatim Record (11 November 1992). Riigieelarve seaduse eelnõu esimene lugemine. [The first reading of the draft State Budget Act] Available at: http://web.riigi kogu.ee/ems/stenograms/1992/11/t92111105.htm [last retrieved January 2009]
Riigikogu Verbatim Record (20 January 1993). Seaduse "Eesti Vabariigi 1993. aasta riigieelarve kohta" seaduse eelnõu teine lugemine. [The second reading of the draft State 1993 Budget Act] Available at: http://web.riigikogu.ee/ems/stenograms/1993/01/t93012002.htm [last retrieved January 2009]
Riigikogu Verbatim Record (26 January 1993). Seaduse "Eesti Vabariigi 1993. aasta riigieelarve kohta" eelnõu teise lugemise jätkamine. [Continuation of the second reading of the draft State 1993 Budget Act] Available at: http://web.riigikogu.ee/ems/stenograms/1993/01/t93012603.htm [last retrieved January 2009]
Riigikogu Verbatim Record (9 February 1993). Seaduse "Eesti Vabariigi 1993. aasta riigieelarve kohta" eelnõu kolmas lugemine. [The third reading of the draft State 1993 Budget Act] Available at: http://web.riigikogu.ee/ems/stenograms/1993/02/t93020904.htm [last retrieved January 2009]
Riigikogu Verbatim Record (14 April 1993). Riigieelarve seaduse eelnõu esimene lugemine. [The first reading of the draft State Budget Act] Available at: http://web.riigikogu.ee/e ms/stenograms/1993/04/t93041411.htm [last retrieved January 2009]
Riigikogu Verbatim Record (12 May 1993). Riigieelarve seaduse eelnõu teine lugemine. [The second reading of the draft State Budget Act] Available at: http://web.riigikogu.ee/ems/stenograms/1993/05/t93051214.htm [last retrieved January 2009]
Riigikogu Verbatim Record (9 June 1993). Maksukorralduse seaduse eelnõu esimene lugemine. [The first reading of the draft Taxation Act] Available at: http://web.riigikogu.ee/ems/stenograms/1993/06/t93060917.htm [last retrieved January 2009]
Riigikogu Verbatim Record (25 August 1993). Maksukorralduse seaduse eelnõu teine lugemine. [The second reading of the draft Taxation Act] Available at: http://web. riigikogu.ee/ems/stenograms/1993/08/t93082501.htm [last retrieved January 2009]
Riigikogu Verbatim Record (28 September 1993). Vabariigi Presidendi poolt tagasisaadetud maksukorralduse seaduse uus käsitelu. [Renewed deliberation of the Taxation Act sent back by the President of the Republic] Available at: http://web.riigikogu.ee/ems/steno grams/1993/09/t93092821.htm [last retrieved January 2009]
Riigikogu Verbatim Record (7 December 1993). Maksukorralduse seaduse eelnõu esimene lugemine. [The first reading of the draft Taxation Act] Available at: http://web.riigikogu.ee/ems/stenograms/1993/12/t93120728.htm [last retrieved January 2009]
Riigikogu Verbatim Record (16 December 1993). Maksukorralduse seaduse eelnõu teine lugemine. [The second reading of the draft Taxation Act] Available at: http://web. riigikogu.ee/ems/stenograms/1993/12/t93121629.htm [last retrieved January 2009]
Riigikogu Verbatim Record (10 November 1993). 1994. aasta riigieelarve seaduse eelnõu teine lugemine. [The second reading of the draft State 1994 Budget Act] Available at: http://web.riigikogu.ee/ems/stenograms/1993/11/t93111025.htm [last retrieved January 2009]
Riigikogu Verbatim Record (12 October 1994). Seaduse "1995. aasta riigieelarve" eelnõu esimene lugemine. [The first reading of the draft State 1995 Budget Act] Available at: http://web.riigikogu.ee/ems/stenograms/1994/10/t94101204.htm [last retrieved January 2009]
Riigikogu Verbatim Record (4 May 1995). Tulumaksuseaduse muutmise seaduse eelnõu (1 SE ja 21 SE) teine lugemine. [The second reading of the draft Amending Act of In-

come Tax Act (1 SE and 21 SE)] Available at: http://web.riigikogu.ee/ems/stenograms/1995/05/t95050406.html [last retrieved January 2009]
Riigikogu Verbatim Record (15 October 1996). Käibemaksuseaduse muutmise seaduse eelnõu (385 SE) esimene lugemine. [The first reading of the draft Value Added Tax Act (385 SE)] Available at: http://web.riigikogu.ee/ems/stenograms/1996/10/t96101505.html [last retrieved January 2009]
Riigikogu Verbatim Record (22 November 1995). Tulumaksuseaduse muutmise seaduse eelnõu kolmas lugemine. [The third reading of the draft Income Tax Act] Available at: http://web.riigikogu.ee/ems/stenograms/1995/11/t95112209.html [last retrieved January 2009]
Riigikogu Verbatim Record (8 October 1996). Riigieelarve seaduse muutmise seaduse eelnõu (163 SE) esimene lugemine. [The first reading of the draft State Budget Act (163)] Available at: http://web.riigikogu.ee/ems/stenograms/1996/10/t96100804.html [last retrieved January 2009]
Riigikogu Verbatim Record (15 October 1996). Käibemaksuseaduse muutmise seaduse eelnõu (385 SE) esimene lugemine. [The first reading of the draft Value Added Tax Act [385 SE)] Available at: http://web.riigikogu.ee/ems/stenograms/1996/10/t96101505.html [last retrieved January 2009]
Riigikogu Verbatim Record (22 October 1996). Riigieelarve seaduse muutmise seaduse eelnõu (163 SE) teine lugemine. [The second reading of the draft Amending Act of the State Budget Act (163 SE)] Available at: http://web.riigikogu.ee/ems/stenograms/1996/10/t96 102206.html [last retrieved January 2009]
Riigikogu Verbatim Record (20 May 1997). Riigieelarve seaduse muutmise seaduse eelnõu (163 SE) teise lugemise jätkamine. [The continuation of the second reading of the draft Amending Act of the State Budget Act (163 SE)] Available at: http://web.riigikogu.ee/ems/stenograms/1997/05/t97052015.html [last retrieved January 2009]
Riigikogu Verbatim Record (11 February 1998). Riigieelarve seaduse eelnõu (618 SE) teise lugemise jätkamine. [The continuation of the second reading of the draft State Budget Act (618 SE)] Available at: http://web.riigikogu.ee/ems/stenograms/1998/02/t98021104-08.html#P667_130401 [last retrieved January 2009]
Riigikogu Verbatim (17 March 1998). Maksukorralduse seaduse muutmise seaduse eelnõu (626 SE) esimene lugemine. [The first reading of the draft Amending Act of the Taxation Act (626 SE)] Available at: http://web.riigikogu.ee/ems/stenograms/1998/03/t98031708-02.html#P104_11270 [last retrieved January 2009]
Riigikogu Verbatim Record (20 May 1997). Riigieelarve seaduse muutmise seaduse eelnõu (163 SE) teise lugemise jätkamine. [The continuation of the second reading of the draft Amending Act of the State Budget Act (163 SE)] Available at: http://web.riigikogu.ee/ems/stenograms/1997/05/t97052015.html [last retrieved January 2009]
Riigikogu Verbatim Record (8 April 1998). Riigieelarve seaduse eelnõu (618 SE) teise lugemise jätkamine. [The continuation of the second reading of the draft State Budget Act (618 SE)] Available at: http://web.riigikogu.ee/ems/stenograms/1998/04/t98040810-02.html#P99_12231 [last retrieved January 2009]
Riigikogu Verbatim (14 April 1999). Vabariigi Presidendi poolt välja kuulutamata jäetud riigieelarve seaduse uuesti arutamine. [Renewed deliberation of the State Budget Act not proclaimed by the President of the Republic] Available at: http://web.riigikogu.ee/ems/stenograms/1999/04/t99041404-04.html#P246_45691 [last retrieved January 2009]
Riigikogu Verbatim Record (19 May 1999). Vabariigi Presidendi poolt välja kuulutamata jäetud riigieelarve seaduse teistkordse menetlemise teine lugemine. [The second reading of the renewed proceedings of the State Budget Act not proclaimed by the President of

the Republic] Available at: http://web.riigikogu.ee/ems/stenograms/1999/05/t99051908-05.html#P275_50880 [last retrieved January 2009]
Riigikogu Verbatim Record (15 June 1999). Riigikogu kodukorra seaduse § 104 muutmise seaduse eelnõu (125 SE) esimene lugemine. [The first reading of the draft Amending Act of § 104 of the Riigikogu Procedure Act (125 SE)] Available at: http://web.riigikogu.ee/ems/stenograms/1999/06/t99061511-04.html#P110_6910 [last retrieved January 2009]
Riigikogu Verbatim Record (19 October 1999). Käibemaksuseaduse § 13 muutmise seaduse eelnõu (164 SE) esimene lugemine. [The first reading of the draft Amending Act of § 13 of the Value Added Tax Act (164 SE)] Available at: http://web.riigikogu.ee/ems/steno grams/1999/10/t99101905-02.html#P100_20031 [last retrieved January 2009]
Riigikogu Verbatim Record (15 November 2000). Käibemaksuseaduse § 13 muutmise seaduse eelnõu (539 SE) esimene lugemine. [The first reading of the draft Amending Act of § 13 of the Value Added Tax Act (164 SE)] Available at: http://web.riigikogu.ee/ems/stenograms/2000/11/t00111508-10.html#P597_123468 [last retrieved January 2009]
Riigikogu Verbatim Record (24 October 2001). Eesti Vabariigile välislaenude võtmise ja välislaenulepingutele riigigarantiide andmise seaduse muutmise seaduse eelnõu (870 SE) esimene lugemine. [The first reading of the Amending Act of the Foreign Borrowing by the Republic of Estonia and State Guarantees for Foreign Loan Agreements Act (870 SE)] Available at: http://web.riigikogu.ee/ems/stenograms/2001/10/t01102406-27.html#P1315_264502 [last retrieved January 2009]
Riigikogu Verbatim Record (10 November 1999). Tulumaksuseaduse eelnõu (143 SE) esimene lugemine. [The first reading of the draft Income Tax Act (143 SE)] Available at: http://web.riigikogu.ee/ems/stenograms/1999/11/t99111007-17.html#P1645_364699 [last retrieved January 2009]
Riigikogu Verbatim Record (24 november 1999). Tulumaksuseaduse eelnõu (143 SE) teine lugemine. [The second reading of the draft Income Tax Act (143 SE)] Available at: http://web.riigikogu.ee/ems/stenograms/1999/11/t99112409-11.html#P1787_255328 [last retrieved January 2009]
Riigikogu Verbatim Record (24 October 2001). Tulumaksuseaduse ja sotsiaalmaksuseaduse muutmise seaduse eelnõu (857 SE) teine lugemine.[The second reading of the draft Amending Act of the Income Tax and Social Tax Act (857 SE)] Available at: http://web.riigikogu.ee/ems/stenograms/2001/10/t01102406-08.html#P518_102936 [last retrieved January 2009]
Riigikogu Verbatim Record (20 November 2001). Eesti Vabariigile välislaenude võtmise ja välislaenulepingutele riigigarantiide andmise seaduse muutmise seaduse eelnõu (870 SE) teine lugemine. [The second reading of the draft Amending Act of the Foreign Borrowing by the Republic of Estonia and State Guarantees for Foreign Loan Agreements Act (870 SE)] Available at: http://web.riigikogu.ee/ems/stenograms/2001/11/t01112009-02.html#P40_3800 [last retrieved January 2009]
Riigikogu Verbatim Record (5 December 2001). Riigieelarve seaduse muutmise ja sellest tulenevalt teiste seaduste muutmise seaduse eelnõu (773 SE) teine lugemine. [The second reading of the draft Amending Act of the State Budget Act and related Acts (773 SE)] Available at: http://web.riigikogu.ee/ems/stenograms/2001/12/t01120510-16.html#P1397_364847 [last retrieved January 2009]
Riigikogu Verbatim Record (12 December 2001). Vabariigi Presidendi poolt väljakuulutamata jäetud Eesti Vabariigile välislaenude võtmise ja välislaenulepingutele riigigarantiide andmise seaduse muutmise seaduse uuesti arutamine. [Renewed Deliberation of the Amending Act of the Foreign Borrowing by the Republic of Estonia and State Guarantees for Foreign Loan Agreements Act not proclaimed by the President of the Republic]

Available at: http://web.riigikogu.ee/ems/stenograms/2001/12/t01121211-04.html#P22 7_52607 [last retrieved January 2009]
Riigikogu Verbatim Record (19 December 2001). Riigieelarve seaduse muutmise ja sellest tulenevalt teiste seaduste muutmise seaduse eelnõu (773 SE) teise lugemise jätkamine. [The continuation of the second reading of the draft Amending Act of the State Budget Act and related Acts (773 SE)] Available at: http://web.riigikogu.ee/ems/stenograms/2001/12/t01121912-07.html#P362_82991 [last retrieved January 2009]
Riigikogu Verbatim Record (19 March 2002). Riigieelarve seaduse muutmise ja sellest tulenevalt teiste seaduste muutmise seaduse eelnõu (1000 SE) esimene lugemine. [The first reading of the draft Amending Act of the State Budget Act and related Acts (1000 SE)] Available at: http://web.riigikogu.ee/ems/stenograms/2002/03/t02031908-04.html#P14 1_19152 [last retrieved January 2009]
Riigikogu Verbatim Record (9 April 2002). Riigieelarve seaduse muutmise ja sellest tulenevalt teiste seaduste muutmise seaduse eelnõu (1000 SE) teine lugemine. [The second reading of the draft Amending Act of the State Budget Act and related Acts (1000 SE)] Available at: http://web.riigikogu.ee/ems/stenograms/2002/04/t02040910-01.html# P27_1 491 [last retrieved January 2009]
Riigikogu Verbatim Record (17 April 2002). Riigieelarve seaduse muutmise ja sellest tulenevalt teiste seaduste muutmise seaduse eelnõu (1000 SE) teise lugemise jätkamine. [The continuation of the second reading of the draft Amending Act of the State Budget Act and related Acts (1000 SE)] Available at: http://web.riigikogu.ee/ems/stenograms /2002/04/t02041711-11.html#P481_89338 [last retrieved January 2009]
Riigikogu Verbatim Record (14 May 2002). Vabariigi Presidendi poolt välja kuulutamata jäetud riigieelarve seaduse muutmise ja sellest tulenevalt teiste seaduste muutmise seaduse uuesti arutamine. [Renewed deliberation on the Amending Act of the State Budget Act and related Acts not proclaimed by the President of the Republic] Available at: http://web.riigikogu.ee/ems/stenograms/2002/05/t02051414-03.html#P396_112418 [last retrieved January 2009]
Riigikogu Verbatim Record (18 June 2002). Riigieelarve seaduse muutmise ja sellest tulenevalt teiste seaduste muutmise seaduse eelnõu (1103 SE) esimene lugemine. [The first reading of the draft Amending Act of the State Budget Act and related Acts (1103 SE)] Available at: http://web.riigikogu.ee/ems/stenograms/2002/06/t02061818-05.html#P12 9_20588 [last retrieved January 2009]
Riigikogu Verbatim Record (20 June 2002). Riigieelarve seaduse muutmise ja sellest tulenevalt teiste seaduste muutmise seaduse eelnõu (1103 SE) teine lugemine. [The second reading of the draft Amending Act of the State Budget Act and related Acts (1103 SE)] Available at: http://web.riigikogu.ee/ems/stenograms/2002/06/t02062018-04.html# P10 1_17829 [last retrieved January 2009]
Riigikogu Verbatim Record (11 December 2002). Palgaseaduse, tulumaksuseaduse, sotsiaalmaksuseaduse, kogumispensionide seaduse ja maksukorralduse seaduse muutmise seaduse eelnõu (1215 SE) teine lugemine. [The second reading of the draft Amending Act of Wages Act, Income Tax Act, Social Tax Act, Funded Pensions Act and Taxation Act (1215 SE)] Available at: http://web.riigikogu.ee/ems/stenograms/2002/12/t0212 1111-21.html#P1276_292489 [last retrieved January 2009]
Riigikogu Verbatim Record (30 April 2003). Õiguskantsleri ettepanek 1. jaanuaril 2003. aastal jõustunud maksukorralduse seaduse § 163 lõike 2 kooskõlla viimiseks Eesti Vabariigi põhiseadusega. [The Proposal of the Legal Chancellor to bring § 163 Section 2 of the Taxation Act into conformity with the Constitution of the Republic of Estonia]

Available at: http://web.riigikogu.ee/ems/stenograms/2003/04/t0304 3004-06.html#P 423 _77171 [last retrieved January 2009]
Riigikogu Verbatim Record (11 December 2003). Riigieelarve seaduse ja tulumaksuseaduse muutmise seaduse eelnõu (137 SE) esimene lugemine. [The first reading of the draft Amending Act of the State Budget Act and the Income Tax Act (137 SE)] Available at: http://web.riigikogu.ee/ems/stenograms/2003/12/t03121111-10.html#P527_102268 [last retrieved January 2009]
Riigikogu Verbatim Record (5 June 2008). Käibemaksuseaduse § 15 muutmise seaduse eelnõu (224 SE) esimene lugemine. [The first reading of the draft Amending Act of the Value Added Tax Act (224 SE)]. Available at: http://www.riigikogu.ee/?op=steno &stcommand=stenogramm&date=1212649500#pk2271 [last retrieved January 2009]
Protocol of the Constitutional Committee of the *Riigikogu* (17 April 2003). Available at: http://web.riigikogu.ee/ems/sarosbin/mgetdoc?itemid=031110007&login=proov&passwo rd=&system=ems&server=ragne11 [last retrieved January 2009]

Verbatim Records of the Supreme Council of the Soviet Republic of Estonia and the Republic of Estonia

Verbatim Record of the Supreme Council, 22 August 1990. Available at the Parliamentary Library of Estonia.
Verbatim Record of the Supreme Council, 18–21 February 1991. Available at the Parliamentary Library of Estonia.
Verbatim Record of the Supreme Council, 3–5 September 1991. Available at the Parliamentary Library of Estonia.
Verbatim Record of the Supreme Council, 9–12 September 1991. Available at the Parliamentary Library of Estonia.
Verbatim Record of the Supreme Council, 16–19 September 1991. Available at the Parliamentary Library of Estonia.
Verbatim Record of the Supreme Council, 14–17 October 1991. Available at the Parliamentary Library of Estonia.
Verbatim Record of the Supreme Council, 16–19 March 1992. Available at the Parliamentary Library of Estonia.
Verbatim Record of the Supreme Council, 10–13 August 1992. Available at the Parliamentary Library of Estonia.

Archival documents

Archival document no. RA-23-24-1-5. Estonian State Archive. Eesti Vabariigi Põhiseaduslikule Assambleele esitatud ekspertide arvamused. [The opinions of experts submitted to the Constitutional Assembly of the Republic of Estonia]
Archival document no. R-23-24-1-6, pp. 294–295. Estonian State Archive. EV Põhiseadusliku Assamblee toimkondade ettepanekud ja apellatsioonid. [The proposals and appellations of the committees of the Constitutional Assembly of the Republic of Estonia]

Finanzsoziologie

Herausgegeben von Jürgen G. Backhaus

Band 1 Jürgen G. Backhaus (ed.): Essays on Fiscal Sociology. 2005.

Band 2 Jürgen G. Backhaus (ed.): Fiscal Sociology. Public Auditing. 2007.

Band 3 Helge Peukert: Rudolf Goldscheid: Menschenökonom und Finanzsoziologe. 2009.

Band 4 Ringa Raudla: Constitution, Public Finance, and Transition. Theoretical Developments in Constitutional Public Finance and the Case of Estonia. 2010.

www.peterlang.de

Peter Lang · Internationaler Verlag der Wissenschaften

Carolin Metzner

Johann Caspar Bluntschli

Leben, Zeitgeschehen und Kirchenpolitik
1808–1881

Frankfurt am Main, Berlin, Bern, Bruxelles, New York, Oxford, Wien, 2009.
174 S., 2 Abb.
Schriften zum Staatskirchenrecht.
Herausgegeben von Axel Frhr. von Campenhausen, Christoph Link und Jörg Winter. Bd. 46
ISBN 978-3-631-59679-1 · geb. € 41,80*

Die Arbeit befasst sich mit der Biografie des Schweizer Rechtsgelehrten Johann Caspar Bluntschli (1808–1881). Die Untersuchung verfolgt das Ziel, das bislang einseitig auf den Juristen Bluntschli fokussierte Interesse auf den Freimaurer und Protestanten Bluntschli zu lenken, um sein Lebenswerk einer umfassenden Würdigung zuzuführen. Im Blickpunkt steht das kirchenpolitische Wirken Bluntschlis im deutschen Protestantismus des ausgehenden 19. Jahrhunderts. Neben dem Lebensweg Bluntschlis beschäftigt sich die Studie mit der Freimaurerei, dem Deutschen Protestantenverein und den Auffassungen Bluntschlis zum Verhältnis von Staat und Kirche.

Aus dem Inhalt: Biografie Bluntschlis · Wesen und Geschichte der Freimaurerei · Haltung der Kirchen gegenüber Freimaurern · Deutscher Protestantenverein · Kulturkampf · Verhältnis von Staat und Kirche